Macroeconomic Policy in Fragile States

Macroeconomic Policy in Fragile States

Edited by

RALPH CHAMI, RAPHAEL ESPINOZA,
AND PETER MONTIEL

OXFORD
UNIVERSITY PRESS

OXFORD
UNIVERSITY PRESS

Great Clarendon Street, Oxford, OX2 6DP,
United Kingdom

Oxford University Press is a department of the University of Oxford.
It furthers the University's objective of excellence in research, scholarship,
and education by publishing worldwide. Oxford is a registered trade mark of
Oxford University Press in the UK and in certain other countries

First Edition published in 2021

Impression: 2

Published in the United States of America by Oxford University Press
198 Madison Avenue, New York, NY 10016, United States of America

British Library Cataloguing in Publication Data
Data available

Library of Congress Control Number: 2020950500

ISBN 978–0–19–885309–1

DOI: 10.1093/oso/9780198853091.001.0001

Printed and bound by
CPI Group (UK) Ltd, Croydon, CR0 4YY

Contents

Foreword

Picture a child born today to a villager in Somalia or Laos, or another fragile state. Think about her prospects in life. As a reader of this book, you are probably worried: Will she have clean water and enough to eat? Will she be safe from violence? Will she be able to go to school? To work? To live better than her parents?

It depends—on leadership in her country, and on support from the international community.

Stabilizing fragile and conflict-affected states is among the world's most difficult challenges. And it is one of the most pressing—not only for the people of those countries, but for all of us. Supporting these states is critical to challenges like ending the COVID-19 pandemic, fighting climate change, reducing global poverty, and ameliorating some of the causes of involuntary migration.

Working with fragile states at the IMF, and throughout my career, I learned that no two countries are the same. Knowledge of each country's people and history is necessary, in addition to understanding its political economy.

Ralph, Raphael, Peter, and the contributors to this book have studied fragile states and their problems from many angles, taking a broad view of the macroeconomy. They have identified the most pressing challenges and provided a comprehensive and timely set of solutions. It is both a menu of options for policymakers seeking to address these states' urgent needs, and a manual for how to execute them.

In additional to wisdom born of deep experience and analytical rigor, the authors bring a humility and humanity that recognizes the unique qualities of each country, and the enormity of the challenges they face. And the discussion is enriched by country case studies showing both policy successes and failures, and lessons learned.

Informed by this perspective and the ongoing pandemic, the IMF is implementing a strategy to improve the quality and effectiveness of its engagement with these countries. We have responded quickly to a crisis like no other, with nearly $2 billion in new lending to 12 fragile or conflict-affected states, which will help catalyze donor support. And the IMF is also granting debt relief to 21 fragile states, home to about 313 million people.

We are changing our lending facilities to allow for quicker and better targeting of financial support, and adapting our policy advice and technical assistance to account for the peculiarities of the crisis. Some of these changes will doubtless outlast the pandemic.

The Fund and our most vulnerable member states are on a journey toward a greener, fairer, smarter recovery—and a safer, brighter future for that child born today, and all those to come.

This book helps us get there.

Kristalina Georgieva
Managing Director
International Monetary Fund

Preface

The concept of state fragility is often taken to capture a situation in which a country's governmental apparatus is of limited effectiveness in delivering a broad range of public services. Although the provision of security is essential, other public goods are also important, in particular those that promote social cooperation (such as laws that are fair and consistent with personal freedom), those that provide some basic social insurance (such as disaster relief and healthcare, which is particularly important to address the COVID-19 pandemic), and those that create the conditions for economic prosperity.

From our perspective, a *failed* state is then one that fails to deliver along all four of these dimensions, and a *fragile* state is one that faces a high probability of becoming a failed one. A fragile state is therefore not necessarily an ineffectual one; while a state's inability to deliver basic public goods may certainly be grounds for citizen disaffection and therefore for social upheaval, a repressive state that minimizes crime and makes the trains run on time may only temporarily be suppressing a social explosion.

Setting macroeconomic policy is especially difficult in fragile states. Political legitimacy concerns are heightened, raising issues such as who the policymakers are, what incentives they face, and how the process of policymaking is likely to work under limited legitimacy and high uncertainty both about the macroeconomic environment and about policy effectiveness. In addition, fragility expands the range of policy objectives in ways that may constrain the attainment of standard macroeconomic objectives. Specifically, in the context of fragility policymakers also need to focus on measures to mitigate fragility itself; that is, they need to address issues such as regional and ethnic disparities in economic outcomes and access to public services, youth unemployment, and food price inflation. Sociopolitical developments around the world have thus pushed policymakers to expand their toolkit to improve the effectiveness of macroeconomic management in the face of these constraints.

The chapters in this book address these issues, by giving an analytical context from which policymakers can build to answer the questions they face in fragile situations as well as by providing lessons drawn from empirical analyses and case studies, leveraging the extensive experience of the contributors. It is our hope that this volume will further stimulate thinking on policymaking in fragile states and promote the importance of that work.

We acknowledge the generous support of DFID which allowed this work to happen, as well as the support of the institutions that hosted us: the IMF Institute for Capacity Development, Fiscal Affairs Department, Research Department, and European Department, and Williams College.

Our acknowledgments also go to the contributors of the volume: Daron Acemoglu, Christopher Adam, Sarthak Agrawal, Ramzy Al-Amine, Giorgia Albertin, Nabila Assaf, Katherine Baer, Adolfo Barajas, Timothy Besley, Francesca Caselli, Warren Coats, Paul Collier, Charles Collyns, Mattia Coppo, Phil De Imus, Ibrahim Elbadawi, Michael Engman, Lars Engstrom, Ekkehard Ernst, Connel Fullenkamp, Enrique Gelbard, Jose Gijon, Mark Griffiths, Sanjeev Gupta, Ermal Hitaj, Kareem Ismail, Kevin Kuruc, Chris Lane, MarioMansour Isaac Martinez, Gary Milante, Clara Mira, Hannes Mueller, Anne Oeking, Sailendra Pattanayak, Mehta Paulomi, Andrea Presbitero, Alexandros Ragoussis, Gustavo Ramirez, Thomas Risse, James A. Robinson, Daouda Sembene, Raimundo Soto, Shinji Takaji, Robert Tchaidze, Rima Turk, James Wilson, Michael Woolcock; to the Workshop participants at Oxford: Nathalie Brajard, Sharmini Coorey, Elizabeth Cunningham, Conor Doyle, Chady El-Khoury, Tim Green, Sean Hagan, David Hidalgo, Andy Hinsley, Oussama Kanaan, Adnan Khan, Nick Lea, Viola Lucas, Alexandre Marc, Eva Myers, Sean Nolan, Jonathan Ostry, Sebastian Pompe, David Robinson; and to other colleagues who discussed this project at different stages: Andrew Berg, Chris Papageorgiou, Dominique Desruelle, Ali Mansoor and Abdelhak Senhadji. Kia Penso provided superb help with the editing of the volume.

Of course, we would not have been able do this without the support and patience of our respective families, who tolerated our dedication to this project. They join us in hoping that this volume will contribute to better international understanding of how to improve the lives of our fellow human beings who have to cope with the challenges of living in fragile states.

Ralph Chami, Raphael Espinoza, and Peter Montiel

How this Book Came to Be

I can still recall the day in 2009 when my director walked into my office and asked me to take over as mission chief for Libya. He said, "You are fluent in Arabic, and not much is happening there." At that time, I was head of the regional surveillance division, overseeing 32 countries that comprised the Middle East and Central Asia Department (MCD), at the International Monetary Fund (IMF). True, going by the typical statistics of GDP growth, inflation, and internal and external balances, Libya looked like the poster child of a resource-rich emerging economy. A country three times the size of France but with 11 percent of its population, a fast-growing economy heavily dependent on oil, with well over $100 billion in reserves along with double-digit external and internal surpluses. Masked by these statistics, however, was a more alarming picture of a country lagging behind its comparators on social, institutional, and political indices, with a young population that was also suffering from high unemployment, especially among the youth.

It is not surprising that when the Arab Spring started in neighboring Tunisia and then spread to Libya's neighbor in the west, Egypt, Libya's disenfranchised population would join the quest for voice and inclusion. Over the next four years, I led many missions into Libya with a group of dedicated IMF staff, often in perilous circumstances, working closely with authorities, nongovernmental organizations (NGOs), other international financial institutions (IFIs), as well as other stakeholders to help the country make the transition to a new Libya that would live up to its tremendous potential, thereby delivering the promised prosperity for its people, 42 years in waiting.

The political and security situation, however, was quickly deteriorating, and we were now dealing with a country that was showing signs of fragility, with relentless pressures on its nascent leadership to acquiesce to the multitude and immediate requests by its young population to deliver, even if it meant at the expense of medium-term sustainability.

Our position was to advise the state on how to stabilize the economy in the short term, while leaving room for much-needed structural reforms in the medium term. But that was easier said than done, for many of the tools honed by experience in working on low-income or middle-income countries, let alone in advanced economies, could not be used in such a fragile condition; where the political economy situation was morphing quickly, where different actors appeared and disappeared on the ground, and where the security situation was quickly deteriorating.

We had to tackle issues such as how to design fiscal, monetary, and exchange rate policies in such a situation. How to create trust between the authorities and the society, after many years of mistrust? How to enhance the efficiency of the government, which despite its wealth lacked the capacity to deliver? How to empower the private sector, in a country that suffered from the heavy hand of the state, lacked a constitution, proper definition of property rights, or the ability to enforce the rule of law? One question that I had to grapple with was whether the country was even ready for all the advice that we, among other IFIs and stakeholders, were readily providing.

Unfortunately, by late 2013 the fast-deteriorating political and security situation meant that we could no longer meet in Libya, and our efforts became focused on developing emergency budgets on a six-month rolling basis, awaiting the normalization of the security situation.

However, the civil strife intensified, trumping our efforts to stabilize the economy, and the country was plunged into conflict among its various factions.

At the same time in 2013, I received a phone call from my director who promptly asked me, "Mr. Chami, who is the mission chief for Somalia?" By that time, I was division chief for a number of states, most of them experiencing fragile situations: Egypt, Libya, Somalia, Sudan, South Sudan, and Yemen. I replied, "As you know, Somalia has been offline for 22 years," to which he quickly replied "So, you are now the mission chief for Somalia." Though Somalia lacked Libya's deep central bank resources and was in fact in arrears to the IMF, both states shared a number of characteristics, such as the absence of or inability of the state to deliver public services including security; lack of trust in the state; certain pockets of stability in the middle of chaos; warring factions jostling for power; and a young population in urgent need of meaningful jobs and aspiring for a better future.

Though both countries were fragile in their own way, one stark difference between the situation in Libya and that in Somalia was that while the former was descending into chaos after many years of macroeconomic stability enforced by a predatory state, the other was making its way out of chaos, driven by a society that had decided to cede power to a representative state. Again, the same set of policy issues and design questions that we faced in dealing with Libya were present in the case of Somalia, as well as in other fragile states such as Yemen, among others, even though each of these countries has its own social narrative and experience. What does fragility mean in terms of designing macroeconomic policy? What role does the country's sociopolitical situation play in defining what is possible? How to build trust between the state and society? How should we take fragility into consideration when designing macroeconomic policies for such countries? What does that precisely mean for fiscal, monetary, exchange rate, and financial policies in such countries? When and how should IFIs engage in helping countries facing fragile situations? What lessons can we learn from the successes and failures of countries to exit fragile situations?

Together with my two co-editors, Raphael Espinoza, who has written extensively on macroeconomic management in resource-rich countries, and Peter Montiel, who has had a long and celebrated career in thinking and advising on macroeconomic policy in emerging and developing countries, we set out to answer these questions. We solicited the best expertise on this subject to help. Renowned scholars, who have devoted extensive time and effort to thinking about the role of political economy in fragile sates and highlighted the need to tailor macroeconomic policy to the local situation, have contributed to this book, alongside experts with extensive field experience in fragile states.

Our aim is to help policymakers, practitioners, and others interested in engaging with fragile states by taking stock of what we have learned about the daunting challenge of framing macroeconomic policy in those environments. We hope that the book contributes to developing an understanding about how policy may need to adapt in countries experiencing fragility, especially as the list of such countries continues, alarmingly, to grow.

Ralph Chami

List of Contributors

Daron Acemoglu is an Institute Professor at MIT and an elected fellow of the National Academy of Sciences, the Turkish Academy of Sciences, the American Academy of Arts and Sciences, the Econometric Society, the European Economic Association, and the Society of Labor Economists. He is the author of five books, including *Why Nations Fail: Power, Prosperity*, and *Poverty and The Narrow Corridor: States, Societies, and the Fate of Liberty* (both with James A. Robinson).

Christopher Adam is Professor of Development Economics in the Department of International Development at the University of Oxford, UK. He is an IMF Visiting Scholar under the IMF-DFID program on Macroeconomic Research in Low-Income Countries, a Fellow of the European Development Network, and an associate editor of the *Journal of Development Economics*. He holds a DPhil in Economics from Nuffield College, Oxford.

Sarthak Agrawal is a Research Economist with the Institute for Fiscal Studies in London, working in their Centre for Tax Analysis in Developing Countries. He has a BA in Economics (Hons.) from Shri Ram College of Commerce, University of Delhi and an MPhil from the University of Oxford. His research interests include issues around fragility and conflict, the economics of education, and tax policy in low-income countries.

Ramzy Al-Amine is a Research Analyst in the Front Office of the IMF's Strategy, Policy, and Review department. Previously, he worked in the Middle East and Central Asia department, where he focused on economic issues relating to Maghreb countries. Ramzy is a graduate of the American University of Beirut and holds an MA from Georgetown University. His work focuses on big data, text mining, and data visualization.

Giorgia Albertin is Deputy Division Chief at the African Department of the IMF and mission chief for Guinea. She has extensive experience working on emerging markets and low-income and fragile countries. She was the IMF Resident Representative for Tunisia and worked on capacity building at the IMF Institute. She holds a PhD in Economics from the London School of Economics and Political Science.

Nabila Assaf is the Practice Manager in the Finance, Competitiveness, and Innovation Global Practice at the World Bank, covering the Middle East, Afghanistan, and Pakistan, and was previously part of the Fragility, Conflict, and Violence group. She spent the earlier years of her career in manufacturing, agribusiness, and export development, and translated that experience into private sector development in developing and fragile countries. She holds a master's degree in industrial engineering and management from the University of Washington.

Katherine Baer is an Assistant Director in the Fiscal Affairs Department (FAD). She manages the division in FAD that provides technical assistance in tax and customs administration to more than 80 IMF member countries in the Western Hemisphere and Sub-Saharan Africa. She has also helped design and implement tax and customs reforms in Asia, Europe, and the former Soviet Union, including in crisis countries. Prior to taking up her current position in the IMF she was a Financial Economist in the US Treasury and head of research in the Mexican Tax Administration. Ms Baer has a number of publications in the field of tax administration and holds a PhD from Cornell University.

Adolfo Barajas is a Senior Economist in the Monetary and Capital Markets Department of the IMF, where his primary responsibility is to lead analytical chapters of the Global Financial Stability Report. He has worked in the Institute for Capacity Development, delivering courses on macroeconomics and finance; and in regional departments of the Fund, where he participated in country work and authored chapters of the Regional Economic Outlook. Previously, he has worked as a researcher in the Colombian central bank and at Fedesarrollo, a think tank in Bogotá.

Tim Besley is Sir W. Arthur Lewis Professor of Development Economics at the LSE. His research focuses on the political economy of policy making. A past president of the Econometric Society, International Economic Association, and European Economic Association, his policy experience includes membership of the Bank of England Monetary Policy Committee and the UK National Infrastructure Commission. He served on the LSE- Oxford commission on state fragility, growth, and development.

Francesca G. Caselli is an economist in the World Economic Studies Division of the IMF Research Department. Previously, she worked in the IMF European Department. Her research interests include applied econometrics and international economics. Her recent work focuses on the impact of fiscal rules and the role of anchoring of inflation expectations in the transmission of shocks. Before joining the IMF, she worked at the OECD and visited the Bank of Italy. She holds a PhD in International Economics from the Graduate Institute in Geneva.

Ralph Chami is currently Assistant Director in the Institute for Capacity Development, International Monetary Fund. Most recently, he was Assistant Director and Mission Chief in the Middle East and Central Asia Department (MCD) where he oversaw surveillance and program work on fragile states: Egypt, Libya, Somalia, Sudan, South Sudan, and Yemen. Previously, he was the Chief of the Regional Studies Division in MCD. He is the recipient of the 2014 IMF Operational Excellence Award.

Warren Coats retired from the International Monetary Fund in 2003 as Assistant Director of the Monetary and Capital Markets Department, where he led technical assistance missions to more than 20 countries. He was Assistant Professor of Economics at the University of Virginia from 1970–75 and a director of the Cayman Islands Monetary Authority 2003–10. His most recent books include *One Currency for Bosnia: Creating the Central Bank of Bosnia and Herzegovina* (2007); Building Market Economy Monetary Systems—My Travels in the Former Soviet Union (2020); Afghanistan: Rebuilding the Central Bank after 9/11—My Travels to Kabul (2020); Iraq: An American Tragedy, My Travels to Baghdad (2020); and Palestine: The Oslo Accords before and after, My travels to Jerusalem (2020). He graduated in Economics from UC Berkeley (BA), and the University of Chicago (PhD).

Paul Collier is Professor of Economics and Public Policy, Blavatnik School of Government, Oxford University; Director (with Robin Burgess) of the International Growth Centre; Director (with Dennis Snower) of the ESRC-NIESR network, the Social-Macro Hub. Formerly, Director of the Development Research Department of the World Bank, and of the Centre for the Study of African Economies. He is the author of *The Bottom Billion* (Oxford University Press), *Refuge* (Penguin, with Alex Betts), *The Future of Capitalism* (Penguin) and *Greed is Dead: Politics After Individualism*, 2020, Allen Lane, (with John Kay).

Charles Collyns joined the IMF's Independent Evaluation Office (IEO) as Director in February 2017, after working as Chief Economist at the Institute of International Finance. He served as Assistant Secretary for International Finance at the US Treasury Department from February 2010 to July 2013. Prior to joining Treasury, he worked at the IMF, including as Deputy Director in the Research Department responsible for the World Economic Outlook and Deputy Director in the Western Hemisphere Department. He holds a doctorate in economics from the University of Oxford and a BA from the University of Cambridge.

Mattia Coppo is a Research Officer in the Research Department at the IMF. He has worked as well in the IMF Institute of Capacity Development and Innovation Unit. Before joining the IMF, he has been working at the Royal Bank of Scotland as a risk analyst. He holds a MA in Economics from University College London and Higher School of Economics.

Thomas F. Cosimano is Professor Emeritus from the Mendoza College of Business at the University of a Non-resident Fellow at the Center for Global Development, Washington, D. C. He was Notre Dame. He was a Professor of Finance and Concurrent Professor of Economics and Mathematics at the University of Notre Dame, 1987–2016. He has been a Visiting Scholar at the Institute for Capacity Development until October 2019, International Monetary Fund from 2000–19.

Phil de Imus is a Senior Economist at the IMF's Middle East and Central Asia Department currently working on Somalia. The IMF is supporting the country's efforts to achieve debt relief under the Highly Indebted Poor Country Initiative. He previously worked on other countries and capital markets issues for the IMF. He spent the earlier part of his career at the Federal Reserve Bank of New York and the private sector and holds graduate degrees from the University of Chicago.

Ibrahim Elbadawi is Managing Director of the Economic Research Forum. Previously he was Minister of Finance and Economy of Sudan and he worked for the Dubai Economic Council and the World Bank. His research focuses on macroeconomic policy and foreign exchange rate policy. His latest book is *Understanding and Avoiding the Oil Curse in Resource-rich Arab Economies*, published by Cambridge University Press in 2016. Mr. Elbadawi holds a PhD in Statistics and Economics from North Carolina State University.

Michael O. Engman is a senior economist in the Finance, Competitiveness & Innovation Global Practice at the World Bank. His work covers trade, investment, and technology diffusion in Africa and South Asia. He previously covered trade and economic policy at the

Organisation for Economic Co-Operation and Development, the World Trade Organization, and the European Commission. He holds a PhD in international economics from Sciences-Po in Paris.

Lars Engstrom is a senior economist in the IMF African Department and member of the team covering Togo. He has a wide experience working on low-income and fragile African countries, including as the IMF Resident Representative for Rwanda and Burundi. Prior to this, he worked at the Swedish Ministry of Finance. He did his graduate studies in Economics at the University of Umeå, Sweden.

Ekkehard Ernst is Chief of the Macroeconomic Policies and Jobs Unit at the International Labour Organization, where he analyses the impact of technological change and macro policies on productivity, employment, wages, and inequality. His current focus is on understanding trends in the Future of Work. Together with his team he analyses how artificial intelligence, demographic shifts, globalization, climate change, and political vagaries might unfold in the world of work.

Raphael Espinoza is Deputy Division Chief at the IMF, in the Fiscal Affairs Department. He has worked on several crisis cases (Brexit, the euro crisis, IMF Stand-by Arrangment programs, etc.) as well as in the IMF Research Department and as Lecturer and Director of the Centre for the Study of Emerging Economies at University College, London. He has written a book on *The Macroeconomics of the Arab States of the Gulf* (Oxford University Press, 2013) and several papers on international macroeconomics and finance.

Connel Fullenkamp is Professor of the Practice of Economics and Director of the Economics Center for Teaching at Duke University in Durham, North Carolina. His research interests include the macroeconomic impacts of migrant remittances, financial market development, and financial regulation. He earned MA and PhD degrees in Economics from Harvard University.

Enrique Gelbard is Advisor at the African Department of the IMF and mission chief for Tanzania. Prior to that, he has worked as mission chief for several low- and middle-income countries and conducted analytical work on poverty reduction, fragile states, trade integration, exchange rates, and financial sector development. He obtained his post-graduate degrees in economics from the University of Toronto and Yale University.

Jose Gijon is IMF Resident Representative in Côte d'Ivoire. He has extensive experience working on low- and middle-income African and Middle Eastern countries. He also has expertise on financial sector issues and has previously been in academia and other international organizations. Mr. Gijon holds a PhD from Johns Hopkins University.

Mark Griffiths is the IMF's mission chief to Libya and to West Bank and Gaza. Previously he was mission chief to Georgia (2012–16), Latvia (2008–12) and Macedonia (2005–08). At the IMF he has worked on European transition economies, as well as the Thailand, Indonesia, and Turkey crisis programs. Before joining the IMF Mark held teaching positions at Exeter College, Oxford and at the Virginia Polytechnic Institute. He has a DPhil in Economics from Oxford University.

Sanjeev Gupta is a senior policy fellow at the Center for Global Development. Previously, he was deputy director of the Fiscal Affairs Department of the IMF and has worked in its

African and European Departments. Prior to joining the IMF, Mr. Gupta was a fellow of the Kiel Institute of World Economics, Germany; professor at the Administrative Staff College of India; and secretary of the Federation of Indian Chambers of Commerce and Industry. He has authored/coauthored over 150 papers, many of which are published in well-known academic journals, and has authored/coauthored/coedited 13 books.

Ermal Hitaj is a Senior Economist at the Economics and Market Analysis Department of the European Stability Mechanism. Prior to that he was an Economist in the IMF Strategy, Policy and Review Department, and Africa Department, where he worked on Mali and other West African countries.

Kareem Ismail is the IMF resident representative for Iraq and Yemen. He previously worked in the IMF's Strategy, Policy, and Review Department on emerging markets and low-income countries, and in the African department. During that time, he led the vulnerability exercise for low-income countries, helped design and implement programs including those in fragile states, and co-authored policy papers on IMF lending. He holds a PhD from Johns Hopkins University.

Kevin Kuruc is an assistant professor of economics at the University of Oklahoma. Prior to this, he was pursuing his graduate studies at the University of Texas at Austin where he earned his PhD in May of 2019. During his graduate studies, Professor Kuruc spent time working in, and then consulting for, the Independent Evaluation Office of the IMF.

Chris Lane is an Advisor in the IMF Strategy, Policy and Review Department and chairperson of the IMF Fragile States Task Team. His previous positions include IMF Special Representative to the United Nations, Chief of the Developing Markets Division, and Mission Chief to Liberia and to Mali.

Mario Mansour is the Coordinator of the IMF's Middle East Regional Technical Assistance Center, which provides advisory and capacity development services to IMF Middle East members. Prior to joining the Center in January 2019, Mr. Mansour was Deputy Chief of the Tax Policy Division at the IMF, where he managed the provision of tax policy technical assistance. Mr. Mansour has over 27 years of experience in policy advice and project management; he has advised on taxation in over 40 countries of all income levels and has published on a wide range of taxation issues. Before joining the IMF in 2004, he worked as a tax analyst at the Canadian Department of Finance, and with a private consultancy where he led taxation projects in the Eastern Caribbean and the Middle East.

Isaac Z. Martínez is currently studying his PhD in Economics at the London School of Economics and Political Science. He holds a MA in Economics from the Pontificia Universidad Católica de Chile, where he served as lecturer between 2017 and 2019. His research focuses on the empirical aspects of macroeconomic issues—including optimal fiscal rules, unemployment and salary levels, and employment dynamics in informal markets—as well as the adoption of institutions.

Paulomi Mehta is a research analyst at the IMF. She has worked extensively on projects related to IMF Programs such as the Review of Conditionality, the Low-Income Countries Facilities Review, the Review of Eligibility to Use Fund Facilities for Concessional Financing, and the Efficacy of Fund Programs in Fragile States.

Gary Milante is Programme Director for the Global Registry of Violent Deaths (GReVD) initiative at the Stockholm Director of Studies at the Stockholm International Peace Research Institute. His research deploys a wide array of methods, focusing on making complex problems accessible to policymakers and practitioners, especially as they pertain to the needs of fragile and conflict-affected states. He has served as an advisor to the United Nations, NATO, and various governments, and was lead economist on the *World Development Report 2011: Conflict, Security and Development*. He received his PhD in Economics from the University of California, Irvine.

Clara Mira is the IMF Resident Representative in Uganda. Before that, she held positions at the IMF African department, the IMF Executive Board, the Bank of Spain, and the European Commission. She has extensive experience on surveillance and program countries as well as on regional integration issues. She graduated from the College of Europe in Belgium and the University of Manchester.

Peter Montiel is the Fairleigh S. Dickinson Jr. '41 Professor of Economics at Williams College. He has also worked at the IMF and at the World Bank, and has served as a consultant for the African Development Bank, the Asian Development Bank, and the Inter-American Development Bank, as well as for several central banks. His research is on macroeconomic issues in developing countries. He has written several books and a number of papers in professional journals.

Hannes Mueller is a tenured researcher at the Institute for Economic Analysis (IAE(CSIC)) and an Associate Professor at the Barcelona Graduate School of Economics. His fields of interest are political economy, development economics, machine learning, and conflict studies. His work has been published in leading journals in economics and political science and he has provided expert opinion on fragility for the World Bank, the UN, and others. His recent work is using features extracted from text and satellite images to forecast and nowcast armed conflict and violence.

Anne Oeking is an economist in the IMF's Asia and Pacific Department, currently on an external assignment at the ASEAN+3 Macroeconomic Research Office in Singapore. She holds a Master's Degree in Economics from the University of Amsterdam and a PhD in Economics from the University of Duisburg-Essen, Germany. She has published on a range of topics, mainly in the field of international macroeconomics and international finance.

Sailendra Pattanayak is currently a Deputy Division Chief in the Fiscal Affairs Department of the IMF. He has extensive experience in the public financial management area and the wider public sector. Since joining the IMF in 2006, he has advised a wide range of countries, of all income levels, on public financial management and fiscal transparency. Before joining the IMF, he held senior positions in the Indian federal government, including at the ministry of finance. He has written several papers on public financial management and has led analytical projects at the IMF on a broad range of fiscal issues, including the development of standards and guidance material in the area of fiscal transparency.

Andrea F. Presbitero is Associate Professor of Economics at the Johns Hopkins University School of Advanced International Studies (SAIS) and member of the Money & Finance Research (MoFiR). He is on leave from the International Monetary Fund, where he was a

Senior Economist in the Research Department's Macro-Financial Division. He is an applied economist whose research covers financial intermediation, development finance, and international finance. His work has been published in the Review of Financial Studies, the Journal on International Economics, and the Journal of Development Economics. He is Associate Editor of the Journal of Financial Stability and Economia (LACEA).

Alexandros Ragoussis is a Senior Economist at the International Finance Corporation, World Bank Group, and a Fellow of the German Development Institute. In past years he has written extensively in the field of private sector development, and international economics and policy, and has held positions at the OECD and the German Development Institute, and taught economics at the University of Sydney and at Sciences-Po, Paris. He studied engineering and geography in Athens and Brussels, and holds a PhD in economics from the University of Sydney.

Gustavo Ramirez is an IMF Economist in the Middle East and Central Asia Department. He has worked on Yemen for the past 18 months. Prior to that, he worked on several sub-Saharan African countries, some of them in conflict or post-conflict. He has also worked on Latin American countries at the World Bank and the UN Economic Commission for Latin America and the Caribbean (ECLAC). He graduated from Georgetown University and is a Colombian national.

Thomas Risse is Professor of International Politics at the Otto Suhr Institute of Political Science, Freie Universität Berlin, Germany. His most recent publications include *Effective Governance Under Anarchy. Institutions, Legitimacy and Social Trust in Areas of Limited Statehood* (Cambridge University Press, 2021, with Tanja A. Börzel) and the *Oxford Handbook of Governance and Limited Statehood* (Oxford University Press, 2018, ed. with Tanja A. Börzel and Anke Draude). Risse received his PhD in political science in 1987 from the University of Frankfurt, Germany. He has taught in the United States at Cornell, Yale, Stanford, and Harvard universities as well as the University of Wyoming, in Europe at the University of Konstanz, Germany, and the European University Institute, Florence, Italy.

James A. Robinson is a University Professor at the Harris School for Public Policy, one of only nine University Professors at the University of Chicago. He is also Institute Director at The Pearson Institute for the Study and Resolution of Global Conflicts. He is co-author with Daron Acemoglu of *Economic Origins of Dictatorship and Democracy* and *Why Nations Fail.* Their latest book is *The Narrow Corridor* (2020).

Daouda Sembene is a Distinguished Nonresident Fellow at the Center for Global Development. He served as a senior economic advisor to the President of Senegal. He was previously an Executive Director of the IMF, where he represented 23 African countries. He began his career at the World Bank in Washington, before joining the IMF. His research interests include: poverty, growth, fragility, trust, development finance and global governance. He holds a PhD in development economics from American University. He co-edited and contributed to the book *Race to the Next Income Frontier—How Senegal and Other Low-Income Countries Can Reach the Finish Line* (IMF, 2018).

Raimundo Soto is associate professor of economics, Pontificia Universidad Católica de Chile. He received his PhD in Economics from Georgetown University. Professor Soto has published extensively on long-term growth, resource curse, institutions, and exchange rate misalignment. His current research focuses on policy reforms in conflict-affected countries. His volume on *The Economy of Dubai* was published by Oxford University Press in 2016. He served as president of the Chilean Economic Association between 2009 and 2010.

Shinji Takagi is Distinguished Research Professor at the Asian Growth Research Institute, Kitakyushu, Japan and Professor Emeritus of Economic at Osaka University. From 2013 to 2018, he was Assistant Director at the IMF's Independent Evaluation Office, where he managed projects to evaluate, among other things, the IMF's engagement in fragile states and the euro area crisis. Professor Takagi obtained his PhD in economics from the University of Rochester.

Robert Tchaidze a national of Georgia, joined the IMF in 2002. He has worked on a wide range of countries and issues, and currently is a Resident Representative in West Bank and Gaza. He taught at the International School of Economics in Tbilisi, Georgia in 2007–9 and has been a member of its Governing Board since then. He holds a PhD in Economics from Johns Hopkins University.

Rima Turk is a Senior Economist in the IMF Strategy, Policy and Review Department. Before that, she was a tenured Associate Professor in finance at the Lebanese American University. Her cross-country research on macro-financial linkages, the bank competition-stability nexus, and corporate governance, among others, is published in peer-reviewed journals.

James Wilson hold a PhD from the University of Oxford, where his research concentrated on the CFA Franc monetary zones in Western and Central Africa. Prior to this, he spent five years working at Soros Fund Management as an investment analyst looking at the global financial sector. He received a BA and MPhil in Economics from the University of Cambridge.

Michael Woolcock is Lead Social Scientist in the World Bank's Development Research Group, where he has worked since 1998. For 14 of these years he also been a (part-time) Lecturer in Public Policy at Harvard Kennedy School of Government. His research explores the various ways in which social institutions interact with development outcomes; its current focus is on strategies for enhancing implementation capability and assessing complex interventions. An Australian national, he has a PhD in Sociology from Brown University.

List of Illustrations

Figures

Tables

Boxes

1

Macroeconomic Policy Issues in Fragile States

A Framework

Ralph Chami, Mattia Coppo, Raphael Espinoza, and Peter Montiel

1. What Is Fragility?

State fragility is one of the most pressing development challenges of our time. About half of the world population living in extreme poverty resides in fragile states. Fragile states could also be among the worst affected by the COVID-19 crisis, increasing the risk of conflict and instability. Motivated by this, several organizations have been pushing a research agenda to understand how state fragility must be accounted for in the design of policies: see for example OECD (2013); World Bank (2011); United Nations-World Bank (2018); IMF (2018); LSE-Oxford Commission on State Fragility, Growth and Development (2018). The objective of this volume is to bring this research to the area of macroeconomic policy, which has received less attention.

In broadest conceptual terms, the concept of state fragility, which has come into widespread use by both the international community and academics, refers to a situation in which a country's governmental apparatus is of limited effectiveness in delivering a broad range of public services. However, the concept of "limited effectiveness" is vague and can cover a broad range of state limitations. Indeed, no state has ever existed that can be described as fully effective; every state can, in principle, be placed along a continuum of effectiveness. At one extreme of what is observed are states in the high-income countries of Northern Europe that continually top the charts of international governance indicators. At the other are completely "failed" states, a term that refers to situations in which a country's central authority has completely broken down, in the sense that it lacks the coercive power to enforce national laws and that it fails to provide even the most basic of public goods at the national level, chief among them being security of person and property.

The views expressed in this chapter are those of the authors and do not necessarily represent the views of the IMF, its Executive Board, or IMF management.

Ralph Chami, Mattia Coppo, Raphael Espinoza, and Peter Montiel, *Macroeconomic Policy Issues in Fragile States: A Framework* In: *Macroeconomic Policy in Fragile States*. Edited by: Ralph Chami, Raphael Espinoza, and Peter Montiel, Oxford University Press (2021).
DOI: 10.1093/oso/9780198853091.003.0001

Indeed, the provision of security through a monopoly of the legitimate use of force is what Weber identified as the defining characteristic of the state. But other roles of the state are surely relevant in assessing state effectiveness. At a minimum, we would include among these the provision of essential public goods that promote social cooperation (a well-defined corpus of effectively enforced laws that are perceived as fair and as consistent with an acceptable level of personal freedom), that provide a modicum of social insurance (for example, disaster relief), and that create the conditions for economic prosperity (for example, the provision of physical infrastructure as well as the infrastructure for health and education). We therefore define "failed" states as those that fail to deliver along all four of these dimensions.[1]

From our perspective, it is this "failed state" extreme that gives meaning to the notion of state fragility. Fragility is a derivative term defined by reference to potential state failure; that is, *a fragile state is one that faces a high probability of becoming a failed one*, typically as the result of civil conflict.[2] A fragile state is therefore not necessarily an ineffectual one; while a state's inability to deliver basic public goods may certainly be grounds for citizen disaffection and therefore for social upheaval, a repressive state that minimizes crime and makes the trains run on time may only temporarily be suppressing a social explosion. Fragility therefore arises when the central authority is perceived as illegitimate either because it is ineffectual or repressive, when the underlying conditions exist for the central authority to be challenged, and when the results of that challenge are likely to result in civil conflict that culminates in state failure.

It is worth noting that the usefulness of the concept of state fragility has not been without its critics, and that the distinction between fragility and failure has not always been clearly drawn. In Chapter 4, for example, Risse questions the usefulness of the concept, and argues for a distinction between fragility and limited governance, showing that limited state capacity at the national level may not necessarily coincide with widespread governance failures within a country's territory, and also that pockets of governance failures can exist in what are normally considered to be highly capable states.

There is also no general consensus on the specific definition of state failure which, as we have indicated, we take to be the concept ultimately underlying the notion of fragility. In the literature, for example, the term "failed state" is often used as a synonym for a fragile or weak state, and even when failure has been

[1] Our four-dimensional definition is similar to that of the OECD (2009), which defines failed states as "countries that lack the essential capacity and/or will to fulfil four sets of critical government responsibilities: fostering an environment conducive to sustainable and equitable economic growth; establishing and maintaining legitimate, transparent, and accountable political institutions; securing their populations from violent conflict and controlling their territory; and meeting the basic human needs of their population."

[2] Stewart and Brown (2010), as well as Mueller (2018), interpret fragility as meaning that a state is at risk of failure and thus as a concept that indicates future risks.

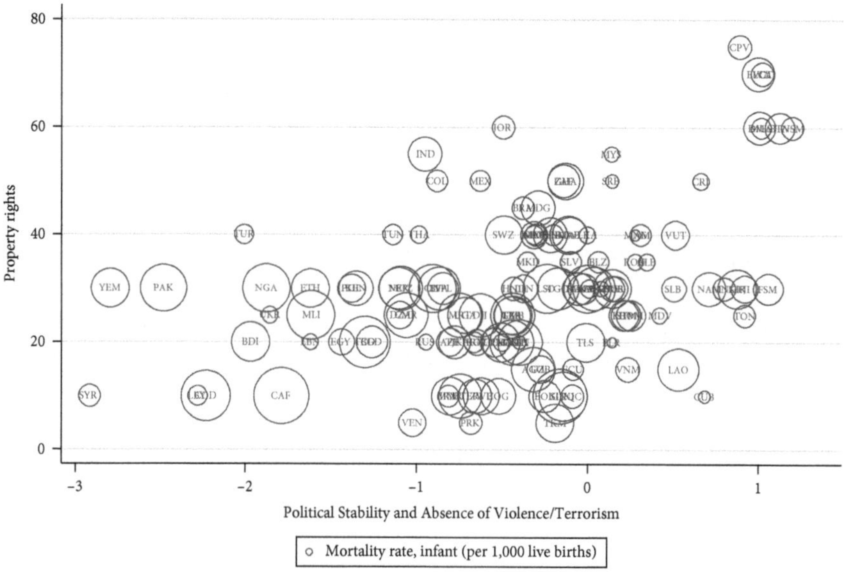

Only low- and middle-income countries included
1990–2016 averages.
The size of the bubble corresponds to the average mortality rate in the period

Figure 1.1 Relationship between Different Indicators of State Capacity
Source: World Development Indicators

identified as the worst extreme in the fragility continuum, it is not always made clear whether this refers to one, some, or all of the dimensions (for example, institutional or economic) along which state ineffectiveness can manifest itself. We note in passing that the importance of this latter point can be exaggerated, because the dimensions of state failure identified in the literature tend to be associated with each other. For example, when we use (1) the World Bank Political Stability and Absence of Violence/Terrorism Estimate as a proxy for security, (2) the infant mortality rate as a proxy for the provision of basic public goods such as health and education, and (3) property rights as a proxy for the quality of economic institutions, we find that there is a strong correlation among them that persists through time (Figure 1.1).[3] Despite these concerns, it is fair to say that a consensus has emerged on the views both that fragility is best

[3] Similarly, Besley and Persson (2014) show that three important aspects of development—the absence of political violence, state capacity (measured as an equally weighted sum of fiscal capacity, legal capacity, and collective capacity), and per capita income—are correlated with each other at the country level, as the result of common economic, political, and social drivers and two-way positive feedbacks.

understood as a multifaceted concept that encompasses multiple dimensions of the state and society, and that fragility and failure are indeed distinct concepts.[4]

Susceptibility to state failure clearly poses severe challenges for social policy. If fragility reflects an ineffective state, then the crucial challenges are how to improve state effectiveness and how to implement desirable policies with an ineffective government. If it instead arises because a repressive state is precariously keeping the lid on a potentially explosive social situation, then the challenge becomes how to design policies that can improve social wellbeing without potentially blowing the lid off the social cauldron. Because the social costs of state failure are so high (see United Nations-World Bank, 2018), an overriding concern is reducing fragility, either by improving state effectiveness if the first case applies, or by adopting measures intended to alleviate social tensions in the second case.

The set of policies in question potentially includes policies of very different types, including reform of the security apparatus, of political and economic institutions, legal and judicial reforms, civil service reform, social policies addressing the needs of disadvantaged populations, and more narrowly economic policies intended to promote economic prosperity. Risse (Chapter 4) argues that the priority should be on governance-building, which focuses on results and outcomes, rather than on institutions, because blueprints for these are rarely available and "Western'" blueprints also assume a consolidated statehood.

Several of these issues are addressed in this book, although its main focus is on macroeconomic policies—broadly understood—in fragile states.[5] Its intent is to explore both what is desirable and what may be possible in designing a wide range of such policies in countries that suffer from state fragility. Its perspective is that the fragile context creates special circumstances that require modifications to conventional policy advice, perhaps because macroeconomic institutions have to be constructed from the ground up, perhaps because existing institutions lack credibility and/or implementation capacity, perhaps because social tensions limit the range of specific policies that can be considered, perhaps because persistent fragility has created urgent social needs that call for drastic rethinking of policy priorities.

Moreover, every fragile situation is likely to be different, suggesting that considerations such as those just listed will differ from country to country. How to tailor policy design to idiosyncratic country contexts is therefore a recurring challenge in fragile states. Using the words of Carment et al. (2011),

[4] Carment at al. (2011), for example, distinguish between first-generation studies on fragility, which identified fragility with conflict, and second-generation approaches which recognize that fragility is a multi-faced concept that may be analytically useful in non-conflict situations.

[5] The reader is referred to other volumes for a discussion of post-conflict peace operations (Paris and Sisk, 2009), for proposals for civil service reform (UNDP, 2018), for economic reconstruction (del Castillo, 2008), for the analysis of political and economic institutions to reduce conflict (Collier, 2009), and for social and development policy (World Bank, 2011; Naudé et al., 2011).

"understanding of context in fragile states is a prerequisite of effective and properly sequenced engagement, an indication that fragility manifests itself in different forms that require different types of intervention."

In the remainder of this chapter we examine some empirical indicators that have been employed to identify and measure fragility, review some stylized facts of macroeconomic performance in fragile states, examine the broad range of challenges that fragility poses for macroeconomic policy, and summarize the policy lessons that emerge from the volume.

2. Measuring Fragility

The two main indicators of state fragility used by researchers—and by the contributors to this volume—are the Country Policy and Institutional Assessment (CPIA) index of the World Bank and the Fragile States Index published by the Fund for Peace and Foreign Policy.

The World Bank defines fragility as a severe development challenge that encompasses weak institutional capacity, poor governance, and political instability, often linked to conflict and violence (World Bank, 2010). The CPIA thus rates 73 countries against a set of 16 criteria grouped in four clusters: (i) economic management; (ii) structural policies; (iii) policies for social inclusion and equity; and (iv) public sector management and institutions. The criteria are focused on "the key factors that foster growth and poverty reduction, with the need to avoid undue burden on the assessment process" (World Bank, 2016). Annual data have been publicly available since 2005; however, an index to allocate resources to low-income countries, the International Development Association (IDA) Resource Allocation Index, has been used internally at the World Bank since the 1990s. The index was not originally designed to serve as an indicator of state fragility (Rocha De Siqueira, 2014), but extended use for that purpose by donors has made it an anchor for fragile state analysis. The World Bank's Harmonized List of Fragile Situations, that is also the basis for the African Development Bank, Asian Development Bank, and IMF lists of fragile states, is made of the countries with a CPIA score below 3.2 or of countries where peacekeeping operations are ongoing.

The second widely used indicator is the Fragile States Index (FSI), which consists of five groups of indicators that are collected through a proprietary tool, the Conflict Assessment System Tool (CAST). After extensive content analysis, data produced by the CAST are assessed and reviewed by experts. Its main advantage is that content analysis allows "measurement of concepts that are difficult to measure with other methods, especially in the area of fragile states" (Fabra Mata and Ziaja, 2009). Other, less widely used indicators are also available, and are summarized in Table 1.1 (see also Fabra Mata and Ziaja, 2009, for a comprehensive review of indictors of fragility).

Table 1.1 Fragility Indicators Overview

	Starting date	Frequency	Country coverage	Concept measured and its definition
CPIA (World Bank)	2005	Annually	95 economies (includes regions, and income levels)	*Fragile states:* "... the term used for countries facing particularly severe development challenges: weak institutional capacity, poor governance, and political instability. Often these countries experience ongoing violence as the residue of past severe conflict." (World Bank, 2010)
Fragile/Failed State Index (Fund for Peace)	2006	Annually	178 countries	*State failure:* "A state that is failing has several attributes. One of the most common is the loss of physical control of its territory or a monopoly on the legitimate use of force. Other attributes of state failure include the erosion of legitimate authority to make collective decisions, an inability to provide reasonable public services, and the inability to interact with other states as a full member of the international community." (Fund for Peace, 2009)
State Fragility Index (Centre for systemic peace)	1995	Annually	167 countries with populations greater than 500,000 in 2017	*State fragility:* "The State Fragility Index and Matrix [...] rates each country according to its level of fragility in both effectiveness and legitimacy across four dimensions: security, governance, economic development, and social development."
the Index of State Weakness in the Developing World (Brookings Institution)	2008	One off	141	*State weakness:* "We define weak states as countries that lack the essential capacity and/or will to fulfill four sets of critical government responsibilities: fostering an environment conducive to sustainable and equitable economic growth; establishing and maintaining legitimate, transparent, and accountable political institutions; securing their populations from violent conflict and controlling their territory; and meeting the basic human needs of their population." (Rice and Patrick, 2008, p. 3)
Global Conflict Risk Index (European Commission)	2016	Every 6 months	138	

OECD Fragility Framework Authority Legitimacy and Capacity framework	2015	biannual—intermittent	58		
CIFP Fragility Index (Country Indicators for Foreign Policy)	2007	One off	192		*Fragility:* "Fragility is a measure of the extent to which the actual institutions, functions, and processes of a state fail to accord with the strong image of a sovereign state, the one reified in both state theory and international law." (Carment et al., 2011, p. 84)
Peace and Conflict Instability Ledger (University of Maryland's Center for International Development and Conflict Management)	2008	2008 and 2010	160		*State instability:* "[E]vents that create significant challenges to the stability of states. These include revolutionary wars, ethnic wars, adverse regime changes, and genocides or politicides." (Hewitt et al. 2008, p. 5)

Source: Ziaja, 2012.

Although many authors recognize the value for social scientists of indices that measure fragility, common critiques are that the underpinnings of the measurements are often not supported by the literature and that they tend to confuse symptoms and causes (Besley and Persson, 2011). For example, it is unclear whether variables such as child mortality or conflict should be used to measure fragility, when they might actually be a consequence of fragility instead (Ferreira, 2017; Glawion et al., 2019). Moreover, it is ambiguous whether "the fragility captured in these indices is attributed to the society as a whole or only to the state and its institutions" (Khan, 2017) and if it should be "measured on an absolute scale or [. . .] relative to a society's expectations" (Ziaja, 2012).

In addition, though these indices tend to agree on which countries should be at the top or at the bottom of the list, the situation in the middle of the rankings is more fuzzy (Gutiérrez et al., 2011). This problem might stem from a too simplistic aggregation of several hardly unidimensional sub-indicators, which are assigned the same weight without considering which of them are "necessary" or "sufficient" conditions, or considering how one category—for example, factors related to the strength of the economy—may be able to compensate for shortcomings in other categories, such as violence (Fabra Mata and Ziaja, 2009; Nay, 2013; Glawion et al., 2019). Certain indices are time-invariant and do not anticipate deterioration of conditions, but rank countries as fragile according to past failures (Ziaja, 2012; Mueller, 2018). Other critiques revolve around subjectivity and cultural bias inherent to the selection of the sub-indicators, often lacking theoretical underpinnings, with choices narrowed down because of lack of data availability (Fabra Mata and Ziaja, 2009; Ziaja, 2012).

Different country coverage and time span make comparison difficult, but in Figure 1.2 we document the correlation between some of the indicators. Fabra and Ziaja (2009) argue that the high correlation among these indices "reflects that, within their conceptual boundaries, they do measure some aspects of 'state fragility,'" but another reason could be that these indicators often use similar data sources.

It is finally worth recalling that most of these indicators are in an "infant" stage, and they come with "cautionary notes warning against the immediate transfer of index scores into policies" (Faust et al., 2015). It is therefore necessary to know the context and the information used before aggregation, because fragility is a multidimensional concept that can hardly be reduced to a simple raw number. Nevertheless, as Glawion et al. (2015) point out, these indicators still have a discursive value, which can help to "create order and steer priorities."

Using different indicators, it appears that the number of fragile states has remained roughly constant or has even increased. There is also wide agreement on the view that fragility tends to be a persistent phenomenon: few countries graduate from fragility. Figure 1.3 also shows that state fragility manifests itself in all parts of the globe, including Africa, the Middle East, Oceania, and Southeast Asia and at both middle- and low-income levels.

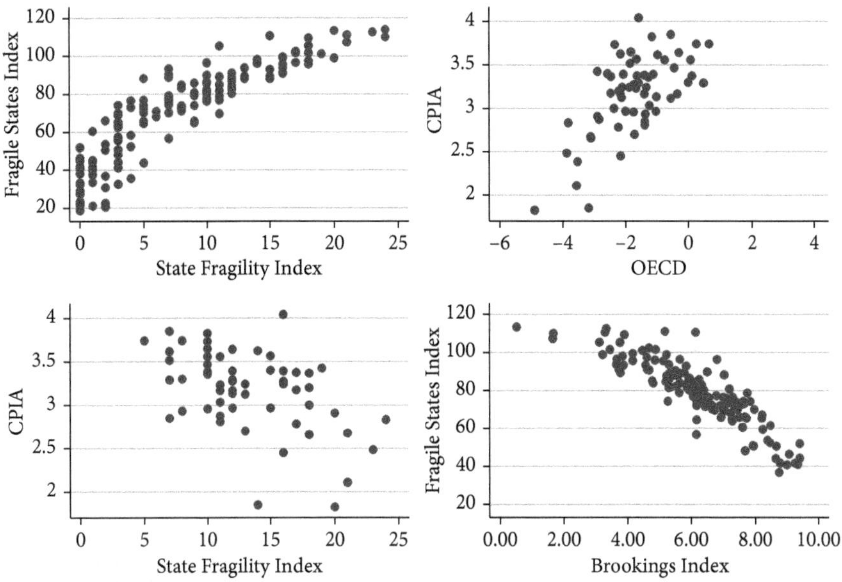

Figure 1.2 Fragile Indicators Correlations

Source: World Development Indicators Country Policy and Institutional Assessment, 2019; Fund for Peace fragile state index, 2019; Brookings Index of State Weakness in the Developing World, 2019; Centre for Systemic Peace State fragility index, 2019; OECD state of fragility report, 2019

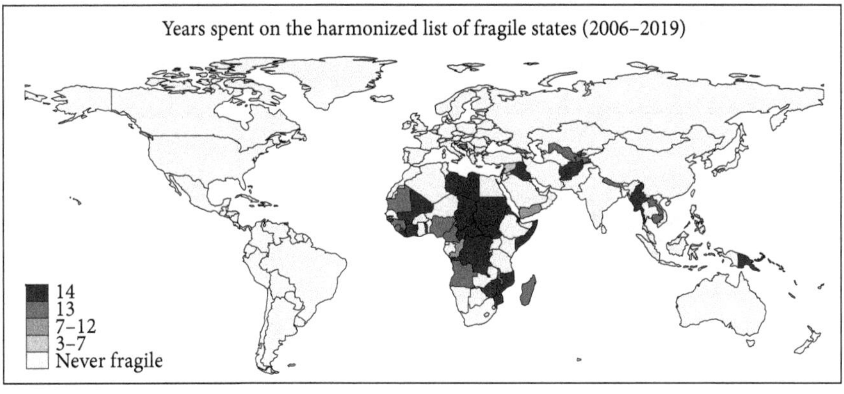

Figure 1.3 Time Spent Being Fragile

(World Bank, 2019 http://pubdocs.worldbank.org/en/709631582764857310/FCSListFY06toFY19.pdf)

3. Macroeconomic Characteristics of Fragile States

State fragility can be both a cause and an outcome of weak governance and poor macroeconomic performance. Institutional quality is correlated with fragility and with income (Figure 1.4.C). Risse (Chapter 4) and Sembene (Chapter 5) highlight

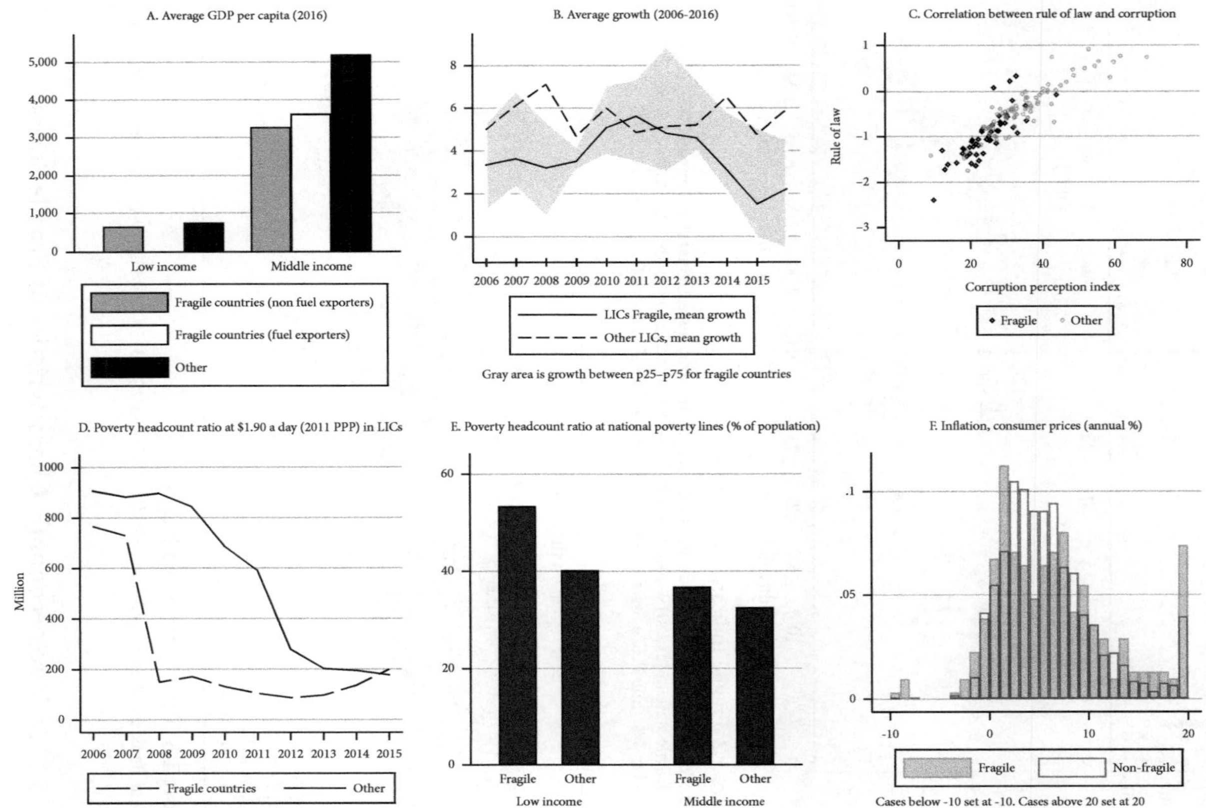

Figure 1.4 Macroeconomic Characteristics of Fragile States

Source: World Bank, IMF, and authors' calculations.

the importance of institutions. In fact, Risse notes that an appropriate institutional setting coupled with social trust and legitimacy can be sufficient for the delivery of public goods, even in the presence of a weak state apparatus. This is why more than half of people living in conditions of extreme poverty now live in fragile states (Figure 1.4.D). Without seeking to demonstrate causality, this section presents a few stylized facts that highlight the poor performance suffered by fragile states.

First, within specific income groups, fragile states are poorer in per capita terms than nonfragile states in the same income group—that is, they tend to be located at the lower end of the income distribution for the group. Not surprisingly, therefore, as shown in Figure 1.4. A–B below, low-income fragile states have lower GDP per capita and tended to grow at lower rates on average than even other low-income countries. Macroeconomic conditions can also be more unstable, as witnessed by the more frequent occurrence of high inflation (Figure 1.4.F) and high growth volatility (Assaf, Engman, Ragoussis, and Agrawal, Chapter 6). As we argue later, a fragility trap tends to reinforce the low-income trap.

The roots of this weak performance may reflect both the countries' economic structure as well as poor domestic policies. Fragile states rely heavily on commodity production for export. Fragile states' exports are thus less sophisticated, with lower value added, and more subject to fluctuations in the terms of trade (Elbadawi, Soto, and Martinez, Chapter 14). In addition, the formal sector tends to be small as a share of the economy, and in turn to consist largely of small firms that are unable to exploit economies of scale. Firms suffer more frequently from power outages, from water insufficiency, and from the need to cover security costs, and even then, losses to crime and theft are more common (Assaf and others, Chapter 6). Entrepreneurship is thus generally weak in fragile situations. Enterprises tend to be younger and tend to start operations without formal registration, which can be explained by the high costs of registering a company. Thus, three-quarters of workers operate in the informal sector, either as self-employed or as employees in informal micro and small enterprises (Chapter 6). As a result, fragile states tend to have small, or almost nonexistent, middle classes.

Weak state capacity is most obvious when the size of government revenues and government spending is measured. Governments in fragile states have difficulty collecting taxes (Figure 1.5.A) and they rely heavily on commodity revenues, especially in middle-income countries (Figure 1.5.B). Though all low-income countries raise a large share of their revenues from import duties, fragile countries rely differentially more on such duties. The chapters by Besley and Mueller (Chapter 9), Milante and Woolcock (Chapter 10) and Baer, Gupta, Mansour, and Pattanayak (Chapter 11) provide a wealth of additional facts on the fiscal performance of fragile states.

At the same time, the political demands arising from fragility create spending pressures in the form of a large and downward-inflexible government wage bill, for military spending but not only (Figure 1.5.C). Spending tends to be politically

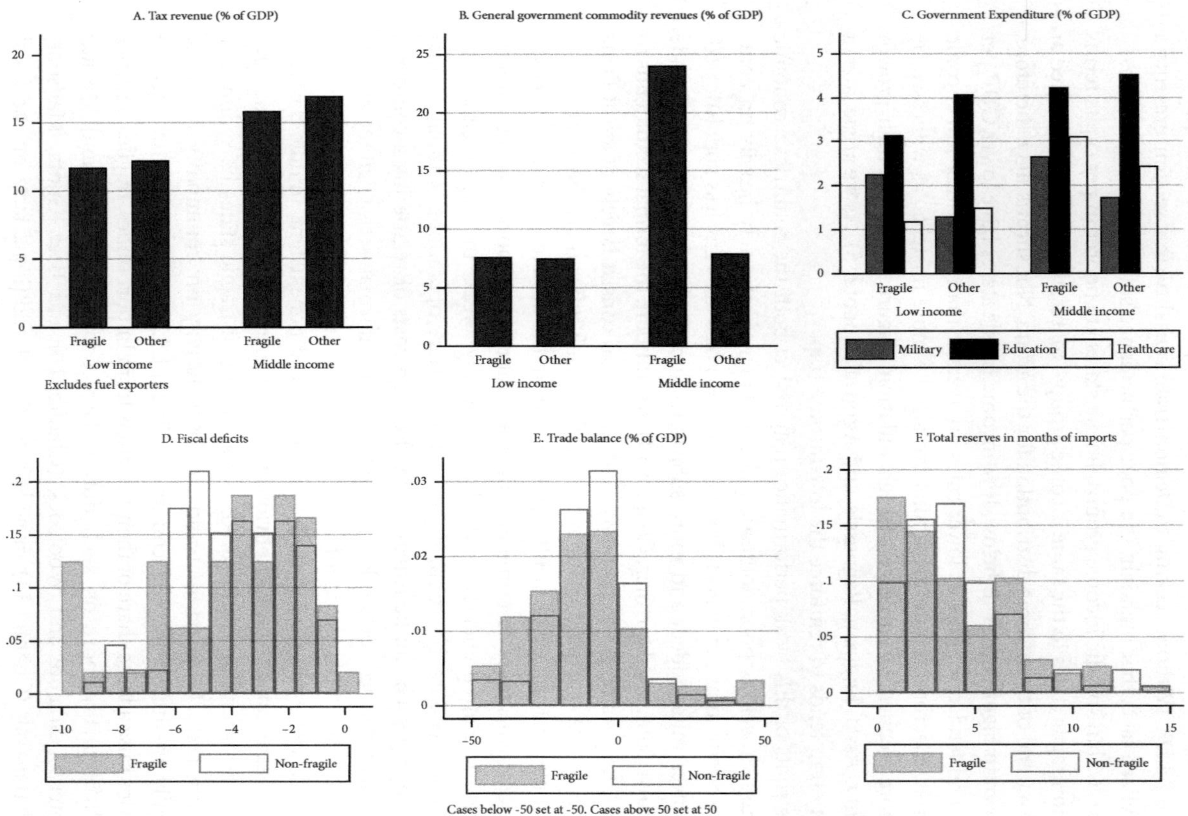

Figure 1.5 Fiscal and External Situation in Fragile States

Source: World Bank, IMF, and authors' calculations.

difficult to contract when fiscal resources become scarce, resulting is a strong pro-deficit bias that is restrained chiefly by the availability of external grants and concessionary financing. This situation can lead to more extreme fiscal and external deficits (Figure 1.5.D–F).

It is thus unsurprising that the financial sector in these countries is underdeveloped. In Chapter 7 in this volume, Barajas, Chami, and Fullenkamp find that fragile states show on average lower levels of financial development than other countries: bank credit to the private sector is 20 percentage points of GDP lower in fragile states; stock markets in fragile states are half the size of those in other countries; access to banking by households and firms is about half of what it is in the rest of the world. Risk-averse banks in fragile states seem to shun long-term investments and prefer lending to the government as well as short-term financing of working capital for select borrowers. Banks in fragile situations tend to demand high levels of collateral in lending to the private sector. Reflecting these characteristics, interest rates on loans to the private sector tend to be high in fragile situations (Assaf and others, Chapter 6).

Finally, fragile states have weaker and more volatile external positions. They tend to receive significantly less foreign direct investment (FDI) as a share of GDP than other low-income countries, and half of FDI flows to fragile states are concentrated on the top 10 recipients (Lomoriello, 2018). Remittances accounted for 45 percent of total financial flows to fragile states, but again the top five recipients received 70 percent of all remittances. Official Development Assistance (ODA) is also a major source of external flows in fragile states, representing up to 10 percent of GDP in some cases (Caselli and Presbitero, Chapter 16). Chami, Ernst, Fullenkamp, and Oeking (Chapter 15) find that while remittance flows to fragile countries have been relatively stable, ODA and FDI flows have been quite volatile, potentially heightening vulnerability to external shocks in fragile states through this mechanism.

4. Macroeconomic Policy Challenges in Fragile States

The previous section highlighted some stylized facts showing how extreme the economic situation of fragile states can be. However, weaker economic conditions do not necessarily require changing theories and principles of policy making. An important question is thus: does fragility per se pose specific macroeconomic policy challenges beyond those that are associated with low incomes or with commodity dependence? Evidence from the IMF, which is the organization with the most experience of macroeconomic programs, strongly supports a positive answer to this question:

Based on a sample drawn from the IMF's 2018 *Review of Conditionality*, Collyns, Kuruc, and Takagi (Chapter 17 in this volume) show that programs implemented in fragile countries have lower completion rates and weaker performance on structural reform objectives than those in nonfragile countries at similar income levels. Performance is especially weak in growth and inflation outcomes, because fragile states are less likely to meet the targets agreed under the program.

Reasons for such discrepancy can be found in another chapter in this volume; Lane, Turk, Hitaj and Mehta (Chapter 18) present evidence that concessional programs did not work well in fragile states, in particular because of civil unrest and/or coups d'état. They argue that the challenging political environment is the reason that prior actions and other types of ex ante conditionality tend to reduce the probability of program completion for fragile states.

The difference in performance could be due to the effect of both macroeconomic conditions as well as broader political and governance factors. Starting with the latter, conflict over rents can frustrate structural economic reforms (Acemoglu and Robinson, Chapter 2). A poor general institutional environment, political fractionalization, a production structure that makes the economy especially susceptible to large shocks, coupled with weakened coping mechanisms in the private sector, and poor macroeconomic institutions (including obscure and unstable budgetary processes and a central bank with limited resources and capacity, both of which are likely to be associated with low credibility of macro policies), also suggest that the macroeconomic stabilization challenges in fragile states would tend to be especially severe.

Turning to macroeconomic factors, the evidence shown in this volume is that fragility changes the way the macroeconomy operates. Specifically, fragility influences the impact of financial flows on macroeconomic outcomes—a key element in any stabilization program—as would be expected, given earlier findings that the effects of flows depend on the structure of the economy (Chami and others, Chapter 15). In particular:

- ODA leads to growth accelerations in nonfragile countries, but not in fragile states.
- Remittances, which lower the frequency of growth accelerations and increase that of employment slowdowns in nonfragile countries, fail to have either of those effects in fragile states.
- The effect of FDI and ODA on inequality and poverty in fragile countries is favorable, but less so than in nonfragile countries, and remittances have no impact on these variables in fragile contexts.
- In nonfragile countries, FDI, ODA, and remittances all influence the sectoral allocation of employment (FDI increases employment in manufacturing; ODA and remittances increase employment in construction and public service), but those effects are absent in fragile states.

Finally, fragility also influences outcomes at the microeconomic level, with macroeconomic consequences (Assaf and others, Chapter 6). Efficiency issues exist both for private and public investment: the empirical analysis in Caselli and Presbitero (Chapter 16) shows that fragility is consistently associated with a lower probability of project success, even controlling for project and country factors and a large set of fixed effects.

5. A Framework to Understand Fragility

But why exactly do fragile states pose special macroeconomic challenges? The answer to this question appears to be that fragile states tend to find themselves in a self-reinforcing *fragility trap* that is a special and more severe case of a poverty trap. Though certainly not all countries that were poor, say, at the end of the Second World War have remained poor, remaining poor appears to be the most likely outcome for poor countries (Quah, 1993). One interpretation of this experience is that there exist vicious circles (*poverty traps*) that link low incomes back to an inability to grow. Although the evidence for poverty traps is not very conclusive (Easterly, 2006), several economic theories have been particularly influential (see also gray circle in Figure 1.6): [6]

(i) Escaping poverty requires investment, but funds are lacking when incomes and savings are low, when risks are high, and when access to external finance is limited (Kuznets, 1966; Sachs, 2005; Galor and Zeira, 1993);

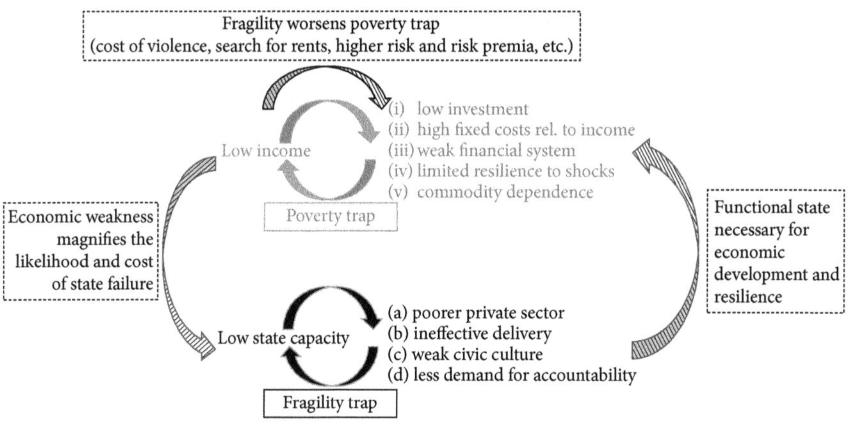

Figure 1.6 The Poverty Trap and the Fragility Trap

[6] Azariadis and Stachurski (2005) provide a survey of this literature.

(ii) Increasing returns to scale are essential to long-term growth (Romer, 1986; Lucas Jr., 1993), but the large fixed costs that must be incurred to take advantage of economies of scale make it difficult to start on this path at low initial income levels (Rosenstein-Rodan, 1943: Murphy et al., 1989);
(iii) The financial system is weaker in poorer countries, but the capacity for the financial system to lend is also essential for agents to invest and for economies to grow (King and Levine, 1993; de Gregorio, 1993).
(iv) Economic shocks lead to setbacks which can be persistent (Ramey and Ramey, 1995), and resilience is difficult to build at low income levels;
(v) Poverty tends to create commodity dependence, and commodity prices tend to suffer from secular declines (Prebish, 1950; Singer, 1950; Harvey et al., 2010) as well as from extensive volatility.

The fragility trap can be thought of as a second vicious circle, one that focuses specifically on the relationship between the state and society (see black circle in Figure 1.6).[7] The trap emerges because state capacity requires at least the voluntary cooperation, and in many cases the active engagement, of the citizenry in state-building activity, including paying taxes and developing accountability mechanisms. Because this engagement is costly to the private sector, it will be forthcoming only when society expects the state to act in the public interest by fulfilling its function of delivering public goods. If it fails to do so, it will lose legitimacy and with it the support of the public, which in turn makes it difficult for the state to deliver public goods, thereby further undermining its legitimacy, and so on. Several theories of the fragility trap are discussed in this volume:

(a) The theory of endogenous fiscal capacity (Besley and Persson, 2013; Besley and Mueller in Chapter 9) emphasizes that investments in state structures (such as monitoring, administration, compliance) depend on economics, on institutions, and on the extent to which the government benefits from a growing private economy.
(b) The "long route of accountability" argues that state capacity depends on the feedback loop between the citizenry's support for state building (via taxes but also politics), the quality of "compacts" with public goods providers, and effective delivery (World Bank, 2004). This feedback loop can become vicious if "leakages" (graft, corruption, state capture) weaken its different links (Milante and Woolcock in this volume).

[7] The fragility trap is closely related to the conflict trap, identified by Collier et al. (2004). But as mentioned earlier, conflict is a *realization* of the risk implicit in the concept of fragility. As a result, fragility is a broader concept than conflict, and thus the fragility trap is also broader than the conflict trap.

(c) The civic culture hypothesis underlines how coordination issues between agents affect the efficiency of the state as well as the relationship between state and society (Collier in Chapter 3; Bisin and Verdier, 2017).
(d) The Red Queen theory argues that a state builds its authority and society increases its demand for accountability when the contest for power between the two actors is on a balanced path, with neither the state nor society eventually dominating in the contest (Acemoglu and Robinson in Chapter 2; Acemoglu and Robinson, 2019).

The key to the challenges posed by fragility is that the two vicious circles are likely to interact in ways that magnify the difficulty of escaping the traps they pose. To see how, extend the standard poverty trap in the top part of the figure by incorporating the role of fragility. Fragility is likely to reinforce the poverty trap by increasing risks in the economic environment, increasing the operational costs of enterprises, and promoting a search for rents as an alternative to low-yielding productive activity. This additional clockwise arrow (hatched arrow) on the top of the loop illustrates that theories (i) to (v) are magnified by the link between political instability and economic weakness. Several chapters of this book (Adam and Wilson; Assaf, Engman, Ragoussis, and Agrawal; Elbadawi, Soto and Martinez; Barajas, Chami, and Fullenkamp) indeed argue that low or inefficient investment, high fixed costs relative to income, economic volatility, weak financial systems, and commodity dependence are all likely to be magnified by political instability.

Because a functional state is necessary for development and resilience, when a country is caught in a fragility trap the weakness of the state magnifies the poverty trap through its effects on political uncertainty and instability. Thus, the fragility trap at the bottom of the figure affects the poverty trap at the top. This feedback from fragility to poverty is captured by the hatched counterclockwise arrow on the right-hand side of the figure. But because economic weakness magnifies the problem of low state capacity by making it more difficult for the state to muster the resources with which to operate, the poverty trap in turn tends to magnify the severity of the fragility trap. This influence is captured by the hatched counter-clockwise arrow on the left-hand side of the figure, running from the poverty trap to the fragility trap.[8]

The macroeconomic policy challenge facing fragile states is thus especially severe because the low-welfare situation in which these economies find themselves

[8] This presentation is related to earlier discussions of the poverty trap. For instance, Collier (2007) and Acemoglu (2009, Ch. 4) include economic explanations (geography, natural resources) as well as political economy theories (conflict trap; institutional theories) of the poverty trap. The vicious circle presented by the LSE-Oxford Commission on State Fragility, Growth and Development (2018) links in one circular loop the interdependencies insecurity → weak economy → vulnerability to shocks → fractured societies → distrusted governments → weak institutions, and back to insecurity. Besley and Mueller also note in their chapter that "many of the dimensions reinforce each other but there is no obvious clear-cut causal structure."

is sustained by several strong self-reinforcing mechanisms. To better understand the nature of this challenge, it is useful to dig into what is meant exactly by vicious circles and traps. The notion of a vicious circle refers to the process by which multiple iterations over the loop lead to convergence to an *equilibrium*: when the iteration over the loop is done many times, it doesn't matter what the starting point is. The system is also stable because *small* shocks do not affect where the system converges to. A trap also requires that several *stable equilibria* coexist, which happens when the links in the vicious circle are sufficiently nonlinear. In that case initial conditions may determine which equilibrium is achieved. The specifics of the nonlinearities, for instance the strength of each link in the vicious circle, determine whether there are multiple equilibria and how far apart they are from each other. For instance, Andrimihaja et al. (2011) explicitly relate the savings rate to the effectiveness of the state, and obtain multiple equilibria in a Solow model.

5.1 Feedback Loops

The main practical interpretation of this theory for our volume is that macroeconomic policy can strengthen or weaken the feedback loops, and thus either remove the bad equilibrium or move it closer to the good equilibrium. For instance: international aid could remove the link between saving and investment (theory (i)); trade openness, financial liberalization, currency devaluations, could help leverage trade and overcome the fixed costs due to small markets (theory (ii)); conservative fiscal arrangements can reduce the costs of economic vulnerability (theory (iii)); diversification policies can reduce the costs of commodity dependence (theory (iv)).

We cannot know a priori whether such policies are strong enough to overcome the forces underlying the different poverty traps. However, the failure of traditional structural adjustment programs based on aid and trade and financial liberalization documented by Easterly (1999), as well as the chapters in this volume finding that success is less likely in fragile states (Collyns and others, Chapter 17; Lane and others, Chapter 18) show that addressing poverty traps requires more than implementing orthodox macroeconomic policies.

Similarly, structural policies, especially fiscal capacity building, could work on the fragility vicious circle by affecting the strength of its different components. Steps to increase government revenues can increase fiscal capacity (theory (a); see Baer and others in Chapter 11). Reducing corruption, improving efficiency of ODA, improving the delivery of services can help build the long route of accountability (theory (b); Caselli and Presbitero's chapter as well as Andrews et al., 2017). Changing the narratives, building vanguards, can help coordinate agents in an equilibrium where civic culture leads to a stronger state (theory (c); see Collier in

Chapter 3). Designing economic institutions which widen the corridor as in the chapter by Acemoglu and Robinson can make sure that the country enters the virtuous circle of state-societal development (theory (d)).

5.2 Initial Conditions and Shocks

A second focus of analysis is what determines the initial conditions and what shocks can be strong enough to move the system from one equilibrium to another. In poverty trap models, initial endowments in human and physical capital, culture, institutions, and taxes are natural candidates. Shocks strong enough to move a country from one equilibrium to another include discovery of natural resources (van der Ploeg and Venables, 2011), major trade liberalization (Grossman and Helpmann, 1991); technological change, but also wars, domestic political events, and the engagement of external actors.

In the political-economy vicious circle, initial conditions include the macroeconomic structure, especially the extent of urbanization, the skill composition of labor supply of labor demand, comparative advantage and trade openness (Acemoglu and Robinson, Chapter 2). Shocks could include changes in institutions or leadership (Collier's Pivotal Moment in Chapter 3), or the global environment (the fall of the Berlin wall, technology). Section 6.2 delves into these questions in more detail.

5.3 Interventions with Perverse Effects

Finally, the presentation allows us to highlight the possibility that actions designed to address one specific vicious circle can have negative effects on others, either by affecting the strength of the loops or shifting initial conditions. Because these perverse effects are very difficult to anticipate and are not systematically supported by empirical analysis, they explain Collier's emphasis on the Knightian uncertainty facing policy makers. Among the perverse effects to look for, macroeconomists should pay particular attention to those economic policies that affect the costs and benefits of mobilizing violence. This implies monitoring the impact of policies on inequality, social inclusion, political equilibria, and so on. In addition, care should be taken that policies seeking to address governance issues and the fragility trap (such as decentralization) do not jeopardize economic development.

The next section develops broad policy principles that may be appropriate to follow when such complex traps interact. These principles must recognize (i) the extreme costs of fragility and thus the huge benefits of preventing conflict and escaping the fragility trap (Mueller, 2018); (ii) the benefits but also the limitations of policies that attempt to cut feedback loops (for example, aid flows intended to close financing gaps; Easterly, 1999); (iii) the difficulty in identifying and thus replicating the mechanisms that allow a system to move from one equilibrium to another one (Collier, Chapter 3); (iv) the difficulty in identifying the deep causes of the fragility trap and thus intervening on the initial conditions of vicious circles; (v) the risks of perverse effects just mentioned.

6. Policy Lessons: a Primer

The key issue explored in this book concerns the policy options that may be available to the international community in order to ameliorate the welfare consequences of fragility for the populations of fragile states. Based on the contributions to the volume, in this section we consider potential responses to this challenge in three increasingly specific steps: (1) General principles for policy engagement, (2) Policies to escape fragility, and (3) Macroeconomic policies to manage fragile economies.

6.1 General Principles

Taking Risks and Being Flexible Are Worth It

Because conflict is so costly, minimizing the risk of conflict is a priority. The United Nations-World Bank (2018) *Pathways for Peace* report estimates that for every dollar invested in prevention, about 16 dollars are saved in the future. Minimizing the risk of conflict may require more risk-taking from international agencies that have traditionally preferred tried and tested approaches. However, policymaking in fragile settings must acknowledge that the unknown unknowns (Knightian uncertainty) probably dominate the known risks. Collier, in this volume, suggests that a progressive and flexible approach with regular monitoring ("feeling a way across a river, stone by stone") is needed in such settings.

Giving Advice in Context

Fragile states may require different treatment from nonfragile ones, but they are also likely to require different treatment from each other: there is no unique "fragile" policy package, because every fragile situation is fragile in its own way. This heterogeneity shows the need to understand the country's specific context, and to tailor policy design to that context, taking into account the possibility that inappropriate policy advice could magnify fragility or–at the extreme–push the country into state failure. It is also important that outsiders put themselves "in the shoes of their interlocutors." Policymakers in fragile states may internalize better the risks and costs of conflict.

Don't Let the Best Be the Enemy of the Good

"Best practice" as recognized elsewhere may be of limited relevance in the context of fragility. Institutions must be designed in recognition of the past history and the economic, political, and cultural legacies of specific countries. Coats (Chapter 12) notes for instance that the key for external advisors is to work with what they have and not just try to import ready-made institutions. This principle is not always respected in practice. As noted in the chapter by Lane and others (Chapter 18), the evidence suggests that IMF programs, in particular, have in practice often treated fragile states almost like any other developing country rather than requiring distinctive treatment.

A Need for International Cooperation

Addressing the multiple self-reinforcing mechanisms that make fragility difficult to escape is likely to require more diverse expertise and greater resources than any single agency can mobilize. Coordinating assistance and policy advice with various international bodies is always wise, in order to maximize the benefit of any resources provided and to help fill gaps in counterpart capabilities (Collyns and others, Chapter 17). Moreover, where there is political resistance to reforms or specific policy measures, coordinating policy advice is necessary since conflicting advice undermines itself. Collaboration, however, is not easy to achieve when the receiving government does not have the capacity to coordinate the donors, which is why outside actors should consider designating one or two lead agencies to play this role.

Sustained and Patient Engagement

A familiar observation is that sustained and patient engagement by the international community is necessary, for a variety of reasons. First, it may take time–as well as repeated interactions–for the authorities to come to trust the advice received from foreign agencies. Second, successful transitions require a concerted effort to forge domestic coalitions that make agreements with external actors credible, to ensure that potential losers do not become roadblocks to reform. In other words, reforms require domestic ownership. The extensive use of prior actions in the IMF program conditionality in fragile states may be an indication precisely of the perceived absence of such ownership (Lane and others, Chapter 18). Third, fragility means that the situation on the ground may change frequently, and external advisors need to learn how to adapt their policy recommendations to those changes. In particular, the types and timing of engagement by the international community may both be vitally important. The chapter by Collier in this volume emphasizes that a certain amount of social learning will be required to prepare the way for the adoption of significant reforms, and the likely success of such reforms may depend on their timing; that is, reforms that may be successful at pivotal moments may not fare as well outside of such moments. Finally, in many fragile situations, domestic capacity development, which takes time, may be an important area in which the international community can make positive contributions. As noted by Collyns and others (Chapter 17), authorities in post-conflict states widely acknowledge that the IMF has played a crucial role in building capacity at the central bank and the ministry of finance during the early phases of reconstruction.

6.2 Escaping from Fragility

In discussing the more specific content of policy advice, it is useful to distinguish between policy initiatives specifically intended to move a country away from a fragile equilibrium and policies intended to improve macroeconomic outcomes in fragile situations.[9] We discuss the former in this section, and the latter in the section that follows.

Collier (Chapter 3) highlights that fragility tends to be locally stable (this is, in effect, the meaning of the "fragility trap" discussed previously), but that there may be pivotal moments at which time the adoption of measures to escape from fragility may be possible. Such moments may arise as the result of a belated but sincere recognition on the part of the authorities that past policies have been misguided (sustained engagement by the international community may help to produce such a moment), of a change in leadership to one with a new narrative, or of a shock that, because of the country's limited resilience, becomes magnified into an economic crisis.

At such moments, a change in policy regime featuring the wholehearted and sustained implementation of some subset of the specific macroeconomic policies described in lesson 3 will be possible.[10] What is essential is that the change in regime be clearly communicated to the public, and that it be backed up by some "visible, quick wins" that help build confidence and credibility. The case studies on the Middle East provide some examples of "quick wins" (Griffith, de Imus, Ismail, Ramirez, Tchaidze, and Al Amine, Chapter 19). In Yemen, in the second half of 2018, IMF policy advice, together with foreign financing and increased central bank issuance of letters of credit, helped break the uncontrolled depreciation of the exchange rate, steadied domestic inflation, and increased the availability of essential food imports. In Libya, the IMF helped the country reach agreement on a

[9] Given the feedback loops discussed previously, we would expect both that improved macro outcomes would assist in reducing fragility (e.g., by improving the state's fiscal capacity) and that policies to reduce fragility would make possible improved macroeconomic outcomes (for the latter, see, for example, Chapter 8 in this volume, by Chami, Cosimano, Espinoza, and Montiel).

[10] We say, "some subset," because given the heterogeneity of fragile states, the specific components of macroeconomic policy that should be given priority will differ from case to case.

national budget. Though advice to depreciate the exchange rate was resisted, the authorities did take measures to reduce pressures on the exchange rate by introducing a tax on foreign exchange purchases and increasing the availability of foreign exchange.

Implementing the change in regime and delivering "quick wins" is likely to require an infusion of external resources; for example, to stabilize the exchange rate, to reform the budgetary process and/or the central bank and, perhaps most importantly, to finance the quick delivery of public goods that had previously been lacking. This is where the international community can help with both funds and expertise. Such assistance is likely to prove fruitless outside of pivotal moments, however, because it is essential that the authorities own the reforms.

Acemoglu and Robinson (Chapter 2) emphasize that moving out of fragility toward becoming a robust nation-state is not just about empowering the state at any cost, since in the case of a predatory state, strengthening the state may simply result in despotic behavior. Instead, it involves a complex interaction between the state and society, such that empowering and mobilizing society are important to ensuring a strong and inclusive state. That includes building coalitions that co-opt potential losers as part of the new equilibrium. Intervention by the international community—to the extent it is limited to dealing with the state—is likely to be most effective when state and society have reached a point of recognizing each other's needs and roles—a pivotal moment—where social learning ensures past mistakes are recognized and both society and state are ready to engage forward.

The chapters in this volume that analyze country case studies in the Middle East and Sub-Saharan Africa also offer several insights in this regard. Gelbard, Albertin, Engstrom, Gijon and Mira (Chapter 20) point to the role of political inclusiveness in building resilience in Côte D'Ivoire, Rwanda, and Uganda, all cases in which explicit efforts were made to give political voice to social groups that had previously been in conflict, though constraints on executive power remain rudimentary in these cases.

6.3 Managing Fragility: Macroeconomic Policies

While specific initiatives to emerge from fragility such as those discussed above have received much attention in the literature, improving macroeconomic outcomes in fragile contexts has not. But better macroeconomic outcomes are critical not only to improve economic wellbeing for those living in fragile states, but as an additional means of fostering escape from fragility. As Akmeemana and Haque (2019) put it: "Nothing is more crucial to peace than the emergence of an economy that provides incentives for co-operation and collective action among those with the power to mobilize violence." In this section we summarize some lessons from this book for macroeconomic management in the context of fragility.

A first requirement for the formulation of macroeconomic policy in the context of fragility is that policymakers and their advisors have appropriate information about the state of the economy. Such information is indispensable to assessing macroeconomic conditions and providing a consistent macroeconomic framework for policy design, critical steps for the design of policy and the mobilization of external finance. Griffith and others (Chapter 19) highlight challenges in this area in the five Middle Eastern fragile case studies that they consider. In the absence of technical capacity to generate such information at the national level, there is a potentially important role for outside agencies that have a comparative advantage in constructing coherent macroeconomic frameworks on limited information.[11]

A second key point recognized throughout this volume is that the design of institutions and the formulation of policy under the special circumstances of fragile states is likely to require emphasis on different objectives or modifications to conventional policy advice:

- Formulating policies in fragile settings calls for paying special attention to their distributional and social consequences. Social tensions often limit the range of policies that can be considered, and urgent social needs may trump other considerations, not only for humanitarian reasons, but to avoid a greatly heightened risk of state failure. This question is tackled specifically, by extending a standard macroeconomic model to account for the probability of failure, in Chami, Cosimano, Espinoza, and Montiel (Chapter 8).
- Recognizing what is feasible must take into account not just the capacity, but also the honesty of the bureaucracy. Measures to reduce corruption (which must be specific to each setting) should also carry a high priority to increase the likelihood that specific policies will be implemented. Corruption indeed undermines the effective implementation of a variety of policies. For example, the judicial process may be damaged by corruption; the delivery of public goods may be undermined not just by the lack of resources but also by the siphoning off of such resources by actors in the public sector for their own ends (Milante and Woolcock, Chapter 10); regulation of the financial sector may be weakened by corruption (Coats, Chapter 12); and so on. Caselli and Presbitero (Chapter 16) also find that project success rates increase with stronger control of corruption, showing that polices targeted at curbing corruption could contribute to increasing aid effectiveness because control of corruption is weaker in fragile than in other developing countries.
- Fragility is often accompanied by severe deficiencies in domestic macroeconomic institutions. In many fragile situations—especially in post-conflict

[11] Collyns and others (Chapter 17) note that IMF involvement (albeit in the form of programs) has been highly effective in mobilizing official development assistance in fragile countries.

states—it may be necessary for these institutions to be developed from the ground up. But even where such institutions are in place in some form, they may close to nonfunctional, lacking capacity or suffering from an extreme shortage of credibility (Coats, Chapter 12).

- Third, in designing specific macroeconomic policies in fragile states, it is important to recognize that "conventional" policy advice may not only fail to yield the expected beneficial results but may run the risk of actually aggravating fragility. Examples include
- Financial assistance to predatory states that encourages additional predation and/or rent-seeking, and programs imported without local ownership that impede social learning. Chami and others (Chapter 15) find that on average ODA undermines country stability in fragile states.
- Structural reforms, such as trade and financial liberalization, that create losers and run the risk of starting a vicious circle of lack of "trust" (Sembene, Chapter 5).
- Fiscal interventions that disproportionately place the burden of adjustment on disaffected sectors and risk creating unrest that, in the fragile context, could trigger a move from fragility to failure.
- Nontransparent privatization of state-owned assets that are perceived as transfers to favored elites and are likely to reinforce the perception of government corruption.

These observations provide the justification for a broad agenda to build macroeconomic policy *capacity* in fragile environments. It is critical in such contexts to get the key macroeconomic institutions and policy regimes "right," where "right" means that the institutions are capable of delivering what they are intended in all countries to deliver, even if their specific design—and the specific policies they implement—are tailored to the circumstances of the specific country.[12] In other words, what is universal for such institutions is function, and what is specific is form.

The key institutions in question involve the formulation of the public sector budget, which determines fiscal policy outcomes, the governance of the central bank, which manages monetary and exchange rate policy, and the institutional

[12] Gelbard and others (2015) investigated the role of macroeconomic policies in escaping fragility (building resilience). They used panel data to estimate the probability of surpassing the World Bank's resilience threshold, using a logit model. They found significant effects for a set of political, institutional, and macroeconomic variables. The political variables included political stability and the strength of constraints on the executive. Regulatory quality was the significant institutional variable, and macroeconomic variables included the strength of fiscal institutions, revenue mobilization, public spending on education and infrastructure, low inflation, and the avoidance of exchange rate misalignment. They used a GMM approach to attempt to avoid endogeneity. Interestingly, natural resource abundance did not help explain performance relative to the threshold, but the extended presence of an IMF program did help to build resilience.

framework for the operation of the private financial sector. In turn, the functions that these institutions are expected to perform are:

- In the case of the public sector budget, the provision of certain public goods (e.g., security, a well-functioning legal system, infrastructure, health, and education), while avoiding debt crises and fiscal procyclicality.
- In the case of the central bank, price stability, the stabilization of the economy in the face of shocks to the macroeconomic environment, and a well-functioning exchange rate mechanism.
- In the case of the private financial sector, the provision of undistorted saving incentives, the allocation of investment to socially productive activities, and the means for the private sector to smooth consumption in the face of shocks.

These functions are critical to create an environment in which the private sector can thrive. Efforts to improve public financial management (PFM) and central bank governance, as well as to implement mechanisms to enhance the transparency and accountability of the fiscal and monetary authorities, should be high on the reform priority list, as should the provision of an institutional and regulatory framework within which the domestic financial sector can develop.

6.3.1 Fiscal Policy

Reforms in the fiscal area should be intended to ensure that the government provides an appropriate supply of public goods, that it raises revenues fairly and efficiently, that it does not itself become a source of macroeconomic instability, and that it contributes to macroeconomic stabilization if possible. Fragility poses special challenges to achieving these objectives, because implementing the necessary fiscal reforms is not simply a technocratic problem: raising revenue depends heavily on voluntary compliance, and this is undermined when the very legitimacy of the state is in question, administrative capacity is weak, the economy is dominated by small and opaque firms, and where a variety of other characteristics of the fragile context are present.

External policy advice should therefore provide support for context-specific domestic revenue mobilization as well as for context-specific mechanisms for designing and monitoring the level and composition of spending. As noted by several authors in this volume, delivering legitimacy-enhancing public goods and enhancing the transparency and accountability of public expenditures can make an important contribution to escaping the fragility trap.

Concretely:

- On the revenue side, the chapter by Baer and others (Chapter 11) draws an important implication from this requirement: in fragile states, among the tax system objectives of revenue, efficiency, and equity, the raising of revenue may need to take priority in the short term. The authors suggest not only how this short-term focus can be implemented in fragile situations, but also how more ambitious goals for fiscal reform can be implemented as resilience improves. Success is certainly possible. In Rwanda, the revenue-to-GDP ratio doubled from 9.1 percent in 1996 to 18.5 percent in 2018 (Gelbard and others; Chapter 20).

- On the expenditure side, an important point that is not typically a factor in nonfragile circumstances needs to be recognized: the social returns to the provision of public services should be perceived as consisting not just of the direct welfare benefits to the recipients, but also of the contribution that such provision can make to social cohesion. In other words, inclusiveness needs to be taken into account both in the allocation of spending among different public goods and in the allocation of specific public goods among different segments of society. Similarly, the true social costs of well-targeted subsidies (in the form of their social opportunity costs) may be overstated in a fragile context if such subsidies make an important contribution to social cohesion.

The volatility of the fragile environment also heightens the urgency of building effective stabilization policies. In the fiscal area, this means that fiscal institutions and budgetary processes should be designed first, to "do no harm"—that is, to prevent fiscal policy from itself becoming a source of macroeconomic instability, and second, to behave countercyclically. The first means limiting the size of fiscal deficits to what is consistent with fiscal sustainability, and the second means managing budget deficits so as to stimulate the economy when it would otherwise contract and to contract it when it would otherwise over-expand. This is a challenging agenda for many countries, fragile or otherwise. In fact, pro-deficit bias exists, and fiscal policy tends to be procyclical, even in many nonfragile low-income countries.

Concretely:

- Besley and Mueller (Chapter 9) point to independent fiscal councils as an institutional innovation that could play a key role in supporting both fiscal sustainability and countercyclicality in fragile states. Fiscal councils have been created in many countries, but design is important because they need both to be independent and to have access to sufficient analytical capacity. External agencies can provide significant assistance on these design issues.
- A related, but separate idea, is to create institutions in commodity-dependent economies that would perform the role that sovereign wealth funds (or "rainy day" funds) perform elsewhere—specifically, to help stabilize fiscal policy outcomes in the face of volatile natural resource revenues, so that volatility in such revenues does not get transmitted to the economy through a

fiscal response. Again, how to design such institutions such that the resources they accumulate in good times are protected in the political fragmentation that characterizes fragile states remains an open question. Adaptation to local conditions and political realities would again seem to be crucial.

Because of perceived deficiencies in public sector expenditure management, ODA in many fragile states tends to be channeled through nongovernmental organizations, rather than through the government budget. Elbadawi, Soto, and Martinez (Chapter 14) point to a potential problem with this situation: an attempt to buttress the government's legitimacy in an effort to escape the fragility trap by increasing public sector spending on the provision of public goods may not have the desired effect if, with limited domestic revenue mobilization and restricted ODA financing for the government, that spending increase has to be financed by debt. The reason is that if the private sector is forward-looking, it may anticipate a future sovereign debt crisis as the result of debt accumulation. Put differently, the "small wins" that can be achievable by improved public good provision in the short term must not come at the expense of compromising the government's perceived ability to deliver public goods in the future because of tightening budget constraints. In principle, we want to identify policies that give the biggest bang in terms of current legitimacy for the least future constraints. This identifies an important potential role for the international community in a pivotal moment: when public expenditure management becomes reliable, ODA financing of increased public good provision may be able to make an important contribution to escaping the fragility trap. Indeed, Gelbard and others (Chapter 20) note that donor support, including debt relief, played an important role in providing fiscal space for priority spending in Rwanda and Uganda.

6.3.2 Monetary and Exchange Rate Policy

Price stability is essential to facilitate private sector planning and promote an efficient allocation of resources. This requires a credible nominal anchor that can only be provided by the central bank. Adam and Wilson (Chapter 13) document the variety of exchange rate and monetary regimes chosen by central banks in fragile states, including monetary unions, dollarized systems, hard and soft pegs, and some versions of floating regimes, although none of the persistently fragile states has moved to inflation targeting. Adam and Wilson point to a common challenge, however: given the limitations that the government faces in resource mobilization, central banking in many such countries tends to be characterized by fiscal dominance. That is, monetary policy is dominated by the government's demand for seigniorage revenue. This creates a tradeoff between the need to raise seigniorage revenues for the government and the desire to stabilize prices.

In the extreme, this situation can worsen fragility. If the country maintains a fixed exchange rate, a shock that reduces the government's resources (for example, an adverse terms-of-trade shock in a resource-dependent economy) may induce the government to demand more seigniorage financing. This excessive money creation can worsen balance of payments pressures, and if the central bank attempts to protect its reserves by imposing restrictions on external payments, it can give rise to a parallel market for foreign exchange, a fertile terrain for rent-seeking and corruption. Griffith and others (Chapter 19) cite foreign exchange rents as the largest source of rents in Libya, for example. Under a more flexible exchange rate regime, the attempt to generate additional seigniorage revenues results in higher inflation, but this in turn shrinks the monetary base and thus decreases seigniorage revenue. To sustain such revenues, money issuance is increased further, but this in turn results in an inflationary spiral with dramatic costs that can undermine the government's political legitimacy. Limiting the risk that fiscal dominance poses to monetary stability is thus critical.

Concretely:

- Making the central bank independent, in a *de facto* and not just *de jure* sense, from the central government is essential. There is a broad literature that describes the mechanisms (legal standing, central bank budget, governance) for doing this but actual practice must depend on the county's specific circumstances. Coats (Chapter 12) emphasizes that it is essential that central bank laws conform to the local legal tradition and practice and that they be drafted in close cooperation with the authorities that will implement them. Political considerations, in terms of its financial relationship with the treasury and the design of notes, also cannot be ignored.
- The governance of an independent central bank needs to take into account political and social divisions. Specifically, it is important that the bank be truly independent of politics, and that policy decisions made by the bank not be perceived to be governed by the interests of specific social groups. This may require, for example, diverse representation in the central bank's governing Board. Reforms to make the central bank transparent and to hold it accountable for its contribution to the country's macroeconomic performance can build credibility (and thus macroeconomic stability) as well as engender trust in government

When domestic circumstances are such that effective central bank independence is not a feasible outcome, the alternative is dollarization, that is, the abandonment of the domestic currency, which is sometimes necessary, especially after conflict, because it ensures price stability.[13] But dollarization causes the government to have to forego seigniorage revenue entirely, making other types of

[13] As Adam and Wilson document, dollarization may in any case be the outcome if fiscal dominance and fiscal profligacy create a hyperinflationary crisis and currency substitution.

revenue mobilization that much more urgent, and it also means that the central bank has no independent monetary or exchange rate policy, and is thus prevented from playing a stabilizing role in the economy. In that case adjustment to shocks, especially external shocks, requires *internal* devaluations that can be extremely painful.

As discussed by Adam and Wilson in Chapter 13, in fragile states that retain an independent currency, the IMF has often advocated monetary policy regimes that feature reserve money programs (RMPs). RMPs consist of the imposition of a floor on the central bank's net international reserves combined with a ceiling on its net domestic assets, intended to prevent excessive money financing of the government and thus to reinforce fiscal stabilization objectives. RMPs, which place high weights on price stability and fiscal control (including via a cash budget mechanism) can play a decisive role in anchoring inflation (and inflation expectations) in the aftermath of periods of weak economic performance and often incoherent macroeconomic management that stems from environments of fragility.

This limited and nondiscretionary approach to monetary policy is not just feasible in such environments, but may be optimal when fiscal and monetary institutions are weak and the monetary transmission mechanism is broken, particularly in dollarized economies. However, RMPs are not without deficiencies: (i) RMPs do not work well when confronted with supply shocks; (ii) RMP performance is vulnerable to instability in the money multiplier; (iii) RMPs add volatility to interest rates when the demand for money is unstable, which hinders financial development; and (iv) RMPs contribute to the volatility of the exchange rate when balance of payment flows are volatile, because they may restrict central bank intervention in the foreign exchange market (Adam and Wilson, Chapter 13).[14]

Many central banks in developing countries seek to stabilize the exchange rates while conducting an independent monetary policy. They are able to do so in the short term because international capital mobility can be very limited, especially in fragile states. Fixing the exchange rate to use it as a nominal anchor is a reasonable approach when price stability is an important objective and the central bank is institutionally weak, causing it to lack anti-inflationary credibility. But for such a strategy to be effective, exchange rate misalignment must be avoided by adjusting the officially determined rate when the underlying equilibrium real exchange rate is perceived to have sustainably changed, both to avoid the macroeconomic distortions that are created by a misaligned rate and to resist the temptation to

[14] Some of these issues could be addressed even in the context of a reserve money program, for example, by formulating the credit ceiling on the basis of a nominal GDP target instead of a strict inflation objective, allowing for some output stabilization in the face of supply shocks.

restrict foreign exchange trading, which would be likely to create parallel markets and increase the scope for fragility-reinforcing corruption.

Unfortunately, tracking the equilibrium real exchange rate is a tall order, especially in unstable fragile situations.[15] Thus, as institutional reforms in the central bank and a central bank track record of generating subdued inflation contribute to the bank's anti-inflationary credibility, the scope for exchange rate flexibility increases. This is not just a matter of central bank readiness, however; it requires developing the market infrastructure for the emergence of a competitive foreign exchange market, which in turn is likely to require a competitive domestic banking system (see section 6.3.3). The exchange rate regime thus needs to respond to the specific characteristics of the fragile environment. Indeed, there is no convergence of fragile states on a single dominant exchange rate regime, as documented by Adam and Wilson.

6.3.3 The Domestic Financial Sector

Fragility seems to not only heighten the sensitivity of the economy to shocks, but also to reduce the power of coping mechanisms for private agents, with the consequence that economic crises can lead quickly to costly political crises, potentially culminating in state failure. This points to the importance of fostering financial development and financial inclusion in fragile states, both to facilitate borrowing and lending that allow the financing of investment and the smoothing of consumption, as well as to trade risks. As noted in the chapter by Assaf and others (Chapter 6), "The financial sector constitutes the underlying backbone of the private sector and is particularly vulnerable in [fragile state] contexts, therefore should constitute a top priority on the policy agenda to support resilience of the private sector, particularly in terms of financial stability and integrity." The chapter by Barajas, Chami, and Fullenkamp in this volume (Chapter 7) provides some empirical estimates of the possible contribution that eliminating financial development underperformance could make to economic growth in individual fragile states, concluding that growth rates could be boosted by between 0.6 percent and 1.2 percent annually in their sample of fragile states.

Moreover, a healthy financial sector may also influence fragility more directly because, as Barajas, Chami, and Fullenkamp also note in Chapter 7, financial development has been shown to reduce income inequality and alleviate poverty, potentially helping to ameliorate the social fragmentation that contributes to fragility.

Unfortunately, building a robust and efficient domestic financial sector poses a special challenge in fragile states, because both the institutional and regulatory underpinnings that such a sector requires are likely to be weak, and because

[15] Estimates by Couharde et al. (2017) show that fragile states are more likely than nonfragile economies to have an overvalued currency.

uncertainty in the environment, and the associated prevalence of small and weak firms in the private sector, increase the cost of financial intermediation and inhibit the growth of the financial sector. Indeed, as shown in Figure 1.6, the relationship between the financial sector and private economic activity represents another vicious cycle that tends to sustain fragility: small and weak private firms operating in an unstable environment tend to stunt the development of a robust and efficient domestic financial sector, but, in turn, the absence of a robust and efficient domestic financial sector makes it more challenging for the private sector to thrive and for private firms to grow.[16]

There are obvious ways to intervene to try to break this negative feedback loop, though implementing such measures is much easier to say than to do. First, it is hard to envision an adequately functioning domestic financial system without minimum levels of property rights, sufficiently appropriate accounting and disclosure standards, a judicial system that allows impartial and reasonably inexpensive enforcement of financial contracts, an adequate regulatory and supervisory structure for the banking system, and sufficient capacity on the part both of bank staff as well as potential borrowers. Reform of institutions on which financial intermediation relies, and investment in capacity building for financial sector personnel are of first-order importance in allowing a well-functioning domestic financial sector to emerge. This subsequently needs to be buttressed by regulatory and supervisory mechanisms to cope with moral hazard and competitive issues in the financial sector. Again, this will require both resources and technical assistance.

Second, reform of fiscal and monetary policies that reduce the risk of sovereign debt crises, that mute the transmission of terms-of-trade shocks to the domestic economy through the public sector budget, that reduce the risk of currency crises and/or high inflation, and that allow fiscal and monetary policies to play a countercyclical role, are complementary to the development of the domestic financial system, because they promote stability in the domestic economy and thereby reduce the cost of financial intermediation. Thus, success in other areas of reform makes financial development more likely.

Third, as documented by Barajas, Chami, and Fullenkamp, policies for social inclusion and equity tend to enhance financial depth and financial inclusion. Thus, not only is financial development likely to improve wellbeing and reduce fragility by improving economic performance and reducing social divisions, but

[16] There are actually two issues here: avoiding domestic financial repression and promoting financial development. Financial repression—often adopted for fiscal reasons—not only tends to promote fragility indirectly by undermining economic performance, but also directly through the administrative allocation of credit in the banking system, which creates scope for corruption and favoritism, undermining trust in economic institutions.

policies that directly address the social fragmentation that contributes to fragility are in turn likely to contribute to financial development.[17]

7. Conclusions

As our discussion in this chapter suggests, the good news is that, while fragility may be self-reinforcing, positive macroeconomic feedback loops are also possible in the fragile context. Such loops may operate, for example, not only in a direction from success in fiscal and monetary reforms to success in financial development, but also in the other direction: a larger and more sophisticated domestic financial system is likely to increase the demand for base money and increase seigniorage revenue at a given rate of inflation, it is likely to create an expanded market for government debt among domestic banks, and by strengthening the private economy, it is also likely to increase the government's tax revenues, allowing it to finance larger levels of public services. A larger and more sophisticated domestic financial sector will enhance the effectiveness of monetary policy by increasing the reach of the formal financial sector through financial inclusion, and by creating a liquid market for short-term government debt instruments, allowing the central bank to move away from RMPs to the use of market-determined domestic interest rates as its primary policy instrument. Finally, a larger and more competitive domestic financial system creates the basis for a competitive foreign exchange market, allowing the exchange rate regime to move in a more flexible direction.

Heterogeneity in fragile situations is, of course, likely to influence what can be accomplished in the area of macroeconomic reform in specific country cases. But even if conflict or capacity constraints prevent the immediate implementation of reforms to macroeconomic institutions, there are steps that can be taken in the meantime. Having policy recommendations and a revised strategy ready for when the conflict is over and/or capacity building has been accomplished, for example, could be very helpful when the time is ripe—that is, when a pivotal moment arrives. Moreover, because it may often be easier to build the parts of those institutions that are less political or are more independent, and where the work is more technical (such as statistical offices in both the government and the central bank), that may prove to be the most feasible entry point for reform efforts. In such cases, turnover may be high, so the focus needs to be on reforms that are easy to pass on to successor staff, including easily accessible manuals for local staff.[18]

[17] Barajas and others (Chapter 7) note that significant government ownership of financial institutions is associated with financial underdevelopment. Thus, transferring bank ownership to the private sector may be an additional policy instrument when the institutional environment satisfies the conditions described above.

[18] In contrast, success in reforming public financial management may prove more elusive because the government may have an interest in less transparency.

As noted in the chapter by Assaf and others, when reforms of public financial management are delayed, there may be other ways to increase the provision of goods typically provided by the public sector: increased private provision of water, power, health, education, and transportation. This might entail implementing reforms that may potentially be more feasible in the short term than reforming public financial management, such as liberalizing the provision of licenses, reducing the role of state-owned enterprises to give more room for the private sector to operate, and developing the means of fostering public-private partnerships to improve service delivery. These are themselves challenging reforms with their own complex political economy dimensions, and it is unclear whether they are likely to be more or less feasible than reforms to public financial management. However, in some cases the need for service delivery may be sufficiently dire to allow smaller changes of this type when wholesale public sector reform is stymied by political stalemates or capacity constraints.

Finally, the challenges involved in building a well-functioning domestic financial sector and implementing the institutional reforms required to construct an effective stabilization (fiscal and monetary) policy framework suggest the need to improve the functioning of other mechanisms for coping with volatility. There is evidence that ODA flows, especially important in the fragile setting, have not been countercyclical (Caselli and Presbitero, Chapter 16). Mechanisms to make them more so are certainly worth exploring, but this may pose difficult coordination problems for donors and may therefore not be easily implemented. Fragile states also rely heavily on remittance flows, which are known to be countercyclical (see Chami et al., 2008). Thus, any steps the donor community could take to reduce the costs of effective remittance flows can constitute an important contribution to allowing citizens of fragile states to cope with economic volatility.

In short, macroeconomic management in fragile situations is undoubtedly a daunting task, requiring both a level of commitment by the domestic authorities as well as intense and sustained engagement by the international community, in the form not just of the provision of resources when the circumstances are right but also of institution-building, policy advice, and investments in human capital. There are steps that can be taken even before pivotal moments arrive, but when they do, reforms may generate positive feedback loops that make escaping from fragility a self-reinforcing process.

References

Acemoglu, D. 2009. *Introduction to Modern Economic Growth*. Princeton, NJ: Princeton University Press.

Acemoglu, D. and J. Robinson. 2019. *The Narrow Corridor. States, Society and the Fate of Liberty*. New York: Penguin Random House.

Akmeemana S. and T. Haque. 2019. "Cameron and Collier on Fragile States: Anything New? Devpolicy blog. https://www.devpolicy.org/cameron-collier-fragile-states-anything-new-20180618/ (last accessed July 16, 2020).

Azariadis C. and J. Stachurski. 2005. "Poverty Traps," in P. Aghion and S. Durlauf (Eds.), *Handbook of Economic Growth*. Amsterdam: Elsevier.

Besley, T. and T. Persson. 2011. *Pillars of Prosperity: The Political Economics of Development Clusters*. Princeton, NJ: Princeton University Press.

Besley, T. and T. Persson. 2013. "Taxation and Development," in A.J. Auerbach, R. Chetty, M. Feldstein, and E. Saez (Eds.), *Handbook of Public Economics* Vol. 5, 51–110. Amsterdam: Elsevier.

Besley, T. and T. Persson. 2014. "The Causes and Consequences of Development Clusters: State Capacity, Peace, and Income." *Annual Review of Economics*, 6(1): 927–49.

Bisin, A. and T. Verdier. 2017. "On the Joint Evolution of Culture and Institutions." No. w23375. National Bureau of Economic Research.

Carment, D., S. Prest, and Y. Samy. 2011. "The Causes and Measurement of State Fragility," in W. Naudé, A.U. Santos-Paulino, and M. McGillivray (Eds.), *Fragile States: Causes, Costs, and Responses*. Oxford: Oxford University Press.

Chami, R., A. Barajas, T. Cosimano, C. Fullenkamp, M. Gapen, and P. Montiel. 2008. *Macroeconomic Consequences of Remittances* (p. 259). Washington, DC: International Monetary Fund.

Collier, P., Hoeffler, A., and Söderbom, M. 2004. "On the Duration of Civil War. *Journal of Peace Research*, 41(3): 253–273.

De Gregorio, J. 1993. "Credit Markets and Stagnation in an Endogenous Growth Model." IMF Working Paper 93/72, International Monetary Fund, Washington, DC.

Di John, J., 2010. "The Concept, Causes and Consequences of Failed States: A Critical Review of the Literature and Agenda for Research with Specific Reference to Sub-Saharan Africa." *The European Journal of Development Research*, 22(1): 10–30.

Easterly, W. 1999. "The Ghost of Financing Gap: Testing the Growth Model Used in the International Financial Institutions." *Journal of Development Economics*, 60(2): 423–38.

Easterly, W. 2006. "Reliving the 1950s: The Big Push, Poverty Traps, and Takeoffs in Economic Development." *Journal of Economic Growth*, 11(4): 289–318.

Fabra Mata, J. and S. Ziaja. 2009. *Users' Guide on Measuring Fragility*. German Development Institute.

Faust, J., J. Grävingholt, and S. Ziaja. 2015. "Foreign Aid and the Fragile Consensus on State Fragility." *Journal of International Relations and Development*, 18(4): 407–27.

Ferreira, I.A. 2017. "Measuring State Fragility: A Review of the Theoretical Groundings of Existing Approaches. *Third World Quarterly*, 38(6): 1291–309.

Fund for Peace. 2009. *Failed States Index FAQ*.

Galor, O. and J. Zeira. 1993. Income Distribution and Macroeconomics. *The Review of Economic Studies*, 60(1): 35–52.

Gelbard, D., P. Jacoby, R. Hussain, F. Xu, F., and D. Mulaj. 2015. *Building Resilience in Sub-Saharan Africa's Fragile States*. African Department, International Monetary Fund, Washington, DC.

Glawion, T., L. De Vries, and A. Mehler. 2019. "Handle with Care! A Qualitative Comparison of the Fragile States Index's Bottom Three Countries: Central African Republic, Somalia and South Sudan." *Development and Change*, 50(2): 277–300.

Grossman, G.M. and E. Helpman. 1991. "Trade, Knowledge Spillovers, and Growth." *European Economic Review*, 35(2–3): 517–26.

Gutiérrez, F., D. Buitrago, A. González, and C. Lozano. 2011. "Measuring Poor State Performance: Problems, Perspectives and Paths Ahead. Crisis State Research Centre Report," London, London School of Economics and Political Science.

Harvey, D. I., N.M. Kellard, J.B. Madsen, and M.E. Wohar, M.E. 2010. The Prebisch-Singer Hypothesis: Four Centuries of Evidence. *The Review of Economics and Statistics*, 92(2): 367–77.

Hewitt, J.J., J. Wilkenfeld, and T.R. Gurr (Eds). 2008. *Peace and Conflict 2008*. College Park: Center for International Development and Conflict Management, University of Maryland.

IMF (International Monetary Fund). 2018. *The IMF and Fragile States: 2018 Evaluation Report*. Washington DC: International Monetary Fund.

Khan, M.Z. 2017. The Fallacies of State Fragility Indices, IIs There a Fragility Trap? Working paper, Submission for BIISS Monograph: *The Fallacy of State Fragility Indices: Is There a 'Fragility Trap'?*

King, R.G., and R. Levine. 1993. Finance and Growth: Schumpeter Might be Right. *The Quarterly Journal of Economics*, 108(3): 717–37.

Kuznets, S. 1966. *Modern Economic Growth*. New Haven, CT: Yale University Press,.

Lomoriello, R.S. 2018. "What Sources of External Development Finance are Available to Fragile Contexts?" in *States of Fragility 2018*. Paris: OECD, chap. 6.

LSE-Oxford Commission on State Fragility, Growth and Development. 2018. Escaping the Fragility Trap. London: International Growth Center.

Lucas Jr, R.E. 1993. "Making a Miracle." *Econometrica: Journal of the Econometric Society*, 251–72.

Mueller, H., 2018. Fragility in the Data. LSE-Oxford Commission on State Fragility, Growth and Development.

Murphy, K.M., A. Shleifer, and R.W. Vishny. 1989. "Industrialization and the Big Oush." *Journal of Political Economy*, 97(5): 1003–26.

Naudé, W., A.U. Santos-Paulino, and M. McGillivray. 2011. *Fragile States: Causes, Costs, and Responses*. Oxford: Oxford University Press.

Nay, O. 2013. "Fragile and Failed States: Critical Perspectives on Conceptual Hybrids." *International Political Science Review*, 34(3): 326–41.

OECD (Organisation for Economic Co-Operation and Development). 2009. *Preventing Violence, War and State collapse: The Future of Conflict Early Warning and Response*. Paris: OECD Publishing.

OECD. 2013. *Fragile States 2013: Resource Flows and Trends in a Shifting World*. Paris: OECD Publishing.

Paris, R., and T.D. Sisk (Eds). 2009. *The Dilemmas of Statebuilding: Confronting the Contradictions of Postwar Peace Operations*. Oxford: Routledge.

Prebish, R. 1950. "The Economic Development of Latin America and its Principal Problems." UN document no. E/CN. 12/89/Rev. 1. Lake Success. New York: United Nations.

Quah, D. 1993. "Galton's Fallacy and Convergence in Models of Distribution Dynamics." *Scandinavian Journal of Economics*, 95: 427–43.

Ramey, G. and V.A. Ramey. 1995. "Cross-Country Evidence on the Link Between Volatility and Growth." *The American Economic Review*, 85(5): 1138–51.

Rice, S.E. and S. Patrick. 2008. *Index of State Weakness in the Developing World*. Washington, DC: Brookings Institution.

Rocha De Siqueira, I. 2014. "Measuring and Managing 'State Fragility': The Production of Statistics by the World Bank, Timor-Leste and the G7+. *Third World Quarterly*, 35(2): 268–83.

Romer, P.M. 1986. Increasing Returns and Long-Run Growth. *Journal of Political Economy*, 94(5): 1002–37.

Rosenstein-Rodan, P.N. 1943. Problems of Industrialisation of Eastern and South-Eastern Europe. *The Economic Journal*, 53, 202–11.

Sachs, J.D. 2005. "Can Extreme Poverty Be Eliminated?" *Scientific American*, 293(3): 56–65.

Singer, H. 1950. "The Distribution of Gains between Investing and Borrowing Countries." *American Economic Review, Papers and Proceedings*, 40(1950): 473–85.

Stewart, F. and G. Brown. 2010. *Fragile States: CRISE Overview 3*. Centre for Research on Inequality, Human Security and Ethnicity (CRISE), Oxford.

United Nations-World Bank. 2018. *Pathways for Peace: Inclusive Approaches to Preventing Violent Conflict*. Washington, DC: World Bank.

UNDP (United Nations Development Programme). 2018. Supporting Civil Service Restoration and Reform. New York: United Nations Development Programme.

Van der Ploeg, F. and A.J. Venables. 2011. "Harnessing Windfall Revenues: Optimal Policies for Resource-Rich Developing Economies. *The Economic Journal*, 121(551): 1–30.

World Bank. 2004. World Development Report 2004: Making Services Work for Poor People. Washington, DC: World Bank.

World Bank. 2010. Fragile and Conflict-Affected Countries: Definitions of Fragility and Conflict. Washington, DC: World Bank.

World Bank. 2011. World Development Report 2011: Conflict, Security and Development. Washington, DC: World Bank.

World Bank. 2016. *The World Bank Group A to Z 2016*. Washington, DC: World Bank.

Ziaja, S. 2012. "What Do Fragility Indices Measure? *Zeitschrift für vergleichende Politikwissenschaft*, 6(1): 39–64.

2

Building Inclusive States

A Simple Framework

Daron Acemoglu and James A. Robinson

1. Introduction

There is currently a large consensus that a prerequisite for economic development is some level of state effectiveness or "capacity." The lack of this capacity creates a syndrome which is referred to as "fragility." A fragile country is one with a "weak" state, unable or unwilling to raise resources, provide public goods, and govern effectively. Fragile states lack a social contract and tend to be unaccountable and not trusted by citizens.[1] This creates an environment with poor economic incentives and the potential for disorder and, in the limit, civil war.

We contrast such a fragile state to one that is defined by two conditions. The first condition is a state with capacity—"strength"—possessing a monopoly of violence and able to raise taxes, regulate society, and provide public goods. The second condition is a political regime where power is broadly distributed and there is representation and accountability—a situation where society also has "strength." When either of these two conditions fails, we say the state is prone to be fragile (in the terminology of Acemoglu and Robinson, 2012, it is "extractive").

Fragility means that a state may collapse into conflict and civil war. This is obvious if only condition 1 fails. For example, historic Somali society never created any centralized political or state institutions at all, and attempts to create them, first during the military government of Siad Barre between 1969 and 1991, and then subsequently with the help of the international community, have been unsuccessful. Though the recent period is often described as one of "state collapse," it would be closer to the truth to say that Somalia never really had a modern state. In consequence it was prone to a great deal of instability and conflict. This was true of the traditional society (Lewis, 1961) and for the past 30 years. But it would also be true to say that Somali society was very democratic. Indeed, Lewis titled his book *A Pastoral Democracy*. At a local level Somali society had a great deal of participation and accountability and adult men collectively

[1] As emphasized by the British government's Commission on State Fragility, Growth and Development https://www.theigc.org/research-themes/state/fragility-commission/

Daron Acemoglu and James A. Robinson, *Building Inclusive States: A Simple Framework* In: *Macroeconomic Policy in Fragile States*. Edited by: Ralph Chami, Raphael Espinoza, and Peter Montiel, Oxford University Press (2021). © International Monetary Fund.
DOI: 10.1093/oso/9780198853091.003.0002

made decisions. The Somalis never managed to combine this accountability with centralized political institutions. Fragility is perhaps even more obvious when both conditions 1 and 2 fail. Take a country like Colombia, where the state has been persistently unable to collect taxes, or provide infrastructure or basic public goods (Robinson, 2016; Uribe, 2017). At the same time elections have been riven by fraud (Acemoglu et al., 2013; Chaves et al., 2015), and society fragmented by clientelistic ties and unable to engage in collective action or formulate programmatic goals. Colombia has had an ongoing civil war since 1948 and for much of this period has been the homicide and kidnapping capital of the world.

Though 2017 did see the successful signing of a peace agreement with the Marxist rebel groups the FARC (Revolutionary Armed Forces of Colombia), a non-trivial achievement, this is only the most recent of a long string of peace agreements with various armed groups, none of which has ended the conflicts. Perhaps more surprisingly, fragility can result when only condition 2 fails, as it has done in China's history. Though China has had a centralized state for over 2000 years and important elements of capacity, such as the famously meritocratic bureaucracy, it has completely lacked any mechanisms of accountability. Though the capacity of the state has allowed public goods to be provided in certain periods and has occasionally facilitated sustained economic expansion, for example during the Song dynasty and since Deng Xiaoping's reforms in 1978, it has also been periodically subject to widespread revolts and state collapse.

The critical question is how do you develop a polity where both the state and society are strong? How do societies exit from fragile states and build something more effective? In this chapter we develop a simple framework of the emergence of nonfragile, "strong" states, drawn from Acemoglu and Robinson (2019).

A prime motivation for a state to develop strength is the desire to control society. For example, Anderson (1974) argued that the collapse of feudalism in Western Europe in the wake of the Black Death meant that elites lost a large number of instruments which they had previously used to extract rents and exercise authority. In response they built absolutist states to re-exert their control in new ways. But this elite project sets off a contest in which society fights back.

Sometimes the state definitively wins this contest, as it did in China after the establishment of the Qin dynasty in 221 BC. But this leads not to a strong state, but to a state we shall call a Despotic Leviathan. Sometimes society permanently wins this conflict, as it did in Somalia, so that no state forms or at best only a very weak state forms—a situation we call an Absent Leviathan. But in a narrow corridor between excessive state and society power, we can have a balance of power. When this balance is attained, the state and society continually compete, both getting stronger in the process, which we call the Red Queen Effect, and this effect undergirds the emergence of strong states. This is a different type of state, what we shall denote a Shackled Leviathan. Crucially, such a state is not shackled by constitutions or clever designs, but by society.

In the next section we develop this theory in more detail and elaborate on the existence of the three types of state, Despotic, Absent, and Shackled, and we introduce a phase diagram that summarizes the framework in an intuitive way.

This turns out not to completely exhaust the possibilities, and in Section 3 we introduce the notion of a Paper Leviathan, a particular type of state-society relation which characterizes many fragile states. Section 4 begins to use our framework to discuss policy. The key idea here is that fragile states are outside the corridor. The key policy problem is twofold; first, how to make the corridor wider so that it is easier to get into; second, how to get into the corridor. An important feature of our framework is that what you need to do to get into the corridor differs greatly depending on where you are relative to it. If a polity is in the basin of attraction of an Absent Leviathan, for example, the challenge will be to strengthen the state but make this compatible with allowing society to control it. If a polity is on the other side of the corridor, closer to the Despotic Leviathan, then the main problem will be to make society stronger.

It should be clear that our framework has very different implications than a lot of popular social science. For example, a leading argument as to how you create inclusive states and exit from fragility was developed by Huntington (1968) and recently elaborated by Fukuyama (2011). This argument insists that a country must develop the state first and then modernization creates democracy and makes the governance of the state more inclusive. Our framework suggests that this is an unlikely outcome. Creating a state in the context of a narrow distribution of political power will create an institution which can be used to repress any nascent demands of society and this is perhaps one of the reasons that the empirical evidence does not support the modernization hypothesis (Acemoglu et al., 2008).

2. The Narrow Corridor and the Red Queen

The creation of inclusive states is the outcome of a game between state elites and society (Acemoglu and Robinson, 2017, for a formalization). One of the great theorists of this game was James Madison, the main architect of the US Constitution. In Federalist #51 he famously wrote:

> In framing a government... the great difficulty lies in this: you must first enable the government to control the governed; and in the next place oblige it to control itself.

Most discussion of this quotation focuses on "oblige it to control itself," where Madison stressed both democratic control and also checks and balances and constitutional design. But we begin by emphasizing his emphasis on the fact that the government must "control the governed." The initial constitutional framework of the United States was the Articles of Confederation, which came into force in 1781. Under these rules the United States, as a state, was very weak. There was no president or national tax system, and individual states maintained the right to print their own currency and levy their own customs. Power was very decentralized, and it coalesced into radical movements which the central state could not contain (Breen, 2011; Holton, 2008).

In the winter of 1787–88, for example, the federal government had been unable to raise resources to repress Shay's rebellion in Massachusetts, which eventually had to be put down by the state militia. The project of Madison and the so-called Federalists was to solve this problem by strengthening the central state. They planned to take away the rights of individual states to print money and set customs, and to create a national fiscal system and a strong executive in the president. That way they'd be able to pay George Washington's army.

The project of the Federalists was a response to an organized and belligerent society. But when the blueprint for a new set of rules emerged from Philadelphia in the summer of 1788, society pushed back. Most obviously, the Constitution lacked any notion of rights. People were not going to put up with that and even in the face of Madison, Hamilton, and Jay's brilliantly designed propaganda campaign for the Constitution (the Federalist Papers), they forced the Bill of Rights onto the table.

Indeed, Madison had to agree to this to get himself elected as a Representative of his home state of Virginia. The Constitution strengthened the state against society. The Bill of Rights strengthened society against the state. This was still a pretty weak state. There would be no income tax until the twentieth century and the Constitution reserved for the individual states any power not specifically allocated to the federal state. But it was also a pretty weak society; there was still slavery and women were also second-class citizens in many ways. But the key thing was that there was a balance between the power of the state and the power of society. The United States was in the corridor.

The contest between state and society didn't stop with the Constitution and the Bill of Rights. It is ongoing. As the state tries to accumulate authority and power and takes on new roles, it threatens society which reacts by demanding accountability and control to make sure that the power of the state does not work against its collective interest. This dynamic interplay between state and society unleashes the Red Queen Effect whereby, as in *Alice through the Looking Glass*, where Alice and the Red Queen must run faster and faster to stay in the same place, state and society must run faster and faster to stay balanced and in the corridor.

Though this contest keeps state and society in balance, in doing so it creates a much stronger state and a much stronger society. The strength of the state doesn't just allow it to contain a more organized society; it also allows it to provide a lot more public goods and services. That it can do this doesn't mean that it will—it is the strength of society that forces the state to act in the collective interest.

It is useful to dwell here on exactly what we mean by "strength." In terms of the state, this usage is well established in the social science literature, and we discussed it at the start. Our main contribution here is to argue that the strength of the state rests on the strength of society. This strength is manifested in the ability to act collectively, but also in the way society coheres and identifies and in what it demands.

The response of US society to the Federalists' project was not a demand for parochial favors or concessions, but a collective appeal for rights, even if for the moment these rights were limited to white men. The programmatic nature of this demand forced the state to react with rules which applied in the same way to white men. Just as the strength of the state rests on the strength of society, so the opposite is also true. When the state provides public goods and rules that apply to all then it creates incentives for society to identify and organize in particular ways.

Nevertheless, as we've discussed, this balance that the United States achieved in the late eighteenth century is difficult to achieve (the corridor is narrow) and few societies have achieved it. Our description of the game between state and society in the United States suggests why: the balance is contingent on many factors, and can easily get out of kilter with one side getting the upper hand, as we saw with the Qin state. For example, in the wars of independence in South America, society was also energized in many ways. But in the postwar settlements, state elites managed to craft states that were more autocratic and less participatory than in the United States. Simón Bolivar's constitution of Bolivia, for example, featured a president for life who would nominate his successor. It's not that US elites didn't have the same ideas; at the Constitutional Convention in Philadelphia Alexander Hamilton proposed that the president and senators should serve for life. The difference in the United States was that they couldn't get away with it. The reason for that is clear: colonial society in Latin America was already more hierarchical than that in the United States, where the early colonial period had seen the contested emergence of participatory legislative assemblies; there was nothing to compare with these in Latin America (Acemoglu and Robinson, 2012). Elites had more power in Latin America, and they were able to craft institutions that were outside the corridor.

Elites don't always get the upper hand, of course. Precolonial Africa, for instance, was characterized by an incredible number of anti-elite institutional devices which made it very difficult to create hierarchy or centralized institutions. The lineage and clan structures of the Somalis are only one such example. Others include: the nature of social norms and witchcraft accusations amongst the Tiv of Nigeria (Bohannan, 1958); the division of villages into competing moieties in Igboland (Green, 1947); the existence of various types of autonomous checks and balances, such as secret societies in Sierra Leone (Little, 1965, 1966). In precolonial Africa the balance of power tipped not toward state elites but toward society.

We depict these different outcomes in Figure 2.1. On the horizontal axis is plotted the power of society. The vertical axis codes the power of the state. The bold loci distinguish the narrow corridor where state and society are balanced and the Red

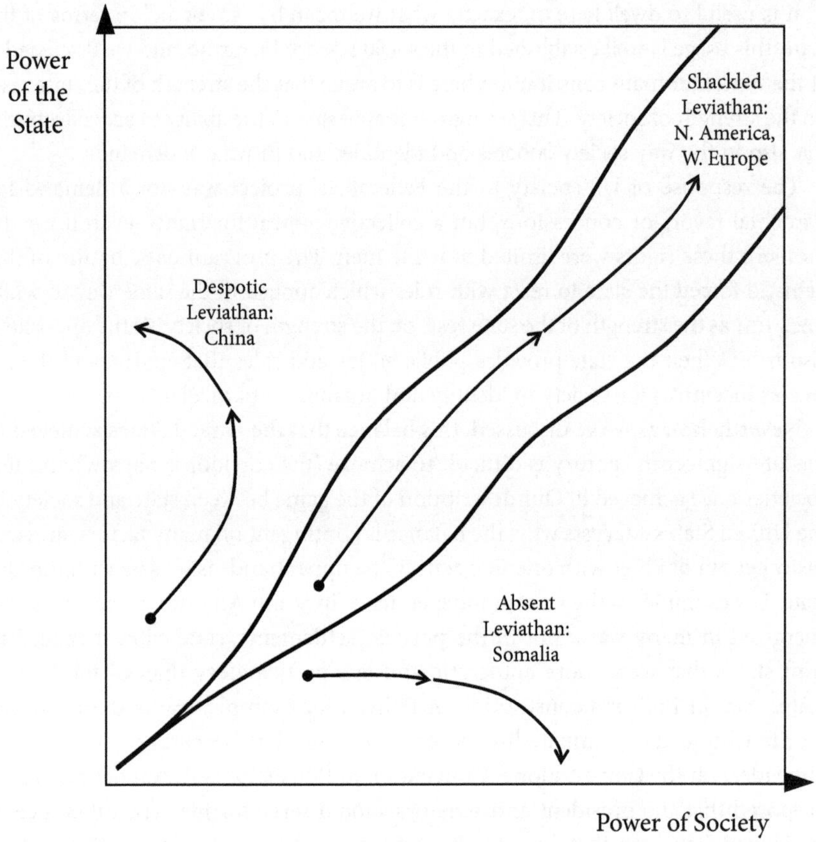

Figure 2.1 The Narrow Corridor

Queen Effect comes into operation. In this case the dynamics take a polity toward the top right of the diagram, where both state and society are strong. Yet if a polity is outside of the corridor, it veers off towards either an Absent or Despotic Leviathan.

There are a few important things to observe about this diagram. Though in the Despotic case one might have thought state elites could freely create a very powerful state, what the framework reveals is that such a state is always weaker than a Shackled state. The reason is that the strength of the state is acquired in competing with society. If society is vanquished, as in Qin China, then the state can easily dominate it without the need to acquire great strength and so it does not bother to accumulate it. Another important result of the framework is that in a sense Migdal (1988) is right when he argues that the state is weak because society is strong. This is true in the Somali case. But what Figure 2.1 shows is that a truly strong state emerges when society is very strong. In a sense the problem in Somalia is that while society is strong and organized, it is not organized in a way that allows it to use its strength to control an emergent state. If it could, then the virtuous dynamics of the Red Queen Effect would come into play. Finally, it is good to note that this framework departs significantly from the elite-centric framework of much of the literature on state formation, with its emphasis on stationary bandits etc. (Sánchez de la Sierra, 2020). Our view is that it is never in the self-interest of elites to create inclusive states; they have to be forced to do so by the pressure of society. This implies that most existing political economy theories of fragile states (such as Besley and Persson, 2011) are incomplete because they focus only on various types of elite strategies without conceptualizing the role of society in forcing the state to become stronger.

3. Paper Leviathans

Figure 2.1 implies that all societies are within the basin of attraction of one of the three types of states we have outlined; Despotic, Absent, and Shackled Leviathans. But in fact these are not the only possibilities. We can also have incompetent, weak, but still unaccountable and cruelly despotic states. This situation, which we call a Paper Leviathan, is common in Latin America, Africa, and parts of Asia. It can be stable, in the sense that society is not strong enough to credibly challenge state elites and such elites do not want to develop state strength for one of two reasons: First, elites may be able to exploit state weakness to their benefit—as former Brazilian President Gertulio Vargas supposedly put it: "To my friends everything, to my enemies the law." Second, because building the state may set off what we call the "mobilization effect"—a process whereby society becomes more organized in response.

To see this effect, recall our discussion of the Red Queen Effect in the US case. Here the state-building project of the Federalists triggered a reaction from society which had significant effects on what the state actually ended up looking like, and the Federalists had to give up on some of their goals. If state elites had anticipated that, then it might have deterred them from initiating the state building project to start with. This is the essence of the mobilization effect. Go back to the Colombian case we discussed in the introduction. Why is it that Colombia has such a dreadful road network? As Uribe (2017) documented, for 200 years the Colombian state has failed to construct a proper road between Mocoa, the capital of the department of Putumayo and the rest of the country. Why? Though his evidence does not definitively reveal a Machiavellian design, it is clear that an effect of the absence of roads in peripheral Colombia is to create a very parochial society unable to organize together and focused on private goods and favors for itself. This is a very different type of society than that which demanded the Bill of Rights in the United States. This parochial society is very easy for elites in Bogotá to manage with some well-chosen subsidies and concessions. Colombian elites are worried that broader provision of public goods will create a very different type of society, one much more mobilized at a national level, more difficult to control, and much more difficult, possibly impossible, to buy off. They do not want the Red Queen Effect to get into motion (see Robinson, 2016).

4. Getting into the Corridor

Let's now return to our discussion of fragility. Fragile states are outside the corridor in Figure 2.1. This framework suggests that the right way to think about how to cope with fragility, and how to design policy to reduce fragility, is how to trigger a movement into the corridor. We can break this into two parts. First, the wider the corridor, the easier it is to get into. So the first question is what factors or policies influence the width of the corridor? The second question is, holding the position and width of the corridor constant, what strategies can help get you into it?

4.1. The Width of the Corridor

It is useful to think of the corridor's width in terms of various types of structural factors. For instance, consider a specific corridor: South Africa. Historically, in the years of Apartheid before 1994, South Africa was out of the corridor and well into the despotic part of Figure 2.1. Apartheid, though it had an intellectual rationale in the separate development of white and black people, was at heart a huge system of labor repression (see Feinstein, 2005). This system was institutionalized through the Bantustan system and the creation of black "homelands" and pass laws and through the Color Bar which blocked Africans from becoming skilled workers. This system benefitted all whites but had some severe tensions. For one, it forced white business-people to pay high wages for skilled white laborers who did not face competition from Africans. In the second half of the twentieth century, however, the situation began to change. As the economy became more industrialized, partly in response to externally imposed sanctions, labor coercion became less profitable because unskilled labor became less and less important while the dearth of black skilled workers became more and more costly. Apartheid became less profitable for whites. At the same time repression became less internationally acceptable with evolving notions of universal human rights, and this is where the sanctions came from. The power of this agenda was supported by the international community at the end of the Cold War. Apartheid South Africa had been staunchly anti-communist, but suddenly that didn't matter anymore. Nelson Mandela was released from prison only three months after the fall of the Berlin Wall. All these factors made the corridor wider in South Africa. Sustaining a despotic state is costly, and whether whites wanted to do it depended on the costs and benefits. These moved against the

Apartheid state in the 1980s and made it more likely that the country would get into the corridor, but it didn't make it inevitable, as we'll see.

The nature of our argument here immediately suggests several other factors that plausibly influence the width of the corridor. The idea that the structure of the economy mattered in South Africa obviously has broader implications. For example, natural resource dependence tends to narrow the corridor. The width of the corridor can also depend on globalization, but how it influences this depends on your comparative advantage. For example, the nature of comparative advantage probably narrowed the corridor in many developing countries in the late nineteenth century. In countries like Guatemala, which could advantageously specialize in exporting labor-intensive tropical crops like coffee, there were large benefits to repressing labor. This encouraged the rise of more despotic institutions, making the corridor narrower (Acemoglu and Robinson, 2012, chapter 12). At the same time, for countries with different comparative advantages, say in manufacturing, the resulting process of urbanization and the emergence of modern factories created the incentives and opportunities for society to become more mobilized, thus making the corridor wider.

As the example of sanctions against South Africa suggests, the width of the corridor also depends on the nature of legitimacy in the international state system. In October 2017, the World Health Organization (WHO) appointed Zimbabwe's then-President Robert Mugabe its "goodwill ambassador" for noncommunicable diseases, declaring that he could use this position "to influence his peers in his region." Yet Mugabe had adopted policies that led not just to severe economic decline in his country, but also to a collapse in public good provision—including public goods in the health sector. In 2008–09 an outbreak of cholera in the country led to almost 100,000 cases and 4,300 fatalities. This was blamed by the World Health Organization (WHO) itself precisely on the lack of public goods provision such as the "Environment (no toilets or latrines, lack of safe water/no working boreholes, sewage in the streets) [and] Limited access to health care (lack of transport/distance to hospital)" (WHO, 2009). How on earth could Mugabe then be appointed, by the same institution, to such an incongruous role? The answer is the nature of sovereignty in the international system. A president of a sovereign state, even if he maintains power through fraud and violence, as Mugabe did until he was removed from power by his own army, is respected by the international system.

4.2. Strategies for Entering the Corridor

Taking as given the position and width of the corridor, the second question is what does a polity which is outside of the corridor have to do to get into it? One thing we have already mentioned, which is evident from Figure 2.1, is that the task is very

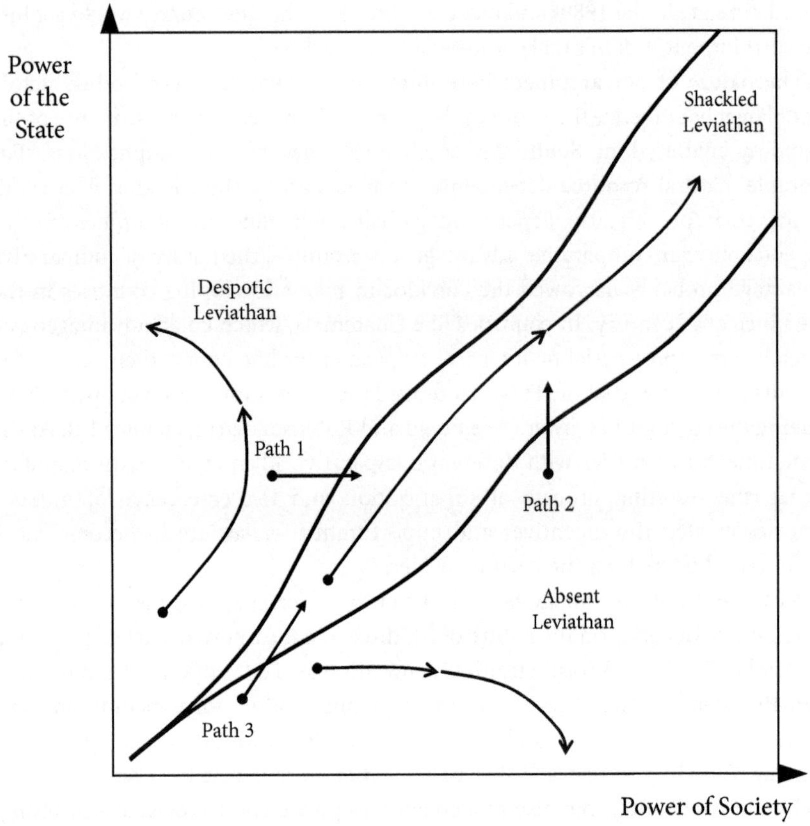

Figure 2.2 Doors into the Corridor

different depending on where you are. To emphasize this, examine Figure 2.2, where we plot three arrows. Path 1 moves a polity from the orbit of the Despotic Leviathan into the corridor. To the left of the corridor the state dominates society, you have to reduce this imbalance. To the right of the corridor the typical problem is that society is stronger than the state (as in our Somalia example). You need to develop a stronger state, but one which people will cooperate with because they think they can control it. This is Path 2. With a paper Leviathan you have to try to set off the mobilization effect so that society gets stronger and the state responds to this by accumulating capacity so that both society and state move together and the Red Queen starts to work. This is represented by Path 3.

4.2.1. Three Heuristics

We now present four examples of relatively successful transitions, if not into the corridor, then at least in the direction of the corridor. They correspond to paths

1–3 in Figure 2.2. In each case we emphasize what we call an "heuristic"—a general property of the strategy used to deal with specific problems, which we believe has some broader utility.

Path 1: Create coalitions that make credible agreements to make sure that potential losers do not become roadblocks.

In our framework it is natural to think of both the strength of the state and society as inputs into a "production function" that generates surplus (Acemoglu and Robinson, 2017). Surplus is higher when both are strong. Thus, from a situation where the state is despotic, if credible agreements could be made, both elites and society could be made better off by moving along Path 1. A clear difficulty from the elite point of view is whether or not society can credibly commit not to use its strength in ways which make the despotic elite worse off.

One can think of the transition from Apartheid in South Africa in exactly these terms. Earlier we emphasized how domestic structural change began to make Apartheid less attractive economically, particularly for manufacturers, while at the same time making it less acceptable in the international state system. Nevertheless, Apartheid could have persisted. That it did not was because the African National Congress (ANC), representing the disenfranchised, managed to strike a deal with the white governing National Party. A key part of the deal involved agreeing to let the whites keep the assets they had accumulated under Apartheid. On the extensive margin, however, things would be radically different. South Africa got into the corridor through a negotiation that credibly changed the balance of power and made institutions more inclusive. Part of the agreement was constitutional; for example, the restrictions on the uncompensated redistribution of land. But constitutions can be rewritten and even ignored, so this could not be the whole answer to the problem of how the deal was credible. The solution to the credibility problem was to make sure that black political elites had a vested interest in maintaining white property rights intact. This was achieved by part of the policy of Black Economic Empowerment (BEE). The critical part of this policy was the stipulation that white businesses had to take on board black owners. The threshold level of black ownership started gradually and was then increased. But black people had little capital so they could not buy shares outright. To be BEE compliant, therefore, companies made deals with Africans, selling the shares at a discount and usually financing the transaction themselves. As it turned out, most of these black partners were politically connected ANC elites. The current president, Cyril Ramaphosa, became a multimillionaire through these deals. Though in fact the deals started spontaneously before the transition, when white businesses realized that a way to protect their property rights was to give black elites a vested interest in them, the ANC institutionalized the policy. This was needed because whites faced a collective action problem which the ANC solved for them.

Econometric evidence (Santos-Villagrán, 2016) suggests that BEE deals improved firms' profitability and increased their investment. The rest of BEE was a far more radical affirmative action plan to promote the inclusion and social mobility of black people.[2]

The comparison here to Zimbabwe is interesting. The agreement made between the whites and blacks in South Africa in 1994 has been broadly respected, but that made in Zimbabwe fell apart. The constitutional strategy was the same, reconfirming that simply writing things into the constitution doesn't solve commitment problems. There was no Zimbabwean BEE. Why not? Here the width of the corridor mattered. The Zimbabwean corridor was much narrower because the economy was more agricultural and there was far less industry. In fact, in 1980 at the time of Zimbabwe's independence, there were a mere 50 firms listed on the Salisbury (to become Harare) stock exchange. This meant that the redistribution of shares and ownership titles was infeasible in Zimbabwe; therefore, compromise and coalition building to achieve a balance of power were much harder.

It's not all structures of course. Coalition building and deal-making necessitate innovation. People have to see things in different ways and people must be willing to compromise. Here there seems to have been a critical difference between Nelson Mandela and Robert Mugabe.

Path 2: Build on existing balances of power in society and scale them up.

Societies which are in the basin of attraction of the Absent Leviathan are there because society keeps the state weak. Typically, at a local level, people have developed norms or institutions which block hierarchy from emerging. The trick to getting into the corridor for a society like Somalia, which has these features, is not to override these local norms and institutions but to build on them and institutionalize them in ways that can be scaled up.

In the introduction we pointed out that historically, Somalia had never developed centralized political authority. In his discussion of this history, Lewis emphasizes that the clan was the fundamental way that society was organized ("As Somalis themselves put it, what a person's address is in Europe, his genealogy is in Somaliland," Lewis, 1961, p. 2). But he also emphasized contract, or *heer*;

> Its closest equivalents in English are compact, contract, agreement or treaty in a bilateral sense. Thus several men or parties are said to be of the same *heer* when their relations are regulated by an agreement... As need arises the terms of contracts are abrogated, existing treaties modified or rescinded, and new

[2] BEE is related to the strategies used by Chinese Township and Village Enterprises in the 1980s and 1990s; these gave shares to local politicians so that they had a vested interest in the property rights of the firms (see Che and Qian, 1998).

> agreements made. The majority of *heer* agreements binding groups relate principally to collective defense and security and to political cohesion in general.
> (Lewis, 1961, pp. 161–2)

The notion of *heer*, and the fundamental egalitarianism of Somali society, provided the basis for a process of state formation.

In the northwest of the country, in what was formerly British Somaliland (where Lewis had done his research), the Somali National Movement (SNM) led the movements towards autonomy and independence (even if not recognized by the international community). The Barre government persecuted the Isaaq clan family, who formed the core of the SNM. As early as 1981 in its political manifesto "A Better Alternative" the SNM proposed "a new political system built upon Somali cultural values . . . which elevated the Somali concept of *heer* or inter-family social contract in which no man exercised political power over another except according to established law and custom" (Bradbury, 2008, pp. 63–4).

After the Barre government collapsed in 1991, Somaliland became de facto independent and under the control of the SNM. Since then there has been a remarkable process of bottom-up state formation. To understand how this happened we have to go back to Lewis's emphasis on contract. Somali society was very used to negotiation and agreement, even if there was conflict as well. Clan elites tapped into this tradition and organized a series of conferences, which often lasted for months, to try to build consensus within the Isaaq clan family (about 80 percent of the population of Somaliland) and then with the other clans. In 1988 the SNM had already formed a *Guurti*, consisting of a council of clan elders, to advise them. It was not a traditional institution, but an innovation, and it proved to be the basis of what now is the upper house of the Somaliland legislature. After 1991 the SNM found it could not govern or provide order without the cooperation of clan elders, and in 1993 at Boroma it convened a conference to plot the constitutional future of the country. At this conference there were 150 clan elders and the aim was "to fashion a form of government that accommodated the clan system within a modern structure of government" (Bradbury, 2008, p. 99). It designed a constitution with an elected president and a bicameral legislature, both houses of which were to represent the clans.

Boroma was only the most important of a whole series of conferences. Another, the Sanaag Grand Peace and Reconciliation Conference, was held in October 1993.

> The peace process in Sanaag utilized customary practices and institutions of peacemaking. Elders of diya-paying groups met in assemblies (*shir*), together with religious leaders and [Sultans], and created new political treaties (*heer*) between clans. (Bradbury, 2008, p. 102)

Early reinforcement of the authority of elders seems to have been important in stopping warlordism from emerging. It took until 2001 to finally agree on a constitution and ratify it in a plebiscite.

In the meantime, the conference at Boroma had elected Mohammed Egal to be the first president. Egal was a shrewd political operator who immediately struck a deal with a group of mostly expatriate businessmen to get a $3 million loan in exchange for favorable economic opportunities. He used the money to begin demobilizing armed militias, a legacy of the war against Barre. Egal also used the resources and customs receipts from the port of Berbera to strengthen his political control; at another conference in Hargeysa in 1997 he both got himself re-elected and the constitution adjusted so that while the upper house was to be a clan-based House of Elders, the lower chamber was to be based on direct universal suffrage elections. Most commentators interpret this initiative as an attempt by Egal to strengthen his personal control at the expense of clan elites. Egal systematically strengthened the state, for example banning local revenue-generating checkpoints in 2000 (only the central government could levy taxes) and he began to centrally appoint local governors, disrupting de facto clan control: "By using a discourse related to state and constitution, the government tried to keep the opposition in check. By using a discourse related to clan institutions, the opposition tried to displace the government's legitimacy" (Renders, 2012, p. 222). Interestingly the constitutions stipulated that only three political parties could run candidates for the lower chamber or the presidency. This was an explicit attempt to stop the political fragmentation which had bedeviled the country in the 1960s when hundreds of clans and sub-clans began forming parties. The three eligible parties were those who got the most votes in local elections which were more open.

The incentives to start this process were obviously to rebuild the state and to provide order and some basic public goods. They were also economic. Just across the Red Sea is Saudi Arabia and the Gulf states, which are large markets for Somali livestock exports, particularly during the Hajj when several million people descend on the Islamic holy cities. Acharya et al. (2017) show that the Somaliland state organized to provide public goods, both in terms of animal health, and also to restrict piracy so that exports took place.

The Somaliland experience is not anomalous. One can interpret the successful economic and political development as caused by the ability of Tswana elites to build legitimate institutions from the bottom up (Acemoglu and Robinson, 2012, chapter 14). More recently the experience of attempts by outsiders to build state authority in Afghanistan and Iraq suggests that this works when it begins with the already existing legitimate local political institutions (see Malkasian, 2013; Murtazashvili, 2018).

Another interesting example of the resilience, effectiveness, and legitimacy of local institutions comes from post-civil war Sierra Leone. The post-colonial national state in Sierra Leone suffered from all of the syndromes that plagued independent Africa (see Reno, 1995; Acemoglu and Robinson, 2012, chapter 12). It was autocratic, unaccountable, and had little organizational capacity. At the local level, however, the story was very different. there are many instruments that society uses to control power. The postcolonial state left intact the system of paramount chiefs which the British had created in the 1890s. Yet the British, as in most of Africa, simply recognized the "facts on the ground" and the authority of existing elites and "ruling families." Even the method of electing chiefs, the so-called "Tribal Authority" seems to have been modelled on pre-existing institutions. Subsequently neither the British, nor post-independence governments, were able to seriously manipulate these institutions, mostly because they seem to have retained legitimacy and the support of local people. The obvious reason for this is that people have norms and institutions that can make sure chiefs are accountable. These include the secret societies, such as the Poro. They also include landowning families that have deep roots and de facto power. Chiefs themselves only have land to the extent that they are themselves part of a landowning family. They have no control over the land of others. The legitimacy of these institutions was evident at the end of the civil war in 2002. Though there was a great deal of pressure from outsiders to radically change these local political institutions, this was ignored by the Sierra Leone government who reconstituted the system pretty much as it had been before the war.

What were the consequences? Sierra Leone isn't yet a "development miracle" but it certainly is a "stability miracle." Guns have gone and you can travel anywhere in the country in safety. The current homicide rate is lower than that of the United States. Our hypothesis is that this is because the balance of power at the local level creates a legitimate political order that allowed demobilized combatants to be reintegrated into society. Stability has also been aided by the post-civil war decentralization, which has aided power-sharing between the two major political parties. The Sierra Leone People's Party (SLPP), which is strong in the south, and the All People's Congress (APC), strong in the north. The SLPP could win in the south, and show they could govern well (Myerson, 2014), which is one of the reasons that they won the 2018 presidential election. However, even if the APC lost national power, they can still govern northern councils. So far Sierra Leone has not gone along the same route as Somliland and completely re-imagined national institutions from the bottom up, but the balance of power at the local level has addressed fragility.

Path 3: Harness the mobilization effect to trigger the Red Queen.

What can you do in a situation like the one that Bogotá, the capital city of Colombia, found itself in early the 1990s? Homicide rates were at about the national average of 80 per 100,000, the highest in the world. People were so afraid of being carjacked or robbed that nobody stopped at a red light at night. When you drove you hid money in different parts of your vehicle, just in case. The rich hired bodyguards and lived in fear of being kidnapped. Parks and public places were deserted. There were constant power cuts.

The weak state and the weak society were exactly what you would expect with a Paper Leviathan. In 1994 Antanas Mockus was elected mayor of Bogotá. He was a mathematics and philosophy professor from the National University of Colombia. He reached the critical realization that the solution to Bogotá's problems was not to fear the mobilization effect, but to harness it. He aimed to build state capacity to trigger social mobilization and at the same time stimulate social mobilization to get the state and state functionaries to react. Liliana Caballero, his chief of staff, described their philosophy as "to not have the citizens go around the state asking for a favor, asking for their rights, but rather the administration going around the citizen that should be at the center."

In Bogotá, the main administrative building was known colloquially as "the humiliator" signifying the indifference with which a Paper Leviathan treats its citizens. How could it get away with that? Because local politics was clientelistic, with politicians exchanging money, jobs, and contracts for votes. Society was fragmented and reduced to "patients of the state" as Auyero (2012) puts it. Mockus' gamble was that if he could jolt society out of this equilibrium, he could break the clientelistic grip. To do this he had to change the way people thought about the rules, to convince them of the value of public goods and acting in the collective interest. He first hired 20 mime artists who walked the streets of Bogotá and made fun of people who crossed the street on a red light, threw litter on the floor or broke the rules. This was such a success that he hired 400 more. He distributed 350,000 thumbs up and thumbs down cards so that Bogotanos could either approve or disprove of behavior on the street. He developed a whole set of ideas which he used to try to get people back into the empty public spaces, like parks. Women were particularly affected by the insecurity, so he introduced a "Night for Women"; for four hours men had to remain at home so that only women would be on the street. It was policed by more than 1,500 policewomen.

This mobilization pushed the state to deliver, and from the other end Mockus pushed the state. The average amount of time it took to pay a bill, which had previously been one and a half hours, fell to just five minutes. There were huge improvements in public good provision. Between 1993 and 2003, for instance, the proportion of households who had access to piped drinking water increased from 79 percent to 100 percent. For access to sewage, the proportion increased from 71 percent to 95 percent. Perhaps most consequential for people's welfare, the homicide rate fell by almost three quarters to just 22 per 100,000 by the time Mockus left office.

The strategy that Mockus used was adapted to Medellín by Sergio Fajardo, first when he was mayor there between 2004 and 2008 and then as governor of

Antioquia between 2012 and 2016. He took the radical step of trying to integrate Medellín's outlying areas, the "comunas" into the city by building a series of dramatic escalators.

5. Conclusions

Fragility (and lack of capacity) of the state in many parts of the world is a vital problem for prosperity, peace, and stability. But stability and state capacity cannot be engineered by international organizations (or even by clever constitutional designers). The only way fragility can be avoided is by building inclusive states, that is, Shackled Leviathans, which means moving into the narrow corridor. This is not easy, but it has been done in the past and it can be done again, even if some factors make it significantly more challenging for a society to move into the corridor as our comparison between South Africa and Zimbabwe makes clear. Recognizing the problem and identifying what facilitates (both in terms of structural factors and coalition building) such a move are critical. We have emphasized two main things here. First, the nature of the problem critically depends on the initial conditions of the society. The problem facing the ANC in South Africa, for example, was a very different one from the one facing the SNM in Somaliland at precisely the same time. Different movements in Figures 2.1 and 2.2 are required, and different strategies are appropriate and feasible in different contexts. We provided three ideas, "heuristics," which we abstracted from successful cases of moving towards the corridor. Though there is much to learn, our simple framework gives a way of conceptualizing the challenge of escaping from fragility.

References

Acemoglu, D., S. Johnson, J.A. Robinson, and P. Yared. 2008. "Income and Democracy", *American Economic Review*, 98: 808–42.

Acemoglu, D. and J.A. Robinson. 2012. *Why Nations Fail.* New York: Crown.

Acemoglu, D. and J.A. Robinson. 2015. "Paths to Inclusive Political Institutions," in J. Eloranta, E. Golson, A. Markevich, and N. Wolf (Eds.), *Economic History of Warfare and State Formation*. New York: Springer.

Acemoglu, D. and J.A. Robinson. 2017. "The Emergence of Weak, Despotic and Inclusive States," NBER Working Paper #23657.

Acemoglu, D. and J.A. Robinson. 2019. *The Narrow Corridor.* New York: Penguin.

Acemoglu, D., J.A. Robinson, and R. Santos-Villagrán. 2013. "The Monopoly of Violence: Theory and Evidence from Colombia." *Journal of the European Economics Association*, 11(1): 5–44.

Acharya, A., R. Harding, and J.A. Harris. 2017. "Security in the Absence of the State," unpublished paper, Stanford University.

Anderson, P. 1974. *Lineages of the Absolutist State*. London: New Left Books.

Auyero, J. 2012. *Patients of the State: The Politics of Waiting in Argentina*. Durham, NC: Duke University Press.

Besley, T. and T. Persson. 2011. *Pillars of Prosperity*. Princeton, NJ: Princeton University Press.

Bohannan, P. 1958. "Extra-Processual Events in Tiv Political Institutions," *American Anthropologist*, 60: 1–12.

Bradbury, M. 2008. *Becoming Somaliland*. Oxford: James Currey.

Breen, T.H. 2011. *American Insurgents, American Patriots: The Revolution of the People*. New York: Hill & Wang.

Chaves, I., L. Fergusson, and J.A. Robinson. 2015. "He Who Counts Wins: Determinants of Fraud in the 1922 Colombian Presidential Elections," *Economics and Politics*, 27(1): 124–59.

Che, J. and Y. Qian. 1998. "Insecure Property Rights and Government Ownership of Firms," *Quarterly Journal of Economics*, 113(2): 467–96.

Feinstein, C.H. 2005. *An Economic History of South Africa: Conquest, Discrimination and Development*. New York: Cambridge University Press.

Fukuyama, F. 2011. *The Origins of Political Order*. New York: Farrar, Straus, and Giroux.

Green, M.M. 1947. *Ibo Village Affairs*. London: Sidgwick and Jackson.

Holton, W. 2008. *Unruly Americans and the Origins of the Constitution*. New York: Hill & Wang.

Huntington, S.P. 1968. *Political Order in Changing Societies*. New Haven, CT: Yale University Press.

Lewis, I.M. 1961. *A Pastoral Democracy: Study of Pastoralism and Politics Among the Northern Somali of the Horn of Africa*. Oxford: Oxford University Press.

Little, K.M. 1965. "The Political Function of the Poro. Part I." *Africa*, 35(4): 349–65.

Little, K.M. 1966. "The Political Function of the Poro. Part II." *Africa*, 36(1): 62–72.

Malkasian, C. 2013. *War Comes to Garmser*. New York: Oxford University Press.

Migdal, J. 1988. *Strong Societies and Weak States*. Princeton, NJ: Princeton University Press.

Murtazashvili, J. 2018. *Informal Order and the State in Afghanistan*. New York: Cambridge University Press.

Myerson, R. 2014. "Democratic Decentralization and Economic Development," https://home.uchicago.edu/~rmyerson/research/decent.pdf (last accessed July 16, 2020).

Renders, M. 2012. *Consider Somaliland: State-Building with Traditional Leaders and Institutions*. Leiden: Brill.

Reno, W. 1995. *Corruption and State Politics in Sierra Leone*. New York: Cambridge University Press.

Robinson, J.A. 2016. "La Miseria en Colombia," *Desarollo y Sociedad*, 76(1): 1–70.

Sánchez de la Sierra, R. 2020. "On the Origin of States: Stationary Bandits and Taxation in Eastern Congo," Volume 128, Number 1, 32–74. *Journal of Political Economy*.

Santos-Villagrán, R. 2016. "To Share in to Keep: Ownership Transfers to Politicians and Profitability in Post-Apartheid South Africa," https://sites.google.com/site/rjsantosvillagran/research (last accessed July 16, 2020).

Uribe, S. 2017. *Frontier Road: Power, History, and the Everyday State in the Colombian Amazon*. Hoboken, NJ: John Wiley & Sons.

World Health Organization. 2009. "Cholera Country Profile: Zimbabwe," https://www.who.int/cholera/countries/ZimbabweCountryProfileOct2009.pdf (last accessed July 16, 2020).

3

Transition Programs

A Theory of the Scaffolding Needed to Build out of Fragility

Paul Collier

1. Introduction

A fragile state is typically in a locally stable but dysfunctional sociopolitical equilibrium that traps the economy in stagnation and repeated economic crisis. This makes the objective of an International Financial Institution (IFI) Program quite distinct from that in a society that is normally successful but has stumbled into a macroeconomic crisis. In the latter, the predominant objective is to restore normality through a period of expenditure restraint. In the former, macroeconomic crisis may be an opportunity to disrupt the dysfunctional political equilibrium—what the Report of the Commission on State Fragility Growth, and Development refers to as a "pivotal moment."

This difference makes complex the task of designing a Program in a fragile state. A successful Program is likely to be distinctive: not only different from those in advanced economies that hit macroeconomic crisis, but different from those in other fragile countries that are not at pivotal moments.

The premise of this chapter is that both fragility and "normality" are locally stable equilibria. The core task facing a fragile state is *transition* between these equilibria. I set out three recent developments in theory each of which is useful in understanding this transition. Their common generic concept can be thought of as a "scaffold": an apparatus that becomes irrelevant once a country arrives within the gravitational pull of the desired locally stable equilibrium, but which is essential for the transition from the initial equilibrium. Because "scaffolds" are commonly discarded once the new equilibrium is reached, little can be learnt from the observable characteristics of "normal" countries that is pertinent for the escape from fragility. Hence, we should expect the macroeconomic theory needed to underpin a Program designed to help a fragile state escape the condition, to be radically different from that underpinning a "normal" Program.

Section 2 sets out the overarching concept of the "syndrome of fragility" introduced in the Report of the Commission on State Fragility, Development and Growth. It shows how a series of distinctive and interdependent sociopolitical

Paul Collier, *Transition Programs: A Theory of the Scaffolding Needed to Build out of Fragility* In: *Macroeconomic Policy in Fragile States.* Edited by: Ralph Chami, Raphael Espinoza, and Peter Montiel, Oxford University Press (2021). © International Monetary Fund.
DOI: 10.1093/oso/9780198853091.003.0003

characteristics and their economic consequences lock some societies into a dysfunctional but locally stable equilibrium. In the following sections I delve into two of these characteristics that are particularly critical for IFI Programs, each of which is amenable to specific types of "scaffolding." Section 3 sets out in detail a diagnosis of why the state is ineffective. It incorporates basic insights from the social psychology of motivation in teams into an economic theory of the rational behavior of public employees. As in section 2, it shows why ineffectiveness is a locally stable condition, in the process, providing an explanation as to why it has been impervious to the vast donor expenditures on "capacity building." I use the theory to set out the scaffolding needed to escape the condition and draw its implications for IFI Programs. In section 4 I discuss a second fundamental characteristic of fragility: radical (Knightian) uncertainty. Having been dismissed by macroeconomics since the 1950s, Knightian uncertainty has recently been rediscovered, but the valuable new insights have yet to be applied to fragility. I attempt to do this, drawing out the implications for IFI Programs. Section 5 concludes.

2. The Syndrome of Fragility

The predominant international narrative explaining fragility is that it is the result of some "root cause," usually a past injustice perpetrated by the government, that must be corrected. This is both misleading and unhelpful. It is misleading because fragility is a set of interdependent characteristics that lock a society into a dysfunctional but stable equilibrium. As a matter of logic, as in any aspect of public policy, the solution to the problem need bear no relation to its cause. It is unhelpful because it casts the government in the role of the guilty party. Not only does this inevitably undermine a cooperative relationship; in many respects, governments of fragile states are, in fact, helpless victims of the syndrome.

2.1 The Syndrome of Characteristics

Typically, a fragile state has six distinctive characteristics. First, the society is fractured into oppositional identities with little or no overarching shared identity that might set differences in a context of cooperation. Shared identity did not exist prior to colonization; the colonial authorities were incapable of building it; and post-Independence leaders have not built it. Instead, struggles for power have been organized around inherited subnational identities. Second, the state lacks legitimacy with a substantial group of its own citizens. Third, the state lacks the capacity to perform basic functions such as taxation, security, the rule of law, and the provision of economic infrastructure. Fourth, households and firms face existential uncertainties that discourage irreversible decisions and shorten horizons. Fifth, there are few formal private sector enterprises and so the workforce is not organized into entities that can reap economies of scale and specialization, leaving the population unproductive and hence poor. Finally, the polity and the economy are frequently hit by shocks against which they have little resilience.

Each of these characteristics not only differentiates a fragile state from a conventional situation, but differentiates one fragile state from another. Further, the characteristics reinforce each other. Because the society is fractured into oppositional identities, the state is typically regarded by parts of society as captured by one identity group, undermining its legitimacy. Lacking legitimacy with many citizens, the state cannot rely upon willing compliance, and struggles to motivate the public sector workforce, so that basic functions cannot be properly performed. This in turn further undermines legitimacy. The risks posed by the lack of legitimacy, and the inadequacy of basic state functions, combine to discourage the formation and attraction of formal enterprises. In turn, the paucity of formal enterprises, together with the lack of legitimacy, expose the society to shocks, and the incapacity of the state limits the ability to cushion them. In turn, the frequency and severity of adverse shocks keeps derailing attempts to escape from fragility.

Once fragility is recognized as such a syndrome, it has clear and important implications. One is that strategies of escape are highly constrained and so more complex than macroeconomic management in conventional settings, both for governments and for the IFIs. Programs in fragile states should be both highly distinctive, and highly context-specific.

The other is that fragility is highly persistent. Much of the time a fragile state is in a stable political equilibrium that IFI intervention cannot alter. An IFI cannot by itself heal social rifts, and the composition of the government may merely exacerbate those rifts. An IFI cannot confer legitimacy on the state in the eyes of its own citizens, even if it can sometimes do so with bilateral donors. An IFI cannot build state capacity unless a government genuinely wants that capacity: the Fiscal Affairs Department of the IMF has been "building capacity" in African tax administrations for several decades, yet the ratio of tax revenue to GDP has not increased. An IFI Program can, for its duration, reduce existential uncertainties, but as I will argue, this is often at the expense of increased post-Program uncertainty. An IFI Program cannot increase foreign direct investment (FDI), unless the government itself can establish credibility with investors. Only the final aspect of fragility, a lack of resilience, is reduced by an IFI Program, but I will again argue that even this is more limited that usually recognized.

2.2 Implications for Program Design

An implication of this frustrating litany of limitations, is that IFIs should no longer connive at the pretence that progress is always possible everywhere.

Unambiguously, what fragile states need is transformative change. But for much of the time an IFI is not in a position to overcome the sociopolitical obstacles to transformation.

Programs come with finance and policy change: both are intended to restore sustainability, but the two components can be both complements and substitutes. Finance and reform are complements when the finance enables a sequence to be implemented, both politically and practically. They are substitutes when finance is used to avoid necessary change. To date, the solution adopted by the IFIs to this potential for tension has been conditionality: the government wants to avoid change, but agrees to some as the price of the finance. In the conventional Organisation for Economic Co-operation and Development (OECD) context this approach is appropriate. The cause of the unsustainability is either an adverse shock or a temporary deviation from a satisfactory path: once normality is restored, the society will be back on this path. But fragile states are not on such a path, and the Program may be an opportunity for the fundamental change. However, IFI Program conditionality cannot force an unwilling government into implementing such change. Instead, it risks inducing a theatrical performance in which the government publicly commits to changes that it intends to frustrate.

Hence, Programs for fragile states should be tailored to three distinct circumstances. Distinguishing between the three is an important matter of two professional assessments, both sociopolitical. The first is whether the situation is potentially a pivotal moment in which the government may be willing to face the reality that past policies have failed and a new approach must be embraced. In sections 3 and 4 I will set out objective criteria which can help to guide this assessment. If the situation is judged not to be pivotal a Program is likely to encounter the above scenario of theater. Both by mitigating the crisis provoked by past policies, and by shifting the responsibility for painful corrective actions from the government to the IFIs, under these conditions a Program impedes social learning and so, *ceteris paribus*, is unhelpful. Nevertheless, a Program may be necessary if without it the society is at significant risk of imploding into open disorder. But in this case, the objective of the Program should be to preserve order rather than force through radical reforms for which there is neither political appetite nor social acceptance. Arguably, the ambitious IFI Program in Yemen may have triggered the collapse into disorder. Hence, this risk of disorder needs to be assessed both in determining whether a Program is justified despite the lack of potential for serious reform, and in determining the content of any Program.

In combination, the two assessments generate three distinct situations:

(1) The crisis is not a pivotal moment and there is little risk of implosion without a Program: the best strategy is therefore to avoid a Program. Being solely responsible for undiluted consequences of how the country has been run, is the best context for social learning;

(2) the crisis is not a pivotal moment but without a Program there would be a significant risk of implosion: the best strategy is to proceed with a cautious and modest *Stabilization Program* which recognizes that there is limited scope for reform; and
(3) the crisis is potentially a pivotal moment: the best strategy is to engage through a distinctive style: a *Transition Program.*

2.2.1 Programs for Fragile States That Are Not Coincident with Pivotal Moments

Such Programs should be less ambitious about change. The typical situation will be an order-threatening crisis to which the government is neither willing nor able to respond adequately without IFI assistance. Conditionality is inherent to such Programs, but in imposing it, IFIs risk taking the primary responsibility for announced policies. The infamous photograph of the Managing Director of the IMF standing over President Suharto as he signed the Indonesia Program, exemplifies this transfer of authority and responsibility. By casting governments in the role of entities in need of external restraint, this inevitably reinforces the external narrative of domestic mis-governance, and denies government the autonomy necessary for credible external communication. Regardless of what it says, the government's agreement to the Program is interpreted not as a free choice, but as the price it is willing to pay in order to get the money. It is presumed that it would rather have the money without the policies. Since the Program is temporary, while it reduces near-horizon investor fears, it may thereby intensify longer-horizon fears.

Quite evidently, in many contexts, not just those of fragile states, this accurately reflects the nature of the situation: the country is in a crisis because the government has mismanaged the situation. But the domestic narrative is controlled by the government, and may deviate considerably from that apparent to an external audience. The government signs an agreement concerning policy change in return for IFI finance. The IFI Program enables the government temporarily to cede responsibility for policy. This, for example, was the situation in the UK in 1976, and in Nigeria in 1986. The gain in terms of the rapid, temporary improvement in macroeconomic management comes at the price of reduced social learning. Almost invariably, a Crisis Program involves sharp reductions in living standards. The proposition that the reduction would have been even sharper without the Program is overly complex in the context of practical politics and the government is most certainly not going to make it. Hence, typically the misery is attributed to the IFI policies of adjustment, rather than to the preceding policies that caused the crisis. As a result, the society learns the wrong lesson. As with other forms of social learning, this lesson sets in as a narrative and can be highly persistent. The exemplar, is that the legacy of the Nigerian Structural Adjustment Program of 1986 is still setting Nigerian policy in 2018, as President Buhari adamantly resists the policies needed to accommodate the 2014 fall in the global oil price. The lesson of Nigeria is that Crisis Programs should be designed so as not to impede social learning. A highly difficult implication is that once a crisis begins, it should be left to unfold sufficiently for citizens to recognize that something painful is happening that cannot be blamed on foreign agencies. A further difficult implication is that support should only be available once a government has fully and repeatedly explained to its citizens the mistakes it has made that have led to the crisis. It should be quietly explained to the government that the more it tries to blame the crisis on bad luck or foreign malevolence, the more delayed will be any Crisis Program.

2.2.2 Programs during Pivotal Moments

Programs during pivotal moments are arguably going to be the most important activity of IFIs during the coming decades. Being capable of supporting these opportunities to the maximum extent possible should be the IFI priority. IFI engagement with fragile states should be such that they are able to identify potential moments, and respond swiftly and at scale. Inevitably, pivotal moments are more easily seen in retrospect. But given these uncertainties, IFI responses should be guided by the asymmetric consequences of type 1 and type 2 errors. The costs of missing a pivotal moment are likely to far exceed those of providing temporary support in an environment that turns out not to be receptive.

The modalities of an IFI Transition Program are advice, practical support, finance, and communication. I consider them in pairs.

2.2.3 Advice and Practical Support

The strategy contained in a Program is advice to government. What both variants of opportunity have in common is that any strategy must at all times respect the distinctive constraints implied by the syndrome of fragility. The most significant of these constraints is the lack of state capacity: regardless of what policy change is desirable, little can be implemented. Policy change must fit into existing capacity.

Regardless of the substance of any proposed change, there is liable to be an asymmetry in the consequences of failure and success that is distinctive to fragility. Because the syndrome of fragility is persistent, a state that is fragile is likely to have a long history of being so, which has left a legacy of despondency and the psychological condition of "learnt helplessness." People expect proposed changes to fail, and this belief tends to be self-fulfilling. Psychologically, people tend to shift their identity towards success and away from failure. Public officials are typically demoralized by decades of failure, and this reduces their identification with the state—which in turn is damaging for the performance of public organizations. An implication is that there is a premium on success; it helps to reset expectations.

For this reason, an IFI program in a fragile state should not begin with a diagnosis of what is wrong—many things are wrong—but with an assessment of the effective capacity for implementing change. On the basis of an honest and prudent assessment of this capacity, the IFIs and bilateral donors should jointly and severally commit to accepting the principle of ruthless prioritization: any Program must be feasible given capacity. But feasibility requires more than being within bureaucratic capacity. A Program is only feasible if it also satisfies the other constraints implied by fragility. The social fragmentation into oppositional identities, and the lack of state legitimacy, imply that any change initiated by government, however benign, is liable to be misinterpreted and opposed by significant groups. Hence, there needs to be some realistic assessment of the likelihood that a proposed change may be derailed by political opposition.

Because fragile states are shock-prone, horizons are rationally short. Consequently, citizens and politicians will judge Programs by effects that are quick and visible, rather than by prospects of long-term improvement.[1] Conventional Programs that deliver the standard sequence of pain now for benefit later are unlikely to endure to the stage at which gains are reaped. Hence, a successful Transition Program is likely to be a sequence of easily implemented steps, each of which rapidly generates some visible improvements. The magnitude of the improvements may be less important than their sign and their speed. Initially, the choice set for feasible policies that generate such payoffs may be very limited but early successes may slacken the constraints sufficiently so that the set of feasible policies expands more rapidly than it is being depleted, and gradually comes to include changes that matter for the long term. The set of policies that in sequence enable the society to escape the fragility trap to a better local equilibrium, may well be trivial or even irrelevant once in the vicinity of that new equilibrium: they are scaffolding that achieves the transition.

Because the government will only wholeheartedly implement changes that it has embraced, all such changes must be within its locus of control. Hence, the process that generates a Transition Program cannot be a negotiation. IFI staff can help a government think through options by working with government staff on an initial menu of such options, and helping clarify the data that enable assessments of packages that would be macro-feasible. Possibly, there should also be limited financial support so that governments can hire individuals who could work for it. But any such external support should be clearly embedded within the domestic political process. Were the IFIs to find themselves negotiating with a consultancy company, it would evidently be even more damaging than negotiating directly with government.

[1] The work of David Laibson suggests that preferences are better described by now-bias, rather than by a high discount rate.

In contrast to a conventional Program, the actions to be taken by the government should not be specified over a three-year horizon. Some pre-commitments may be useful, but the immediate crisis atmosphere must first be alleviated to provide the government with the space to think strategically. It will then face many unknowns and so need to plan change on a step-by-step basis as initial changes that yield quick and visible success open opportunities for further change. The purpose of the Program is to support a transition between locally stable equilibria. By their nature, such transitions are times of extreme Knightian uncertainty: the future course of events is not well predicted by behavior during the recent past. In such a context, many actors—including opponents of fundamental change—will make mistakes, and these unanticipated events will create new opportunities. The famous Chinese metaphor of "feeling a way across a river, stone by stone" aptly captures a sensible decision calculus for such transitions, as does the Facebook management maxim, "move fast and break things."

2.2.4 Finance and Communication

The finance provided for a Program to reduce the risk of disorder in a fragile state is conceptually a form of conflict prevention. The purpose of finance for a Transition Program is quite different. In the context of crisis, it can greatly increase the scope for quick, visible wins. Typically, during the onset of crisis the government is inflicting painful adjustments on the population that reduce its popularity. In fragile states the government does not have the trust of citizens; consequently, such unpopularity can be terminal for those in government espousing change. Sacrifices by citizens for a better future will indeed be needed, but these may need to follow after a phase of actions that build trust.

Here I consider only communication of IFIs with government. External communication is taken up in section 4. Governments of fragile states typically hold two related and highly dysfunctional beliefs: a lack of responsibility for failure, and helplessness. Crises are blamed either on chance events, or on enemies within or outside the country. Helplessness is used to explain the persistence of failure. In the sense discussed further below, these beliefs are sustained by narratives that need to be countered. The standard psychological approach to countering them is not direct contradiction, since this gets filtered out, but to make officials aware of nuance and counter-examples. The aim is for the officials themselves to respond to further crises by more nuanced explanations. Achieving this change in thought processes typically takes a few months. This is longer than a single IFI mission visit, but remarkably short relative to the long history of failed past engagement.

One implication is that all IFI staff who engage with officials in fragile states should be trained in these standard psychological techniques of influence. A second is that officials are helped to see situations in a more nuanced way if they come to know and trust officials from countries that have recently successfully implemented change.

3. The Sinews of State Effectiveness

I now address in more detail the characteristic that the state is ineffective.[2] It cannot raise taxes; it cannot provide practical security; it cannot enforce the rule of law; and it cannot provide the basic economic infrastructure of energy and connectivity needed for firms to function properly.

The IFIs have misdiagnosed this condition as a lack of "capacity," defined technically as missing skills. Ineffectiveness is, however, fundamentally a sociological and psychological condition rather than a technical one. The ability of institutions to function depends primarily upon the motivation and cooperation of the teams employed to undertake their mandates: the skills of individuals are endogenous. Often, functionality will also depend upon the degree of willing compliance by citizens: tax administration is more effective if people accept their obligation to pay tax.

Few fragile states are actually short of staff. They are, however, acutely short of *motivated* staff. Two solutions have been attempted, one from economists, the other from lawyers. Both are direct applications to fragile states of approaches that have become internationally standard in OECD contexts. I will suggest that in fragile states they have had only limited success because neither addresses the real problem.

3.1 Building Motivation in Public Organizations

Economists have viewed the problem through the lens of Principal-Agent Theory. Public employees need to be rewarded with incentives tied to monitored performance. The generic drawbacks of this approach are well understood. Most monitoring schemes can be gamed: employees deliver what is monitored at the expense of what is not monitored. Most public sector work depends upon cooperation in various teams, often ill-defined, and differentiated rewards are demotivating because they weaken group identity.

Lawyers have viewed the problem through the lens of obligations and decision procedures specified in contracts. Globally, contracts have become much more specific, and hence longer, and the room for discretion has been reduced. Directors specify verifiable criteria that determine decisions, and their staff become implementers of these rules. For example, in Britain over the past 25 years, the proportion of workers who say that they have significant discretion over the content of their work has declined by 40 percent. As with monitored incentives, the generic drawbacks of this approach are well understood. The reduction in autonomy is demotivating, and also forfeits the use of tacit knowledge that cannot be verified: all contracts are intrinsically incomplete.

[2] This section draws on Collier (2016, 2018).

These economic and legal strategies for improving the performance of public officials are designed for a public sector that is already working fairly well—as it is in the locally stable OECD equilibrium. This gives little guide to how they might work in the very different equilibrium that characterizes fragile states. In principle, their effects could be much better or much worse, but regardless of what the effects are, it is evident that they have not been designed to address the fundamental challenge of transition.

In the OECD countries the public sector had already built a reasonably motivated workforce. The new techniques have had some modest successes by tightening up on the slack inevitable even when an approach dependent upon intrinsic motivation and peer pressure is overall successful. Their generic problems have arisen because this bedrock of motivation has inadvertently been somewhat weakened. But in fragile states the bedrock has never been built. In consequence, sometimes the strategies may work better in fragile states: there is less bedrock to undermine. For example, the reduction in autonomy may not matter if staff have not been using their autonomy to further the mandated functions of the organization. But equally, they may work even worse because there is no safety net of social motivation. For example, monitored incentives may induce far more diversion of effort when previously unmonitored tasks have been performed merely due to inherited routine rather than from a sense of purpose. Irrespective of the net balance of these positive and negative effects, each of the generic strategies makes the fundamental task of building purposive teams more difficult because, as in OECD contexts, they undermine trust, team spirit, and engagement with purpose.

Economists are manifestly correct in thinking that people are not willing to work without appropriate financial reward, but wrong if they insist that this is the sole motivation that needs to be considered. People are also motivated by ("incentivized by"), the peer esteem and self-respect that come from accomplishing a task that fulfils a recognized purpose. Similarly, lawyers are right in thinking that the tasks that need to be accomplished should be clearly specified in the job, but wrong if they insist that this can be sufficient to fulfil the goals of the organization. A public organization cannot fulfil its mandate unless most staff accept the necessary tasks as part of their own purposive goal.

How then can this process of internalization be accomplished? All public institutions are organized into hierarchies. The leader has some powers of command and control but these are insufficient to accomplish the mandate. However, an implication of the hierarchy is that the leader is also the nodal actor in a social network, with asymmetric power of communication with those staff within his mandate. He communicates through what he says and what he does.

The communication task of the leader is to address the compliance problem through creating a sense of obligation among his staff. The goal is to create obligations that are sustainably performed by all staff because they are recognized as *reciprocal*. This is the new locally stable equilibrium to which a fragile state needs to transition. A fundamental neurological reason for the efficacy of reciprocity is that Oxytocin release, the trigger for trust, is *reciprocal*. We also know that reciprocity is reinforced by anger: this is the response when an action by *i* that benefits *j*, *and is intended to be reciprocated*, is not in fact reciprocated. Across human societies, this instinct develops in childhood: what matters is not *i*'s action of help, but how the intention behind the actions is understood. As with all complex understanding, this depends upon language. In virtually all human societies a generic package of beliefs circulates, implanted by narrative speech acts reinforced by visible actions, that can be made specific for the leader's purpose through effective communication. This belief system consists of three distinct beliefs. One concerns identity: the individual is a member of the group, getting utility directly from the sense of belonging to it and being esteemed by its members. The second concerns causality: there is some task which if everyone in a group performs it, all will benefit. The third concerns norms: if *i* performs the task and *j* benefits, *j* should reciprocate, while if *j* does not reciprocate, he should lose esteem within the group.

Virtually all humans are socialized during childhood into receptivity of this generic package: this is why "minimal group" experiments have proved to be so alarmingly effective. Internalization of mandated purpose on a public organization depends upon a leader harnessing this predisposition by inculcating a specific package of beliefs about identity, causality, and norms among his staff.

Starting from a situation in which few staff work as desired, generating reciprocity among a staff faces a severe coordination problem. If the desired effort is individually costly, nobody has an incentive to perform it. Overcoming the coordination problem involves two distinct stages. In the first stage a "scaffold" is erected using a specific and often complex set of speech acts that initiate the process of behavioral change. In the second stage, once change has spread across the organization, it can be maintained by the generic package without the scaffold. Then, however, analysis of such a self-sustaining equilibrium gives no insight into how it has been built. That is why the analysis of the efficacy of small interventions in successful public organizations cannot be used as a guide to what works in fragile states: OECD states are post-scaffold; fragile states are pre-scaffold.

A new sense of obligation to perform a reciprocal action, *x*, begins with the leader generating three interlocking beliefs among his staff, each by specific speech acts:

D "I am the communicator-in-chief of this organization"

E "If each of us does *x* it will benefit us"

F "People who belong to this organization esteem members who do *x*"

Belief *D* starts with a minimal but strategically important assertion of a fact. But for strategic purposes the leader needs to ensure that his communications are understood as generating common knowledge: "I, the head of this organization, am communicating with all you." It then adds salience to the objective characteristic of membership. Since change is easiest if started in small subgroups, membership of these sub-units must become salient. The most straightforward and minimalist mechanism for conferring identification on membership is to give the group a name. Attaching a name to an entity makes it easier for the brain to recognize it as a concept: this applies not just to groupings of people but quite generally to comprehension of the world. But for complex concepts, such as the collective intentionality that creates the mental concept of a human group, language is essential: naming gives a group identity.[3] As discussed in the following paragraphs, this can be reinforced by conferring a special purpose.

Belief *E* is a crucial causal proposition that persuades by explaining the rationale for the individually costly action. The first necessary condition for compliance is that in aggregate, the individual costs of action x should be perceived to be less than the common benefit: x is collectively rational. Articulated purely as a narrative, the proposition must be compatible both with prior beliefs about causality and any recalled consequences of past common action by some group with which members of the network are familiar. In a sub-unit of a public organization, making this belief credible may depend upon a national leader having credibly communicated why particular public sector mandates are vital for national progress.

Belief *F* sets an additional criterion for membership of the organization: the action e, of conferring esteem on other members of the group who perform action x. Action e is far less costly than action x. But the enforcement of action e in turn depends upon a further action, r: the recognition of common membership. I assume that action r is costless, and directly confers utility on the recipient because it indicates belonging, which is intrinsically valuable. Since it is costless to give and valuable to receive, it triggers the generic package that enforces reciprocity. But awarding r carries the potential cost that if a staff member gives it to someone who has not performed the modestly costly action e, and so will not be regarded as a member of the group by others, then he himself may not receive r from other members. Consequently, a further necessary condition for the leader to be able to generate compliance is that the cost of foregoing r from other members of the group exceeds the gain from receiving r from those excluded. Given these conditions, through the common knowledge generated by *F*, the receipt of r from other members of the group depends upon participating in esteem-conferring behaviour.

[3] Barrett (2017), pp. 97 and 135.

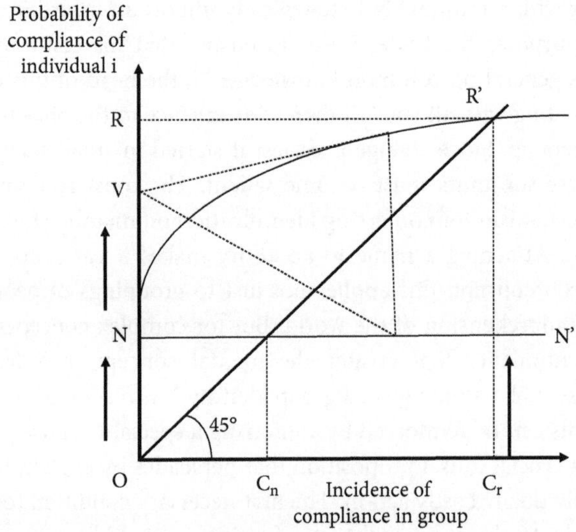

Figure 3.1 Generating Social Pressure for Compliance
Source: Author, modified from Fehr and Falk (2002).

A third necessary condition for the leader to be able to generate compliance is that the value of belonging to the organization should exceed the cost of action *e*. The value of belonging is the sum of the *r* conferred by the other members of the organization. Evidently, the leader may also specify nonbehavioral criteria for shared identity. In conjunction, the criteria unite yet distinguish the group.

With these beliefs in place, members of the organization now face a trade-off between self-interest and esteem. Performing action *x* is privately costly, but it will rationally be rewarded by other members of the group with the utility-increasing action *e*. A fourth necessary condition for compliance is that the cost of action *x* is less than the benefit from the *e*-actions that confer esteem on those who perform *x*.

Figure 3.1 is a modified version of Fehr and Falk (2002), figure 6. The vertical axis shows the probability that actor *i*, the representative member of the group, will comply with action *x*. The horizontal axis shows the incidence of compliance in the group. Prior to communication, compliance would confer a utility loss for *i*, and there is no sense of obligation to others. Hence, regardless of the incidence of compliance, *i* does not put any effort into *x*: *i*'s compliance schedule is coincident with the horizontal axis. The speech acts *D+E+F*, subject to the above conditions, shift *i*'s compliance schedule upwards to *N–N'*. As drawn, the power of esteem generated by this narrative package is modest, yielding only a modest increase in the equilibrium incidence of compliance to c_n.

But now that some people are performing action *x*, the more powerful forces of reciprocity generated by the generic belief system kick in. This twists *i*'s compliance schedule upwards, from *N–N'* to *N–R'*, raising the equilibrium incidence of compliance to c_r. At the eventual equilibrium, R', social pressure consists of two distinct components: N, the initial pressure from the speech acts $D+E+F$, and $R–N$, the pressure from reciprocated actions. As depicted, the latter is by far the stronger component: the equilibrium is self-sustaining. But getting to the new equilibrium from the initial equilibrium at the origin depended upon the specific communication by the leader: the scaffold.

Hence, *reciprocal obligations rest upon a prior well-defined domain of reciprocity*. That is, there has to be a bounded group within which each actor knows the criteria for membership, and its implied esteem-conferring actions. For common action, shared knowledge is insufficient: shared knowledge must become common knowledge.[4]

Finally, I consider steps which speed the passage from new beliefs to changed actions. In a large public sector, not everybody will change their behaviour at once: some must change first. A leader has, therefore, to provide a credible answer to the questions “Why me?” and “Why now?”

3.1.1 The “Why Me?” Problem

Most decisions are not simultaneous: members of the organization take them sequentially. For those decisions that are simultaneous and high in frequency, such as the daily work routine, coordinating change is intrinsically difficult. Expectations of how others will behave today are likely to be more strongly influenced by the weight of past behaviour than by any new communications from the leader. But the leader always has the option of transforming such decisions from being simultaneous by combining the new obligations with a proposed sequence in which they should be adopted within the organization.

Where decisions are sequential, whether intrinsically or by transformation of a simultaneous process, expectations of subsequent decisions will be set predominantly by those early in the sequence. This can make the passage from new obligations to new actions either far more difficult, or far easier, depending upon whether the sequence is private, shared, or common knowledge.

Consider the case in which the sequence of decision is randomly assigned as private knowledge. Further assume that the process of decision itself is unobservable: all that can be observed is the action x, should it be performed. In this structure, the first person in the decision sequence faces no social pressure to perform x. The decision *not* to do x is not observed as a decision: what is observed is merely that nobody has done x. People do not know how many people have reached this as a decision. Hence, the first person in the sequence rationally chooses not to perform the costly action x. The second person in the sequence faces precisely the same decision problem as the first, with precisely the same

[4] See Thomas et al. (2014).

information. Evidently, the outcome of this sequential decision situation is that nobody performs *x*. Further, it gradually becomes manifest that this is the outcome of decisions. Once this becomes common knowledge, the group has inadvertently coordinated on the decision not to do *x*.

To address this problem, the leader needs to generate three further beliefs.

H "The sequence in which staff should take their decision about *x* is $S_1 \ldots S_n$'"

I "Staff 1, 2, 3.. are the "Vanguard" whose decision will determine the outcome and so they are especially worthy of esteem"

J "The rationale for choosing and announcing this sequence is *z*."

Belief *H* reveals, and perhaps changes, the order of decision. If the leader is to propose a purposive sequence, one evident way of signalling that the sequence is fair is for him to put himself first in the sequence. Belief *I* confers a new identity, the Vanguard, upon those first in the sequence. Membership of the Vanguard comes with its own package of recognition, linked to esteem-conferring behaviour. Belief *J* provides a rationale, both for the sequence itself and for making it public. Because the action is privately costly, the most obvious rationale for the chosen sequence might be that those best able to bear the cost should be the first to perform it: by placing himself first in the Vanguard, the leader reinforces his legitimacy. The rationale for making it public follows from how it transforms the decision calculus.

Consider the decision problem of the person assigned to be first in the sequence. In contrast to the previous situation, now all eyes are on him: other members rationally know that his decision will be decisive in determining whether the group reaches a collectively good outcome and that non-adoption is a decision. Who should the leader choose as the first member of the group in the sequence? Unless overruled by manifest constraints, the answer to this is evident: to reinforce the narrative of purposive sequence with credible action, the leader must put himself as the first in the sequence. For other members of the selected sub-group, the new and unavoidably salient identity of "Vanguard" created by *I* thereby gears up the potential loss of esteem.[5] The effect of the package *H*+*I*+*J* is shown in Figure 3.1 as the upward shift in *i*'s compliance schedule, *i* having now been identified as a member of the Vanguard, from *N* to *V*. As the Vanguard is gradually expanded, the esteem associated with being a member of it diminishes: as drawn if fades to zero, so that the compliance schedule ends up being twisted from *N–R*' to *V–R*', with no change in the eventual equilibrium but a more rapid move toward it.

[5] The strategy has been proposed by Collier and Venables (2015), as a means of increasing the pressure for the gradual closure of the global coal industry.

3.1.2 The "Why Now?" Problem

Whereas the "Why me?" problem is how to publicly identify the sequence of decision and to provide a credible rationale for it, the "Why now?" problem is how to provide a credible rationale for why *the next time* the decision is taken, it should be different from previous decisions. Why is now the right time to change, given that it inflicts individual costs on each decision taker?

Belief *E* is not in itself sufficient to provide a convincing answer to this question. Belief *E* is merely a necessary condition: if action *x* will not ultimately advantage the group it will clearly not be adopted. But there may be many actions which if we all did them would advantage the group at individual cost. Hence, Belief *E* needs to be reinforced by a new sense of timeliness: for some reason, the group has reached a *pivotal moment*. Logically, this can be either because the past has suddenly become unsustainable, or because the future has suddenly presented the group with new options. Thus, crisis and opportunity are the options for a credible narrative that addresses the "Why now?" problem. Of these, crisis has the advantage in that the urgency of change can more readily be made apparent. Implicitly or explicitly, delay will inflict high costs. A new opportunity may in itself be insufficient: it succeeds in answering the question "Why not yesterday?" but it does not provide a satisfactory answer to " Why now, rather than later?"

In effect, the crisis option is for the leader to communicate the pair of beliefs {*K*, *L*}:

K: "our past behaviour has become unsustainable."

L: "if we delay change, the costs will be much higher."

3.2 Implications for IFI Programs

In considering Program design it is useful to distinguish between two contexts. One is a Program that is not coincident with a pivotal moment: the rationale for the Program is not to support transformation, but to reduce the risk of the society collapsing into disorder. The other is a pivotal moment, whether a crisis or a change of leadership.

If the realistic assessment of the context is that the purpose of the Program is to reduce the risk of disorder, the implication for state institutions is that little can be achieved. The scope for "capacity building" is limited, and is likely to result in failures that reinforce the psychology of hopelessness. To date, practical IFI support for strengthening the civil service in fragile states has focused on "capacity building" through training individual members of staff. If the above analysis is correct, this is largely forlorn, because skill acquisition and utilization are endogenous to team-based motivation. Assessments suggest that the skills acquired are seldom used. In such contexts it may be better not to try than to try and fail.

If, however, there is a reasonable basis for regarding the moment as pivotal, then strengthening the key sinews of the state should become a prime focus of the Program. All IFI Programs depend upon the state for implementation. Without a state that is much more effective, fragile societies will remain fragile. Consequently, strengthening the civil service is an integral objective of a Transition Program. In furthering this objective, IFIs can potentially deploy the four modalities: advice to political leaders on how they themselves can improve the civil service; the provision of practical support to strengthen capacity; finance; and their own direct communications with civil servants.

3.2.1 Advice and Practical Support

To date, the typical Program advice to political leaders has been over-ambitious and conventional. Over-ambition has been driven by the manifest need for far-reaching change, but there is little capacity to implement change and rapid success is important. Realistically, many ministries will be headed by people in a position to frustrate change and so grand reforms are unlikely to be feasible. Program design has been conventional in reflecting the fashions in OECD public sector reform: monitored incentives and more detailed job specification. If the above analysis is correct, while these may yield modest success, they are liable to be counterproductive.

The above analysis implies that the advice for civil service reform that a Transition Program would recommend would be to create Vanguards. These are small units that could become prestigious identities, matched by an important and feasible purpose, within which a big-push approach is taken to changing the norms of their members. The objective is to build new peer group norms that self-police group performance: esteem is reciprocally bestowed for effortful tasks that are aligned with that purpose. Political leadership has the vital role in this process of bestowing prestige and purpose on the Vanguard units. Once one or two Vanguard units are operating successfully, the approach can rapidly be scaled by promoting the staff of the Vanguard units to head other important units, spreading the new norms more widely. Vanguards are the scaffolding that enables the transition to a more effective state. *Whether a government is willing to attempt a Vanguard strategy can then be used as a practical criterion for assessing whether the moment is potentially pivotal.*

If the right strategy is Vanguards, then there is a clear role for practical support to focus on making Vanguard units successful as rapidly as possible. There might be something to be learnt from Tax Inspectors without Borders, which embeds tax inspectors from an OECD country in a unit of a local tax office to work as part of the team, doing the job alongside local colleagues. Evaluated experiments in concentrating foreign staff in Vanguard units and tapering them out, might show which approach was most effective in sustainably resetting norms.

3.2.2 Finance and Communication

A fragile state typically requests a Program when it has run out of money. The Vanguard approach need not be costly, but some additional pay for the members of a Vanguard unit is likely to be a credible signal that political leaders indeed regard its purpose as important, and its members as special. As the Vanguard units are scaled up, this becomes a significant cost, but if they work then expenditure is a sound investment: the state has to become more effective. The use of a Vanguard unit is then a legitimate part of a Transition Program.

In respect of IFI communication, the agencies are well placed themselves to bestow prestige and encourage a sense of purpose in Vanguard units, and the high frequency of interaction with government during a Program provides many opportunities for this to be sustained until it takes root.

4. Fragile States and Knightian Uncertainty

Following 50 years of neglect, the analysis of Knightian uncertainty has recently returned to macroeconomics as a consequence of the 2008 crisis. For the study of fragile states this is fortuitous because, as implied by the syndrome discussed above, existential uncertainty is inherent and salient to the condition and so more important than in societies that are not fragile.

In the 1950s, economists dismissed Knightian uncertainty as an influence on economic decision taking (Kay and King, 2020). Decision takers converted uncertainty into objectively quantified risks in which all available information was efficiently used to produce unbiased forecasts. This was highly convenient for economic analysis, but it rests on two untenable assumptions. One is that the underlying economic process generating observable data is stable, so that the past is in principle a reliable guide to the future. Even for the advanced economies, macroeconomists are now rather less confident about this assumption than they once were. But for states that are currently fragile, the futures generated should the fragility syndrome persist, and should it escape the syndrome and become a conventional economy are evidently fundamentally different. Moreover, the escape from fragility is a unique future event, entirely contingent upon other future events unique to the society, and so itself cannot be predicted on the basis of past data. The transition is inherently both unknowable and fundamentally important. Further, during the transition the country is not within the behaviour patterns of either the initial or the eventual local equilibria. The other mistaken assumption adopted in the 1950s was that economic actors were able to assimilate past data efficiently so that actors already "know the model," or asymptote to it through Bayesian updating. Neuroscience and psychology established the human brain does not work like this, but the assumption was justified by the proposition that although unsophisticated actors were "ambiguity averse"—that is, they avoided decisions when faced with uncertainty—sophisticated actors would recognize that such aversion was a costly "bias." Because those decisions critical for macroeconomic analysis, namely investment, were taken by businesses, Bayesian updating appeared to be a reasonable characterization of the decision processes important for the macro economy. However, recent experimental research has tested this Bayesian assumption and found it to be precisely wrong. Far from sophisticated actors being more willing than others to convert uncertainty into risk, they display stronger "ambiguity aversion."[6]

As Kay and King (2020) argue, faced with the need to take decisions in the context of radical uncertainty, people would be *irrational* to adopt Bayesian updating and have evolved to rely on some plausible narrative account of "what is going on." Explanations of past events that circulate within a network of similar actors and provide a reassuring basis for converting uncertainty into risk. Such narratives are radical simplifications of a highly complex reality around which actors coordinate. Depending upon the context, such coordination around a narrative can have two very different outcomes. One is that since it is a simplification, at some point it grossly mis-forecasts outcomes, resulting in a crisis. The other is that the coordinated behaviour becomes self-fulfilling.

Narratives have these features even in highly-sophisticated markets, but in fragile states they are of the essence. Not only do fragile states abound in Knightian uncertainty; the small size of their economies does not justify substantial expenditures by formal private actors better to understand them. These are the archetypical environments in which economic actors rely upon narratives as the basis for their decisions. The recent history of investor sentiment in developing countries abounds in such narratives: investor-oriented phrases such as "Asian Tigers," "BRICS," "Emerging Markets," "Frontier Markets," "the Hopeless Continent," and "Africa Rising" were simplified explanations of the recent past that became widely accepted in investor circles and were presumed to have predictive power.

Humans have an innate appetite for explanation: narratives readily fill the void left by Knightian uncertainty. Fragile societies have an evident default-option narrative set by their accumulated history of failure: they are "basket cases." This is reinforced by the extensive marketing of images of catastrophe on which the business models of the development NGOs are dependent. The implied explanation of past failure is that there is some unalterable characteristic of the society that dooms it to further failure. Such narratives add a further twist to the syndrome of fragility because they are self-fulfilling. One reason that emerging market investment in fragile states has increased far more than OECD investment is that emerging market firms are immunized against the "basket-case" narrative

[6] As Hong et al. (2018) show, precisely contrary to Bayesian theory, the more sophisticated the economic actor, the more does uncertainty discourage irreversible decisions.

since it was recently falsified in their own societies. They also operate based on a narrative, but it is more likely to be "We know what will happen here because they are us 40 years ago."

4.1 Program Design to Counter Knightian Uncertainty

An implication of the pervasive nature of Knightian uncertainty and the "basket case" narrative in fragile states, is that communication is a fundamental part of public policy.

Narratives are generated and spread by communication within networks. Owing to the structure of networks, the power of communication is commonly highly concentrated among a few nodal actors. In consequence, nodal actors have strategic power: they can influence narratives to achieve their objectives. IFIs and the leaders of fragile states are often the communicators-in-chief in the economic networks pertinent for a fragile state. This power is increasingly recognized even in the context of macroeconomic policy in OECD societies, a striking example of a self-fulfilling narrative being Draghi's "Whatever it Takes" speech.

In considering Program design it is useful again to distinguish between Transition Programs intended to assist pivotal moments, and Stabilization Programs with the more modest objective of averting disorder.

4.1.1 Stabilization Programs

Recall that the justification for these Programs is that without them there is a significant danger of collapse into disorder. Because much of the Knightian uncertainty comes from fear of government, an IFI Stabilization Program directly changes the narrative by placing bounds on government actions. It thereby reduces the "fat tails" of events that actors most fear. However, as discussed above, this gain comes at a high price in reduced social learning. This is compounded by the near-permanent economic crises in fragile states that lead to near-permanent IFI Programs, contrasting with the rarity of Programs in OECD and Emerging Market countries. In the latter, it is evident that the government has been guilty of serious errors and so, temporarily, it is acceptable for it to be subject to IFI policy conditions. However, in crisis-prone fragile societies, Program conditionality implies that policy is being set by the IFIs on a near-continuous basis, fundamentally undermining the accountability of government to citizens. This suggests that in contexts where the chance of initiative fundamental change is negligible, Programs should be as minimal as possible, subject to the need to avert disorder.

4.1.2 Transition Programs

As discussed, pivotal moments constitute the peak of Knightian uncertainty: the strategy is to shift the country between local equilibria. Because policy For a more extended discussion of the use of narratives in policy transition see Collier and Tuckett (2021). conditionality is detrimental to strategies for pivotal moments, Programs out of Fragility cannot directly reduce uncertainty by requiring the government to refrain from damaging actions: the IFIs can no longer play the role of the backstop to fears of government. In their place, governments can themselves communicate through narratives and signalling actions that complement each other. Narratives can reset the ideas around which actors coordinate; signalling actions can enhance the credibility of what is said. Once actors behave in accordance with the new ideas, the new, locally self-reinforcing equilibrium is achieved: the communication is the scaffolding that becomes redundant. But typically, in fragile states official communication has not been used for such a purpose. It has commonly been focused on short-term issues concerning politically salient individuals. An important role of IFIs is to help leaders communicate more strategically.

Narratives have played an important role in some of the remarkable past transitions out of fragility. They address uncertainty by providing an account of events around which actors can coordinate. Botswana was once one of the poorest countries in the world. Like many such countries, it discovered a valuable natural resource, but often such discoveries have reinforced fragility rather than enabled escape. Prudent macroeconomic policies were the proximate explanation for success. But the critical mass of public support that enabled the government of a functioning multi-party democracy to sustain prudence had to be built by communication. The signature narrative of the founding president, Seretse Khama, was "We are poor and so we must carry a heavy load." This message was readily understood as "We must be patient." By pre-empting the more typical resource-discovery narrative of "We're now rich and can have what we want," it protected a generation of technocrats to invest diamond revenues.

Signalling actions which reveal that the government is willing to bear costs to implement its strategy enhance the credibility of its narratives. For example, although the government can no longer use the IFIs to make its commitments credible, it can build its own commitment technologies. Helping a government to do so is a valuable part of a Program that leaves an institutional legacy. The British strategy post-2010 of establishing an independent Office of Budgetary Responsibility may be a useful model. The government publicly committed itself to independent expert assessment of the viability of its budgets. In the preparatory phase of the budget, this assessment would be confidential: a liaison between the Office and the Treasury. Once the Budget was revised and publicly released, the Office would issue a final public assessment. By establishing the Office, the government created a credible commitment technology which enabled the sovereign borrowing to be tapered over the course of a decade, without ever encountering a crisis of confidence. Although the IFIs cannot insist on the creation of equivalent institutions, they can encourage and facilitate them. Commitments to IFIs can also be part of the solution, but they only work to reveal type if they are manifestly freely chosen by government.

Pivotal moments occur in two ways: a change of leader, and a crisis. Though nearly all pivotal moments are of this form, neither new leaders nor crises inevitably create pivotal moments. They are visible signs of a potential opportunity rather than infallible indicators that one has occurred. These two opportunities to launch a process of transformation—new leader and crisis—may call for different IFI responses.

In fragile states, changes of leader are unlikely to be seen as fully legitimate: the state lacks legitimacy with part of its population and so lacks resort to legitimating processes. But this can sometimes enhance the opportunity for policy change: a new leader may need to adopt a narrative of radical change to justify what began as an opportunistic power grab. New leaders can disown the past, and this is a huge advantage. Further, citizens are typically uncertain as to the true intentions of a new leader and so are looking for guidance. This is the context in which communication by a leader is at its most effective: it is much easier to reset a narrative than if an existing leader announces change. It is in consequence, a wasting asset. With a new leader, quiet advice on options is useful, but the imperative is that choices are seen by citizens as those of the leader.

Crisis invites a new narrative that mistakes have been made, so that past beliefs can be challenged. The imperative is to maximize social learning: citizens must clearly associate the costs involved in the crisis with prior choices that the government has made, or with past modes of social behavior. Consequently, the government must take full responsibility for past errors and be seen by citizens to be responsible for the Program. *Whether the government is willing to do this, and understands why it is important for resetting ideas, is a second practical criterion for assessing whether a crisis is a pivotal moment.*

5. Conclusion

To date, IFI Programs in fragile states have lacked a distinctive, differentiating design from those in conventional settings. Fragile states are different from secure states, facing an existential danger of collapse into disorder that cannot be dismissed. I have built on the Report of the Commission of State Fragility, Growth, and Development to develop a taxonomy of fragility, using its concepts of the syndrome of fragility and pivotal moments. Fragility is a syndrome because it is a locally stable equilibrium; some moments are pivotal because events make escape from the syndrome easier.

To date, donor strategies and IFI Programs have implicitly been based on a vision of some desirable future state: that state is essentially the characteristics of a successful OECD country. The contrast between that desired state and the present reality is then used as the diagnostic for action. The result is a strategy that cannot be implemented and so deepens the sense of failure.

I have proposed an alternative strategy. The starting point is the need for an experience-based judgment as to "what is going on"; specifically, whether the current opportunity for a Program coincides with such a pivotal moment. If it does not, then a Program is highly unlikely to shift the country out of its locally stable equilibrium, and so should not be designed around the ambition to do so. Because Programs with substantial conditionality impede social learning, which is the fundamental adaptive process on which progress will depend, it is questionable whether they are worth doing, except in situations where in their absence there is a significant danger of collapse into disorder.

Where there is a reasonable prospect of a pivotal moment, the priorities for a Program should be to support the transition to a better local equilibrium. Because this is by its nature a process facing heightened radical uncertainty, a Transition Program cannot be fully specified as a sequence of reforms. Rather, the strategy should be to develop a coherent and credible narrative explanation of strategy that justifies a few initial actions that are easily done. The strategy in essence has two components. One is a few easy, visible, and quick-win actions that build confidence and credibility: Program finance can make it easier to find such quick wins by reducing the need to cut public spending. The hope is that the improved confidence and credibility, together with unpredicted events, open other opportunities that are then swiftly seized. Along with this sustained focus on the short term, which buys time, the other component of a Transition Program is a ruthlessly prioritized focus on reforms that can be begun at once but will take time to bear fruit. These are the strengthening of key state institutions, and a reset of ideas among citizens, public officials, and investors. I have suggested that a viable way of strengthening state institutions is the strategy of Vanguard units; ideas can be reset through the strategic use of communications. All three types of action—quick wins, Vanguard units within vital state functions, and communication to reset ideas—are "scaffolding"; they are necessary for the transition, but become redundant once the new equilibrium is achieved. By their nature, Transition Programs do not resemble conventional Programs designed for countries already in the neighbourhood of that better equilibrium.

This approach may seem wildly unorthodox, but it is strikingly consistent with the latest fundamental research on appropriate policy responses to radical macroeconomic uncertainty set out in Kay and King (2020). They summarize their analysis in four propositions. Rational policy should not reflect an attempt to optimize, but to build a credible account of "what is going on" that justifies feasible initial actions. The challenge is a unique event so that probabilistic forecasts based on past observations are not warranted. Improvements are achieved through group adaptive behaviour—social learning—not adherence to immutable socioeconomic laws. Finally, group decision-taking is set by communication by means of narratives. Neither John Kay nor Mervyn King would claim to have any knowledge whatsoever of fragile states: their focus is modern macroeconomic theory. Yet the task of rethinking public policy in fragile states may turn out to be the ideal-typical context for their analysis.

References

Barrett, L. 2017. *How Emotions Are Made: The Secret Life of the Brain*. New York: Houghton Mifflin Harcourt.

Collier, P. 2016. "The Cultural Foundations of Economic Failure: A Conceptual Toolkit." *Journal of Economic Behavior and Organization*, 126(B): 5–24.

Collier, P. 2018. "Rational Social Man, Speech Acts, and the Compliance Problem." Blavatnik School of Government WP25:2018.

Collier, P., and Tuckett, D., 2021, "Narratives as a Coordinating Device for Reversing Regional Disequilibrium", *Oxford Review of Economic Policy*, 37.1.

Fehr, E. and A. Falk. 2002. "Psychological Foundations of Incentives." *European Economic Review*, 46: 687–24.

Hong, S., M. Ratchford and J.S. Sagi. 2018. "You Need to Recognize Ambiguity to Avoid It." *Economic Journal*, 128: 2480–506.

Kay, J. and M. King. 2020. *Radical Uncertainty: Decision-making for an Unknowable Future. London*: Bridge Street Press.

Thomas, K., O.S. Haque, S. Pinker, and P. DeScioli. 2014. "The Psychology of Coordination and Common Knowledge." *Journal of Personality and Social Psycholo*gy, 107: 657–76.

4

Building Governance Capacity in Areas of Limited Statehood

Thomas Risse

For more than 20 years, Somalia has topped the list of "failed states" in almost every available dataset. The country is usually portrayed as in permanent turmoil, where civil war prevails, and rebel and terrorist groups freely roam. A closer look at the country reveals a more complex picture, however. While fighting and violence prevail in the province of Central Somalia and particularly in the capital of Mogadishu, the rest of the country remains remarkably quiet. The province of Somaliland has developed into a quite successful quasi-state run by tribal groups and their chiefs (Bakonyi and Stuvoy, 2005; Bryden, 2004; Richards, 2014).

At the same time, few would probably portray Germany as a "failed state," and rightly so. Yet, in the fall of 2016, the city of Berlin gave up on policing Görlitzer Park in the Kreuzberg district, one of the city's major areas of drug distribution.[1] The same holds true for many inner-city districts in the wealthiest countries of the world.

These two contrasting examples serve to illustrate that, first, "areas of limited statehood" are to be found everywhere and are certainly not confined to what the literature erroneously calls "fragile" or "failed" states (for example, Rotberg, 2003, 2004). Areas of limited statehood, where central government authorities lack the capacity of implementing and enforcing central decisions (the law) and/or lack the monopoly over the means of violence, are ubiquitous in the contemporary international system. Second, however, areas of limited statehood are neither ungovernable nor ungoverned. There is no linear correlation between degrees of statehood, on the one hand, and the provision of public goods and services, on the other (Lee et al., 2014). Instead, we find an enormous variation that includes badly governed places but also "good governance" in areas of limited statehood, sometimes separated only by a few blocks (Krasner and Risse, 2014).

I thank Ralph Chami and the participants of the workshop on "Macroeconomic Policy in Fragile States," Blavatnik School of Government, Oxford University, December 10–11, 2018, for very helpful comments on the draft of the chapter. Research for this chapter has been funded by a generous grant of the German Research Foundation (Deutsche Forschungsgemeinschaft) in the framework of the Collaborative Research Center 700 "Governance in Areas of Limited Statehood."

[1] See http://www.bz-berlin.de/berlin/friedrichshain-kreuzberg/berliner-polizei-gibt-am-goerlitzer-park-auf (last accessed December 12, 2016).

Thomas Risse, *Building Governance Capacity in Areas of Limited Statehood* In: *Macroeconomic Policy in Fragile States.* Edited by: Ralph Chami, Raphael Espinoza, and Peter Montiel, Oxford University Press (2021). © International Monetary Fund. DOI: 10.1093/oso/9780198853091.003.0004

Effective governance—both public service provision and rule-making—in areas of limited statehood depends on three factors and their interplay: first, the legitimacy and social acceptance of the governors by those being governed; second, social trust relations within communities; and, third, the adequate design of governance institutions including financial resources. The "fragile states" framework conflates areas of limited statehood and the presence or absence of effective governance and, thus, cannot even address the question under which conditions governance can be effective in areas of limited statehood.

It follows that international financial institutions such as the International Monetary Fund (IMF) or the World Bank should focus on building governance capacity in areas of limited statehood rather than further engaging in state-building, which has failed in recent decades despite the investment of substantial resources. Building governance capacity involves changing the perspective from constructing state institutions to a focus on policy outcomes with a view of engaging existing local capacities, whether state or non-state.

This does not imply, however, that international financial institutions should not engage central state institutions. But it matters a lot how well governed the central state is (think Mali and Niger vs Chad and Sudan). If the central state is autocratic and/or predatory, building state capacity will only make a bad situation worse by encouraging rent-seeking as well as repressive behavior. Yet, if the central government is constrained, at least to some extent, by the rule of law and by democratic institutions, but lacks the capacity to implement and enforce decisions, then capacity-building might actually help improve governance in areas of limited statehood. I discuss various scenarios in this context.

The chapter proceeds in three steps: first, I define central concepts such as (limited) statehood and governance, which includes a critique of the "state fragility" paradigm. Second, I report findings from a twelve-year collaborative project on the conditions of effective governance in areas of limited statehood (see for example, Risse et al., 2018; Krasner and Risse, 2014; Börzel and Risse, 2021). Third, I develop policy conclusions with a focus on building governance capacity in areas of limited statehood. Throughout the chapter, I will illustrate my arguments with empirical examples from Sub-Saharan Africa, Central Asia, and Latin America.

1. Governance in Areas of Limited Statehood: Conceptual Clarifications

This section introduces the central concepts of the chapter, namely "areas of limited statehood" and "governance."[2]

[2] The following represents a condensed version of Börzel et al., 2018.

1.1 Areas of Limited Statehood

The concept of "limited statehood" requires clarification (the present discussion builds upon Risse, 2011; for a more comprehensive argument see Börzel and Risse, 2021: ch. 2). First, I briefly elucidate what I mean by statehood and "the state" as opposed to other forms of political order. Second, I clarify my understanding of "limited statehood" and distinguish it from other concepts such as "weak," "fragile," or "failed" states.

One can distinguish two conceptualizations of statehood (for the following see also Eriksen, 2011). The first is based on the *functions* that states are supposed to perform. From this point of view, functioning states are essentially service providers: from security to health, education, and a clean environment. Most of the scholarly literature on "fragile" and "failed" states, the various datasets measuring degrees of statehood, as well as the state-building programs of development agencies and international organizations are based on such functional understandings of statehood (for example, Rotberg, 2003, 2004; Carment, 2003; Carment et al., 2015; Messner et al., 2015). As a result, this literature often engages in tautological reasoning. States are fragile, because they do not meet basic human needs or do not control their territory. Because they are fragile, they fail to satisfy human needs or to maintain a monopoly over the means of violence. Such conceptualizations are not only analytically useless; tautological reasoning also leads to bad policy advice. Functional conceptualizations, apart from leading to tautologies, also tend to confuse definitional issues and research questions. If we define the state through the functions it performs, a poorly performing state is no longer a "state" at all, strictly speaking. Such conceptualizations often conflates regime type (democracy, autocracy, etc.) and statehood. They prevent us from asking the questions we should be most interested in: under which conditions do states or other types of polities perform well by providing rule structures and delivering goods and services? How much statehood is necessary for effective governance?

A second understanding of state and statehood is *institutional* and conceptualizes the state as a particular type of organizational structure. Max Weber has provided the quintessential definition: "A compulsory political organization with continuous operation (*politischer Anstaltsbetrieb)* will be called a 'state' insofar as its administrative staff successfully upholds the claim to the *monopoly* of the *legitimate* use of physical force in the enforcement of its order" (Weber, 1978, p. 54). Accordingly, the state constitutes an authoritative rule structure, a *Herrschaftsverband* with the capacity to rule hierarchically in the sense of expecting obedience to its commands. This is an institutional understanding of the state and of statehood as a hierarchical rule structure. States command what Stephen Krasner calls "domestic sovereignty," that is, "the formal organization of political authority within the state and the ability of public authorities to exercise effective control within the borders of their own polity" (Krasner, 1999: 4). It does not imply that states rule hierarchically via command and control all the time, only that statehood implies the ability to do so (for such understandings see Fukuyama, 2004, 2012; Holsti, 2004; Jackson, 1990; Krasner, 1999, 2018).

This understanding allows a clear distinction between statehood as an institutional structure of authority, on the one hand, and the kind of governance it provides, on the other. The latter is an empirical not a definitional question. For example, control over the means of violence is part of the definition. Whether this monopoly over the use of force actually provides security for the citizens as a public good and irrespective of one's race, gender, or kinship, becomes an empirical question. The claimed capacity to govern hierarchically is part of the definition, but whether this ability exists and is used to provide collective goods and services, is an altogether different question. Last not least, statehood in this understanding has nothing to do with regime type (democracy, autocracy).

The meaning of "limited statehood" follows from this conceptualization. While areas of limited statehood still belong to internationally recognized states (even the failed state Somalia still commands international sovereignty), it is their domestic sovereignty that is severely circumscribed. Areas of limited statehood then constitute those parts of a country *in which central authorities (governments) lack the ability to implement as well as enforce rules and decisions and/or in which they do not command a legitimate monopoly over the means of violence.*

The ability to enforce rules or to control the means of violence can be restricted along various dimensions, such as territorial, that is, with regard to a country's territorial spaces; or sectoral, that is, with regard to policy areas. The opposite of "limited statehood" is not "unlimited" but "consolidated" statehood: those areas of a country in which the state enjoys the monopoly over the means of violence and the ability to make and enforce central decisions most of the time. Consolidated states, which command more or less sufficient domestic sovereignty over most of the territory, in most policy areas, and so on, are the exception to the rule in the contemporary international system, covering mostly the "global North" of highly industrialized and democratic states.

At the other end of the spectrum, we find "failed states," countries where areas of limited statehood cover the entire territory and most of the population, as well as encompassing most policy areas most of the time. Somalia, the Democratic Republic of the Congo, Yemen, Libya, Iraq, and Afghanistan constitute prominent examples of "failed states" in the current international system.

The vast majority of contemporary states exhibit areas of limited statehood with regard to parts of the territory, particular policy areas, parts of the population, or combinations thereof. The Brazilian state, for example, can certainly not be regarded as failed or fragile, but state authorities do not command the capacity to enforce the law in the favelas of Rio de Janeiro or in vast areas of the Amazon.

With regard to policy areas, the People's Republic of China—*the* rising power of the twenty-first century—has rather strict environmental laws on the books, but still contains some of the most polluted areas of the world, indicating a lack of law enforcement (Man, 2013).

If we conceptualize limited statehood in a configurative way, areas of limited statehood are an almost ubiquitous phenomenon in the contemporary international system, but also in historical comparison (Esders et al., 2018). After all, the state monopoly over the means of violence has only been around since the nineteenth century (see, for example, Osiander, 2001; Thomson, 1994). For centuries, states have fought against mercenaries and pirates so as to seize the means of violence from the various contenders. As Charles Tilly argued, state-making was war-making and war made the state (Tilly, 1985, 1995).

In sum, rather than the Weberian consolidated state with a strong and independent bureaucracy, areas of limited statehood are the default condition in the current global system and historically. It follows that the binary distinction between state and non-state actors becomes problematic. This distinction usually rests on the assumption that state actors enjoy international and domestic sovereignty while non-state actors do not. However, the ability to rule hierarchically is not confined to states; many non-state actors, from warlords to local chiefs, do so, too (Arjona, 2016; Förster and Koechlin, 2018; Baldwin, 2016). Both state and non-state actors govern in areas of limited statehood and it is often less than clear who the "governors" are in particular places.

Moreover, areas of limited statehood are mostly not anarchic in the Hobbesian sense where life is "nasty, brutish, and short" (Hobbes, 1987 (1652): ch. 13). They are neither ungovernable nor ungoverned. There is no supreme authority governing these spaces, but the international system as well as areas of limited statehood are full of rules, regulations, and institutions, both formal and informal. Some areas of limited statehood are reasonably well governed, while others are not and the provision of basic collective goods and services is lacking. Just because the Brazilian police cannot enforce the law in many favelas of Rio de Janeiro does not mean that all Brazilian favelas are crime-infested places per se. Some are reasonably well governed, while others are not.

1.2 Governance

"Governance" became almost a fashion term in the social sciences during the 1990s and the 2000s. Several handbooks of governance including global and transnational governance have been published since then (Bevir, 2011; Levi-Faur, 2012b; Hale and Held, 2011; Schuppert and Zürn, 2008).

In its most general version, governance refers to all modes of coordinating social activity in human society. Williamson, for example, distinguished between governance by markets and governance by hierarchy (that is, the state), later scholars added governance by networks to this list (see, for example, Williamson, 1975; Rhodes, 1997; Kooiman, 1993; see overview in Levi-Faur, 2012a). However, such a broad understanding that identifies governance with any kind of social ordering does not appear useful for the purpose of this chapter. After all, we want to know how collective goods and services can be provided in the absence of a well-functioning state and how politics as the regulation of public affairs for a society works: "Who gets what, when, how?" to quote Harold Laswell (Laswell, 1936).

As a result, I use a somewhat narrower concept. By *governance*, I mean the various *institutionalized modes of social coordination to produce and implement collectively binding rules, and/or to provide collective goods.* This conceptualization follows closely the understanding of governance that is widespread within the social sciences (see, for example, Mayntz, 2004, 2009; Benz, 2004; Schuppert and Zürn, 2008). Governance covers ruling by the state ("governance by government"), governance via cooperative networks of public and private actors ("governance with government"), as well as rule-making by non-state actors or self-regulation by civil society ("governance without government"). Clarifying the concept of governance also requires answering three traditional political science questions (see Dahl, 1961): Who governs? How is governance taking place? What results from governance?

The "Who" question concerns the actors of governance. We find various combinations of state and non-state actors governing areas of limited statehood. State actors include the national or local governments (irrespective of their limited capability to enforce decisions in areas of limited statehood), international (intergovernmental) organizations, and foreign governments including their multiple agencies. Non-state actors encompass (international) non-governmental organizations (INGOs) and multi-stakeholder partnerships, business actors, but also local chiefs, so-called "traditional" authorities and even violent non-state actors, such as rebel groups and warlords.

The "How" question refers to the modes of governance. Consolidated states have the ability to rule hierarchically, that is, to authoritatively enforce the law, ultimately through policing and "top down" command and control. Hierarchical rule can take place through coercion, but it can also invoke voluntary compliance, the more the political order as well as the governors are considered legitimate in the sense of social acceptance by the governed (Hurd, 1999). Moreover, consolidated states also have the capacity to cast a "shadow of hierarchy," that is, to incentivize other actors to provide governance so as to avoid hierarchical coordination by the state. It is precisely this ability to enforce decisions, which is lacking in areas of limited statehood. However, hierarchical rule is not absent in areas of limited statehood. External intervenors establishing trusteeships, violent non-state actors including warlords, rebel groups, or terrorist groups, as well as "traditional" authorities and local chiefs, often rule hierarchically in areas of limited statehood.

Much more common, however, are non-hierarchical modes of social coordination in areas of limited statehood. The contemporary social science literature has discussed these as "new" modes of governance or the privatization of authority (see, for example, Cutler et al., 1999; Grande and Pauly, 2005). Nonhierarchical modes of governance can be distinguished according to the underlying logic of action. The logic of consequentialism assumes utility-maximizing actors with given preferences whose cost-benefit calculations can be affected through modes of governance. Accordingly, this mode of governance involves creating and manipulating incentives and "benchmarking." Positive incentives, but also sanctions, are meant to affect the cost-benefit calculations of the relevant parties and to induce the desired behavior. Non-hierarchical governance includes the give and take of bargaining processes.

Non-hierarchical modes of governance also encompass interactions following the logics of appropriateness and of communicative action (March and Olsen, 1998; Risse, 2000) including non-manipulative communication, persuasion, and learning. These modes of governance aim at challenging fixed interest and preferences so that actors are induced in a socialization process to internalize new rules and norms. For example, many non-state justice institutions in areas of limited statehood contain strong elements of deliberative processes (Risse, 2018).

Finally, the "what" question: Governance is supposed to provide collectively binding rules as well as collective goods. Simply curbing negative externalities of private goods' production does not qualify as governance (while setting up rules to avoid negative externalities does, see below). One can then distinguish three types of governance contributions:

- direct delivery of collective goods and services, such as security, public health, education, clean environment, and the like. I follow the usual definition of public goods as characterized by non-exclusive access and/or non-rivalry in consumption. At least one of these conditions has to be present for a good to qualify as collective or common;
- formulation and implementation of collectively binding rules for regulating social life (such as human rights) and the delivery of collective goods and services; and
- establishment of institutions regulating the rule-making itself and coordinating the governance contributions of others.

But how and under what conditions is effective governance possible with regard to these three dimensions? I tackle this question in the following section.

2. Explaining Effective Governance in Areas of Limited Statehood

"Effectiveness" means in this context that binding rules and collective goods are actually delivered in areas of limited statehood—for as many people as possible.

One could call it the "problem-solving" capacity of governance under conditions of limited statehood.

2.1 The "Governance Puzzle"

As argued above, areas of limited statehood are neither ungoverned nor ungovernable. Somebody governs almost everywhere and most of the time, whether state or non-state actor, whether external-international or local-national. But how effective is governance under conditions of limited statehood? The short answer is that it varies hugely. The following examples might suffice here.

2.1.1 Security Governance

The following graph displays the number of violent incidents in Somalia, the quintessential failed states, from 1990–2010 (see Figure 4.1). Armed conflict mostly occurs in the province of Central Somalia, around the capital of Mogadishu and along the main infrastructure roads. The provinces of Somaliland and Puntland are almost completely devoid of violence. Yet, the condition of limited statehood is all-pervasive throughout Somalia.

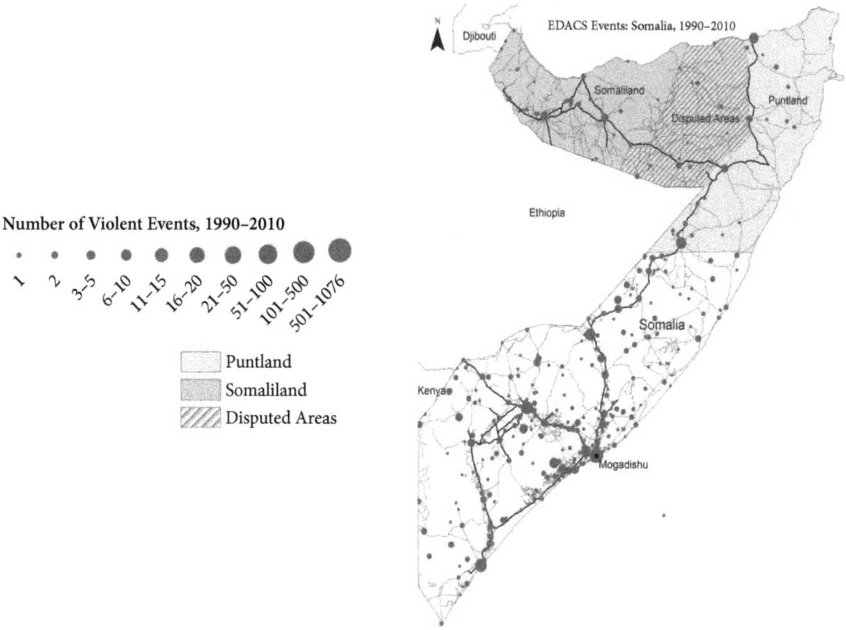

Figure 4.1 Number of Violent Events in Somalia, 1990–2010

Source: Event Data on Armed Conflict and Security (EDACS), http://www.conflict-data.org/edacs/index.html, last access February 28, 2018. Courtesy of Sven Chojnacki. See Chojnacki et al., 2012.

To cut a long story short: civil wars and other forms of violence do occur more often in areas of limited statehood than in areas of consolidated statehood. At the same time, most areas of limited statehood remain peaceful, even if the state lacks a monopoly over the means of violence. Limited statehood does not equal civil war (Risse and Stollenwerk, 2018).

2.1.2 Rule of Law and Human Rights

Figure 4.2 displays data for a joint indicator for human rights and the rule of law, on the one hand, and for statehood, on the other (for the statehood measurement see Stollenwerk, 2018a; Börzel and Risse, 2021, ch. 2). Each dot represents the human rights/rule of law values for one particular state. Statehood values of 0.9–1.0 represent consolidated statehood, while values >0.5 represent very fragile as well as failed states. Most areas of limited statehood are located within the 0.5–0.9 range.

The fitted value line appears to suggest that rule of law and human rights protection correlate with statehood. Although this holds true for consolidated as well as completely failed statehood, the variation among medium levels of statehood is enormous. At statehood levels of 0.7, for example, there are countries with systematic human rights violations, but also countries where the values for the

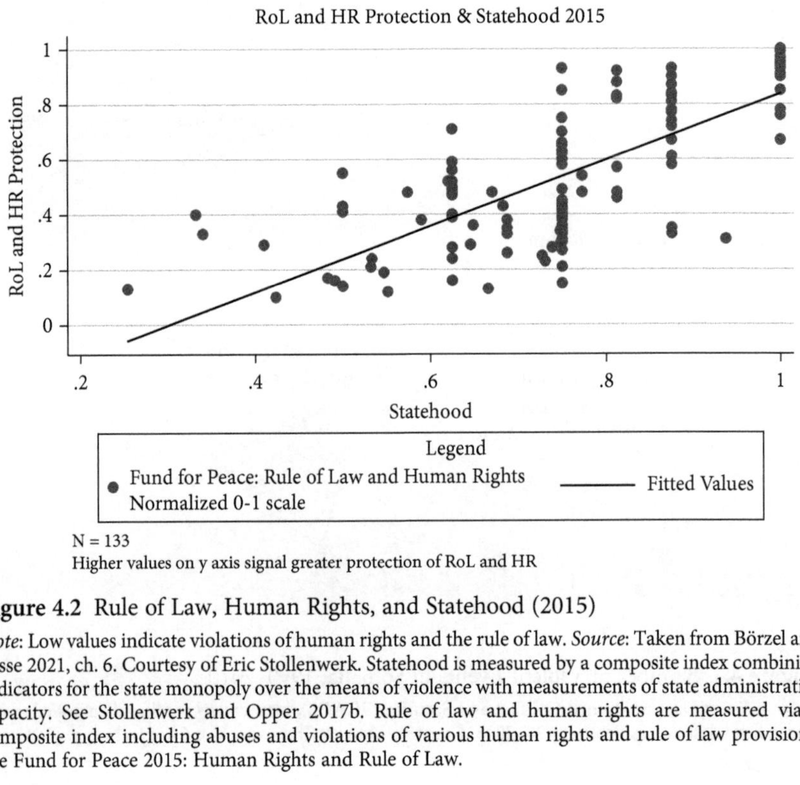

Figure 4.2 Rule of Law, Human Rights, and Statehood (2015)

Note: Low values indicate violations of human rights and the rule of law. *Source*: Taken from Börzel and Risse 2021, ch. 6. Courtesy of Eric Stollenwerk. Statehood is measured by a composite index combining indicators for the state monopoly over the means of violence with measurements of state administrative capacity. See Stollenwerk and Opper 2017b. Rule of law and human rights are measured via a composite index including abuses and violations of various human rights and rule of law provisions. See Fund for Peace 2015: Human Rights and Rule of Law.

rule of law and human rights are equal to those for consolidated democracies. The task is to explain this variation (see Börzel and Risse, 2013, for a discussion).

2.1.3 Public Service Delivery

A similar picture emerges if we look at other public services such as basic subsistence or public health. Figure 4.3 depicts the prevalence of undernourishment and statehood using the same indicators for statehood as in Figure 4.2. Figure 4.4 does the same for infant mortality and statehood. The findings are (almost always) the same, no matter what kind of measurements for public service delivery we use: Consolidated states manage to do a rather good job in public services, as is to be expected. Completely failed states are failing in this respect on average (even though we have rather well-governed areas of limited statehood in failed states such as Somalia; see, for example, Schäferhoff, 2014 with regard to public health in Somaliland). What is striking is the variation pertaining to the middle category of countries with many areas of limited statehood where central state authorities are still capable of performing some basic functions, but are too weak to provide public services across the board (for similar findings see Lee et al., 2014). How can this "governance puzzle" be explained?

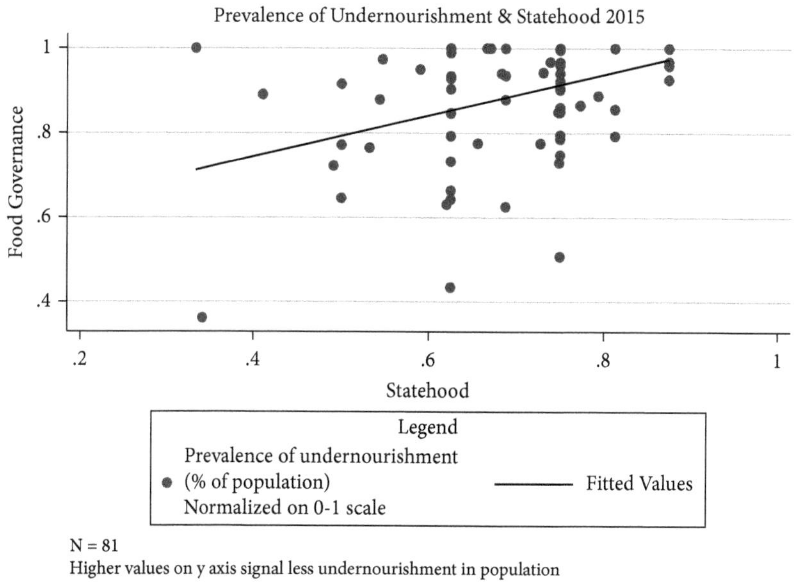

Figure 4.3 Undernourishment and Statehood 2015

Note: Each dot represents the value for one country. N = 54; higher values on y-axis signal less undernourishment in population.

Sources: Börzel and Risse 2021, ch. 7. Courtesy of Eric Stollenwerk. Data taken from Global Hunger Index; for details see Stollenwerk and Opper 2017b; Stollenwerk and Opper 2017a: 6–7. For the statehood indicators see ibid.

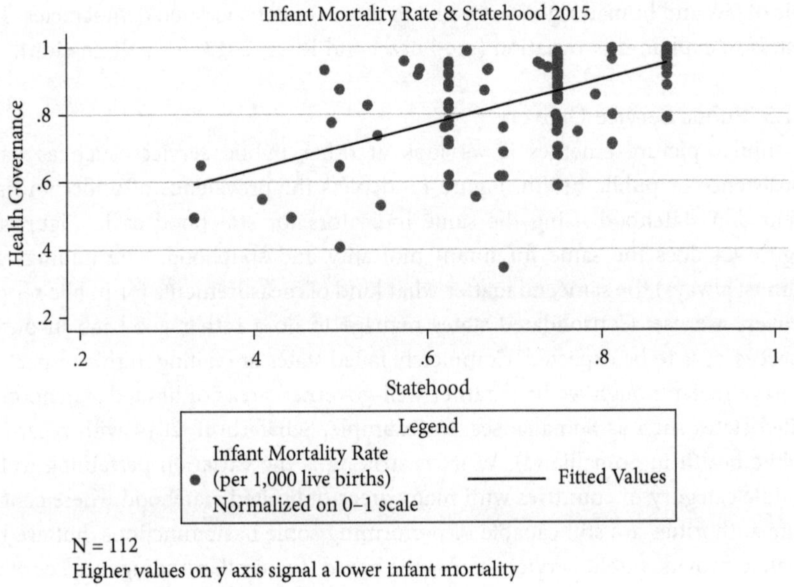

Figure 4.4 Infant Mortality and Areas of Limited Statehood (2015)

Note: Each dot represents the value for one country. N = 112. Higher values on y-axis signal lower infant mortality.

Sources: Börzel and Risse 2021, ch. 7. Courtesy of Eric Stollenwerk. World Bank data, for details see Stollenwerk and Opper 2017a: 7. For the statehood indicators see Figure 4.1.

2.1.4 The Triad: Legitimacy, Institutional Design, and Social Trust

Effective (problem-solving) governance in areas of limited statehood can be explained by the combination of three factors (see Figure 4.5), namely

- empirical legitimacy or social acceptance of the governors;
- institutional design of the governance arrangements; and
- social trust among (imagined) communities.

2.1.5 (Empirical) Legitimacy or Social Acceptance

"Legitimacy" can be understood as the "license to govern" or the "right to rule" (Schmelzle, 2015, following Max Weber). The focus here is on "empirical" legitimacy, that is, the social acceptance of the governors and/or the governance institutions by those being governed or ruled. Empirical legitimacy has to be distinguished from "normative legitimacy," that is, the rightfulness of an order according to some normative criteria.[3] The greater the empirical legitimacy of governors or of governance institutions, the more we can expect

[3] Note that even very autocratic rulers whose normative legitimacy is more than questionable, can be socially accepted as rightful rulers by the population. An example has been President Putin.

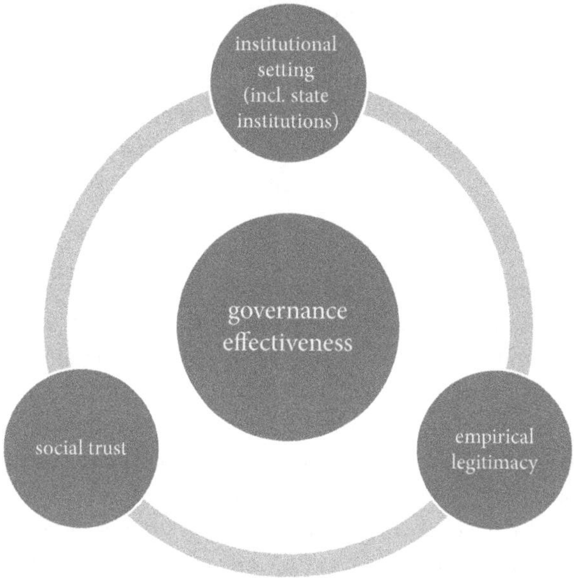

Figure 4.5 What Makes Governance Effective in Areas of Limited Statehood?

voluntary compliance with (costly) rules by those being governed (Hurd, 1999; Scharpf, 1997).

Empirical legitimacy or social acceptance matters hugely for the effectiveness of governance in areas of limited statehood (see Krasner and Risse, 2014 for details). In fact, as Berti argues, particularly violent non-state actors often provide governance in the areas which they rule, to gain legitimacy (Berti, 2018; see also Jo, 2015), in the eyes of both the local population and the international community. The same holds true for business actors as governors (Börzel and Deitelhoff, 2018) and for external governors international organizations such as the IMF or the World Bank, foreign aid agencies, but also international NGOs (Krasner and Risse, 2014). At the same time, lack of legitimacy—both domestic and international—also explains why massive military state-building interventions mostly fail (Lake, 2016, 2018a).

Legitimacy constitutes a decisive scope condition for the effectiveness of governance in areas of limited statehood. Moreover, the causal arrows between empirical legitimacy and the effectiveness of governance in areas of limited statehood point in both directions. On the one hand, legitimacy bestowed on the governors or the governance institutions leads to voluntary compliance with costly rules, which is particularly relevant in areas of limited statehood where the enforcement capacities of the state are notoriously weak. The delivery of collective goods and services by the various governors also requires at least some degree of legitimacy in order to be effective. On the other hand, effective governance tends to increase the legitimacy of the governors and the governance institutions. Thus, output-based legitimacy matters in areas of limited statehood (Scharpf, 1999; see also Schmelzle, 2015). In sum, legitimacy and effectiveness form, to some degree, a virtuous cycle in a similar way as Levi and Sachs have argued for consolidated states (Levi and Sacks, 2009; discussion in Schmelzle and Stollenwerk, 2018; for a thorough quantitative and qualitative treatment see Stollenwerk, 2018b).

2.1.6 Social Trust

Social trust, understood here as risk-taking by engaging in cooperative actions with others in the absence of complete information about their motives and interests (Börzel and Risse, 2016; Draude et al., 2018), serves as another powerful driver for the effectiveness of governance under conditions of limited statehood. As Ostrom in particular has shown, social trust among local community members helps them to overcome collective action problems within and between social groups (Ostrom, 1990, 2000) and, thus, enables effective governance. Thus, social trust can solve the governance problem, making "cooperation under anarchy" possible, which is particularly relevant for areas of limited statehood. The main challenge here is to scale up social trust from the personalized relations within local communities to generalized trust among larger entities.

Social trust not only contributes to effective governance in areas of limited statehood; it also enhances the legitimacy of the governors, particularly those embedded in the various communities. Finally, non-exclusive forms of social trust help prevent the outbreak of violence in areas of limited statehood and are a precondition for effective service delivery.

2.1.7 Design of Governance Institutions

The design of governance institutions also matters for the effectiveness of governance in areas of limited statehood. To begin with, institutions must be "fit for purpose," that is, functionally capable of performing the task that they are built to accomplish (see Koremenos et al., 2001). Moreover, the make-up of institutions for governance in areas of limited statehood must be flexible enough to adapt to local conditions, and this includes built-in learning capacities (Beisheim and Liese, 2014; Beisheim et al., 2014). Institutions also facilitate non-hierarchical modes of governance, which complement and substitute for hierarchical coordination based on statehood (Risse, 2018).

In particular, socially inclusive governance institutions serve as arenas for discourse in areas of limited statehood, enabling deliberative modes of governance and preventing the arbitrary exercise of power. Inclusive governance institutions not only contribute to the effectiveness of governance under conditions of limited statehood; they also foster both legitimacy and social trust. The experience of fair, impartial, and inclusive governance institutions is particularly relevant for building generalized trust in the absence of well-functioning states (Börzel and Risse, 2016).

2.2 But What about the State?

Effective governance in areas of limited statehood does not require a well-functioning state. Rather, the triad of (empirical) legitimacy, social trust, and adequate, well-resourced institutional design can substitute for weak state capacity—and this substitution is sustainable; however, one should not throw out the baby with the bathwater. Statehood still matters for building islands of governance, particularly when it comes to broadening access to collective goods and services. Basic security and administrative infrastructure are essential preconditions for effective governance by non-state and external governors. NGOs, multi-stakeholder partnerships, and companies are unable or reluctant to provide such basic services. External state governors, but also warlords, rebel groups, and other violent non-state actors may engage in peace-keeping and peace-making (see Arjona et al., 2015). They contribute to state-building in the sense that international as well as violent non-state actors hold a monopoly over the means of violence in the areas they control. They also set up basic administrations to coordinate external and domestic resources necessary for service delivery. Though statehood does not have to reside with state actors, non-state actors with the capacity to control the monopoly over the use of force and to set and enforce collectively binding rules have to accept the public responsibility to use their statehood to serve the public interest rather than seek rents (Jacob et al., 2018). The incentives to do so often come from external consolidated statehood and from international law. Home-country regulations keep multinational companies and international NGOs honest. International law entails governance obligations for non-state actors if they want to acquire (international) legitimacy (Krieger, 2018).

In short, some minimum degree of statehood—with regard to the monopoly over the means of violence and basic infrastructure—is probably necessary to provide effective governance with regard to more complex tasks and to enable other (non-state and external) actors to step in as governors. However, we should not forget that states with enough capacity to enforce decisions are often part of the problem, not part of the solution. Consolidated statehood that is unconstrained by the rule of law, including the protection of human rights, amounts to autocratic rule. Moreover, even weak state governments often act as spoilers trying to prevent other governors from stepping in with regard to rule-making and service delivery, for example, to generate rents (Börzel and Thauer, 2013). Many states with and in areas of limited statehood are predatory states (Reno, 2015). It follows that simply strengthening state capacity does not do the trick, as the European Union (EU) has learned the hard way from the Western Balkans to the Southern Caucasus (Börzel et al., 2009; Börzel and Van Hüllen, 2014). If central state actors are rent-seeking or corrupt, strengthening the state makes them more effective in being so. This point is particularly relevant for policy conclusions.

3. Policy Recommendations: Governance-Building Rather than State-Building

The policy community usually discusses the problems of limited statehood in the context of the "state fragility" paradigm. As argued above, this concept not only suffers from a functional rather than institutional understanding of statehood and conflates statehood with governance. It is also rather state-centric in that it tends to ignore the governance contributions of actors other than the state. Yet, as argued above, we find many external/international as well as non-state governors in areas of limited statehood providing rules as well as public goods and services. Weak statehood does not imply weak or insufficient governance.

Analyzing areas of limited statehood under the "state fragility" paradigm resulted in the state-building concept as the main remedy (see Brozus, 2011; Brozus et al., 2018 for the following). State-building became the dominant approach to tackling the problem of failed or fragile states. State-building was understood as mainly institutional transfers of mostly Western (democratic) state institutions to areas of limited statehood, sometimes coupled with military interventions to uphold a monopoly over the means of violence and to restore peace (for thorough critiques see Lake, 2016; Woodward, 2017). Afghanistan and Iraq became the defining examples for Western-led comprehensive state-building. The Afghanistan intervention involved up to 130,000 troops from 43 different countries in 2011, as well as hundreds of international state and non-state actors. At the time, Afghanistan was the single largest recipient of official development assistance in the world: billions of dollars and euros were spent (Brozus et al., 2018, p. 588). In the late 2010s, Afghanistan has become one of the symbols of the failure of state-building efforts (see Paris, 2011, 2013; for a more nuanced discussion see Böhnke et al., 2015).

The leading international financial institutions also followed the state-building paradigm. The IMF is no exception. Capacity development is described as a "core mandate" that accounts for almost a third of the IMF's budget. The website describes capacity building in a rather state-centric way; for example, the IMF advises "finance ministries on how to raise revenue (that) enables governments to provide better public services such as schools, roads and hospitals."[4]

I am not arguing that capacity development is the wrong approach per se; as suggested in the section on design of governance institutions, adequate

[4] https://www.imf.org/external/np/ins/english/capacity_about.htm (last accessed October 14, 2018).

institutional design "fit for purpose" is one of three factors accounting for effective governance. As such, institutional design requires both sufficient—material and intellectual—resources and administrative capacity, irrespective of who the governors are and whether or not the central state is included. At the same time, simple institutional transfers irrespective of local political, socio-economic, or cultural conditions usually do not do the trick. They often result in institutions that are empty shells leading to systematic decoupling of formal institutional norms, rules, and procedures, on the one hand, and informal rules and behavioral practices, on the other (see DiMaggio and Powell, 1991).

Rather, capacity development needs to be embedded in a broader approach which might be labeled "governance-building" rather than state-building (Brozus, 2011; Brozus et al., 2018, pp. 594–6). Governance-building focuses on results and outcomes rather than institutions. It works bottom-up rather than top-down thereby taking local ownership seriously rather than employing it as a rhetorical device (Beisheim et al., 2018, pp. 216–17). When external actors such as international organizations and foreign aid agencies concentrate on governance-building, they are as goal-oriented as state-builders, in that they are aiming at improvements with regard to security, human rights, the rule of law, democracy, and a variety of public services. The difference is that institutional blueprints are rarely available in areas of limited statehood to promote these goals. Moreover, most (Western) blueprints assume well-functioning and consolidated statehood as a background condition which—again—is missing in areas of limited statehood.

If governance-building rather than state-building is the goal, what does this mean for international financial institutions such as the IMF or the World Bank?[5] First, we need to distinguish between direct and more indirect modes of governance-building. International financial institutions such as the World Bank can engage directly with governance actors—whether state or non-state—in areas of limited statehood. Particular efforts should be made to engage non-state actors who are committed to the common good. It is noteworthy in this context that the equation we are used to in democratic consolidated states—public = state actors and private = non-state actors—does not work per se in areas of limited statehood. In many cases, non-state actors such as NGOs, religious communities, traditional authorities (see Baldwin, 2016, companies (Thauer, 2015), but even rebel groups and warlords in some cases (see, for example, Jo, 2015; Arjona et al., 2015) might be more committed to governance and the provision of public services than state actors. This is not to say that the latter should be simply ignored. But external governance providers who are entitled to

[5] I thank Ralph Chami for important insights on the following.

work with non-state actors should analyze very carefully with whom to cooperate in areas of limited statehood.

As argued above, the focus should be on goal attainment rather than institution-building. Good institutional design of governance arrangements is important, but blueprints and "one-size-fits-all" solutions will fail. What is more, simply transferring institutions from the global North to the global South leads more often than not to governance disasters. At best, such transfers result in the decoupling of institutional rules from behavioral practices. Rather, governance institutions—whether in finance, the public health sector, education, or with regard to environmental policies—have to be adjusted to local contexts. Even more important, local social acceptance by the citizens matters hugely for governance effectiveness. No effects without legitimacy! This requires buy-in and local ownership in the sense of co-designing governance.

With regard to more indirect governance-building, what about international financial institutions, such as the IMF, that can only work with states and cannot bypass them by working directly with local actors in areas of limited statehood? Should they pack up and go, leaving the state and national governments to their own devices? Far from it!

Here, three scenarios can be distinguished:

1. Predatory as well as autocratic states with areas of limited statehood.
2. Failed states where limited statehood covers the entire territory as well as most policy areas and where central governments do not exercise much control, whether autocratic or not.
3. Reasonably well-governed and inclusive, but still weak states with areas of limited statehood.

Note that none of these "states" qualify as consolidated democracies in the Western sense or what North et al. have called "open access orders" (North et al., 2009). They are altogether "limited access orders" in their terminology, but it is important to distinguish variations here, because this matters hugely for what can be done from the outside.

With regard to scenario 1, there seems to be very little that international financial institutions such as the IMF can do to promote governance-building and sound macroeconomic policies in areas of limited statehood. Predatory or autocratic states are usually captured by rent-seeking elites using state resources to stabilize their rule and their clientelistic networks (Erdmann, 2013). As a result, budget aid and other means of capacity-building will only increase the exploitative and/or repressive capabilities of governments; for example, helping such governments to mobilize more revenue will only increase "bad governance" rather than improve conditions. Examples include Syria and Sudan until very recently.

Concerning scenario 2, that is, completely failed states, similar lessons apply. Though the IMF might help prevent complete chaos through various measures, its tools mostly assume that there is at least some residual and functioning statehood. With regard to failed states, the restoration of peace and security and some degree of the (state) monopoly over the means of violence is necessary before measures can be effective. International financial institutions have very few tools to aid that process. Moreover, many failed states are more likely to be stabilizable from the periphery rather than from the center, as, for example, in Somalia or the Democratic Republic of Congo. In Somalia, what remains of the central government has been engaged in fighting with different rebel groups including terrorists for decades, mainly in the area surrounding the capital, Mogadishu (see Figure 4.1); by contrast, the provinces of Somaliland and, to some degree, Puntland have developed into rather decently governed areas of limited statehood (see for example Bradbury, 2008; Bryden, 2004; Menkhaus, 2006/2007). What is of utmost importance here is to prevent the chaos and anarchy of Central Somalia from spilling over into these islands of stability. Similar stories can be told from other failed states (for the Democratic Republic of the Congo see for example Lake, 2018b).

For the IMF and other international financial institutions, which have to work through the state in order to improve governance in areas of limited statehood, scenario 3 appears to be the one to concentrate on (see also Chapter 3 in this volume). Many of these states—most of them labelled "partly free" by Freedom House and other datasets[6] - are characterized by ruling coalitions composed of both corrupt rent-seekers as well as elites committed to the rule of law, participatory rule (if not democracy), and other "liberal" values.[7] If the IMF and others want to improve governance in such states with areas of limited statehood (think Mali, Sierra Leone, Liberia, Niger, to name just a few examples in Sub-Saharan Africa), they need to design policies strengthening the latter groups against the former thereby altering the domestic balance of power in favor of the more "liberal" elites. In such cases, capacity-building matters, if and when it strengthens the effectiveness of state administrations constrained by the rule of law. As argued above, such effective "residual" statehood with regard to the provision of macroeconomic policies is crucial as an enabler of good governance in areas of limited statehood. Studies on the EU's efforts to combat corruption in the Southern Caucasus demonstrate that external actors can indeed play a crucial role here—provided that there are domestic groups with whom they can align (see for example Börzel et al., 2009; Börzel and Van Hüllen, 2014, 2015). Georgia has been such an example. To be sure, such efforts from the outside will not transform weak states into consolidated democracies. But they can be significant in

[6] See https://freedomhouse.org/ (last accessed March 24, 2019).

[7] I put "liberal" in quotation marks here because one should not confuse their beliefs with Western values.

providing areas of limited statehood with the financial resources and macroeconomic infrastructure so as to enhance the provision of public goods and services.

In sum, areas of limited statehood are not basket cases for the dustbin of history. Nor are they likely to be overcome by the relentless forces of economic modernization. They are here to stay. But this does not imply that external actors, such as the IMF, cannot support good governance and the provision of public goods in such areas. They have to concentrate their forces on weak states that have a reasonable chance of using their residual statehood toward enabling effective governance and service provision. These are states where the rule of law and inclusive institutions are supported by at least some domestic groups—whether state, business, or (public) interest groups—and where these groups can be strengthened from the outside. International financial institutions can support them through advice, capacity development, communication, and programs tailored to their particular needs. If these measures can help to move areas of limited statehood closer to at least some of the sustainable development goals, this would be quite an achievement.

References

Arjona, A. 2016. *Rebelocracy. Social Order in the Colombian Civil War*. Cambridge: Cambridge University Press.

Arjona, A., N. Kasfir, and Z. Mampilly (Eds.). 2015. *Rebel Governance in Civil War*. Cambridge: Cambridge University Press.

Bakonyi, J. and K. Stuvoy. 2005. "Violence and Social Order Beyond the State: Somalia and Angola." *Review of African Political Economy* 32(104): 359–82.

Baldwin, K. 2016. *The Paradox of Traditional Chiefs in Democratic Africa, Cambridge Studies in Comparative Politics*. Cambridge: Cambridge University Press.

Beisheim, M., A. Ellersiek, and J. Lorch. 2018. "INGOs and Multi-Stakeholder Partnerships," in T. Risse, T.A. Börzel, and A. Draude (Eds.), *The Oxford Handbook of Governance and Limited Statehood* (pp. 210–30). Oxford: Oxford University Press.

Beisheim, M. and A. Liese (Eds.). 2014. *Transnational Partnerships. Effectively Providing for Sustainable Development?* Basingstoke: Palgrave Macmillan.

Beisheim, M., A. Liese, H. Jannetschek, and J. Sarre. 2014. "Transnational Public Private Partnerships and the Provision of Services in Areas of Limited Statehood in South Asia and East Africa: Institutional Design Matters." *Governance*, 27(4): 655–73.

Benz, A. 2004. *Governance—Regieren in komplexen Regelsystemen*. Wiesbaden: VS Verlag für Sozialwissenschaften.

Berti, B. 2018. "Violent and Criminal Non-State Actors," in T. Risse, T.A. Börzel, and A. Draude (Eds.), *The Oxford Handbook of Governance and Limited Statehood* (pp. 272–90). Oxford: Oxford University Press.

Bevir, M. (Ed.). 2011. *The SAGE Handbook of Governance*. London: Sage.

Böhnke, J.R., J. Koehler, and C. Zürcher. 2015. Assessing the Impact of Development Cooperation in North East Afghanistan 2007–2013. Final Report. Bonn and Berlin: Federal Ministry for Economic Cooperation and Development.

Börzel, T.A. and N. Deitelhoff. 2018. "Business," in T. Risse, T.A. Börzel, and A. Draude (Eds.), *The Oxford Handbook of Governance and Limited Statehood* (pp. 250–71). Oxford: Oxford University Press.

Börzel, T.A., Y. Pamuk, and A. Stahn. 2009. "Democracy or Stability? EU and US Engagement in the Southern Caucasus," in A. Magen, M. McFaul, and T. Risse (Eds.), *Democracy Promotion in the EU and the EU Compared* (pp. 150–84). Basingstoke: Palgrave Macmillan.

Börzel, T.A. and T. Risse. 2013. "Human Rights in Areas of Limited Statehood: The New Agenda," in T. Risse, S.S. Ropp, and K. Sikkink (Eds.), *The Persistent Power of Human Rights. From Commitment to Compliance* (pp. 63–84). Cambridge: Cambridge University Press.

Börzel, T.A. and T. Risse. 2016. "Dysfunctional State Institutions, Trust, and Governance in Areas of Limited Statehood." *Regulation & Governance* 10(2): 149–60.

Börzel, T.A. and T. Risse. 2021. Effective Governance Under Anarchy. Institutions, Legitimacy, and Social Trust in Areas of Limited Statehood. Cambridge: Cambridge University Press.

Börzel, T.A., T. Risse, and A. Draude. 2018. "Governance in Areas of Limited Statehood: Conceptual Clarifications and Major Contributions of the Handbook," in T. Risse, T.A. Börzel, and A. Draude (Eds.), *The Oxford Handbook of Governance and Limited Statehood* (pp. 3–25). Oxford: Oxford University Press.

Börzel, T.A. and C. Thauer (Eds.). 2013. *Business and Governance in South Africa*. Basingstoke: Palgrave Macmillan.

Börzel, T.A. and V.Van Hüllen. 2014. "State-Building and the European Union's Fight against Corruption in the Southern Caucasus: Why Legitimacy Matters." *Governance* 27(4): 613–34.

Börzel, T.A. and V.Van Hüllen (Eds.). 2015. *Governance Transfer by Regional Organizations. Patching Together a Global Script*. Basingstoke: Palgrave Macmillan.

Bradbury, M. 2008. *Becoming Somaliland*. Bloomington, IN: Indiana University Press.

Brozus, L. 2011. "Applying the Governance Concept to Areas of Limited Statehood: Implications for International Foreign and Security Policy," in T. Risse (Ed.), *Governance Without a State? Policies and Politics in Areas of Limited Statehood* (pp. 262–80). New York: Columbia University Press.

Brozus, L., C. Jetzlsperger, and G. Walter-Drop. 2018. "Policy," in T. Risse, T.A. Börzel, and A. Draude (Eds.), *The Oxford Handbook of Governance and Limited Statehood* (pp. 584–603). Oxford: Oxford University Press.

Bryden, M. 2004. "State-Within-a-Failed-State: Somaliland and the Challenge of International Recognition," in P. Kingston and I.S. Spears (Eds.), *States-Within-States: Incipient Political Entities in the Post-Cold War Era*. Basingstoke: Palgrave Macmillan.

Carment, D. 2003. "Assessing State Failure: Implications for Theory and Policy." *Third World Quarterly* 24(3): 407–27.

Carment, D., J. Landry, Y. Samy, and S. Shaw. 2015. "Towards a Theory of Fragile State Transitions: Evidence from Yemen, Bangladesh and Laos." *Third World Quarterly* 36(7): 1316–32.

Chojnacki, S., C. Ickler, M. Spies, and J. Wiesel. 2012. "Event Data on Armed Conflict and Security: New Perspectives, Old Challenges, and Some Solutions." *International Interactions*, 38(4): 382–401.

Cutler, C.A., V. Haufler, and T. Porter (Eds.). 1999. *Private Authority and International Affairs*. Albany, NY: State University of New York Press.

Dahl, R. 1961. *Who Governs: Democracy and Power in an American City*. New Haven, CT: Yale University Press.

DiMaggio, P.J. and W.W. Powell. 1991. "The Iron Cage Revisited: Institutional Isomorphism and Collective Rationality in Organizational Fields," in W.W. Powell and P.J. DiMaggio (Eds.), *The New Institutionalism in Organizational Analysis* (pp. 63–82) .Chicago and London: University of Chicago Press.

Draude, A., L. Hölck, and D. Stolle. 2018. "Social Trust," in T. Risse, T.A. Börzel, and A. Draude (Eds.), *The Oxford Handbook of Governance and Limited Statehood* (pp. 353–72). Oxford: Oxford University Press.

Erdmann, G. 2013. "Neopatrimonialism and Political Regimes," in N. Cheeseman and D. Anderson (Eds.), *Routledge Handbook of African Politics* (pp. 59–69). London and New York: Routledge.

Eriksen, S.S. 2011. "'State Failure' in Theory and Practice: The Idea of the State and the Contradictions of State Formation." *Review of International Studies* 37(1): 229–47.

Esders, S., L. Hölck, and S. Rinke. 2018. "Histories of Governance," in T. Risse, T.A. Börzel, and A. Draude (Eds.), *The Oxford Handbook of Governance and Limited Statehood* (pp. 31–147). Oxford: Oxford University Press.

Förster, T. and L. Koechlin. 2018. "'Traditional' Authorities," in T. Risse, T.A. Börzel, and A. Draude (Eds.), *The Oxford Handbook of Governance and Limited Statehood* (pp. 231–49). Oxford: Oxford University Press.

Fukuyama, F. 2004. *State Building: Governance and World Order in the Twenty-First Century*. Ithaca, NY: Cornell University Press.

Fukuyama, F. 2012. *The Origins of Political Order. From Prehuman Times to the French Revolution*. New York: Farrar, Straus, and Giroux.

Grande, E. and L.W. Pauly (Eds.). 2005. *Complex Sovereignty. Reconstituting Political Authority in the Twenty-First Century*. Toronto: Toronto University Press.

Hale, T. and D. Held (Eds.). 2011. *Handbook of Transnational Governance*. Cambridge: Polity Press.

Hobbes, T. 1987 (1652). *Leviathan*. Frankfurt/Main: Suhrkamp.

Holsti, K.J. 2004. *Taming the Sovereigns. Institutional Change in International Politics*. Cambridge: Cambridge University Press.

Hurd, I. 1999. "Legitimacy and Authority in International Politics." *International Organization* 53(2): 379–408.

Jackson, R.H. 1990. *Quasi-States. Sovereignty, International Relations, and the Third World*. Cambridge: Cambridge University Press.

Jacob, D., B. Ladwig, and C. Schmelzle. 2018. "Normative Political Theory," in T. Risse, T.A. Börzel, and A. Draude (Eds.), *The Oxford Handbook of Governance and Limited Statehood* (pp. 564–83). Oxford: Oxford University Press.

Jo, H. 2015. *Compliant Rebels. Rebel Groups and International Law in World Politics*. Cambridge: Cambridge University Press.

Kooiman, J. (Ed.). 1993. *Modern Governance. New Government-Society Interactions*. London: Sage.

Koremenos, B., C. Lipson, and D. Snidal (Eds.). 2001. *Rational Design: Explaining the Form of International Institutions. Special Issue of International Organization*. Cambridge: Cambridge University Press.

Krasner, S.D. 1999. *Sovereignty. Organized Hypocrisy*. Princeton, NJ: Princeton University Press.

Krasner, S.D. 2018. "Theories of Development and Areas of Limited Statehood," in T. Risse, T.A. Börzel, and A. Draude (Eds.), *The Oxford Handbook of Governance and Limited Statehood* (pp. 29–47). Oxford: Oxford University Press.

Krasner, S.D. and T. Risse (Eds.). 2014. *External Actors, State-Building, and Service Provision in Areas of Limited Statehood. Special Issue of "Governance"*. Hoboken, NJ: John Wiley.

Krieger, H. 2018. "International Legal Order," in T. Risse, T.A. Börzel, and A. Draude (Eds.), *The Oxford Handbook of Governance and Areas of Limited Statehood* (pp. 543–63). Oxford: Oxford University Press.

Lake, D.A. 2016. *The Statebuilder's Dilemma. On the Limits of Foreign Intervention*. Ithaca, NY: Cornell University Press.

Lake, D.A. 2018a. "Coercion and Trusteeship," in T. Risse, T.A. Börzel, and A. Draude (Eds.), *The Oxford Handbook of Governance and Limited Statehood* (pp. 293–311). Oxford: Oxford University Press.

Lake, M. 2018b. *Strong NGOs and Weak States. Human Rights Advocacy and Gender Justice in the Democratic Republic of Congo and South Africa*. Cambridge: Cambridge University Press.

Laswell, H.D. 1936. *Politics: Who Gets What, When, How?* New York: Whittlesey House.

Lee, M., G. Walter-Drop, and J. Wiesel. 2014. "Taking the State (Back) Out? A Macro-Quantitative Analysis of Statehood and the Delivery of Collective Goods and Services." *Governance* 27(4): 635–54.

Levi-Faur, D. 2012a. "From 'Big Government' to 'Big Governance?'" in David Levi-Faur (Ed.), *The Oxford Handbook of Governance* (pp. 3–18). Oxford: Oxford University Press.

Levi-Faur, D (Ed.). 2012b. *The Oxford Handbook of Governance.* Oxford: Oxford University Press.

Levi, M. and A. Sacks. 2009. "Legitimating Beliefs: Sources and Indicators." *Regulation and Governance* 3(4): 311–33.

Man, J.Y. (Ed). 2013. *China's Environmental Policy and Urban Development.* Cambridge, MA: Lincoln Institute of Land Policy.

March, J.G. and J.P. Olsen. 1998. "The Institutional Dynamics of International Political Orders." *International Organization* 52(4): 943–69.

Mayntz, R. 2004. "Governance im modernen Staat," in Arthur Benz (Ed.), *Governance—Regieren in komplexen Regelsystemen* (pp. 65–76). Wiesbaden: VS Verlag für Sozialwissenschaften.

Mayntz, R. 2009. *Über Governance: Institutionen und Prozesse Politischer Regelung.* Frankfut: Campus.

Menkhaus, K. 2006/2007. "Governance Without Government in Somalia. Spoilers, State Building, and the Politics of Coping." *International Security* 31(3): 74–106.

Messner, J.J., N. Haken, P. Taft, H. Blyth, K. Lawrence, S. Pavlou, et al. 2015. *Fragile States Index: The Book.* Washington, DC: The Fund for Peace.

North, D.C., J.J. Wallis, and B.R. Weingast. 2009. *Violence and Social Orders. A Conceptual Framework for Interpreting Recorded Human History.* Cambridge: Cambridge University Press.

Osiander, A. 2001. "Sovereignty, International Relations, and the Westphalian Myth." *International Organization* 55(2): 251–87.

Ostrom, E. 1990. *Governing the Commons. The Evolution of Institutions for Collective Action.* Cambridge: Cambridge University Press.

Ostrom, E. 2000. "Collective Action and the Evolution of Social Norms." *The Journal of Economic Perspectives* 14(3): 137–58.

Paris, R. 2011. "Ordering the World: Academic Research and Policymaking on Fragile States." *International Studies Review* 13(1): 58–71.

Paris, R. 2013. "Afghanistan: What Went Wrong?" *Perspectives on Politics* 11(2): 538–48.

Reno, W. 2015. "Predatory States and State Transformation," in S. Leibfried, E. Huber, M. Lange, J.D. Levy, and J.D. Stephens (Eds.), *The Oxford Handbook of Transformations of the State* (pp. 730–44). Oxford: Oxford University Press.

Rhodes, R.A.W. 1997. *Understanding Governance. Policy Networks, Governance, Reflexivity and Accountability*. Buckingham and Philadelphia: Open University Press.

Richards, R. 2014. *Understanding Statebuilding: Traditional Governance and the Modern State in Somaliland*. Farnham: Ashgate.

Risse, T. 2000. "'Let's Argue!' Communicative Action in World Politics." *International Organization* 54(1): 1–39.

Risse, T. 2011. "Governance in Areas of Limited Statehood: Introduction and Overview," in T. Risse (Ed.), *Governance Without a State? Policies and Politics in Areas of Limited Statehood* (pp. 1–35). New York: Columbia University Press.

Risse, T. 2018. "Hierarchical and Non-Hierarchical Coordination," in T. Risse, T.A. Börzel, and A. Draude (Eds.), *The Oxford Handbook of Governance and Limited Statehood* (pp. 312–32). Oxford: Oxford University Press.

Risse, T., T.A. Börzel, and A. Draude (Eds.). 2018. *The Oxford Handbook of Governance and Limited Statehood*. Oxford: Oxford University Press.

Risse, T. and E. Stollenwerk. 2018. "Limited Statehood Does not Equal Civil War," in K. Eikenberry and S.D. Krasner (Eds.), *Civil Wars, Violence, and International Responses. Special Issue of Daedalus, 147 No. 1* (pp. 104–15).

Rotberg, R.I. (Ed.). 2003. *State Failure and State Weakness in a Time of Terror*. Washington, DC: Brookings Institution Press.

Rotberg, R.I. (Ed.). 2004. *When States Fail. Causes and Consequences*. Princeton, NJ: Princeton University Press.

Schäferhoff, M. 2014. "External Actors and the Provision of Public Health Services in Somalia—Task Complexity Matters." *Governance*, 27(4): 675–95.

Scharpf, F.W. 1997. *Games Real Actors Play. Actor-Centered Institutionalism in Policy Research*. Boulder, CO: Westview.

Scharpf, F.W. 1999. *Governing in Europe. Effective and Democratic?* Oxford: Oxford University Press.

Schmelzle, C. 2015. *Politische Legitimität und zerfallene Staatlichkeit*. Frankfurt am Main: Campus.

Schmelzle, C. and E. Stollenwerk. 2018. "Virtuous or Vicious Circle? Governance Effectiveness and Legitimacy in Areas of Limited Statehood, Special Issue." *Journal for Intervention and Statebuilding* 12(4): 449–67.

Schuppert, G.F. and M. Zürn (Eds.). 2008. *Governance in einer sich wandelnden Welt. PVS - Politische Vierteljahresschrift. Sonderheft 41*. Wiesbaden: VS Verlag für Sozialwissenschaften.

Stollenwerk, E. 2018a. "Measuring Governance and Limited Statehood," in T. Risse, T.A. Börzel, and A. Draude (Eds.), *The Oxford Handbook of Governance and Limited Statehood* (pp. 106–27). Oxford: Oxford University Press.

Stollenwerk, E. 2018b. A Virtuous Circle of Governance? The Interplay Between Effectiveness and Legitimacy in Areas of Limited Statehood. PhD. Dissertation, Departmant of Political and Social Sciences, Freie Universität Berlin, Berlin.

Stollenwerk, E. and J. Opper. 2017a. *Codebook. The Governance and Limited Statehood Dataset. SFB Governance in Areas of Limited Statehood.* Berlin: Freie Universität Berlin.

Stollenwerk, E. and J. Opper. 2017b. *The Governance and Limited Statehood Dataset, version March 2017. SFB 700.* Freie Universität Berlin.

Thauer, C.R. 2015. *The Managerial Sources of Corporate Social Responsibility. The Spread of Global Standards.* Cambridge: Cambridge University Press.

Thomson, J.E. 1994. *Mercenaries, Pirates, and Sovereigns. State-Building and Extraterritorial Violence in Early Modern Europe.* Princeton, NJ: Princeton University Press.

Tilly, C. 1985. "War Making and State Making as Organized Crime," in P.B. Evans, D. Rueschemeyer, and T. Skocpol (Eds.), *Bringing the State Back In.* Cambridge: Cambridge University Press.

Tilly, C. 1995. *Coercion, Capital, and European States, AD 900–1992.* Vol. 2. Cambridge, MA: Basil Blackwell.

Weber, M. 1978. *Economy and Society.* Berkeley, LA: University of California Press.

Williamson, O.E. 1975. *Markets and Hierachies: Analysis and Anti-Trust.* New York: The Free Press.

Woodward, S.L. 2017. *The Ideology of Failed States. Why Intervention Fails.* Cambridge: Cambridge University Press.

5

The Role of Trust in Rebuilding Countries in Fragile and Conflict Situations

Daouda Sembene

1. Introduction

There is broad recognition of the potential of trust to facilitate cooperation, enhance economic efficiency, and boost institutional performance. Trust could contribute to these outcomes notably by coordinating interactions between social and economic agents; however, reaping these benefits in countries in fragile and conflict-affected situations (FCS countries) may prove challenging, because relations between various segments of society are typically undermined by mistrust and distrust, with an adverse, all-encompassing impact on economic, social, and institutional development.[1] To rebuild FCS countries, trust must therefore be nurtured with a view to not only managing and resolving conflict, but also to shaping positive development outcomes. But before nurturing trust, it matters first to fully grasp what it is. What are its characteristics? How is it built or earned?

1.1 What Is Trust?

As discussed in Sembene (2007), finding common ground on the definition of trust remains a challenge, partly because trust is a multifaceted concept with direct relevance to multiple disciplines, including psychology, sociology, philosophy, economics, law, political science, history, health care, anthropology, and computer science. Various dictionaries provide a range of definitions that typically characterize trust as a firm reliance on the integrity or the ability of a person or a thing; a certainty in another party's trustworthiness, reliability, and honesty; confident expectations of something; and a condition in which one is free from doubt. Along these lines, trust has been characterized as a confidence in the other party's goodwill or predictability in one's expectations (Luhmann, 1979; Zucker, 1986;

[1] As discussed in this book, definitions of fragility vary across the literature and institutions. For practical purposes, this chapter refers to fragile and conflict-affected countries as those included in the World Bank's Harmonized List of Fragile Situations.

Daouda Sembene, *The Role of Trust in Rebuilding Countries in Fragile and Conflict Situations* In: *Macroeconomic Policy in Fragile States.* Edited by: Ralph Chami, Raphael Espinoza, and Peter Montiel, Oxford University Press (2021).
DOI: 10.1093/oso/9780198853091.003.0005

Ring and van de Ven, 1992). The concept of trust as predictability is meant to refer to the situation in which one party (person or group) estimates that another party will act in a certain way and is thus confident that their predictions about the behavior of the other will come true.

By coordinating social interaction, predictability-based trust promotes cooperation, which is given precedence over confrontation or opportunistic behavior (La Porta et al., 1997; Gambetta, 2000).[2] However, the underlying assumption of the existence of common values that can generate convergent goals or a sense of community has been questioned, especially in the context of relations between organizations which may have different values and goals and be subject to pressures from different constituencies (Hardy et al., 1998). Similarly, the idea of goodwill-based trust raises various questions on the origin, foundation, and signaling of goodwill that prompt divergent answers. Among critics of the concepts of predictability- and goodwill-based trust, some have proposed definitions that attempt to capture other aspects of trust, including the expectation from each party that others will not engage in opportunistic behavior and the expectation of favorable outcomes, which is in turn based on the expected action of another party (Hardy et al., 1998; Chami and Fullenkamp, 2002; Bhattacharya et al., 1998; Sembene, 2007).

1.2 What Are the Characteristics and Sources of Trust?

Despite the numerous and heterogeneous definitions of trust, most authors seem to agree on various characteristics of trust. First, there is a consensus that trust is a desirable property of the relationships among individuals, organizations, and institutions. Its importance is reinforced by its ability to facilitate positive outcomes. Its desirable features include its ability to promote cooperation, which may be preferable to competition under certain circumstances. Second, a noticeable feature relates to the situation- and person-specific nature of trust and its relationship with vulnerability (Bhattacharya et al., 1998). A party's level of trust can evolve depending on the actions taken by other parties and on the expected outcomes and consequences of these actions. Third, another key facet of trust relates to vulnerability. Indeed, trust implies an implicit acceptance of being vulnerable to the actions of the trusted party coupled with an expectation that the latter will act favorably to one's interests. Fourth, trust involves uncertainty and risk, which must not be confused with vulnerability. The relation between trust and risk remains subject to controversy: some authors consider trust as a way to reduce risks associated with economic transactions, while others argue that

[2] The literature has stressed the importance of making a distinction between trust-based interactions and power-based interactions, which produce different forms of cooperation.

trust constitutes a risk to effective transactions between partners (Fisher, 1991; Ring and Van de Ven, 1992). In any case, trust can arguably play a positive role in countries in fragile and conflict situations by reducing the level of risk arising from uncertainty and incomplete and asymmetric information among key domestic and external actors. Fifth, trust can be a functional equivalent of power because the latter can also ensure predictability in coordination. Trust and power can exert similar effects on a party's decision to act in an expected way. An actor can indeed act as another party expects, not on the basis of trusting relationship, but out of fear of the power of the other party or possibly of another actor. Nonetheless, the use of power reduces synergy, even though it may increase predictability and serve the purposes of the dominant party. Finally, trust differs from trustworthiness (Chami and Fullenkamp, 2002). Different parties that do not trust one another can be provided with incentives to act in a trustworthy way. Unlike trust, trustworthiness does not necessarily include cooperation-promoting incentives.

Although some authors argue that trust emerges spontaneously (see for instance Sabel, 1993), many studies undertaken across the literature provide explanations about the sources of trust. Trust is deemed to originate, among others, from the institution of relevant procedures (Zucker, 1986); norms of equity that define the degree to which one party judges that another will fulfill its commitments and that the relationship is equitable (Van de Ven and Walker, 1984); the exhibit of appropriate symbols (Lewis and Weigert, 1985); successful and repeated transactions between parties observing the norms of equity (Dasgupta, 1988; Ring and Van De Ven, 1992); and a communication process in which shared meanings develop to support non-opportunistic behavior (Hardy et al., 1998).

This chapter explores the role played by trust in the process of rebuilding FCS countries. It focuses on the role of trust in the relationships maintained by public officials in these countries with domestic and external stakeholders. The next section analyzes the implications of the trust deficit in FCS countries for the functioning of domestic institutions. More specifically, the section explores how trust—or the lack of thereof—interacts with political legitimacy, weak governance, social exclusion, taxation, and financial sector development. The third section discusses how trust matters for effective engagement of multilateral institutions in FCS countries. The fourth section concludes.

2. Trust and Domestic Institutions in FCS Countries

A widely shared conviction among specialists is that FCS countries suffer from a large deficit of interpersonal as well as intra- and inter-organizational trust. Available evidence appears to confirm this. For instance, while about 28 percent of World Values Surveys respondents do not "trust very much or not at all" their neighborhood, and three out of four respondents expressed the "need to be careful toward most people" in both fragile and nonfragile countries, there are striking differences from individual countries' perspectives.[3] Among FCS countries, the proportion of people who don't trust their neighborhood very much and those who do not trust it at all ranges from about 35 percent in Lebanon and Zimbabwe to 65 percent in Haiti. Similarly, 15 percent or less among respondents feel that most people can be trusted in Palestine, Lebanon, and Zimbabwe, while this rate is more than 23 percent, on average, in nonfragile countries.

In light of this evidence, the next section discusses how this trust gap affects the ability of domestic institutions in FCS countries to shape socially desirable political and development outcomes. While acknowledging that domestic institutions are multidimensional, the focus here is on political and economic institutions.

2.1 Trust and Political Institutions

States have the primary responsibility to build inclusive societies, but governments in many FCS countries find it challenging to fulfill this responsibility.

Indeed, fragility is reflective of a country's inability to maintain social cohesion, as noted by Marshall and Elzinga-Marshall (2017). Given the endemic lack of trust in public officials amid fragility and conflict, citizens tend to be reluctant to engage constructively in government-sponsored state-building processes. The trust deficit may originate in various political and institutional factors, depending on the specific circumstances of these countries; however, the focus of this section is on exploring the role played by state illegitimacy and governance weaknesses.

2.1.1 Trust and Political Legitimacy

Available evidence suggests that distrust in government can be exacerbated by the actual or perceived lack of legitimacy and accountability of FCS country authorities. Figure 5.1 plots the degree of fragility and political legitimacy of 167 countries based on the Fragility Index and Political Legitimacy Score compiled by Marshall and Elzinga-Marshall (2017).[4] Using the indicators on which the political legitimacy score is based as a proxy for regime and governance inclusion, a number of noteworthy trends can be detected. First, six out of eight countries broadly assessed to be of "extreme state fragility" display a score that signals at best moderate fragility in the area of political legitimacy. These six countries are

[3] The World Values Survey database covers 59 countries of which 7 are included in the World Bank's FY19 Harmonized List of Fragile Situations: these 7 are Haiti, Iraq, Lebanon, Libya, Palestine, Yemen, and Zimbabwe.

[4] The State Fragility Index ranges from 0 (No fragility) to 25 (Extreme fragility). The Political Legitimacy score is based on five indicators that serve as a proxy for regime and governance inclusion and are related to factionalism; political discrimination against ethnic groups; political salience of elite ethnicity; polity fragmentation; and exclusionary ideology of ruling elite (see Data Appendix).

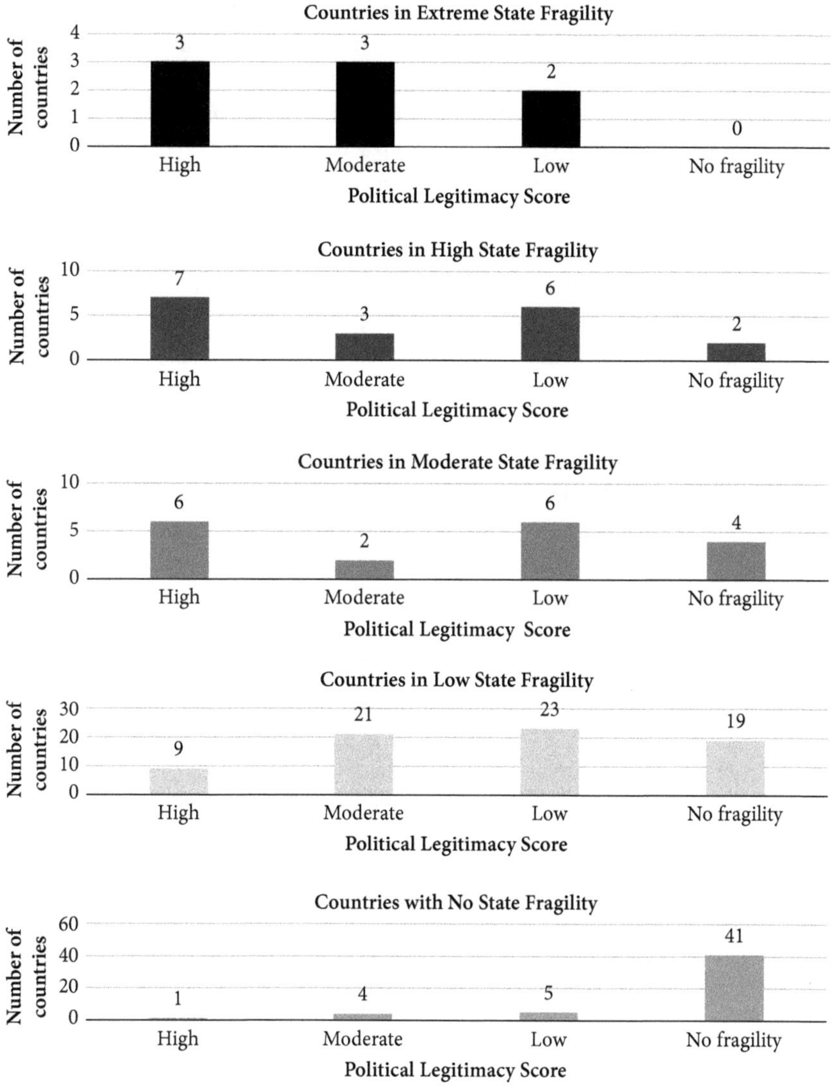

Figure 5.1 Fragility and Political Legitimacy
Source: Marshall and Elzinga-Marshall (2017).

Democratic Republic of Congo, Central African Republic, South Sudan, Sudan, Burundi, and Yemen. Second, out of 26 countries broadly assessed to be of "high fragility" or "extreme fragility," 10 enjoy "low or no fragility" with respect to political legitimacy, while most remaining countries display at best high fragility in this area. In contrast, only 16 among the remaining 141 countries that show, at worst, moderate signs of fragility are assessed to be of "high or extreme fragility" in the area of political legitimacy.

Overall, the data suggest that the more severe the fragility index of a country is, the worse its political legitimacy score is likely to be. Thus, improving the ability of FCS country authorities to achieve greater social cohesion calls for efforts to enhance citizens' perceptions of the political legitimacy and accountability of FCS countries rulers, which in turn requires overcoming the deficit of public trust in government. This is consistent with the conclusions reached by the Commission on State Fragility, Growth and Development (2018) and Acemoglu and Robinson (2019), suggesting that fragility tends to be associated with the lack of accountability; members of society are reluctant to cooperate with people who escape their influence and control. Indeed, government officials in most FCS countries are not selected on the basis of democratic and transparent electoral processes. Rather, their ranks tend to include unaccountable strongmen such as military and militia leaders who opportunistically grab de facto power amid the weak security environment and political instability.

In this connection, the literature unsurprisingly provides evidence of a strong nexus between fragility and autocracy. For instance, Marshall and Elzinga-Marshall (2017) document a positive correlation between the spike in autocratic regimes and the increase in armed conflicts around the world between post-colonial periods and the end of the Cold War. If anything, electoral competition in a situation of fragility often contributes to fueling conflict between ruling and opposition parties, as noted by BenYishay et al. (2017).

2.1.2 Trust and Governance

Beyond political illegitimacy, other potential root causes of public distrust of government officials in FCS countries impede inclusive state-building and require strengthening the governance framework to facilitate exit from fragility and conflict. These include corruption, rent-seeking behavior, regulatory capture, and social exclusion.

Clearly, distrust of authorities in FCS countries may result from regulatory capture, rent-seeking behavior, or corrupt practices by members of national and local governments, parliaments, and the judiciary. When adopted by public officials, such behavior and practices tend to undermine trust by weakening people's confidence in the disinterestedness of their actions. They reduce potential opportunities for citizens and government officials to undertake successful joint nation-building initiatives. This situation can be worse when the private sector is also suspected of engaging in trust-destroying activities. According to Abramov (2009), corruption in the public and private sector adversely affects the trust of local communities in conflict and post-conflict areas. Yet trusting relations between these communities, government, and the private sector are a prerequisite for effective public-private partnerships.

Abramov (2009) suggests that public-private partnerships must help promote principles of good governance in conflict areas, so as to help businesses and government build trust and regain credibility among local communities. More generally, the Commission on State Fragility, Growth and Development (2018) considers that a positive evolution of politics and security in FCS countries requires turning distrust of government into conditional trust, notably by addressing rent capture in both the public and private sectors and strengthening political governance amid distrust in public administration.

Moreover, social exclusion of vulnerable segments of the population undermines trust in government by weakening the social contract. It is often driven by a number of factors that tend to constrain state-building in countries in fragile or conflict situations. These include ethnic tensions, religious differences, and social norms and institutions that may provide some segments of the population all but a subjective rationale for trusting public officials. In addition, disparities in income and unequal access to opportunities tend disproportionately to affect women and the youth, thereby exacerbating social exclusion. Because de facto leaders are more likely to be middle-aged and older male members of the political and military elite, women and the youth in FCS countries are frequently disenfranchised and endowed with little or no political power and typically face high rates of unemployment and illiteracy.

2.2 Trust and Economic Institutions

To cope successfully with situations of conflict and fragility, FCS countries need to improve their economic institutions as much as their political institutions. Ultimately, a sustainable exit from conflict and fragility entails rebuilding their capacity to restore and preserve macroeconomic stability and make steady progress toward their development objectives. To this end, it is critical to enhance the effectiveness of institutions tasked with securing these outcomes, notably the tax administration and financial sector authority. This section examines the role of trust in laying the foundations for improved tax collection and financial sector development.

2.2.1 Trust and Taxation

Traditional economic models of tax compliance assume that taxpayers make strategic decisions based on rational considerations of financial gains and losses.[5] Taxpayers comply with tax laws if the probability of detection is high and the resulting fines are severe. Otherwise, they are incentivized to pursue tax avoidance by under-declaring their assets and claiming undue deductions. More recent theories, however, have emphasized the role of trust in tax compliance. Building

[5] See Kirchler (2007).

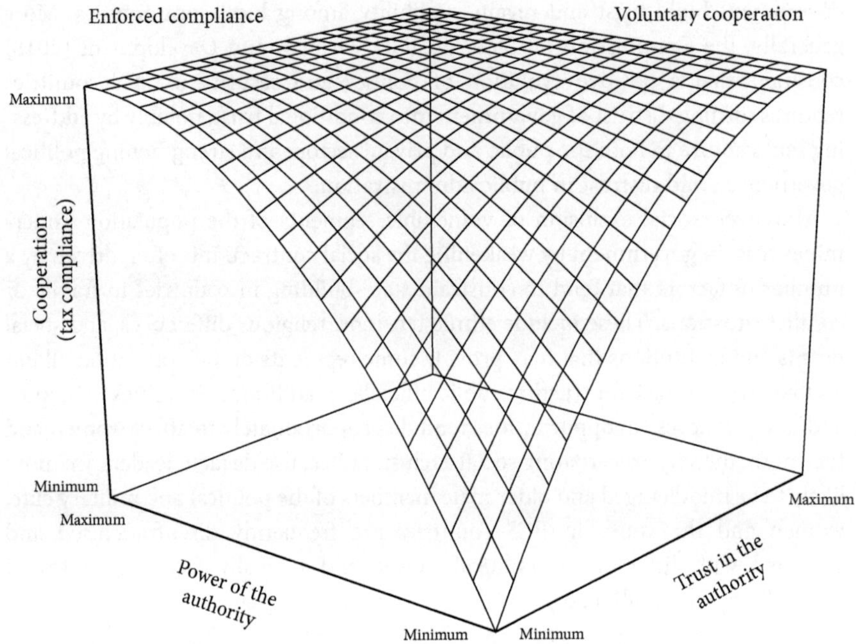

Figure 5.2 The Slippery Slope Framework
Source: Kirchler, Hoelzl, and Wahl (2008).

trust in tax authorities has been featured in proposed solutions to overcome tax compliance challenges.

As illustrated in Figure 5.2 by Kirchler (2007), and Kirchler et al. (2008) using the "Slippery Slope Framework," trust is found, along with the power of authorities, to help solve the social dilemma that is induced by the tension between individual short-term self-interest (avoiding tax payments) and collective long-term interest (securing tax revenue needed for the provision of public goods). The concept of trust in authorities refers to psychological determinants of tax compliance; notably, taxpayers' views about the clarity and transparency of tax laws and regulations and the integrity of the tax authorities. By contrast, the concept of the power of authorities relates to economic determinants and is defined by taxpayers' perception of authorities' capacity to identify and punish tax evaders.

Drawing on the existing literature, Gangl et al. (2015) extend the "Slippery Slope Framework" to analyze the ramifications of the mutual interaction of coercive and legitimate power with reason-based and implicit trust. Reason-based trust derives from the taxpayer's rational expectations that the tax authorities do not pursue their own self-interest, while implicit trust results from instinctive and automatic compliance with social practices and norms that support the perceived trustworthiness of tax authorities. Tax authorities may earn

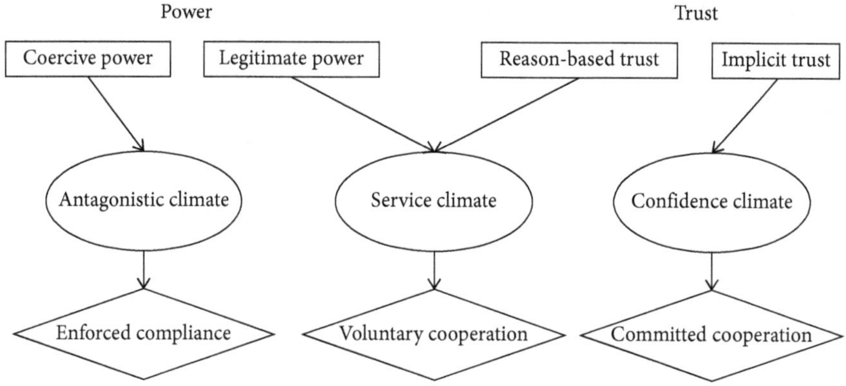

Figure 5.3 The Extended Slippery Slope Framework
Source: Gangl, Hofmann and Kirchler (2015).

taxpayers' trust if their power is viewed as legitimate and their approach to ensuring tax compliance is not based on coercion. Conversely, taxpayers' voluntary cooperation may prove elusive in the event that tax authorities choose to exercise coercive power. Gangl et al. (2015) make the following assumptions, as illustrated in Figure 5.3:

- Coercive power and implicit trust are mutually decreasing each other.
- Legitimate power and reason-based trust are mutually amplifying each other.
- Coercive power and reason-based trust are related through legitimate power.
- Legitimate power and implicit trust are related through reason-based trust.

Based on these assumptions, a number of conjectures can be made in the context of FCS countries. First, the level of implicit trust in tax authorities tends to be weak in FCS countries amid rulers' prevalent use of illegally backed coercive power. In the absence of the rule of law in the context of fragility, people in such societal settings are often subjected by tax authorities to abusive tax collection schemes and expropriation proceedings. Under these circumstances, social norms provide little basis for them to have sympathy for tax authorities and comply with their directives.

Second, taxpayers in FCS countries have little incentive to nurture reason-based trust, owing to the perceived lack of legitimacy of the power exercised by tax authorities. As previously noted, the large majority of FCS countries that are assessed to be of "high or extreme fragility" typically enjoy poor ratings with respect to political legitimacy. This is because de facto rulers in these countries gain and maintain power through political violence and repression rather than democratic elections.

Third, systematic recourse to coercive and illegitimate power in FCS countries creates a vicious circle of mistrust and distrust among the population in general and taxpayers in particular. In turn, this contributes to fueling taxpayers' reluctance to fulfilling their tax obligations and complying with directives provided by tax officials. Tax noncompliance is worsened by the inability of tax administrations to effectively secure tax collection because of their capacity weaknesses.

Weak fiscal performance is consequently endemic in FCS countries partly because of taxpayers' trust deficit; hence, governments are unable to mobilize domestic revenue needed to finance their development objectives. Reversing this trend therefore requires prior efforts to establish trusting relations between citizens and tax authorities.

2.2.2 Trust and Financial Sector Development

The finance literature has long highlighted the role of trust in facilitating financial transactions and promoting financial sector development. This emphasis has increasingly grown since the inception of the asymmetric information theory in the 1980s.[6] Where there are informational asymmetries, financial markets naturally tend to factor in the degree to which agents can be trusted, as this has a bearing on the efficiency of resource allocation and transaction costs as well as the optimality of pricing decisions (Bossone, 1999). Information asymmetry is thus likely to lead to unfavorable financial development outcomes, particularly in FCS countries, where financial market imperfections are prevalent and the level of trust between agents is relatively low.[7]

Extensive evidence is available on the role of trust in financial sector development, but little is known about how it matters in FCS countries and how it compares with its role in their non-fragile peer countries. The answer requires better understanding the distinctive features of financial systems in FCS countries and the implications of trust deficit for financial development and inclusion.

2.2.2.1 Distinctive Features of Financial Systems in FCS Countries

Drawing on the experience of Africa, Financial Sector Deepening (FSD) Africa (2017) reveals a number of distinctive features of fragility-affected states, particularly in the development and performance of the financial sector. First, FCS countries tend to have more shallow financial systems than other countries, notably in terms of credit depth. The banking sector dominates the financial industry, and capital markets are embryonic or nonexistent. Furthermore, the proportion of adults in these countries who have access to a bank account is only about 14 percent compared to 23 percent in Africa.

[6] See Greenwald and Stiglitz (1987).

[7] Available evidence suggests that fragility is rooted in informational asymmetries and high transaction costs. For instance, FSD Africa (2017) reaches this finding in the case of fragile African countries.

Second, financial exclusion is typically more prevalent in FCS countries relative to other peers. According to FSD Africa (2017), it affects 80 percent of the population in Cameroon, Chad, Democratic Republic of the Congo, Sierra Leone, and Sudan and over 90 percent in Burundi and Niger. This is corroborated by Barajas et al. (2019) who underscore the large differences in financial inclusion between fragile states and other countries: they find that fragile states significantly lag behind other countries when it comes to the use of accounts, credit to households, and credit to firms, while being likely to enjoy more limited access to finance.

Third, the regulatory framework is significantly weaker in FCS countries than in non-fragile countries. Analyzing the World Bank's Doing Business indicators, Leo et al. (2012) estimate that African fragile states have, on average, an Ease of Doing Business ranking of 171 (of 182 countries) compared with an average ranking of 117 for non-fragile states in the continent.

Fourth, economic agents tend to display lower levels of risk tolerance and trust in fragile states. Such behavior fuels fragility and can be motivated by a variety of factors, including informational asymmetries, financial infrastructure bottlenecks, high informality, and regulatory weaknesses. It is noteworthy that this specific feature is affected by the aforementioned ones, each of which plays a specific role in constraining the level of trust among financial sector actors, including individuals, business representatives, and government officials.

2.2.2.2 Implications of Trust Deficit for Financial Development and Inclusion

Undoubtedly, the weaknesses of financial systems in FCS countries are likely to affect these countries' development potential, notably through their impact on trust. According to Bossone (1999), societies in early stages of economic development, with strong ties among members, can enjoy relatively low financial transaction costs. Though many FCS countries typically have economies at early stages of development and with undeveloped financial systems, interactions between citizens and businesses tend to be tainted with distrust and mistrust, which inflates financial transaction costs. Combined with infrastructure bottlenecks and weak capacity, these high costs reduce the incentives of banks and other financial sector agents to engage in financial intermediation and initiatives conducive to financial development.

In consequence, some market failures and distortions are likely to emerge that keep financial intermediaries from efficiently fulfilling their role by serving as "bridges of trust."[8] First, intermediaries may be reluctant to engage in trust-based

[8] In the words of Bossone (1999), financial intermediaries act as "bridges of trust" between agents, with their efficiency being reflected in their ability to contain the costs associated with this task.

transactions, while revealing a preference for other types. Accordingly, the most popular activities carried out by financial industry operatives in FCS countries include collecting savings, holding government securities, and providing currency exchange services. In contrast, financial intermediation schemes that are reliant on some of form of trust in individuals, businesses, and government are viewed as unattractive and are only made available at a prohibitive cost.

Furthermore, the financial industry in FCS countries has strong incentives to over-charge customers and consumers for financial services irrespective of their reliance on trust. This results notably from the magnitude of transaction costs and risks associated with doing business in FCS countries, which leads industry players to adopt aggressive business models primarily focused on the quest for short-term investment returns. Yet, the authorities in FCS countries are often unable to prevent such practices amid weak supervision and regulation of the financial sector.

Finally, financial exclusion may be a natural outcome, with the financial industry denying access of "untrustworthy" segments of the population to financial services. As noted by FSD Africa (2017), individuals and enterprises tend to rely on trusted social and business networks amid increased fragility. Beyond the trust factor, risk management in FCS countries' financial industry is further complicated by the high degree of informality.

It comes as no surprise, then, that the interest of the development community in promoting financial inclusion in FCS countries has continuously grown in recent years. Deeper financial markets and services that are accessible to broad segments of the population are found to help reduce poverty and income inequality, address vulnerability, and resolve conflict in FCS countries (FSD Africa, 2017).

3. Trust and International Institutions in Countries in Fragile and Conflict Situations

As discussed in Sembene (2007), trust between government officials and IMF staff exerts a positive influence on the likelihood that a country will achieve its policy objectives. This favorable outcome channels notably through the ability of trust to improve the quality of the design, the efficiency of negotiation, and the effectiveness of implementation of an IMF-supported program.

More generally, while supporting empirical evidence on the overall benefits of trust in these relationships is not always readily available, it is widely acknowledged that international institutions are poised to benefit greatly from trusting relations with government officials in their member countries, particularly those in fragile or conflict situations. The more trusted these institutions are, the more traction their advice has across their membership. In this connection, current threats to multilateralism provide a good illustration of the potential implication of public distrust for the effectiveness and fate of multilateral institutions.

This section explores the specific case of the IMF and FCS countries in Sub-Saharan Africa, based on my previous work on trust-related issues and my personal experience as a former IMF official. It also discusses other determinants of trust in the IMF in fragile and conflict situations, notably the business model of the institution, its internal policies, and the focus of its advice.

3.1 How Trust Affects IMF Engagement in FCS Countries

This section draws on my experience as a former IMF Executive Director representing 23 Sub-Saharan African countries, 10 of which are included in the World Bank's FY19 Harmonized List of Fragile Situations. These are Central African Republic, Chad, Comoros, Democratic Republic of the Congo, Republic of Congo, Côte d'Ivoire, Djibouti, Guinea-Bissau, Mali, and Togo.[9] Because about half of our constituency's members were deemed in fragile or conflict situations, IMF engagement in this context was a key priority for our office. We worked with our Board colleagues as well as IMF management and staff to put fragility and security-related issues high on the IMF agenda.

As underscored by Sembene (2007), several factors contribute to determining the level of trust in IMF staff, including the perceived quality, timing, and origin of IMF advice as well as their handling of sensitive information. Indeed, it appears that the authorities shape conjectures, perceptions, and expectations about the quality and impact of IMF policy advice including on the basis of the outcomes of past IMF engagement in their own country and across the membership. This history in turn affects their level of trust in IMF staff; so does any suspicion that the provision of a specific piece of policy advice stems from pressures by other domestic and external stakeholders. Country authorities expect the IMF, as their trusted and confidential advisor, to safeguard the confidentiality of information that they provide to the institution and that they deem not suitable for public access; therefore, their trust in IMF staff can also be undermined in the event of a leak if they suppose that it occurred because of mishandling of this information by IMF personnel. IMF internal review and transparency policies have greatly contributed to reducing this risk.

3.2 The IMF's Business Model

FCS countries have long been treated by their multilateral partners as business-as-usual cases, but they have increasingly benefited in recent years from efforts to

[9] Madagascar was also included in the list in FY17 when I took over as IMF Executive Director.

tailor development assistance to their specific circumstances. Several multilateral institutions have embarked on this route, mindful of the need to embrace adaptive changes to their institutional culture. The IMF has pursued similar efforts although it faces daunting headwinds in trying to adapt its business model to better serve FCS countries. Indeed, its Independent Evaluation Office finds that initiatives that were taken in the past to adapt IMF policies and practices to these countries have not been sufficiently bold or adequately sustained (IEO, 2018).[10]

Under these circumstances, recalibrating the business model of the IMF to meet the needs arising from conflict and fragility is critical to build trust and enhance the effectiveness of its engagement in affected countries. And clearly, there is a broad convergence of views on this imperative. But in practice, it has proven quite challenging to forge a consensus within the IMF, and its Board in particular, on the role of the institution in member countries in fragile and conflict situations. While some argue against the IMF acting as a "development institution" and advocate primary reliance on the institution's catalytic role, others call for strong and protracted IMF financial assistance in FCS countries.

In any case, the IMF is, at this juncture, obligated under its Articles of agreement to provide only balance of payments financing—rather than development financing—according to predetermined access policies. Yet, the scope of IMF engagement, and its financing in particular, has an inherent impact on the level of trust in the institution. Moreover, access policies that are deemed to result in inadequate access to IMF financial resources may adversely affect the perceptions and views of FCS country officials as to the reliability and trustworthiness of the institution. That said, it is noteworthy that the catalytic role of the IMF can help affect this potential impact when played in an effective manner.

3.3 IMF Internal Policies

Internal policies and processes of multilateral institutions may have ramifications on their ability to build trust in FCS countries. These are most notably expressed through their effect on the morale and dedication of staff who are assigned to these countries and experience working conditions more difficult than do their colleagues covering non-fragile states. At the IMF, human resources policies have a potential effect on the level of trust in the institution by influencing the quality and experience of staff members assigned to FCS countries. For instance, these policies influence the selection of resident representatives who, as the face of the IMF in their host countries, can play a critical role in facilitating relations of trust between the two parties.

[10] See IEO (2018) evaluation on the IMF and Fragile States.

Yet until recently, staff has had little—if any—incentive to work in FCS countries, even as their safety and physical integrity are more under threat. Unlike staff of other multilateral institutions, staff members at the IMF receive no specific reward in terms of career development for their work in FCS countries. As a result, efforts to build trust have been undermined by the limited presence of experienced and skilled staff and the subsequent high turnover among FCS country teams.

Under these circumstances, there is scope for the IMF to enhance the trusting relations maintained with public officials by taking steps to provide incentives for high-quality and experienced staff members to work in these countries, as recommended by the IEO (2018).

Another potential constraint on IMF trust-building initiatives relates to the institution's policies on field presence in high-risk locations, which are more stringent than those implemented by many other peer institutions. Following the tragic loss of the IMF Resident Representative in Agfhanistan, the risk-aversion is understandable but may constrain the IMF's ability to engage in trust-building policy dialogue in many FCS countries.

Finally, it is noteworthy that a number of other IMF internal policies may affect the scope of trusting relations with FCS countries. These include policies related to external communication, diversity, and access to resources.

3.4 The Focus of IMF Advice

In my experience, the focus of IMF advice has a significant bearing on the ability of the institution to maintain trusting relations with FCS country authorities. The reason is that a number of core areas of IMF expertise intrinsically raise critical trust-related issues, as illustrated by the three following examples. First, IMF advice in the area of debt restructuring is prone to raising a number of trust-impacting issues. The recent cases of Chad and the Republic of Congo are illustrative. Because the IMF routinely expresses its strong attachment to the principle of uniformity of treatment of debtors and creditors, any perceived noncompliance with this principle has the potential to fuel distrust in the institution, particularly from concerned government officials. Unsurprisingly, such perceptions may easily emerge in the presence of informational asymmetries during debt restructuring negotiations. Fortunately, the potential loss of trust in the IMF is likely to be offset once a debt restructuring deal is secured with concerned creditors and an IMF-supported program approved by the IMF Board, as has been the case with these two countries.

Second, recent IMF work has put an increasing focus on corruption and bad governance in member countries, including those in fragile and conflict situations. Such focus may be legitimate in many of the FCS countries where these ills are prevalent and often macrocritical, but one of its potential side effects is to undermine parallel initiatives aimed at strengthening the role of the IMF as a trusted, confidential advisor. Clearly, backlash against the potential of the IMF to nurture trust can be expected, especially when the institution is perceived as not making enough effort to fully apprehend the role played by the eventual lack of political goodwill and capacity weaknesses respectively in explaining the scope and resilience of corruption. In this connection, some FCS country officials have expressed their feeling of being stigmatized by the recurrent emphasis put on corruption during policy discussions with IMF staff and in ensuing public statements.

Third, trust in the IMF appears to be dependent on the focus—or lack thereof—of IMF advice on the financing of growing security spending. Amid growing security threats in many FCS countries, the IMF has granted them greater flexibility, on a case-by-case basis, to address peace and security needs by allowing their budgets to accommodate related spending increases. However, it has been faced with the dilemma of seeking to build trust in these countries, while advocating fiscal consolidation amid an explosion of security spending and unmet financing needs for basic public services. At the same time, the authorities have called on the IMF to provide them with more access to its resources, with a view to addressing security and commodity price shocks. These calls have generally triggered a positive response from the IMF, notably in favor of FCS countries in Central Africa, but the resources thereby made available might not have helped to fulfill the full trust-building potential of IMF financing.

4. Conclusion

This chapter explores the role of trust in the relationships maintained by public officials in FCS countries with domestic and external stakeholders. It discusses how the trust deficit in these countries affects the functioning of domestic institutions. More specifically, the chapter analyzes the interaction between trust, or the lack of thereof, with political legitimacy, weak governance, social exclusion, taxation, and financial sector development. It also explores how trust matters for effective engagement of international institutions in FCS countries, building on the IMF's experience in Sub-Saharan Africa.

From the theoretical and empirical evidence reported in this chapter, it appears that the ability of FCS country authorities to achieve greater social cohesion could be improved through efforts to enhance the political legitimacy and accountability of government in FCS countries, which in turn requires overcoming the deficit of trust in government. Beyond political illegitimacy, there are other ills that need to be addressed as they can potentially impede inclusive state-building. These include corruption, rent-seeking behavior, regulatory capture, and social exclusion.

This chapter surveys the literature to examine the role of trust in tax compliance. In this respect, building trust in tax authorities has been featured in proposed solutions to overcome tax compliance challenges. Similarly, the role of trust in financial sector development is investigated, including how it matters in FCS countries and how it compares with peers in non-fragile countries. In this connection, it has attempted to better understand the distinctive features of financial systems in FCS countries and the implications of trust deficit for financial development and inclusion.

Finally, the chapter explores how trust affects engagement of multilateral institutions in FCS countries through a case study of the IMF and FCS countries in Sub-Saharan Africa, based on my personal experience as a former IMF Executive Director. It provides a detailed analysis of specific determinants of trust in the IMF, notably the business model of the institution, its internal policies, and the focus of its advice.

More broadly, the focus of this last section is a reminder of the importance for multilateral institutions to rebuild trusting relations with their membership, particularly in FCS countries. It is especially needed at a time when the relevance of international institutions, as perceived by their membership, is at risk, and when isolationist agendas, acting as both a root cause and consequence of distrust in multilateralism, are gaining popularity.

Strengthening the effectiveness of international institutions is a responsibility that the latter share with their member states, but capitals cannot be always trusted to fulfill their roles. As a matter of fact it may often be in their own political interest to withdraw support from multilateral organizations, including through untimely contributions, delays in critical decisions, and breaches of previously agreed rules and practices.

Under these circumstances international institutions should primarily rely on their own efforts and understand that their fate will ultimately be determined by their ability to rebuild public trust. Progress on this latter front could be achieved by promptly adapting to the current global context and addressing legitimate concerns expressed by their individual members, especially those like FCS countries whose voices may be too rusty to be heard.

Now is also the time for multilateral bodies to embark on long-overdue reforms needed to strengthen their governance and accountability frameworks, adopt twenty-first-century communication strategies, and make further progress toward transparency. Fostering greater collaboration among international institutions could help them overcome current headwinds facing them. It also contributes to enhancing their effectiveness as they leverage each other's comparative advantage and resources. Finally, strong leadership matters at least as much as all of the above. Here it is needless to say that transparent selection of their heads can only help multilateral organizations in the public eyes. Regrettably, many of them continue to underperform in this area, to say the least.

The global context has now changed and the current health crisis has accelerated this trend; repeating past mistakes could prove devastating. Failure to adapt quickly to the new order exposes international institutions to the risk of losing trust, and ultimately their relevance, particularly in FCS countries, which need them the most.

References

Abramov, I. 2009. "Building Peace in Fragile States—Building Trust is Essential for Effective Public-Private Partnerships." *Journal of Business Ethics*, 89: 481–94. https://link.springer.com/article/10.1007/s10551-010-0402-8 (last accessed July 16, 2020).

Acemoglu, D. and J.A. Robinson. 2019. "Building Inclusive States: A Simple Framework," Chapter 2 in this volume.

Barajas, A., R. Chami, and C. Fullenkamp. 2019. "The State of Finance in Fragile States," Chapter 7 in this volume.

BenYishay, A., L. Mueller, and P. Roessler. 2017. "Impact Evaluation of the Niger Participatory and Responsive Governance: Baseline Report." *AidData Research Consortium*; November. https://www.aiddata.org/publications/impact-evaluation-of-the-niger-participatory-responsive-governance-project-baseline-report (last accessed July 16, 2020).

Bhattacharya, R., T.M. Devinney, and M.M. Pillutla. 1998. "A Formal Model of Trust Based on Outcomes." *The Academy of Management Review*, 23(3): 459–72.

Bossone, B. 1999. "The Role of Trust in Financial Sector Development." Policy Research Working Paper 2200. World Bank, Washington, DC.

Chami, R. and C. Fullenkamp. 2002. "Trust as a Means of Improving Corporate Governance and Efficiency." IMF Working Paper WP/02/33. International Monetary Fund, Washington, DC.

Commission on State Fragility, Growth and Development. 2018. *Escaping the Fragility Trap*. London: International Growth Centre.

Dasgupta, P. 1988. "Trust as a Commodity", in D. Gambetta (Ed.), *Trust: Making and Breaking Cooperative Relations* (pp. 49–72). Oxford: University of Oxford.

Fisher, R. 1991. "Beyond Yes", Harvard Program on Negotiation, Cambridge, Massachusetts.

FSD (Financial Sector Deepening) Africa. 2017. *Financing the Frontier: Inclusive Financial Sector Development in Fragility-Affected States in Africa*, February 2017 Report published in partnership with and Mercy Corps.

Gambetta, D. 2000. "Can We Trust Trust?" in D. Gambetta (Ed.), *Trust: Making and Breaking Cooperative Relations* (pp. 213–37). Oxford: University of Oxford.

Gangl, K., E. Hofmann, and E. Kirchler. 2015. "Tax Authorities' Interaction with Taxpayers: A Conception of Compliance in Social Dilemmas by Power and Trust." *New Ideas in Psychology*, 37: 13–23.

Greenwald, B. and J.E. Stiglitz. 1987. *Money, Imperfect Information and Economic Fluctuations*. No. w2188. National Bureau of Economic Research.

Hardy, C., N. Phillips, and T. Lawrence. 1998. "Distinguishing Trust and Power in Interorganizational Relations. Forms and Facades of Trust," in C. Lane and R. Bachmann (Eds.), *Trust within and between Organizations. Conceptual Issues and Empirical Applications* (pp. 64–87). Oxford: Oxford University Press.

IEO (Independent Evaluation Office). 2018. *The IMF and Fragile States*. Washington, DC: International Monetary Fund.

Kirchler, E. 2007. *The Economic Psychology of Tax Behavior*. Cambridge: Cambridge University Press.

Kirchler, E., E. Hoelzl, and I. Wahl. 2008. "Enforced versus Voluntary Tax Compliance: The 'Slippery Slope' Framework." *Journal of Economic Psychology*, 29(2):210–25.

La Porta, R., F. Lopez-de-Silanes, A. Shleifer, and R. Vishny. 1997. "Trust in Large Organizations." *The American Economic Review*, 87(2): 333–8, Papers and Proceedings of the Hundred and Fourth Annual Meeting of the American Economic Association.

Leo, B., V. Ramachandran, and R. Thuotte. 2012. Supporting Private Sector Growth in African Fragile States: A Guiding Framework for the World Bank Group in South Sudan and Other Countries, Center for Global Development, Washington, DC.

Lewis, J.D. and A. Weigert. 1985. "Trust as a Social Reality." *Social Forces*, 63(4): 967–85.

Luhmann, N. 1979. *Trust and Power*. New York: Wiley.

Marshall, M.G. and G. Elzinga-Marshall. 2017. *Global Report 2017: Conflict, Governance and State Fragility*. Vienna, VA: Center for Systemic Peace.

Ring, P.S. and A.H. Van De Ven. 1992. "Structuring Cooperative Relationships between Organizations." *Strategic Management Journal*, 13: 483–98.

Sabel, C.F. 1993. "Studied Trust: Building New Forms of Co-operation in a Volatile Economy," in Richard Swedberg (Ed.), *Explorations in Economic Sociology* (pp. 104–44). New York: Russel.

Sembene, D. 2007. "Give Trust a Chance—A Model of Trust in the Context of an IMF-Supported Program." IMF Working Paper WP/07/42, Washington DC.

Sembene, D. 2017. "African Strategies to Boost Growth and Combat Poverty and Inequality." United Nations DESA Expert Group Meeting on Strategies for Eradicating Poverty to Achieve Sustainable Development for All, May 8–11. https://www.un.org/development/desa/dspd/wp-content/uploads/sites/22/2017/04/Daouda-Sembene-African-strategies-to-boost-growth-and-combat-poverty-PPT-Presentation-1.pdf (last accessed July 16, 2020).

Sembene, D. 2015. "Poverty, Growth, and Inequality in Sub-Saharan Africa: Did the Walk Match the Talk under the PRSP Approach." IMF Working Paper WP/15/122, Washington DC.

Sembene, D., S. Issoufou, and A. Mansoor (Ed.). 2018. Race to the Next Income Frontier—*How Senegal and Other Low-Income Countries Can Reach the Finish Line*. Washington DC: International Monetary Fund.

Van de Ven, A.H. and G. Walker. 1984. "The Dynamics of Interorganizational Coordination." *Administrative Science Quarterly*, 29: 598–621.

Zucker, L.G. 1986. "Production of Trust: Institutional Sources of Economic Structure." *Research in Organizational Behavior* 8: 53–112.

Data Appendix: State Fragility Index and Matrix 2016

The State Fragility Index and Matrix 2016 compiled by Marshall and Elzinga-Marshall (2017) lists all 167 independent countries in the world in which the total country population is greater than 500,000 in 2016. The Fragility Matrix scores each country on both Effectiveness and Legitimacy in four performance dimensions: Security, Political, Economic, and Social, at the end of the year 2016. Each of the Matrix indicators is rated on a four-point fragility scale: 0 "no fragility," 1 "low fragility," 2 "medium fragility," and 3 "high fragility," except the Economic Effectiveness indicator, which is rated on a five-point fragility scale (including 4 "extreme fragility"). The State Fragility Index, then, combines scores on the 8 indicators and ranges from 0 "no fragility" to 25 "extreme fragility." A country's fragility is closely associated with its state capacity to manage conflict, make and implement public policy, and deliver essential services, and its systemic resilience in maintaining system coherence, cohesion, and quality of life, responding effectively to challenges and crises, and sustaining progressive development.

Fragility Indices

- **State Fragility Index** = Effectiveness Score + Legitimacy Score (25 points possible)
- Effectiveness Score = Security Effectiveness + Political Effectiveness + Economic Effectiveness + Social Effectiveness (13 points possible)
- Legitimacy Score = Security Legitimacy + Political Legitimacy + Economic Legitimacy + Social Legitimacy (12 points possible)
- **Political Legitimacy ("polleg") Score**: Regime/Governance Inclusion, 2016. Sources: Polity V, 2016; Ted Robert Gurr, Monty G. Marshall, and Victor Asal, Minorities at Risk Discrimination 2016 (updated by Monty G. Marshall); and Ted Robert Gurr and Barbara Harff, Elite Leadership Characteristics 2016 (updated by Monty G. Marshall). In the 2007 report, four indicators were used to determine the Regime/Governance Inclusion score: Factionalism (Polity V, parcomp value 3 = 1); Ethnic Group Political Discrimination against 5 percent or more of the population (Discrimination: POLDIS values 2, 3, 4 = 1); Political Salience of Elite Ethnicity (Elite Leadership Characteristics: ELETH values 1 or 2 = 1); and Polity Fragmentation (Polity V, fragment value greater than 0 = 1). To these indicators, the authors have added Exclusionary Ideology of Ruling Elite (Elite Leadership Characteristics: ELITI value 1 = 1). Political Legitimacy Score is calculated by adding these five indicators; scores of 4 or 5 (rare) are recoded as 3. Note: Countries coded in the Polity V dataset as an "interregnum" (that is, total or near total collapse of central authority, −77) for the current year are scored 3 on the Political Effectiveness indicator.

6

The Private Sector in Fragile Situations

Nabila Assaf, Michael Engman, Alexandros Ragoussis, and Sarthak Agrawal

1. Introduction

Creating the conditions that would allow private investment and commerce to take root is essential to set economies in fragile situations on a positive, long-term growth trajectory. This matters greatly because the world's poor are increasingly concentrated in fragile situations. In 2002–13, the incidence of extreme poverty fell in 104 countries and rose in 27 countries. Most of the countries that experienced a rise in poverty levels were also classified as fragile or conflict-affected.[1] By 2030, it is estimated that roughly half of the world's population that lives in poverty will be based in fragile situations. The private sector in fragile situations currently produces a small fraction—or approximately 1 percent—of global output, trade, and foreign investment. In 2017, Finland received more foreign direct investment (FDI) than the total amount received by 36 fragile or conflict-affected states as per the World Bank Group classification.

This study of the private sector in fragile situations identifies common government failures and market failures that prevent the private sector from realizing its potential. Severe political turbulence or sudden conflict can wipe out businesses or lead to cycles of severe contraction. Many businesses resort to operating in the informal economy. Businesses that do operate in the formal economy are strikingly often sole proprietors. Coping mechanisms tend to be costly and cumbersome, resulting in depressed productivity levels. To foster the private sector's contribution to stability, economic policymakers and the development community need to focus on both resilience and economic growth. A combination of institutional and regulatory reforms, risk-sharing instruments, and public investments can help to advance this agenda. Institutional and market characteristics should inform priorities for development interventions.

This paper has benefitted from comments from Raphael Espinoza, Leonardo Iacovone, John Speakman, and participants at a conference on Fragility in Oxford hosted by IMF and Oxford University on December 10–11, 2018. The findings, interpretations, and conclusions expressed in this chapter are entirely those of the authors. They do not necessarily represent the views of the International Bank for Reconstruction and Development/World Bank, the International Finance Corporation, and their affiliated organizations, or those of their Executive Directors or the governments they represent.

[1] Poverty defined with respect to the international poverty line of $1.90/person per day.

Nabila Assaf, Michael Engman, Alexandros Ragoussis, and Sarthak Agrawal, *The Private Sector in Fragile Situations*
In: *Macroeconomic Policy in Fragile States.* Edited by: Ralph Chami, Raphael Espinoza, and Peter Montiel,
Oxford University Press (2021). © International Monetary Fund.
DOI: 10.1093/oso/9780198853091.003.0006

The debate about the role of the private sector in conflict situations tends to generate opposing views. The development community generally acknowledges its importance and counts on its mobilization for economic growth. Yet, private interests can also be a cause of conflict or social tension. A history of foreign interference, weak governance, or political views may fuel skepticism over the motivations and criticism over the outcomes of economic activities. This paper seeks to inform this debate by providing a comprehensive picture of private economic activity at the micro and macro levels by treating fragility as a continuum rather than a binary concept. The objectives are to provide a broad assessment that helps reduce misconceptions, and approach private enterprises as transformative partners in trajectories towards stability. Governments should seek to address common failures to allow private enterprises to fulfill that role. This agenda constitutes one of the great development challenges of our time.

The paper is structured as follows. Section 2 looks at the role that the private sector plays in fragile situations, covering common outcomes of private participation. Section 3 then studies characteristics of enterprises and markets to present the typical business environment in fragile situations. Section 4 finally draws some general policy conclusions from the preceding analysis and discusses approaches that development practitioners may consider in addressing the failures.

2. The Private Sector and Its Role in Building Resilience

Peace, fragility, and conflict are hard to delimitate. The terms cover a range of situations from countries with weak institutions and high risk of conflict to actual events of violence or war. The set of countries that are severely affected by fragility and conflict is broadly consistent across classifications but is also heterogeneous in its characteristics. As this paper will show, there is no single point of fragility where a consistent change is observed in economic outcomes across countries.

The private sector contributes in many ways to the foundations of social stability and resilience. For example, businesses generate employment and income, pay taxes, and directly provide necessity goods and services such as food, water, health, education, and transportation. The private sector forms the backbone of resilience of local populations during periods of conflict. Collectively, the private sector can make a difference in times of transition. Business associations have at times shown leadership by being directly involved in the process of peace-building. The informal private sector is also essential for income generation because of the relative ease of entry and low requirements for education, capital, skills, and technology, although most people enter the informal economy out of a need to survive and to have access to basic income-generating activities rather than by choice. But in situations where law and order have collapsed, some private sector actors may also act in harmful ways. The outcome depends on the economic interests of businesses and their owners; and the political, security, and governance context in which they operate.

2.1 The Boundaries of Peace, Fragility, and Conflict Are Fluid

Fragility can be both the cause and the outcome of conflict. Fragile situations often evolve into violent conflict, which bring about protracted periods of instability. The dynamics of "conflict" and "fragility" tend to affect states simultaneously. Yet the two remain conceptually and practically distinct. Fragility is broadly defined as a state of significant government failure to fulfill the basic needs of its citizens—whether through lack of capacity or desire. The definition centers on the potential for adverse outcomes and the absence of fundamental structures that ensure continuity and stability. Conflict is, by contrast, an actual series of events: violent collisions between specific parties that could extend to a continuous state over time.

Country lists drawn up by institutions to define fragility, including by the World Bank Group's list of fragile countries, share similarities in their scope and methods. They tend to classify countries categorically—as fragile or non-fragile—which conceals fundamental differences among them. This paper refrains from using definite statements on fragility and does not classify countries as fragile or non-fragile. It considers countries within the entire fragility spectrum using a continuum that synthesizes social, economic, and political outcomes produced annually by the Fund for Peace's Fragile States Index (FSI) (see Figure 6.1). This chapter thus refers to "fragile situations" more broadly as countries and territories with higher FSI without providing a cutoff point. The FSI is a composite index made up of cohesion (security apparatus, factionalized elites, group grievance); economic (economic decline, inequality, human flight/brain drain); political (state legitimacy, public services, human rights/rule of law); and social (demographic pressure, refugees or internally displaced persons [IDPs], external interventions) indicators estimated for 178 countries (see description in Annex 1).

The countries that are most severely affected by fragility and conflict are currently concentrated mainly in Sub-Saharan Africa, South Asia, and the Middle East and North Africa. For countries with an FSI above 90, which covers a total of 32 countries, 22 are in Sub-Saharan Africa; four in the Middle East and North Africa (Iraq, Libya, Syria, Yemen); three in South Asia (Afghanistan, Bangladesh, Pakistan); two in East Asia (North Korea and Myanmar); and one in the Caribbean (Haiti). Approximately half of the countries officially designated by the World Bank Group as Fragile and Conflict States (FCS) are in Sub-Saharan Africa. In the World Bank Group's Harmonized List of Fragile Situations in 2019, the 36 countries and territories had a combined population of 515 million inhabitants with a median population per country not much different from the countries outside the list (7.4 million versus 8.9 million). The countries that are

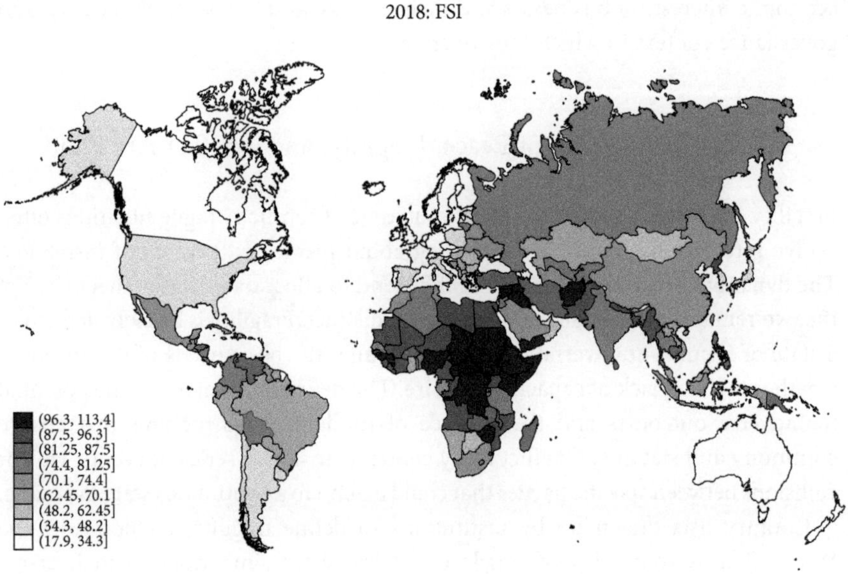

Figure 6.1 The Fragile States Index in 2018, by Country
Source: Illustrations using data from Fund for Peace (2018). (editor: Intervals to be rounded)

most severely affected by fragility outside Sub-Saharan Africa are typically in postconflict transition, or in a deep state of fragility with sporadic episodes of conflict.

Failures that affect economic activity occur at various points along what we refer to as "the fragility continuum" and tend to be highly heterogenous. There is no single point where a consistent change is observed for multiple economic variables. Regression discontinuity tests for different economic outcomes at different intervals of fragility reject the existence of a fragility level that captures multidimensional change in markets (see Figure 6.2).[2] However, using the FSI to describe the continuum, two smaller concentrations of kink points emerge. The first occurs around values of 65–70 where discontinuities are observed in terms of export orientation, access to technology, and financial markets. This level of fragility corresponds to the situation in countries like Mexico, Brazil, or Vietnam. The second occurs around values of 90, where discontinuities are more likely in terms of arms imports and tax revenue but also volume of exports

[2] Following a simple approach, discontinuities are tested in the intercept and slope between level of fragility and different economic outcomes at several thresholds of fragile states index. The basic equations are: Y + a0 + a1*(x−k) + b1*D*(x−k) + a2*(x−k)^2 + a3*D*(x−k)^2 + [...] where Y = outcome; X = Running variable (FSI); K = "kink point" in regression discontinuity (RD) terms, that is, in our case it is the level of fragility where; D = Dummy variable indicating that a a country is fragile according to the threshold. Regressions are run globally rather than locally because of limitations in the size sample.

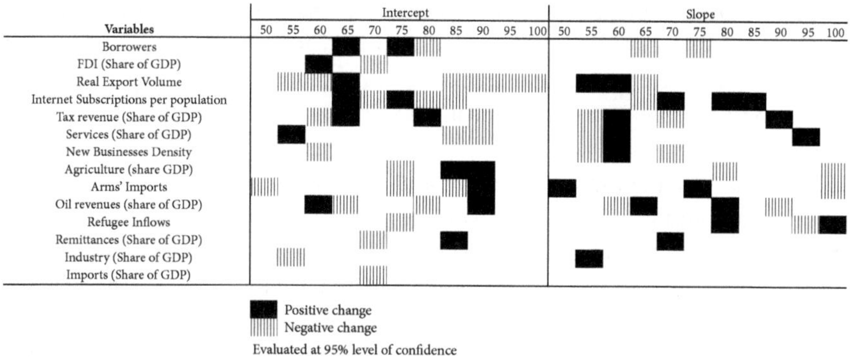

Figure 6.2 Discontinuities in economic variables at various levels of fragility
Source: Authors' calculations

and reliance on agriculture and natural resource sectors, which are intuitive. It corresponds to the fragility levels of Angola, Bangladesh, or Rwanda. The picture is noisy, and little can be inferred from it.

2.2 The Private Sector Has a Critical Role to Play in Strengthening Economic and Social Resilience

Economic activity often shapes the dynamics of a conflict. In general, low income and low growth rates are the strongest predictors of conflict. This reflects the smaller economic benefit of the peace dividend in these settings and the strongly negative impact of conflict on poverty reduction. Evidence abounds to support this point. For example, the poorest quintile of countries are 18 times more likely to experience conflict over a decade compared with the richest quintile (Fearon and Laitin, 2003; Collier and Hoeffler, 2004; Roesch, 2014). A decline of 1 percentage point in gross domestic product (GDP) is associated with a greater likelihood of war by 2 percentage points (Miguel et al. 2004). A doubling of the initial GDP is associated with a lowering of the risk of reverting to conflict in the first decade of peace from 40 percent to 31 percent, suggesting that the poorest post-conflict societies suffer from a higher risk of relapse (Fearon and Laitin, 2003; Collier et al., 2008).

The link between economic activity and stability elevates the role of private enterprises in fragile situations above and beyond their role as contributors to economic growth. Businesses, particularly domestic ones, contribute to socio-economic resilience in two main ways. First, they generate the jobs, income, and taxes that sustain the economy. Second, they directly provide goods and services that contribute to communities' resilience, including food, water, health, education, and transportation. The latter role is particularly prominent in many countries or subregions where the state may be absent, or too weak to play a satisfactory role, such as in Somalia, parts of Pakistan, or Nigeria. Thus, even in contexts of negative growth and failing economic fundamentals, the private sector collectively contributes to the foundations of social stability and resilience.

2.2.1 As an Engine for Job Creation and Income Generation

Creating and sustaining jobs is perhaps the most visible and effective contribution businesses make to stability. Jobs generate local income, including in conflict-affected communities, and help lift local populations out of poverty. Jobs, whether formal or informal, are essential to maintaining resilience and reducing incentives to engage in conflict. Informal subsistence agriculture and trading activities represent important sources of income and livelihoods for populations in fragile situations. A handful of large investments—typically in domestic backbone services and in natural resource extraction—tend to consolidate future growth and formal employment. The preservation of these jobs and livelihoods can act as a disincentive for conflict. Private businesses also generate income for governments through taxes, duties, and fees that can then be reinvested in social services and reconstruction needs, although governments in fragile situations tend to have less capacity to raise income, especially beyond taxes imposed on trade.

2.2.2 As a Provider of Necessity Goods and Basic Services

Situations of active conflict are where the contribution of the private sector to resilience stands out. Even under pervasive uncertainty and the collapse of public institutions, private enterprise "continues by other means" (Keen, 1998). Its distinctive features include the circumvention of the formal economy for the provision of basic goods and services, the growth of illicit supply chains, alongside an array of activities that can contribute to conflict dynamics such as pillage, predation, extortion, and deliberate violence to control resources. In these situations, the harm exacerbated in the absence of institutional oversight is more often emphasized. The vital role of the private sector in sustaining formal and informal networks for the distribution of food, health, or power is often overlooked.

Yemen is an example of the three-way nexus between conflict, the private sector, and resilience. Amid full-fledged war and a fractured state providing limited services, the private sector plays a key role in providing energy, water, healthcare, and food supply and distribution. Disruption and damage from the conflict have dramatically decreased the availability of electricity and fuel. The private sector stepped in with the supply of small-scale solar power equipment, which is now widely adopted throughout the country. Over the past five years, about US$1 billion has been invested in solar photovoltaic systems with market penetration at around 75 percent of households in urban areas, and 50 percent in rural areas (World Bank, 2017). A total of 180 private hospitals, tens of thousands of enterprises and farms, and 180,000 water pumps operate with energy from this source. Food, healthcare, and water supply are also heavily dependent on private sector activity because of the breakdown in public services.

Even where active conflict has subsided, the private sector's contributions remain critical even as they tend to emerge as complements to the state. The transition process towards stability and prosperity requires stronger government legitimacy. It is often built through public provision of increased security, basic services, and necessity goods. Private enterprises can nevertheless help close critical gaps by building basic infrastructure and establishing or restoring backbone services. In some fragile situations, private providers may even be the primary providers of health and education services and essential foodstuffs.

The telecommunications sector is one example where improved service provision is largely driven by private providers. In Afghanistan, mobile cellular telephone subscriptions per 100 citizens increased from less than 1 in 2003 to 61 in 2015. In Sierra Leone, the rate improved from 2.4 in 2003 to 89.5 in 2015. Myanmar illustrates the importance of private as opposed to public capital. As late as 2013, Myanmar had only 4.4 million mobile subscribers served exclusively by the government-owned monopoly provider. After the sector was opened to private and foreign investment, subscriber numbers exploded, and it reached 45 million in only two years. This growth was driven by Ooredoo and Telenor and it has transformed the way people access information, communicate, and trade.

The benefits to local communities extend beyond commercial activities. In the Palestinian Territories, the private real estate investment of Rawabi was behind the first planned town in the territory. Starting in 2010, it now provides housing for up to 40,000 people, and financing for infrastructure and schools. The private investor coordinated the development with the Palestinian Authority and in some respects substituted for its role by financing what typically would be public infrastructure, such as the building of schools and water supply, and even negotiating directly with Israeli authorities for permissions.

Some sectors in the economy may flourish even in the absence of functioning government. Somalia is an intriguing example: since the 1990s, local entrepreneurs have compensated for the lack of effective public governance by "importing governance" from foreign institutions in areas such as airline safety and currency control. Clans and other informal social networks uphold traditional customs and laws. But what might work for one sector does not necessarily apply to all. In some critical areas the private sector has made little progress. The Somali road system is limited and in poor condition, which partly explains the growth in private airlines, and the quality of most privately provided education and healthcare is relatively low.

However, the private sector needs support if it is to fill the vacuum of what are normally government functions, because a purely private approach has limitations in equity and access for the poor. For instance, during periods of intense conflict in Yemen, food has continued to be available and almost exclusively imported and distributed by the private sector. But tragically, the prices of most foodstuffs have left them beyond reach of the most vulnerable households. In the Palestinian Territories, the housing development provided much needed housing in an area with high demand, but it was only affordable for the middle class. The *hawala* system, while providing affordable, accessible, and reliable financial transfers, may not comply with international anti-money laundering and combating the financing of terrorism regulations. Combining the capacity of the private sector with policies that address reach and equity constraints, as well as mitigating against harm, is imperative to address the challenges of fragile situations.

2.2.3 As a Partner and Source of Leadership During Transition

Most private enterprises have an important stake in peace and the process of peace consolidation. They often play a role in that process before, during, and after a conflict. Larger enterprises and industry associations can make substantial contributions by setting examples of conduct, negotiating concessions, and consolidating international partnerships. In Sri Lanka, for example, industry associations initiated joint activities among enterprises from different ethnic groups. In Colombia, enterprises worked on urban employment programs and related education and social services. Bogotá's participatory policies empowered the business community, among others, through action boards (Juntas de Acción Comunal) to decide how city budgets would be spent in the neighborhoods they represented, including identifying projects for education and social services; and awarding contracts to small local enterprises. Numerous examples show that enterprises can bring diverse groups together through employment or trade and thereby help reduce social tensions.

Participation by the business community in conflict prevention has reaped rewards in contexts such as the Caucasus region, Kenya, Nepal, the Philippines, Rwanda, South Africa, Sri Lanka, and Uganda. In South Africa, a movement led by business leaders facilitated the country's transition from apartheid to a multiracial state. The Consultative Business Movement initiated broad-based bilateral consultations with political parties, civil society, and the media, and convened a process that led up to the 1991 National Peace Accord, which put in motion the country's transition to democracy (Ganson, 2017). In this case, the private sector was able to act as a stabilizing agent in the transition because it occupied the space between the apartheid regime and the African National Congress, and thus could credibly promote dialogue, trust-building, and consensus-building. In Kenya, following post-election violence in 2008, the Kenya Private Sector Alliance intervened to help end the political crisis and has thereafter continued to engage in peacebuilding activities by funding peace forums, preventing incitement, and disseminating conciliatory narratives. It negotiates privately with political leaders, organizes presidential debates, and maintains political neutrality (Austin and Wennmann, 2017). These examples illustrate the private sector's interest in stability, and leadership driven often not only by commercial but also social, cultural, and ethical concerns.

2.3 Some Private Enterprises Can Do More Harm than Good

There may be strong incentives for some enterprises to act in harmful ways that contribute to conflict dynamics in situations where law and order are weak. The same is true of governments, religious leaders, and political activists; no single actor has a monopoly on virtue. The response by businesses to conflict depends on the opportunities, challenges, and incentives they face. Local businesses may develop operations in the informal economy or seek to capture opportunities for profit from illicit activities during a conflict. Multinationals may find themselves supporting functions beyond their legitimate role, such as public security.

The type of economic activity makes a difference in how sensitive private actors are to conflict. Enterprises engaged in low-tech, high-value commodities, for example, are more indifferent to the external environment, provided these commodities can still be extracted during a conflict (Keen, 2009). A minority of businesses, most of which have a direct stake in the outcome of a power struggle, are also more profitable during a conflict and therefore may have an interest in preventing any restoration of peace. This may include businesses that make high profits from trading in food at times of artificially high food prices, or private military companies (PMCs) whose business is war (O'Brien, 2000). Recent decades have seen a sharp increase in the number of PMCs and their activities can be extensive.

By contrast, enterprises that suffer severe adverse effects from the economic downturn of conflict—for example, those in industrial and agricultural production or the services sector—have the strongest interest in stability (Keen, 2009). The tourism, telecoms, finance, retail, and transportation industries, to mention only a few, have plenty of practical incentives to work more for peace than for war (Oetzel et al., 2010). These are also precisely the businesses that support the livelihoods of the largest parts of nonmilitary populations in situations of conflict.

Countries dependent on primary commodity exports are more vulnerable to the outbreak of civil war (Collier and Hoeffler, 2004; Fearon, 2005). A natural resource bonanza may not only trigger conflict but also prolong the conflict by providing finance to various parties to the conflict (Ross, 2004). According to the United Nations, the exploitation of natural resources has been directly or indirectly associated with 40 percent of all intrastate conflicts in the past six decades (UNEP, 2009). In the Democratic Republic of Congo, for example, there are close links between armed factions and natural resource extraction: some business entities with close ties to rebel forces have encouraged armed interventions against business rivals.[3] But abundant natural resources have not destabilized countries like Australia, Canada, and Norway. The strength of public institutions and the level of inequality in the society are indicators of the extent to which natural resource extraction will affect political stability.

The size and ownership of private enterprises also affect their interaction with conflict. Because of multiple institutional failures, local businesses in conflict situations tend to be family-owned and mobilize finance through family and kinship networks. They manage risks through close relationships with those who have coercive power, often involving informal payments in return for protection. They tend to use political connections to keep new entrants out of the market. Many private businesses in conflict-prone countries or fragile situations tend to be owned by politicians, members of the military-intelligence nexus, and other leaders of authorities with coercive power. The so-called private sector may be owned and controlled by individual public officials and this creates its own issues: calls to "privatize the private sector" are common in many low-income countries and fragile situations.

The incentives for cooperation with ruling authorities and the nature of the interaction differ according to the size and ownership of the company. Small and medium-sized enterprises tend to have low capacity, be isolated, and make little profit that could be of legitimate or illegitimate interest to state actors. Therefore, they have limited interaction with formal ruling authorities. Large domestic enterprises, by contrast, represent bigger streams of revenue and therefore may be captured and controlled by ruling elites. In this case, there is either full alignment between large enterprises and political elites, or enterprises may be entering agreements with authorities to secure space to operate in a mutually beneficial way. Large local enterprises are often more comfortable navigating the complex domestic political and economic environment than foreign enterprises, because they do not face the same accountability or reputation costs.

Multinationals in most industries are sensitive to actions that give rise to reputational risk and adverse consumer reaction. Public scrutiny generates certain incentives to uphold ethical, environmental, and social standards in their operations and supply chains. This is particularly the case for branded consumer goods. However, local enterprises may have less scope to exit a market if they do harm and they may therefore be disciplined by the fact that they serve their local communities. Some multinationals may cause unintentional harm because of poor understanding and accounting for the impact of their operations on local communities; a claim that local actors cannot make over outcomes of their operations. To avoid such pitfalls, many multinationals adopt corporate policies

[3] Braud, 2006.

of concepts such as "do no harm" or "conflict sensitivity"; both of these concepts originated in the development and humanitarian community.

3. Entrepreneurs and Markets in Fragile Situations

To what extent do the characteristics and performance of businesses differ in more fragile situations? What are the common government and market failures that contribute to these differences? And what are the most common coping mechanisms and their associated costs? The following analysis seeks to answer these questions by assessing the responses from formal enterprises in the World Bank Group's Enterprise Survey.[4] This database includes responses to more than 150 questions from 135,000 formal enterprises in 139 countries collected between 2006 and 2018. It is one of the most comprehensive and geographically diverse sources of enterprise-level data that is available to a public audience. Informal businesses represent a significant share of the economies of most fragile situations (more below) and they are also key to fostering economic and social resilience. But cross-country data sources are few and informal businesses tend to have low levels of productivity. Those that do grow tend ultimately to register and join the formal economy. Formal businesses are essential for growth and as a source of information on the performance of the private sector at large.

The analysis adopts the FSI published by the Fund for Peace as its measure of fragility because it is objective and allows for an analysis of fragility as a continuous rather than binary concept (See Annex 1 for a comparison of the FSI with the World Bank Group's Country Policy and Institutional Assessments [CPIA]).[5] The FSI comprises some economic variables that could correlate with some of the enterprise characteristics and market conditions of the analysis. However, an analysis that excludes these variables nevertheless finds the results to be robust (see Annex 2). The following analysis presents the results against the full FSI but controls for the level of income throughout the analysis. A summary table of means, medians, and standard deviations is presented in Annex 3 for each studied variable and for different sets of FSI values.

The FSI theoretically spans from 0 (entirely robust) to 120 (entirely fragile). Speakman and Rysova (2015) used the enterprise survey dataset and the CPIA classification to compare enterprise characteristics in fragile versus non-fragile

[4] The survey data is representative (and not just a sample) of the non-agricultural, non-extractive, non-financial private sector. The data was retrieved in August 2018 on www.enterprisesurveys.org. Enterprise surveys in another 41 countries are due in 2019, including for Equatorial Guinea, Haiti, Kosovo, Lao People's Democratic Republic, Suriname, São Tome and Principe, Tajikistan, and Ukraine.

[5] The Fragile States Index is generated by the Fund for Peace on an annual basis and is accessible on www.fundforpeace.org/fsi/.

states in different geographical regions. This paper builds upon those findings but avoids the issues around classification. The objective of the analysis is to generate stylized facts and illustrate trends across the spectrum of countries: from peaceful countries with strong institutions to turbulent countries with weak institutions—that is the "fragility continuum."

3.1 Enterprise Characteristics and Performance

Formal enterprises in fragile situations are scarce, and many commence operations in the informal sector. First, entrepreneurship as measured by new business density—or the number of formal business registrations as a share of the population—is generally low in fragile situations. There are on average more than 6 business registrations per 1,000 people in countries with an FSI below 40 compared to less than 2 business registrations per 1,000 people in countries with an FSI above 90 (see Figure 6.3). It is only Iraq, Rwanda, and Timor-Leste among the countries frequently referred to as "fragile or conflict-affected," and which have FSIs above 90, that show more than one new business registration per 1,000 citizens.

Second, enterprises tend to be younger in fragile situations (see Figure 6.4). They also employ on average somewhat fewer workers, but the degree of

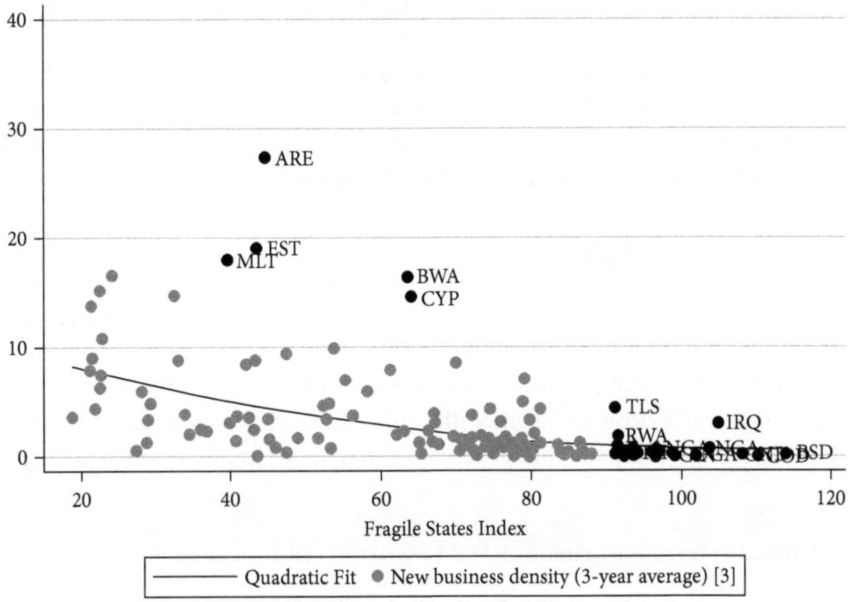

Coeffient on FSI controlling for income = –.0913 [p-value = 0]

Figure 6.3 New Business Density (3-Year Average)
Source: World Bank (2018a), World Bank (2018b), Fund for Peace (2018).

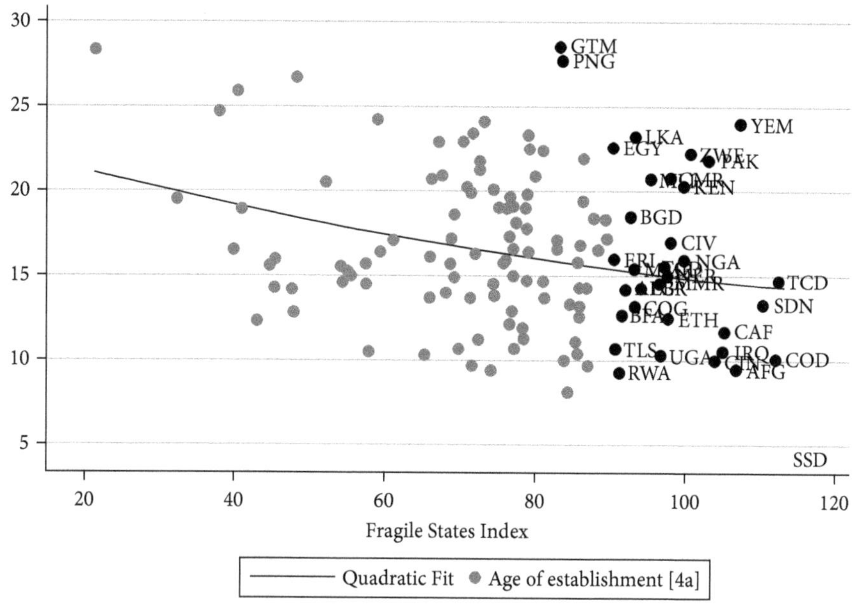

Coeffient on FSI controlling for income = –.0479 [p-value = .034]

Figure 6.4 Age of Establishment
Source: World Bank (2018a), World Bank (2018b), Fund for Peace (2018).

heterogeneity increases along the FSI. Papua New Guinea and (pre-civil war) Yemen have among the oldest enterprises in the dataset, whereas Afghanistan, the Democratic Republic of the Congo, Iraq, and South Sudan have among the youngest enterprises. The effects of conflict and violence on market entry and exit could be one explanation for the relative youth of enterprises in many fragile situations.

Third, more formal enterprises in fragile situations start operations without a formal registration, though the heterogeneity is again pronounced (see Figure 6.5). Indonesia is an outlier with more than two-thirds of its formal enterprises starting out in the informal sector; elevated levels of informality at start are seen in Nigeria, Uganda, Iraq, Angola, and Gabon. The enterprises in fragile situations that started without a formal registration but ultimately registered also stayed informal longer than their equivalents in countries with stronger institutions (see Figure 6.6). However, there is no discernable difference in the FSI 60–120 group of countries. Generally higher transaction costs are associated with company registrations in fragile situations, as is extensively covered in the World Bank's annual Ease of Doing Business survey. Formality may carry higher perceived costs (such as taxation, harassment by officials) than benefits (government support, access to financial services). The productivity of informal enterprises is often too low for them to thrive in the formal sector, so they remain informal indefinitely (La Porta and Shleifer, 2014).

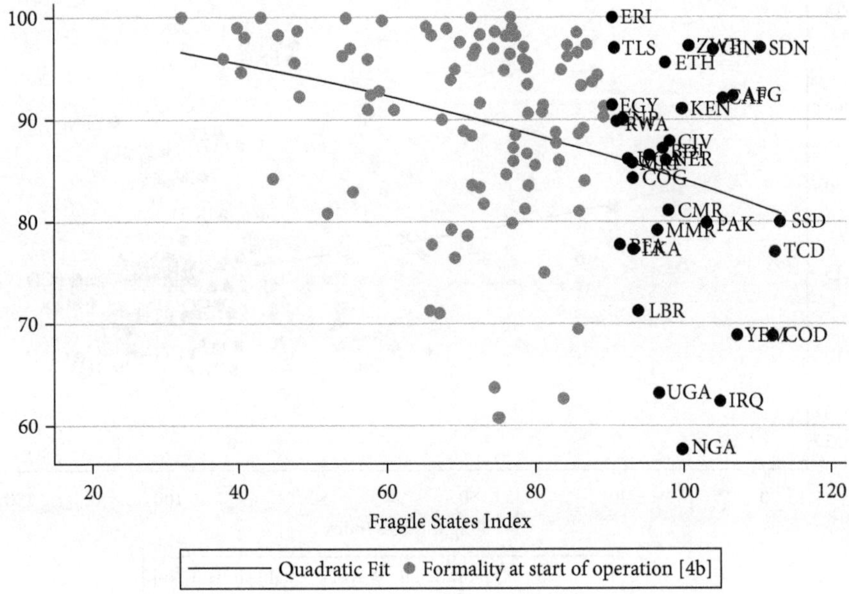

Coeffient on FSI controlling for income = –.2141 [p-value = 0]

Figure 6.5 Formality at Start of Operation
Source: World Bank (2018a), World Bank (2018b), Fund for Peace (2018).

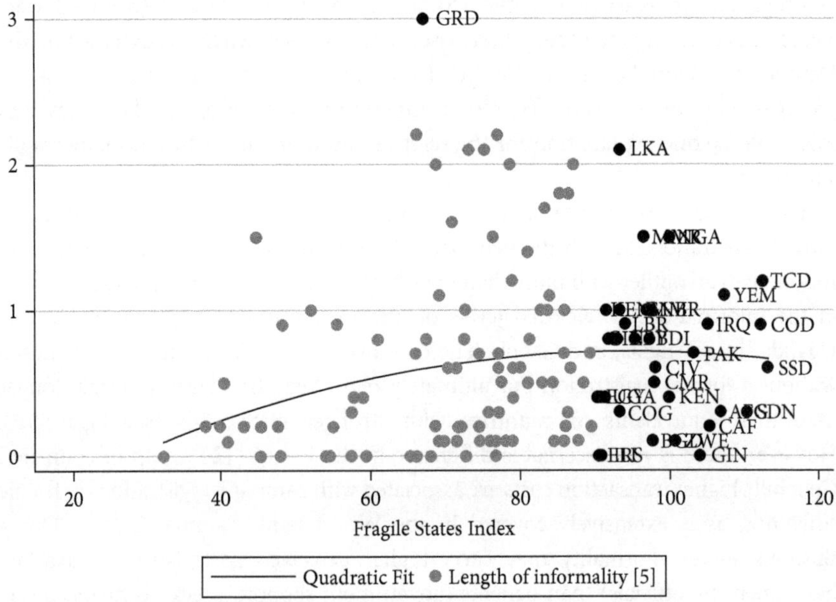

Coeffient on FSI controlling for income = .0085 [p-value = .028]

Figure 6.6 Length of Informality
Source: World Bank (2018a), World Bank (2018b), Fund for Peace (2018).

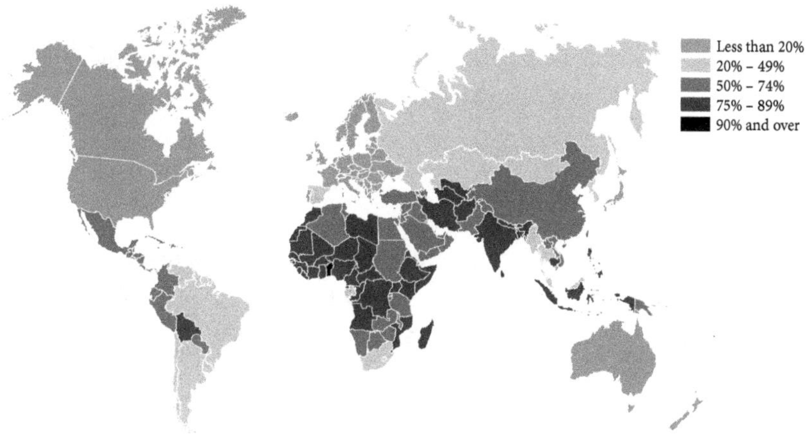

Figure 6.7 Informal Employment in Total Employment, excl. Agriculture
Source: World Bank (2018a), ILO (2018), Fund for Peace (2018).

There is no authoritative source of cross-country data on the number of informal enterprises in the world but the International Labour Organization publishes cross-country estimates on the share of informal employment in total employment. Figure 6.7 presents an illustration of informal employment in economies, excluding the agriculture sector.[6] There is a strong negative correlation between income per capita and informal employment in total employment. Three-quarters or more of the labor force in most countries that are often classified as fragile situations operate in the informal sector. Many of these workers are either self-employed or work in informal micro- and small enterprises. Informal enterprises tend to be small and highly unproductive compared to small formal enterprises and, in particular, relative to the larger formal enterprises (La Porta and Shleifer, 2008).

Owners of formal enterprises in fragile situations are significantly more exposed to financial risk at the personal level than owners in countries with more robust institutions. The level of personal risk exposure for formal entrepreneurs increases drastically with the level of fragility of the host country. The share of enterprises classified as sole proprietorship increases on average by about 8 percentage points for every 10-point move up the FSI (see Figure 6.8). For example, in countries with an FSI around 40, the average share of sole proprietorship is just above 10 percent. In the most fragile situations (FSI > 90) it is on average five to seven times as high. From a low of 1 in 5 enterprises in Mauritania to more than 4 in 5 enterprises in Niger and Cameroon; and more than 9 in 10 enterprises in Iraq, Timor-Leste, and Myanmar.

[6] This divide widens further with the inclusion of employment in agriculture (not included here).

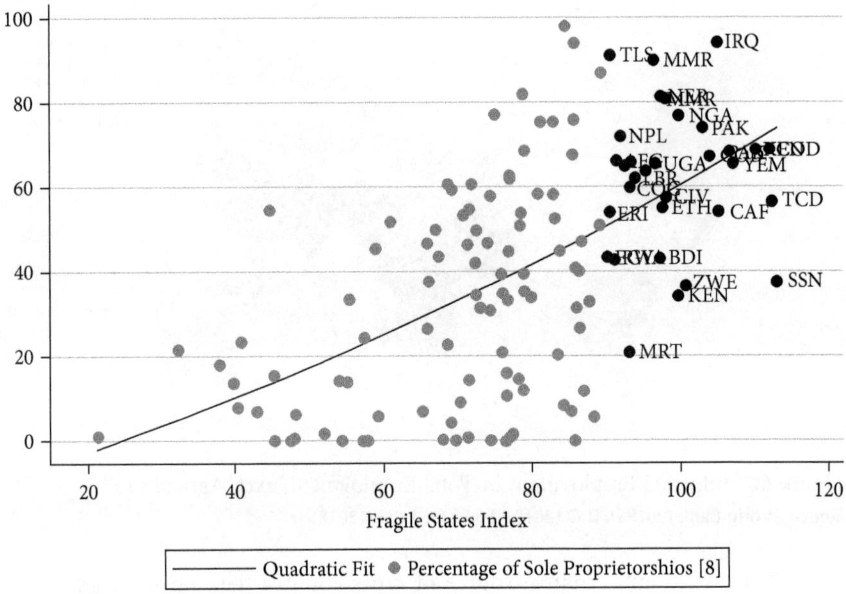

Coeffient on FSI controlling for income = .9132 [p-value = 0]

Figure 6.8 Sole Proprietorship (% of Total)
Source: World Bank (2018a), ILO (2018), Fund for Peace (2018).

A sole proprietorship is an unincorporated enterprise owned and managed by one individual (without partners) without distinction between the enterprise and individual: thus, s/he is entitled to all profits and responsible for all debts, losses, and liabilities. In other words, in the most difficult and risky environments to do business, you also find the highest share of business leaders directly personally liable to the performance of the enterprise. This has implications for their growth potential because it may impede the owner's willingness and ability to make capital investments, finance working capital, hire full-time workers, expand operations, and so on.

Enterprises in fragile situations generally use less of their production capacity, exhibit slightly lower and more unpredictable growth rates of sales and labor productivity, but have slightly higher, but more unpredictable, growth rates of employment.[7] First, real annual sales growth decreases slowly along the FSI while the range of outcomes increases, reflecting increasing uncertainty and volatility (see Figure 6.9). There are several negative outliers in the bottom third (80 < FSI < 120) of the index, as would be expected with the concentration of countries affected by conflict and other shocks. Several emerging economies record high real

[7] Growth figures in employment, sales, or productivity, in the World Bank Enterprise Survey are calculated on the basis of self-reported recall values, therefore come with strong caveats in terms of reliability. Recall values tend to be systematically higher than real records.

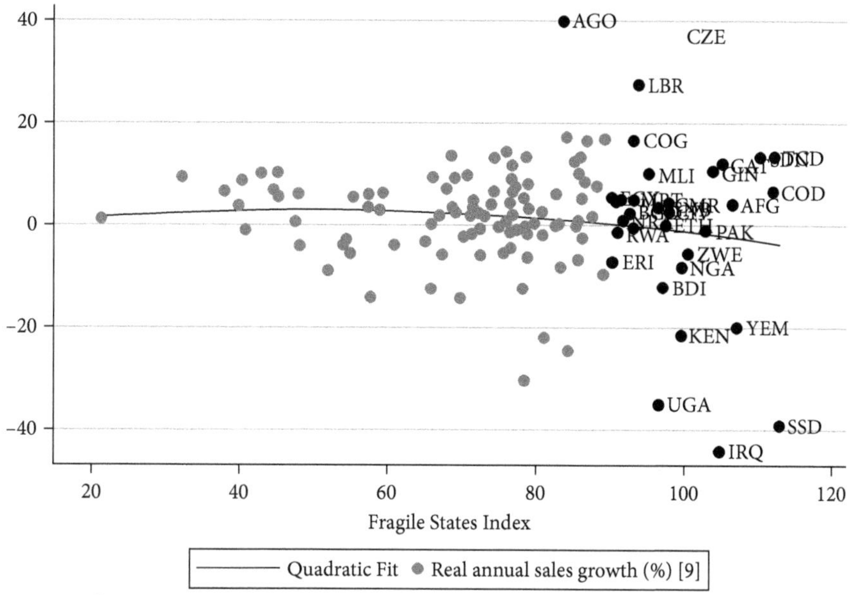

Coeffient on FSI controlling for income = –.0369 [p-value = .528]

Figure 6.9 Real Annual Sales Growth (%)
Sources: World Bank (2018a), Fund for Peace (2018).

annual sales growth rates but there are more than a dozen countries suffering a loss of 10 percent or more. Notable outliers include Iraq (−43 percent), South Sudan (−40 percent), Uganda (−35 percent) and Cameroon (−31 percent). In addition, Lao People's Democratic Republic, Kenya, Tanzania, and Yemen all experienced an average of 20–25 percent sales losses for the year surveyed.

Second, the annual employment growth rate increases on average along the FSI and so do the swings in recruitment and retrenchment (see Figure 6.10). For example, no country with an FSI below 50 saw average annual employment losses of more than 1 percent. However, in the group of countries with FSI above 90, Eritrea (−7 percent), Yemen (−5 percent), and Zimbabwe (−4 percent) experienced large annual employment losses. On the flip side, companies in about a dozen countries with FSI above 90 also increased annual headcounts on average by 10 percent or more, including Liberia, Chad, and South Sudan. Thus, both the upside and downside for businesses can be extreme as they struggle to manage political and economic turbulence. This seems to indicate that there is scope for rapid catchup in fragile situations once the internal and external conditions are conducive. Sri Lanka's tourism industry offers an example: during the decade up to 2009, which marked the end of the country's lengthy armed conflict, the number of tourist arrivals was stagnant with fluctuations around half a million annual arrivals. By 2012, the number of tourist arrivals had doubled to exceed

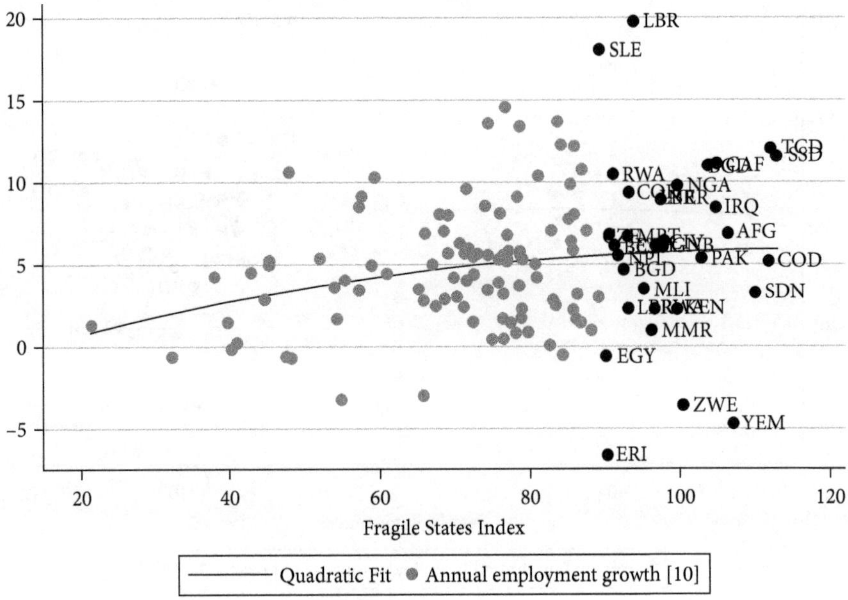

Coeffient on FSI controlling for income = .0539 [p-value = .011]

Figure 6.10 Annual Employment Growth
Sources: World Bank (2018a), Fund for Peace (2018).

1 million, and by 2016, the number had doubled again to exceed 2 million tourist arrivals (SLTDA, 2018).

Third, average capacity utilization rates start to decline at around FSI > 70 (Figure 6.11). The difference may seem modest but a 5-percentage point difference as the average between the countries with the higher and the lower FSI scores offers a real advantage in a competitive industry. Djibouti, Mauritania, Sierra Leone, Yemen, and Zimbabwe reported the lowest rates of capacity utilization (52–58 percent) in the 139 surveyed countries. However, enterprises from Myanmar (90 percent), Mali (84 percent), Liberia (82 percent) and Afghanistan (81 percent) also reported particularly high capacity utilization rates, which could reflect low initial production capacities caused by capital destruction during conflict, or low capital investments resulting from economic embargo.

Finally, the growth in annual labor productivity is on average negative for enterprises in countries with an FSI above 60 (Figure 6.12). Overall, the results are increasingly negative the more fragile the country. The number of negative outliers also increases with fragility. Iraq and South Sudan experienced extreme drops of nearly 50 percent. Thus, volatility increases, and sometimes drastically, along the FSI. It is also worth noting that the fitted lines of annual employment growth and annual labor productivity growth slope in different directions, which could be a sign that enterprises in fragile situations are more likely to employ more

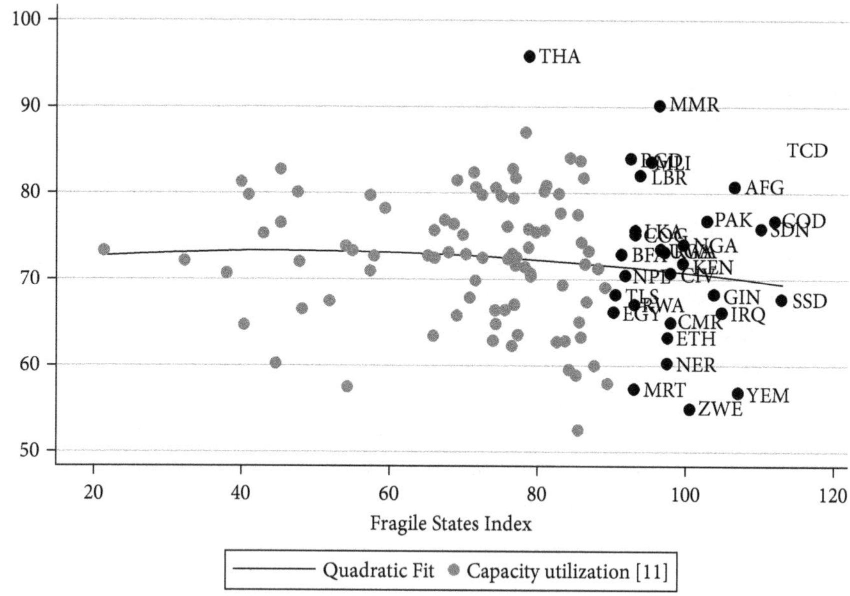

Coeffient on FSI controlling for income = –.054 [p-value = .243]

Figure 6.11 Capacity Utilization

Sources: World Bank (2018a), Fund for Peace (2018).

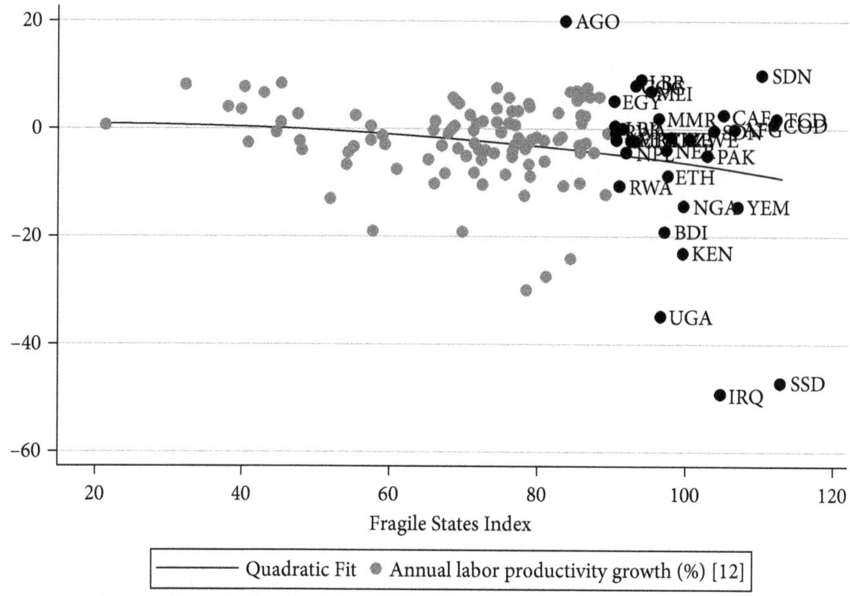

Coeffient on FSI controlling for income = –.081 [p-value = .118]

Figure 6.12 Annual Labor Productivity Growth (%)

Sources: World Bank (2018a), Fund for Peace (2018).

staff rather than improve performance of those already employed during periods of expansion. This could be linked to low levels of human capital at the managerial level.

In summary: (a) there is a relatively low density of formal enterprises in fragile situations where most of the labor force operate in the informal economy; (b) formal enterprises in fragile situations are generally younger and many start out in the informal economy; (c) enterprises in fragile situations have lower growth rates (often negative) and operate at relatively low capacity utilization rates; (d) annual labor productivity growth rates are on average close to zero and often negative in fragile situations but employment growth is relatively high; (e) enterprises in fragile situations experience greater swings/shocks to their operations; and (f) enterprises owners in fragile situations predominantly run their businesses as sole proprietorships, which highlights the elevated personal risk of entrepreneurship in these countries. Overall, the degree of heterogeneity in the results increases with the degree of fragility.

3.2 Distinguishing Factors of Markets in Fragile Situations

This section studies markets' characteristics in fragile situations and how they differ in some fundamental respects. It looks at evidence of market diversification and openness to trade, volatility in the macro-economic environment, common market failures, and at how most governments in fragile situations generally struggle to provide public goods.

3.2.1 Markets in fragile situations tend to be inward-looking and structurally undiversified

Agriculture remains the most important sector in terms of employment and livelihoods in most fragile situations, with nonfarm entrepreneurs predominantly concentrated in the trade/services sector (see Speakman and Rysova, 2015; Ragoussis and Shams, 2018). Natural resource rent dependence is in low single digits for nearly all countries with robust institutions (FSI below 40) but countries with relatively weak institutions (such as those with FSI above 90) generate on average 15–20 percent of GDP from natural resource rents (World Bank, 2018a, 2018b). This matters: many social and economic grievances are linked to the competition for land and natural resources. There is little evidence that productive land is scarcer in fragile situations, but land records tend to be incomplete and insecure, which increases the risk of expropriation and conflict.

Governments in fragile situations, and more generally in low-income countries, raise a relatively high proportion of their revenue from import duties because these are easier to administer than taxes on direct consumption, labor, or income. The applied tariff rate (weighted mean for manufacturing goods) increases along

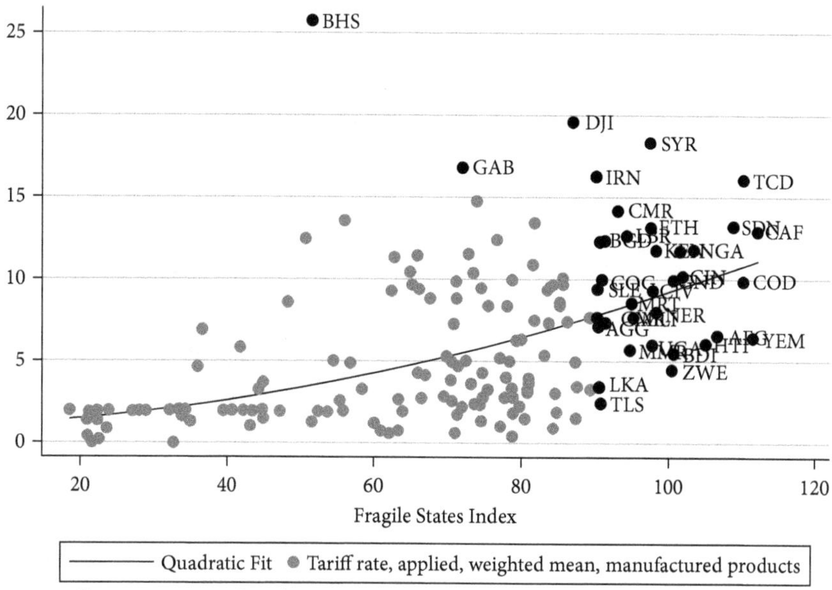

Coeffient on FSI controlling for income = .0996 [p-value = 0]

Figure 6.13 Tariff Rate, Applied, Weighted Mean, Manufactured Products (%)
Source: World Bank (2018a), Fund for Peace (2018), UN COMTRADE (2018).

the FSI (see Figure 6.13). It is on average 10 percent in countries with an FSI around 100, or four times the average in countries with an FSI around 40. Para-tariffs are also higher in low-income countries than in high-income countries, but the evidence is more circumstantial because they tend to change and often go unannounced.

The average shares of enterprises that export "directly" and "directly or indirectly" drop steeply along the FSI: or by approximately three-quarters between the two ends of the fitted trend lines (Figures 6.14–6.15). For example, the share of enterprises exporting directly or indirectly (>10 percent) drops from nearly 1 in 4 in countries with FSI around 40, to 16 percent in countries with FSI around 70, to 9 percent in countries with FSI around 100 (Figure 6.16). The share of enterprises with internationally recognized quality certifications, which can be considered as a proxy for export readiness, also drops by two-thirds between the two ends, or from nearly 30 percent to less than 10 percent. Few enterprises in fragile situations enjoy the institutional support structures—public or private—that enable or allow them to comply with technical standards and sanitary and phytosanitary requirements applied to many product categories in global markets. So enterprises in fragile situations are simultaneously relatively protected by tariffs from international competition at home and facing great restrictions on exporting to potential markets abroad. As a result, producers tailor their goods and services

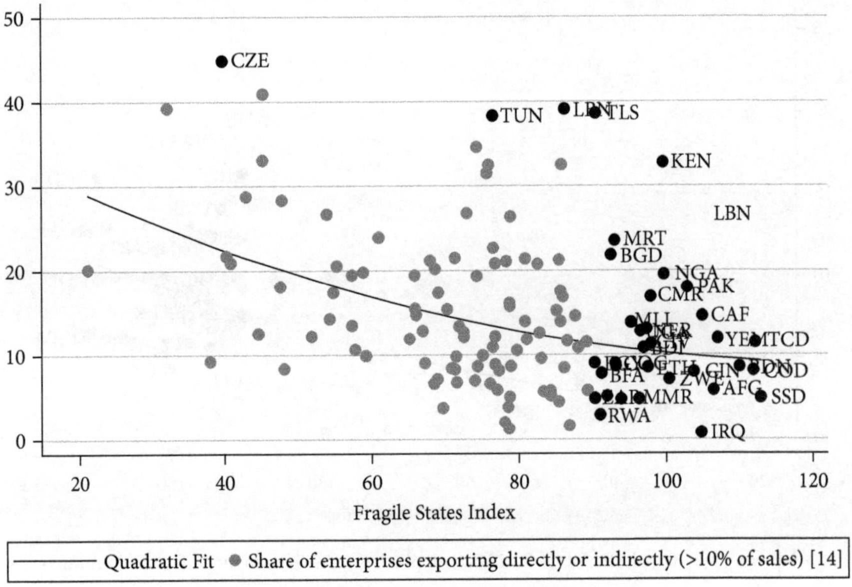

Coeffient on FSI controlling for income = –.1751 [p-value = 0]

Figure 6.14 Share of Enterprises Exporting Directly or Indirectly
Source: World Bank (2018a), Fund for Peace (2018), UN COMTRADE (2018).

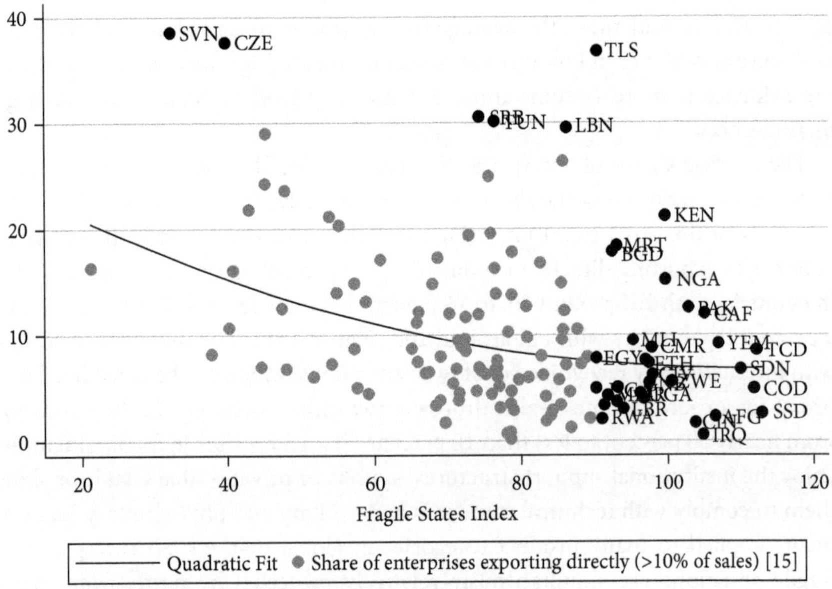

Coeffient on FSI controlling for income = –.1498 [p-value = 0]

Figure 6.15 Share of Enterprises Exporting Directly
Source: World Bank (2018a), Fund for Peace (2018), UN COMTRADE (2018).

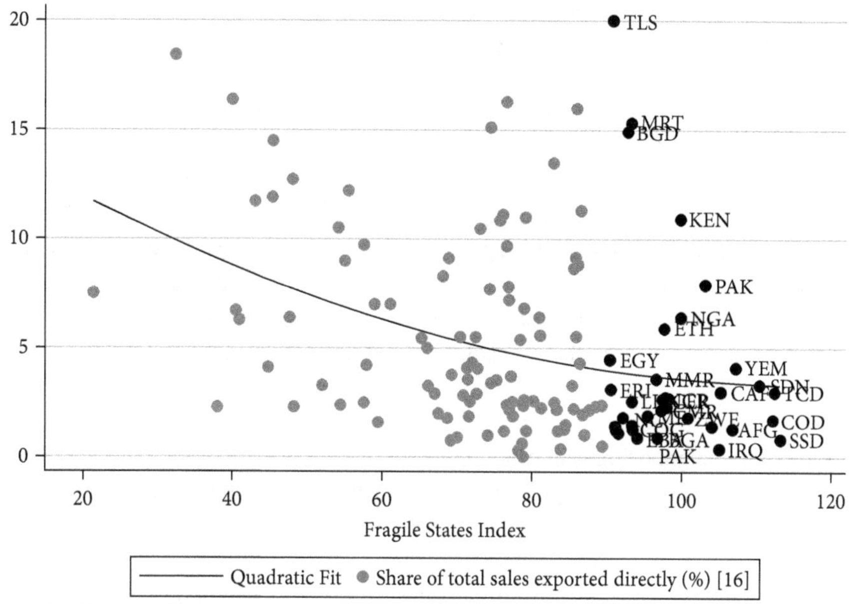

Coeffient on FSI controlling for income = –.0688 [p-value = .004]

Figure 6.16 Share of Total Sales Exported Directly (%)
Source: World Bank (2018a), Fund for Peace (2018), UN COMTRADE (2018).

to domestic consumers. When exporting, they tend to export to neighboring countries, which often impose lower technical barriers to trade and tariff rates.

Trade and FDI have acted as important engines for growth and development in many low-income countries, especially in those that have been able to leverage efficiency-seeking private investment to supply foreign markets thanks to labor cost advantages. Bangladesh is an example with exports of readymade garments growing from US$0.6 billion in the year ending March 31, 1990, to US$5.7 billion in the year when the Multi Fiber Agreement was phased out in 2004; and exports exceeded US$30 billion in the year ending March 31, 2018.[8] But enterprises in many fragile situations fail to serve export markets beyond primary goods as they struggle with macroeconomic volatility and the lack of institutional support structures to take advantage of preferential market access abroad. Linkages with international markets can help raise the productivity of domestic enterprises, which in turn raises living standards; trading with neighbors may, in some circumstances, promote stability (Box 6.1). Exports bring in foreign exchange that, together with remittances from workers in foreign countries and overseas

[8] www.bgmea.com.bd/home/pages/tradeinformation

Box 6.1 Fragility and Neighborhood Effects

A country's neighborhood can exacerbate fragile situations through historical and colonial legacies, interstate interventions, population displacement, competition for natural resources or access to the sea, etc. But neighbors also offer opportunities for stability through cultural affinity, labor mobility, trade and investment, and political leverage. The channels of transmission—cultural, economic, and political—act as opportunities and risks in different regions and at different points in time. Recent empirical work has sought to estimate the "spatial lag" of fragility—to summarize the fragility of one's neighbors in space—calculated using hybrid contiguous and distance weights describing the fragility experienced by neighbors. Similarly to the neighborhood fragility index, the neighboring economic opportunity mirrors countries' own volume of economic activity onto proximate country values. Standardized values, or z-scores of the two, allow for comparisons based on relative positions in the distribution of values across countries.

The gaps between neighborhood opportunity and neighborhood stability stand out in an illustration of standardized scores for select countries. The gaps highlight the complex nature of relationships between neighbors and the ambivalent role that regions play. For example, Yemen's neighbors are stable and prosperous, which offers opportunity for the Yemeni economy, if it was not embroiled in violent conflict with one of the neighbors. Fragile situations in Asia appear better positioned to perceive its region as an opportunity because of what the indices show (market size and political stability) and what they conceal (less random division of geographic boundaries).

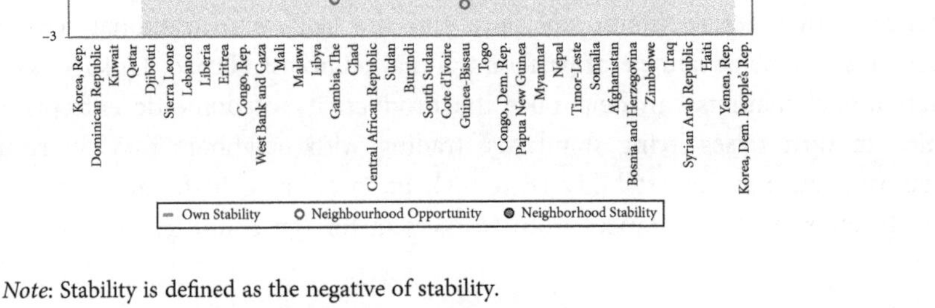

Note: Stability is defined as the negative of stability.

Source: Calculations on FSI, neighborhood FSI and Neighborhood Market Size Index (2016).

development assistance, helps to pay for most imports of vital needs such as transport vehicles, medication, food products, and energy, which domestic enterprises in many fragile situations do not produce. In addition, domestic markets in fragile situations tend to be small for most goods categories because of low incomes and unequal distribution of purchasing power, with a small or almost nonexistent traditional middle-class. Annex 3 highlights that countries that are among the most fragile on average trade less as a share of GDP and receive much less FDI as a share of GDP. Being fragile thus means being less connected to the global economy and to the opportunities it offers.

The degree of export diversification declines along the FSI (see Figure 6.17). An export diversification index constructed by the IMF (2017), where higher values denote less diversification, has a positive correlation of 0.5 with the FSI. Export diversification still declines linearly with the FSI after controlling for income. Specialization leads to gains from trade; but it also makes countries more vulnerable to terms-of-trade shocks. Collier and Hoeffler (2004) has shown that a deterioration in the terms of trade is an important predictor of conflict. Al-Marhubi (2000) also found that countries with more diversified export baskets experience not only lower output volatility but also higher average growth than most other small states.

There is a negative correlation between export quality and fragility (see Figure 6.18). Export quality falls as product quality declines. An increase in fragility is also accompanied by a rise in heterogeneity in export quality. This matters because quality is more important than price as a determinant of a country's success in penetrating export markets (Banerjee et al., 2006).

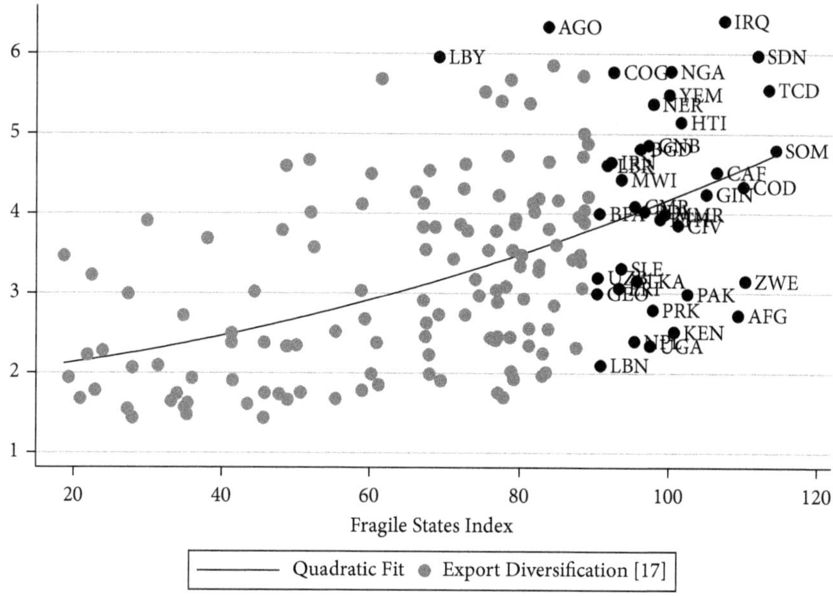

Coeffient on FSI controlling for income = .0291 [p–value = 0]

Figure 6.17 Export Diversification

Source: IMF (2017), Fund for Peace (2018).

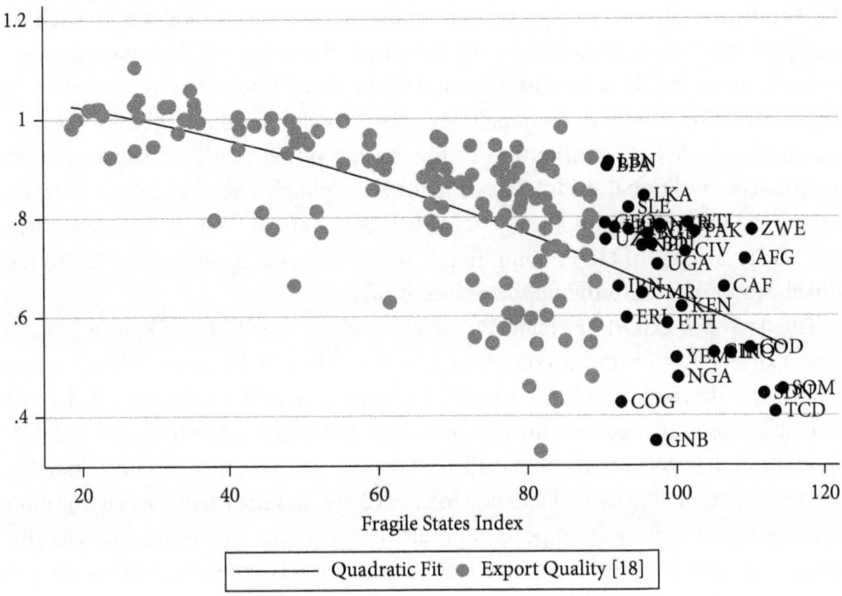

Coeffient on FSI controlling for income = –.0047 [p–value = 0]

Figure 6.18 Export Quality
Source: IMF (2017), Fund for Peace (2018).

3.2.2 Markets in fragile situations tend to operate in contexts of high macro-economic volatility

Investors and enterprises in fragile situations deal with a great deal of uncertainty as highlighted by macroeconomic indicators. Simultaneously high volatility of most core economic indicators creates an investment climate that is much more unpredictable (and risky) than the sum of these fundamental parts would indicate. For example, economic growth rates are more volatile in countries in the bottom-third of the FSI (see Figure 6.19). This is partly due to greater fluctuations in exports and fixed capital formation where the coefficients of variations for countries with FSI around 50 are approximately half of that of countries with FSI around 100. The enterprise survey data display a strong negative decline in the share of enterprises that buy fixed assets along the FSI. For example, the difference between countries around FSI=50 and FSI=90 is approximately 15 percentage points, which highlights a substantial difference in capital intensity.

The volatility of inflation (coefficient of variation) for countries with an FSI around 100 is on average five times as high as in countries with an FSI around 50 (see Figure 6.20). Likewise, interest rates in countries with an FSI around 90 (or 110) is on average twice (or three times) as high as in countries with an FSI around

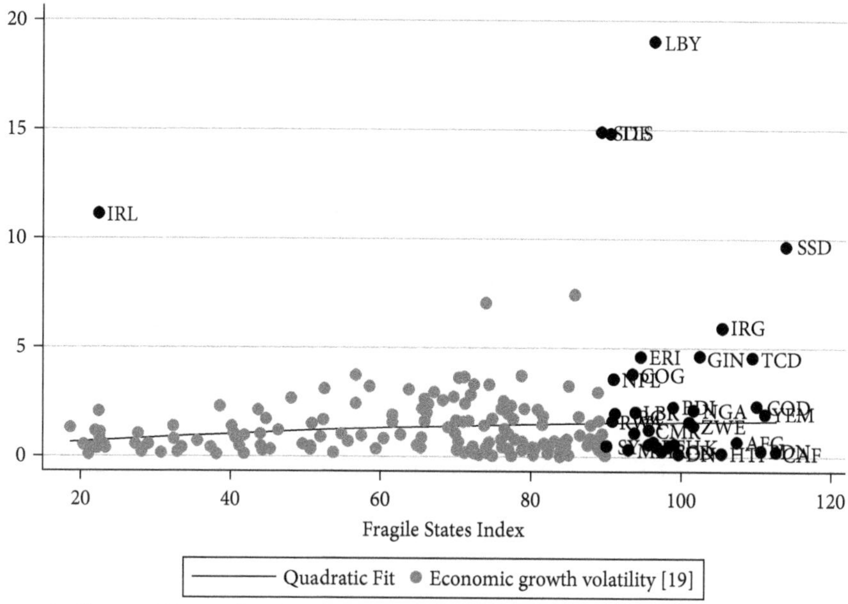

Coeffient on FSI controlling for income = .0155 [p-value = .062]

Figure 6.19 Economic Growth Volatility
Sources: World Bank (2018b), Fund for Peace (2018).

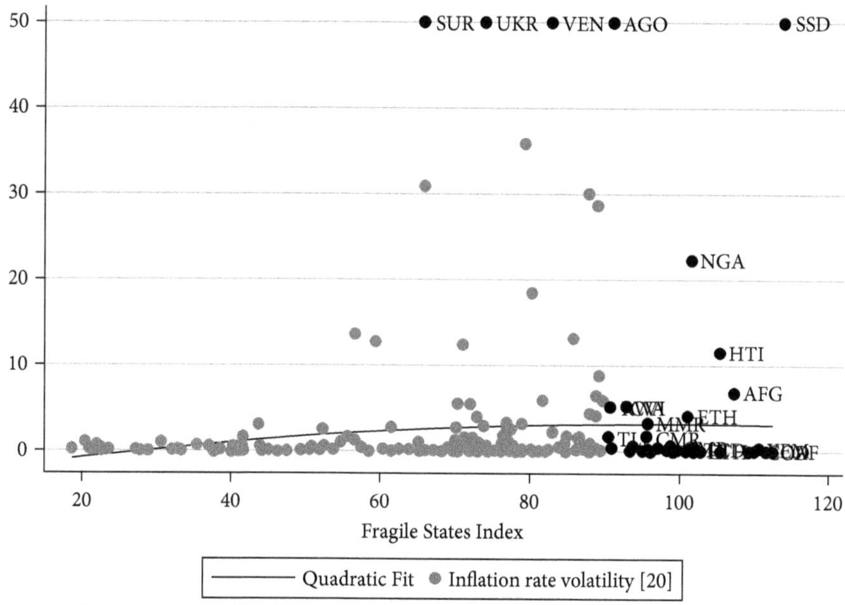

Coeffient on FSI controlling for income = .0986 [p-value = .757]

Figure 6.20 Inflation Rate Volatility
Sources: World Bank (2018b), Fund for Peace (2018).

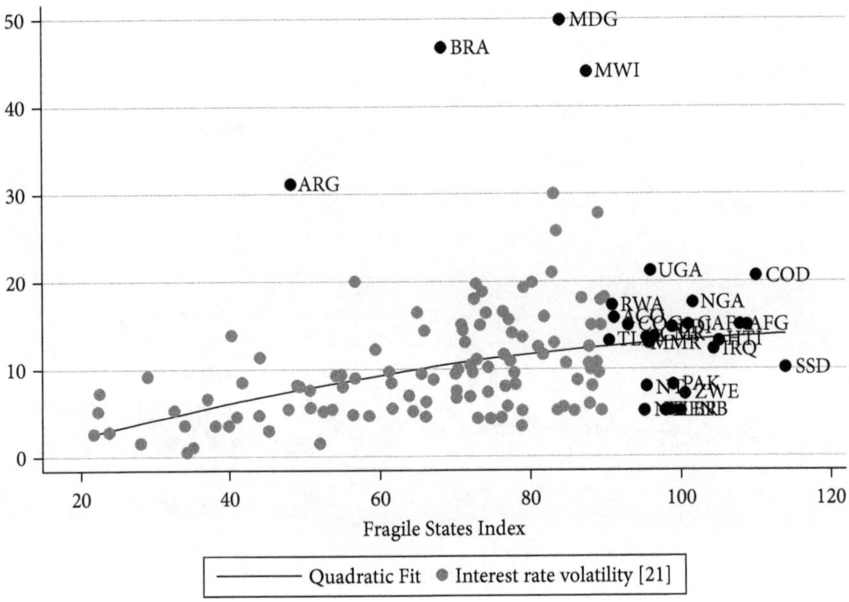

Coeffient on FSI controlling for income = .1263 [p-value = 0]

Figure 6.21 Interest Rate Volatility
Sources: World Bank (2018b), Fund for Peace (2018).

50 (see Figure 6.21). The ratios for exchange rate volatility are approximately of the same proportion (see Figure 6.22). Thus, any financial model employed for a new investment in a fragile situation will need to factor in uncertainty that may make standard financial modeling techniques in investment decisions seemingly irrelevant.

Gonzalez et al. (2013) has studied the effect on enterprises from the high volatility of economic growth in Russia, which is characterized by relatively long and deep slumps—similar to what is often found in fragile situations. The authors found that protracted slumps not only eliminate the least efficient enterprises; they also sweep aside many new and relatively efficient ones, which impedes economic diversification.

3.2.3 Markets in Fragile Situations Are Often Missing or Distorted

Missing or incomplete markets—as when goods or services are demanded but not supplied, or only partially supplied—are common market failures in fragile situations. Access to finance is a particularly frequent complaint for which there is also abundant survey data. Financial and capital markets are generally undeveloped in fragile situations and they tend to serve a relatively small share of private enterprises despite evidence of strong demand. Figure 6.23 illustrates the quite drastic reduction in enterprises' use of bank loans and lines of credit along the FSI. The share of enterprises in countries with more robust institutions that have a

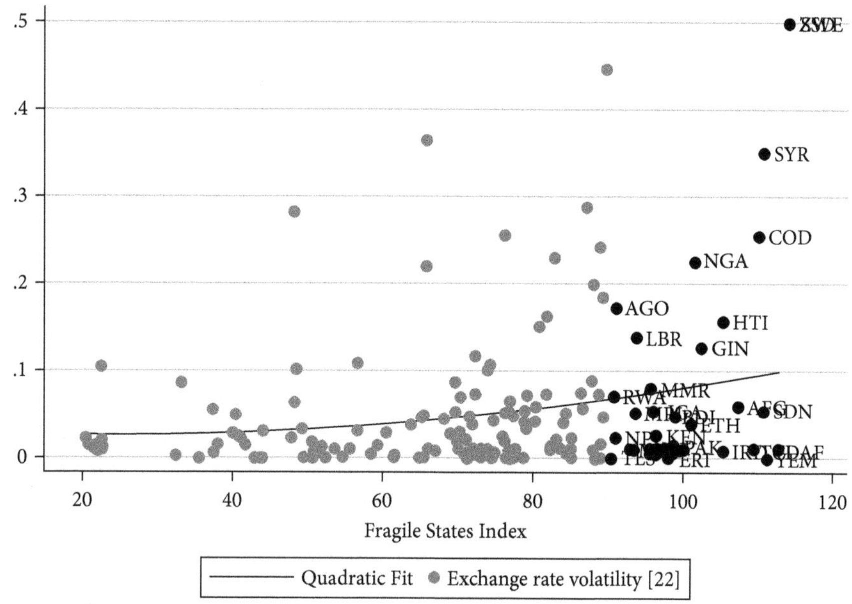

Coeffient on FSI controlling for income = .0014 [p-value = .005]

Figure 6.22 Exchange Rate Volatility
Sources: World Bank (2018b), Fund for Peace (2018).

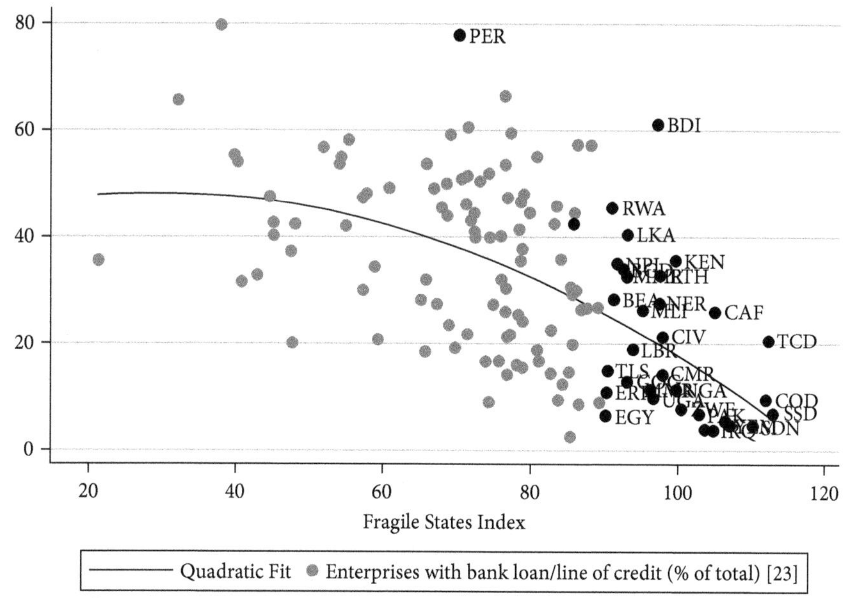

Coeffient on FSI controlling for income = .4677 [p-value = 0]

Figure 6.23 Enterprises with Bank Loan/Line of Credit (% of Total)
Source: World Bank (2018a), World Bank (2018b), Fund for Peace (2018).

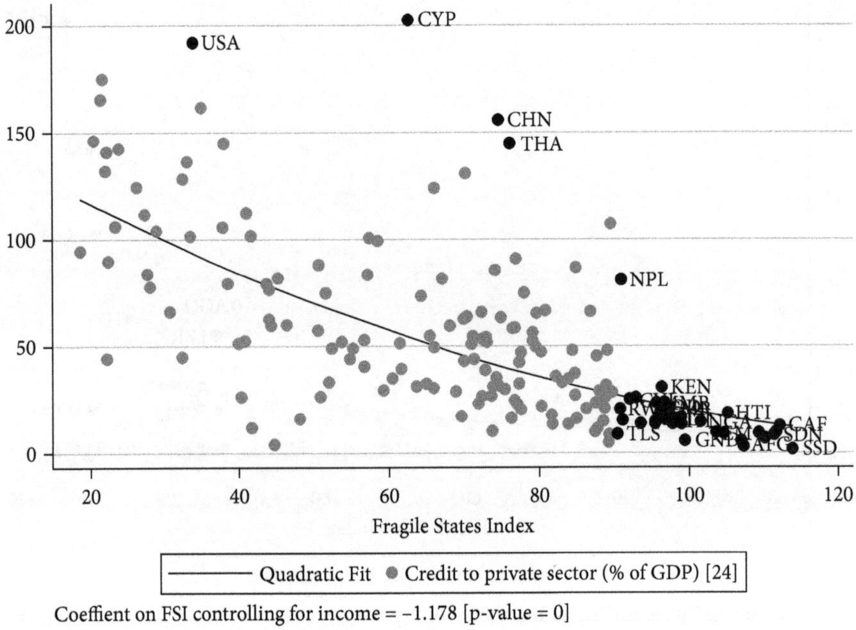

Figure 6.24 Credit to Private Sector (% of GDP)
Source: World Bank (2018a), World Bank (2018b), Fund for Peace (2018).

bank loan or a line of credit drops from 50 percent in countries with FSI around 50 to 20 percent in countries with FSI around 100. Likewise, the proportion of the population borrowing from a commercial bank is close to 50 percent in countries with FSI around 40 compared to closer to 5 percent in countries with FSI higher than 100. As a result, credit to the private sector as a share of GDP is three (four) times as high in countries with an FSI around 60 (40) compared to around 100 (see Figure 6.24). The supply of banking and financial services is thus serving only a segment of the potential market. The share of enterprises that identify access to finance as a major constraint increases with the host country's degree of fragility.

The share of enterprises using banks to finance investments or working capital drops continuously along the FSI (see Figure 6.25). Roughly one-fifth of surveyed enterprises in countries with FSI around 100 use banks. Instead, most enterprises in fragile situations depend on internal sources of finance for investments and working capital, with banks financing less than 2 percent of national investments in countries with FSI above 100 (see Figure 6.26). Thus, risk-averse banks seem to shun long-term investments and prefer short-term financing of working capital of select creditors.

The demand for loans increases along the FSI by roughly 15 percentage points between the ends of the trend line. This could partly be because equity markets are less developed in fragile situations. There is an increase in the share of enterprises that report rejected loan applications along the FSI but there is large variation in

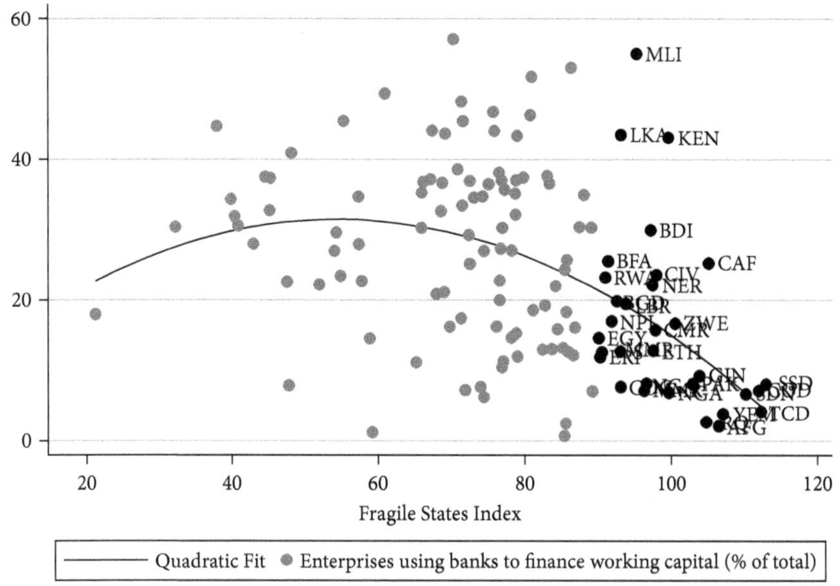

Coeffient on FSI controlling for income = –.2359 [p-value = 0]

Figure 6.25 Enterprises Using Banks to Finance Investments (% of Total)
Source: World Bank (2018a), World Bank (2018b), Fund for Peace (2018).

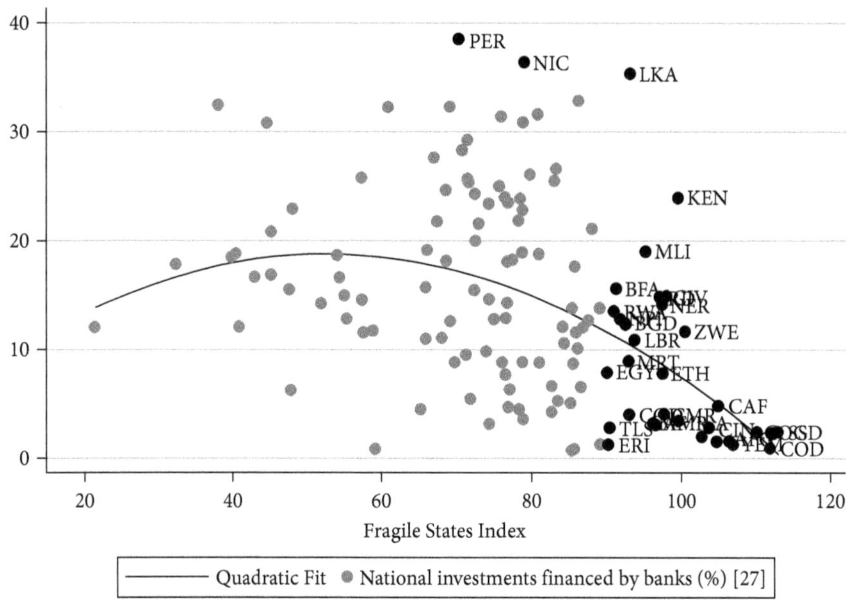

Coeffient on FSI controlling for income = –.1654 [p-value = 0]

Figure 6.26 National Investments Financed by Banks (%)
Source: World Bank (2018a), World Bank (2018b), Fund for Peace (2018).

the data. It could partly be explained by the value of collateral that is imposed on loans. There is approximately a 50 percentage points increase in the value of collateral to loan between the two ends of the trend line. Collateral requirements are common: most loans to enterprises that are taken in fragile situations require collateral. There is a steady increase by roughly 20 percentage points of loans requiring collateral along the trend line. About 85 percent of loans in countries with an FSI around 100 use collateral. Collateral between 100 percent and 300 percent of the loan amount is standard while figures over 200 percent are common. It exceeds 350 percent in a handful of fragile situations, according to the surveys.

Finally, the interest rate on loans of surveyed enterprises increases along the FSI. The trend line for the nominal interest rate is on average less than 20 percent although there are countries where it exceeds 50 percent. Interest rates might not rise by much, perhaps because of the increased possibility of strategic default, with interest rates higher in countries with limited facilities for contract enforcement. Thus, lenders seem to resort to more stringent requirements on collateral as opposed to increasing rates (Ray, 1998).

The implication of missing markets—for example for banking and financial intermediation—is lower-than-potential growth rates. And there are many contributing factors. Information asymmetries in credit markets may be pronounced with a lack of functioning credit registries and unique personal identification numbers in fragile situations. Government ownership of banks and financial intermediaries, in addition to political influence in credit allocation decisions, may distort credit markets and build inefficiencies in the banking system. Various forms of market control through regulation may stymie competition and credit growth. On the positive side, the past decade has seen a high degree of technology-driven innovation catalyzed by rising penetration rates of mobile internet services in low-income countries. Though the enterprise survey dataset still highlights a drastic digital divide along the FSI—with relatively depressed internet penetration rates and use of digital communication by enterprises (e-mail and websites) in fragile situations—there is hope that this divide will be bridged in time.

3.2.4 Negative Externalities from Weak Rule of Law and Governance Are Common in Fragile Situations

The presence of legal institutions to uphold the rule of law is essential for the functioning of a modern economy because it creates constraints on individual and institutional behavior through publicly disclosed legal codes and processes. The rule of law in fragile situations is often compromised, however: access to legal recourse tend to be low, due process lengthy and costly, and decisions more arbitrary; corruption may add another level of unpredictability. The World Bank (2018c) reports that in Timor-Leste, Papua New Guinea, and Cambodia the cost of resolving a commercial dispute in court is higher than the claim value.

And even if the claim value exceeds the cost of contract enforcement it may take more than 1600 days on average to go through the process in Afghanistan, Suriname, and Guinea-Bissau. Hoffmann and Lange (2016) present an in-depth analysis of how enterprises in many fragile states rely on personal and social networks as well as on arrangements with nonstate governance actors rather than dysfunctional state institutions for arbitration and enforcement of traditional or tribal law. Weak rule of law and poor governance increase negative externalities because third parties—both citizens and competitors—often are adversely affected by the decisions of enterprises.

Environmental degradation and pollution can be costly to a society. When an effluent treatment plant for industrial waste water management is shut at night in Haiti to save on running costs and factory management dumps the effluent in a local river or lake, there are many losers: farmers, fishermen, consumers of drinking water from local wells, among others. When a garment factory building collapses in Bangladesh, killing workers because of lax enforcement of national building codes, the entire garment industry suffers as international buyers alter their supply chains to avoid reputational damage. And when Somali authorities fail to enact and enforce legislation against anti-money laundering and terrorist financing, the local industry for financial remittances operates underground and consumers suffer from more unreliable transactions.

Corruption deters investment—especially to foreign and efficiency-seeking investors—and it amplifies the risks associated with other institutional and regulatory weaknesses. Informal payments to sort out petty transactions such as obtaining a permit or avoiding a fine, let's say, or underestimating the value of a consignment by a customs official, may be perceived by some incumbents as the grease that lubricates the wheels, especially if it is predictable; however, it has a negative effect on the overall economy. Dealing with corruption is costly, time-consuming, and risky—especially in highly corrupt environments where the outcome is uncertain because most or all parties pay some form of bribes (see Figure 6.27). The number of enterprises that report corruption as a major constraint to doing business rises steadily with the FSI. The many corruption-related questions in the World Bank Enterprise Survey offer consistent evidence that there is a strong positive correlation between corruption and the degree of fragility.

Figure 6.28 illustrates that practices of informal enterprises often act as a major constraint to formal enterprises and they tend to increase with the host country's degree of fragility. The fitted line shows that as many as two-thirds of enterprises report these practices as a major constraint in countries such as Benin, Cameroon, Chad, and Niger. Formal and more productive enterprises often adjust their own business practices to compete in domestic markets where informal competitors may have drastically different costs of operation. For example, during a recent business roundtable discussion in Islamabad with large manufacturers, some

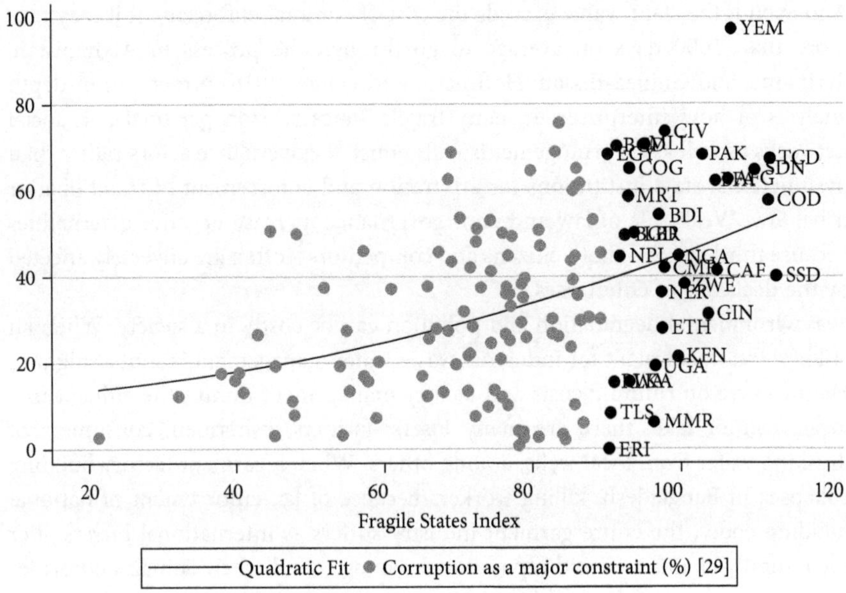

Coeffient on FSI controlling for income = .4896 [p-value = 0]

Figure 6.27 Corruption as a Major Constraint (%)

Source: World Bank (2018a), Fund for Peace (2018).

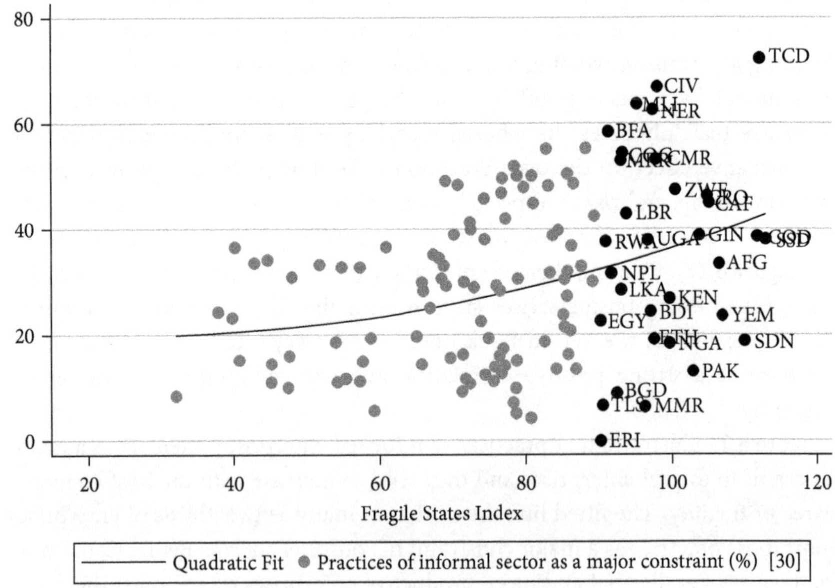

Coeffient on FSI controlling for income = .0155 [p-value = .001]

Figure 6.28 Practices of Informal Sector as a Major Constraint (%)

Source: World Bank (2018a), Fund for Peace (2018).

business leaders admitted off the record that they operated three or four informal plants for every formal plant. They argued that it was necessary to stay beyond the reach of confiscatory tax officials and inspectors. They also argued that any enterprise that broke this pattern would go out of business with operating profits seldom exceeding 10 percent and taxes and official fees often exceeding 40 percent. However, in fragile situations, as presented in section 2.3, formal enterprises are generally smaller and more focused on serving the domestic market, whereas the informal sector is relatively large, so there is more overlap in the market space in which they compete.

3.2.5 Government Policies to Address Market Failures Are Less Effective in Fragile Situations

A government failure is a situation in which a public intervention meant to correct a market failure creates inefficiency and leads to a misallocation of resources. Common measures include various forms of taxation, subsidies, and price controls as well as regulations that give local or national authorities the right to supply a market with a monopoly. The enterprise survey covers basic services that often are provided by state-owned enterprises that may enjoy monopoly rights. The supply of basic services such as water and electricity can serve as proxy for the prevalence of government failure. Figures 6.29–6.30 illustrate the share of enterprises that experience water insufficiencies and the frequency of occurrence increase along the FSI. In countries like Malawi and Yemen, most enterprises experience water insufficiencies. In countries with an FSI above 90 more than 1 in 5 enterprises report water insufficiency on average. Climate change, combined with growing populations in many fragile situations, increases the strain on water resources. Poor governance of water makes the situation worse.

Electricity is another scarce resource in many fragile situations. Figures 6.31–6.32 highlight how it remains a serious constraint to many enterprises. Losses to electrical outages quadruple on average between countries with an FSI around 60 and an FSI around 80. It then more than doubles again as the FSI reaches 100. It is difficult to exaggerate the crisis of electricity shortages in Cameroon, Pakistan, and Yemen, where the average enterprise lost between 20 percent and 34 percent of sales to electrical outages. Companies report that outages are frequent and last much longer on average the higher the FSI.

A surprising number of governments in fragile situations use their scarce resources to pay subsidies—often for energy/fuel—and many also impose some form of import and export controls or national price controls. These policies may appear tempting in the short term in countries that rely on a few scarce resources for income, especially in cases of international price fluctuations. Commodities such as cocoa, coffee, cotton, flour, gum Arabic, and copper have been targeted in fragile situations. Expropriation and forced nationalization of private property have also reduced output drastically in many cases and hurt the overall economy. Domestic

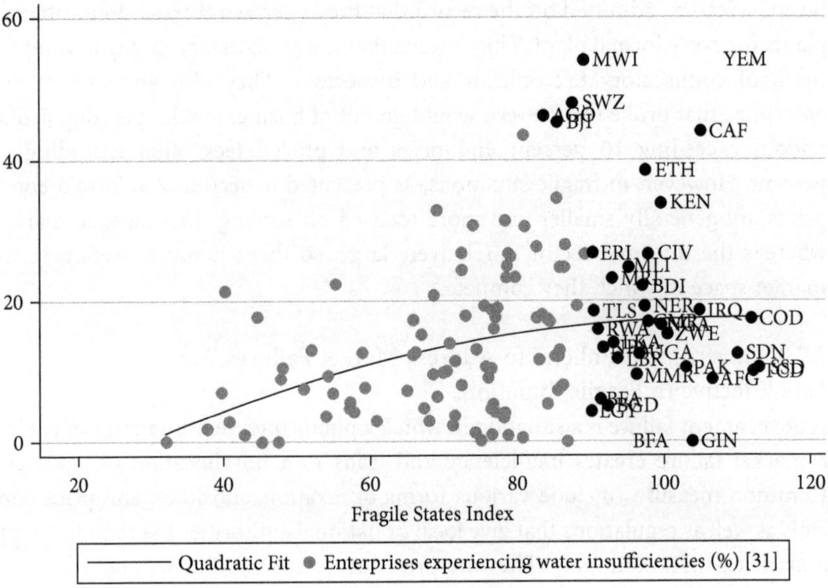

Coeffient on FSI controlling for income = .2377 [p-value = 0]

Figure 6.29 Enterprises Experiencing Water Insufficiencies (%)
Sources: World Bank (2018a), Fund for Peace (2018).

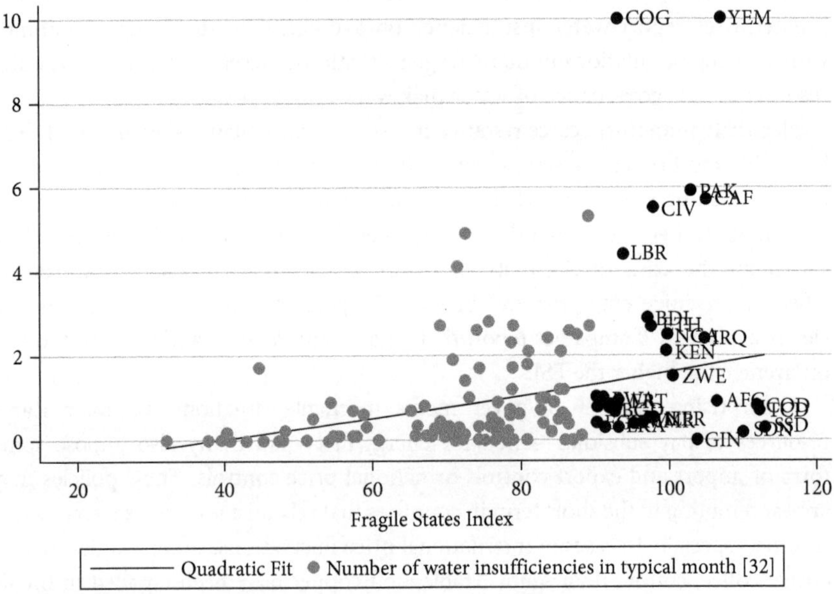

Coeffient on FSI controlling for income = .0387 [p-value = 0]

Figure 6.30 # of Water Insufficiencies in Typical Month
Sources: World Bank (2018a), Fund for Peace (2018).

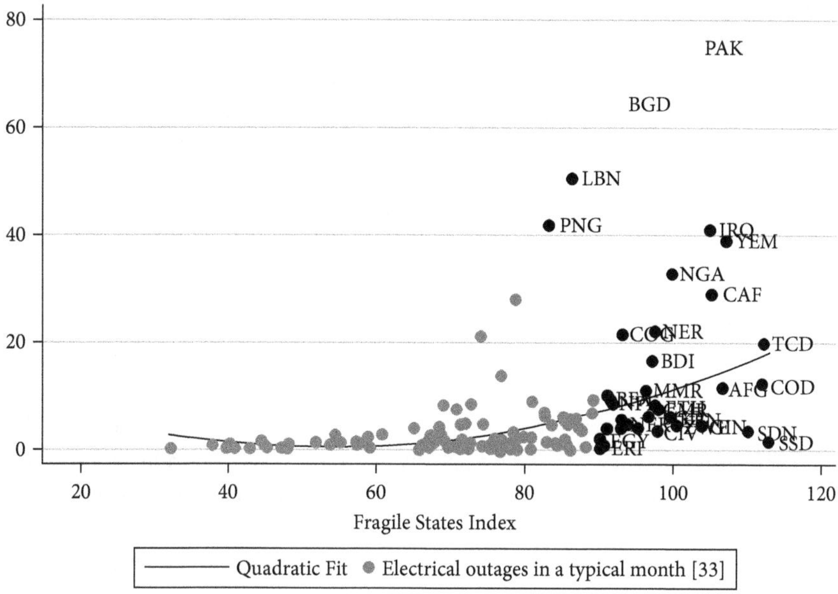

Coeffient on FSI controlling for income = .2962 [p-value = 0]

Figure 6.31 Electrical Outages in a Typical Month
Sources: World Bank (2018a), Fund for Peace (2018).

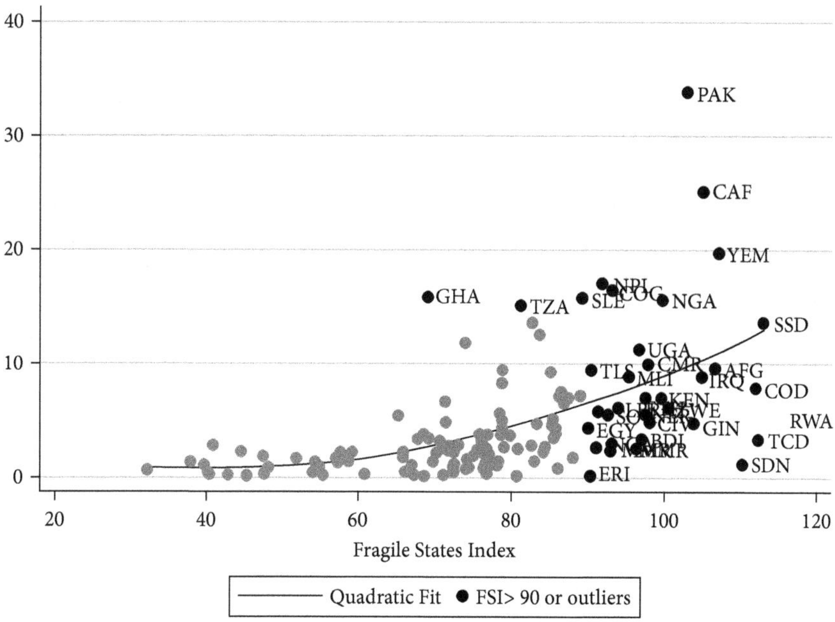

Figure 6.32 Losses due to Electrical Outages (% of sales)
Sources: World Bank (2018a), Fund for Peace (2018).

and especially foreign investors tend to vote with their feet. The Governments of Venezuela and Zimbabwe are two examples where widespread nationalization campaigns have been implemented in the past two decades. Both countries have also dealt with collapsing output, mass emigration, and hyperinflation.

3.3 Select Coping Mechanisms and Associated Costs

The previous sections presented some of the business challenges that are common in fragile situations. The political and macroeconomic environments tend to bring a high degree of volatility to virtually every major variable that affects an investment decision. Enterprises that operate in these uncertain business environments adopt coping mechanisms—that is, ways to manage, adapt to, or act on external or internal stress—to survive or thrive. Many coping mechanisms add to the cost of doing business. Others entrench the reliance on informal institutions and social arrangements that impede the emergence of a modern economy.

Insecurity and private solutions: The proportion of enterprises identifying crime and theft as a major constraint nearly doubles between the two ends of the FSI.[9] Even in countries with the most robust institutions, 1 in 5 enterprises cite crime and theft as a major constraint. Furthermore, beyond an FSI of 65 the heterogeneity increases quite significantly as more countries deal with significant levels of crime and theft. Most of the enterprises in a dozen countries consider theft and disorder to be a serious constraint to their business. But it is the gravity rather than the prevalence of losses that matter once crime and theft are afflicting enterprises. The national cost of crime—measured in terms of the proportion of total sales lost to activities of theft and vandalism—increases at an increasing rate with the extent of fragility (Figure 6.33). In countries such as Afghanistan, the Democratic Republic of the Congo, Cameroon, Lesotho, Samoa, and Sierra Leone between 4 percent and 6 percent of national sales are lost on average to theft and vandalism (Figure 6.34). And this share would be much higher in countries with large-scale conflict, which we have no comparable data for. The so-called peace dividend can be significant.

Many enterprises pay for some form of security independently of their host country's degree of fragility (see Figure 6.35). With a few exceptions, most enterprises in countries with an FSI below 50 pay for security, and heterogeneity then increases greatly as FSI increases. One-fifth or fewer of enterprises in countries such as Iraq, Jordan, and Uzbekistan report that they pay for security. By contrast, four-fifths or more of enterprises in countries as diverse as Afghanistan, Australia, and India report that they pay for security. The literature highlights informal solutions common in many countries. The average enterprise expenditure on security rises drastically with

[9] The enterprise survey does not pose any question on violence, destruction, and damage because it would only apply in conflicts, so the closest proxy is crime and theft/vandalism.

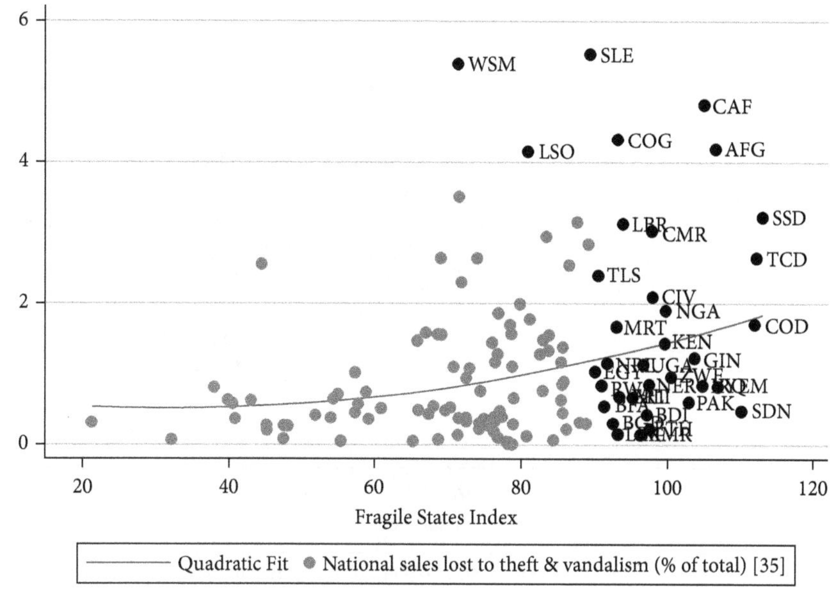

Coeffient on FSI controlling for income = .0183 [p-value = .001]

Figure 6.33 National Sales Lost to Theft and Vandalism (% of total)
Source: World Bank (2018a), Fund for Peace (2018).

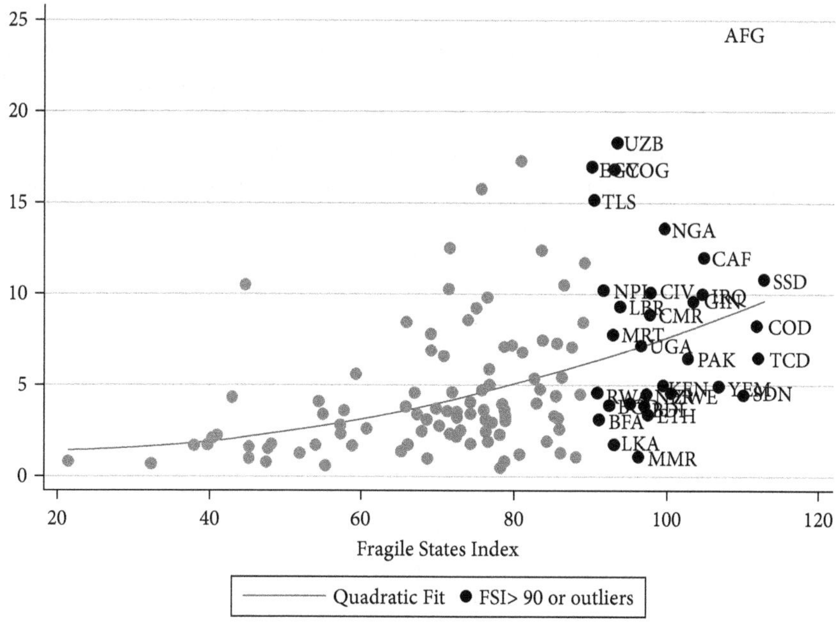

Figure 6.34 Share of Sales Lost to Theft/Vandalism (%)
Source: World Bank (2018a), Fund for Peace (2018).

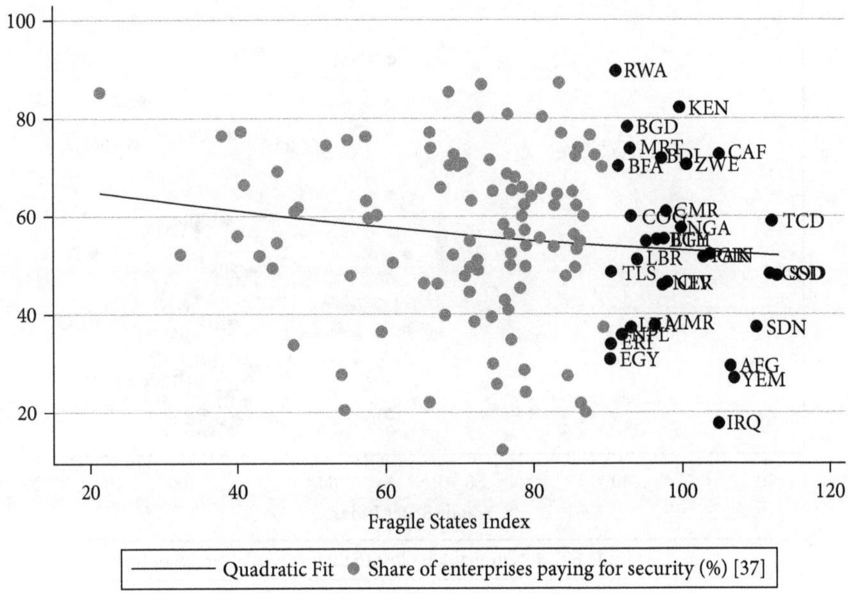

Coeffient on FSI controlling for income = –.1496 [p-value = .083]

Figure 6.35 Share of Enterprises Paying for Security (%)
Source: World Bank (2018a), Fund for Peace (2018).

increasing fragility. Enterprises clearly step in when governments fail to uphold law and order, and it can be very costly. In many fragile situations, enterprises on average spend more than 5 percent of their sales value to boost security. In a handful of countries, they spend more than 10 percent (see Figure 6.36). The variation is high in the sample: even at the high end of the spectrum there is great diversity. Enterprises in Cambodia, the Democratic Republic of the Congo, Sierra Leone, and Timor-Leste reported the highest expenses on security.

Utilities and private solutions: As highlighted in section 3.2, enterprises in fragile situations face various forms of shortages of essential utility services such as electricity and water. The natural coping mechanism for enterprises facing electricity shortages is to buy (or rent) electricity generators if they can afford to do so (see Figure 6.37). Enterprises in Afghanistan, the Central African Republic, and the Democratic Republic of the Congo get two-thirds or more of their electricity from generators and there is a fourfold increase of the fitted line between FSI around 40 and FSI around 100 (see Figure 6.38). Thus, a fair number of enterprises in countries with robust institutions also own generators but very few need to use them much. This matters because electricity produced by a diesel generator is much costlier than electricity supplied by power grids. In countries where petrol and diesel are subsidized by the government this puts a strain on the national treasury. In countries where petrol/diesel prices reflect international market rates and incorporates taxes it can be detrimental to doing business.

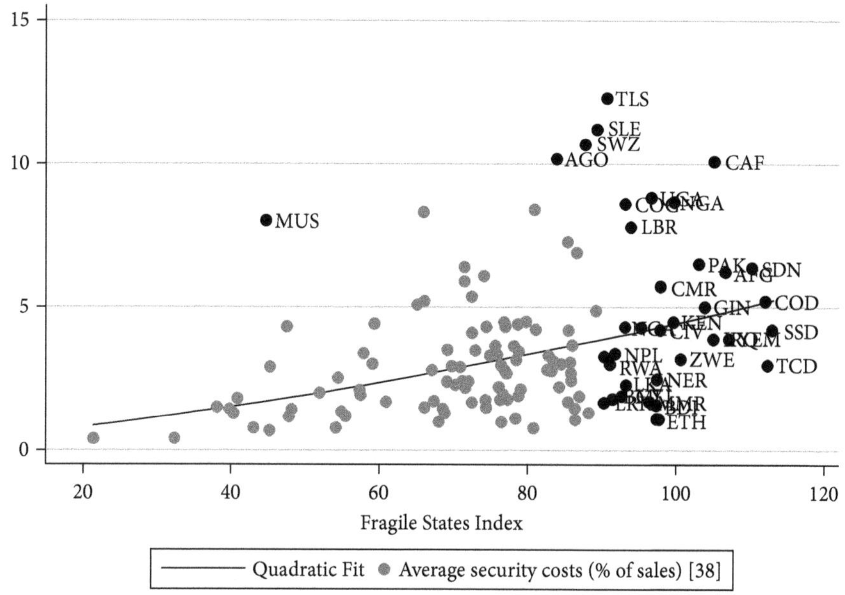

Coeffient on FSI controlling for income = .0479 [p-value = 0]

Figure 6.36 Average Security Costs (% of Sales)
Source: World Bank (2018a), Fund for Peace (2018).

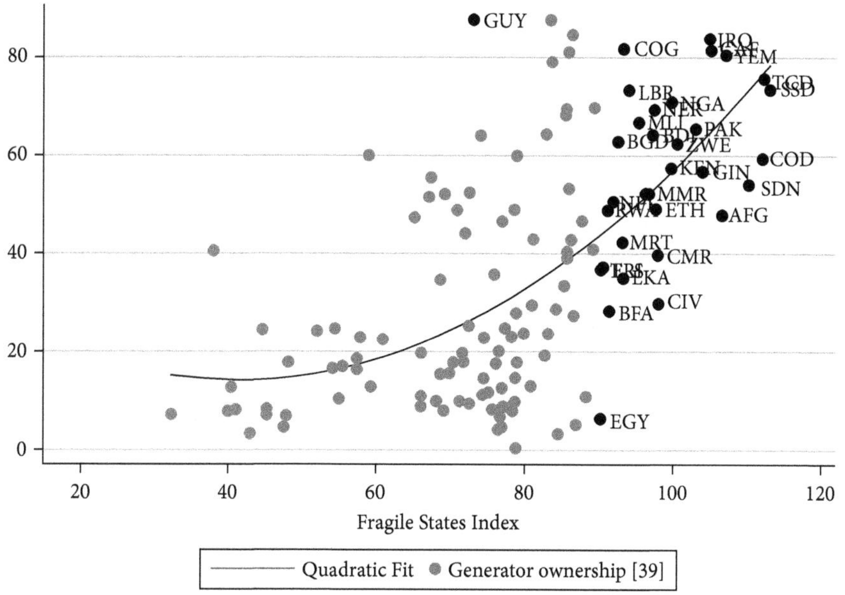

Coeffient on FSI controlling for income = .8100000000000001 [p-value = 0]

Figure 6.37 Generator Ownership
Source: World Bank (2018a), Fund for Peace (2018).

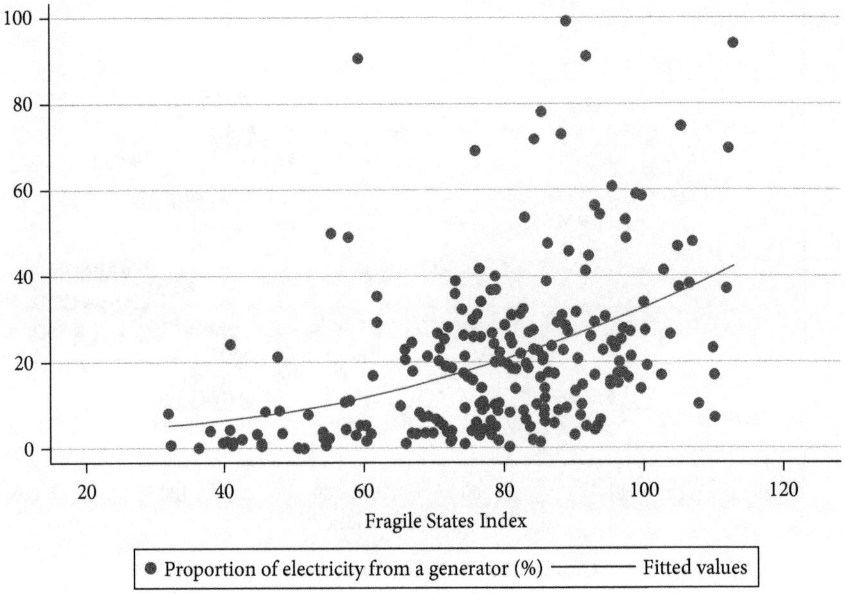

Figure 6.38 Electricity Generated by Generators
Source: World Bank (2018a), Fund for Peace (2018).

For example, in an informal survey of hotel operators in Madagascar, the cost of operating a diesel generator often equaled one-third of the revenue from a room in a two- or three-star hotel. The scarcity of grid electricity and the requirement of running a generator to manage routine operations discriminate especially against micro- and small enterprises because many cannot afford one. And this does not factor in the time and cost of connecting to the national power grid, which, as the World Bank Group's annual Ease of Doing Business survey illustrates, can be extremely burdensome in fragile situations. The worst capitals in which to get an electricity connection are in Yemen, South Sudan, Somalia, Eritrea, Venezuela, Madagascar, Central African Republic, Burundi, and the Republic of Congo. In many of these countries a connection can take between half a year and one-and-a-half years to obtain (Madagascar, Liberia, Venezuela, Guinea-Bissau, Burkina Faso) and cost 50–177 times per capita income (Chad, Venezuela, Uganda, Sierra Leone, Burundi). It is often even slower and costlier in secondary and tertiary towns and in rural areas, if available at all.

4. Public Policies for Private Sector Resilience and Growth in Fragile Situations

The previous sections underscored the volatility and uncertainty that private enterprises face in fragile situations. Private businesses that operate in contexts of failing public institutions and markets struggle to operate and grow. Those that deal with political turbulence and conflict may be wiped out or face cycles of severe contraction. Many businesses resort to operating in the informal economy. Those that operate in the formal economy are, strikingly often, sole proprietors, which leaves the financial exposure to a single individual. Coping mechanisms tend to be costly and cumbersome, leaving productivity levels low and produced goods and services locally uncompetitive.

Domestic businesses have a strong stake in their host communities and a strong role in upholding socio-economic resilience. We argue that policymakers in fragile situations who want to boost growth through private sector activity need to work on parallel work streams. First, they should seek to strengthen the resilience of the existing domestic private sector, given its role as a contributor to the socioeconomic welfare of the communities in which they do business, and as a channel for future recovery. Second, they need to design and adopt policies that promote growth opportunities where these can be found, and which respond to the unique and ever-changing context.

A broad and adaptive range of policy instruments is needed to support the objectives of resilience and growth. The heterogeneity between and within fragile situations makes it difficult to generalize too much or assume that a development model that has been effective in one situation would be effective in another situation. Public policies should support resilience where populations are under pressure and where the collapse of private enterprise would contribute to a cycle of deteriorating socioeconomic outcomes. But there are normally some growth opportunities and private enterprise should be the channel for recovery when possible. Public policies supported by development partners should be conflict-sensitive and avoid financing bad actors. They should account for how they interplay with the political economy and reduce the risk that new investments exacerbate conflict or directly lower social and environmental standards.

This section discusses policy responses to the types of market failures and enterprise risks identified in the preceding analysis, balancing both the resilience and the growth promotion agenda although they are not mutually exclusive. The policy responses are covered under: (i) efforts to strengthen institutions, regulations and policies; (ii) risk-sharing mechanisms; and (iii) public investments. The appropriate combination of public policies will depend on the idiosyncrasies and dynamics of the political context, the quality of existing institutions, fiscal constraints, and so on. It is important to factor in the sociopolitical context and private interest groups, including information about the potential winners and losers, in crafting the policies so as to avoid fueling the dynamics of tension or conflict.

4.1 Improving Predictability and Quality of the Business Environment

The business environment in fragile situations is typically complex, uncertain, and opaque. Reforming it is often high on the policy agenda but the reform process and capacity-building efforts can go on for years without tangible results. It may be hampered by the complexity of the task, insufficient political will, and the array of parties whose interests are in opposition to the reforms because of potential loss of rents. Policymakers must make difficult choices of where to focus, given the multitude of laws, regulations, and practices across numerous government authorities and agencies.

The financial sector is critical for private sector development because it supports the resilience of the private sector, which includes financial stability and integrity. Maintaining central bank supervisory functions, compliance with anti-money laundering and terrorism financing controls, correspondent banking, business continuity planning, and risk management constitute an essential policy agenda. It is the subject of another chapter in this book and is not covered further here.

The more visible aspects of the general business environment—where business owners, investors, and entrepreneurs interact with the state—are frequently the focus of reforms to promote economic growth. The scope of the reforms is often framed around the World Bank Group's Ease of Doing Business indicators that serve as proxies for assessing the overall business environment. They provide a clear framework for action and the measuring of results. These efforts can be important for creating momentum and changing perceptions. For example, Afghanistan focused on Doing Business reforms and achieved "top performer" status in the Doing Business 2019 report. Djibouti achieved the same feat for two consecutive years. Afghanistan's Doing Business ranking is 167 out of 190 economies, and Djibouti, while faring better at 99, still has a relatively low ranking. Both countries sought to signal to investors that their governments were intent on improving the overall business environment. But these reforms are not likely to have significant short-term effects on the day-to-day experience of businesses.

Policymakers who formulate a business environment reform agenda focused on resilience may focus on the aspects of the business environment that affect most enterprises daily, and which serve to reduce the uncertainty that characterizes that environment. These may not be captured by the Ease of Doing Business indicators. For instance, the inspection regime or municipal licensing of small retail and services may be useful starting points. These are common public-private interfaces that often act as channels for corruption, and which, as shown in section 3, tend to have higher incidence levels in fragile situations. Policy measures that ensure consistency of treatment—through reduced discretion, automation, transparency, and time limits—are a priority in environments where unpredictability and uncertainty prevail, where corruption is rampant, and where institutions are weak (Mahmood and Slimane, 2018). Improving predictability of treatment—for example, having clear maximum time limits and a grievance mechanism—may be more important than improving average or typical treatment, such as reducing the average time to receive a permit. Weak institutional capabilities also demand that business rules, regulations, and their enforcement be well suited to the capacity of both businesses and regulators. In environments where most enterprises are informal with few employees, business regulations may be of little consequence to their daily experience; but reducing hurdles to opening and running a formal business may contribute to a growth agenda.

There is value in nurturing an organized, diverse, and capable private sector institutional landscape. Private sector demand for good governance can help ensure that the reform agenda is maintained and improvements in the business environment are sustained, and can even act as a force for recovery and reconciliation. Companies that act in concert are more effective in peacebuilding efforts because they can amplify their voices, pool their resources, and spread the risk of engagement (Miller et al., 2019). This is an argument for fostering civil society and private sector institutions such as business membership organizations, professional associations, and cooperatives. These institutions act as counterparts to authorities and agencies that regulate the private sector and can create a positive dynamic around policymaking by being active participants in notice and comment exercises around new regulations and acting as a sounding board on new strategies. On the other hand, where these organizations suffer from poor governance themselves they can sometimes act as mouthpieces for the interests of a narrow elite and act as a barrier to reforms.

4.2 Facilitating Market Entry in Weak Public or Private Service Delivery Contexts

A resilience-focused policy agenda may seek to strengthen sectors that play a key role in providing goods and services, with a growth-oriented policy agenda aimed at catalyzing opportunities and pioneer investments. As discussed in section 2, the breakdown of public services delivery in fragile situations can leave no choice or option but reliance on private delivery. This goes beyond the provision of goods and services typically provided by the private sector to increase the supply of water, power, health, education, and transportation. Private enterprises in fragile situations suffer from poor reliability and availability of services, including power and water (discussed in section 3), reflecting the poor service level to the population at large. Policy actions that facilitate entry into these markets to complement public services or substitute for poor public service delivery might entail liberalizing provision of licenses, reducing the role of state-owned enterprises, and issuing regulations to enable concessions or other forms of public-private partnerships. These are challenging reforms with complex political economy dimensions, but in some cases may unfold because of a public sector vacuum. Somaliland, discussed in section 2, is one of the most prominent examples of the expanded role of the private sector because of such a vacuum.

Opportunities to catalyze investment through pioneer investors are typically rare, and when they do arise they may raise issues about tradeoffs between attracting early investment and an open competitive environment. Open competition may be a long-term goal, but where a high level of investment is demanded under risky conditions, it may be worth offering pioneer investors an advantage. In 1996, the Palestinian Authority granted Paltel a 20-year license to build, own, and operate the telecommunications network, aiming to secure the investment and provision of land line, ISP, and mobile phone services, with exclusivity for 10 years. Without this time-limited monopoly, investment in the sector may have been slow or not materialized. But shifting to a competitive environment requires a strong regulatory framework (World Bank, 2016). Provided that regulatory capacity can be developed, and that exclusive licenses include clear and definite sunset clauses and appropriate pricing, this type of public policy which concedes open competition in the short term can be beneficial in overcoming risk aversion in new and uncertain markets.

The most active pioneer investors are generally domestic, diaspora, or neighboring country investors. Except in resource-rich economies, which can attract multinationals, investors in fragile situations are often South-based investors within the region, who can leverage their familiarity with the local context, are more experienced in these environments and better equipped to cope with the risks (Ragoussis and Shams, 2018). Though these investors are more likely to be able to assess and cope with the risks, there may still be a risk gap that needs to be overcome by additional measures.

4.3 Risk-Sharing Instruments to Mitigate Exposure to Higher Volatility and Risk

Section 3 illustrated how private enterprises in fragile situations face more volatile and uncertain market conditions. Business and investment guarantees and other types of risk-sharing instruments can promote investment and growth by limiting exposure to risks that are difficult to quantify, including adverse government actions and security risks. Guarantees are less used as a development instrument than public investment. They could be used more effectively to limit risks to investors in fragile situations where there is potential for growth. The risks may be high and there are negative perceptions about how far they can go.

Political risk insurance (PRI), such as that offered by the Multilateral Investment Guarantee Agency (MIGA), typically serves cross-border rather than local investors. PRI is not necessarily viewed by foreign investors as the best way to mitigate risk, particularly South-based investors. MIGA (2010) analyzed political risk in fragile situations and found that most investors used informal means of risk mitigation (such as engagement with local governments) rather than PRI. South-based investors were found to be half as likely to use PRI as North-based investors. Domestic investment is seldom covered by these policies though domestic investors represent an important source of capital in fragile situations. In the Palestinian Territories, MIGA operated a trust funded guarantee facility which was underused for years. In 2008, MIGA took the decision to change eligibility rules, allowing coverage for domestic investors. This decision resulted in the rapid commitment of the US$26 million fund, guaranteeing more than US$100 million of investments primarily in the industrial and energy sectors.

These more innovative PRI products are exceptions rather than the rule. In a recent positive development, the MIGA risk facility under the IDA18[10] private sector window (PSW), provided US$500 million to enable MIGA to broaden its reach in fragile situations. MIGA has since issued guarantees in Afghanistan, Myanmar, and Sierra Leone, using the first loss guarantee under the MIGA risk facility of the PSW. The value of the guarantees is just US$37 million so there is still a long way to go to utilizing the facility. Likewise, the IDA18 PSW also includes a US$1 billion risk mitigation facility administered by the International Finance Corporation (IFC). It provides project-based finance without sovereign indemnity to crowd in private investment in large scale infrastructure and public-private partnership projects. Beyond PRI, the risk mitigation facility also provides liquidity financing guarantees to backstop state-owned enterprise payment obligations. To date the risk mitigation facility has yet to be used, which highlights the challenge of identifying suitable investments in fragile situations and of deploying these instruments effectively.

Other types of guarantee instruments are needed to bring risk-sharing approaches within reach of small domestic businesses coping with risks in fragile situations. The analysis in section 3 demonstrated that most private enterprises in fragile situations are sole proprietors who per definition are vulnerable to internal and external shocks. Yet, there are few policy interventions designed to mitigate these risks for this segment of the private sector that is crucial to socioeconomic resilience. A partial credit guarantee reduces the risk exposure of financial institutions serving small and medium-sized enterprises and underserved segments. It acts as a risk-sharing mechanism in countries with very low financial intermediation and where access to finance is limited by the risks faced by financial institutions in lending in a context of volatility, uncertainty, and poor rule of law, and by the inability of potential borrowers to offer collateral or other personal guarantees. IFC has used the PSW blended finance facility to fund small loan guarantee programs in West Africa. In Afghanistan, a Credit Guarantee Facility is fully subscribed and covers more than 50 percent of private sector lending to micro-, small, and medium enterprises. Trade insurance and export

[10] IDA18 is the 18th Replenishment of the International Development Association.

guarantees can enable access to markets for buyers and sellers, but often comes at a high price in fragile situations. Temporarily buying down the cost of these products for businesses could support recovering businesses under certain conditions.

Another form of instrument where there is scope for product innovation is service performance guarantees. They could offer investors a guaranteed minimum level of service for services such as licensing, power, water, logistics, and security within a specified physical area, such as a special economic zone (see Center for Global Development). Any penalties resulting from not meeting the service standards could be paid out from a fund financed from tenant fees, which could be backed by a sovereign guarantee. This type of product could be considered in strong recovery contexts, where the main obstacle to investment was assessed to be a persistent negative perception despite an improvement in the level of risk and service delivery.

Guarantee products create contingent liabilities. The value of private leveraged finance needs to justify these liabilities, which would be borne by the government, development partners, or other agencies. Given that risks can materialize in ways that affect a broad set of actors, care must be taken to design these products in a manner that doesn't undermine macro-fiscal or financial sector stability.

4.4 Public Investment to Support Nascent Growth Opportunities

Fragile situations are associated with inefficient factor markets, underdeveloped financial markets, low capital, labor and total factor productivity levels, and, in cases of extreme violence, sudden loss of human capital. When these failures are combined with the elevated risks borne by small-scale sole proprietors with limited coping mechanisms, public investment is needed to address some of them. The aim should be to mitigate risks, support the resilience of private enterprises operating in these contexts, and seed future recovery and growth.

One common approach is the use of grants for small enterprises to overcome external shocks or heightened risks related to conflict, climate, and disaster. Affected businesses typically have limited access to credit, as discussed in section 3, and modest capital to finance their recovery or growth. Grants, often requiring a commensurate match from the beneficiaries, can be small and linked to sectors with a close link to the provision of goods, services or jobs in fragile situations. For instance, emergency resilience grants were provided in Yemen to farmers and fishermen to support food production and jobs within conflict-affected communities. The grants reached more than 3,000 small enterprises producing food and jobs in conflict-affected provinces, and over 44,000 people benefited from employment, including women and IDPs. In Somalia, matching grants provided under the Somaliland Business Fund with funding from external development partners reached hundreds of enterprises, supported the employment of more than 2,000 people, and led to startups in several underserved sectors and new markets. Savvy implementation partners, including United Nations agencies and national institutions well versed in the local environments, are often crucial to the success of these grant programs. The Somalia and Yemen grant programs offered an opportunity to introduce farmers and fishermen to new resilience-supporting technology, including drip irrigation and solar powered water pumps on farms, global positioning system guidance on fishing boats, small windfarms in remote communities, with strong replication by non-grantees demonstrating potentially high positive externalities of this approach.

Public investment can be used to spur financial inclusion, which is typically limited in fragile situations. Micro- and small enterprises are particularly unlikely to have access to credit. Where some microfinance or small and medium enterprise finance channels exist, they can be destroyed in times of conflict and war. In Yemen, the microfinance industry, which before the war served more than 120,000 active borrowers with a portfolio at risk under 2 percent, was heavily damaged by the conflict. Many microfinance institutions found themselves unable to collect on loans because a high number of borrowers had become IDPs or otherwise unable to pay, with portfolio at risk soaring into double digits (SFD, 2015). The World Bank provided a grant to nine microfinance institutions to cover their operating costs of sustaining their operations though the crisis. The 9 microfinance institutions extended loans to 85,000 clients during the project period, including 7,000 new borrowers.

Public investments in support of small enterprise resilience and recovery may be made not only in businesses, but also in public and shared goods along value chains. Low capital productivity and higher risk mean businesses are less likely to invest. Shared goods along a value chain can substitute for individual enterprise investments and increase utilization rates. Common examples include collection and distribution centers along agribusiness value chains, data platforms on market prices, marketplaces, shared tooling and equipment, and support for sector organization. These types of public investments may be beneficial as part of spatially focused growth programs. World Bank Group projects have supported value chain recovery and development such as gemstones in the Federally Administered Tribal Areas in Pakistan, gums and resin and fisheries in Somaliland, raisin and pomegranate production in Afghanistan, and cocoa, beef, and tourism in Madagascar, to name a few.

Countries with high levels of displacement also raise the question of public policies to address the needs and impacts of the forcibly displaced. This topic goes beyond the scope of private sector development policies, but the dynamics between return of refugee and IDP populations and business resilience and recovery are important both from the perspective of forced displacement and the private sector development agenda. The Syrian conflict and refugee crisis is an example in which rebuilding human capital is crucial to recovery. A recent study on Syrian businesses showed that the losses of workers, managers, and business relationships caused by the loss of customers or suppliers were reported among the greatest adverse effects of the conflict on businesses still operating in Syria (after access to electricity and fuel). Nearly 50 percent of businesses reported loss of skilled workers as a major or severe problem; loss of customers, suppliers, managers, and unskilled workers were also notable. Rebuilding the private sector in Syria will demand policies that rebuild human capital and supply chain relationships.

These policies can get a head start with the forcibly displaced populations in host countries. Education, training, and employment opportunities provided to refugees in host communities can strengthen attributes that facilitate their successful return. Some displaced Syrians have capital assets and have the potential to re-establish businesses if they return. A survey of diaspora business leaders indicated that most have an interest in returning to Syria if conditions improve (70 percent) and most are currently investing either in Syria or neighboring countries (World Bank, 2017). Designing policies that leverage the assets and capabilities of the diaspora is an underexploited opportunity for policymakers.

References

Al-Marhubi, F. 2000. "Export Diversification and Growth: An Empirical Investigation." *Applied Economics Letters*, 7(9): 559–62.

Austin, J.L. and A. Wennmann. 2017. "Business Engagement in Violence Prevention and Peace-Building: The Case of Kenya." *Conflict, Security and Development*, 17(6): 451–72. doi: 10.1080/14678802.2017.1401840

Banerjee, A.V., R. Benabou, and D. Mookherjee (Eds.). 2006. *Understanding Poverty*. Oxford: Oxford University Press.

Collier, P. and A. Hoeffler. 2004. "Greed and Grievance in Civil War." *Oxford Economic Papers*, 56(4): 563–95. doi: 10.1093/oep/gpf064

Collier, P., A. Hoeffler, and M. Söderbom. 2008. "Post-Conflict Risks." *Journal of Peace Research*, 45(4): 461–78. doi:10.1177/0022343308091356

Fearon, J. 2005. "Primary Commodity Exports and Civil War." *Journal of Conflict Resolution*, 49(4): 483–507.

Fearon, J.D. and D.D. Laitin. 2003. "Ethnicity, Insurgency, and Civil War." *American Political Science Review*, 97(1): 75–90. doi:10.1017/s0003055403000534

Ganson, B. 2017. "Business in the Transition to Democracy in South Africa: Historical and Contemporary Perspectives." Peace Research Institute Oslo, CDA Collaborative, and Africa Centre for Dispute Settlement.

Gonzalez, A.S., L. Iacovone, and H. Subhash. 2013. "Russian Volatility: Obstacle to Firm Survival and Diversification." Policy Research Working Paper 6605. Washington, DC: World Bank.

IMF (International Monetary Fund). 2017. "The Diversification Toolkit: Export Diversification and Quality Databases." www.imf.org/external/np/res/dfidimf/diversification.htm (last accessed July 16, 2020).

Keen, David. 1998. *The Economic Function of Violence in Civil Wars.* London: International Institute for Strategic Studies.

Keen, D. 2009. Economic Initiatives to Tackle Conflict: Bringing Politics Back In (Occasional Paper 9). London: Crisis States Research Centre. http://r4d.dfid.gov.uk/Print/Output.aspx?OutputID=180389&Mode=Print (last accessed July 16, 2020).

Mahmood, S.A. and M.A.A. Slimane. 2018. *Privilege-Resistant Policies in the Middle East and North Africa: Measurement and Operational Implications.* Washington, DC: World Bank.

MIGA (Multilateral Investment Guarantee Agency). 2010. *World Investment and Political Risk Annual Survey: Investment Political Risk in Conflict-affected and Fragile Economies.* Washington, DC: World Bank.

Miguel, E., S. Satyanath, and E. Sergenti. 2004. "Economic Shocks and Civil Conflict: An Instrumental Variables Approach." *Journal of Political Economy*, 112(4): 725–53. doi:10.1086/421174

Miller, B., B. Ganson, S. Cechvala, and J. Miklian. 2019. A Seat at the Table, Capacities and Limitations of Private Sector Peacebuilding. CDA Collaborative Learning.

La Porta, R., and A. Shleifer. 2008. "The Unofficial Economy and Economic Development," Brookings Papers on Economic Activity. Economic Studies Program, Brookings Institution, 39(2) (Fall)): 275–363.

La Porta, R. and A. Schleifer. 2014. "Informality and Development." *Journal of Economic Perspectives, American Economic Association*, 28(3): 109–126.

O'Brien, K.A. 2000. "PMCs, Myths, and Mercenaries: The Debate on Private Military Companies." *Royal United Service Institute Journal*, 145(1): 59–64.

Oetzel, J., M. Westermann-Behaylo, C. Koerber, T.L. Fort, and J. Rivera. 2010. "Business and Peace: Sketching the Terrain." *Journal of Business Ethics*, 89(4): 351–73. doi: 10.1007/s10551-010-0411-7

Ragoussis, A. and H. Shams. 2018. "FDI in Fragile and Conflict-Affected Situations", 2017–2018 Global Investment Competitiveness Report. Washington, DC: World Bank.

SFD (Social Fund for Development), Republic of Yemen. 2015 . The Impact of the 2015 Conflict in Yemen on the Local Microfinance Industry.

Speakman, J. and A. Rysova. 2015. *The Small Entrepreneur in Fragile and Conflict-Affected Situations. Directions in Development.* Washington, DC: World Bank.

Ray, D. 1998. *Development Economics.* Princeton, NJ: Princeton University Press.

Roesch, A. 2014. Understanding Poverty Amid Fragility: Moving from Rhetoric to Analysis. USAID Frontiers in Development, USAID.

Ross, M. 2004. "The Natural Resource Curse: How Wealth Can Make You Poor," in I. Bannon and P. Collier (Eds.), *Natural Resources and Violent Conflict.* Washington, DC: World Bank.

SLTDA (Sri Lanka Tourism Development Authority). 2018. www.sltda.lk/node/200 (last accessed July 16, 2020).

UNEP. 2009. *From Conflict to Peacebuilding: The Role of Natural Resources and the Environment.* Geneva: UNEP.

World Bank. 2016. "The Telecommunications Sector in the Palestinian Territories: A Missed Opportunity for Economic Development." Washington, DC: World Bank. https://openknowledge.worldbank.org/handle/10986/24019 (last accessed July 16, 2020).

World Bank. 2017. "Assessment of the Status of Solar Pv in Yemen, WB Project: Republic of Yemen—Restoring and Expanding Energy Access." The Regional Center for Renewable Energy and Energy Efficiency (RCREEE), www.rcreee.org/content/assessment-status-solar-pv-yemen (last accessed July 16, 2020).

World Bank. 2018a. Enterprise Surveys, www.enterprisesurveys.org/ (last accessed July 16, 2020).

World Bank. 2018b. World Development Indicators, https://data.worldbank.org/ (last accessed July 16, 2020).

World Bank. 2018c. Ease of Doing Business, www.doingbusiness.org (last accessed July 16, 2020).

Annex 1

Measuring Fragility

This paper relies on the Fragile States Index (FSI) as its main measurement of fragility. The FSI has been published annually by the Fund for Peace since 2006 and marks countries on 12 indicators of state vulnerability grouped by cohesion and economic, political, and social categories. Each indicator is scored from 0 to 10 and the index is obtained by adding up the values of the 12 indicators. The higher the value of the FSI, the more fragile (and prone to collapse) a state is under this classification. The FSI has three advantages in quantitative work compared to the World Bank's Country Policy and Institutional Assessment (CPIA), which is an alternative benchmark indicator for fragility.[11] First, the dataset on FSI (178 countries) is nearly twice as large as the dataset for CPIA (78 countries). Second, the observations in the FSI have a variation around its mean that is about three times larger than for the CPIA. This is valuable because our approach is to study fragility as a continuous rather than binary concept of fragile versus non-fragile states and the higher variability makes correlations and regression results more precise. Third, the FSI is theoretically more relevant in studies of how vulnerable states are to collapse because it covers both the strength of institutions and impending conflict. Unlike the CPIA, the FSI's 12 components account for both sorts of state failure. The FSI correlates well with indicators of economic, political, press freedom, and rule of law indices, which underscores its theoretical relevance.

The literature has studied the effects of fragility mostly through a binary classification: fragile versus non-fragile. For the CPIA, a cutoff point of 3.2 (out of 4.0) is used where countries with CPIA scores less than 3.2 are defined as fragile. This seemingly arbitrary cutoff point has become a sort of industry standard.[12] No such cutoff is provided for the FSI by the Fund for Peace. However, the Organisation for Economic Co-operation and Development uses a cutoff point of 90 when it applies the FSI for focus on fragile and conflict-affected states. This cutoff point for the FSI can be constructed using the accepted benchmark score of 3.2 for the CPIA. Using a fitted line, the CPIA of 3.2 corresponds to a FSI of 89, with a positive correlation of 0.70 between the two indices (see Figure A6.1). Thus, countries that belong in the fragile and conflict-affected situations category according to the World Bank classification will on average have an FSI of 90 or higher. This paper refrains from using definite statements on fragility and does not classify countries as fragile or non-fragile. It more broadly refers to countries as having more or less strong (robust or fragile) institutions.

Fragility as defined by the FSI is strongly and negatively correlated with political (−0.91) freedom. Some of the correlation is explained by the fact that 3 out of 12 sub-indicators that constitute the FSI cover political variables. But the deterioration is still striking (see Figures A6.1.1–A6.1.2). There is only one country (X) with a political freedom score above six among countries with an FSI above 100. Likewise, there is only one country (Y)

[11] The FSI and CPIA differ in their presumptions. The former relies primarily on measuring outcomes of fragility—such as media coverage of events or various poverty data—whereas the latter attempts to measure policy inputs.

[12] The World Bank Group is currently reviewing this methodology with the aim of improving it.

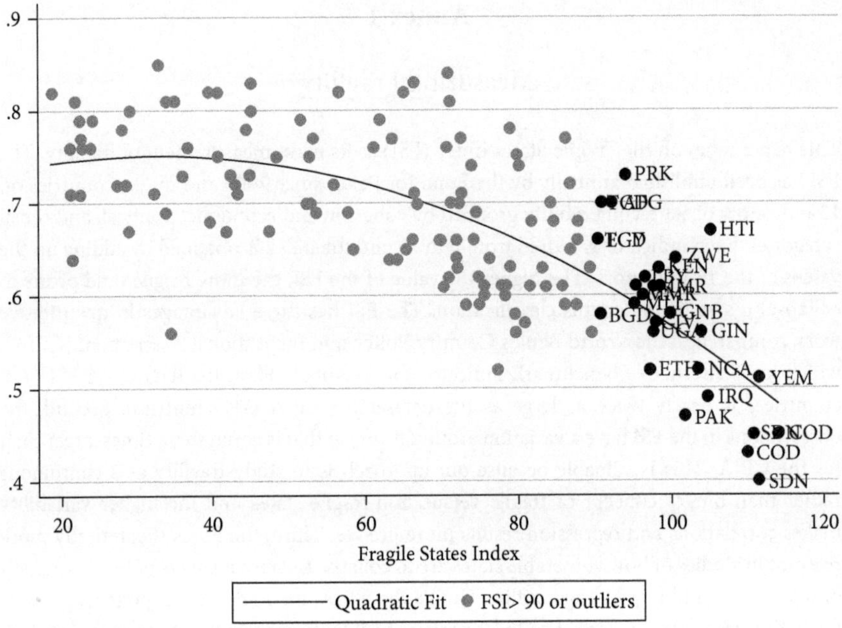

Figure A6.1 Political Freedom

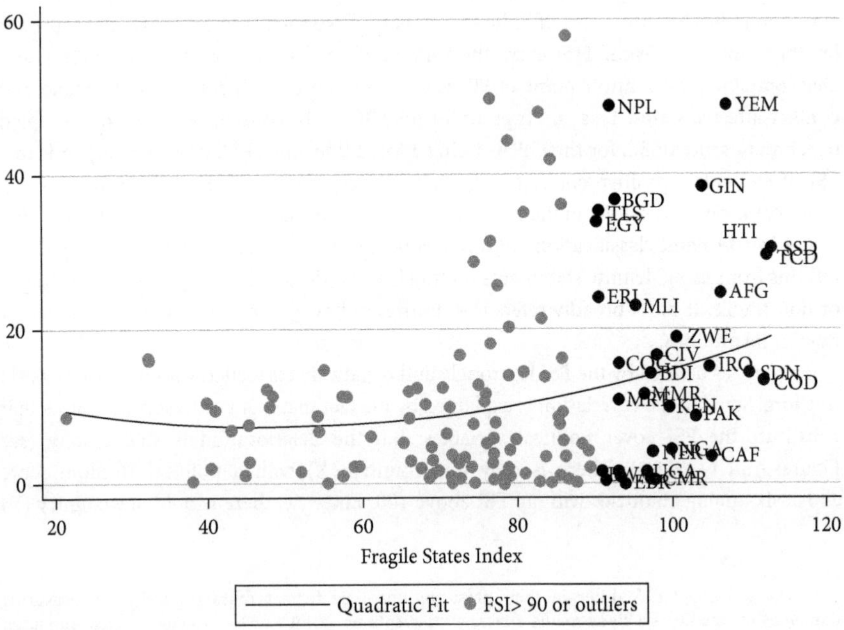

Figure A6.2 Political Instability

with a political freedom score below six among countries with an FSI below 70. But there is an elevated degree of heterogeneity in the sample. Several countries that lack basic political freedom are also politically stable (at least in the short and medium term). More interesting, however, is that there are few, if any, countries that are politically free and at the same time politically unstable.

Annex 2

Correlations with FSI Controlling for Income, and Correlations with FSI without Its Economic Components

Table A6.1 Correlations with FSI Controlling for Income, and Correlations with FSI without Its Economic Components

Variable	Correlation FSI (Total)		Correlation FSI (non-Economic)		Figure
	β	p-value	β	p-value	
New business density (3-year average)	-0.0938541	0	−0.0912613	0	3
Age of establishment	−0.0507425	0.028	−0.0479438	0.034	4a
Formality at start of operation	−0.2152805	0	−0.2141252	0	4b
Length of informality	0.00857713	0.032	0.00852797	0.028	5
Percentage of Sole Proprietorships	0.94130526	0	0.91324039	0	8
Real annual sales growth (%)	−0.0387003	0.519	−0.0369248	0.528	9
Annual employment growth	0.05522578	0.011	0.05393293	0.011	10
Capacity utilization	−0.0672282	0.157	−0.054043	0.243	11
Annual labor productivity growth (%)	−0.0842867	0.113	−0.0810391	0.118	12
Tariff rate, applied, weighted mean, manufactured products (%)	0.1028821	0	0.09955938	0	13
Share of enterprises exporting directly or indirectly (>10% of sales)	−0.1784744	0	−0.1751024	0	14
Share of enterprises exporting directly (>10% of sales)	−0.1527159	0	−0.1497737	0	15
Share of total sales exported directly (%)	−0.0697699	0.004	−0.0688439	0.004	16
Economic growth volatility	0.01680253	0.047	0.01545082	0.062	19
Inflation rate volatility	0.12839365	0.694	0.09857841	0.757	20
Interest rate volatility	0.13395943	0	0.12634116	0	21
Exchange rate volatility	0.00147728	0.003	0.00138447	0.005	22
Enterprises with bank loan/line of credit (% of total)	−0.4927623	0	−0.4677	0	23
Credit to private sector (% of GDP)	−1.2296015	0	−1.1780399	0	24
Enterprises using banks to finance investments (% of total)	−0.2510021	0	−0.2358858	0	25
Share of investments financed internally (%)	0.17276184	0.007	0.16349361	0.008	26
National investments financed by banks (%)	−0.1789438	0	−0.1653763	0	27

Enterprises using banks to finance working capital (% of total)	0.51318369	0	0.48962634	0	28
Corruption as a major constraint (%)	0.29621247	0	0.28083666	0.001	29
Practices of informal sector as a major constraint (%)	0.25849711	0	0.2377042	0	30
Enterprises experiencing water insufficiencies (%)	0.04149081	0	0.03872448	0	31
Electrical outages in a typical month	0.30705225	0	0.29621751	0	33
National sales lost to theft & vandalism (% of total)	0.02012754	0	0.01828533	0.001	35
Share of enterprises paying for security (%)	−0.1482275	0.094	−0.1496038	0.083	37
Average security costs (% of sales)	0.05159258	0	0.04789706	0	38
Generator ownership	0.85518451	0	0.80998098	0	39

Annex 3

Summary Table

Table A6.2 Summary Table

	FSI<45			45<FSI<70			70<FSI< 95			95<FSI		
	Aver	Med	δ	Aver	Med	δ	Aver	Med	δ	Aver	Med	δ
GDP per capita (US$)	41,769	44,125	21,574	14,863	11,324	12,720	4,198	2,877	5,069	1,180	729	1,271
FDI/GDP (%)	6.6	2.8	17.3	8.1	3.9	26.9	5.1	3.4	6.3	3.0	1.8	4.6
Trade/GDP (%)	110	85	81	105	99	43	83	78	37	59	56	28
New Business Density (annual reg./1,000 citizens)	5.7	4.2	4.7	5.1	3.2	5.4	1.3	0.7	2.5	0.7	0.2	1.1
Agriculture/GDP (%)	2.2	1.6	1.9	5.1	3.5	5.2	14.7	11.3	10.9	26.8	23.8	13.1
Tax/GDP (%)	19.3	20.2	6.8	17.6	18.5	8.2	16.5	15.3	7.1	10.2	9.2	4.9
Industry/GDP (%)	24.7	24.5	6.2	29.3	24.6	16.3	29.3	26.9	13.9	25.9	22.4	14.5
Volatility of Growth (Standard Deviation)	1.8	1.3	1.8	2.8	2.1	2.9	2.7	1.6	5.6	3.7	1.9	6.0
Credit to Private Sector (% of GDP)	108.4	105.0	45.0	62.0	55.4	39.7	36.4	28.9	26.7	13.8	12.5	10.5
Firms identifying corruption as major constraint (%)	2.7	2.5	1.4	6.4	4.5	5.9	7.9	6.8	6.3	7.8	7.4	5.7
Firms identifying informality as major constraint (%)	15.6	16.8	7.5	11.8	11.6	7.1	13.0	11.7	8.6	9.0	5.0	8.9
Percent of firms having Bank Loans	51.5	48.0	15.1	41.8	43.9	12.8	34.1	33.4	17.0	16.0	11.0	13.3
Percent of firms using Banks to finance investments	28.4	30.5	13.2	31.7	32.7	14.0	23.9	22.0	14.0	13.2	9.2	12.0
Age of Firm	21.2	21.6	5.7	15.7	14.9	4.3	15.8	15.4	4.5	14.1	14.4	5.9
Formality at start of Operations (% of firms)	96.4	97.8	4.2	92.2	96.1	9.0	88.8	90.5	10.0	82.8	86.5	12.6
Years to Formality	0.3	0.2	0.4	0.6	0.2	1.1	0.9	0.6	1.0	0.7	0.6	0.5
Percent of firms experiencing water insufficiency	6.1	4.1	6.8	10.6	8.4	9.5	17.7	15.8	12.6	21.7	18.8	14.3
Number of water insufficiencies per month	0.2	0	0.5	0.6	0.2	1.1	1.3	0.6	1.8	2.6	1.8	2.9
Number of electrical outages per month	0.5	0.5	0.4	2.6	1.0	5.0	4.9	1.7	9.0	20.7	12.3	21.4
Average proportion of electricity from generator, if used	4.5	2.0	6.6	14.5	8.4	15.7	21.8	19.2	18.2	33.4	26.6	20.3
Capacity Utilization	73.4	72.4	8.2	74.4	75.3	5.9	71.6	72.3	7.4	71.0	71.8	8.8
Real Annual Sales Growth (%)	7.4	8.6	4.1	2.0	3.2	6.9	4.4	4.2	11.0	(0.3)	3.0	15.3
Annual Employment Growth (%)	3.5	4.3	3.0	4.8	4.7	3.3	6.0	5.6	4.1	6.6	6.4	5.2
Annual Labor Productivity Growth (%)	3.6	3.8	3.3	(2.2)	(1.6)	6.3	(0.8)	(0.8)	10.0	(5.7)	(4.0)	15.0
Volatility of Inflation (Standard Deviation)	3.4	1.2	6.7	25.8	4.3	115.4	71.4	6.4	719.3	74.3	16.71	141.6

Volatility of Exchange Rate (Standard Deviation)	0.06	0.05	0.04	0.05	0.03	0.06	0.06	0.04	0.08	0.10	0.05	0.25
Interest Rate (%)	6.2	5.4	4.1	11.4	9.3	7.8	13.3	12.2	7.5	21.4	14.4	58.8
Export Diversification Index	2.2	2.0	0.7	3.1	2.7	1.3	3.7	3.6	1.1	4.2	4.1	1.2
Export Quality Index	1.0	1.0	0.1	0.9	0.9	0.1	0.7	0.8	0.2	0.7	0.7	0.1
Percent of firms exporting directly or indirectly	19.3	16.3	11.7	12.2	12.1	6.5	8.9	7.2	7.1	6.0	4.9	4.9
If there is a loss, then % of sales lost due to Crime, Theft and Vandalism	4.7	3.7	3.9	4.4	1.7	6.7	5.0	2.6	6.4	3.6	2.1	4.1
Firms identifying crime, theft & vandalism as major constraint (%)	22.2	21.1	11.9	18.7	14.0	14.8	22.7	21.4	15.3	29.6	27.8	19.1
Security Expenses (% of total sales)	1.6	1.4	1.9	2.3	2.0	1.5	3.5	2.9	2.2	4.2	3.2	2.6

7

The State of Finance in Fragile States

Adolfo Barajas, Ralph Chami, and Connel Fullenkamp

1. Introduction

The level of financial market development is an important aspect of fragile states that needs to be better understood.[1] Financial development has been shown to promote economic growth at the national, industry, and individual firm levels, as well as productivity growth and capital accumulation.[2] It has also been shown to reduce income inequality and is strongly associated with poverty alleviation (Beck et al., 2007). Therefore, if the financial markets of fragile states are underdeveloped, financial development has the potential to help these states deal with both the symptoms and the sources of their fragility.

At the same time, however, fragility may interfere with the process of financial development. Financial markets and financial activity rely critically on well-functioning institutions that protect property rights and provide a minimum of certainty, on an environment that fosters trust among economic agents, and on policymakers with the competence and will to provide stable macroeconomic conditions. It stands to reason that fragile states, where these ingredients are scarce, are likely to face a unique challenge in developing their financial institutions and markets.

This chapter will provide a description of the state of development of financial activity in fragile states, aiming to answer the following questions: How does the degree of financial development differ, if at all, from that in other countries? How heterogeneous is the group of fragile states with respect to financial development? How well has financial inclusion advanced in these countries? To the extent that some countries are relatively further along than others, could one identify factors that may help to explain these differences? In particular, does fragility appear to be associated with the level of financial performance of a country? And finally, to the extent that finance is relatively underdeveloped, what are the likely costs—for example, in terms of long-term growth—that these countries have had to bear?

[1] The views expressed in this chapter are those of the authors and do not necessarily represent the views of the IMF, its Executive Board, or IMF management.

[2] See, for example, Beck et al. (2000) and Levine (2005).

Adolfo Barajas, Ralph Chami, and Connel Fullenkamp, *The State of Finance in Fragile States* In: *Macroeconomic Policy in Fragile States.* Edited by: Ralph Chami, Raphael Espinoza, and Peter Montiel, Oxford University Press (2021).

DOI: 10.1093/oso/9780198853091.003.0007

The analysis in this chapter is based on indicators that have been used extensively in the literature to capture the degree to which financial services and activities are present in an economy and the extent to which they are disseminated and made available to the population. Several aspects will be highlighted. Section 2 focuses on financial depth and inclusion. Financial depth primarily reflects the scale of financial sector activity relative to the size of the economy, either in banking or in capital markets. Country-level indicators of financial inclusion reflect the extent to which financial services are available and how broadly they are used throughout the economy. Section 3 examines a more recently constructed set of composite indicators of financial development, which aims to provide a holistic measure along three main dimensions: depth, access, and efficiency. These composite indicators also measure institutions (including banking institutions and some nonbank institutions) and markets.

While sections 2 and 3 make simple comparisons between fragile states and other countries, section 4 goes one step further. Recognizing that financial development is driven to some extent by longer-term, non-policy structural characteristics, such as the level of income, demographic characteristics and other factors, the section makes use of a benchmarking exercise that allows comparison between the levels of different indicators and their expected value given the country's structural determinants of financial development. Thus, each country is compared to a hypothetical median country that shares its structural characteristics but is not necessarily a fragile state. The resulting comparison allows one to assess to what extent the different fragile states can be said to be under- or overperforming relative to their structural peers. The relationship between country fragility and these benchmarked measures of financial performance is then examined using cross-country regressions. Section 5 uses coefficient estimates of the growth impact of different measures of financial depth and development to evaluate whether there are sizable growth costs to financial underdevelopment in certain fragile states. Section 6 concludes.

2. Financial Depth and Inclusion: Individual Measures

The main data source for indicators on financial depth and inclusion is the World Bank Global Financial Development Database (GFDD), which collects data from multiple sources[3] since 1960 for a broad cross-country sample, covering more than 160 countries. Based on the levels of two commonly used indicators of

[3] The principal sources that feed into the GFDD are the IMF International Financial Statistics and Financial Access Survey; and the World Bank World Development Indicators, Enterprise Surveys; and the Global Findex.

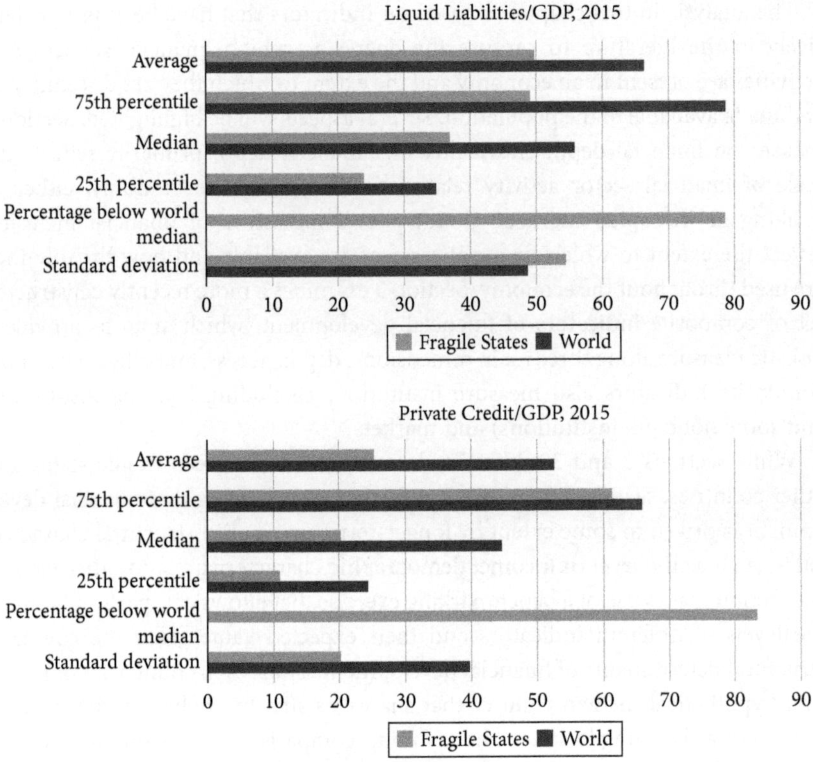

Figure 7.1 Financial Depth in Fragile States

banking depth in 2015,[4] the banking systems' liquid liabilities (M2) and credit to the private sector, both measured as a percentage of GDP,[5] it is apparent that fragile states as a group lag behind the rest of the world (Figure 7.1).

Although some countries such as Nepal and Lebanon register levels of banking depth well above the world median, the bulk of fragile states lie in the lower tail of the distribution, with 80 percent of them below the world median (Figure 7.2) and more than 90 percent lying below the top quartile.[6]

For the most part, these differences have been widening over time. When the increases in these indicators over the past two decades are compared, there are visible differences between fragile states and the rest of the world. Between 1995

[4] This year was the most recent for which there was data availability for a broad group of countries.

[5] Both have been used extensively in the literature and have been found to be positively and significantly related to long-term real GDP growth in numerous empirical studies (see for example, Levine, 2005), although more recent studies suggest a nonlinear relation (Arcand et al., 2015).

[6] For the definition of fragile states used in the descriptive analysis, we use the World Bank's Harmonized List of Fragile Situations, which yields a set of 55 countries that have been in a fragile situation for at least one year since 2006. However, in section 4 we present econometric results using alternative definitions of fragility.

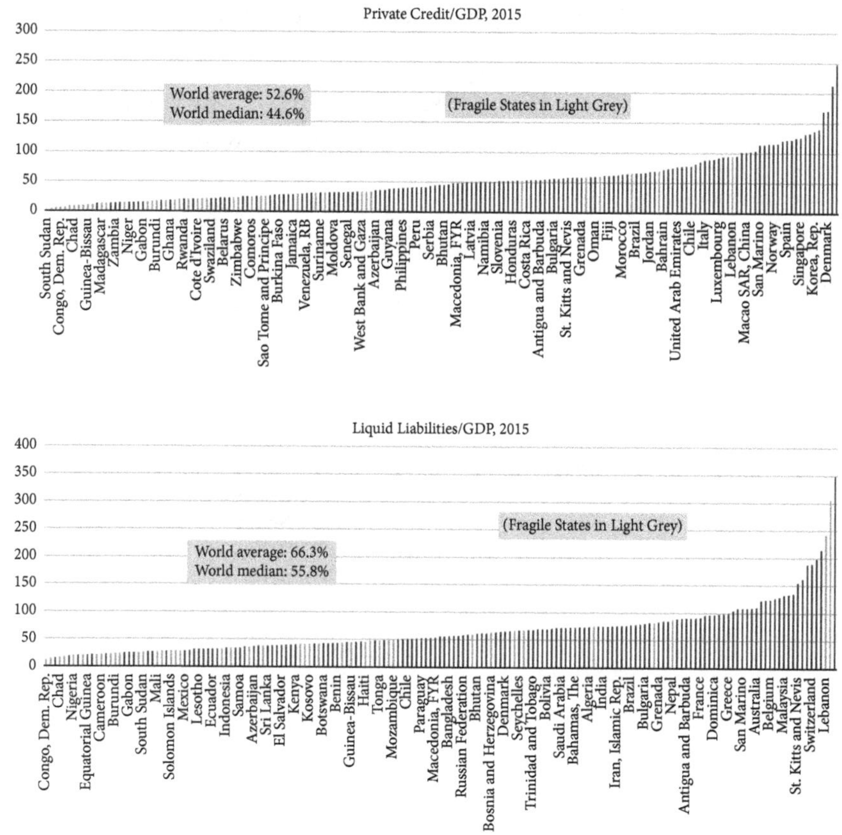

Figure 7.2 Banking Depth Throughout the World

and 2015, the median country increased its liquid liabilities-GDP ratio by 1.08 percentage points per year, while the median fragile state did so by 0.69 percentage points. Over a 20-year period, this would amount to a difference of over eight percentage points. For the private credit-GDP ratio, the differences are slightly greater; 0.87 compared to 0.43 percentage points, for an accumulated difference of more than 9 percentage points[7] over 20 years (Table 7.1).

Of course, there is considerable diversity within the fragile states group. Some have experienced impressive increases in financial depth. For example, Lebanon had the second-largest annual growth in the liquid liabilities-GDP ratio, by 6.2 percentage points; and Cyprus had the largest increase in the private credit-GDP ratio, by 7.2 percentage points, and Cambodia increased private credit-GDP by 3.1 percentage points per year. It also appears, however, that the adverse effects of the

[7] Based on simple regressions for the 20-year change of financial depth on a fragile state dummy, the difference between fragile states and other countries is significant at the 10 percent level for private credit but not for liquid liabilities.

Table 7.1 Changes in Financial Depth: Comparing Fragile States to the World

	Annual increase 1995–2015		Global Financial Crisis: Total change 2007–10	
	World	Fragile States	World	Fragile States
Liquid liabilities/GDP				
Average	1.29	1.06	5.60	3.79
Median	1.08	0.69	5.41	2.73
Private credit/GDP				
Average	1.18	0.72	6.21	3.50
Median	0.87	0.43	4.68	1.99

Sources: Global Financial Development Database and authors' calculations.

Table 7.2 Stock Market Depth, 2015

	Fragile States	World
Stock Market Capitalization/GDP		
Average	19.1	60.6
Median	23.4	45.1
Number of countries	3	56
Percentage < World median	100.0	...
Stock Market Value Traded/GDP		
Average	1.6	40.3
Median	1.4	9.0
Number of countries	3	56
Percentage < World median	100.0	...

Source: Global Financial Development Database and authors' calculations.

Global Financial Crisis on financial deepening were particularly strong among fragile states. During 2007–10, average and median changes in both measures of depth were lower by more than 2 percentage points for fragile states (Table 7.1). A global shortage of US dollar liquidity, which was one of the main international consequences of the financial crisis, may have affected fragile states' banking systems disproportionately, restricting the growth of lending in these countries.

In terms of stock market depth, the gaps between fragile states and the rest of the world appear to be even more pronounced. Many fragile countries—22 in all—lack stock markets altogether. Another 16 countries have stock markets, but no publicly available data on listings, turnover, or trading volume. Only in three fragile states are the indicators available and reported amounts of trading suggest sufficiently liquid markets to merit including in the sample. Based on this limited sample, the size of domestic stock markets (capitalization-GDP ratios) and, particularly, their level of activity (value traded-GDP ratios) are far below what is typical for the world sample of 56 countries (Table 7.2).

Regarding financial inclusion, four different measures of use of financial services are examined: two for households and two for firms. The household indicators are obtained from the 2017 Global Findex survey of over 150,000 households in over 140 countries,[8] and here the focus is on two questions: whether the household holds an account in a formal financial institution, and whether it received a loan from a formal financial institution in the previous 12 months. The firm-level indicator refers to questions from the World Bank Enterprise Survey of 135,000 firms in 139 countries; however, unlike the Global Findex, it is conducted in a non-synchronous manner, that is, at different times for different countries. Therefore, for each country the most recent observation available since 2010 was selected, and two questions from the survey were examined: whether the firm currently had a loan or line of credit with a formal financial institution, and whether it viewed lack of access to finance as a major constraint to its business prospects.

There are also visible gaps in financial inclusion when fragile states are compared to the world. Average and median levels for fragile states are well below the corresponding world benchmarks for the first three indicators (usage of accounts, credit to households, and credit to firms), and the fourth indicator shows that firms in fragile states are much more likely to feel constrained by a lack of access to finance (Table 7.3).

3. Composite Measures of Financial Development

In addition to comparing measures of individual aspects of financial development, one can also draw on efforts that have been made to construct composite, or multi-dimensional measures. One such effort is that of Svirydzenka (2016), which aims to reflect three dimensions of financial development—depth, access, and efficiency—for two groups of providers of financial services: institutions (both bank and nonbank) and markets. Through a principal components procedure, individual indicators are aggregated into nine separate measures,[9] and ultimately aggregated into an overall financial development index, *FD*. It is a relative measure, indicating where a country stands in a given point in time relative to the maximum level achieved in the sample. For example, in 2016 the value of the index was 0.24 for Nigeria, implying that it was at 24 percent of the country-year observation with the highest level of financial development. Disaggregating to the service-provider level, one sees that in terms of its institutional development

[8] See Demirgüç-Kunt et al. (2018) for details.

[9] These measures are: overall financial development (FD); institution development (FI); market development (FM); institution depth, access, and efficiency (FID, FIA, FIE); and market depth, access, and efficiency (FMD, FMA, FME). See Svirydzenka (2016) for details on the methodology and the data used to construct the composite measures.

Table 7.3 Financial Inclusion, Latest Figure Available

	Percentage of households who have:				Percentage of firms who:			
	An account at a formal financial institution		A loan from a Formal Financial Institution		Have a loan or line of credit from a formal financial institution		Report lack of access to finance as major constraint	
	World	Fragile States	World	Fragile States	World	Fragile States	World	Fragile States
Average	58.1	28.4	12.2	7.8	33.9	24.8	25.8	33.4
Median	55.3	25.0	10.9	5.2	32.8	20.6	22.1	37.6
25th percentile	32.7	15.0	7.3	3.6	21.5	9.4	13.2	15.0
75th percentile	86.3	37.1	16.4	8.6	46.9	33.4	38.8	46.6
Percentage below world median[1]		90.9		78.8		70.0		65.6
Standard deviation	29.3	15.8	7.0	6.2	17.3	17.4	16.6	19.3

Note: The two indicators for households are taken from the 2017 Global Findex Survey, and the two indicators for firms are taken from the most recent available figure from the World Bank Enterprise Survey since 2010.

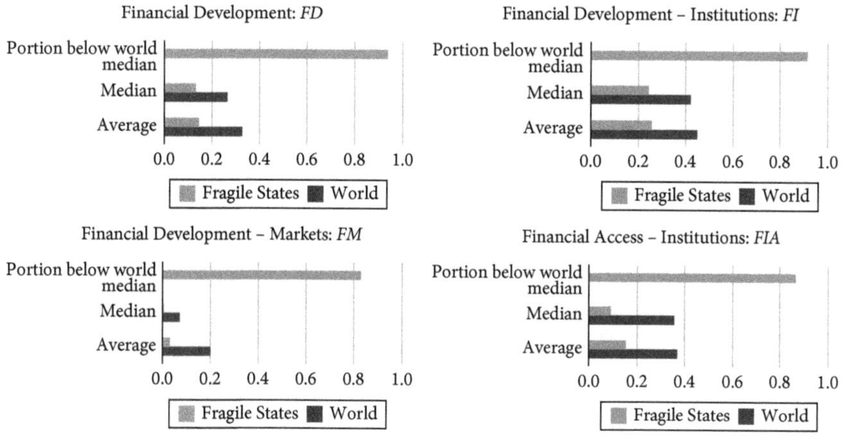

Figure 7.3 Composite Financial Development Indicators, 2018
Source: IMF Financial Development Database and authors' calculations.

(*FI* = 0.26), El Salvador was not as far behind as it was in its market development (*FM* = 0.20). One could disaggregate further to see, for example, how this country fares on institution depth (*FID*) or market efficiency (*FME*). Time series of the composite indicator are available from 1980. Similar to the financial depth indicators covered in section 2, the overall indicator *FD* has been shown to have a positive but nonlinear impact on long-term economic growth (Sahay et al., 2015a).

The more holistic assessment that these measures make possible confirms the substantial gap in financial development by fragile states documented in the previous section, which used selected individual indicators. In 2016 the median fragile state registered a value of 0.13 in the overall development index, about half the world median (Figure 7.3). Gaps in market development appear to be greater than in institutions, and an index reflecting the access of individuals and business to banking services through physical branches and presence of automated teller machines (*FIA*) shows an even wider gap; the world median for access is more than 3½ times that of fragile states.

4. Fragile States Compared to their Structural Benchmarks

The previous sections have shown that across several dimensions, actors, and aspects of financial development, fragile states currently lag the rest of the world. To a large extent, this may not be a fair comparison, because fragile states may not share certain characteristics of other countries—beyond the circumstances determining the fragility itself—that could either benefit or hinder financial development.

One such characteristic is income level, which has long been recognized as a significant determinant of financial depth. This is illustrated in Figure 7.4, where a

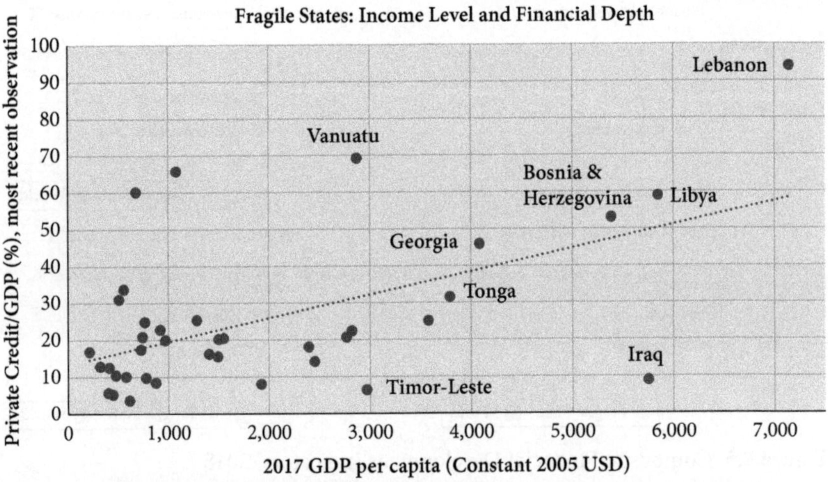

Figure 7.4 Fragile States: Income Level and Financial Depth
Sources: World Bank Global Financial Development Database and authors' calculations.

positive relationship is visible between level of income and private credit-GDP among fragile states. Most fragile states are also low-income countries, and their low level of financial depth and development may reflect this fact. Nonetheless, some fragile states are not low-income countries and may either underperform (Tonga and Iraq, for example) or overperform (Lebanon and Libya) relative to the level of depth predicted solely by their income level.

It has been recognized that there are structural or non-policy factors, apart from income level, that play a role in financial development. Thus, there has been an effort to isolate the impact of these factors, effectively benchmarking a country's financial development to a hypothetical peer country sharing its structural characteristics. As described in detail in Feyen et al. (2019), the benchmarking exercise consists of two steps. First, quantile regressions are run for each of 46 indicators of financial depth, inclusion, or performance on a set of structural explanatory variables reflecting income level, demographics, and special circumstances that affect financial development. Note that although some of these structural determinants may be correlated, to some extent, with fragility, they are not intrinsically associated with it.[10] Then the predicted median (as well as the 25th and 75th percentiles) from this regression provides a structural benchmark against which the indicator in a given country at a given time can be compared. Thus, if the observed value of the indicator is above or below the structural

[10] The full set of structural variables includes economic development (GDP per capita and its square); population factors (total population and its density); demographic factors (young and old age dependency ratios); "special circumstances" (dummies for oil exporters, offshore financial centers, transition countries, and landlocked countries); and the global cycle (time fixed effects).

benchmark, one can say that the country is overperforming or underperforming relative to what is typical for countries of similar structural characteristics.[11]

The relevant question then is, now that we have established from a broad set of indicators that financial development in fragile states lags that of the rest of the world, how do fragile states fare relative to their structural benchmarks? Focusing on seven indicators—three on inclusion, two on banking depth,[12] and two on stock market depth—the overall picture of underperformance becomes less clear. Although on banking depth and inclusion in 2016 at least half of fragile states are seen to underperform their structural benchmarks, there are still many countries that overperform (Table 7.4). For example, Mozambique overperforms its structural benchmark for accounts per thousand adults by 190, for the percentage of firms with a line of credit by 1 percentage point, and for private credit-GDP by 13 percentage points.

The sample of fragile countries for which benchmarking of stock market variables was undertaken is very small, but it also hints at a mix between under- and over-performance. For example, Iraq overperformed its capitalization-GDP ratio by 2.5 percentage points and its turnover ratio by 14 percentage points. Nigeria, by contrast, underperforms these ratios by 29 percentage points and 6 percentage points respectively.

Fragile countries can therefore be grouped into varying levels of performance relative to the structural benchmarks. Based on the five indicators for depth and inclusion, an overall measure of underperformance is constructed as the sum of the share of indicators for which the gap is negative. If a country underperforms on both depth indicators, then it receives a value of 1.0 for depth. If it underperforms on all three inclusion indicators, it receives a value of 1.0 for inclusion. Thus, a country that underperforms on all five indicators receives a maximum of 2.0. Likewise, a country overperforming on all indicators receives a value of 0.0. Values between 0 and 1 indicate that the country underperforms on some indicators, but overperforms on others.

Out of the 45 fragile states included in the benchmarking exercise, all but 8 exhibit underperformance on at least one of the 5 indicators of banking depth and inclusion. Twenty-four show relatively broad underperformance (index of 1.0 or greater), and a group of seven countries underperforms on most, if not all, measures (Table 7.5).

Although the comparison reveals substantial variation in performance gaps across fragile states and the existence of relative overperformance of some fragile states in some measures, the benchmarking exercise by itself does not suggest a strong relation between fragility and financial under- or over-performance.

[11] The Finstats database created by Feyen et al. (2019) provides observed values as well as estimated structural benchmarks for each of the 46 indicators.

[12] Note that deposits-GDP is shown here rather than the liquid liabilities-GDP shown in section 2. They are similar indicators, and only deposits-GDP was benchmarked in the Finstats database.

Table 7.4 Fragile States: Gaps with Respect to Structural Benchmarks

	Accounts Per Thousand Adults, Commercial Banks	Percent of Firms With Line of Credit, All Firms (%)	Domestic Bank Deposits/GDP (%)	Private Credit/GDP (%)	Stock Market Capitalization/ GDP (%)	Stock Market Turnover Ratio (%)	Percent of Adults with an Account at a Formal Institution (%)
All countries							
Number of countries	31	34	41	41	3	2	34
Average	−4.5	1.3	11.6	2.0	−21.6	3.9	3.0
Standard deviation	364.8	13.4	32.9	16.1	21.4	14.2	11.5
Countries with Gaps >0							
Number of countries	12	17	23	18	1	1	18
Percentage	38.7	50.0	56.1	43.9	33.3	50.0	52.9

This table summarizes statistics for the gap between the observed value and the structural benchmark for each indicator estimated in the FinStats database *i.e.*, the expected median. Thus, a positive (negative) gap indicates over (under) performance relative to a country's structural benchmark. For each indicator and country, the most recent available observation was taken, usually corresponding to 2016 or 2017. The average difference with respect to the rest of the world refrs to the coefficient of a regression of each country's gap on a fragile states dummy variable.

Source: FinStats 2019 Database and authors' calculations.

Table 7.5 Fragile States: Index of Underperformance in Bank Depth and Inclusion

	Number of countries	Countries
Value of the index	45	
Lowest performance		
2.00	5	Central African Republic, Chad, Guinea, Sudan, Timor-Leste
1.67	2	Madagascar, Mauritania
1.50	8	Angola, Cameroon, Congo, Dem. Rep., Micronesia, Myanmar, Nigeria, Sierra Leone, Yemen
1.33	1	Malawi
1.17	1	Congo, Rep.
1.00	7	Cambodia, Djibouti, Guinea-Bissau, Haiti, Kiribati, Papua New Guinea, Sao Tome and Principe
0.67	5	Bosnia and Herzegovina, Burundi, Croatia, Lao PDR, Lebanon
0.50	5	Comoros, Eritrea, The Gambia,Libya, Tajikistan
0.33	3	Liberia, Nepal, Uzbekistan
0.00	8	Cote d'Ivoire, Georgia, Mali, Mozambique, Solomon Islands, Togo, Tonga,Vanuatu
Highest		

This table shows the countries associated with various values of an index measuring the degree of underperformance relative to structural benchmarks in five measures of financial depth and inclusion. A value is assigned for depth and for inclusion corresponding to the proportion of indicators in each category that have a negative sign (for underperformance). If all five indicators are negative, then a value of 1.0 is assigned for depth and another for inclusion, for an overall value of 2.0. Similarly, an overall value of zero indicates that the country is overperforming on all indicators reported. Values between zero and 2.0 indicate that there is underperformance on some indicators, overperformance on others. For each indicator and country, the most recent available observation was taken, usually corresponding to 2016 or 2017.

Source: FinStates 2019 Database and authors' calculations.

But we searched for evidence of such a relationship by running panel and cross-sectional regressions of the estimated performance gaps for all countries on different measures of fragility.[13] The measures of fragility employed in different specifications included a fragility dummy variable as well as several different continuously measured indexes. In addition, specifications were estimated that used some of the individual component indicators that comprise the Country Policy and Institutional Assessment (CPIA) index as the fragility variable.

The results of the regression exercise, presented in Table 7.6, reveal that fragile states are more likely to underperform, particularly with regard to financial

[13] We report the results for these simple regressions with the fragility dummy as the sole explanatory variable. However, the results are virtually unchanged when the size of the government, the inflation rate, and the size of trade are included as control variables.

Table 7.6 Performance Gaps in Financial Depth and Inclusion and Fragility

		Accounts Per Thousand Adults, Commercial Banks	Percent of Firms With Line of Credit, All Firms (%)	Domestic Bank Deposits/ GDP (%)	Private Credit/GDP (%)	Percent of Adults with an Account at a Formal Institution (%)
Fragile Situations		−225.08	−4.62	3.39	−0.11	−2.87
		(3.43)***	(1.88)*	(1.34)	(0.06)	(1.28)
	Observations	1,375	229	5,515	5,477	405
Fragile States Dummy (CPIA)		−182.48	−6.98	7.34	0.47	−7.46
		(6.89)***	(2.88)***	(3.73)***	(0.47)	(2.81)***
	Observations	514	117	879	882	142
State Fragility Index		−22.62	−0.05	−0.67	0.66	0.34
		(2.80)***	(0.18)	(2.74)***	(4.21)***	(2.35)
	Observations	553	99	1,449	1,445	171
Fragile States Index		−7.91	0.07	−0.31	0.21	0.10
		(4.15)***	(0.92)***	(4.63)***	(3.85)***	(1.81)*
	Observations	586	105	880	883	174
CPIA - Overall index		132.14	9.60	−1.81	8.79	8.93
		(4.37)***	(3.52)***	(1.27)	(8.49)***	(2.35)***
	Observations	500	116	851	851	136
Structural policies component		15.79	6.54	−7.88	4.34	8.75
		(0.56)	(2.84)***	(6.25)***	(4.47)***	(2.74)***
	Observations	505	118	862	862	137
Public sector management & institutions		175.89	7.35	0.48	7.44	11.19
		(6.22)***	(2.83)***	(0.37)	(7.73)***	(3.20)***
	Observations	505	118	862	862	137
Policies for social inclusion & equity		161.51	10.01	2.53	9.61	10.77
		(6.06)***	(4.07)***	(1.97)**	(10.40)***	(3.39)***

	Observations	500	117	857	857	137
Economic management		54.18	6.00	0.40	5.40	−0.37
		(2.54)***	(3.09)***	(0.41)	(7.52)***	(0.13)
	Observations	505	118	862	862	137

This table summarizes regression results of the performance gap of each financial depth or inclusion indicator on different indicators of fragility: (i) a dummy for fragile states; (ii) the State Fragility Index (SFI) compiled by the Center for Global Policy, George Mason University; (iii) the Failed States Index (FSI), constructed by the Fund for Peace; (iv) the composite Country Policy and Institutional Assessment (CPIA) indicator, constructed by the World Bank; and (v) individual CPIA components. The SFI ranges from 0 (best) to 24 (worst); the FSI ranges from 0.0 (best) to 12.0 (worst); and the CPIA ranges from 1.0 (worst) to 6.0 (best). The failed states dummy is defined as a CPIA score of less than 3.2. The performance gap is measured as the difference between the observed level of each indicator and its structural benchmark, as estimated by Feyen and others (2019). T-statistics are shown in parentheses with 10 percent (*), 5 percent (***), and 1 percent levels of significance indicated.

Sources: FinStats Database, the World Bank, the Center for Global Policy, and authors' calculations.

inclusion.[14] The top row of the Table is a panel regression in which a fragile situations dummy takes the value of 1.0 only in periods deemed to be fragile for a given country. Therefore, a country can move in and out of fragility within the sample. This regression shows that, on average, fragile situations are associated with fewer accounts, by 225 per thousand adults, and 4.5 percentage points less for firms with credit.[15] However, they are associated with average performance on private credit to GDP, domestic banks deposits, and percentage of account holding.

For comparison purposes, similar regressions were run on three alternative definitions of fragility.[16] The first is a Fragile States dummy derived from the Country Policies and Institutional Assessment (CPIA) indicator, constructed for a subsample of lower-income, IDA-eligible countries,[17] and which defines fragility as registering a score of 3.2 or less. The second is a State Fragility Index compiled by the Center for Global Policy, George Mason University, and the third is, the Failed States Index constructed by the Fund for Peace.

Based on this analysis, a more nuanced pattern emerges. When the State Fragility Indicator and the Failed States Indicator, constructed for a broad sample of 162–177 countries, are the fragility measures, Table 7.6 shows that there is a clear association between fragility and underperformance in accounts per thousand adults and the deposit-GDP ratio, though the association with firms with credit or adults with accounts is weak, and the association with the private credit-GDP ratio is positive.

The results become stronger when the CPIA overall index is considered; in contrast to the previous dummy variables, it is a continuous variable that reflects the degree of fragility.[18] Also, recall that it is measured for a subsample of lower-income countries. Within this sample, fragility is now clearly associated with lower performance on all three measures of financial inclusion and on the pre-eminent financial depth variable, the credit-GDP ratio, although again positively related to deposits-GDP. Thus, fragility appears to have more clear-cut implications for financial inclusion and financial development for the group of lower-income countries.

Comparing the different subcomponents of the CPIA, one observes that the factors related to policies for social inclusion and equity have the clearest beneficial impact across the board on financial depth and inclusion. A unit increase in the index is associated with increases by 162 in accounts per thousand adults, by

[14] Regressions for the stock market indicators were not reported, due to the very small coverage of fragile states in the sample.

[15] Similar results are obtained in cross-section regressions in which the explanatory variable is a dummy variable that takes the value of 1.0 for a country that experienced fragility in at least one year since 2006, or a continuous variable expressing the percentage of years a country spent in fragile situations.

[16] See Fabra Mata and Ziaja (2009) for an overview of fragility indicators.

[17] The sample initially comprised 55 countries, but it has since been expanded several times, to 73 countries currently (see https://datacatalog.worldbank.org/dataset/country-policy-and-institutional-assessment).

[18] Note that an increase in the Country Policy and Institutional Assessment reflects a decline in fragility; therefore, a positive sign in table 6 implies that greater fragility is associated with underperformance.

over 10 percentage points in firms with credit and adults with accounts, and by close to 10 percentage points in the credit-GDP ratio as well, all increases over and above the effect of structural characteristics of the economies. The ratio of deposits to GDP is also increased by 2.5 percentage points.

To summarize, the analysis of this section shows that the findings of sections 2 and 3, financial underperformance of fragile states relative to the rest of the world, continue to be true after accounting for structural characteristics—such as a country's income level—that are certain to affect financial development as well. Not only do fragile states tend to underperform compared to similar peer countries, the degree of underperformance is associated with the degree of fragility. Furthermore, the analysis highlights the importance of policies for social inclusion and equity, which tend to have the clearest impact on both financial depth and financial inclusion. That said, it is also critical to recognize the heterogeneity within the fragile states, with some countries actually overperforming in relation to their structural benchmarks. This evidence suggests that although fragility tends to be associated with lower financial performance, the circumstances leading to fragility may not affect financial markets or institutions uniformly.

5. Growth Costs of Financial Underdevelopment in Fragile States

The previous sections showed that many fragile states underperform on various measures on financial development relative to world medians and even relative to levels that would be expected of countries sharing their structural characteristics that play a key role in either permitting or impeding financial activity. Drawing on recent studies estimating long-term growth regressions that have used some of the financial indicators examined here as explanatory variables, it is possible to calculate potential growth costs of financial underdevelopment in fragile states. This section conducts two such exercises, one relating to private credit-GDP and another using the comprehensive financial development index *FD*.

On private credit-GDP, Arcand et al. (2015) estimate a nonlinear impact of finance on long-term growth, very strong at low initial levels of financial depth, but weakening as depth increases, and eventually becoming negative for countries with the highest levels of depth, generally above 100 percent of GDP. As of 2015, Lebanon at about 94 percent of GDP was the only fragile state approaching this level; all others could presumably benefit from higher growth by increasing their financial depth. The estimation of growth costs uses the Arcand et al. (2015) coefficients to estimate additional annual real GDP growth rates that could be obtained by increasing private credit-GDP either to match the country's structural benchmark or to reach the world median level of 44.6 percent.

Table 7.7 Estimated Growth Costs of Financial Underdevelopment: Private Credit–GDP

Estimated coefficients[1]				**World median**				
Linear term	**3.628**			**Value:**	**0.446**			
Square term	**–2.021**			**Growth impact:**	**1.2160788**			
	Growth costs, relative to:		Gaps with respect to:		Private credit-GDP		Estimated Growth Impact	
	Benchmark	World Median	Benchmark	World Median	Observed	Benchmark	Observed	Benchmark
	(Percentage points of annual growth in real per capita GDP)							
	(1)	(2)	(3)	(4)	(5)	(6)	(7)	(8)
Angola	0.043	0.705	–0.014	–0.292	0.154	0.168	0.511	0.553
Cameroon	0.022	0.689	–0.008	–0.287	0.159	0.167	0.527	0.550
Congo, Dem. Rep.	0.251	1.033	–0.077	–0.394	0.052	0.129	0.183	0.434
Eritrea	0.165	0.812	–0.054	–0.327	0.119	0.173	0.404	0.569
Micronesia, Fed. Sts.	0.098	0.426	–0.039	–0.192	0.254	0.292	0.790	0.888
Guinea	0.297	0.891	–0.097	–0.351	0.095	0.192	0.325	0.622
Gambia, The	0.279	1.023	–0.086	–0.391	0.055	0.141	0.193	0.473
Guinea-Bissau	0.134	0.799	–0.044	–0.323	0.123	0.168	0.417	0.551
Haiti	0.263	0.662	–0.096	–0.277	0.169	0.264	0.554	0.817
Madagascar	0.109	0.763	–0.036	–0.311	0.135	0.171	0.453	0.562
Central African Republic	0.017	0.818	–0.005	–0.329	0.117	0.123	0.398	0.415
Myanmar	0.193	0.461	–0.077	–0.206	0.240	0.318	0.755	0.948
Mauritania	0.585	1.115	–0.186	–0.418	0.028	0.215	0.101	0.686
Malawi	0.113	0.860	–0.036	–0.342	0.104	0.140	0.356	0.469
Nigeria	0.140	0.743	–0.047	–0.304	0.142	0.189	0.473	0.613
Libya	0.199	0.382	–0.084	–0.175	0.271	0.355	0.834	1.033
Papua New Guinea	0.359	0.688	–0.132	–0.286	0.160	0.292	0.528	0.887

Sudan	0.309	0.901	−0.101	−0.354	0.092	0.193	0.315	0.624
Sierra Leone	0.344	1.034	−0.107	−0.394	0.052	0.159	0.182	0.526
Sao Tome and Principe	0.575	1.215	−0.176	−0.446	0.000	0.176	0.001	0.576
Chad	0.118	0.881	−0.037	−0.348	0.098	0.135	0.335	0.454
Timor-Leste	0.414	0.936	−0.137	−0.365	0.081	0.218	0.280	0.694
Yemen, Rep.	0.350	1.018	−0.110	−0.390	0.056	0.166	0.198	0.548

[1] Taken from Arcand, Berkes, and Panizza (2015). Corresponds to the results of the panel data regressions reported in their Table 5, Column 4 and used to show the marginal effect of finance on growth in their Figure 4.

This table shows the fragile states that underperform on private credit-GDP relative to their structural benchmark, and calculates the estimated impact on average per capita real GDP growth derived from the gap relative to the benchmark (Column 1) and relative to the world median (Column 2). The respective gaps relative to the benchmark and to the world median are shown in Columns 3 and 4. Columns 5 and 6 show the observed and bechmark levels or private credit-GDP, and columns 7 and 8 show the estimated growth impact, evaluated at the observed and benchmark levels, respectively.

Source: Finstats 2019, Global Financial Development Database and authors' calculations.

Table 7.7 summarizes the results for the 23 fragile states found to underperform relative to their structural benchmark. Some countries—Angola and Cameroon, in particular—are very close to their benchmark, and for these the estimated impact of falling short is relatively small. However, all could boost their per capita real growth rates substantially—by between 0.6 and 1.2 percentage points per year—by achieving the world median. Finally, although the growth impacts stemming from underperformance relative to the benchmark may seem small, when accumulated over an extended period they can make a notable difference in income per capita, up to 12 percent over two decades. Combined with the finding in section 2 that fragile states appear to have been falling behind in financial development over the past two decades, a continuation of this trend would increase the potential growth costs.

A second exercise repeats the analysis for the overall financial development indicator, *FD*. It uses coefficient estimates from Sahay and others (2015b), who find a similar nonlinear relationship between growth and *FD*. As there is no

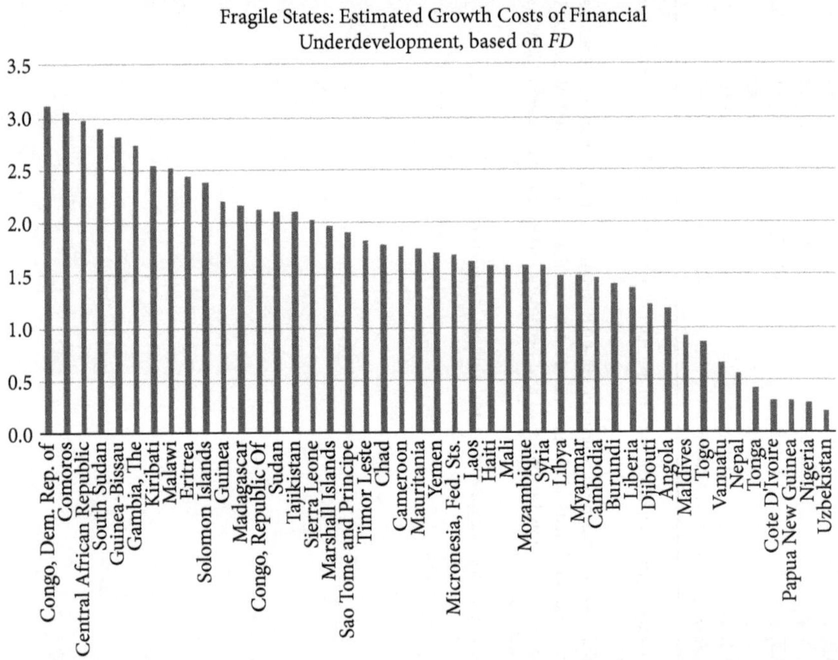

Figure 7.5 Fragile States Estimated Growth Costs of Financial Underdevelopment, based on FD.

This figure shows the fragile states that underperform on the overall financial development index FD relative to world median, and calculates the estimated impact on average per capita real GDP growth derived from the gap relative to the median. The estimated growth impact is calculated using coefficients from panel data growth regressions reported by Sahay and others (2015), Table B.1, Column 1.

Source: IMF Financial Development Database, and authors' calculations.

corresponding benchmarking of *FD*, the comparison is done for each country relative to the 2016 world median of 0.26. Figure 7.5 shows the results for all 45 fragile states falling short of this level. In general, the estimated impacts tend to be greater using this measure, primarily because the observed gaps relative to the rest of the world are greater than in individual depth measures such as private credit-GDP. Many countries could increase per capita GDP growth by up to 2 percentage points per year, but presumably there is a much greater challenge in reaching the world median in overall development than in depth alone.

6. Conclusions and Recommendations

This chapter has provided a description of the current state of financial development of fragile states, based on the best available methods of measurement. In general, we find that financial markets in fragile states are markedly underdeveloped, and financial inclusion is low, relative to both the full sample of countries and relative to other low- and middle-income countries. This is particularly true of equity markets. Indeed, we believe that this chapter establishes the financial underdevelopment of fragile states as an important stylized fact. An equally important stylized fact revealed by our benchmarking and regression exercise is that fragility is negatively related to financial performance, in terms of development and especially in terms of inclusion. We have also used benchmarking methods to estimate how much the underdevelopment of financial markets in fragile states is costing them, in terms of economic growth.

In contrast to our main conclusion, however, we also find that there are several examples of financial markets in some fragile states which are more highly developed or have achieved higher financial inclusion than their peers. This heterogeneity of financial development among fragile states may seem somewhat surprising at first, but we argue that this reflects the diversity within fragility itself. Fragility is associated with many different circumstances and contexts, and each fragile state has its own history that makes its case distinctive.

Although this chapter has focused on description, this is the first step in revealing interesting questions for future research into financial development in fragile states. Establishing the main stylized facts mentioned above—the very low level of financial development in fragile states, and the negative relationship between fragility and financial performance—naturally prompts a search for explanations. Thus, one of the first tasks for future research is to investigate why financial markets tend to be significantly underdeveloped in fragile states. Embedded within this task is the challenge of estimating causality between financial development and country fragility. Do underdeveloped financial markets contribute significantly to fragility, or does fragility retard or perhaps even reverse financial development? Describing and measuring the various pathways through which financial (under-)development and country fragility affect each other should be high on the research agenda, especially given the observations in the introduction of this chapter regarding the role of finance in economic development and poverty alleviation.

For example, one possible pathway that could explain the lack of financial development in fragile states has been suggested by Barajas et al. (2013). These authors show that an excessive level of government involvement in the financial sector—usually in the banking industry, since many countries' financial systems are bank dominated—leads to financial underdevelopment. A review of the extant data on government ownership of banking system assets does show significant government involvement in the banking systems of fragile states. Although 28 fragile states do not have data, of the remaining 26 fragile countries where such data is available, 19 of them report that at least 5 percent of all banking system assets are held in institutions that are majority government-owned or government-controlled. Twelve countries report that at least 10 percent of banking system assets are in government-owned or government-controlled banks, and in seven countries, the share of assets is at least 20 percent. In addition, the finding in section 4 that fragility seems to be positively related to the bank deposits-GDP ratio could be an indicator of a greater degree of financial repression in fragile states. These data suggest that the link between government ownership of banks, financial underdevelopment, and fragility is worth looking into.

Another potential source of insight into the relationship between fragility and financial development is the set of exceptions or outliers discovered in this chapter: countries that are fragile yet have at least one relatively developed financial market. The specific stories behind each of these exceptions could reveal much about the interaction between fragility and financial development. For example, a fragile country's (relatively) developed financial market could be a legacy from a time before the country was fragile. This may describe the story of a country such as Lebanon. If this is the case, then the country's financial history could inform us about how fragility affects a developed financial market, from which we can also make inferences about how fragility affects nascent markets. And a case in which a financial market developed in spite of—or perhaps even more interesting, because of—country fragility would also be richly informative. Thus, learning from the exceptions uncovered in this chapter should also be high on the research agenda.

Finally, information problems are also likely to be a major cause of financial underdevelopment in fragile states. Asymmetric information problems, in which one potential party to a contract has an informational advantage over the other potential party, can prevent successful contracting and hence limit financial development of all types. But lack of information also includes situations of risk and uncertainty, in which any potential party to a financial contract lacks sufficient information about potential costs and benefits of a financial relationship to be willing to make financial commitments. In environments with asymmetric information and high uncertainty, opportunities to save and invest are limited, or have prohibitively high transactions costs. In addition, this environment discourages the trust that is essential to successful contracting, and increases risk aversion as well. As a result, new financial products and institutions are difficult to launch, and people restrict their financial participation to the informal financial sector.

Although every country faces information problems that restrict the development of their financial markets, fragile states are likely to be afflicted with particularly severe information problems that make financial development especially challenging. Indeed, FSD Africa and Mercy Corps (2017) argues that asymmetric information problems are themselves a source of fragility. The other drivers of fragility, such as conflict, are also significant sources of uncertainty that are specific to fragile states. Thus, finding effective ways to combat the information problems should also be a priority of future research. In particular, finding a way to determine which sources and types of information problems must be mitigated first in fragile states, and which ones can be dealt with later, would itself be a significant contribution to our understanding of financial development in fragile states.

In addition to enhancing our overall understanding of the causes and consequences of fragility, the study of financial development in fragile states will pay significant dividends for at least one other important area of research as well. In the introduction of this chapter, we raised the issue that fragile states are likely to lack many of the key ingredients or preconditions thought to be necessary for financial market development. Because of this, fragile states may turn out to be important laboratories or proving grounds for financial development policy ideas. Fragile states are likely to be some of the least hospitable environments for financial development. Therefore, if researchers can find effective methods to promote financial development in fragile states, these methods may prove to be successful in nonfragile contexts also.

References

Arcand, J-L., E. Berkes, and U. Panizza. 2015. "Too Much Finance." *Journal of Economic Growth*, 20(2): 105–48.

Barajas, A., R. Chami, and R. Yousefi. 2013. "The Finance and Growth Nexus Re-examined: Do All Countries Benefit Equally?" IMF Working Paper 13–130. Washington, DC: International Monetary Fund.

Beck, T., A. Demirgüç-Kunt, and R. Levine. 2007. "Finance, Inequality and the Poor." *Journal of Economic Growth*, 12(1): 27–49. https://doi.org/10.1007/s10887-007-9010-6 (last accessed July 16, 2020).

Beck, T., A. Demirgüç-Kunt, R. Levine, and V. Maksimovic. 2000. "Financial Structure and Economic Development: Firm, Industry, and Country Evidence." World Bank Policy Research Paper no. WPS 2423. World Bank, Washington, DC. http://documents.worldbank.org/curated/en/955641468761673605/Financial-structure-and-economic-development-firm-industry-and-country-evidence (last accessed July 16, 2020).

Demirgüç-Kunt, A., L. Klapper, D. Singer, S. Ansar, and J. Hess. 2018. *The Global Findex Database 2017: Measuring Financial Inclusion and the Fintech Revolution.* Washington, DC: World Bank.

Fabra Mata, J. and S. Ziaja. 2009. *User's Guide on Measuring Fragility.* Bonn, Germany: United Nations Development Programme.

Feyen, E., K. Kibuuka, and D. Sourrouille. 2019. "Finstats 2019: A Ready-to-use Tool to Benchmark Financial Systems across Countries and over Time," World Bank, Finance and Markets Global Practice. Washington, DC.

FSD Africa and Mercy Corps. 2017. "Financing the Frontier: Inclusive Financial Sector Development in Fragility-Affected States in Africa," https://responsiblefinanceforum.org/wp-content/uploads/2017/04/Financing-the-Frontier-Inclusive-Financial-Sector-Development-in-Fragility-Affected-States-in-Africa.pdf (last accessed July 16, 2020).

Levine, R. 2005. "Finance and Growth: Theory and Evidence," in Philippe Aghion and Steven Durlauf (Eds.), *Handbook of Economic Growth.* Amsterdam: Elsevier.

Sahay, R., M. Čihák, P. N'Diaye, A. Barajas, R. Bi, D. Ayala, et al. 2015a. "Rethinking Financial Deepening: Stability and Growth in Emerging Markets," Staff Discussion Note 15/08. Washington, DC: International Monetary Fund.

Sahay, R., M. Čihák, P. N'Diaye, A. Barajas, S. Mitra, A. Kyobe, et al. 2015b. "Financial Inclusion: Can it Meet Multiple Macroeconomic Goals?" Staff Discussion Note 15/17. Washington, DC: International Monetary Fund.

Svirydzenka, K. 2016. "Introducing a New Broad-Based Index of Financial Development," IMF Working Paper 16/05. Washington, DC: International Monetary Fund.

8

The Challenge of Macroeconomic Stabilization in Fragile States

Ralph Chami, Thomas F. Cosimano, Raphael Espinoza, and Peter Montiel

1. Introduction

State fragility is an important obstacle to development. Not only are the lives of populations that are exposed to conflict dramatically altered, but violence, the risk of conflict, and the lack of capacity and legitimacy of the state also change the incentives and the ability of private and public actors to plan ahead. Such planning is indispensable for societies seeking to enter the narrow path of development.

There are several possible definitions of state fragility, as witnessed by the different contributions in this volume. In this chapter, we focus on state fragility understood as the government's vulnerability to failure—defined as a situation of state collapse in which the government is unable to deliver a broad range of public goods that contribute to economic wellbeing, typically as the result of social conflict. Such vulnerability constrains the choices that governments in fragile states make with respect to a broad range of policies: governments fear that policy changes can trigger loss of support, political instability, and eventually state failure. In particular, state fragility can thus lead to a reluctance on the part of policymakers to undertake policies that would benefit the economy as a whole but would distribute benefits unequally or would impose costs on some specific segments of society.

Macroeconomic stabilization is an example of policies of this type. Stabilization is welfare-enhancing for society as a whole both directly, by reducing the uncertainty and risks that are associated with an unstable macroeconomic environment, as well as indirectly, by facilitating activities that contribute to promoting growth. Yet stabilization often requires an unequal sharing of burdens and/or

We are grateful for comments from and helpful discussions with Christopher Adam, Paul Collier, Dominique Desruelle, Mark Griffith, Raimundo Soto, and from the participants at the Oxford Workshop on Macroeconomic Policy in Fragile States. The views expressed in this chapter are those of the authors and do not necessarily represent the views of the IMF, its Executive Board, or IMF management.

Ralph Chami, Thomas F. Cosimano, Raphael Espinoza, and Peter Montiel, *The Challenge of Macroeconomic Stabilization in Fragile States* In: *Macroeconomic Policy in Fragile States.* Edited by: Ralph Chami, Raphael Espinoza, and Peter Montiel, Oxford University Press (2021).
DOI: 10.1093/oso/9780198853091.003.0008

the imposition of costs on some groups.[1] While a reluctance to impose such costs in a fragile context creates an effect of fragility on macroeconomic policy choices, causation between fragility and macroeconomic policymaking can also run in the opposite direction: poor macroeconomic policy choices may ultimately generate state fragility by creating economic conditions under which relatively small adverse shocks to the economy can give rise to concentrated economic hardships, which then provide the trigger for social strife and state failure.

In this chapter we explore the potential interactions between state fragility and macroeconomic policy. Our objective is to investigate how objective economic circumstances may interact with distortions in policy formulation to create a path toward state fragility, and how state fragility may in turn affect subsequent macroeconomic policy.

We develop a standard open economy of a dependent-economy (as in Khan and Montiel, 1987; Devarajan and Go, 1998) intended to represent a macroeconomic environment that is likely to be characteristic of low-income countries with the potential to become fragile states, and we allow macroeconomic policies to be determined endogenously in the model as the outcome of a policymaker maximization problem. Our framework seeks to capture certain features of the economy that tend to be common across countries commonly considered to be in fragile circumstances:

- On the supply side, the economy is comprised of three sectors. The first sector specializes in the production of exports (including primary commodities). It is assumed this sector uses domestic labor and capital as inputs. The export sector provides an important source of government revenue but the rest of the economy constitutes the larger home goods sector, which in practice may represent a large urban informal sector as well as subsistence agriculture. A persistent wage gap between the two sectors contributes to income inequality. It has it source in a friction preventing the efficient allocation of labor across sectors. The third sector produces public goods with the labor of public servants. This sector provides scope for employees in the public sector to collect rents as well as for the public sector to engage in featherbedding, that is, hiring workers for purely political reasons who do not meaningfully contribute to public sector output.
- On the demand side of the economy we consider the separate roles of the government, the central bank, and the private sector. We assume that fragility increases sovereign risk to such an extent that the government is unable to borrow domestically and is effectively shut out of international private financial markets. It can, however, receive grants and concessional

[1] This has given rise to a literature that interprets macroeconomic outcomes as the result of "wars of attrition" among competing groups.

funding from official sources. The authorities in charge of the government budget use those resources as well as taxes levied on both sectors to produce public goods that increase the wellbeing of the private sector, but they also divert some of them for their own consumption. The central bank in this economy is not independent: the policy levers it manages are controlled by the finance ministry. The central bank issues base money to purchase foreign exchange and extend credit to the government. Because it is subservient to the finance ministry, the bank simply supplies the credit demanded by the government. Its management of reserves depends on the foreign exchange regime implemented in the country. We assume that the regime consists of a managed float,[2] because the central bank lacks the resources to implement an official peg (Adam and Wilson in this volume analyze in detail how monetary and exchange rate arrangements tend to evolve in fragile states, as a function of conflict and fiscal capacity in particular).

- The private sector earns labor income, as well as the after-tax profits generated by the export sector and any profits generated by the home goods sector. Because the sector is opaque from the perspective of foreign creditors, like the government it does not have access to the private international financial market. It holds domestic liquid assets to facilitate its conduct of transactions as well as to save for a rainy day (there is no currency substitution possible).

We develop our fragile-state framework in two steps:

First, we explore the implications of this hypothesized structure of the economy for the behavior of macro variables over time, conditioned on exogenously chosen and permanent values of policy variables. The equilibrium of the model is analyzed using its representation in terms of Internal Balance—External Balance; see also Montiel (1999).

In a second step we endogenize the choice of policy variables, taking into account that an important element of fragility is that such choices are affected by both the likelihood of state failure and the objective of the policymaker in increasing her own consumption. To analyze the role of such political distortions, we solve the model under the objectives of three different policymakers: the political policymaker, the technocratic policymaker, and the social planner.

[2] Fragile states are heterogeneous with respect to their exchange rate arrangements. Using the World Bank's classification of fragile states, 9 of 34 countries whose exchange rate regimes were classified according to the IMF's 2016 Annual Report on Exchange Rate Arrangements and Exchange Restrictions maintained a floating exchange rate. Of the remainder, eight belonged to currency unions, six maintained dual exchange rate regimes, six were dollarized, three maintained crawling pegs, one operated a conventional peg, and one operated a currency board. We adopt the modal regime here.

More precisely, the model is solved under three objective functions, reflecting three different institutional setups:

(i) A "political" policymaker who takes the risks of failure into account (because she expects to bear at least some of its costs), who has a shorter policy horizon than desirable and who puts excessive weight on public goods (perhaps as a way of distributing resources to members of favored groups);
(ii) A "technocratic" policymaker, who maximizes intertemporal utility of the representative agent with the correct discount rate as well as the correct social value of public goods, but doesn't understand the risk of failure and thus does not treat fragile situations differently from any macroeconomic program.
(iii) The "social planner," who understands the risk of failure and places a high weight (in proportion of the cost of failure) to avoiding state failure. The social planner also understands what drives the risk of failure, uses the appropriate social discount rate and the correct social value of public goods, and chooses policy accordingly.

The model assumes that the probability of state failure is a function of the government's capacity to deliver favors through public employment, as well as of the economic situation as summarized by the rate of inflation. The cost of state failure is an exogenous parameter. Where this cost is large enough, a social planner would choose policies intended to avoid failure altogether (see UN-World Bank, 2018, for a discussion of large benefits of conflict prevention). More generally, however, the costs of failure imply that the probability of failure will influence the policy choices made by a social planner.

The rest of the chapter is organized as follows: Section 2 presents our macroeconomic model. Section 3 interprets the model in terms of an internal balance-external balance equilibrium; Section 4 clarifies the model dynamics; and Section 5 shows some comparative static results on its long-term equilibrium. Section 6 is the heart of our analysis. It explains how the model accounts for different policymaking objectives, explains how it is solved, and discusses its results. Section 7 concludes on the policy implications.

2. The Model

2.1 Production Structure

There are three private goods in the model: an exportable good; an importable good; and a nontraded, or "home" good. The domestic economy produces the exportable and home goods, but there is no domestic production of importables. Production of exportables and home goods uses capital and labor, and is subject to a multiplicative TFP shock. There is a fixed capital stock in both the exportables and home goods sectors, so labor is the only variable factor of production and is therefore subject to diminishing marginal productivity:

$$y_x = A_x X(K_x, L_x), \text{ with } K_x \text{ fixed and } X_2 > 0, X_{22} < 0 \tag{1a}$$

$$y_h = A_h H(K_h, L_h), \text{ with } K_h \text{ fixed and } H_2 > 0, H_{22} < 0 \tag{1b}$$

Labor is homogeneous, and the total supply of labor is exogenous.[3] The supply of labor available to the private sector is the total labor supply L net of labor employed by the public sector L_g:

$$L_h + L_x = L - L_g \tag{2}$$

The former is exogenous and the latter a policy variable. For reasons we do not model (for example, costs of migration from rural to urban areas), labor employed in the private sector cannot instantly reallocate itself between the two private production sectors. Because the sectoral reallocation of labor takes time, the nominal wage can differ between the two private production sectors in the short run. Over time, however, workers move from the low-wage private sector to the high-wage one, according to:

$$\dot{L}_x = -\dot{L}_h = \varphi(w_x - w_h) \tag{3}$$

with $\varphi(0) = 0$ and φ an increasing function, and where w_h and w_x are respectively the real wages (measured in terms of the consumer price index) in the home and in the exportable sectors. This restricted labor mobility will imply different wages in these two sectors until the reallocation process is completed.[4]

We assume that firms in the exportable and home goods sectors are always on their labor demand curves. This allows us to write the nominal wage in each sector as:

$$W_x = P_x A_x X_2(L_x) \tag{4a}$$

$$W_h = P_h A_h H_2(L_h) \tag{4b}$$

where P_x and P_h are respectively the domestic currency prices of the exportable and home goods. In the case of the former, we assume that the law of one price holds continuously for internationally traded goods, so $P_x = SP_x^*$, where S is the nominal exchange rate (units of domestic currency per unit of the foreign

[3] The number subscript on a function refers to a partial derivative. A letter subscript on a variable refers to the sector. A dot over a variable refers to a time derivative. A * superscript on a variable refers to the foreign country.

[4] This wage heterogeneity could also affect the transition probability from the fragile to the failed state because it provides a proxy for domestic inequality measures between workers in rural and urban areas. This is an area of research for the future.

currency) and P_x^* is the foreign currency price of the exportable good. We assume that the economy in question is small, and therefore faces exogenously-determined values of P_x^* and P_z^*, where z refers to the imported good. We denote the economy's terms of trade as $\rho = P_x^*/P_z^*$ and set $P_x^* = 1$, so $P_x^* = \rho$.

The government also engages in production. It hires L_g workers and uses them to produce goods G for its own consumption according to the production function:

$$C_g = G(L_g), \tag{5}$$

with $G_1 > 0$ and $G_{11} < 0$, where subscripts denote the variable to which the partial derivatives apply. To attract labor the government pays a real wage w_g, which it sets as a policy variable and which must satisfy $w_x > w_g > w_h$. Importantly, the government is not necessarily a profit maximizer, so this wage may be set such that $w_g > G'()$.

The government hires workers who would otherwise be employed in the home goods sector to produce goods for itself. As discussed below, the weight given to the government's own consumption in its objective function serves as an index of policymaker self-interest (e.g. through corruption) in our model.

2.2 Demand Side

2.2.1 The Government

The government pays interest at the nominal rate i on the credit D previously extended to it by the central bank. It collects as revenues a share t_x of total export sales, receives nominal transfers TR from the central bank, and nominal grants AID^* (denominated in foreign currency) from abroad.[5] The time path of this grant funding is assumed to be exogenous.[6] The effective share of export revenues that the government can capture depends on the official tax rate τ_x and the efficiency of its tax administration, which we capture through a shift parameter ω. Thus we can write:

$$t_x = t_x(\tau_x, \omega), \text{ with } t_{x,1}, t_{x,2} > 0.$$

Because the government is perceived as a high-risk debtor by foreign private creditors in the absence of tangible collateral, it faces an effectively infinite risk premium for borrowing from such creditors and is therefore unable to borrow from private international capital markets. There is no operative domestic bond

[5] Alternatively, the government may simply own the exportables sector. The modifications this would require in the equations that follow are described in footnotes 7 and 8.

[6] AID^* is meant to capture total resource transfers received by the public sector from abroad. Thus, it can be interpreted as including disbursements of new concessional loans in excess of debt service due on previous concessional borrowing.

market, so the government also cannot issue bonds to the domestic private sector. It can therefore finance deficits only by borrowing from the central bank. Its flow budget constraint is given by:

$$\dot{D} = P\ w_g L_g + iD - t_x S p y_x - TR - SAID^* \tag{6}$$

where $\dot{D}$ is the rate of increase of nominal central bank credit to the government, and P is the domestic consumer price index.[7]

2.2.2 The Central Bank

The economy possesses its own currency, issued by a central bank. There is no domestic banking system. The central bank prints the domestic currency to acquire foreign exchange reserves and to provide financing to the government. Decisions about the scale of such financing are made by the finance ministry, not the central bank itself; that is, the central bank is not independent. The bank's balance sheet is given by:

$$M = SF^* + D, \tag{7}$$

where F^* is the foreign-currency value of the central bank's stock of foreign exchange reserves. We impose a non-negativity constraint on reserves, so $F^* \geq 0$. The rate of growth of the money supply is therefore:

$$\dot{M} = S\dot{F}^* + \dot{S}F^* + \dot{D}, \tag{8}$$

Note that $\dot{F}^*$ can be negative as long as the non-negativity constraint on the stock of reserves is respected. The central bank's balance sheet in equation (7) embeds the assumption that the central bank has no net worth, so it must transfer its profits, plus any capital gains on its reserve holdings, to the central government. These transfers can therefore be written as:

$$TR = i^* SF^* + iD, \tag{9}$$

where i^* is the interest rate that the central bank can earn on its foreign exchange reserves.

2.2.3 The Consolidated Public Sector

To consolidate the public sector (that is, to merge the accounts of the government with those of the central bank), substitute equations (8) and (9) into the government's budget constraint (6). These operations yield:

[7] If the government owns the export sector the term $t_x S p y_x$ would be replaced by $S p y_x - P\ w_x L_x$.

$$\dot{M} = Pw_gL_g + S\dot{F}^* - t_xSpy_x - i^*SF^* - SAID^*, \tag{10}$$

Intuitively, the consolidated public sector spends on hiring labor to produce public goods and on the accumulation of assets in the form of foreign exchange reserves. The resources it has available for these purposes consist of tax revenues, interest on central bank reserves, and foreign grants. The excess of spending over these revenues is financed by printing money.

2.2.4 The Private Sector

The private sector owns the firms that produce exportable and home goods (as mentioned before, we can allow the government to own the exportable sector in a fairly straightforward manner). On the financial side, the private sector is opaque to foreign private creditors; therefore, like the government, it cannot borrow in private international financial markets. It can, however, acquire financial claims on the rest of the world, but only by accumulating foreign currency; it cannot acquire foreign interest-bearing assets. The private sector owns no interest-bearing assets, its nominal disposable factor income is therefore given by:[8]

$$Y = (1 - t_x)Spy_x + P_hy_h + Pw_gL_g.^8 \tag{11}$$

The private sector derives utility from consuming importable and home goods:

$$U = U(C_z,\ C_h), U_1, U_2 > 0, \tag{12}$$

where C_z and C_h denote private consumption of importable and home goods respectively. We assume that utility from consumption of private goods is Cobb-Douglas in the two types of private good consumption, with expenditure shares θ and $1 - \theta$ respectively for importable and home goods. The consumer price index (CPI) therefore becomes:

$$P = S^\theta P_n^{1-\theta}, \tag{13}$$

where P_z, the domestic currency price of importables, is equal to SP_Z^*, and where without loss of generality we have set $P_Z^* = 1$. Letting real private consumption measured in units of the consumption bundle be denoted C, private demand for importable and home goods is therefore given by:

$$C_z = \theta CP/S \tag{14a}$$

$$C_h = (1 - \theta)CP/P_h \tag{14b}$$

[8] If the government owns the export sector the term $(1 - t_x)Spy_x$ would be replaced by Pw_xL_x.

To spend on consumption, the private sector must incur transaction costs. In analogy with "shoe-leather costs," we assume that those costs are borne in the form of home goods. We assume that transaction costs per unit of consumption are decreasing in the ratio of liquid assets to total consumption. Letting transaction costs per unit of consumption be denoted by *t*, total transaction costs can therefore be expressed by the function:

$$t = t(M/P)C \text{ with } t_1 < 0 \text{ and } t_{11} > 0, \tag{15}$$

where *M/P* represents the real value (in units of the consumption bundle) of the (as yet unspecified) liquid assets held by the private sector. The assumption is that larger holdings of liquidity per unit of transactions reduce transaction costs, but they do so at a decreasing rate as the ratio of liquid assets to spending increases. The private sector acquires liquid assets by saving. Its nominal budget constraint is therefore given by:

$$\dot{M} = Y - Pt(M/P/C)C - PC, \tag{16a}$$

The left-hand side of this equation represents nominal liquid asset accumulation and the right-hand side is nominal saving (we will consider how *C* is determined below). After taking into account that the private sector optimizes its demand for liquidity by trading off the shoe-leather costs with the opportunity cost of holding money, the real (flow) demand for money is

$$\dot{M}/P = Y/P - \left(1 + t\left(h(\pi)\right) + \pi h(\pi)\right)C. \tag{16b}$$

Notice that inflation thus reduces the real income of the private sector through two channels: by inducing the sector to economize on its holding of liquidity, it increases the transaction costs $t\left(h(\pi)\right)$ associated with private consumption. In addition, it forces the private sector to incur an inflation tax $\pi h(\pi)$.

3. Internal and External Balance

Equilibrium in this model requires that the market for home goods clears. Because only the domestic private sector buys such goods, the equilibrium condition in this market is given in nominal terms by:

$$P_h y_h(L_h) = [1 - \theta + t\left(h(\pi)\right)]CP \tag{17}$$

It will be useful to define an "importables real exchange rate" as $e = \frac{S}{Ph}$. In this case, using (13), the relative price of the consumption bundle in terms of importables is given by $P/S = e^{\theta-1}$, and in terms of home goods by $P/P_h = e^{\theta}$. We can therefore write equation (17) in units of home goods as:

$$y_h(L_h) = [1 - \theta + t\Big(h(\pi)\Big)]Ce^{\theta} \tag{17a}$$

This is the economy's "internal balance" condition. For a given value of π, it establishes a *negative* relationship between real consumption and the real exchange rate—that is, an increase in real consumption increases the demand for home goods, and given the short-term fixed supply of such goods, this requires a decrease in e—an appreciation of the real exchange rate—to clear the market for home goods. The relationship between the real exchange rate and real consumption in home goods market equilibrium is given by:

$$e = \left[\frac{y_h(L_x)}{[1 - \theta + t\Big(h(\pi)\Big)]C}\right]^{1/\theta} \tag{18}$$

This relationship is depicted as the curve IB in Figure 8.1. Its slope is:

$$\frac{de}{dC} = -\frac{e}{\theta C} < 0.$$

We derive the corresponding "external balance" condition, in foreign currency units, by summing the budget constraints of the public and private sectors (10) and (16a)—see Annex for details:

$$\dot{F}^{*} = \rho y_x(L_x) - (\theta Ce^{\theta-1}) + i^{*}F^{*} + AID^{*}.$$

This equation sets the current account surplus, given by the right-hand side of the equation, equal to the rate of reserve accumulation. Under a unified floating exchange rate, this rate of reserve accumulation is an exogenous policy variable. It is convenient to rewrite this equation as:

$$\Omega_0 = \rho y_x(L_x) - \theta Ce^{\theta-1},$$

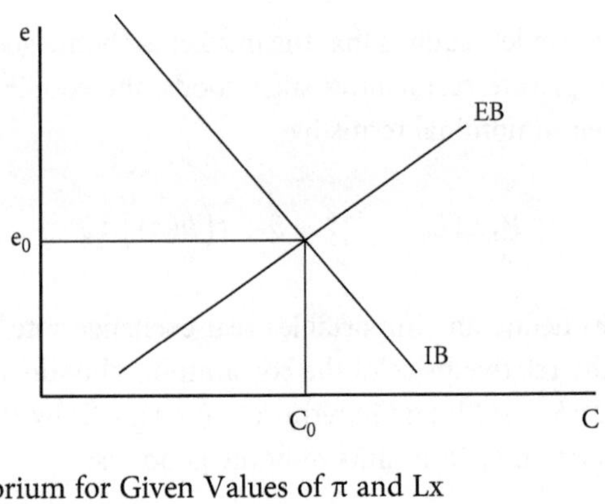

Figure 8.1 Equilibrium for Given Values of π and Lx

where $\Omega_0 = \dot{F}^{\star} - (i^{\star}F^{\star} + AID^{\star})$ captures the joint effect on the external balance condition of all of the exogenous variables in the equation above. The external balance relationship between the real exchange rate and consumption is given by:

$$e = \left[\frac{\theta C}{\rho y_x(L_x) - \Omega_0}\right]^{\frac{1}{1-\theta}} \tag{19}$$

Its slope in *(e, C)* space is given by:

$$\frac{de}{dC} = \frac{1}{1-\theta}\left(\frac{e}{C}\right) > 0$$

Since $0 < \theta < 1$, this equation yields a *positive* relationship for the external balance between C and e in *(e, C)* space, as shown by the curve EB in Figure 8.1.

Equations (18) and (19) can be solved for equilibrium values of e and C, conditional on π, L_x, and the exogenous variables in the model. The equilibrium real exchange rate is given by:

$$e^{*} = \frac{y_h(L - L_g - L_x)\theta}{\left[\left[1-\theta + t\left(h(\pi)\right)\right]\left[\rho y_x + i^{*}F^{*} + AID^{*} - \dot{F}^{*}\right]\right]}. \tag{20a}$$

with:

$$\frac{1}{e}\frac{\partial e}{\partial L_x} = \ < 0$$

$$and\ \frac{1}{e}\frac{\partial e}{\partial \pi} = \frac{-1}{\left[1-\theta + t\left(h(\pi)\right)\right]}\frac{\partial t}{\partial \pi} < 0$$

That is, the equilibrium real exchange rate appreciates as labor is allocated to the export sector and away from the home goods sector, essentially because this reallocation reduces the supply of home goods, therefore raising their relative price. An increase in the inflation rate causes an equilibrium real appreciation through a similar mechanism: because higher inflation increases transaction costs, and such costs are incurred in the form of home goods, higher inflation reduces the supply of such goods and causes their relative price to increase. We also have:

$$\frac{\partial \frac{1}{e}\frac{\partial e}{\partial \pi}}{\partial \pi} = \frac{1}{\left[1-\theta + t\left(h(\pi)\right)\right]^2}\left[\frac{\partial t}{\partial \pi}\right]^2 - \frac{1}{\left[1-\theta + t\left(h(\pi)\right)\right]}\frac{\partial^2 t}{\partial \pi^2} > 0$$

The equilibrium level of consumption, in turn, is:

$$C^* = \frac{y_h[e^*]^{-\theta}}{\left[1-\theta + t\left(h(\pi)\right)\right]}. \tag{20b}$$

with:

$$\frac{1}{C}\frac{\partial C}{\partial L_x} = -\left[\frac{y_h'(L_x)}{y_h(L_x)}L_x + \theta\frac{de}{dL_x}\frac{L_x}{e}\right]L_x^{-1}$$

and:

$$\frac{1}{C}\frac{\partial C}{\partial \pi} = -\frac{1}{\left[1-\theta + t\left(h(\pi)\right)\right]}\frac{\partial t}{\partial \pi} - \theta\,\frac{1}{e}\frac{\partial e}{\partial \pi} < 0$$

The effect of labor reallocation to the exportables sector on real consumption depends on whether such reallocation increases or decreases the value of home goods production measured in units of the consumption bundle (the numerator of equation 20a). Holding the inflation rate constant, labor reallocation into exportable goods production has an ambiguous effect on real consumption. Holding the real exchange rate constant, shifting more labor into exportables production means removing labor from home goods production and therefore reducing the supply of home goods, requiring a reduction in real consumption to maintain equilibrium in the home goods market. However, this labor reallocation causes an appreciation of the real exchange rate, as shown above, which increases the relative price of the home good in terms of the consumption bundle, thereby making an increase in real consumption compatible with home goods market equilibrium.

An increase in the inflation rate affects real consumption through two channels: first, because it increases transaction costs, it reduces the supply of home goods, requiring a decrease in consumption to create a matching decrease in the demand for such goods. On the other hand, the real appreciation caused by higher inflation makes home goods relatively more expensive, and with constant expenditure shares in consumption, that means that each unit of real consumption generates a smaller demand for home goods. The latter means that an *increase* in real consumption would be required to sustain equilibrium in the home goods market. However, because the "crowding out" effect of higher transaction costs on real consumption is one-for-one, while the relative price effect is less than one-for-one, the former dominates, and higher inflation therefore reduces real consumption.

4. Dynamics

Because labor re-allocation across sectors is imperfect, employment in the export sector is a state variable. In addition, the model dynamics also require tracking the level of inflation. The two dynamic equations of the model are:

$$\dot{L}_x = \varphi[\rho\alpha_x Ax(L_x)^{\alpha_{x-1}} e(\pi, L_x) - \alpha_h A_h(L - L_g - L_x)^{\alpha_{h-1}}]e^{-\theta}(\pi, L_x). \tag{21}$$

where the wage differential has been replaced by the difference in labor productivities across sector; and

$$\dot{\pi} = \left[\frac{\partial h}{\partial \pi} C^* + h(\pi)\frac{d\,C^*}{d\pi}\right]^{-1}\left[w_g L_g + \left(\Omega_0 - t_x\rho y_x(L_x)\right)e^{1-\theta}(\pi, L_x) - \pi h(\pi)C^* - h(\pi)\frac{d\,C^*}{dL_x}\dot{L}_x\right]. \tag{22}$$

which represents the dynamics of the domestic inflation rate. This condition states that the inflation rate will increase when the public sector budget deficit

$$def = w_g L_g + (\Omega_0 - t_x\rho y_x(L_x))e^{1-\theta}$$

exceeds the amount that can be financed at the current inflation rate by the inflation tax $\pi\, h(\pi)C^*$ plus seigniorage created by the increase in real money demand (occurring when consumption changes because of labor reallocation: $h(\pi)\frac{dC^*}{dL_x}\dot{L}_x$.)

The phase diagram of the model near the steady state is shown in Figure 8.2 (see Annex for the derivations). Intuitively, the condition $\dot{L}_x = 0$ is the equilibrium condition that wages be equalized in the home and export sectors. Inflation affects

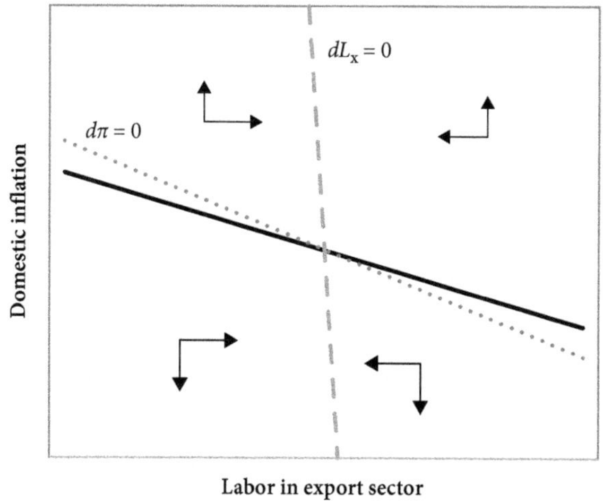

Figure 8.2 Phase Diagram Near the Steady State

the labor market because of the shoe-leather costs of inflation: when inflation increases, transaction costs increase. Because these costs are borne in the form of home goods, the internal balance schedule shifts to the left as shoe-leather transaction costs reduce the "effective" supply of home goods. As a result, the real exchange rate appreciates for a given level of real consumption (equation 20a). To maintain equilibrium in the home goods market, the real exchange rate has to appreciate to stimulate home goods production and reduce home goods consumption. The appreciation of the real exchange rate stimulates home goods production by shifting labor from the export sector to the home sector. Thus, the relationship between inflation and labor is downward sloping (dotted locus in Figure 8.2).

The condition $\dot{\pi} = 0$ near the steady state is also shown in Figure 8.2. The analytical representation of this schedule is complex because of non-linearities and because there are multiple effects of inflation on labor allocation at the steady state. However, the main effect of labor allocation on inflation is that a larger export sector supports fiscal revenues and reduces the need for seigniorage, thus lowering inflation. This explains why the dashed locus in Figure 8.2 is downward sloping near the steady state.

Employment in the exportable sector is a state variable, whereas the inflation rate is a "jump" variable. Away from the steady state, the system moves along a negatively-sloped saddle path. As exportable employment adjusts toward its steady-state value from below, the increase in exportables production causes the government's tax revenue to increase, reducing the fiscal deficit and the pressure on the central bank to print money, thereby resulting in a reduction in inflation. This mechanism operates in reverse, causing inflation to increase along the saddle path, when exportable employment approaches its steady-state value from above.

5. Steady-State Comparative Statics

We are interested in examining the macroeconomic consequences of the types of exogenous shocks that low-income fragile states often experience, such as supply shocks (e.g. weather-related shocks), a deterioration in their terms of trade, as well as in exploring the macroeconomic consequences of foreign assistance and of policy choices that the governments of such states may make. In this section we start by analyzing the long-term effects of these shocks thanks to comparative statics on the equilibrium conditions.

5.1 Comparative Statics with Respect to A_h

We begin by considering the steady-state effects of productivity shocks. Recall that the dynamic behavior of L_x is given by equation (21), while inflation dynamics are given by equation (22), and that around the steady-state, $\dot{\pi} = \dot{L}_x = 0$. An increase in productivity of home production increases real wages in the home sector. For a given inflation rate, labor has to move to the home sector to equalize wages, and as L_h increases, L_x decreases. Thus, the $dL_x = 0$ (dashed) locus in Figure 8.2 shifts to the left. The increase in productivity of home goods production causes the real exchange rate to depreciate as the supply of home goods increases. This reduces the real cost of the public wage bill when compared to foreign receipts. In addition, consumption increases, which increases the base for the inflation tax. Thus, the dotted locus moves downwards.

The equilibrium effect is to reduce steady-state inflation. The change in the share of labor allocated to the home sector is ambiguous because less inflation means that shoe-leather costs are diminished, which reduces the need to produce "shoes,"[9] but the net effect can be shown to be a decrease in labor in the home sector for the parameter values given in section 6b.

5.2 Comparative Statics with Respect to A_x (or ρ)

An increase in productivity (or in the relative price) of exports production increases real wages in the export sector. For a given inflation rate, labor has to move to the export sector to equalize wages: L_x rises and L_h falls. Thus, the dashed locus in Figure 8.4 moves to the right.

Additional export revenues should overall reduce the fiscal deficit ($t_x \rho y_x (L_x)$ increases), although the real exchange appreciation that follows tends to increase the wage bill when compared with the domestic value of foreign receipts (e falls). As a result, the need to monetize deficits is reduced. In addition, the increase in overall productivity increases domestic consumption and, thus, real money demand and the receipts from the inflation tax ($\pi h(\pi) C$ increases). The increase in the productivity of export production thus reduces inflation for a given L_x, and the dotted locus moves downwards. The net effect of the increased export sector productivity is thus to move labor to the export sector and reduce the inflation rate.

5.3 Comparative Statics with Respect to Foreign Currency Financing of the Budget

Foreign currency financing of the budget can increase when official reserves are used ($F^{*\prime} < 0$), when (net) interest revenues on net foreign assets increase, or when official assistance increases. Such an improvement in foreign currency financing reduces the need to monetize fiscal deficits. Thus, the dotted locus shifts downwards while the dashed locus is unaffected, resulting in higher export-sector

[9] This effect is what explains that the dashed locus is upward sloping instead of being vertical.

employment and lower inflation: because the shoe-leather costs of inflation are paid using home goods, which require labor in the home sector, the reduction in inflation also allows more labor to be allocated to the export sector.[10]

5.4 Comparative Statics with Respect to Public Wages and Public Employment

An increase in public wages that worsens the fiscal deficit needs to be financed by money creation. Thus, the dotted locus shifts upwards. Inflation increases and export-sector employment falls: the movement along the dashed locus reflects the fact that higher shoe-leather costs reduce the labor supply that can be allocated to the export sector.

This effect is reinforced when public employment increases, both because the vertical shift in the dotted locus is magnified (more spending to be financed through seigniorage), and because an increase in L_g reduces L_h directly (recall that $L_h = L—L_g\_L_x$), shifting the dashed locus to the left. The reduction in labor supply also appreciates the real exchange rate further, worsening the wage bill.

6. Fragility and Policymaking

6.1 Objective Function

We now solve the full model with endogenous policy. First, we will assume that the policymaker's utility can be represented by a version of the following expression:

$$W = \int_0^{\infty} P(L_{g,t}, \pi_t\ )\ e^{-\beta t} K + \Big(1 - P(L_{g,t}, \pi_t)\Big) e^{-\beta t} [kC]^{\xi}\ C_g^{1-\xi} dt \tag{23}$$

where $P(L_g, \pi)$ is the probability of state failure, K a parameter that captures flow welfare under a situation of state failure, C is the basket of private consumption goods, C_g is the total production of public goods, 1-ξ is the weight in the utility function given to production of public goods (and ξ is the weight given to private consumption goods), β is a discount rate. The probability of state failure is modelled as a simple logistic function of public employment and inflation:

[10] Notice the contrast with standard "Dutch disease" analyses of the effects of aid. Why the difference? The answer lies in our assumptions that i) An inflow of aid does not affect spending by the domestic government, but simply alters the way it finances its fiscal deficit—specifically, that it reduces the need for central bank financing, and ii) Transaction costs are incurred in home goods. By lowering inflation, an increase in aid thus effectively increases the supply of home goods, reducing their relative price and inducing labor to move to the export sector.

Use a logit probability model for the probability of failure.

$$P(L_g, \pi) = \frac{1}{1 + exp[a_0 + \ a_1[L_g - \ L_g^*] + a_2[\pi - \ \pi^*]]}.$$

where a_0, $a_1 > 0$, $a_2 < 0$ are parameters and L_g^* and π^* are the long-run values of L_g and π. The likelihood of state failure is increasing in inflation because inflation hurts real savings and incomes and is a good summary statistic of the degree of economic turmoil. The likelihood of state failure is also decreasing in public employment because public employment is a vehicle through which a policy-maker can provide benefits to individuals who might otherwise create civil unrest.[11]

We consider three different policymakers. How their objective function relates to the representative agent's welfare function is essential to the discussion of how state fragility affects macroeconomic policymaking.

6.1.1 The Political Policymaker

This policymaker understands the risks of state failure, and thus maximizes utility with a functional form similar to that presented in equation (23). However, she has a short policy horizon. This is captured by a discount rate βp that is set higher than the representative agent's discount rate ($\beta p > \beta$). In addition, this policymaker places large weight in her utility on public sector production, either because of distorted policy incentives or because of graft. This is modeled with a parameter ξ that serves as an indicator of this distortion, in the form of the diversion of resources for the production of public goods. The objective function she maximizes is thus

$$W^P = \int_0^\infty P(L_{g,t}, \pi_t) \ e^{-\beta p \ t} K + \Big(1 - P(L_{g,t}, \pi_t)\Big) e^{-\beta p \ t} C_t^{\ \xi} \ C_{g,t}^{1-\xi} dt \qquad (23a)$$

6.1.2 The "Technocratic" Policymaker

This policymaker doesn't understand the risk of failure and thus does not treat fragile situations differently from any macroeconomic program. However, her discount rate β correctly captures the representative agent's preferences and the technocrat faces no incentives to artificially expand public sector production (that is, she can completely ignore the political reality of featherbedding and corruption), so that she places the correct weight on the production of public goods. The objective function she maximizes is

[11] Public employment can be used, for example, to provide jobs to former combatants or militias, to distribute rents across a population, etc. We do not model specifically how political support is determined, but the reader is referred to Chapter 14 in this volume for a model of political support.

$$W^T = \int_0^\infty e^{-\beta t} C_t^{\xi_T} C_{g,t}^{1-\xi_T} dt \tag{23b}$$

6.1.3 The "Social Planner"

This policymaker maximizes the utility of the representative agent with the correct social discount rate β and with the correct weight on the production of public goods ξ_T, as with the technocratic policymaker, but in addition takes into account the probability of state failure.

$$W^S = \int_0^\infty P(L_{g,t}, \pi_t)\, e^{-\beta t} K + \Big(1 - P(L_{g,t}, \pi_t)\Big) e^{-\beta t} C^{\xi_T} C_g^{1-\xi_T} dt \tag{23c}$$

6.2 Solution Method and Calibration

The complete setup takes the form of a Ramsey problem, whereby a policymaker chooses a policy instrument in order to maximize a welfare objective, taking into account the behavior of the private sector and budget constraints (see similar problems in, for instance Barro, 1979, and Chari et al., 1994). More specifically, after private decisions and budget constraints are solved for and substituted in, the policymaker maximizes her welfare criterion (equation 23a, 23b or 23c) subject to the labor market adjustment (equation 21) and to the equation linking inflation dynamics to fiscal deficits (equation 22). For simplicity in our case, we will take the policy instrument to be the level of public employment L_g.

The difficulty in solving the model lies in the non-linearity of these two equations. These are first linearized so that the Maximum Principle can be applied to the following Hamiltonian

$$H\Big(t, x(t), y(t), \lambda(t)\Big) \doteq f\Big(t, x(t), y(t)\Big) + \lambda(t) \cdot G(t, x(t), y(t)).$$

where the optimal control $\hat{y}(t)$ is public employment L_g and the linearized system of differential equation for the vector of state variables $x = (L_x, \pi)$ is $\dot{x}(t) = G(t, x(t), \hat{y}(t))$, where G is linear, as presented in the Appendix. In addition, an initial condition linking the costate variable at time 0 to the marginal utility at time 0 is necessary to solve the model.

That theoretical solution is solved numerically by Chebyshev approximation of the functional equations (the decisions are functions of the two states, L_x, and π). The calibration is presented is Table 8.1.

Table 8.1 Calibration

A_h	A_x	A_g	α_h	α_x	α_g	L_g^*	$\bar{L}$
0.95	1	0.6	0.64	0.66	0.6	0.05	1
w_g	θ	τ_0	τ_1	F	REM	C_g	$\frac{dF}{dt}$
0.68	0.4	0.1	-5	0.2	0.2	0.1	0.02

6.3 Results

We start by discussing the labor allocation by the private sector as well as the fiscal policy decision for L_g. The optimal employment allocation across sectors for the "political" policymaker is shown in Figure 8.3. Labor is misallocated initially, with the export sector unable to expand as much as it would need to eliminate intersectoral wage differentials. As a result, the marginal productivity of labor, as well as wages, is higher in the export sector. This sector slowly attracts workers and grows, whereas the home sector shrinks. In our illustrative calibration, public employment is around a third of the labor force, and the optimal "political" policymaker's decision does not vary much with time (Figure 8.3).

More importantly, Figure 8.4 shows how state fragility can affect the fiscal policy decision. Public employment is much higher if it is decided by the "political" policymaker (Scenario 1), since that policymaker potentially personally benefits from the production of goods for her own consumption and, given her higher discount rate, puts less weight on the future fiscal and inflationary pressures generated by the additional spending associated with increased public employment. Although the level of public employment is high, which would contribute to reduce fragility, the probability of state failure is also highest for the "political" policymaker, because large fiscal deficits are monetized and lead to higher inflation now and in the future (see Figure 8.5), which increases the probability of failure. This effect dominates the direct effect of public employment on the probability of failure.

The "technocratic" policymaker (Scenario 2) implements a conservative fiscal plan, lowering public employment. The fiscal deficit is small, inflation is low, and the production of private goods is the highest among the three scenarios (Figure 8.5). The probability of state failure is overall lower than under the "politician" policymaker (Figure 8.5), although it is higher than what could be achieved if the probability of state failure is explicitly acknowledged before the fiscal decision is taken.

Indeed, the probability of state failure is lowest when the social planner chooses policies. The social planner trades off inflation against public employment and present versus future utility with the appropriate weights. As a result, the level of public employment chosen by the social planner (Scenario 3) lies between the two extremes (see Figure 8.4). Fiscal deficits and inflation are higher, and the

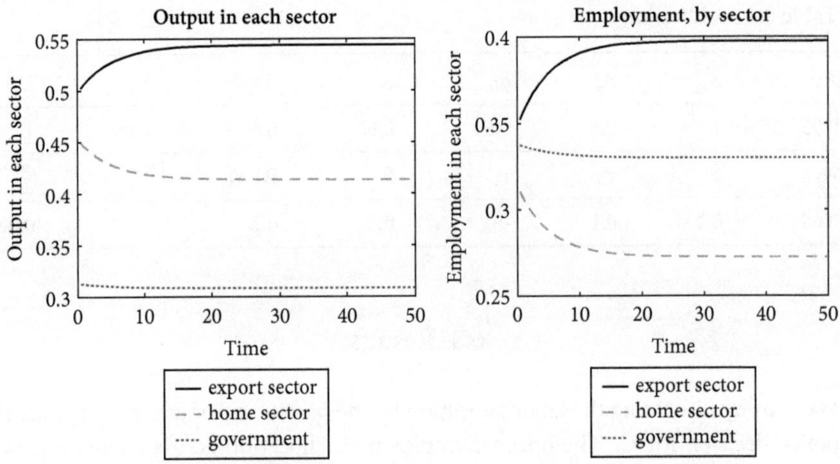

Figure 8.3 Employment Allocation and Output, by Sector; Political Policymaker Optimal Plan

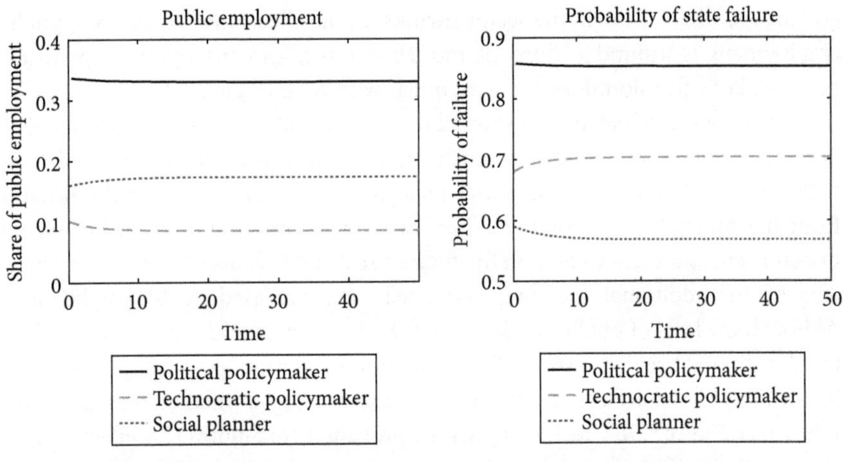

Figure 8.4 Public Employment and Probability of State Failure; by Scenario.

Note: Scenario 1: political policymaker; Scenario 2: technocratic policymaker; Scenario 3: social planner

production of private goods is lower, than under the technocratic policymaker, but the reduction in the probability of failure brought about by large public employment is worth the utility cost of inflation and lower private consumption.

Our model allows us to make welfare comparisons among policy regimes. Under our calibration, expected social welfare, as represented by the "true" welfare function (23.c), is 16.4 under the "political" policymaker, 168.6 under the "technocratic" policymaker, and 194.7 under the social planner. While technocratic policy advice can potentially achieve significant improvements welfare, ignoring the risk of state failure can be costly. Modifications to "technocratic" advice in the

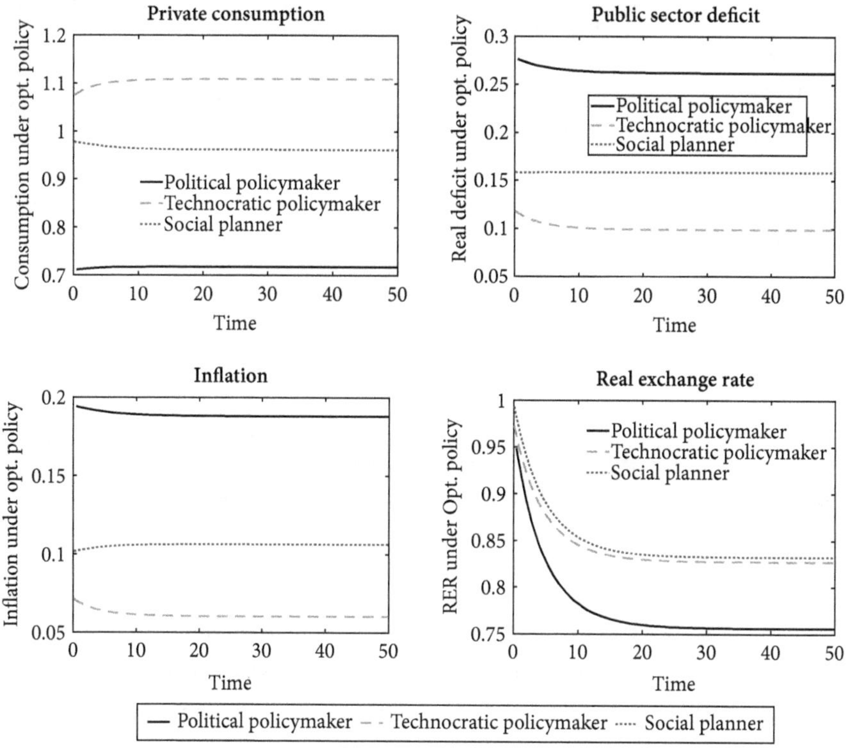

Figure 8.5 Macroeconomic Outcomes

direction of reducing fragility can improve welfare. In our specific simulations, this involves moderating ambitious plans for reducing inflation by tolerating higher levels of public employment as a means of reducing social tensions.

How can the international community reduce the risk of state failure? We ran some comparative statics exercises, increasing the value of international aid so that more resources are provided to the budget. Figure 8.6 shows that the political policymaker increases her direct consumption, because her budget constraint is relaxed. By contrast, the social planner reduces public employment. Foreign aid reduces the pressure to monetize deficits, so additional aid contributes to moderating inflation. As a result, the probability of state failure falls, and, given the shape of the logistic function, the marginal benefit of public employment in reducing the probability of state failure decreases. As a result, the social planner's choice for public employment is lower when foreign aid is higher, which benefits not only the fiscal accounts but also the private sector.

This comparative statics exercise shows how the model can provide insights into the interactions between macroeconomic imbalances and fragility. In addition, it underlines that a benevolent policymaker should take advantage of additional fiscal space to reduce macroeconomic instability. Spending most or all of additional

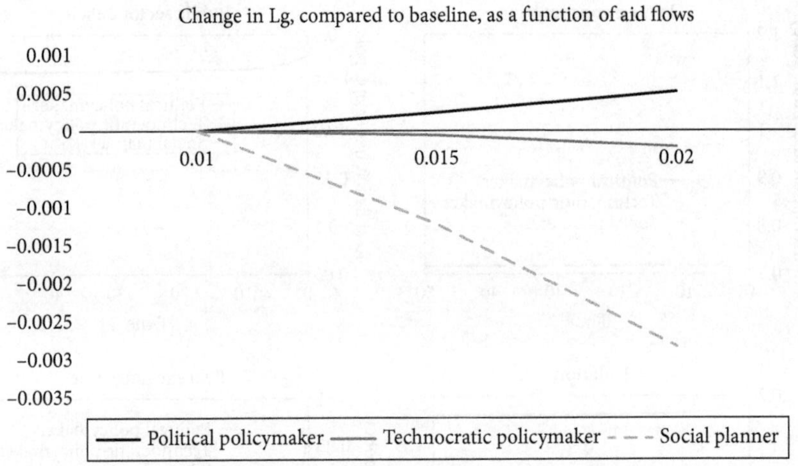

Figure 8.6 Steady-State Public Employment—Comparative Statics with Respect to Foreign Aid

resources on direct policymaker consumption or on the public wage bill is unlikely to be the interior solution chosen by a benevolent policymaker. Revealed preferences are important for the international community intent on assessing whether a pivotal moment (in the sense of Collier in this volume) is at hand.

7. Summary and Conclusions

How should macro-fiscal policy advice account for the risk that a fragile state can descend into full-blown state failure? Our chapter intends to provide some insight on this question, based on a standard "dependent-economy" macro model, extended so as to account for the lessons the international community has learned about engagement in fragile states, in particular those lessons of most relevance for macro economic policy: (i) taking context as the starting point, and aligning advice with local conditions; (ii) prioritizing prevention; (iii) recognizing the links between political, security, and development objectives; (iv) acting fast but staying engaged long enough to give success a chance (see OECD, 2007 and Chapter 1 in this volume).

The model we propose accounts for the macroeconomic context of fragile states (lesson (i)), in particular the lack of fiscal space, nonexistent markets for domestic and international borrowing from private creditors, fiscal dominance in the setting of monetary policy, dependence of fiscal accounts on export revenues, and misallocation of labor, typically with excess labor in the non-tradable and the government sectors.

In addition, our chapter focuses on what understanding the local priorities and prioritizing prevention means for macro-policy making (lessons (ii) and (iii)). We investigate optimal fiscal policy under different objective functions, and find that although it is true that distorted policy incentives and graft under "political" policymaking tend to result in oversized public sectors that crowd out private activity and reduce private welfare, prioritizing prevention of failure can justify moderating fiscal adjustment—relative to what would be done under a purely technocratic solution that ignores fragility—as long as the fiscal path is sustainable.

Our chapter proposes an explicit, simple, and practical way to formalize within macro models the links between the political and security objectives of the international community and the macroeconomic objectives of stabilization programs. Our suggestion is to make explicit in the objective function the probability and the cost of the state failure. In particular, the probability of state failure can be expressed as a function of a range of policy variables and economic outcomes. Future work should delve into this model specification, looking in particular at the importance of social inclusion, inequality, and inflation as determinants of state failure, building on the extensive literature on the drivers of conflict (Collier and Hoeffler, 2004 ; Collier et al., 2009; Celiku and Kraay, 2017; see also survey in Blattman and Miguel, 2010).

Our findings highlight the difficulty in interpreting what drives fiscal decisions in fragile states. Distinguishing between graft and distorted policy incentives, which may be justified if the risk of conflict is high, needs local expertise. In the same vein, understanding how macro policies can affect fragility requires a knowledge of the cultural, historical, and social drivers of fragility, as well as an understanding of the effect of macro policies on the political economy equilibrium.

But even with the best knowledge of the country and the most detailed understanding of the impact of policies, the risks posed by macroeconomic adjustment are likely to be high. In the face of Knightian uncertainty, acting fast but remaining engaged is essential, and monitoring the effect of policy at a disaggregated level and with sufficient frequency also seems important. Taking policy steps that support state-building is essential. This is the object of the next three chapters in this volume.

References

Barro, R.J. 1979. "On the Determination of the Public Debt." *Journal of Political Economy*, 87(5, Part 1): 940–71.

Blattman, Christopher, and Edward Miguel. 2010 "Civil War." *Journal of Economic Literature*, 48(1): 3–57.

Celiku, B. and A. Kraay. 2017. "Predicting Conflict." World Bank Policy Research Working Paper 8075. Washington, DC: World Bank.

Chari, V.V., L.J. Christiano, and P.J. Kehoe. 1994. "Optimal Fiscal Policy in a Business Cycle Model." *Journal of Political Economy*, 102(4): 617–52.

Collier, P. and A. Hoeffler. 2004. "Greed and Grievance in Civil War." *Oxford Economic Papers*, 56(4): 563–95.

Collier, P., A. Hoeffler, and D. Rohner. 2009. "Beyond Greed and Grievance: Feasibility and Civil War." *Oxford Economic Papers*, 61(1): 1–27.

Devarajan, S., and D.S. Go. 1998. "The Simplest Dynamic General-Equilibrium Model of an Open Economy." *Journal of Policy Modeling*, 20(6): 677–714.

Khan, M.S. and P.J. Montiel. 1987. Real Exchange Rate Dynamics in a Small, Primary-Exporting Country. Staff Papers, *IMF Economic Review*, 34(4): 681–710.

Montiel P.J. 1999. "Determinants of the Long-Run Equilibrium Real Exchange Rate," in L.E. Hinkle and P.J. Montiel (Eds.), *Exchange Rate Misalignment: Concepts and Measurement for Developing Countries*. Oxford: Oxford University Press.

OECD (Organisation for Economic Co-Operation and Development). 2007. *Principles for Good International Engagement in Fragile States*. Paris: OECD Development Assistance Committee.

UN-World Bank. 2018. *Pathways for Peace: Inclusive Approaches to Preventing Violent Conflict*. Washington, DC: World Bank.

Annex

Demand for Liquidity

Just as the private sector has to decide its allocation of consumption between importables and home goods conditional on C, it also has to determine its demand for liquidity conditional on C. To examine this decision, note that the change in the private sector's holding of liquid assets is given by *(PLQ)' = PLQ' + P'LQ*. Using this in (16a), we can rewrite the sector's budget constraint in real (consumption-bundle) terms as:

$$\dot{LQ} = Y/P - \Big(t(LQ/C)C + \ \pi LQ\Big) - C, \tag{16b}$$

where $\pi = \frac{d(P)}{dt}/P$ is the (actual and expected) domestic rate of inflation. The private sector chooses LQ to maximize its real income, which allows it to maximize its consumption opportunities. It does so by minimizing the term in parentheses in (16b). The first-order condition for this minimization is $t'(LQ/C) + \pi = 0$. Inverting this equation to solve for LQ yields:

$$LQ = h(\pi)C, \text{with } h(\pi) = t^{-'}(\pi) \text{ and therefore } h' = -t'' < 0. \tag{17}$$

Substituting for LQ in (16b) we can therefore write the private sector's budget constraint as:

$$\dot{LQ} = Y/P - \Big(1 + t\Big(h(\pi)\Big)C + \pi h(\pi)\Big)C. \tag{16c}$$

Derivation of External Balance Condition

To derive the external balance condition, note that by summing the budget constraints of the public and private sectors (10) and (16a) we can derive the version of Walras' Law for our model:

$$\begin{aligned}(\dot{SF^*}) =& [\dot{M} - (P\dot{LQ})] + [P_h y_h(L_x) - [1 - \theta + t\ (h(\pi))]CP] \\ &+ [S\rho y_x(L_x) - SC_g^* - \theta PC + i^* SF^* + S(AID^*)].\end{aligned}$$

Using (17a) this becomes:

$$S\dot{F^*} = [\dot{M} - P\dot{LQ}] + [S\rho y_x(L_x) - SC_g^* - \theta PC + i^* SF^* + S(AID^*)].$$

It will be useful to express this in foreign currency units, by dividing by S:

$$\dot{F^*} = [\dot{M} - P\dot{LQ}]/S + [\rho y_x(L_x) - C_g^* - \theta Ce^{\theta-1} + i^* F^* + AID^*]. \tag{19}$$

The left-hand side of this equation is the overall balance of payments expressed in units of foreign currency, while the right-hand side consists of two terms: the flow excess supply of money and the current account balance. To derive the model's external balance condition we therefore need to specify the form in which the private sector chooses to accumulate liquid assets. As a point of departure, suppose that $PLQ = M$ — that is, that liquidity services can only be provided by domestic currency. In this case $\dot{M} = (\dot{PLQ})$, and the first term on the right-hand side of (19) disappears. Expressing the result in foreign currency units the external balance condition becomes:

$$\dot{F}^{*} = \rho y_x(L_x) - (\theta C e^{\theta-1} + C_g^{*}) + i^{*}F^{*} + AID^{*}.$$

Linearization of the Dynamic Equations Driving the State of the Economy

A first-order approximation to (21) is:

$$\dot{L}_x = \left(\frac{\partial \dot{L}_x}{\partial L_x}\right)(L_x - L_x^{*}) + \left(\frac{\partial \dot{L}_x}{\partial \pi}\right)(\pi - \pi^{*}) + (\partial \dot{L}_x/\partial L_g)(L_g - L_g^{*}) \qquad (21')$$

Because $\partial \dot{L}_x/\partial L_x$ and $\partial \dot{L}_x/\partial \pi$ are both negative, the slope of the curve in (L_x, π) space that satisfies $\dot{L}_x = 0$ must be negative. We add the change in government employment, so that the government's problem can account for its impact on the private sector. This curve is depicted as the dashed line in Figure 8.4. To the right of the dashed line $(L_x - L_x^{*}) > 0$, so this means:[12]

$$\dot{L}_x > 0 \text{ for } (\pi - \pi^{*}) \leq -\left[(\partial \dot{L}_x/\partial L_x)/(\partial \dot{L}_x/\partial \pi)\right](L_x - L_x^{*})$$

That is, employment in the export sector decreases (increases) when we are to the right (left) of the dashed line.

A first-order approximation of the change in inflation is

$$\dot{\pi} = (\partial\, \dot{\pi}/\partial L_x)\ (L_x - L_x^{*}\ ) + (\partial \dot{\pi})/\partial \pi)(\pi - \pi^{*}) + (\partial\, \dot{\pi}/\partial L_g)(L_g - L_g^{*}). \qquad (22')$$

Where $(\partial \dot{\pi}/\partial L_x) = 0.0068$ and $(\partial \dot{\pi}/\partial \pi) = 0.2350 > 0$ at our simulated steady state values $(L_x^{*}, \pi^{*}) = (0.3830, 0.0402)$. $-(\partial \dot{\pi}/\partial L_x)/(\partial \dot{\pi}/\partial \pi)$ is the slope of the dotted line in the phase diagram shown in Figure 8.4. This slope is negative).$-(\partial \dot{\pi}/\partial L_x)/(\partial \dot{\pi}/\partial \pi) = -0.0926$ at the steady state values $(L_x^{*}, \pi^{*}) = (0.3830, 0.0402)$. We also have:

$$\dot{\pi} > 0 \text{ for } (\pi - \pi^{*}) > -(\partial \dot{\pi}/\partial \dot{\pi} L_x)/(\partial \dot{\pi}/\partial \pi)(L_x - L_x^{*}).$$

Thus, inflation increases when the economy is above the dotted line in the figure and decreases below it. The upshot is that the simulated dynamic system contains a saddle path in the vicinity of the steady state, depicted as the solid line in Figure 8.4, in which export sector employment dominates. This means that the economy follows a saddle path in which domestic inflation is the jump variable.

[12] We set the government employment term to zero to simplify this discussion.

9

Fiscal Capacity and State Fragility

Timothy Besley and Hannes Mueller

> It is shortage of resources, and not inadequate incentives, which limits the pace of economic development. Indeed the importance of public revenue from the point of view of accelerated economic development could hardly be exaggerated.
>
> Nicholas Kaldor, "Taxation for Economic Development," *Journal of Modern African Studies*, 1963

> [T]he fiscal history of a people is above all an essential part of its general history. An enormous influence on the fate of nations emanates from the economic bleeding which the needs of the state necessitates, and from the use to which the results are put.
>
> Schumpeter, *The Crisis of the Tax State*, 1918

1. Introduction

There are many dimensions to state fragility, but a weak capacity of the state to raise revenue is a key feature. Technical support is often provided to increase revenue generation as, for example, when a country reforms its value-added tax (VAT) system. International organizations like the IMF, as well as donors, play a key role in assisting with the more technical aspects of revenue mobilization.

Raising taxes is not only a technical issue but a political and social one. Low tax revenue not only reflects the tax system or a weak economy but also an incompetent and corrupt bureaucracy, lack of cohesiveness in the operation of the state, and a weak civic culture in the population. Studying revenue goes well beyond the narrower concern that without tax revenues, the state cannot support its citizens. It lies at the heart of the compact between a state and its citizens. The task of raising fiscal capacity in this context therefore needs to pay attention to these dimensions to succeed.

We thank the participants of the workshop on Macroeconomic Policy in Fragile States in Oxford in December, 2018, for useful feedback on this project and on an earlier draft. We also thank Lavinia Piemontese and Sacha Dray for excellent research assistance and comments. All errors are ours.

Timothy Besley and Hannes Mueller, *Fiscal Capacity and State Fragility* In: *Macroeconomic Policy in Fragile States.* Edited by: Ralph Chami, Raphael Espinoza, and Peter Montiel, Oxford University Press (2021). © International Monetary Fund.
DOI: 10.1093/oso/9780198853091.003.0009

The capacity to mobilize revenues can come from three main sources: first, the economy has to be conducive to levying taxes, so having a larger formal economy with large firms will generally make compliance easier; second, there needs to be investment in the monitoring and compliance that make it feasible to collect taxes owed; third, citizens have to be willing (at least to some degree) to comply with the demands of the tax system, because relying exclusively on monitoring and compliance is costly. Even though the tax share tends to increase with income, it is well known that countries raise different levels of revenue per capita even controlling for GDP.

Unlike low levels of revenue mobilization, fragility is hard to define and measure. This is because fragility is essentially a statement about risks, that is, the risk of failure when put under stress. But failure is not easy to define in the context of the multidimensional responsibilities of states, so measuring the risk of failure is complicated. Commonly used approaches, including the Country Policy and Institutional Assessment used in this volume, harness aggregates (typically weighted sums) of many indicators to capture fragility. These aggregated approaches have the advantage of giving the measurement a broad base but the disadvantage of being less transparent and generating the tendency to evaluate fragility ex post. For example, a country will tend to be labelled as fragile *after* it has experienced the outbreak of armed conflict in its territory or a dramatic decline of its GDP.[1]

Here we follow IGC (2018) which argues that there are six key symptoms of fragility in general:

(i) Weak state capacity: a failure to invest in fiscal, legal, regulatory and spending capabilities of government;
(ii) A weak private sector: economies are characterized by a large informal sector with few large firms and poor legal structures in place, which hampers taxation;
(iii) Lack of security: the state is not able to provide security from disruptive actors (such as organized criminals or militias) throughout its territory;
(iv) Weak resilience: the economy often relies on few sectors and is subject to external shocks which threaten political stability;
(v) Low levels of state legitimacy: society suffers from low levels of trust and reciprocal compliance; and

[1] For a discussion of the Country Policy and Institutional Analysis and its relationship with future risks see Celiku and Kraay (2017). In their recent report, the Organisation for Economic Co-operation and Development (2018) tried to avoid this problem and instead framed fragility as a combination of risks and coping capacities through a principal component analysis of more than 40 variables. However, fragility even in this dataset should be regarded as much an evaluation of realized failures (a fall in the growth rate) as a measure of unrealized risks.

(vi) Polarized societies: prevalence of oppositional identities whether ideological, ethnic, linguistic, or religious. Different polities display these symptoms to differing degrees. Moreover, countries that have functioned effectively for long periods of time may occasionally display some of these symptoms.

The symptoms of state fragility are best thought of as lying on a continuum with multiple dimensions. Underlying causes are more complex still. Many of the dimensions reinforce each other and there is no clear-cut causal structure. Although it is important to keep the wider picture in mind, it can be useful to examine a specific aspect of state effectiveness as we will do here. By unpacking issues around revenue mobilization, we will gain wider insights into fragility problems and the specific challenges that need to be addressed to create a more effective state.

Taking this to heart, this chapter looks at the challenge of building fiscal capacity and discusses how it is related to contemporary concerns about state fragility. It will argue that these two lines of thinking have strong commonalities and that by learning about one specific weakness in the way that the state works—poor revenue-raising capacity—we learn a lot about how states function effectively in general. Therefore, a key message developed here is that it is essential to move beyond purely technocratic approaches to revenue mobilization and to incorporate an appreciation of the political and social dimensions of fiscal capacity.

The chapter is organized as follows. Section 2 reviews some important background elements. It discusses some of the relevant ideas in the literature on the role of institutions, civic culture, and state capacity. In section 3, we look at some evidence drawn mainly from correlations that we use to build a narrative and argue that increasing fiscal capacity is related to the development of the state, society, and the economy. Section four discusses some policy conclusions and suggests that a new conceptual approach is needed for international engagement on problems of low fiscal capacity and state fragility. We suggest that much greater attention has to be paid to political economy.

2. Institutions, Norms, and Culture

Stressing the importance of political institutions has now become an established line of argument in explorations of the factors that are conducive to economic development. Seminal historical work by North (1990) and North and Weingast (1989) envisages building institutions that restrain the state as the *sine qua non* of economic development. Recent studies in political economy, such as North et al. (2009), Acemoglu and Robinson (2012), and Besley and Persson (2011) stress the role of building political institutions which create greater cohesiveness as lying at the heart of state effectiveness. There is now a large body of supporting evidence (see Acemoglu et al., 2005) that institutions affect the path of economic development.

One key issue is how far institutions are codified into rules and formal structures. Mapping these has certainly provided valuable insights into correlates of state performance. Less easy to measure are the more informal aspects of institution building such as how far people choose to *behave* cooperatively within a set of rules; these aspects relate to norms and beliefs about how an institution will work. Increasing attention has been paid to this (Acemoglu and Robinson, 2018; Bisin and Verdier, 2017) and it leads to a greater interest in the role of culture in making states function effectively. This links to an older literature in political science which gives a key role to transformations in civic culture in explaining how governments work (see, for example, Almond and Verba, 1963, and Lipset, 1960).

A good illustration of the importance of civic culture is the study of diplomatic parking tickets by Fisman and Miguel (2007). Diplomats to the UN in New York come from different countries but face the same institutional environment in New York. Until 2002, diplomatic immunity protected UN diplomats from parking enforcement actions. Fisman and Miguel show that diplomats from countries with high levels of corruption (on the basis of survey-based indicators) accumulated significantly more unpaid parking violations. And the effect is large: diplomats from the most corrupt countries accumulated about 80 percent more parking tickets than diplomats from the least corrupt countries. This is a striking variation in behavior, purely driven by the different cultural backgrounds of these diplomats.[2]

In the context of fiscal capacity, Besley (2019) discusses three roles for civic culture (see also Levi [1988] for historical evidence). First, it has a direct impact on fiscal capacity because tax compliance increases when individuals regard it as their duty to pay taxes. Second, civic culture reacts to the investments of the government. For example, tax compliance increases when public goods are provided and falls when the elite uses the state to extract resources.[3] Third, there is a complementarity between being a civic-minded citizen and the proportion of such citizens in the population as a whole. It is more attractive to be civic-minded when there are more civic-minded citizens around. This leads to a self-reinforcing cultural dynamic that is affected by government policy.

[2] The article also finds that diplomats of the best-behaving countries were converging toward bad behavior over time but that the enforcement of ticket fines after 2002 reduced parking violations dramatically. Both of these results show that the institutional framework matters for behavior.

[3] From a modeling perspective, civic-minded citizens are like motivated agents in the sense of Besley and Ghatak (2005); they respond positively if their preferences are aligned with the government objectives and negatively otherwise.

The two approaches, building institutions and building a civic culture, are increasingly seen as complementary; here we highlight these complementarities and draw policy conclusions from them. Interestingly, this is in line with two old traditions in social science. The first follows Hobbes (1651) who envisaged state building as the expansion of formal state authority and the capacity to project power in the form of a *Leviathan*. This vision is often contrasted with the contractarian approach of Locke (1690) and Rousseau (1762), which views the state as a nexus of reciprocal obligations and where voluntary compliance is key to state power. Both approaches give a role for institutions in restraining state power.

State capacity has three core dimensions (for a brief summary see Besley and Persson, 2014). Fiscal capacity is the capacity of the state to raise revenue. Most government activities require revenues from a tax system with the power to enforce payment of statutory taxes. This must be underpinned by the recruitment and training of tax inspectors and investing in systems of monitoring and compliance. Fiscal capacity acts in conjunction with legal capacity and collective capacity but is also influenced by civic culture and the level of per capita income.

Legal capacity is the capacity of the state to secure private property rights to the ownership of physical and human assets. Policies of effective market support require a series of costly and durable investments. For example, public land and property registries have to be built, and functioning court systems require trained officials and a number of courts on top of written statutes.

Collective capacity augments markets, mostly by supplying public goods. But policies to limit inequality also belong in this category, as do paternalistic policies to counter imperfect individual decisions. Stretching the concept further, the regulation of externalities also increases the benefits of using markets. As with market support, increasing collective capacity requires investments. For example, running an effective public health system is enhanced by investments in delivery, trained personnel, structures, and equipment.

Here our primary focus is on fiscal capacity. Weak fiscal capacity contributes to state fragility in several ways. First, it encourages government to use sources of tax revenue which can undermine trust in government; for example, resorting to the use of the inflation tax or finding other less transparent and arbitrary ways of acquiring resources. This weakens legitimacy. Using more selective forms of taxation can also enhance polarization between taxpayers and others. This weakens cohesion. Low levels of fiscal capacity make it more difficult to use government debt as a source of smoothing shocks but also because broad-based taxation is more stable. This reduces resilience. In extreme cases, natural resource-based taxation tends to fluctuate because price shocks make intertemporal management of public resources much more challenging.

As we explain, building state capacity is partly a function of making investments in the working of the state. It is facilitated by having a constellation of relevant supporting institutions. It is also affected by the complexion of society, particularly the extent of oppositional identities and the strength of civic culture. We present some evidence that these dimensions of state functioning are associated with fiscal capacity building and relate them to debates about state fragility.

3. Country Experiences

In this section, we discuss some of the evidence of the link between state fragility and fiscal capacity grouped under three headings: state, society, and the economy. Fragility affects all of these, and we discuss some of the main theoretical ideas as well as the links to evidence based on country experiences. This review of the evidence will frame the discussion of policy implications.

3.1 The State

3.1.1 Institutions and State Capacity

The state operates in a framework of institutions that serve two core functions: allocating access to power and regulating its use. The latter plays a key role in shaping whether the state is used for common purposes or is captured by sectional or private interests. Legitimacy comes both from constraints on power as citizens and from the acquisition of power. Elected leaders often claim legitimacy via having a mandate from the people, a claim which is less compelling for those who rule by force or have inherited power.

Some symptoms of state fragility are a direct consequence of institutional conditions. For example, lack of institutional cohesion can result in low levels of state capacity. This is because the incentive to invest will be greatest when the state is used for common purposes (Besley and Persson, 2009, 2011). Consequently, there is a robust correlation between fiscal and legal capacity and weak executive constraints across a range of measures (Besley and Persson, 2009) and this also holds for fiscal capacity for a sample of countries in the twentieth century even when country fixed effects are included (Besley et al., 2013).

Lack of institutional cohesion also matters for security. Besley and Persson (2011) present theoretical and empirical evidence that weak executive constraints are associated with a higher risk of conflict. This makes sense from a theoretical point of view: incentives to fight are likely to be strongest when the state can be used for private rather than common interests. So we would expect weak executive constraints to increase political instability, further weakening incentives to invest in state capacity (Besley and Persson, 2010). Moreover, those who acquire power after a period of conflict may lack legitimacy.

Table 9.1 provides a summary of the resulting empirical relationship between cohesive institutions (executive constraints) and state failures such as the collapse

Table 9.1 Failures and Executive Constraints

	weak executive constraints		strong executive constraints		t-test	t-test*
	obs	mean	Obs	mean		
10% drop in GDP per capita	4170	3.86%	1979	1.11%	7.23	4.41
20% drop in GDP per capita	4410	1.52%	2017	0.40%	4.85	2.92
fall in life expectancy	5656	1.45%	2222	0.50%	4.38	1.08
increase in child mortality	5102	1.22%	2145	0.47%	3.52	1.72
start of armed conflict	6095	3.20%	2417	1.03%	7.09	2.62
start of civil war	6627	1.39%	2611	0.27%	6.37	2.93
start of refugee outflow	4976	2.07%	2397	0.42%	6.86	2.54
start of purge	4924	6.15%	2225	1.71%	10.13	4.47

Notes: "t-test" reports the t-test on a difference in means. "t-test*" reports the t-test on the coefficient of regression of the respective variable on weak executive constraints controlling for ln(GDP per capita). The years after the onset of a failure episode is set to missing to and all independent variables are lagged by one year to prevent the most obvious reverse causality problems. "10% drop in GDP per capita" is a drop in GDP per capita of more than 10 percent in the past 5 years. "20% drop in GDP per capita" is a drop in GDP per capita of more than 20 percent in the past 5 years. "fall in life expectancy" is a fall by more than half a year within a 5-year period. "increase in child mortality" is an increase from one year to the next. "armed conflict" is defined by more than 25 battle related deaths within a year. "civil war" are more than 0.08 battle related deaths per 1000 population in a year. "refugee outflow" is a year in which the country generates refugees. "purge" is an episode with purges. The table categorizes episodes of bad outcomes with the political institution in place in the year before the start of the episode. "strong executive constraints" are years of xconst=7 before the start of the respective episode. "weak executive constraints" are years of xconst<7 before the start of the respective episode. Data on executive constraints is from PolityIV. Data on GDP, population, child mortality and life expectancy is from the World Bank. Data on armed conflict and civil war is generated from UCDP/PRIO data on battle-related deaths presented in Pettersson and Eck (2018). Data on refugees is from the UNHCR. Data on Purges is from the Cross-National Time-Series Data Archive by Banks and Kenneth (2017).

of GDP or the outbreak of armed conflict and the use of purges. The table shows simple summary statistics for the occurrence of failures in country/years with weak and strong executive constraints. On all dimensions, failure is more likely for countries with weak executive constraints.[4] As the last column of Table 9.1 shows, this holds even when controlling for GDP levels.

Two further background factors bear on the incentives to invest in state capacity. The first is the underlying state of polarization, typically rooted in religious and/or ethnic divisions. We return to this in section 9.4. The second factor is access to natural resources and aid revenues. Natural resources weaken the demand for tax revenue from other sources and hence blunt the incentive to invest in fiscal capacity. Such resources also make capturing the state more valuable and hence can fuel conflict and political instability.

[4] Accordingly, Besley and Mueller (2018d) model executive constraints as a fail-safe mechanism of the state.

The state of institutions, availability of natural resources, and polarization lie behind all dimensions of state capacity, affecting incentives for the state to be more or less cohesive and, hence, to invest. Many of these are also factors that lie behind fragility and can generate dynamics towards a negative but stable equilibrium (in conflict studies this negative equilibrium has come to be known as the "conflict trap") (Besley and Persson, 2011, ch. 5).

Different dimensions of state capacity can be complements in the sense that investing in one dimension of state capacity can increase investment returns in another (Besley and Persson, 2009). To see this effect, consider the following example. Suppose a government contemplates an investment to encourage participation in the formal labor market. In a low-income country, this may, for example, be a legal framework supporting the formal sector. Such investment in legal capacity is more attractive after an investment in fiscal capacity raises the effective tax rate on labor—it now yields additional tax revenues, which can be used for lower tax rates or more collective consumption. But the complementarity runs both ways. The investment in legal capacity supporting formal sector employment encourages a fiscal capacity investment that improves labor income tax compliance, because the broader tax base implies more revenues.

Such complementarities can explain why governments make simultaneous investments in different state functions. But they also suggest that project-by-project appraisal of individual state capacity investments could seriously understate their benefits. This calls for a holistic look at the economy and state capacity to evaluate the value of state investment. This is important from a modeling perspective; standard models of optimal taxation either abstract from what is done with the revenues or even assume that total transfers need to sum to zero, that is, there is no public good provision. Such models also rarely look at complementarities between the use to which tax revenues are put and tax policies.

Figure 9.1, from Besley and Persson (2011), illustrates that development goes hand in hand with an expansion of state capacity over different dimensions. The y-axis shows the share of income tax in the total tax take, a result of investments in fiscal capacity, and the x-axis is an index that captures the ability of the state to enforce contracts, a result of investments in legal capacity.

Clearly, both of these dimensions are correlated with each other and improve as income per capita increases. Most of the high-income countries have managed to invest in both aspects of state capacity. Figure 9.1 also reveals a distinct group of low-income countries with very low legal capacity; all have also low fiscal capacity and collect less than 40 percent of their taxes as income taxes.

An important case study of the complementarities and why this inhibits the development of state capacity comes from Sanchez de la Sierra (2018) who studies the rise of local armed actors in Eastern Congo, a region typically associated with extreme state fragility. The study shows that armed militia groups in this area develop several aspects of state capacity the moment they become stationary. In

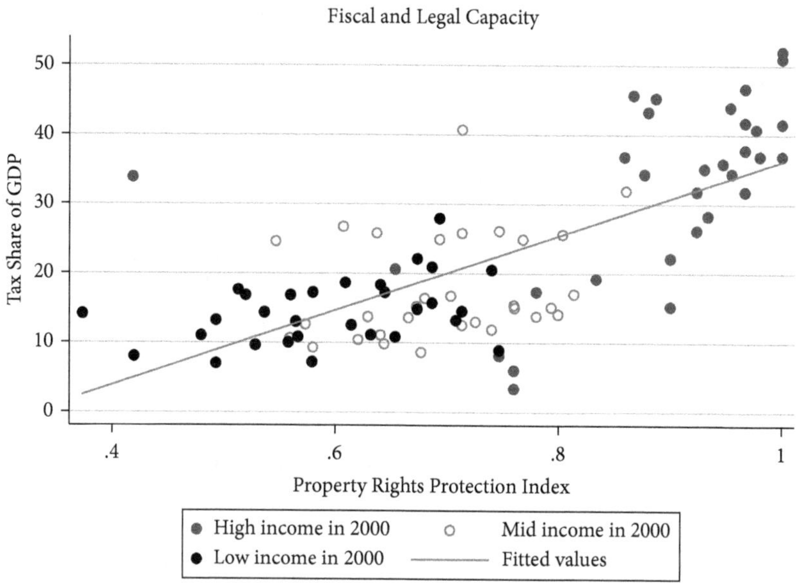

Figure 9.1 Complementarity between Capacities and Income: Income Taxes and Contract Enforcement by GDP

particular, they start to develop a tax system, security, administration, and even provide legal services.

Interestingly, a comparison between the Congolese army and local militias reveals that the militias develop state capacity more vigorously and that this has benefits to the local population. The surveys also reveal that the militias are seen as legitimate (or even more legitimate) compared to the army. One interpretation of these findings is that the Congolese state has not managed to move other aspects of state capacity, like taxation and the provision of legal services, with the army, and this is one reason that it fails to enhance welfare and elicit loyalty from the local population, something that we will return to in section 9.3.2.

3.1.2 Security and Instability

Fiscal capacity is also affected by lack of security, particularly when it leads to conflict and political instability. At the same time the outbreak of political violence is a symptom of state failure and fragility. Thus, the causality between the outbreak of violence and fiscal capacity runs in both directions.[5] On the one hand, higher capacity allows the state to provide security and establish its monopoly of violence. In addition, high state capacity typically means that public services are provided which lowers the incentives to engage in violence for the

[5] See Besley and Persson (2011, table 5.1).

opposition. At the same time challenges to power imply that the incentives to invest in state capacity fall (Besley and Persson, 2010). Political stability encourages governments to use a long planning horizon, which can lead to increased investment in state capacity. A government that is on the brink of collapse will not invest in its own capacity but will use all available resources to cling to power. At the same time, violence has an impact on economic activity, which will tend to discourage investment in state capacity.

We now look at the relationship between security and fiscal capacity using the IMF World Revenue Longitudinal Data (WoRLD) and data from the Uppsala Conflict Data Program (UCDP) Geocoded Event Dataset (GED) which we aggregate to country/year or country/quarter data.[6] We follow Mueller (2016) in defining conflict as violence per capita so that large countries such as India do not appear to be more violent just because of their population size.

Figure 9.2 shows the average income tax revenue per GDP in the period 1990–2016 for two groups of countries: those that experienced a great deal of armed conflict throughout this period and those that were mostly peaceful. The average for fragile countries, illustrated by the red line, is considerably lower. In addition, countries with security problems did not develop this capacity over time.

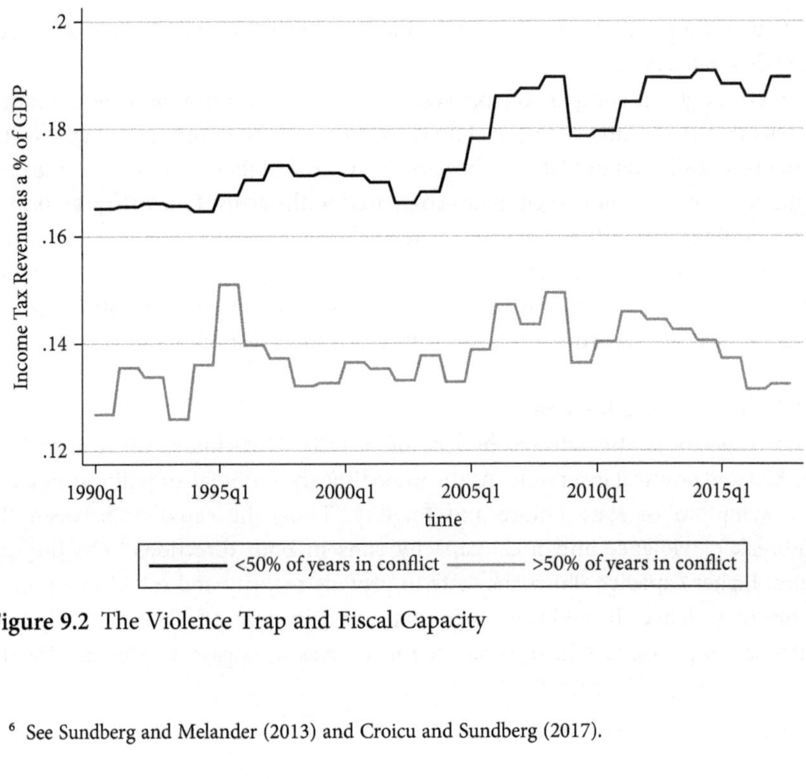

Figure 9.2 The Violence Trap and Fiscal Capacity

[6] See Sundberg and Melander (2013) and Croicu and Sundberg (2017).

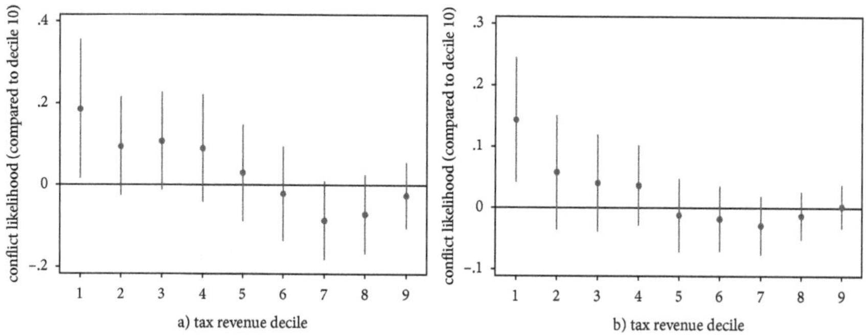

Figure 9.3 Conflict Risk and Fiscal Capacity between and within Country Evidence
Panel a) shows coefficients without controls. Panel b) shows coefficients controlling for country and time fixed effects.

There is a clear upward shift in the average of revenues in the peaceful countries which is absent in fragile countries.

Figure 9.3 exploits both the time series and cross-sectional variation to show that the outbreaks tend to be higher in countries which also fail to raise tax revenues. In Panel A of Figure 9.3 we look at the relationship between the risk of conflict and the revenue decile of a country/year. The propensity to conflict is almost 20 percentage points higher in countries with low tax revenues. This relationship appears to be nonlinear, with conflict being most concentrated in the lowest decile of tax-collecting countries.

Panel B of Figure 9.3 shows that this pattern is not generated by the between-country variation because it is almost identical when we control for country and year fixed effects; that is, the relationship is identified from within-country variation over time. This is important because it suggests that countries tend to stabilize as their revenues increase and that a necessary condition for developing state capacity above a low level is security. Panel B also suggests that it is not global trends in increasing revenue that matter and that a falling propensity to conflict at a country level is driving these results.

Although it is necessary to be circumspect, the patterns in Figures 9.2 and 9.3 are consistent with the ideas that state capacity and conflict reinforce each other and that fiscal capacity can only develop once security is established. And this hints at the possibility of a "conflict trap that is a combination of high conflict and low state capacity."

Regardless of the causal interpretation, the importance of these kind of complementarities in data is a marked feature of fragile countries. The far greater likelihood of conflict in the lowest decile of fiscal capacity suggests that low fiscal capacity could be a key element of the conflict trap.[7] Panel A of Figure 9.3 shows

[7] The trap is very clear in the data we use. Countries that come out of violent episodes have a likelihood of experiencing renewed violence of over 30 percent the first quarter after the end of conflict.

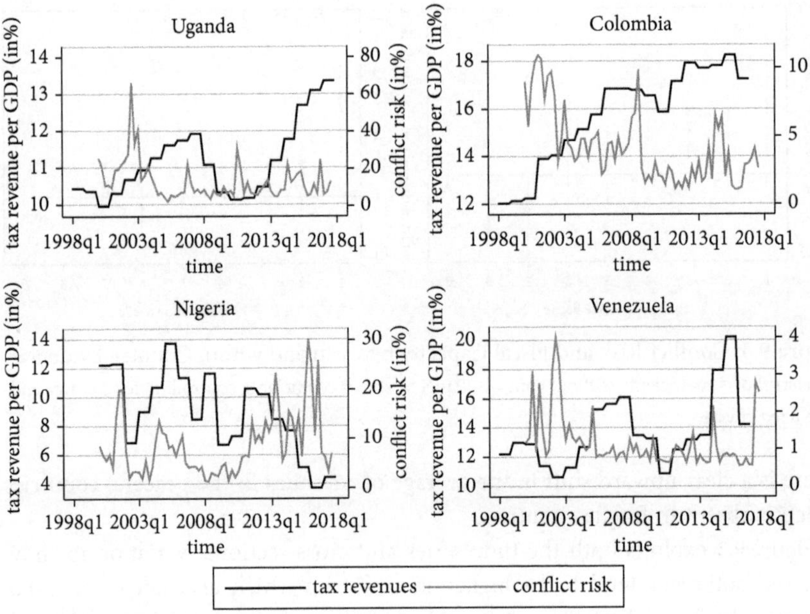

Figure 9.4 Conflict Risk and Fiscal Capacity: Case Studies Data on conflict risk is based on a forecast framework of armed conflict by Mueller and Rauh (2019). Tax revenue data is from the IMF.

that low fiscal capacity and low security correlate and Panel B shows that this is even the case if we control for country fixed effects, which implies that history, geography, and ethnic composition are not solely responsible for this link. Instead, countries seem to be least secure when they have least fiscal capacity. Moreover, panel B suggests that conflict risk drops dramatically with rising fiscal capacity within the same country; that is, escaping the conflict trap is possible, which confirms the findings in Baer et al. (2019) in this volume.

This general picture is further reinforced in Figure 9.4, which is based on four country case studies of how capacity and risk change over time. To get a contemporaneous risk estimate we use the forecasting framework in Mueller and Rauh (2019) to estimate future conflict risk at the quarterly level. In this way we derive a measure of susceptibility to conflict which is not based on an ex post valuation of a situation but captures future conflict risk.[8]

The likelihood is then falling but remains significantly higher up to 10 years after the violence ended. This finding implies that many countries are cycling in an out of violence repeatedly.

[8] This sort of framework is also what political risk insurers like the World Bank's Multilateral Investment Guarantee Agency (MIGA) use to calculate political risk insurance rates. To the best of our knowledge MIGA uses a model based on Goldstone et al. (2010).

The case studies reveal dramatic differences in conflict risk and revenues. Whereas conflict risk in Uganda was extremely high, reaching up to 70 percent during the conflict, it has been much lower in Venezuela; however, there are also interesting changes across time in which Uganda and Colombia show clear positive and long-lasting trends in revenues and negative trends in risk. Venezuela and Nigera, two countries with significant natural resources, do not seem to develop their fiscal capacity during this period; nor do they seem to show any reduction in conflict risk. And indeed, recent events in both Nigeria and Venezuela suggest that the two countries are failing in their ability to provide security.

Figure 9.4 suggests that Uganda and Colombia are making moves towards exiting their conflict traps. Both countries have increased the share of tax revenues over GDP by 4–5 percentage points in the past two decades. This does not mean that both countries do not face formidable challenges in the coming years but, given that both countries were facing extreme levels of fragility not so long ago, their current situation gives some hope that escaping the conflict trap is possible.

The complex question hence arises of how countries manage to escape from violence. Although it is not the only factor, lack of security is related to a lack of cohesive institutions. Cohesive institutional arrangements make it more likely that the state is used for common purposes and thus reduce the value of fighting for political control. This is consistent with cross-country patterns in the data. But the institutional changes do not necessarily need to take place at the federal level. Mueller and Rohner (2018), for example, find large falls of violence after local power sharing agreements in Northern Ireland. Fetzer and Kyburz (2019) exploit variation in revenue disbursements to local governments, together with data on local democratic institutions in Nigeria. They find a strong link between rents and conflict. Having democratically elected local governments significantly weakens the causal link between rents and political violence.

3.2 Society

Oppositional identities—whether these are ideological, ethnic, linguistic, or religious—are one of the key contributors to state fragility. Here we argue that they contribute directly and indirectly to weak fiscal capacity. The direct channel operates through its consequences for public resource allocation and its indirect channel through weakening the culture of compliance.

Most studies that invoke the importance of societal cleavages take these as fixed. However, this need not be the case. For example, polarization need not be fixed and ethnic identities can be activated for political use.[9] Moreover, shared

[9] For an overview see Fearon and Laitin (2000) and Sen (2007) and for recent evidence see Eifert et al. (2010).

experiences can sometimes bring divided societies together. For example, Depretis-Chauvin et al. (2018) show that shared experiences such as winning a football championship influence the strength of ethnic identities. However, even though it is now widely appreciated that narratives that create a shared sense of purpose are important, relatively little remains known about the dynamics of identity and strategies to bring about social cohesion.

As we discussed in section 9.3.1, it is important to consider that societal changes which support the emergence of an effective social contract between the state and its citizens are a dynamic feature of state development. Moreover, it has a bearing on building fiscal capacity which depends on norms and values as well as the coercive power of the state. A state in which citizens share a sense of common purpose and trust the government to deliver on it is more likely to elicit tax compliance.

The discussion of society and its evolution goes beyond traditional boundaries of economic analysis, which takes preferences and values as fixed.[10] Although norms are discussed in a range of economic applications, they are rarely joined to discussions of state capacity.

3.2.1 Politics and Resource Allocation

Polarized societies can affect political instability; there are many studies which have linked ethnolinguistic and religious cleavages to an increase in the likelihood of violent conflict; for example, Montalvo and Reynal-Querol (2005), Esteban et al. (2012), and Michalopoulos and Papaioannou (2016). In general, more oppositional identities at the core of politics makes it more challenging to organize common interest policies. There is a range of studies that have linked polarization and fractionalization to patterns of public spending, for example Alesina et al. (1999), Hodler and Raschky (2014), and De Luca et al. (2018).

As we have argued, cohesion is important to the incentive to build state capacity. Fractured societies that result in more conflict over public resources are not conducive to revenue mobilization. As Besley and Persson (2011) show in cross-country data, fractionalization is strongly negatively correlated with measures of state capacity, though it is difficult to infer causality from such data.

3.2.2 Compliance

It has long been recognized in the literature on "tax morale" that nonpecuniary motives are important in tax compliance.[11] Following the historical narrative of Levi (1988), Besley (2019) argues that this can be linked to the way in which the state chooses to spend resources. The larger the transfers to favored groups, the

[10] That said, many economists have argued for treating these things as endogenous (see, for example, Bowles, 1998).

[11] See, for example, Luttmer and Singhal (2014) and Torgler (2007).

less likely it is that a broad culture of tax compliance will emerge. It is an issue of trust; citizens must be able to believe that the state will pursue common purposes rather than operating as a private fiefdom of a ruling elite or ethnic group.

Compliance provides a direct link to the idea of legitimacy, that is, the process by which individuals defer to decisions and rules, following them voluntarily out of obligation rather than out of fear of punishment or anticipation of reward (Tyler 2006). It is arguable that core aspects of state capacity, especially of legal and fiscal capacity, are directly related to building norms of voluntary compliance. Levi et al. (2009), for example, demonstrate a link between the extent of the trustworthiness of government and procedural justice and citizens' willingness to defer to the police, courts, and tax department in a wide range of African societies. More generally, this makes clear that effective states are built on the back of "civic cultures" which can facilitate the operation of state functions.

Reciprocity can be an important part of this. For example, citizens pay taxes as long as the state reciprocates by providing public goods. But if citizens feel that the political elite or the bureaucratic apparatus is stealing money, they have no incentive to pay taxes and corruption erodes state capacity through its effect on legitimacy.

Putting it all together, we would expect the willingness to comply with taxes to be stronger where citizens identify more with the revenue raising collective and where there is greater trust that the state will deliver by providing public goods. We now look at some evidence for this idea in attitudinal data. Specifically, we link national identities, trust in government, and the willingness to pay taxes from two large databases of survey results, the World Value Surveys and the Afrobarometer.[12] The first of these covers a global population while the Afrobarometer only covers Africa. However, given our focus on state fragility, this is arguably a more relevant population.

Both surveys ask questions that capture the attitude of the respondent towards paying tax and also questions on identities. The surveys are repeated cross sections, with the questions being asked over several rounds. We will include country fixed-effects and survey round dummies and hence rely on within-country variation after controlling for any "macro" time effects. We also have access to a range of control variables in the survey such as age, education, gender, and income.

The question that we use to gauge whether attitudes are supportive of tax compliance in the World Value Survey is whether the respondent believes that cheating on taxes is ever justified. To make the interpretation of magnitudes easier we reverse the scale such that only respondents that believe cheating is never justified are coded as 10. The mean of the resulting variable in the World Value

[12] Besley (2019) shows evidence based on combining the European Values Survey and World Values Survey.

Table 9.2 National Identity and Tax Compliance in the World Values Survey Data

VARIABLES	(1) cheating on taxes is not justifiable (1-10)	(2)	(3)	(4)	(5) cheating on taxes is never justifiable
I see myself as citizen of the [country] nation	0.320*** (0.010)	0.326*** (0.010)	0.229*** (0.012)	0.220*** (0.012)	0.062*** (0.002)
I see myself as member of my local community			0.188*** (0.009)	0.118*** (0.010)	0.032*** (0.002)
the government should take more responsability			0.023*** (0.002)	0.025*** (0.002)	0.005*** (0.000)
Observations	149,863	131,918	128,792	128,792	128,792
R-squared	0.008	0.019	0.023	0.145	0.127
Controls	NO	YES	YES	YES	YES
Country/Wave FE	NO	NO	NO	YES	YES

Robust standard errors in parentheses. *** $p<0.01$, ** $p<0.05$, * $p<0.1$. Question on cheating on taxes in columns (1) to (4) is coded from 1 to 10 with a standard deviation of 2.18. In column (5) we code a dummy equal to 1 if the answer is 10 (never justified). Question on national identity is coded from 1 to 4 with a standard deviation of 0.62. All data is from the World Values Survey.

Survey sample is 8.7, i.e. most people believe taxes should be paid. In the Afrobarometer we use three questions surrounding the necessity to pay taxes: (1) whether they think it is wrong not to pay taxes (coded 1–3); (2) whether they have refused to pay fee or tax to government (coded 1–5); and (3) whether they agree to the claim that people must pay taxes (coded 1–5). Again, we find throughout that, by and large, respondents believe taxes need to be paid.

The results in Tables 9.2 and 9.3 show a strong and robust relationship between attitudes towards paying taxes and a stronger sense of national identity, even if one controls for country/round fixed effects. Table 9.2 shows results for the World Value Survey.[13] Column (1) shows the overall correlation between whether the respondent believes that cheating is not justified and national identity. Columns (2) to (4) add fixed effects and controls. Column (5) shows the result if we code a simple dummy that captures whether respondents think that cheating is completely out of the question and therefore receive the top score (10). In all cases the positive relationship with national identity, even when controlling for the strength of local identity, is robust.

[13] These develop some of the empirical findings in Besley (2019) who uses combined data from the World Values Survey and European Values Survey.

Table 9.3 National Identity and Tax Compliance in the Afrobarometer Data

VARIABLES	(1) Wrong: Not paying taxes	(2) Refused to pay fee or tax to government	(3) People must pay taxes	(4) Wrong: Not paying taxes	(5) Refused to pay fee or tax to government	(6) People must pay taxes
Strength of National Identity Relative to Ethnic Identity	0.009*** (0.002)	0.015*** (0.002)	0.014*** (0.004)	0.004* (0.002)	0.008*** (0.002)	0.024*** (0.004)
Observations	82,131	83,638	83,224	82,131	83,638	83,224
R-squared	0.001	0.001	0.001	0.064	0.043	0.047
Controls	YES	YES	YES	YES	YES	YES
Country/Wave FE	NO	NO	NO	YES	YES	YES

Robust standard errors in parentheses. *** $p < 0.01$, ** $p < 0.05$, * $p < 0.1$. Question on whether it is wrong not to pay taxes is coded from 1 to 3 with a standard deviation of 0.67. Question on not paying taxes or fee is coded from 1 to 5 with a standard deviation of 0.8. Question on people having to pay taxes is coded from 1 to 5 with a standard deviation of 1.17. Question on national identity is coded from 1 to 5 with a standard deviation of 1.17. All data is from the Afrobarometer.

Table 9.3 confirms the same pattern with the different sample and questions from the Afrobarometer. Columns (1) to (3) of Table 9.3 do not control for country/wave fixed effects, columns (4) to (6) do. Again, results indicate a positive relationship between national identity and attitudes towards paying taxes. The only exception is the question regarding whether the respondent has refused to pay taxes or a fee before, which tends to be answered positively for individuals with stronger national identities. Although only based on subjective attitudes, these correlations do suggest a link between national identity and compliance.[14]

In Tables 9.4 and 9.5, we consider the link between trust in government and willingness to comply with taxes. The results show some strong patterns in the existing survey data which are consistent with this view. In Table 9.4 we report on the same World Value survey data question as in Table 9.2, except that we now try to explain the willingness to pay taxes through the attitude of the respondent to the government. Confidence in government is significantly correlated with the opinion that cheating on taxes in not justified. Confirming what was shown in Besley (2019), this relationship is not simply a proxy for attitudes regarding government or general trust but seems to be specific to the attitude towards the government.

[14] Blimpo et al (2018) use Afrobarometer data to show a strong positive correlation between electrification, national identity, and attitudes to tax compliance at the subnational level. They instrument electification with the density of power grids at the district level and find strong effects of electrification on the willingness to pay taxes.

Table 9.4 Confidence in Government and Tax Compliance in the World Values Surveys

VARIABLES	(1) cheating on taxes is not justifiable	(2)	(3)	(4)	(5) cheating on taxes is never justifiable
Confidence in the government	0.169*** (0.005)	0.161*** (0.005)	0.170*** (0.005)	0.123*** (0.006)	0.021*** (0.001)
Most people can be trusted			−0.011 (0.011)	0.010 (0.011)	0.019*** (0.002)
The government should take more responsibility			0.008*** (0.002)	0.018*** (0.002)	0.004*** (0.000)
Observations	271,642	230,591	215,471	215,471	215,471
R-squared	0.005	0.014	0.015	0.127	0.120
Controls	NO	YES	YES	YES	YES
Country/Wave FE	NO	NO	NO	YES	YES

Robust standard errors in parentheses. *** $p<0.01$, ** $p<0.05$, * $p<0.1$. Question on cheating on taxes in columns (1) to (4) is coded from 1 to 10 with a standard deviation of 2.18. In column (5) we code a dummy equal to 1 if the answer is 10 (never justified). Confidence in government is coded from 1 to 4 with a standard deviation of 0.94. All data is from the World Values Survey.

In Table 9.5 we look at various measures of the willingness to pay taxes in the Afrobarometer data and two dimensions of attitudes towards the government. The first, shown in panel A, is measuring whether respondents trust the tax department, that is, the institution which is directly in charge of collecting taxes. There is a positive, significant relationship between trust in the tax department and the willingness to pay taxes. This positive relationship is also economically relevant. Moving an individual from low to high trust changes attitudes regarding taxes by up to half a standard deviation. This relationship also holds when we control for country fixed effects and individual controls. In panel B we show similar magnitudes when we look at the corruption of tax officials. Individuals are much less likely to be willing to pay taxes when they think that tax officers are corrupt. This raises an interesting perspective on the role of the tax agency when raising taxes. A population that sees tax officials as corrupt will not be willing to pay taxes and investing in the conduct of these officials is therefore an important part of raising fiscal capacity.

These are only correlations; however, the evidence provided in Weigel (2018) supports the ideas behind the mechanism that we are suggesting. He examines the determinants of payment in a citizen property tax campaign that raised average compliance from 0 percent to 10 percent. Aside from ability to pay, prior beliefs about the legitimacy of the provincial government were the strongest predictor of tax payment. Legitimacy was itself influenced by tax collectors' identities: minority

Table 9.5 Institutional Trust and Tax Compliance in the Afrobarometer

Panel A: Trust and Tax Department and Willingness to Pay

VARIABLES	(1) Wrong: Not paying taxes	(2) Refused to pay fee or tax to government	(3) People must pay taxes	(4) Wrong: Not paying taxes	(5) Refused to pay fee or tax to government	(6) People must pay taxes
Trust Tax Department	0.0575***	−0.0367***	0.189***	0.0544***	−0.0248***	0.179***
	(0.00218)	(0.00255)	(0.00372)	(0.00230)	(0.00277)	(0.00399)
Age and gender controls	YES	YES	YES	YES	YES	YES
Education and corruption controls	NO	NO	NO	YES	YES	YES
Region/ round fixed effects	NO	NO	NO	YES	YES	YES
Observations	85,719	91,931	92,136	85,531	91,686	91,883
R-squared	0.010	0.003	0.030	0.128	0.100	0.135

Panel B: Corruption of Tax Officials and Willingness to Pay

VARIABLES	(1) Wrong: Not paying taxes	(2) Refused to pay fee or tax to government	(3) People must pay taxes	(4) Wrong: Not paying taxes	(5) Refused to pay fee or tax to government	(6) People must pay taxes
Corruption: tax officials	−0.0415***	0.0516***	−0.135***	−0.0366***	0.0286***	−0.118***
	(0.00277)	(0.00335)	(0.00488)	(0.00325)	(0.00414)	(0.00578)
Age and gender controls	YES	YES	YES	YES	YES	YES
Education and corruption controls	NO	NO	NO	YES	YES	YES
Region/ round fixed effects	NO	NO	NO	YES	YES	YES
Observations	81,843	87,471	87,706	81,668	87,250	87,480
R-squared	0.004	0.004	0.011	0.125	0.102	0.119

Robust standard errors in parentheses. *** $p<0.01$, ** $p<0.05$, * $p<0.1$. Question on whether it is wrong not to pay taxes is coded from 1 to 3 with a standard deviation of 0.67. Question on not paying taxes or fee is coded from 1 to 5 with a standard deviation of 0.8. Question on people having to pay taxes is coded from 1 to 5 with a standard deviation of 1.17. Question on trust in the tax department is coded from 0 to 3 with a standard deviation of 1.06. Question on corruption of tax officials is coded from 0 to 3 with a standard deviation of 0.86. All data is from the Afrobarometer.

ethnic citizens were more likely to pay to minority ethnic tax collectors. In addition, Weigel finds that those paying were more likely to trust the government and believed that more would be submitted to the state and used for public good provision. This lines up with the empirical regularities in Tables 9.4 and 9.5.

Weigel also shows that there are knock-on effects of the tax campaign. On average the tax campaign leads individuals to update positively about the legitimacy of the provincial government, indicating a positive feedback loop of state building and citizen tax compliance. Weigel (2019) also finds that the campaign increased political participation by 5 percentage points (28 percent): citizens in taxed neighborhoods were more likely to attend town hall meetings hosted by the government or to submit evaluations of its performance.

In conclusion, we believe that a focus on factors which affect trust in government and a sense of identity may have a role to play in building fiscal capacity in general. This is particularly important in the shadow of state fragility, where weak legitimacy and low levels of trust are endemic. More generally, the kinds of attitudes that we have looked at shape the environment in which tax policy is made and could be an important diagnostic when considering the context for policy reform. Moreover, it reinforces the idea that reforms in policies and institutions which strengthen trust and legitimacy may have important roles to play in building fiscal capacity.

3.3 The Economy

Fiscal capacity depends crucially on the structure and development of the economy. For example, structural changes in the economy facilitate the collection of taxes, particularly as formal employment increases. This means that there are multiple feedbacks between state capacity and income. The typical growth process involves higher incomes as well as structural change (for example, by extending the domain of markets). Higher income will provide a natural boost to investments in some kinds of state capacity. Citizens may more intensively demand goods best produced by the state, creating higher returns to investing in collective capacity and fiscal capacity. Larger prospective tax bases also mean that a given investment in fiscal capacity generates larger revenues. Thus, the marginal return to such investment may increase.

As fiscal capacity expands, it does so typically by creating more broad-based taxation. In most advanced economies it is the personal income tax (including social security contributions) and broad-based consumption taxes that do the heavy lifting in funding the state. These taxes tend to displace reliance on trade taxes (see Besley and Persson, 2013). This tendency toward more broadly based taxation is important because it emphasizes that fiscal capacity building in part mirrors structural change in the economy.

A weak private sector economy with little production at scale, which is a symptom of state fragility, therefore poses an impediment to building fiscal capacity. Kleven et al. (2016) argue that cross-reporting is facilitated by having larger firms play a principal role in complying with taxes. And, as shown in Besley and Persson (2013), an increase in income tax withholding by employers is an important aspect of fiscal capacity investment. Firms are also at the heart of compliance with VAT.

Jensen (2019) shows that the structure of employment matters and that this structure causally affects the strength of the state. He argues that a high employee share is a necessary condition for effective taxation and that increases in employee shares drive the expansion of the income tax base. However, the causality runs in both directions. Assaf, Engman, and Ragoussis (2019) in this volume show that firms in fragile states (based on the Fragile States Index definition) are small, low in productivity, low in growth, and report being constrained by a lack of capital as well as being impeded by volatility in their economic environments.

Some of these issues can be directly traced back to the failure of the state to develop its collective and legal capacity. For example, there is now a large literature that establishes that the weak protection of property rights hinders economic development.[15] Lack of property rights enforcement has the potential to lead to serious distortions of the economy because it can lead to a dramatic misallocation of resources in the private sector towards predation and towards the defense against predation. There is a direct link to the lack of taxation since predation and weak property rights are more likely when governments lack the kind of broad-based taxation that is needed to redistribute efficiently in line with the famous Diamond and Mirrlees efficiency theorem.

Having a strong private sector also requires other investments in state capacity. Firms rely on contract enforcement and protection of property rights. When the state fails to provide these services, then firms may have to invest in security. Given that weak security is a feature of state fragility, this contributes towards the weakness of the private sector by increasing the cost of doing business. In effect this is a tax on business which yields no public revenues. To compound this, Besley and Mueller (2018a) show that where the state fails to provide law enforcement institutions, then firms invest in security, a form of misallocation of resources away from productive ends. This is a particularly serious problem if the most productive firms are affected by crime and Besley and Mueller (2018a) present evidence that this is indeed the case in several countries.

A weak private sector is also tied to a lack of resilience. Looking across countries, Figure 9.5 shows that fiscal capacity is also correlated with GDP

[15] For two theoretically structured overviews of this literature see Besley and Ghatak (2010) and Gonzales (2012).

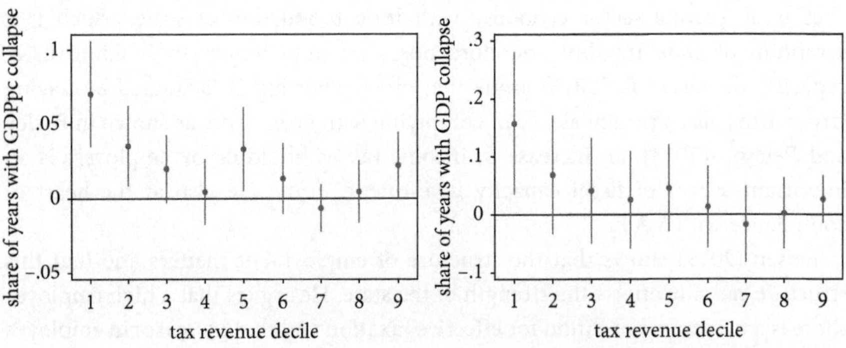

Figure 9.5 Economic Fragility and Fiscal Capacity between and within Country Evidence

Data on GDP is from the World Bank. Data on tax revenue is from the IMF. Both panels show regression coefficients of a regression of a dummy indicating a decline of GDP per capita in the following year of more than 10% on tax revenue decile dummies. The omitted category is decile 10. Panel a) shows coefficients without controls. Panel b) shows coefficients controlling for country and time fixed effects.

declines.[16] When we control for country and time fixed effects in panel B the relationship strengthens, that is, it is not to the effect of fixed country characteristics or world trends. The decile with the weakest fiscal capacity is 15 percent more likely to experience a collapse of GDP. By now, it should be clear that this is because weak fiscal capacity is also correlated with a plethora of other weaknesses in the state and further underlines a range of interdependent issues that comprise fragility.

The link between GDP shocks and fiscal capacity links to a literature that documents higher volatility for emerging markets. Aguiar and Gopinath (2007), for example, argue that this volatility is best modelled as shocks to trend growth, rather than transitory fluctuations around a stable trend. Koren and Tenreyro (2007) show that as countries develop, their productive structure moves from more volatile to less volatile sectors. Exporters of natural resources are often dependent on these resources, have low fiscal capacity and experience dramatic swings in output.[17]

It is important to realize that the link between economy and fragility is mediated by political institutions. Cohesive political institutions, for example, may play a role in reducing volatility caused by policy.[18] Besley and Mueller (2018b) show that countries without strong executive constraints are more volatile and that foreign investors tend to avoid these countries. Political reforms which credibly constrain the government are followed by large increases in foreign

[16] Note that falling GDP will lead to higher revenues per GDP so that this is not a mechanical relationship.

[17] Indeed, the relationship we show in figure 10, panel B is to some degree driven by these countries. This is interesting because it means that producers of natural resources seem to be able to avoid sudden falls in GDP when they have a larger revenue base.

[18] In a related argument Rodrik (1999) makes the observation that a combination of social conflict interactions and external economic shocks can throw countries off their growth path.

investment inflows. There is a link to volatility because foreign firms may be averse to policy risk. There is a direct link to the findings in Besley and Mueller (2018c), Burgess et al. (2015), and Fetzer and Kyburz (2019), who argue that some political institutions are better able to reduce the toxic politics associated with competition for political rents.

Economic and political resilience will also be important in the coming decades in which volatility induced by climate change will, even in the most optimistic scenarios, take a toll on the agricultural output of many countries. According to estimates by Costinot et al. (2016), who also take into account changing production and trade patterns, the most affected countries will be Malawi, Myanmar, Democratic Republic of the Congo, Ghana, Bangladesh, Thailand, Nigeria, and Sudan. These are all countries with relatively low state capacity and weak political institutions. Moreover, violence has recently broken out and intensified in Malawi, Sudan, and Nigeria. Recent political changes in Thailand suggest that the country is dismantling executive constraints.

The bottom line is that the economic conditions that generate a weak private sector are also a factor that inhibits fiscal capacity building. Improving the performance and resilience of the economy therefore has a bearing on fiscal capacity building via this channel.

4. Policy Implications

The key take-away from the discussion so far is that revenue mobilization is linked to building the state, society, and the economy. The thinking that underpins this is allied to a political economy approach which takes the cultural and political context seriously alongside conventional economic thinking. It is therefore essential to move away from viewing creating fiscal capacity as purely technocratic. Advice on tax policy, including methods of auditing and better tax design is valuable, but it has to be located in a wider context, especially in the presence of factors that are symptomatic of state fragility. A radically different approach may still not be necessary; this must be assessed case by case.

4.1 The Policy Challenge in the Face of State Fragility

At first sight, the analysis suggests that engagement with fragile countries is more complex and may require stepping outside of tried and tested frameworks that are deemed to work in standard policy settings.[19] International organizations and

[19] This is also suggested by Baer et al. (2019) who propose a two-stage approach where the first stage of reforms involves "recuperation" reforms, while the second stage focuses on "building progress" reforms.

donors have mandates that steer them towards giving technical advice in their policy dialogue. But it is more difficult to engage when the issues are as much about societal and political issues as they are about economics. Moreover, in the wider sociopolitical context, international actors have much less legitimacy in policymaking when they can disrupt and change political equilibria. Quite often, mandates restrict international engagement so that recommendations on important aspects of fragility, such as weak legitimacy, can appear to be "off limits." Nevertheless, in the contexts that we have been discussing here, some way has to be found to operationalize an approach which is based on political economy and which speaks to the wider range of factors that affect state fragility.

It begins with the way in which fragility is conceptualized and measured. Here we have stressed two factors with direct repercussions for policy. Fragility is a statement about the future, and it is important to evaluate risks when designing policy. If fragility is to be tackled there needs to be a shift away from managing and responding to crises and towards preventing expensive breakdowns.[20] Approaches as they are followed by the Multilateral Investment Guarantee Agency, for example, which uses political risk forecasts in its portfolio choices, could therefore make sense.[21] Second, fragility is multidimensional, so it makes less sense to rely on a single measure of fragility than to think about all of the different dimensions. Surveys which capture the willingness to pay taxes, like the ones conducted by the Afrobarometer, will, for example, provide important clues about the capacity of the state to raise revenues. Opinion polls can give important clues about the constraints that the government faces when implementing reforms and should be part of the evidence base.[22]

How far the preventive approach can be built into the institutional architecture for revenue mobilization in the face of state fragility has not been explored systematically and needs to be part of ongoing engagement. Standard economic models of tax reform take the institutional environment as fixed, with a tendency to focus on revenue implications of varying tax bases and tax rates. This scope is too narrow for the issues that underpin weak fiscal capacity in the shadow of state fragility.

That said, most fiscal reforms are piecemeal and marginal; opportunities for wholesale change are scarce. This is not all bad; with weak bureaucratic capacity, a step-by-step approach is almost certainly to make most sense. This is also not

[20] This approach is also proposed by the United Nations and the World Bank (2017).

[21] See Sundberg et al. (2009) for a discussion. At the time, the Multilateral Investment Guararntee Agency investigated forecast models and settled for Goldstone et al. (2010). See Mueller and Rauh (2018, 2019) for a recent discussion of forecasting.

[22] A very stark example here is the early history of reform of Russia, which faced formidable challenges to its fiscal capacity in the 1990s. Under Gaidar, the government followed considerable fiscal consolidation broadly in line with the technical requirements. However, by 1993, Russians had completely lost faith in the process. According to a poll, only 30.7 percent of respondents supported the free market while 53.2 percent opposed it. The result was a complete reversal of the reforms.

inconsistent with consideration of a broader range of factors. Drawing on the experience of EBRD following the fall of the Berlin Wall provides some pointers as to how a piecemeal (in their case project-based lending) approach can also serve as a catalyst for sustainable institutional change. In that context, improvements in regulation of markets and greater attention to environmental concerns were included as part of assessing the transition impact of individual projects. Moreover, assessment of standard financial returns was augmented using a transition impact "scorecard." Following this idea, widening the ambitions of tax reform programs to include specific institution building goals could be considered systematically, which means factoring benefits in the form of long-term capacity building. We agree with Baer et al. (2019) when they attribute the failure of revenue conditionality to have a significant impact on tax revenue outcomes to weaknesses in basic institutions and administrative capacity, which make it difficult for these states to implement major tax revenue reforms. But this means developing approaches which give a role for promoting these capacities. It also means realizing that a collection of interlinked reforms can create a critical mass for institutional change so that a sequenced reform program can achieve much more than a one-off change.

Many technocratically-minded advisors find it hard to work in second-best environments when it comes to offering advice on building fiscal capacity. There appears to be some truth to the old joke in which the response to the symptoms of state fragility is to advise countries to "behave more like Denmark," that is, to emulate the kinds of fiscal reforms and tax systems that could work in such contexts. Of necessity, this advice is accompanied by a list of reforms so long that the starting point is far away from the desired destination. As Collier (2019) emphasizes, this is a major policy error. You cannot infer the path to building successful states by studying the desired outcome, any more than observing a completed building tells you about the construction process. He argues that we need to focus on the structures—the scaffolding—that supports a country's early efforts to become an effective state.

Realism is important; raising revenues in a context of fragility can be an uphill struggle when other elements that are complements to fiscal capacity are not in place. This is especially true when fragile countries are caught in a vicious cycle in which weak institutions and low provision of public goods reinforce a civic culture that hinders tax collection, and can be exacerbated by a weak, shock-prone economy. It also means being cognizant of political constraints.

Admitting when conditions are not conducive to reform is also essential in some situations. Failing to do so risks disappointment, which can further fuel fragility instead of helping to improve the situation. However, when pivotal moments occur, such as when a new government comes to power with a genuine will for change, it is important to engage, albeit with sensitivity as to the limits set by existing state capacities. The risk is to overload already stretched administrative capacity by developing a long list of reforms which cannot possibly be delivered in reasonable time. Those offering fiscal advice need to be mindful of the strains that may already be present in the system. It is often important to proceed gradually rather than trying to leap too quickly to the ultimate destination; small steps that work can build confidence in weak state institutions.

4.2 Reforming State Institutions

Institutional reform is one way of trying to improve the capacity for revenue mobilization; it many different dimensions, however, and we are mindful here of the limitations of what can be done in the context of a focus on fiscal capacity. Nevertheless, some policy reform options do merit discussion.

4.2.1 Political Institutions

Building institutions that support cohesiveness may be the long-term goal but it cannot be promoted directly within the mandates of most international actors.[23] There is little room to manoeuvre when a country is run by an unaccountable elite with little commitment to the long-term benefits to their fellow citizens from broad-based economic development; but there is still a strong case for focusing on institutions that strengthen transparency and scrutiny of policy in a fiscal context, thereby contributing to building stronger constraints on the executive. Having a clearer role for independent courts in the field of tax policy, including enforcement of tax compliance, can also be important not just for tax policy but as a key component in establishing the rule of law. It is essential that citizens feel that elites are subject to the same level of scrutiny and compliance requirements as they are. The results on compliance above emphasize that weak attitudes towards compliance are associated with a lack of confidence in the state.

When government is failing to produce a coherent broad-based approach to revenue mobilization, pressure for change needs to come from somewhere. Countries vary enormously in the strength of civil society as a means of promoting change. The task therefore often falls to international organizations and aid agencies, even though they lack any form of legitimacy and are not accountable to citizens locally. There are limits to what interventions by external donors can achieve for the long term. None of the successful fiscal states in the world continue to rely on support from outside actors, even though this support can add to their resilience as we saw in Greece and Ireland following the global financial crisis. However, these were inherently temporary measures.

[23] Even if this not the case and the dialogue can include political reform, it is not helpful to use broad-brush categories like "democracy." As argued forcefully in IGC (2018), holding elections in fractured polities with a history of conflict is rarely a recipe for creating better cohesion.

It is problematic for external actors to be overt advocates of political change, whatever their concerns about the behavior of governments towards their citizens. Accusations of neocolonial meddling in the affairs of nations can be close to the surface. But actions around the margin which are linked to revenue mobilization should be considered. Chief among these is the task of building a more effective set of fiscal institutions, to which we now turn.

4.2.2 Fiscal Institutions

Fiscal institutions that emphasize transparency and accountability, such as independent fiscal councils, can play a role in helping to achieve a more cohesive system. For example, giving legislators greater access to fiscal councils, as in the Netherlands or Australia, can strengthen constraints on the executive. In many countries, budgets and other fiscal measures are handed to independent bodies for scrutiny, including scrutiny of the realism of the economic assumptions used to make fiscal projections.

There is, however, a paradox; agencies that enhance transparency and accountability are most needed in situations where they are likely to fail. Political cultures that respect independent advice and a distribution of authority more rarely need this oversight. Courts also act infrequently to overtly restrain what governments do, even though the threat that they will act reduces the need for them to act. There is also evidence of a link between fiscal rules and judicial review. For example, Bohn and Inman (1996) find that heterogeneity in the effectiveness of balanced budget requirements in US states is greatest when they are enforced as constitutional constraints by an independently elected state supreme court. This suggests a potential complementarity between fiscal and legal capacity.

The main lesson from international experience with fiscal institutions is that the details matter in the design of such institutions: the mandate that they are given, how they are held accountable, and the staffing/resources that they are given.[24] Failing to give sufficient prominence and resources to fiscal councils is a sure-fire way of limiting their effectiveness. Although bringing evidence from international experience can be a useful catalyst for change, it is also important to tailor the institutional framework to the specific needs and context of the country in question. For example, in some settings, such work could be a combined responsibility of a central bank and in others it would be the responsibility of a separate authority.

Independent fiscal bodies that hold the government to account for the conduct of fiscal policy and can assist in designing long-term strategies for management of public resources are inevitably part of the "body politic," and it is impossible to hide behind technical design issues. Hence, a careful balance has to be struck

[24] See Beetsma et al. (2018) for discussion of some alternative models.

between being overtly political and supporting government structures. Acting as an agency of restraint and trying to create a longer-term, more strategic perspective is important as a state builds out of fragility. The fiscal architecture can be particularly important in countries with abundant natural resources. Resource price fluctuations can be a particular challenge and could benefit from independent fiscal management to increase legitimacy. And, as we discussed above, resilience is an even larger issue in resource-dependent countries.

Strengthening the internal capacity of revenue authorities of revenue raising institutions is important. Some extremely useful insights have, for example, been gained by innovative experiments in weak institutional contexts like from Pakistan in Khan et al. (2016, 2019) or Brazil in Naritomi (2019). But strengthening capacity has to go beyond technical aspects. Supporting activities which draw attention to noncompliance by elites and multinational businesses can also create a greater sense of trust in government. However, this has to be done in a way that does not accentuate divisions, which is likely when it is a politically motivated process. There are good reasons why revenue authorities in many countries enjoy a degree of autonomy from the political process.

4.2.3 Natural Resources

Quite apart from the challenge of fragility, states with high dependence on natural resources struggle to build fiscal capacity for reasons outlined, for example, in Besley and Persson (2013). They are also among the most conflict-prone, and have struggled to build effective constraints on executive power. Often, as a result of this struggle, repression replaces conflict. Evidence from the World Values Survey suggests that natural resource–dependent governments have lower levels of confidence in government and weaker attitudes towards tax compliance.

There are some standard prescriptions for managing natural resource revenues which apply in all contexts and are not different when there is state fragility. These include trying to achieve macrostabilization benefits by building reserves and developing well-managed sovereign wealth funds. In countries with weak constraints on executive power, such management is made more difficult because it may be difficult to prevent governments from taking a short-term approach to spending accumulated revenues. Worse still, competition to control such reserves can increase the potential for political violence.

A first step towards moving out of fragility is to find ways of better controlling such behavior. This can be achieved in part by increasing fiscal accountability and transparency, as shown, for example, by Fetzer and Kyburz (2019); butthe problem runs much deeper. Easy access to public revenues, whether well-managed or not, prevents the emergence of the kind of social contract that sees the provision of state services as the quid pro quo for compliance with taxation. Finding ways of building broad-based tax systems such as income taxes and VAT is thus important, even when there are natural resources.

4.2.4 The Role of Decentralization

All countries must decide on the balance between taxes raised locally and taxes centrally. In most advanced countries, most taxation is raised centrally. This is logical, given that there are reasons to avoid a race to the bottom from tax competition between jurisdictions. A focus on central government tax raising has history on its side: many strong fiscal states were built on the back of limiting the fiscal capacity of local jurisdictions (see, for example, Dincecco, 2011, 2015). Some modern states, such as the United States, used a federal model of fiscal capacity building; however, fiscal capacity was gradually transferred to a central state because of national emergencies, and this shift became more and more necessary as the economy and commerce became more integrated.

In spite of this historical trend, decentralized settings are a promising testing ground for building fiscal capacity in the face of state fragility. It affords some possibilities for experimentation. Local leaders may also enjoy legitimacy that national leaders lack, and they may preside over less polarized polities. That said, they may not have formal bureaucratic structures in place to raise revenues unless they are encouraged to build them.

Whereas it will often be impossible to advocate cohesive institutions at the national level, it might be possible to prevent fragility by putting in place such institutions locally. The studies by Mueller and Rohner (2018) and Fetzer and Kyburz (2019) both show, in very different contexts, that power sharing and democratic selection at the local level can help diffuse fragility that comes with the distribution of revenues locally.

Whatever the virtues of decentralization, the value of investing locally should be considered as an option which recognizes the difficulty of building cohesion in a central state. However, the scope for this is country-specific and there is no one-size-fits-all solution. It will depend in particular on the traditions and cultures of local governance in the country in question, beyond formal administrative structures. Decentralization is a particularly tricky issue in societies with strong ethnic politics and regional concentration of ethnicities.

4.3 Strengthening the Social Contract

We have emphasized that a large part of building a fiscally successful state lies in strengthening the social contract between state and citizens emphasizing reciprocity whereby increased expenditures with common benefits are delivered in exchange for voluntary compliance. As emphasized in Besley (2019), the role of increasing the strength of state institutions should not be underestimated in this process. Nevertheless, there are also ways of trying to build compliance through shifting norms and modes of engagement between the state and citizens which are pathways towards building fiscal capacity.

Actions to mobilize revenue could be scored by a set of explicit indicators which assist in making a fiscal transition in countries where reforms are hampered by symptoms of state fragility. So the score for fiscal reforms could be based on how far they have elements that increase accountability and administrative competence explicitly. We now discuss some further dimensions of this.

Levi et al. (2009) argue that having a competent bureaucracy can increase quasi-voluntary compliance with the state. This emphasizes that the kind of "teachable moments" that occur in tax bureaucracies can spillover to wider perceptions of the operation of government. Our analysis of the Afrobarometer surveys strongly suggests that perceptions of corruption of tax officers are extremely damaging to the willingness to pay tax. This means training workers in revenue agencies to treat citizens with respect and ensure the maximum transparency of the agency.

Crafting a program of fiscal capacity building to suit the context of state fragility means tailoring the narrative of reform to the context. For example, recognizing that lack of legitimacy stemming from poor accountability for use of public resources and corruption by elites needs to become a standard part of understanding the context for reform. This can be supported by evidence and analysis as we have shown: for example, trying to find ways in survey data of documenting weak compliance cultures based on norms can be a useful diagnostic in setting priorities. A country with low trust in government, weak national identity, and low confidence in the state may need a different approach from that taken where these things are not a feature of the landscape.

Concerns related to legitimacy are not typically part of what tax reform programs advocated by economists think about. Providing links to reforms of public services that demonstrate the merits of higher revenue mobilization can also be important, because a key element of a social contract is forging a link in the minds of citizens between paying taxes and receiving benefits. It is no coincidence that social security systems where retirement benefits are linked to contributions have played a pivotal historical role in fiscal capacity building.

Public services at the micro level need to be designed to move with the tax system. Visible improvements need to happen around people soon after enforced taxes come in. Although there are good reasons for being suspicious of crude efforts at hypothecating revenues to specific ends, there are some issues worth thinking about in the highly second-best world of fragile states. Norms of reciprocity rely on citizens seeing that the state is using revenues for common purposes. There is potential value in programs of reforms to public services rolled out in tandem with revenue raising initiatives, especially in those where the gains from public spending are visible and tangible. The presence of strong local ethnic or regional identities can make this even more important. It can help to improve the mobilization of revenues and may ultimately enhance the legitimacy of government.

These findings are increasingly validated in field work in the face of state fragility. For example, Weigel (2018) emphasizes that tax compliance is a political act and Sanchez de la Sierra (2018) shows that in some regions armed militia are better able to use this insight for themselves than the central government. The government is collecting taxes and providing security but fails to provide other public services. This means that competitors can be seen as legitimate or even as more legitimate than the central government.[25] This effect parallels the literature on building policy legitimacy from the ground up, that is, realizing that each encounter that the citizens have with the police is potentially important in shaping their perception of the state.

An approach that recognizes the need to strengthen the social contract also reinforces the need for organizations such as the IMF to coordinate with other international institutions when it is focusing on tax reforms. Such reforms in the tax system may work better if there is scope to increase security (which means coordinating with security operations) and with projects to improve service delivery.[26] The case of Egypt shows how difficult this is in practice. Reforms on fiscal reforms were accompanied by a World Bank project for social security. However, a government change away from Morsi damaged the project and, according to the national data, poverty has increased. The Egyptian government needs to understand that sharing resources with the population is also a way of building fiscal control.

5. Concluding Comments

This chapter has discussed the specific challenges of building fiscal capacity in the shadow of state fragility. The main message is that fiscal capacity building needs to recognize the social, political, and economic realities of state fragility. This creates both constraints and opportunities for policy reform.

Constraints come from the need to be sufficiently modest in what is being proposed and being sure that it is feasible, given the economic and political realities. Where norms of compliance are weak, it may be much more difficult to build fiscal capacity. However, opportunities come from being able to see the challenge of fiscal capacity building as a much wider activity than purely technical advice on tax policy. Seeing how taxation plays a role in enhancing the social

[25] An extreme version of this insight is provided by Berman et al. (2011) who find in the context of Iraq that the provision of public services even seems to be a relatively cost-effective counterinsurgency strategy.

[26] Research on regional favoritism also makes clear that service delivery has a regional perspective. If ethnicities live concentrated in certain areas, then public services need to be spread to areas where the tax take is to increase.

contract and increases legitimacy is key; so is recognizing the importance of tax revenue authorities as one of the key citizen-state relationships.

Well-designed tax policy can help to facilitate both institutional and cultural change, particularly when initial steps are sustained and there is prolonged and sustained engagement. But the kind of change needed has to be motivated from within polities rather than externally imposed. Moreover, well-meaning external actors will face strong headwinds when conditions are not right. A suitably modest expectation of success is needed, as well as resilience in the face of setbacks, when there is engagement with donor agencies and international organizations. State fragility creates an inherently riskier economic and political environment, and that holds true also for reform efforts to build fiscal capacity. An appropriate assessment of such risks is therefore essential.

References

Acemoglu, D. and J. Robinson. 2012. *Why Nations Fail.* New York: Crown Publishers.

Acemoglu, D. and J. Robinson. 2018. "The Emergence of Weak, Despotic and Inclusive States." Unpublished typescript.

Acemoglu, D., S. Johnson, and J. Robinson. 2005. "Institutions as a Fundamental Cause of Long-Run Development," in P. Aghion and S. Durlauf (Eds.), *Handbook of Economic Growth.* Oxford: Elsevier.

Aguiar, M. and G. Gopinath. 2007. "Emerging Market Business Cycles: The Cycle Is the Trend." *Journal of Political Economy,* 115(1): 69–102.

Alesina, A., R. Baqir, and W. Easterly. 1999. "Public Goods and Ethnic Divisions." *Quarterly Journal of Economics* 114: 1243–84.

Almond, G., and S. Verba. 1963. *The Civic Culture: Political Attitudes and Democracy in Five Nations.* New York: Sage Publications.

Baer, K., S. Gupta, M. Mansour, and S. Pattanayak. 2020. "Building Fiscal Institutions in Fragile States—A Two-Step Approach," in R. Chami, R. Espinoza, and P. Montiel (Eds.), *Macroeconomic Policy in Fragile States.* Oxford: Oxford University Press.

Beetsma, R., X. Debrun, X. Fang, Y. Kim, V. Lledó, S. Mbaye, and X. Zhang. 2018. "Independent Fiscal Councils: Recent Trends and Performance," IMF Working Paper 18/68. International Monetary Fund, Washington, DC.

Besley, T. 2020. "State Capacity, Reciprocity, and the Social Contract," *Econometrica,* 88(4): 1345–9.

Besley, T. and M. Ghatak. 2010. "Property Rights and Economic Development," in D. Rodrik and M. Rosenzweig (Eds.), *Handbook of Development Economics,* Vol. 5. Oxford: Elsevier.

Besley, T. and H. Mueller. 2018a. "Predation, Protection and Productivity: A Firm-Level Perspective." *American Economic Journal: Macroeconomics,* 10(2): 184–221.

Besley, T. and H. Mueller. 2018b. "Volatility, Institutions and Investment." *Journal of the European Economic Association*, 16(3): 604–49.

Besley, T. and H. Mueller. 2018c. "Cohesive Institutions and the Distribution of Political Rents: Theory and Evidence," in Kaushik Basu and Tito Cordella (Eds.), *Institutions, Governance and the Control of Corruption*. Cham, Switzerland: International Economic Association Series, Palgrave.

Besley, T. and H. Mueller. 2018d. "Executive Constraints as Robust Control." Barcelona GSE Working Paper: 1054. Barcelona Graduate School of Economics.

Besley, T. and T. Persson. 2009. "The Origins of State Capacity: Property Rights, Taxation and Politics." *American Economic Review*, 99: 1218–44.

Besley, T. and T. Persson. 2010. "State Capacity, Conflict and Development." *Econometrica*, 78(1): 1–34.

Besley, T. and T. Persson. 2011. *Pillars of Prosperity: The Political Economics of Development Clusters*. Princeton, NJ: Princeton University Press.

Besley, T. and T. Persson. 2013. "Taxation and Development," in A.J. Auerbach, R. Chetty, M. Feldstein, and E. Saez (Eds.), *Handbook of Public Economics*, Vol. 5 (pp. 51–110). Oxford: Elsevier.

Besley, T. and T. Persson. 2014. "The Causes and Consequences of Development Clusters: State Capacity, Peace, and Income." *Annual Review of Economics*, 6: 927–49.

Besley, T.E. Ilzetzki and T. Persson. 2013. "Weak States and Steady States: The Dynamics of Fiscal Capacity." *American Economic Journal: Macroeconomics*, 5(4): 205–35.

Berman, E., J.N. Shapiro, and J.H. Felter. 2011. "Can Hearts and Minds Be Bought? The Economics of Counterinsurgency in Iraq." *Journal of Political Economy*, 119(4): 766–819.

Bisin, A. and T. Verdier. 2017. "On the Joint Evolution of Culture and Institutions." NBER Working Paper No. 23375. Cambridge, MA: National Bureau for Economic Research.

Blimpo, M., J. Tei Mensah, K. Ochieng' Opalo, and R. Shi. 2018. "Electricity Provision and Tax Mobilization in Africa," World Bank Policy Working Paper, 8408. World Bank, Washington, DC.

Bohn, H. and R. Inman. 1996. "Balanced Budget Rules and Public Deficits: Evidence from the U.S." NBER Working Paper, No. 5533. Cambridge, MA: National Bureau for Economic Research.

Bowles, S. 1998. "Endogenous Preferences: The Cultural Consequences of Markets and Other Economic Institutions." *Journal of Economic Literature*, 36(1): 75–111.

Burgess, R., R Jedwab, E. Miguel, A. Morjaria, and G. Padró i Miquel. 2015. "The Value of Democracy: Evidence from Road Building in Kenya." *American Economic Review*, 105: 1817–51.

Celiku, B. and A. Kraay. 2017. "Predicting Conflict." World Bank Policy Research Working Paper, 8075. World Bank, Washington, DC.

Collier, P. 2019. "Transition Programs: A Theory of the Scaffolding Needed to Build out of Fragility," in R. Chami, R. Espinoza, and P. Montiel (Eds.), *Macroeconomic Policy in Fragile States*. Oxford: Oxford University Press

Costinot, A., D. Donaldson, and C. Smith. 2016. "Evolving Comparative Advantage and the Impact of Climate Change in Agricultural Markets: Evidence from 1.7 Million Fields around the Earth." *Journal of Political Economy*, 124(1): 205–48.

Croicu, M. and R. Sundberg. 2017 . "UCDP GED Codebook version 18.1.", Department of Peace and Conflict Research, Uppsala University.

De Luca, G., R. Hodler, P.A. Raschky, and M. Valsecchi. 2018. "Ethnic Favoritism: An Axiom of Politics?" *Journal of Development Economics*, 132: 115–29.

Dincecco, M. 2011. *Political Transformations and Public Finances: Europe, 1650–1913*. Cambridge: Cambridge University Press.

Dincecco, M. 2015. "The Rise of Effective States in Europe." *Journal of Economic History*, 75: 901–18.

Eifert, B., E. Miguel, and D.N. Posner. 2010. "Political Competition and Ethnic Identification in Africa." *American Journal of Political Science*, 54(2): 494–510.

Esteban, J., L. Mayoral, and D. Ray. 2012. "Ethnicity and Conflict: An Empirical Study." *The American Economic Review*, 102(4): 1310–42.

Fearon, J.D. and D.D. Laitin. 2000. "Violence and the Social Construction of Ethnic Identity." *International Organization*, 54(4): 845–77.

Fetzer, T. and S. Kyburz. 2019. "Cohesive Institutions and Political Violence." CGDEV Working Paper 503.

Fisman, R. and E. Miguel. 2007. "Corruption, Norms, and Legal Enforcement: Evidence from Diplomatic Parking Tickets." *Journal of Political Economy*, 115(6): 1020–48.

Goldstone, J.A., R.H. Bates, D.L. Epstein, T.R. Gurr, M.B. Lustik, M.G. Marshall, J. Ulfelder, and M. Woodward. 2010. "A Global Model for Forecasting Political Instability." *American Journal of Political Science*, 54(1): 190–208.

Gonzalez, F.M. 2012. "The Use of Coercion in Society: Insecure Property Rights, Conflict, and Economic Backwardness," in M.R. Garfinkel and S. Skaperdas (Eds.), *Oxford Handbook of the Economics of Peace and Conflict*. Oxford: Oxford University Press.

Hobbes, T. 1651. *Leviathan*. London: Everyman Edition.

Hodler, R. and P.A. Raschky. 2014. "Regional Favoritism." *Quarterly Journal of Economics*, 129(2): 995–1033.

IGC. 2018. *Escaping the Fragility Trap*. Report by the LSE-Oxford Commission on State Fragility, Growth and Development. (London: International Growth Centre IGC).

Khan, A.Q., A.I. Khwaja, and B.A. Olken. 2019. "Making Moves Matter: Experimental Evidence on Incentivizing Bureaucrats through Performance-Based Postings." *American Economic Review*, 109(1): 237–70.

Khan, A.Q., A.I. Khwaja, and B.A. Olken. 2016. "Tax Farming Redux: Experimental Evidence on Performance Pay for Tax Collectors." *Quarterly Journal of Economics*, 131(1): 219–71.

Kleven, H., C.T. Kreiner, and E. Saez. 2016. "Why Can Modern Governments Tax So Much? An Agency Model of Firms as Fiscal Intermediaries," *Economica*, 83: 219–46.

Koren, M. and S. Tenreyro. 2007. "Volatility and Development." *Quarterly Journal of Economics*, 122(1): 243–87.

Levi, M. 1988. *Of Rule and Revenue*. Berkeley, CA: University of California Press.

Levi, M., A. Sacks, and T. Tyler. 2009. "Conceptualizing Legitimacy, Measuring Legitimating Beliefs." *American Behavioral Scientist*, 53(3): 354–75.

Lipset, S.M. 1960. *Political Man*. London: Heinemann.

Locke, J. 1690. *Two Treatises on Government*. London: Everyman Edition.

Luttmer, E.F.P. and M. Singhal. 2014. "Tax Morale." *Journal of Economic Perspectives*, 28(4): 149–68.

Michalopoulos, S. and E. Papaioannou. 2016. "The Long-run Effects of the Scramble for Africa." *American Economic Review*, 106(7): 1802–48.

Montalvo, J.G. and M. Reynal-Querol. 2005. "Ethnic Polarization, Potential Conflict, and Civil Wars." *American Economic Review*, 95(3): 796–816.

Mueller, H. 2016. "Growth and Violence: Argument for a Per Capita Measure of Civil War." *Economica*, 83: 473–97.

Mueller, H. and C. Rauh. 2018. "Reading Between the Lines: The Prediction of Political Violence Using Newspaper Text." *American Political Science Review*, 112(2): 358–75.

Mueller, H. and C. Rauh. 2019. "The Hard Problem of Prediction for Conflict Prevention." CEPR Discussion Paper, DP13748.

Mueller, H. and D. Rohner. 2018. "Can Power-Sharing Foster Peace? Evidence from Northern Ireland." *Economic Policy*, 33(95): 447–84.

Naritomi, J. 2019. "Consumers as Tax Auditors." *American Economic Review*, 109(9): 3031–72.

North, D.C. 1990. *Institutions, Institutional Change and Economic Performance*. Cambridge: Cambridge University Press.

North, D.C. and B.R. Weingast. 1989. "Constitutions and Commitment: The Evolution of Institutional Governing Public Choice in Seventeenth-Century England." *Journal of Economic History*, 44: 803–32.

North, D.C., B. Weingast, and J. Wallis. 2009. *Violence and Social Orders: A Conceptual Framework for Interpreting Recorded Human History*. Cambridge: Cambridge University Press.

OECD (Organisation for Economic Co-operation and Development). 2018. *States of Fragility 2018*. Paris: OECD Publishing.

Rodrik, D. 1999. "Where Did All theGrowth Go? External Shocks, Social Conflict, and Growth Collapses." *Journal of Economic Growth*, 4(4): 385–412.

Rousseau, J-J. 1762. *The Social Contract*. London: Everyman Edition.

Sanchez de la Sierra, R. 2018. "On the Origins of the State: Stationary Bandits and Taxation in Eastern Congo." *Journal of Political Economy*.

Sen, A. 2007. *Identity and Violence: The Illusion of Destiny*. New York: Penguin Books.

Sundberg, R. and E. Melander. 2013. "Introducing the UCDP Georeferenced Event Dataset." *Journal of Peace Research*, 50(4): 523–32.

Sundberg, M., F. Quraishi, and S. Choudhury. 2009. "Linking Political Risk Insurance Pricing and Portfolio Management with Economic Capital Modeling: A Multilateral Perspective?" in K.W. Lu, G. Verheyen, and S.M. Perera (Eds.), *Investing with Confidence: Understanding Political Risk Management in the 21st Century*. Washington, DC: World Bank.

Törgler, B. 2007. *Tax Morale and Tax Compliance: A Theoretical and Empirical Analysis*. Cheltenham: Edward Elgar.

Tyler, T.R. 2006. "Psychological Perspectives on Legitimacy and Legitimation." *Annual Review of Psychology*, 57: 375–400.

United Nations and World Bank. 2017. *Pathways to Peace: Inclusive Approaches to Preventing Violent Conflict*. Washington, DC: World Bank.

Weigel, J. 2018. "The Taxman Cometh: A Virtuous Cycle of Compliance and State Legitimacy in the D.R. Congo." unpublished manuscript.

Weigel, J. 2019. "Building State and Citizen: How Tax Collection in Congo Engenders Citizen Engagement with the State." unpublished manuscript.

10

Fiscal Policy in Fragile Situations

Flying in Fog with Limited Instrumentation[1]

Gary Milante and Michael Woolcock

1. Introduction

Fiscal policy involves raising and using public finance to provide public goods. At a minimum such goods include assuring the security of the state and its citizens, protecting private property from predation, upholding the integrity and legitimacy of the processes by which leaders are selected and held accountable, and (in the modern expansive definition of the state) assuming responsibility for (if not directly providing) key public services such as health, education, and transportation (Boyce and O'Donnell, 2007; Evans and Carnahan, 2015; Andrews, 2008). The choice of which goods to provide is a political one; the choice of how to provide those goods is also often political and complex. Meanwhile, the choices of specific fiscal policy mechanisms to be used to finance and deliver these public goods—that is, how taxes are levied and collected, the architecture of the ministries, procurement, delivery, and so on—are important and a whole volume could be written on them; for the most part, however, these are technical problems.

For present purposes we are interested in the political, complex, and adaptive problems of fiscal policy and responses to them in fragile situations: namely, how or why a group of citizens in control of a government at a moment in time choose to deliver some or all of these public goods.[2] We leave the technical problems of

The findings, interpretations, and conclusions expressed in this chapter are entirely those of the authors. They do not necessarily represent the views of the International Bank for Reconstruction and Development/World Bank and its affiliated organizations, or those of the Executive Directors of the World Bank or the governments they represent. Our thanks to exceptional research assistance from Gulzhan Asylbek Kyzy (SIPRI), though errors remain those of the authors. An earlier version was presented at an authors' conference held at Oxford University, from which we gleaned much useful feedback. We especially thank the editors—Ralph Chami, Rafael Espinoza, and Peter Montiel—for soliciting our contribution and providing helpful suggestions along the way.

[1] Depending on flight conditions, pilots or air traffic control choose between using visual flight rules (VFR) or, where meteorological conditions do not allow, instrument flight rules (IFR). Rarely do pilots fly when they cannot rely on one or the other. In fragile situations, policymakers have limited visibility and weak instruments, yet they must try to fly the plane of fiscal policy nonetheless; needless to say, we recommend caution in such situations.

[2] On the difference between technical and adaptive problems, see Heifetz et al. (2009).

Gary Milante and Michael Woolcock, *Fiscal Policy in Fragile Situations: Flying in Fog with Limited Instrumentation*
In: *Macroeconomic Policy in Fragile States.* Edited by: Ralph Chami, Raphael Espinoza, and Peter Montiel,
Oxford University Press (2021).
DOI: 10.1093/oso/9780198853091.003.0010

specific mechanisms to the side, as there are many other experts who can speak to those. In fragile environments, public goods delivery is often limited to a specific sector, is nonexistent or rare, or the services may be delivered by external actors creating a dual-services problem (Di John, 2011). In other cases, the government is used by those in power (or has been used in the past) for predation on the citizenry, through oppression or corruption (Milante, 2007; Mungiu-Pippidi, 2011; IMF, 2016). In some unusual cases, however, policymakers have broken the cycle of poor performance, managed to reduce leakage and capture, built the capacity to deliver, and thereby actually succeeded in providing public services, seemingly against all odds (Kleinfeld, 2018).

In this chapter we explore some of the possible pathways by which these contrasting outcomes might be attained in the fiscal policy space. We provide an analytical framework for considering how the coherence and credibility of the "social contract" between citizens and the state is shaped by successive interactions at the nexus of revenue generation, expenditure on key public services, and the performance of those services (see also Besley, 2020). Using existing governance data on changes (positive or negative) across five sequential measures of public sector activity (tax collection, government spending, government effectiveness, reduced wastefulness, lowered perceived corruption) from the periods 2005–10 and 2010–15, we endeavor to empirically test the connections between these relationships across a sample of 106 (period 1) and 95 (period 2) countries as they pertain to performance on a key public service outcome (reducing infant mortality). Consistent with our past work (Milante and Woolcock, 2017), our findings show the wide variation in pathways by which performance outcomes can be and are reached: across five rounds of interaction, a country-period observation exists for each of the 32 logically possible pathways, with the highest number in any one category (for example, positive change in all five indicators) being only 8 percent of country-period observations. Not surprisingly then, one can discern only weak aggregate trends, even within a single time period. These findings point to the limits of asking global governance data to provide country-specific policy guidance to fragile states, which should be based on solid theory, experience, and country-specific knowledge. In other words, there is no single "right answer" (silver bullet) about reforms and sequencing that will always lead to improved performance in a simple outcome measure like infant mortality. We see a wide variety of governance reform pathways, with some progress and some setbacks, resulting in a wide variation in performance on the outcome variable.

2. Background: Connecting Fragility and Fiscal Policy

There are important economic and political consequences attached to labeling a country as "fragile"—such as level of funding, the perceived likelihood it will be able to honor financial contracts and international agreements, the credibility of its credit ratings, and so on. Given the stakes, domestically and regionally, one might be surprised to learn that the theoretical, methodological, and empirical foundations on which this crucial designation rests are conspicuously (one might even say disconcertingly) thin: a single aggregate number with a weighted average from 4 clusters of 16 component elements on which country experts have provided their (mostly subjective) verdict and a single objective measure.[3] Even if observers periodically lament this mismatch between the approach we have and the one we need, few have offered a viable alternative, or even an initial basis on which the gap might be narrowed, that would meet the criteria of being analytically sound, politically supportable, and operationally implementable.[4]

In previous work (Milante and Woolcock, 2017), we sought to promote such a discussion by proposing that "fragility" be understood as a fundamentally dynamic and contextually specific construct, rather than a static, discrete and all-encompassing condition, building on the premise that countries with notionally similar "scores" on any given fragility metric at a given point in time could in fact be consequentially different from one another. Specifically, we argued—and demonstrated empirically—that a country's governance trajectory mattered: at a particular point in time, countries A, B, and C could all receive a score of (say) 3.2 on the Country Performance and Institutional Assessment (CPIA) scale and yet be on vastly different journeys, with different pasts and presents, requiring correspondingly different forms and levels of "support" from the international community to guide their possible futures. Country A, for example, might have only recently become "fragile," Country B might have been "consistently fragile" for decades, while Country C might be steadily recovering from a brutal civil war—yet none of this would be apparent if all three countries happened to receive the same "score" and be in the same state of peacekeeping mission, and if this score *alone* were the basis on which fragility designations were made (as is current practice).

If the rules of the game for designation as fragile are ignorant of these trajectories and these rules have knock-on effects on funding, staffing, or engagement, then there is no incentive for political leaders in country to behave differently if they score 3.2 on the CPIA. But given the fundamental differences between A, B, and C, we would expect political leaders in each country to deploy different strategies in their engagements with the international community, reflecting their national circumstances, the historical context of policymaking and governance, domestic political dynamics, and personal interests or proclivities. President A, for example, might seek temporary support that she hopes will quickly restore

[3] The World Bank's current formal criteria for defining a fragile state is scoring less than 3.2 on the CPIA and having had at least one UN peacekeeping mission in the past three years.

[4] We recognize that steps are under way at various international organizations to refine their approach to or identifying state fragility; even so, we suggest these efforts have yet to fully reckon with the specific issues we raise, namely the inherently dynamic and context-specific nature of state fragility.

her country to its historically non-fragile state (yet be frustrated that her country is regarded as analytically indistinguishable from others); Prime Minister B might seek to keep her country just fragile enough to ensure that it continues to receive a steady flow of grants (and thus of personal rents), confident in the knowledge that the singular static metric by which donors assess fragility will enable her to passively resist pesky invocations to "graduate" out of fragility; while Queen C might worry that hard-won development gains from a precariously low base are perennially at risk of unravelling, and so seek support that consolidates the legitimacy of her policy agenda thus far while incrementally seeking to forge a shared national identity between various social groups.[5]

We contend that navigating policy in fragile situations is at least as complicated as flying a plane, which involves knowing more than the current location (including altitude), but also the velocity (speed) and vector (direction of travel) as well as, of course, the surrounding terrain! In our previous work, we created an analytical space wherein the idiosyncrasies of each country's history, culture, social structures, and political economy might be accommodated to discern the specific *ways in which* a fragile state was (and had become, or never ceased being) fragile, and thus what work a corresponding policy response strategy might reasonably attempt within that context. If, as it were, each unhappy country is indeed unhappy in its own way, then the diagnostic instruments by which both a country's fragility status and its fragility response strategies are determined need to be sufficiently sophisticated and analytically grounded to do this important work. At present, we suggest, they are not.

Big questions about fiscal policy in fragile states demand expansive answers, which we do not have. In this chapter we offer instead some preliminary arguments based on initial evidence grounded in a modest analytical framework, one that extends the spirit of our earlier work to a key domain at the nexus of enhancing organizational capability and state-society relations in fragile states. The central idea is that the capability for policy implementation in fragile states can vary quite considerably, especially among key tasks for which governments have clear mandates and responsibilities (even if they are not directly engaged in providing it—for example, education, water, health). The variability we previously observed in country-level fragility over time is, in short, highly likely to be both mirrored at, and a function of, variation in implementation capability at the subnational level and between different sectors/ministries: the very essence of being "fragile" is that the complex tasks[6] required of any specific ministry—such

[5] There are specific countries (and political leaders) corresponding to each of these types, but for present purposes we wish to keep the focus on the underlying analytical issues.

[6] For present purposes, a "complex" task is one that is not only technically difficult but also politically contentious (for example, elections, regulation) and featuring numerous spaces for discretionary action (teaching, social work, collecting taxes); in fragile states its implementation is also likely to be physically dangerous (police reform) and attempted by organizations possessing limited professional capacity.

as security, justice, health—are performed with levels of efficiency and effectiveness that is likely to vary considerably over time. Furthermore, the policy space in which actors are making strategic decisions are difficult to measure or unknown until tried (thus our metaphor of flying in fog). In many cases, these are wicked problems with no readily apparent correct answer (Milante, 2015).

At the heart of this complexity and central to the functioning of the modern state is fiscal policy because services of any kind ultimately have to be paid and accounted for: public revenue has to be generated, contracts to providers have to be written and honored, services must be delivered. In all states, including fragile ones, citizens expect government to contract services through agents; to the extent the service is duly provided at levels above minimal standards and expectations, we argue, and is perceived as an outcome made possible by revenues generated (at least in part) from citizen contributions, it becomes the basis of a virtuous cycle of state-society relations—the so-called "long route to accountability" (World Bank, 2003). In fragile situations, the consolidation of this mechanism is the basis on which a state escapes fragility. The argument goes that for every dollar that makes the circuit from taxpayers to actual delivery of services, trust between citizen and state increases, organizational capability is enhanced, and welfare improves (see Figure 10.1).

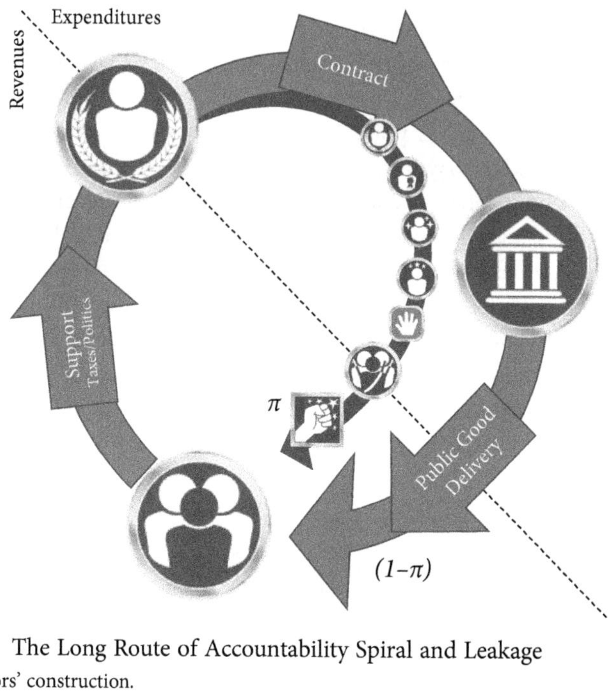

Figure 10.1 The Long Route of Accountability Spiral and Leakage
Source: Authors' construction.

Beyond its intuitive appeal, the three primary components of our spiral enjoy strong empirical support, at least in non-fragile developing countries. A venerable literature in political science (Levi, 1988) and public economics (Besley and Persson, 2013) has long noted that, as Besley and Mueller (this volume) put it, "citizens pay taxes as long as the state reciprocates by providing public goods. But if citizens feel that the political elite or the bureaucratic apparatus is stealing money, they have no incentive to pay taxes and corruption erodes state capacity through its effect on legitimacy." This literature effectively addresses the veracity of the first two segments of our spiral—that is, the centrality of a social contract in which citizens trust the state by paying taxes, and states reciprocate by allocating resources to public goods. Evidence for the final stage, in which such a social contract gives rise to a state that actually delivers minimally effective public services, finds support in a recent global study by Sterck et al. (2018). By assessing how structural factors shape national health outcomes (as measured by disability-adjusted life years, or DALYs) in developing countries, they report that—controlling for GNI per capita, poverty, and regional epidemiological spillovers—10 percent of the variance in health outcomes between low-income countries can be explained by the capacity of public institutions (as measured by the World Bank's World Governance Indicators) to deliver their core functions.[7]

But is it possible to demonstrate empirically that this long route of accountability holds across all three segments of our spiral, and that it holds for fragile states? The essence of life in fragile situations, of course, is that this dynamic—almost by definition—is routinely compromised, as is finding credible entry points along the way for initiating positive alternatives (let alone sustaining them). The more familiar reality in fragile situations (and elsewhere) is that the state is not monolithic; it is composed of politicians and policymakers who contract implementers and firms (that may in fact be themselves), who may or may not deliver (or do so via means involving considerable corruption). And one of the hardest services to provide and to reform is security, which, even if it is delivered in some form, may be only for some (the wealthy) or only for the state itself. When this is how citizens consistently experience their "everyday state" (Corbridge et al., 2005), not just in security but in water and sanitation and education and everything else, it can lead to frustration, desperation and grievance, which in turn can lead to cynicism, conflict and violence (United Nations and World Bank, 2018). Repeated and routinized, it contributes to a vicious cycle (World Bank, 2011).

[7] Related findings are provided by Balabanova et al. (2013), who conclude that effective public institutions, now and especially in the future, will be key to providing good health at low cost in developing countries; and Kumara and Samaratunge (2016), who show that in Sri Lanka (and doubtless elsewhere) a key determinant of the extent to which poor citizens have to pay out of pocket for their health care is the weakness of the formal health care institutions in their community. The vast empirical literature surveyed in Andrews et al. (2017) documents the importance of effective public institutions for the provision of all manner of key public services in developing countries; on education in particular, see World Bank (2018).

3. An Analytical Framework

At the risk of oversimplifying the fiscal policy space, in this chapter we reduce it to the choice between capture (leakage, patronage) of this space by those in power or investing in a long route to accountability for service delivery.[8] At one extreme, complete capture of the state and predation on its own citizens involves the kleptocrat directly buying client power and the support of those necessary to keep control of the state (Milante, 2007; Kleinfeld, 2018). The long route of accountability, on the other hand, is a complex relationship between citizens and whoever controls government at a given moment, one that is mitigated by the institutions, norms, customs, rules, and enforcement mechanisms that facilitate trust between actors and transparently convey information on performance of politicians and policymakers acting on behalf of citizens. (This model is not without criticism; see, among others, Devarajan et al., 2013 for a discussion.)

A possible strategy for more formally assessing these dynamics is to "follow the money"—that is, to track fiscal flows, and the efficiency with which public revenue is used. Unfortunately, we cannot with precision say how much money leaks from this process, both because very few states report at this level of precision and because the actors who would benefit from leakage are those reporting. Even so, for present purposes, let π be the amount of revenue/expenditure that leaks from a given economy (represented by the smaller icons on the arrow inside the circle in Figure 10.1), there must be a cutoff, π^*, where too much graft, corruption and leakage results in a vicious cycle of less support, lower revenues, weaker contracting, less delivery of security, increased grievance and threat of violence, and so on (that is, where $\pi > \pi^*$). There is a clear empirical link between political violence and perceptions of corruption and abuses of power (World Bank, 2011; UN/World Bank, 2018). Because there is relative peace and stability in many countries, we know that these countries operate with a sustainable level of corruption or graft ($\pi < \pi^*$). Furthermore, we observe insecurity, including defense forces that are not fit for the purpose of delivering security for citizens and/or the state in the most fragile places where π is high. In some cases, security is used to protect graft and corruption (Milante, 2007). In subsequent work we hope to derive some basic estimates of the scale of this leakage relative to other government expenditures.

[8] A phrase coined by the *World Development Report 2004: Making Services Work for Poor People* (World Bank, 2003) to distinguish accountability mechanisms between service providers and citizens exerted directly (through everyday "short route" social interactions and feedback) from those enacted indirectly (via "long route" procedures such as elections, oversight, transparency, auditing, reporting and enforcement).

3.1 Investigating the Framework with Current Governance Indicators

Is it possible, using the wealth of governance indicators publicly available, to measure the performance of states in delivering public services[9] and/or to identify leakage and corruption (π) in the system through proxy measures? After all, if policymakers in a fragile situation need to deliver public goods, they ought to be able to use governance indicators to measure the aggregate performance of their own system. (If they cannot be used for this, what *can* they be used for?) For this chapter, we considered more than 450 indicators on "governance."[10] These indicators cover a wide range of dimensions of governance, including government effectiveness, regulatory quality, rule of law, control of corruption, voice and accountability, political stability, violence, human capital, and free flow of information (following dimensions identified by Kaufmann et al., 2008). The associated data are of various types, including input, process, structural, output, and outcome indicators collected from a wide array of administrative sources, expert judgements, household surveys, and assessments made by academics, think tanks, and advocacy organizations. Time and country coverage of most indicators vary, creating challenges in creating a cross-country, longitudinal dataset on performance. Missing values are particularly pernicious in the fragile countries of most interest to us.

As discussed earlier, the instruments that fiscal policy pilots have for measuring governance are often limited, if not absent. There are a number of issues with the measurement of governance that make the use of these indicators challenging. Critiques of these indicators and responses have been discussed at length, and we do not wish to use valuable space to reopen that conversation here.[11] We begin by noting that a measurement of the level of these indicators can do little to shed light on the trajectory and velocity of change on that dimension. Variance in these indicators year on year also show that trend analysis should be highly suspect; even when trends are known, they cannot tell us about expected future change because strategic action by actors is occurring in real time (that is, much more quickly than these indicators can capture). As we noted in previous work, these issues raise questions about seemingly arbitrary discrete cutoffs used for governance indicators (Milante and Woolcock, 2017). Furthermore, real, lasting institutional change is a slow-moving process (Pritchett and de Weijer, 2010), so annual variation in indicators may not be as informative as change over an extended period of time. Because many governance indicators are relatively recent

[9] For an authoritative overview of governance indicators, see Kaufmann et al. (2008). On the uses and usefulness of these indicators (and their associated limits), see Andrews (2008).

[10] The directory of indicators is available from the authors on request.

[11] See Kaufmann et al. (2007) for a discussion of these critiques and responses. For a recent overview of indicators and their values and limitations, see Venger and Miethe (2018).

innovations, the choice of available indicators which can be studied over a decade or more is limited.

Just as the current location of a plane does not tell us about where the plane is going, the level measure of an institutional performance indicator does not tell us about recent direction of change or the rate of change for the institution. Our analysis in previous work on the period 2005–15 showed that there was considerable movement and variation in the trajectories characterizing actual or potential fragile states, with 30 countries (from a sample of 74) moving between the conditions of being "fragile," "marginally fragile," and "not fragile" (Milante and Woolcock, 2017). Only 15 (or half) of these phase transitions were in a positive direction (from "fragile" to "marginally fragile," or "marginally fragile" to "not fragile"). Fragile states are on an array of "journeys"—moving into fragility, deeper into fragility, out of fragility, in and out of fragility in rapid succession, or remaining "stuck" in fragility—that are poorly served by a single discrete threshold. Likewise, we can say little about a jet at 13,000 feet—it may be on the runway at El Alto, on ascent from Charles de Gaulle, on approach at Bole, or in trouble in the Himalayas.

Despite the challenges of measurement, level, and change, we proceed with identifying some instruments to measure performance of the system (just as the policymaker must) to avoid flying blind. From the more than 450 possible indicators described above we selected six input, process, and output measures. For inputs on the revenue and performance side of the spiral, we use the simplest indicators with most coverage: tax effectiveness and government expenditure. Following the spiral around, we next identify indicators to measure performance of governance, and we use expert assessments of bureaucratic quality and wastefulness as measures of government effectiveness. For outputs—the end of the spiral, because corruption is not directly measurable—we use perception of corruption and the simplest, most widely available health indicator—infant mortality—as an output of the system.[12] These indicators, their coverage, and their sources, are summarized in Table 10.1.

In addition to the selected indicators, we considered alternative indicators, including those from: CPIA (transparency, accountability and corruption in the public sector, quality of public administration); the International Country Risk Guide (quality of governance); the Varieties of Democracy (corruption index); Transparency International (Corruption Perception Index); and the Fund for Peace Fragile States Index (public services). Alternatives considered for infant mortality were inequality-adjusted life expectancy (UN Development Programme Human Development Index) and the poverty gap (from the World Bank), but

[12] Following Sterck et al. (2018) we also used DALYs as an outcome variable and find very similar results to those we obtain with infant mortality; further details on this specific analysis are available upon request.

Table 10.1 Indicators: Coverage, Description, and Sources

Indicator	Coverage	Description	Source
Tax Effectiveness	203 countries, 1993–2013	Taxes including social contributions less resource rents	World Markets Online Global Insight Business Conditions and Risk Indicators
Government Expenditure	193 countries, 1980–2017	Government expenditure (% of GDP)	Elbadawi, Soto and Martinez, this volume (World Bank, World Development Indicators)
Bureaucratic Quality	140 Countries, 1984–2016	Expert Assessment	International Country Risk Guide, Political Risk Services
Wastefulness of Government Spending	136 Countries, 2007–16	Executive Opinion Survey	World Economic Forum. Global Competitiveness Report
Corruption Among Public Officials	120–180 Countries, 1996–2016	Expert Assessment	Economist Intelligence Unit
Infant Mortality	197 Countries, All Years	Infant mortality rate (deaths per 1000 births)	World Development Indicators

Source: Compiled by authors.

Table 10.2 Data coverage, Full Data Set

	Period 1	Period 2
	2005–10	2010–15
N	196	196
Full Data	106	95
Missing 1 indicator	51	55
Missing 2 indicators	24	29
Missing 3 or more	15	17

Source: Compiled by authors.

these were not used because they measured similar concepts with limited country or time coverage. Even with these considerations, the data described above, when used for the limited time frame 2005 to 2015, provide full overage for only about 100 countries in each period (see Table 10.2).

Modern jets have extremely complicated instrumentation that relies on complex systems to deliver high-level performance, including high-speed processing for algorithms, high-precision sensors and global positioning systems. We are nowhere near that level of sophistication for piloting fragile states. With the limited instrumentation described above, we are also concerned about comparability between scores for states in our dataset. Is a bureaucratic quality score of −00.75 for Egypt in 2015, for example, comparable to a −0.75 for Bosnia and Herzegovina in 2005? Would a change of +0.1 in bureaucratic quality really make Egypt as effective as Moldova (−0.65) in 2015? Some of these concerns are grounded in similar concerns that have been voiced about whether these indicators are measuring against a global model (should all countries aspire to be Singapore or Denmark?), or more appropriately measured for function within the context (Andrews, 2008). Furthermore, though the absolute or relative level of an indicator of governance may not be informative, the change may still send a valid signal about trends within a particular country context (Venger and Miethe, 2018). To address these concerns and improve our coverage, we use only the direction of the change in the indicator (improvement or decline) over the two periods of interest (2005–10 and 2010–15) and assume that no change is an improvement. (We also reverse the measure of corruption, so that all of the governance indicators move positively in the same direction.) That is to say, a reported positive change in corruption, wastefulness, or bureaucratic quality in the results that follow reflects an improvement; likewise, a negative change in any of these governance indicators represents a decline. Finally, because progress on reducing infant mortality is related to the level of infant mortality, we run a simple linear regression on starting infant mortality (two years before the period of interest) and take the residual; thus a negative value is unexpected progress on reducing infant mortality and a positive value is slower progress than expected.

As noted in Table 10.2, a number of values are still missing, even with this optimal group of indicators selected for the qualities and coverage described above. If we were to drop all country cases from the analysis because of missing values, we would lose 191 cases, many of which would be fragile or conflict-affected; these are most likely to have missing data. However, because we only use change in the indicators, rather than actual values, missing values can be filled in by creating an artificial set of weighted country observations (see Box 10.1). This allows us to create a nearly full and rectangular dataset with 180 country observations for the period 2005–10 and 178 country observations for 2010–15 (see Table 10.3).

Coding the direction of change for each period in each of the five governance indicators of interest (except infant mortality) allows us to code country observations with 32 possible outcomes (5^2) for each period (2005–10 and 2010–15). Countries with improvements across all five indicators for the period 2005–10 (↑↑↑↑↑) comprise group 1 in period 1; countries with a negative change in the first indicator comprise group 2, etc. through to countries with a decline in all five indicators comprising group 32 (see Table 10.3). The ordering of the indicators follows the spiral framework presented in Figure 10.1: Arrow 1: Tax Effectiveness; Arrow 2: Government Expenditure, Arrow 3: Bureaucratic Quality, Arrow 4: Wastefulness of Government Spending; Arrow 5: Corruption Among Public Officials. The distribution column shows the percentage of countries in each group, over both periods, and shows that only group 1, 5, 9, and 14 demonstrate

Box 10.1 Using Agnostic Weights and Direction of Change to Fill Missing Values for Fragile Data

It is not uncommon for fragile states to have missing values in data; after all, fragility is often linked to institutional capacity, and institutional capacity is necessary to create trustworthy statistics—indeed, credible statistics are themselves necessary for the proper functioning of a modern state. Furthermore, by definition, fragile environments are ones with incomplete information, so it is not uncommon for them to have incomplete statistics. In most economic analysis, these country observations are dropped when data are missing, which raises questions about the validity of the statistical analysis to fragile situations and opens the analysis to the "keys under the streetlamp" critique. Despite the paucity of the data (and the quality concerns discussed above), we are trying to include as many fragile situations in our analysis as possible to ensure that the results are relevant.

Because of concerns about level comparability (how well ordered the ordinals are) of indexes and measures of governance, we do not attempt to use or recommend using regressions or other arithmetic analysis on measures of governance (Sanin, 2011). Simply put, we cannot say that an improvement of one unit at one point on an index such as tax effectiveness or bureaucratic quality is the same as an improvement of one unit at another point on the same index, particularly at different times (2005 vs 2015) and between countries, given the subjectivity of how these indexes are created. This is not to say that these numbers are not useful; as ordinal numbers that describe direction of change, they are certainly useful. Because the coding processes underlying them are likely to be consistent within country, the direction of change can also tell us when reform is under way, which is what we are really interested in (even if we cannot say "how much reform"). In other words, it is nonsensical, particularly in fragile states, to say how many units of reform, security, or peace have been accumulated, but we can say which direction of change an indicator has moved in, and we believe that change within a country over time is comparable at least in direction.

Using simply direction of change, rather than amount of change, makes each variable dichotomous—for each governance indicator it has either improved (+) or regressed (−). Allowing for a dichotomous (dummy) variable opens a new possibility with regard to missing values. Rather than ignoring missing values because we do not know their value, we can create an artificial set of country experiences that allows a country with a single missing value to be either (+/−), but agnostically weight each of these cases by 50 percent in any analysis. This can be done for any combination of missing values, weighting each artificial entry accordingly; we limit our imputation to two missing values (maximum 25 percent weight each).

Box Table 10.1.1a Change (Δ) in five measures of fiscal policy with missing data (2005 to 2010)

	Δ Tax Effectiveness	Δ Government Expenditure	Δ Bureaucratic Quality	Δ Wastefulness of Government Spending	Δ Corruption among Public Officials
Chile	−.47	+3.2	+.04	+.08	0
Egypt	.	+1.0	+.04	+.11	0
Gabon	.	+2.3	+.04	.	+.05

Box Table 10.1.1b Artificial dataset with agnostic weights for imputed direction of change (missing) values

	Δ Tax Effectiveness	Δ Government Expenditure	Δ Bureaucratic Quality	Δ Wastefulness	Δ Corruption	Weight
Chile	−	+	+	+	+	1
Egypt1	+	+	+	+	+	.5
Egypt2	−	+	+	+	+	.5
Gabon1	+	+	+	+	+	.25
Gabon2	+	+	+	−	+	.25
Gabon3	−	+	+	+	+	.25
Gabon4	−	+	+	−	+	.25

For example, the actual data are shown for three countries (Chile, Egypt, and Gabon) in Table 10.1.1a. These data have been converted so that it all moves in the same direction—a positive change in corruption is now an improvement in corruption, following the rest of the variables.

If we were using this data as is, we would lose Egypt and Gabon (and 157 other cases) from our analysis. However, we can replace these numbers with direction of change and create artificial entries with agnostic weights, allowing us to use the information we have, despite missing information for these cases. As noted earlier, zero values are coded as improvements. This approach yields an artificial database that is replicated for these same three countries in Box Table 10.1.1b.

This approach saves 159 cases (75 for the period 2005–10; 84 from the period 2010–15) that would be lost due to missing data, many of which would have been fragile states, increasing the relevance for our findings in concluding on the dynamics of government reform in fragile situations.

Table 10.3 Count of Country Observations by Type (Including Artificial Sets for Missing Values)

Group	TypeArrows	Period 1	Period 2	Total Count	Distribution
1	↑↑↑↑↑	20.75	9.25	30	8.4%
2	↓↑↑↑↑	11	6.5	17.5	4.9%
3	↑↓↑↑↑	5.75	7.5	13.25	3.7%
4	↑↑↓↑↑	11	5.75	16.75	4.7%
5	↑↑↑↓↑	14	12.75	26.75	7.5%
6	↑↑↑↑↓	5.75	6	11.75	3.3%
7	↓↓↑↑↑	4.25	5	9.25	2.6%
8	↓↑↓↑↑	6.25	2.25	8.5	2.4%
9	↓↑↑↓↑	12.75	6	18.75	5.2%
10	↓↑↑↑↓	2.25	3	5.25	1.5%
11	↑↓↓↑↑	2.25	5.75	8	2.2%
12	↑↓↑↓↑	3*	7	10	2.8%
13	↑↓↑↑↓	1.5	4.75	6.25	1.7%
14	↑↑↓↓↑	13	13.5	26.5	7.4%
15	↑↑↓↑↓	4.75	4.5	9.25	2.6%
16	↑↑↑↓↓	5.5	7.5	13	3.6%
17	↓↓↓↑↑	2	1.75	3.75	1.0%
18	↓↓↑↓↑	5.25	5.5	10.75	3.0%
19	↓↓↑↑↓	2.75	5	7.75	2.2%
20	↓↑↓↓↑	13.75	4	17.75	5.0%
21	↓↑↓↑↓	3	0.25*	3.25	0.9%
22	↓↑↑↓↓	6	1.5*	7.5	2.1%
23	↑↓↓↓↑	1*	10.75	11.75	3.3%
24	↑↓↓↑↓	1*	5	6	1.7%
25	↑↓↑↓↓	2.5	4.75	7.25	2.0%
26	↑↑↓↓↓	5.25	10.5	15.75	4.4%
27	↓↓↓↓↑	2.5	3.25	5.75	1.6%
28	↓↓↓↑↓	2	3*	5	1.4%
29	↓↓↑↓↓	1.75	4	5.75	1.6%
30	↓↑↓↓↓	3.5	2.25	5.75	1.6%
31	↑↓↓↓↓	2	6.5	8.5	2.4%
32	↓↓↓↓↓	2	3	5	1.4%
		180	178	358	100%

Source: Compiled by authors.

any kind of pooling (more than 5 percent of the observations are grouped in these sets). Of course, some of the distribution is a function of the construction of the artificial sets; it is impossible to tell whether the Republic of Congo had an increase or decrease in measure of wastefulness in the period 2005–10, because of missing data, so it is coded in both groups with 50 percent weight on each. Only six groups (Period 1, groups 12, 23, 24; Period 2, groups 21, 22, 28) indicated by asterisks comprise only "artificial" observations, but there is no apparent relationship

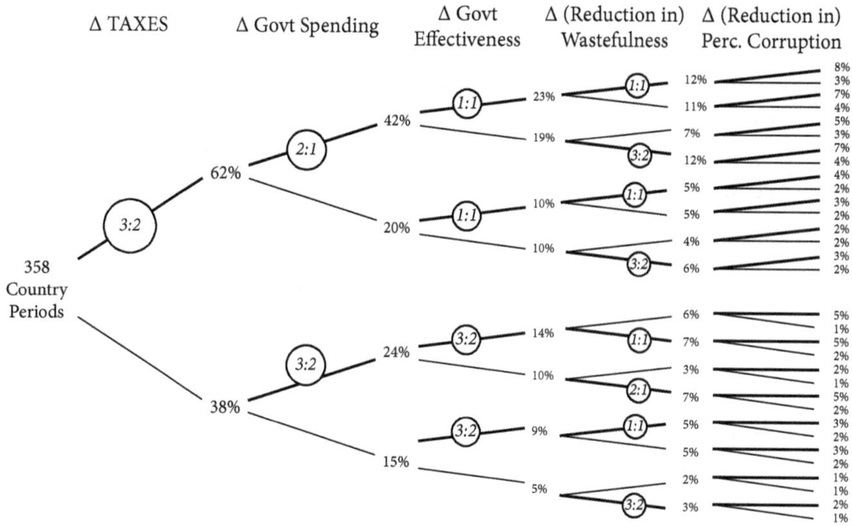

Figure 10.2 Odds Ratios of Increasing/Decreasing Activity Across Given Governance Indicators (both periods (both periods combined, bold lines indicates higher odds-ratio))
Source: A authors' calculations

between missing values that result in these artificial observations and indicator or period (different countries have different missing values on different indicators).

Implicit in the argument about the long route to accountability and the concept of leakage is the relationship between the functions of government following the virtuous spiral around the fiscal policy space: from revenue collection to budgeting and prioritization, to procurement and the perceptions of how money is spent by citizens. This suggests a sort of conditional performance we would expect to prevail through these indicators—where more tax is collected, we would expect to see more expenditure, better quality of delivery, less wastefulness, and decreases in perceptions of corruption from citizens. We therefore unpack the observed incidence data from Table 10.3 into a tree of conditional probabilities (Figure 10.2) following the logic of Figure 10.1.

As the bold lines and odds-ratios indicate, we see some evidence of the virtuous spiral at play. States that improve on tax effectiveness are more likely to increase expenditure; states that increase expenditure are slightly more likely to improve bureaucratic quality. In the latter two indicators we see less evidence of the virtuous spiral at play: there is a limited relationship between wastefulness of government spending and earlier reforms and almost no relationship between perceptions of corruption and earlier reforms. In the following sections we discuss interpretations of each of the indicators, proceeding in order around the spiral from the framework. Where useful, we note correlations between different indicators in the spiral.

3.1.1 Tax Effectiveness

Out of 358 country-period observations, 62 percent saw an increase in tax effectiveness. Increases in tax effectiveness were more prevalent in Period 2 (2010–15, 68 percent of countries saw an increase in tax effectiveness). Following the same sequence of indicators, we consider the conditional probabilities of change for each:

- An increase in tax effectiveness was positively correlated with an increase in government expenditure (68 percent of the cases where tax effectiveness increased saw an increase in government expenditure), particularly in period 1 (81 percent).
- Bureaucratic quality increased in 54 percent of the cases where tax effectiveness increased, particularly in period 1 (59 percent).
- Wastefulness decreased in less than half the cases where tax effectiveness increased (46 percent).
- Citizens' perceptions of corruption largely move in the same direction as increases in tax effectiveness—in period 1 only 71 percent of countries had an increase in tax effectiveness and perceived reforms on corruption. Meanwhile in period 2, 59 percent of the increases in tax effectiveness coincided with perceived reduction in corruption.

While we use this indicator as a proxy measure of tax effectiveness, we remain agnostic as to whether a positive change in taxes collected is overall a positive change. Tax effectiveness here is used as a measure of the relationship between state and citizen (following di John, 2011 and Besley and Mueller in this volume). We assume that the governments were already operating at or near their fiscal budget constraints and that an increase in taxes collected from citizens demonstrates improved state-society relations necessary to collect higher taxes, but we do not know whether this is linked to a promise on how taxes will be spent, good fiscal policy and/or debt, and use or misuse of other revenues.[13]

3.1.2 Government Expenditure

Independent of the change in tax effectiveness, government expenditure increased for most countries in both periods (see Figure 10.2): 77 percent of countries had an increase in government expenditure in period 1 and 54 percent had an increase in Period 2. As Figure 10.2 shows, this increase in government expenditure occurred more often regardless of whether tax effectiveness increased in the same period, though it was slightly higher in countries with increased tax effectiveness, with an odds-ratio of 2:1 for countries with an increase in tax effectiveness

[13] Further, see di John (2011) for discussion on the relationship between other sources of revenues (development aid, natural resource rents) and production, tax collection, and elite bargains.

and a 3:2 odds-ratio for countries with a decline in tax effectiveness. With respect to changes in other indicators along the long route to accountability:

- 56 percent of the cases where government expenditure increased were correlated with an improvement in government effectiveness as measured by bureaucratic quality in both periods.
- Some of the breakdown of the long route to accountability starts to become apparent in the relationship between government expenditure and change in wastefulness. In only 44 percent of the cases where government expenditure increased was there an improvement (reduction of wastefulness). This was particularly pronounced in Period 2 (2010–15), with a reduction in government wastefulness in only 39 percent of the countries that experienced an increase in government expenditure. Countries that otherwise saw positive improvement along the rest of the virtuous spiral but a regression in government wastefulness in 2010–15 included Cambodia, Bangladesh, France, Costa Rica, Albania, Rwanda, Colombia, Bulgaria, and Switzerland.
- An increase in government expenditure was accompanied by an improvement on perceptions of corruption in 69 percent of the cases.

We use government expenditure data used by Elbadawi, Soto and Martinez (this volume). Of course, government expenditure is only what is reported; depending on accounting methods and reporting level, leakage from government systems may not be reported in government expenditure. In such situations, "leakage" (π) can be pervasive yet difficult to observe, particularly if the systems for monitoring are not being used for reporting. Indeed, in many fragile countries, about 80 percent of the budget is executed outside of official Financial Management Information Systems (FMIS) processes, manually added to reporting after the fact, making it impossible to say how much was actually spent on what (Piatti-Fünfkirchen, 2018; see Figure 10.3). This of course raises broader questions about the veracity of global reporting and comparability between country statistics.

Such leakage of government expenditure may be particularly relevant and be of particular concern to the international community for the security sector in fragile states. Leakage from the security sector is especially difficult to observe, partly because of the opacity of expenditures on security, which in turn can be linked to issues such as: classified (secret) budget items; off-budget security items (including some security assistance); anticompetitive bidding; transfer pricing through procurement processes; ghost workers in the military and police; security firms with commercial business without oversight, and so on. Evidence suggests that a one-unit change in the corruption perceptions index results in direct and indirect losses in economic growth of 0.3 percent for low-income countries, implying significant leakage from government expenditure and subsequent effects on economic growth (Menocal and Taxell, 2017). Similarly, perceived corruption is also

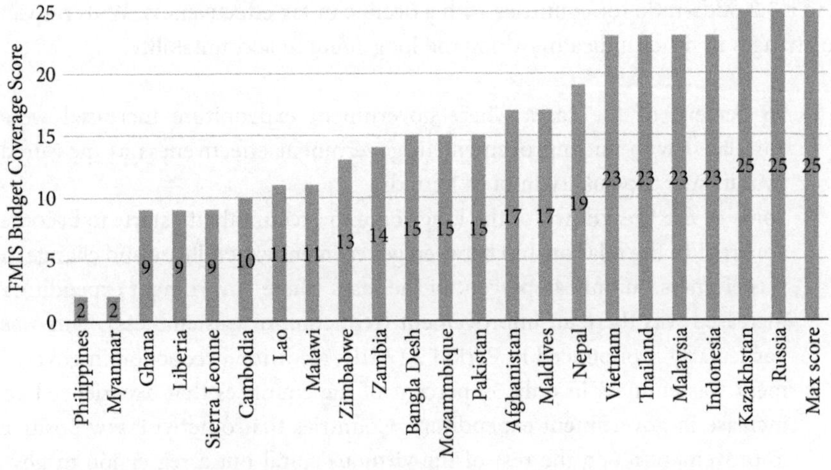

Figure 10.3 Low FMIS Budget Coverage Means Low Expenditure Control
Source: Piatti-Fünfkirchen (2018).

positively associated with security assistance as a percentage of military expenditure; the latter is rarely included in military expenditures recording and, to be sure, there are differences between transfers and in-kind assistance, which cannot be extracted from Security Assistance Monitor. Globally, US security assistance is 2.5 percent of total global GDP of fragile states. In the outlier case of Afghanistan, US security assistance is 41 percent of government expenditure (Afghanistan had an increase in government expenditure in both period 1 and period 2).

3.1.3 Bureaucratic Quality

In 56 percent of the country-period cases we observe an increase in the main measure of government capacity (effectiveness), Bureaucratic Quality, roughly equal (58 percent and 54 percent) in both periods. As discussed above and shown in Figure 10.2, bureaucratic quality increased in more cases where there was a reduction in tax effectiveness. One might attribute this to increased austerity (doing more with less), except that these ratios are consistent whether government expenditure increased or decreased. There is very little relationship between bureaucratic quality and wastefulness; in 50 percent of the cases where bureaucratic quality increased, the perception of wastefulness improved. There is, however, more evidence that perceptions of corruption move in the same direction as bureaucratic quality and government effectiveness. In country-periods where bureaucratic quality increased, perceptions of corruption improved in 68 percent of cases.

3.1.4 Wastefulness of Government Spending

Perceptions of wastefulness of government spending improved in 45 percent of the country-period cases, roughly similar in both periods (48 percent and

42 percent). Perceptions of wastefulness and corruption generally moved in the same direction: in 66 percent of the country period cases where wastefulness decreased, perceptions of corruption declined. Furthermore, definitions of wastefulness may vary by policymakers with different objective functions of government expenditure, including pro-poor growth, inclusive growth, and promotion of employment (Felipe, 2010). Note that there is also limited evidence here for an austerity argument, because changes in both perceptions of wastefulness and corruption were concurrent with increases and decreases in government expenditure.

3.1.5 Corruption among Government Officials

Finally, the last indicator used to assess progress along the virtuous spiral is corruption. In 66 percent of the cases, perceptions of corruption improved (less perceived corruption). These percentages were slightly higher in period 2, suggesting a positive trend over time. Note that the odds-ratios are consistent across nearly every one of the 32 groups shown in the last column of Figure 10.2, suggesting that there is no relationship between earlier outcomes in the nested probability and the change in the perceptions of corruption. This suggests a troubling disconnect between the ability of government to raise revenues and spend them efficiently and actual perceptions of corruption.

4. Discussion: Explaining Variation in Performance of Fragile States in Fiscal Policy and Outcomes

Many factors drive variation in performance across countries. All manner of usual suspects, potentially colluding with one another, can be named: vastly inadequate funding (even in countries notionally flooded with aid, such as Afghanistan[14]); poorly trained or poorly motivated staff; technically flawed policy choices or designs; active (and/or passive) resistance from competing factions or domestic adversaries; misguided advice from (and/or onerous requirements imposed by) international agencies, and so on. For present purposes, our focus has been the management of the fiscal policy space, and in particular security spending and its reporting mechanisms—both in its own right and as a "window" into broader dynamics shaping the nature and extent of the "social contract" between citizens and the state. If the coherence and functionality of the fiscal policy space is a central element of the "long route of accountability" by which the rights of citizens and the

[14] Thomas (2015: table 4.1), for example, shows that despite what can be portrayed by critics as "vast sums" being spent on aid to Afghanistan, the total amount of money—public revenue plus aid—actually available to the Afghan government to pay for its *entire* range of activities is estimated to be $285 per capita (in 2014 US dollars, PPP); in the Democratic Republic of Congo the amount is $112 per capita. By contrast, the UK government has $15,800 per capita and France has $21,300 per capita; even China has five times ($1520 per capita) as much revenue to dispense on services as Afghanistan.

obligations of government are mutually sustained and legitimized, especially in fragile states, then one should expect there to be positive reinforcing connections between the amount of public revenue collected from citizens, the effectiveness of the expenditure of this revenue on public services, and the legitimacy of the state to collect the necessary revenue. We see limited evidence of that relationship around the entire virtuous spiral, as evidenced by Figure 10.2.

We further expect a relationship between this promotion and acceleration of this virtuous spiral and performance of the state on core indicators like health, education or security. In this analysis, we use a nearly universally available outcome indicator to assess delivery of public goods—namely the unexpected change in infant mortality—that is the residual adjusting for starting level of infant mortality and the expected change in a period. A high (negative) residual indicates an unexpected improvement in infant mortality (more children surviving every 1000 live births). Meanwhile a positive residual is a case where performance on reducing infant mortality lagged average performance. We found very little evidence of this over time, as shown by Figure 10.4, where we array the governance indicators from left (most positive change in governance indicators) to right (all declines in governance indicators) and plot this against the average (weighted) residuals on change in infant mortality (again, a negative residual is unexpected progress) for each of the 32 groups. There is a slight positive relationship between governance and reduction in infant mortality for the period 2010–15, but the exact opposite relationship for the period 2005–10. Neither relationship is statistically significant, though the finding of opposite signs across time periods suggests (again) the importance of recognizing the limits of drawing broad policy inferences for fragile states from empirical results drawn from short or singular time frames.[15]

In one sense we were disappointed (though perhaps not entirely surprised) to find almost no consistent relationship between the five governance indicators used here and the outcome of unexpected change in infant mortality. This may have happened for a variety of reasons: perhaps governance reform is simply not related to this outcome, though the literature on new institutional economics contends otherwise;[16] possibly our results are linked to variable selection; perhaps a different choice of governance indicators could show that there was clean

[15] By locating the analysis in two convenient comparable time periods, we ignore political issues of budget creation, planning and delivery of political agendas. Another way to do this analysis would be to define periods based on political regimes and then measure changes in inputs, process, and outcome indicators over the length of that regime. This would include having different outcome indicators depending on priorities of the regime.

[16] Furthermore, we ran the same analysis using disability-adjusted life years from the World Health Organization in place of infant mortality and found similar results: there was actually a negative relationship between performance on these governance indicators and percent change in improvements in disability adjusted life years over time; countries that reduced disability-adjusted life years during this period experienced less government reform.

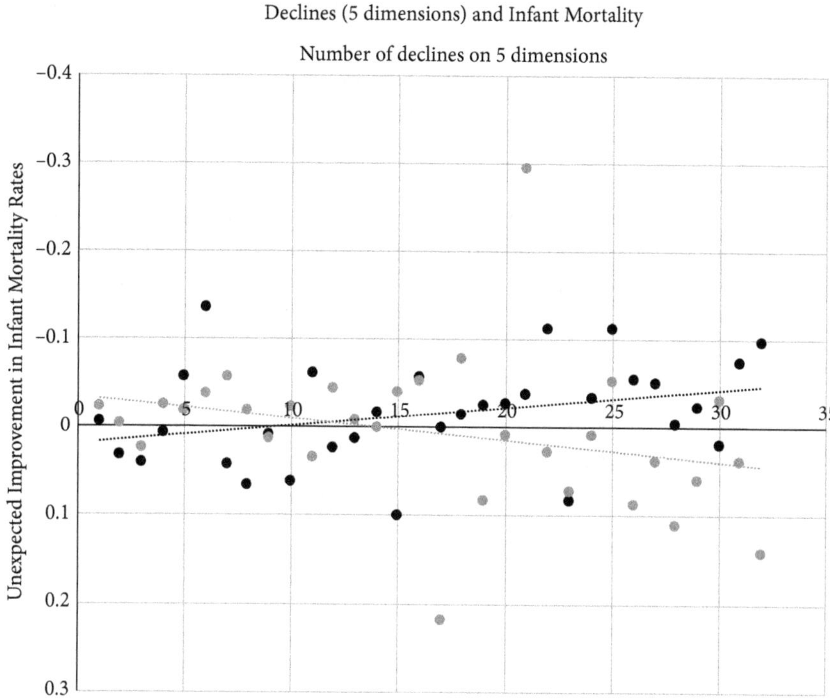

Figure 10.4 No Simple Relationship between Change in Governance and Infant Mortality Outcomes
Source: Authors' calculations

empirical relationship connecting each of the five stages in our spiral. Another reason may be that these indicators measure reform steps that are necessary, but insufficient in themselves to deliver the holistic reform processes that are necessary for improvements—a model allowing for interaction between all of the reforms and progress would need to be constructed (requiring more data and more degrees of freedom than the current data set allows). Or it could be the case, and we suggest that it is, that the complex relationship evidenced by Figure 10.4 says more about the complexity of the challenges of reform in these environments, reforms that must be grounded in local political context, including the realm of the possible and the second-best rather than the best technical solution.

This last interpretation is consistent with the data that underlies Figure 10.4. Though The Gambia, Jamaica, Mauritius, Panama, Namibia, and Singapore all enjoyed positive governance reform in every one of the five indicators discussed above in the period 2005 to 2010, none had better than expected improvements in infant mortality. Meanwhile, during the same period, the best unexpected improvements in infant mortality were in Estonia and China, which experienced setbacks in measures of wastefulness and corruption, respectively. From 2005 to 2015, Belarus made surprising progress on reducing infant mortality, equivalent to China's, and simultaneously retrogressed on every governance indicator except wastefulness, for which there are no data. The simplest interpretation of such complex results is that for Estonia and China, those reforms were not necessary to improve service delivery—whereas in The Gambia and Panama, something else was needed or reduction in infant mortality was not a government priority at that time. Beyond the location, direction, and velocity of change we need to know for each of these indicators what its impact is, but we must also understand the political context (the wind, visibility, terrain) in which each lever is being pushed to know why it is being applied and how it affects performance on the outcome variable. The results in Figure 10.2 show that there are no simple mechanistic relationships in such complex systems; therefore, we should be careful not to propose technical solutions or sequencing that would suggest otherwise.

Another way of showing how difficult sustained reform can be to achieve, regardless of the outcome intended, is to plot performance on reform from period 2 on to performance on reform on period 1 (see Figure 10.5). Countries in the

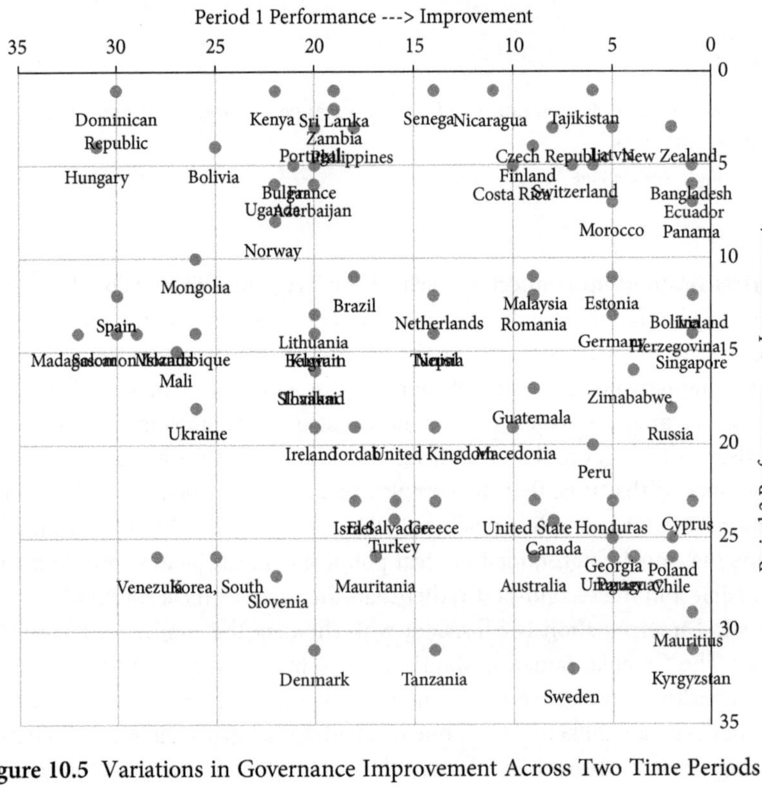

Figure 10.5 Variations in Governance Improvement Across Two Time Periods
Source: Authors' calculations

upper right corner improved significantly on all five areas of governance in both periods. The groupings in period 1 have no bearing on performance in period 2. For example, countries like France, Kuwait, Thailand, and Denmark that had multiple, similar setbacks from 2005 to 2010 have a wide range of outcomes in 2010–15. If there were a relationship between the type of progress or setbacks made in period 1 and the possible outcomes in period 2, we would expect to see vertical patterns by group, but there are none. This suggests that there is no path dependency and supports our claim in earlier work: that over both time and space, there are multiple paths to governance reform and performance improvement in all countries (but especially in fragile states).

Researchers must of course continue to expand and refine the quality of governance data available for understanding and informing policy responses to fragile situations but—at least in this instance—the very essence of state fragility means that our cross-national data on it will be inherently inadequate. It is unrealistic to expect weak states to collect and curate strong data. Moreover, the pressing moral and political imperatives to respond to state fragility also mean that researchers face strong temptations to ask this data to do work it really cannot do. It would be wonderful if the deep policy challenges of fragile states could be redressed by technocratic analysis alone, but such analyses can only ever be part of, not a substitute for, response strategies that take seriously the messy necessity of engaging with local contextual idiosyncrasies (much of which cannot be captured in or reduced to traditional quantitative datasets) and integrating these findings with theory, experience, history, and appreciation of the wide variation in pathways and outcomes that are likely to accompany any response strategy. Our analysis of the fiscal policy space in fragile states in this chapter amply bears out this reality. More and better aggregate data is always welcome, and progress is steadily being made on this front, but at least for the moment policy responses to the particular challenges of particular places must continue to draw on insights and evidence drawn from multiple sources, in multiple forms at multiple levels.

5. Conclusions and Future Research

In principle fiscal policy in all countries is a central component of the "long route of accountability" binding citizens and the state; in fragile states, however, the political dynamics shaping the extent to which this route does in fact lead to incrementally better key services (such as security and health) for citizens—and for which citizens, in turn, give the state due credit—are highly fraught. Using five governance measures across two time periods (2005–10, 2010–15), we have sought to document the wide array of pathways by which the fiscal policy space can and does change.

Consistent with our previous findings on movements in state fragility status over time, the absence of a clear singular empirical story connecting fiscal policy to effective service delivery outcomes suggests that there are multiple paths to effective service delivery—and thus, by extension, multiple points at which breakdowns can (and do) occur. This can be both frustrating and illuminating to policymakers working in fragile situations. It is frustrating because there is no silver bullet or straightforward sequencing by which simply pulling levers X, Y, and Z will yield a desired outcome. It is illuminating, because it opens the solution space to the panoply of reform options available in any given fragile situation. This wealth of possible solutions must be explored; indeed, many of these are likely to come from within the country itself, because phenomena such as corruption and effective health clinics are not uniformly spread across space and sectors: within any country, but especially fragile states, some places and organizational units will be far better and some far worse than others. Where are these places and people, and why do they perform at the high level they do, often against enormous odds? Finding, explaining, and sharing these within-country cases can be an empirically credible, locally legitimate, and even inspiring way forward.[17] Either way, the many pathways open to policymakers each come with their own challenges, pitfalls, advantages, and practicality.

These findings are true generally, but we have endeavored to show that they especially hold in fragile states, which are included in this analysis despite significant data coverage challenges. These findings also suggest the limits of what can be asked of aggregate governance measures in providing context-specific policy guidance in fragile situations; as such, continuing to curate such measures remains a necessary task, but one needing to be closely accompanied by solid theory, experience and context-specific knowledge.

In the coming years, we hope it will be possible to discern with greater accuracy the nature, extent, and location of the leakage in the fiscal policy space, particularly in countries affected by political violence, because a main driver of political violence is perceptions of corruption and abuse of power. If the forging of a coherent and legitimate social contract between citizens and the state is at the heart of reducing fragility, then much remains to be done to identify the particular conditions under which such contracts are initiated and sustained, and how the rightful collection and diligent expenditure of public resources contribute to it. For now, it is enough to show empirically that there are multiple pathways by which this outcome is likely to be obtained; there is no short (or clean or universal) route to this destination.

[17] See Brixi et al. (2015) on the deployment of such an approach for discerning ways to enhance the quality of service delivery in the Middle East and North Africa region.

References

Andrews, M. 2008. "The Good Governance Agenda: Beyond Indicators Without Theory." *Oxford Development Studies*, 36(4): 379–407.

Andrews, M., L. Pritchett, and M. Woolcock. 2017. *Building State Capability: Evidence, Analysis, Action*. New York: Oxford University Press.

Balabanova, D., A. Mills, L. Conteh, B. Akkazieva, H. Banteyerga, U. Dash, et al. 2013. "Good Health at Low Cost 25 Years on: Lessons for the Future of Health Systems Strengthening." *Lancet*, 381: 2118–33.

Besley, T. 2020. "State Capacity, Reciprocity, and the Social Contract." *Econometrica*, 88(4): 1307–1335.

Besley, T. and H. Mueller. (this volume). "Fiscal Capacity and State Fragility."

Besley, T. and T. Persson. 2013. "Taxation and Development," in A.J. Auerback, R. Chetty, M. Feldstein, and E. Saez (Eds.), *Handbook of Public Economics* (pp. 51–110). Oxford: Elsevier.

Boyce, J. K. and M. O'Donnell. (Eds.). 2007. *Peace and the Public Purse: Economic Policies for Postwar Statebuilding*. Boulder, CO: Lynne Rienner Publishers.

Brix, H., E. Lust, and M. Woolcock. 2015. *Trust, Voice and Incentives: Learning from Local Success Stories in the Middle East and North Africa*. Washington, DC: World Bank.

Corbridge, S., G. Williams, M. Srivastava, and R. Véron. 2005. *Seeing the State: Governance and Governmentality in India*. New York: Cambridge University Press.

Devarajan, S., S. Khemani, and M. Walton. 2013. "Can Civil Society Overcome Government Failure in Africa?" *The World Bank Research Observer*, 29(1): 20–47.

Di John, J. 2011. Taxation, Resource Mobilisation, and State Performance. https://eprints.soas.ac.uk/11785/1/WP84.2.pdf (last accessed July 16, 2020).

Evans, S. and M. Carnahan. 2015. "Public Goods for Private Jobs: Lessons from Postconflict Small Island States," in L. Chandy, H. Kato, and H. Kharas (Eds.), *The Last Mile in Ending Extreme Poverty* (pp. 249–74). Washington, DC: Brookings Institution.

Felipe, J. 2010. "Conclusions: How Can Developing Countries Implement an Inclusive-Growth and Full-Employment Strategy?" in *Inclusive Growth, Full Employment, and Structural Change: Implications and Policies for Developing Asia (2nd Ed.)*. London: Anthem Press and Manila: Asia Development Bank, pp. 289–96.

Heifetz, R.A., A. Grashow, and M. Linsky. 2009. *The Practice of Adaptive Leadership: Tools and Tactics for Changing Your Organization and the World*. Cambridge, MA: Harvard Business School Press.

IMF (International Monetary Fund). 2016. "Corruption: Costs and Mitigating Strategies." IMF Staff Discussion Note No. 16/05. Washington, DC: International Monetary Fund.

Kaufmann, D., A. Kraay and M. Mastruzzi. 2007. "The Worldwide Governance Indicators Project: Answering the Critics." Policy Research Working Paper No. WPS 4149. World Bank, Washington, DC.

Kaufmann, D., A. Kraay, and M. Mastruzzi. 2008. Governance Matters VII: Aggregate and Individual Governance Indicators 1996–2007. Policy Research Working Paper No. 4654. World Bank, Washington, DC.

Kleinfeld, R. 2018. *A Savage Order: How the World's Deadliest Countries Can Forge a Path to Security*. New York: Pantheon Press.

Kumara, A.S. and R. Samaratunge. 2016. "Patterns and Determinants of Out-of-Pocket Health Care Expenditure in Sri Lanka: Evidence from Household Surveys." *Health Policy and Planning*, 31(8): 970–83.

Levi, M. 1988. *Of Rule and Revenue*. Berkley, CA: University of California Press.

Menocal, A. and N. Taxell. 2017. "Why Corruption Matters." DFID Evidence Paper, London: Department for International Development.

Milante, G. 2007. *A Kleptocrat's Survival Guide: Autocratic Longevity in the Face of Civil Conflict*. Washington, DC: World Bank.

Milante, G. 2015. "A Thousand Paths to Poverty Reduction," in L. Chandy, H. Kato, and H. Kharas (Eds.), *The Last Mile in Ending Extreme Poverty*. Washington, DC: Brookings Institution Press.

Milante, G. and M. Woolcock. 2017. "New Approaches to Identifying State Fragility." *Journal of Globalization and Development* 8(1).

Mungiu-Pippidi, A. 2011. "Contextual Choices in Fighting Corruption: Lessons Learned." Norwegian Agency for Development Cooperation.

Piatti-Fünfkirchen, M. 2018. "Balancing Control and Flexibility for Improved Service Delivery." Policy Research Working Paper No. 9029. World Bank, Washington, DC.

Pritchett, L., and F. De Weijer. 2010. "Fragile States: Stuck in a Capability Trap?" Background paper for *World Development Report 2011*. Washington, DC: World Bank.

Sanín, F.G. 2011. "Evaluating State Performance: A Critical View of State Failure and Fragility Indexes." *The European Journal of Development Research*, 23(1): 20–42.

Sterck, O., M. Roser, M. Ncube, and S. Thewissen. 2018. "Allocation of Development Assistance for Health: Is the Predominance of National Income Justified?" *Health Policy and Planning* 33: i14–i23.

Thomas, M.A. 2015. *Govern Like Us: US Expectations of Poor Countries*. New York: Columbia University Press.

United Nations and World Bank. 2018. *Pathways to Peace: Inclusive Approaches to Preventing Violent Conflict*. Washington, DC: World Bank.

Venger, O. and T.D. Miethe. 2018. "Volatile Places, Volatile Times: Predicting Revolutionary Situations with Nations' Governance and Fragility Indicators." *Social Indicators Research, 138*(1): 373–402.

World Bank. 2003. *World Development Report 2004: Making Services Work for the Poor*. Washington, DC: World Bank.

World Bank. 2011. *World Development Report 2011: Conflict, Security and Development*. Washington, DC: World Bank.

World Bank. 2018. *World Development Report 2018: Learning to Realize Education's Promise*. Washington, DC: World Bank.

11

Building Fiscal Institutions in Fragile States

A Two-Step Approach

Katherine Baer, Sanjeev Gupta, Mario Mansour, and Sailendra Pattanayak

1. Introduction

Building and/or restoring fiscal institutions in fragile states is central to state-building and economic growth in these countries. Most fragile states struggle to achieve secure and stable tax revenues that can be administered easily, and to administer their budget resources to meet their basic spending needs and deliver basic services. They also face demands to demonstrate transparency and accountability in their use of public funds—especially countries that receive significant grant aid or are resource-rich. Reforms to build fiscal institutions in fragile states need to be sequenced taking into account country-specific circumstances, including absorptive capacity and initial conditions, and reflecting the country's degree of fragility, particularly between the immediate post-conflict/post-disaster stage and a more stable (but still vulnerable) stage.

Based on the IMF's extensive on-the-ground experience providing advice to its member countries, including fragile states, this chapter proposes a two-step approach to building fiscal institutions.[1]

The "first stage" refers to country contexts where the capacity of fiscal institutions is extremely weak, following a period of major conflict (war), political conflict and uncertainty (lack of a government or very frequent changes of government), or immediately after a natural disaster or a pandemic. Because of the country's conditions, a shorter-term and incremental approach is needed to reforming institutions. This will not only help country authorities establish fundamental capacities and obtain the confidence that they can do so but will

The authors would like to thank Gilles Montagnat-Rentier and Victor Mylonas for their significant contributions to this chapter on customs administration issues and on preparation of data, respectively. The views expressed in this chapter are those of the authors and do not necessarily represent the views of the IMF, its Executive Board, or IMF management.

[1] This paper draws from the observations and lessons learned as set out in the IMF Board Paper "Building Fiscal Capacity in Fragile States" (IMF, 2017a).

Katherine Baer, Sanjeev Gupta, Mario Mansour, and Sailendra Pattanayak. *Building Fiscal Institutions in Fragile States: A Two-Step Approach* In: *Macroeconomic Policy in Fragile States.* Edited by: Ralph Chami, Raphael Espinoza, and Peter Montiel, Oxford University Press (2021). © International Monetary Fund.
DOI: 10.1093/oso/9780198853091.003.0011

also provide a sustainable basis for more broad-ranging reforms in a second stage. First stage reforms can perhaps best be understood as being "recuperation" reforms, while second stage as "building progress" reforms.

The "second stage" refers to country contexts where more fiscal institutional capacity has been built: there is a core set of managers and technical experts who can carry out the basic functions of fiscal institutions; there are a core set of laws and regulations backing these institutions; the most basic revenue collection and expenditure management functions are in place; and the largest fiscal vulnerabilities (e.g., collapse in tax revenue, inability to fund basic government services or public sector wages) have been overcome. In this more stable but often still vulnerable phase, a more medium-term approach to building fiscal institutions can be taken.

IMF experience across a broad range of countries suggests that the transition from the first stage to the second stage depends on the situation in each country. There is no one-size-fits-all approach to sequencing the progression from very basic, post-conflict or post-disaster reforms to institutional reforms of a more medium-term nature. A country may remain in the first stage for a long time if there is chronic political instability, a long-term conflict with no end in sight, a lack of resources or a core team to lead the reforms. A country may briefly emerge from the first-stage reform but quickly regress if a conflict resumes, political instability recurs, or because of other factors. Because of this, it is difficult to state with any degree of certainty how long the first and second stage reforms should last. The time frame for each stage and the transition from the first to the second stage of reforms will depend on what happens in each country. The IMF classifies a country as fragile if its three-year average score on the World Bank's Country Policy and Institutional Assessment (CPIA) score is below the 3.2 threshold,[2] or, if the country had a peace-building or peace-keeping operation in the most recent three years.[3] Under this definition, there were 42 fragile states in 2017, among which Sub-Saharan Africa and the Pacific Islands are overrepresented (24 and 8 countries, respectively).[4] Among low- and middle-income countries, one in three was fragile. More than 530 million people (7.3 percent of the world population) lived in fragile states, but they accounted for only 1.7 percent of global GDP, although a significant proportion of them (18 out of 42) were resource-rich countries.

[2] IMF (2011a); IMF (2015); and Gelbard et al. (2015).

[3] Using the average reduces the probability of a country moving in or out of fragility when its annual score is very close to the average.

[4] The list of fragile states in 2017 include: Afghanistan, Burundi, Cameroon, Central African Republic, Chad, Comoros, Côte d'Ivoire, Democratic Republic of the Congo, Djibouti, Eritrea, Guinea, Guinea-Bissau, Haiti, Iraq, Kiribati, Kosovo, Lebanon, Liberia, Libya, Madagascar, Malawi, Maldives, Mali, Marshall Islands, Micronesia, Myanmar, Papua New Guinea, Republic of Congo, São-Tomé and Principe, Sierra Leone, Solomon Islands, Somalia, South Sudan, Sudan, Syria, Tajikistan, The Gambia, Timor-Leste, Togo, Tuvalu, Yemen, and Zimbabwe.

Several characteristics stand out when fragile states are compared with the 82 nonfragile lower- or middle-income countries (labeled as nonfragile states), (Table 11.1). Fragile states tend to have lower economic growth rates than nonfragile states, a larger current account imbalance, and a higher dependence on official development assistance.[5] A significant proportion of fragile states are particularly vulnerable to natural disasters and were among the countries with the highest corruption levels in the world, as measured by the Transparency International Corruption Perception Index. Finally, there is a high incidence of IMF programs among them, reflecting in part their weak macroeconomic performance and vulnerability to external shocks. Virtually all IMF programs have had conditionality to improve revenue performance and enhance the efficiency and transparency of expenditures in fragile states.

It takes a long time to exit fragility. According to several studies, 15 to 30 years may be needed to rebuild a country's institutions after a sharp deterioration, and

Table 11.1 Fragile and Nonfragile States: Selected Indicators (2013–16 average, simple averages in each category of countries, median of the category in parenthesis)

Indicator	FSs	NFSs
GDP per capita (US$, PPP)	3,980 (2,545)	10,479 (9,265)
Real GDP per capita growth (%)	0.28 (1.51)	2.23 (2.39)
Real GDP growth (%)	2.66 (3.77)	3.57 (3.75)
Inflation (%)	8.80 (4.59)	5.86 (3.54)
Current Account Balance (% GDP)	−8.05 (−6.41)	−5.36 (−4.56)
Official Development Aid (% GDP)	13.32 (7.39)	3.01 (1.61)
of which: Grants (% GDP)	8.58 (2.86)	1.78 (0.72)
General Government Gross Debt (% GDP)	47.10 (38.36)	48.11 (43.24)
General Government Net Lending (% GDP)	−4.87 (−3.9)	−3.65 (−3.36)

Note: FS = fragile state: NFS = nonfragile state; PPP = purchasing power parity.

Source: IMF October 2018 World Economic Outlook Database (WEO), IMF World Revenue Longitudina Database (WoRLD), World Bank Development Indicators (WDI) Database.

[5] These differences are statistically significant at the 1 percent level.

not all countries succeed in that time.[6] After having reached the most extreme degree of fragility, the typical country makes rapid progress for about 5 years, during which the CPIA indicators, tax revenue, and security improve steadily; then progress slows down and it takes another 10 years or more to graduate from fragility.

About 30 percent of countries that were fragile in 2008 were no longer so in 2017.[7] None of these fragile states had any security issues immediately before 2008, but half of them had some in the previous decade, confirming that security is a prerequisite for progress and that once security is reestablished (as in Chad, Eritrea, and Timor-Leste), several more years are needed to end fragility.

This chapter is organized as follows: section 2 discusses the approach to designing and implementing revenue and public expenditure reforms in fragile states, as drawn from experience of IMF technical assistance programs. Section 3 discusses the role of fiscal conditionality in IMF programs in helping to build fiscal capacity in fragile states and some recent econometric results. Section 4 concludes.

2. Building Tax Capacity

Fragile states are characterized by low tax ratios (on average 13 percent of GDP against 18 percent in nonfragile countries (Figure 11.1), and frequently extremely low ratios, especially after a conflict (for example, Afghanistan, Chad, Democratic Republic of the Congo, Guinea-Bissau, Iraq, Libya, Myanmar, and Timor-Leste have experienced several years of tax-to-GDP ratios below 3 percent).[8] Resource-rich fragile states fare better, thanks to nontax revenue from the extractive industries.[9] Natural resource revenues have accounted for 11 percent of GDP, on average, in fragile states in recent years.

Two features of tax systems of fragile states are worth noting. First, they collect more from taxes on international trade, which account for a higher share of total taxes than in nonfragile states (23 percent against 14 percent). Second, they rely less than nonfragile states on revenues from domestic taxes on goods and services (such as VAT).[10]

The experience in mobilizing revenue differs somewhat between fragile states that succeeded in exiting fragility, and those that did not (Figure 11.2 and Annex). Before 2008, fragile states that turned successful in the following decade were able

[6] See Cilliers and Sisk (2013), Gelbard et al. (2015), World Bank (2011).

[7] These include Albania, Angola, Bosnia and Herzegovina, Cambodia, Lao P.D.R., Niger, Nigeria, Rwanda, Serbia, Tonga, Uzbekistan, and Vanuatu.

[8] See Mansour and Schneider (2019).

[9] See Crivelli and Gupta (2014), Brun et al. (2015). Nontax revenue from natural resources may stem from a government's share in the equity of the extractive firms, or from licensing fees, recurrent or not, paid by the firms for the exploitation of natural resources.

[10] See Acosta-Ormaechea and Yoo (2012).

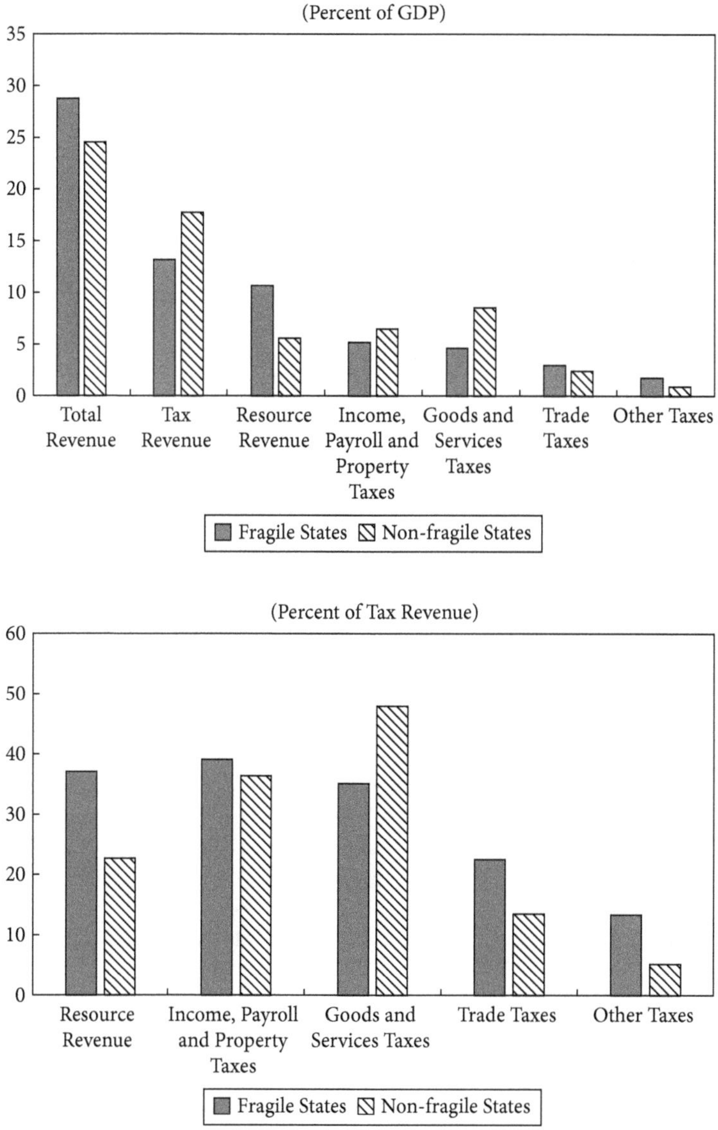

Figure 11.1 Tax Revenue in Fragile and Non-Fragile States

(Simple average for 2013–16)

Top panel. Percent of GDP; Bottom panel. Percent of Revenues

Note: Top panel - Figures for various tax types may not add up given that not all series are available every year for all countries.

Bottom panel - For resource revenues, figures are reported in percent of total revenue (instead of total tax revenue).

to mobilize about 6 percentage points of GDP more revenue than unsuccessful ones, with revenue from natural resources playing an important role in several countries. Angola and Niger raised more than 20 percent of GDP from natural resources in the early 2000s, a share that has fallen significantly since then. Other

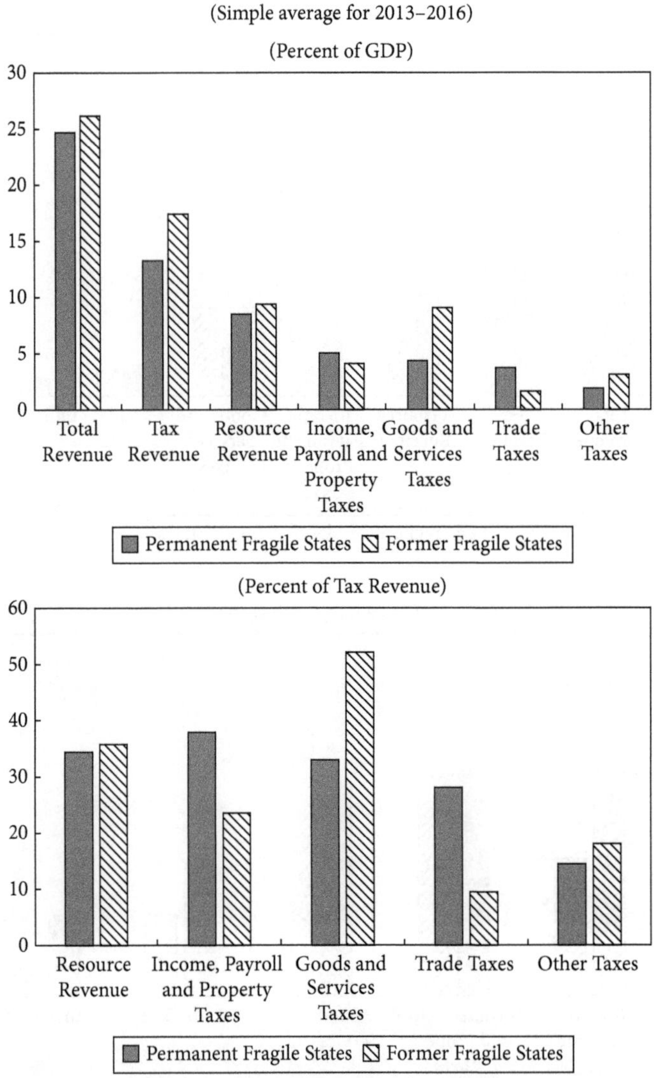

Figure 11.2 Tax Revenues in Permanent versus Successful Fragile States

Note: Top panel - Figures for various tax types may not add up given that not all series are available every year for all countries.

Bottom panel - For resource revenues, figures are reported in percent of total revenue (instead of total tax revenue).

Source: IMF WoRLD, SSA and MENA Databases.

(Simple average, 2013–16) Top panel. Percent of GDP; Bottom panel. Percent of Tax Revenue

countries, such as Cambodia and Rwanda, were able to increase the contribution of natural resource revenues to the budget from initially insignificant levels, as they moved out of fragility.

All successful countries (former fragile states) were able to collect more than 15 percent of their GDP through taxation, and half of them more than 20 percent, at least for some years during the past decade, even if these levels were not sustained for long in some cases (for example, in Angola or Nigeria, where tax revenue collapsed with the fall in oil prices in 2014). This is consistent with the empirical finding that there seems to be a tipping point for tax revenue—about 13 percent to 15 percent of GDP—below which it is very difficult for a country to rebuild its institutions to exit fragility.[11]

The tax composition in successful fragile states, compared with nonfragile states, is characterized by:

- The predominant share of indirect taxation in total taxes, which increases as the situation of the country improves, to reach a level that is comparable to that observed in nonfragile states.
- The relatively small contribution of tariffs, which diminishes over time.

The relationship between taxation and state-building goes deeper than just mobilizing revenue in the medium term.[12] Simplicity, inclusiveness, transparency, and equity of the tax system play an important role in restoring the state's capacity and legitimacy. Therefore, relative to economic efficiency, these objectives may have to be given more weight than they are given in nonfragile countries.[13]

Other objectives assigned to the tax system in nonfragile countries could also be pursued in fragile states. Redistributing income or wealth, or discouraging behavior harming oneself, others, or the environment can sometimes be achieved through simple efficient taxes, such as excises on alcohol or luxury cars. But in other cases, such objectives may be a distraction to rebuilding the basic institutional capacities, and would be addressed more effectively later, as countries become less vulnerable.

A tax system in a fragile state should strive to achieve the following objectives:

- *A small number of taxes:* The limited administrative capabilities should be focused on levying a few effective taxes.
- *A single or very few rates for each tax:* A single rate eliminates bargaining and avoidance possibilities related to the requalification of the tax base.
- *Easy-to-assess tax bases:* Sophisticated tax bases may help reduce economic distortions, but are costly to assess and audit, and may end up opening the way to tax bargaining and avoidance.
- *Few exemptions:* Exemptions create loopholes, through which parallel markets develop, which is especially costly in countries where the informal economy may already be prevalent and undermines both the government's revenue and its legitimacy.
- *A wide recourse to presumptive taxation:* For the tax administration to be able to monitor taxpayers effectively under the standard regime, and for the

[11] See Gaspar et al. (2016). [12] See Besley and Persson (2014), IMF (2018 a).

[13] See Brautigam et al. (2008), Everest-Phillips (2010).

system to be sufficiently inclusive at the same time, it needs to resort to special regimes, in which smaller taxpayers are taxed on a presumptive or lump sum basis.

- *A focus on large taxpayers and easy collection points:* The borders, the large enterprises—especially in extractive industries—and the workers in the civil service and the formal sector are easier for the revenue administrations to monitor, and the design of taxes should take that into account.
- *Preparation for the future:* Even if the tax system of a fragile country cannot comply with the canons of taxation theory, it should preferably be designed in such a way that it can be gradually refined as the situation improves, rather than requiring a complete overhaul.

2.1 First-Stage Reforms: Conflicts and Disaster

The priority should be to use the available administrative capacity on effective collection points. Depending on geography and security, the effective collection points may include:

- The border or, if not the actual border, the checkpoints where goods enter the territory under the control of the government (for example, Afghanistan, Central African Republic);
- the largest enterprises operating in the capital city and other cities under the government's control;
- mining and extraction sites, if any, under the government's control;
- wages in the civil service and possibly in the large enterprises in the formal sector; and
- land, if a cadaster is available.

In post-conflict or crisis situations, reorganizing the tax system around these collection points can help maximize receipts despite administrative weaknesses, keeping in mind that the system will have to evolve toward a design more suited to economic efficiency and other objectives as soon as the situation allows.

Some sectors warrant special consideration because of their special characteristics and their role in economic development. These include banking, telecommunications, and nonrenewable natural resources. In some countries, this list could extend to renewable natural resources, such as forestry and fishing (for example, Cameroon, Central African Republic).

The taxation of banks could be implemented as follows:

- An income tax, which can be calculated as a cashflow tax, that is, based on the difference between the interest received on loans plus the fees received

for services, on the one hand, and the interest paid on deposits plus capital investments, on the other, at a rate approximating a future corporate income tax rate (for example, 20 percent to 25 percent);
- a tax based on the value added of banks, which may be defined either as the sum of the wage bill and cash profits, or as the difference between the interest the bank receives on loans and the interest it pays to depositors, and at a rate approximating the normal rate of a possible future VAT (for example, 10 percent to 15 percent).[14]

Enterprises in the telecommunications sector benefit from an oligopolistic position arising naturally from economies of scale associated with a network industry and from the licensing process required to allocate the spectrum or the access to the physical infrastructure in place. There is a rationale for the telecommunication industry to contribute to the budget through the government's sales of licenses or through specific taxes aimed at recovering part of the oligopoly's rent.

A recurrent tax on telecommunication activity may be preferable to one-time licensing fees, because some telecommunication operators are already licensed, and new entrants may be in a strong bargaining position vis-à-vis the government when they negotiate their access, because they have more information about the future rent and because the government is fragile.

An additional tax on telecommunication could take the form of a turnover tax, to be paid above the common tax applied to other enterprises, and equivalent to an excise on calls. This may be the most convenient tax, though not the least distortive one.[15] Given the importance of telecommunications in the production process, especially for foreign investors, and given the relatively high price elasticity of calls, it is advisable to keep the rate of the additional telecommunications turnover levy at a moderate level, below 20 percent, until a more growth-friendly taxation of rent can be put in place.[16]

A resource-rich country in an emergency situation is inclined to tap extractive industries for more revenue. Trying to increase the contribution of the resource sector by modifying the resource tax law during a period of high fragility can be counterproductive for several reasons:

- Fragility weakens the government's position in designing and trying to impose a different resource-rent sharing arrangement. A new arrangement may be less favorable than previous ones.
- When the fragility of the country is linked to a drop in the world commodity prices, an increase in volumes can be the most effective way to mobilize revenue

[14] See Zee (2004). [15] See Matheson and Petit (2017).
[16] When Guinea introduced a tax representing about 15 percent of the price of calls in 2015, their volume fell by 15 percent.

for the government, until the price rises again. This would require more private investment, which must not be deterred by stricter tax and fee conditions.

- Renegotiation of past sharing agreements creates instability for the investors and conveys the message that any new agreement may be no more definitive. This would weigh on the new investments of the firms already in place, as well as on the confidence of future investors.

However, it may also be the case that the existing tax arrangements are no longer enforceable because of the post-conflict situation. In such cases, it may be useful for the government to replace the pre-existing resource tax by a time-limited simpler tax; for example, an ad valorem royalty based on the gross value of sales by the extractive firms.

Fragile states should limit sectoral provisions. Justified exceptions, if any, would depend on each country's specificities and are likely to remain very limited. Examples of such justified exceptions include:

- Rent sectors, such as high-range hotels and restaurants in a country where the fragile situation discourages new openings, can be subjected to a sectoral levy, additional to the general taxes on income and consumption or to the tax replacing them. This may be of particular relevance in a crisis country, where peacekeeping forces, nongovernmental organizations and technical assistance create high demand for such services. At the same time, it is in the interest of the country to keep the surtax low enough not to deter the aid providers.
- Investments in some sectors can be granted under special conditions, for example, if they involve the construction of infrastructure, such as ports, roads, or pipelines, which will become an economic asset for other agents than the investing firm.

It is important to introduce some sort of income tax. A withholding tax on wages paid to civil servants can be collected at a low administrative cost. To keep it as simple as possible, a single tax rate (for example, about 30 percent) with a sufficiently large tax-free personal allowance (for example, about per capita GDP) can be considered, which would ensure progressivity. Its immediate utility is that it serves as a proxy for a future more comprehensive personal income tax, and as such is a signal toward tax inclusiveness, especially because civil servants may be regarded as a privileged part of the population during a crisis. However, the revenue potential of such a tax remains low, given the narrowness of its base and the fact that civil servants may be able to preserve their net income through offsetting increases in the government's wage bill. At a somewhat higher administrative cost, the same withholding income tax can be applied to the wages distributed by large formal enterprises.

Although property taxation offers only limited scope for revenue in very fragile countries,[17] it has other merits that may make it worth considering, if and where a cadaster is available, which is more likely in middle-income countries (for example, Lebanon). Property taxation may be designed to be simple to administer, and it is among the least distortive taxes. Introducing it early after a crisis, initially at a low rate, paves the way toward an efficient future tax system. The tax can easily be focused on larger property owners, for example by providing a surface allowance. The property tax can be earmarked to local governments.

An issue that arises immediately after an emergency situation is how to treat the pre-crisis legacy. It may have become extremely costly or even impossible to audit or document many claims by taxpayers concerning their liabilities, allowances, or time-dependent tax provision dating from before the crisis, even if the claims are made in good faith. Leaving their treatment unresolved hinders the return to normality and possibly the implementation of an effective emergency tax system, because large taxpayers can be tempted to net their alleged positions vis-à-vis the tax administration before making any post-crisis tax payment (as in Somalia).[18] Options could include a total or partial tax amnesty.

Setting up basic administrative procedures entails establishing processes such as registration, filing, and payment for the major taxpayers and taxes; and at customs, cargo reporting and control, checking the tax base (value in particular), and ensuring that importers pay before goods are released. This approach was followed in South Sudan, for example, before the conflict resumed.[19] In Myanmar, the tax administration reform strategy focused initially on larger taxpayers, to secure a significant percentage of tax revenue and to lay the foundations for progressive strengthening of the tax administration. To restore its tax administration capacities, Somalia's initial step was the establishment of a Large Taxpayers' Office.

Ensuring the continuity of basic operations in the face of crisis and uncertainty can protect against revenue collapses. In Mali, the 2012–14 crisis had only a minor impact on revenue collection largely because of the resilience of the tax and customs departments.[20]

[17] Among 42 fragile states in 2017, only Lebanon collected more than 0.5 percent of GDP from property taxation, and 34 collected no revenue at all.

[18] Countries which have slipped into fragility without experiencing a crisis may experience a low-intensity version of this problem if VAT credits accumulate while the capacity of the tax administration to audit them deteriorates. This creates a liability for the government, often left off-budget, and a loophole in the tax system.

[19] The authorities of South Sudan collected a mere 1.1 percent of GDP in nonoil revenue in 2011–12 (at independence). This subsequently increased to 2.4 percent of GDP in 2012–13, but dropped to 1.8 percent in 2013–14, during the civil conflict. Non-oil revenue increased again to 3.1 percent of GDP in 2014–15 and 6.1 percent of GDP in 2015–16. This increase could have been greater if peace had prevailed.

[20] The March 2012 coup resulted in the pillaging of the customs administration, *Direction Générale des Douanes*, and numerous customs offices, including information technology systems and vehicles.

It is equally important to put in place a basic organizational structure for the tax and customs administration. In South Sudan, this process started with transferring the customs administration from the Ministry of the Interior to the Ministry of Finance and Economic Planning.[21] In Liberia, reforms in revenue administration that started in 2006 included the redesign of the organizational structure of the tax and customs administration, which laid the basis for the establishment of the Liberia Revenue Authority in 2014.

An early focus on obtaining accurate information on the taxpayer base is the foundation for sound tax administration. In Myanmar, while the reform strategy focused initially on larger taxpayers, it aimed to broaden the tax base, by both increasing the number of registered taxpayers and improving compliance with tax obligations, while minimizing the cost of complying with these obligations.

2.2 Second-Stage Reforms: Expansion and Modernization

Modernization programs in fragile states must have a medium-term focus of at least five years and be adaptable to the weak state of the administration, observed progress, and changing circumstances in the country. Reforms need to be clearly sequenced. In this regard, the international community has been focusing on the adoption of explicit medium-term revenue strategies (MTRS) to modernize tax systems in developing countries and in some fragile states. Such a strategy is also intended to help coordinate donor activities in an increasingly active field.[22] While an MTRS approach to tax system reform can be applicable to fragile states, care must be taken to ensure that it is consistent with the government's medium-term fiscal objectives[23] and steer clear of overly ambitious approaches to reform when fiscal institutions are very fragile and when there is uncertain political support for reforming the tax system.

The modernization program must be costed and supported by an appropriate budget. Managers must cope with limited resources, deficient institutions, and wavering political support. Liberia is a good example of commitment to medium-term institutional reform with adequate sequencing. Starting in 2012, Liberia

Imports declined by 16 percent in 2012 because of the Economic Commission of West African States (ECOWAS) embargo and the conflict in the north of the country, which forced the administration to move staff to the south. In this critical context, the DGD opened temporary offices, required use of procedural manuals, and installed a back-up server.

[21] In practice this transfer did not fully occur, in part because of a lack of commitment and no plan for dealing with former combatants who make up the majority of customs staff.

[22] Papua New Guinea is an example of a fragile state where work is ongoing on a medium-term strategy to reform the tax system.

[23] Countries typically prepare a medium-term fiscal framework setting out medium-term fiscal objectives (see also section 3).

approved legislation to establish a revenue authority, and a transition team was formed under strong leadership. Instead of immediately introducing a VAT as a way of modernizing their tax system, the Liberian authorities began by strengthening basic tax and customs operations. Liberia has been supported, and in part financed, by various international donors.

More weight can now be given to non-revenue objectives of tax policy, such as efficiency, equity, and transparency. Starting from weak capacity, strengthening the fiscal institutions is a priority for carrying out the reforms of the tax system during the recovery. The process is facilitated if the following two steps are taken early:

- *Establish a sound legal framework for fiscal management.* Bringing back all tax receipts into the single account of Treasury (even if some remain earmarked),[24] and making the Ministry of Finance responsible for its management is a prerequisite for post-emergency reforms.
- *Establish a central authority responsible for tax reforms:* a single organization responsible for tax policy, tax administration, and customs reforms would help move the reform process forward.

Once these two steps have been taken, policymakers will need to be clear about the characteristics of the tax system that they aim for. However, there needs to be a balance between officials' commitment to a medium-term target for the tax system and the necessary flexibility about the timing to reach it. The adoption and publication of a MTRS may be instrumental in this regard.

The main policy tool for promoting equity is the personal income tax, a revenue source that has increased in recent years in fragile states. Kosovo, for example, expanded the use of income taxes in recent years. However, in most low-income countries (LICs), it remains largely confined to withholding on wages at the level of employers, and primarily from public service employment. Investment income is largely untaxed, partly because of a low savings rate, but also because high-income individuals can hide their wealth effectively, often in foreign countries with bank secrecy laws and low tax rates.

Recent developments may alleviate these constraints, and allow some fragile states to improve the taxation of individuals:

- The"dual income tax (DIT)," which has been adopted in a number of advanced countries, provides a coherent approach to the taxation of personal income in lower-capacity countries (Bird and Zolt, 2010). Under a DIT, wage income is taxed at a progressive rate, and capital income is taxed at a single rate, usually at the lowest marginal rate on wage income. This is often how,

[24] See also section 3.

de facto, the personal income tax works in lower-income countries, though with a patchwork of treatments for different forms of capital income. The DIT offers a way to systematize and more effectively enforce this approach. Furthermore, both the wage tax and most capital income taxes (other than the corporate tax) can be collected through final withholding, provided that the tax base has a simple design. For example, a wage tax that allows for a general deduction, and no itemized deductions, can be withheld at the level of the employer, thus requiring less administrative effort than if the wage earners had to file a tax return.

- Developments in international taxation can prove valuable for fragile states and low-income economies. One strand is the international push for relaxing bank secrecy laws around the world, and strengthening exchange of information (automatically, in due course, for developing countries that are not financial centers); this can provide a strong handle to address evasion by the wealthiest. Another strand in the Group of Twenty (G20)/Organization of Economic Cooperation and Development (OECD) Base Erosion and Profit Shifting (BEPS) project aims at curtailing tax avoidance by multinationals. Country-by-country reporting, for instance, can provide valuable insights into the tax affairs of multinationals operating locally, though subject to strong conditions required to provide such information. Taking advantage of these important developments requires capacity that may exceed that available to many fragile states.

Another key component of a more equitable tax system in fragile states is the taxation of small and micro-enterprises. Their tax treatment should be geared toward easing their transition into the "standard" tax system and creating a sense of fairness by having all citizens contribute to financing government activities. This can involve simple levies on turnover at a rate high enough to encourage transition into the tax system but not so high as to encourage concealment—a difficult balance. Fragile states should resist the (unfortunate but frequent) policy and administrative practices of extending complex tax rules to small and micro-enterprises on the ground that they operate primarily in the informal economy—income concealed in the formal sector often tends to be more significant than the total income that would be subject to tax in the informal sector.

Other noteworthy reforms in the second stage include the introduction, or strengthening, of broad-base consumption taxes, notably the VATs. With proper design, VATs can work well in fragile states that are relatively stable—for example, Kosovo and Mali. In terms of efficiency, their design may depart from that recommended for VATs in high-income countries. For example, the IMF has typically advised that countries define a relatively high registration threshold and use tax exemptions in limited cases as opposed to lower rates—for example, in

Liberia. Though many countries have followed advice on the threshold, experience with VAT exemptions is mixed, and multiple VAT rates are less uncommon today than they were in the early 2000s. Moreover, there are cases where the transition from extreme fragility to less extreme fragility can take a long time, during which advice on whether countries should introduce VAT, and its key design features, should be reconsidered. For example, in Afghanistan and Haiti VAT design evolved over the years, when it became clear that changes in political and security conditions were very slow and affected these countries' administrative capacity to operate a VAT in the domestic economy.

Excises are low-hanging fruit among revenue-enhancing tax reforms in fragile countries. Although the list of excisable products is the same as during the emergency period, with petroleum products, cigarettes and alcohol likely to have the higher potential for revenue, higher rates can be considered during the recovery, as the capacity for fighting the development of parallel markets increases.

During this stage, it is important to strengthen the capacity of the tax and customs administrations' headquarters office so that they can define basic strategies, plan and monitor core operations, and oversee support functions such as information technology (IT) and human resources. In Haiti, the focus has been on clearly delineating the tax administration's headquarters and operational functions, ensuring that the headquarters units are focused on the main tax administration functions, and that the operational offices are organized by taxpayer segments. Unfortunately, the function-based organizational structure has not been approved or implemented, reflecting weak strategic management and high turnover of the tax administration's senior management—recently three tax administration directors were appointed in one year.[25]

Establishing function-based large taxpayer offices (LTOs) and medium-sized taxpayer offices (MTOs) is another important consideration. These offices often serve as pilots for introducing basic core procedures such as taxpayer registration, return filing, and payment monitoring, and help ensure that the bulk of tax revenues are monitored closely. Once established, these procedures can be rolled out to other tax offices and other taxpayer segments. In Liberia, the Liberia Revenue Authority has established an LTO, along with departments that focus on monitoring the compliance of medium, small, and micro taxpayers. The Democratic Republic of the Congo also established an LTO as part of its modernization of its tax administration. In natural resource–rich countries, developing the capacity to audit the oil and mining sectors, and ensuring satisfactory control of exports are high priorities.

[25] High turnover of senior staff, weak headquarters offices, inadequate and unstable financing, and unwieldy office networks are obstacles to effective revenue administration performance in many countries (IMF, 2015).

Strengthening customs operations in the few critical ports is important.[26] International trade in fragile states is conducted through a small number of ports, sometimes through one.[27] Thus, controlling cargo at these ports and monitoring import valuation, exemptions, and relief procedures are essential to securing the tax base. In landlocked countries and those that need to be crossed to access these countries, customs management of transit goods, including exchange of information with neighboring countries, is paramount.[28]

Establishing basic compliance improvement strategies for individual taxes or different taxpayer segments is critical. Kosovo focused on strengthening core tax administration functions (debt collection, audit), managing large taxpayers, and tailoring administrative activities to specific tax risks (synonymous with designing compliance improvement strategies). Building trust and cooperation with taxpayers became a priority of the new compliance improvement approach. Liberia's tax administration has recently established a risk committee, mapped compliance risks, and used an analytical tool (a simplified version of the Australian Tax Office's "Risk Differentiation Framework") to identify the taxpayer's profile and distinguish treatment of taxpayers by groups.

The modernization strategy is not complete without human resource policies that promote performance and integrity. The human resource policy must be based on transparent rules for recruitment, promotion and separation, and reasonable pay. Where such principles have not been adopted, it is important to screen applicants against integrity standards, introduce a compulsory learning assessment after the initial training, require staff to declare assets on a regular basis and conflicts of interest, and implement clear disciplinary procedures with appropriate sanctions in cases of unethical behavior. Instituting training for new officers can have a profound positive impact on the quality of work, as can removal of corrupt officials.

An appropriate IT system is needed to support the core processes described above.[29] This will allow the administration to begin producing periodic operational and management reports. In many fragile states—certainly Haiti, Liberia,

[26] For a more extensive discussion of the issues relating to customs see the IMF Technical Note: Revenue Administration: Short-Term Measures to Increase Customs Revenue in Low-Income and Fragile Countries, by Gilles Montagnat-Rentier, 2019.

[27] The small number of important trading partners and limited intraregional trade facilitate this approach.

[28] Burundi and other East African Community partner states have introduced a "Single Customs Territory" procedure under which taxable imports are cleared at the first port of entry into the Community (usually Dar-es-Salaam, Tanzania for Burundi trade) and circulate duty-paid instead of duty-suspended. The inconvenience of upfront payment of duty and tax has been offset by a significant reduction in transit times.

[29] Customs administrations tend to adopt automated systems at a faster pace, reflecting the transaction-based processing of imports and exports and concentration of collection points. Virtually all customs services in fragile states were equipped early with an automated processing system, many having opted for ASYCUDA, which was developed by UNCTAD.

Mali, and Myanmar, tax IT systems require expansion and upgrades, or need to be implemented from scratch (South Sudan).[30]

Digitalizing operations could help standardize and improve procedures and facilitate control of operations. For customs, this entails the elimination of manual procedures and paper documents. Tax administrations should aim at a leap to a paperless process and should design their automation projects to do so.[31] Digitalization would help improve compliance and reduce evasion. Digital systems can automatically report all outstanding operations to managers, forward reminders to stop-filers, notify a debt due when a duty suspension procedure has expired without action by the declarant, and block operations in relation to incidents that have occurred. Blockchain technology holds substantial promise for improving customs operations by reducing the cost and time taken to clear customs.[32]

Data analysis should be used more intensively to support strategic and operational decisions. Good recent examples include: Côte d'Ivoire, where customs is now operating an automated risk management system that is aligned with updated enforcement data to select shipments for inspection. Comoros and Côte d'Ivoire undertook, in 2017 and 2018, respectively, a mirror analysis to detect and explain gaps between exports from the world and their recorded imports. In Guinea, the use of customs data by the tax administration, in addition to the strengthening of operations, has resulted in a doubling of the number of registered taxpayers at the LTO and the MTO in the first half of 2018.[33]

3. Building Public Financial Management Capacity

Three characteristics of public expenditures in fragile states are noteworthy:

- First, although total public expenditure as a share of GDP in fragile states is marginally higher than in nonfragile states—about 31 percent of GDP compared to 30 percent of GDP (Figure 11.3)—it is significantly lower when grants are excluded. Excluding grants,[34] the average public expenditure of fragile states (during 2013–16) was about 23 percent of GDP compared to 28 percent of GDP in nonfragile states. This is attributable principally to

[30] See IMF 2017a, 2017b.

[31] "Paperless administration" does not mean that all documents should be in the form of electronic messages, which is not possible in many countries yet. Declarations and documents can be presented to the administration using an electronic PDF format.

[32] See Gupta et al. (2017).

[33] Between January and June 2018, the number of registered taxpayers increased from 355 to 656 at the large taxpayers office and from 222 to 482 at the medium-sized taxpayers office.

[34] On average, during 2013–16, the fragile states and nonfragile states received official development assistance of about 14 percent and 3 percent of GDP of which the grants were 8 percent and 2 percent of GDP respectively.

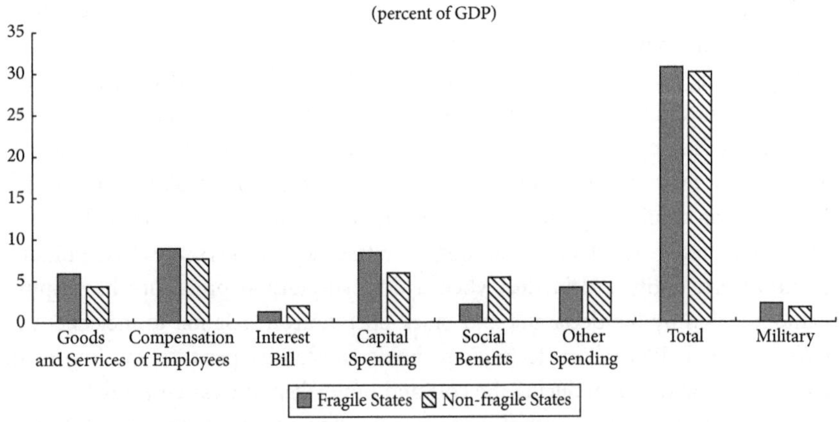

Figure 11.3 Public Expenditure Composition in Fragile States versus Non-Fragile States (Percent of GDP—simple average for 2013–16)

Source: IMF Expenditure Assessment Tool.

their low tax revenues. Many fragile states lack access to financial markets, and donors tend to fund a large proportion of their total expenditure.

- Second, the composition of public spending is different in fragile states, with more resources allocated to wages—representing 29 percent of total expenditure—and less to social benefits such as social assistance and pensions (Figure 11.3). This reflects, in some cases, the need to absorb combatants previously involved in armed conflicts into the military. This could also mean that the public sector is the major employer in the economy. Military spending in fragile states also tends to be higher because some of them continue to experience ongoing conflicts and strengthening security remains a key priority during initial state-building. This reduces the government's ability to spend on goods and services to ensure adequate provision of social services. Interest payments tend to be lower than in nonfragile states because fragile states rely more heavily on concessional or grant financing.
- Third, capital expenditure is higher (in percent of total expenditure) than in nonfragile countries. This reflects the need to rebuild damaged infrastructure and to finance basic public services such as water, electricity, and transportation, which are often lacking. Capital expenditure is the second largest expenditure category, representing nearly 27 percent of total expenditure; it is an area of particular attention for donor support.

3.1 First-Stage Reforms: Conflicts and Disasters

The focus should be on core public financial management (PFM) functions and easy-to-implement measures which do not overburden countries' limited capacity.

The target areas could be identified through diagnostic or strategy defining assessments.[35] Experience shows that fragile states are weak in budget credibility (which also reflects the effectiveness of budget execution), budget preparation, cash management, budget accounting and reporting, and expenditure control including management of arrears. These correspond to the areas with the lowest Public Expenditure and Financial Accountability (PEFA) scores (greatest weaknesses) in the fragile states (Figure 11.4).

Actions that allow fragile states to gain immediate control over the budget, including preparing an annual budget, should receive priority in the first stage. Because many fragile states face the challenge of ensuring fiscal discipline and making the budget an effective policy tool, the link between the government's policy priorities and expenditure allocations remains weak and ad hoc decisions with fiscal implications are taken outside the budget process (see Box 11.1 for example of South Sudan). This undermines budget credibility.[36] Establishing the capacity to prepare a comprehensive cash-based annual budget covering all entities of the central government should be a key goal. A number of measures could be progressively introduced to lay the fundamental building blocks of a

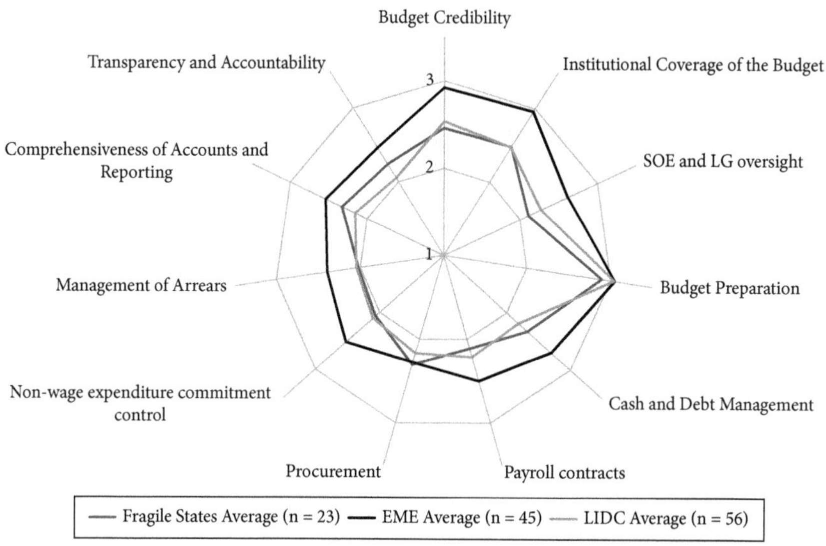

Figure 11.4 Average Public Expenditure and Financial Accountability Scores for Fragile States Compared to Low-Income Countries and Emerging Market Economies
Source: PEFA scores and IMF Staff estimates.

[35] These assessments should be supplemented with other information to understand more clearly the country's readiness to launch specific reforms as part of a public financial management capacity building strategy.

[36] As unbudgeted practices become embedded, budget preparation will be progressively weakened. Spending outside the budget also obfuscates the total picture of what government agencies are spending and conceals the trade-offs between budgeted priorities and unbudgeted contractual commitments.

Box 11.1 Focus of First-Stage Public Financial Management Reforms in Selected Fragile States

Afghanistan. When the Interim Administration took office in January 2002, the fiscal and financial functions of the Ministry of Finance were not operational. Significant efforts were needed to restore fiscal control, rebuild a functioning Ministry of Finance, and gradually improve public financial management (PFM). The approach adopted was to build on the existing structures and initially focus on core PFM reforms. Priority was given to strengthening expenditure controls, fiscal reporting, and accountability, among various measures, by computerizing PFM systems and consolidating the government's bank accounts to move to a treasury single account.

Haiti. There were many weaknesses in PFM when the reform started. Budget execution was cumbersome because fiscal powers were dispersed across line ministries, with very limited fiscal oversight by the Ministry of Finance; fiscal reporting was almost nonexistent; cash rationing was prevalent; and central bank advances to the treasury helped keep the government operating. Given the multitude of donors intervening in the PFM area after 2010, the reforms focused on three critical areas. First, building a macro-fiscal unit to help prepare a credible budget; second, establishing a treasury single account to allow the government to channel available funds more efficiently per the priorities set in the budget for greater development impact; and third, putting in place a fiscal reporting system to account for the use of resources.

Kosovo. Even though there were no PFM systems in Kosovo post conflict, rapid progress was made by targeting some basics, such as establishing a treasury single account with no off-budget funds and an integrated financial management system that all spending agencies at all levels of government could use, using the same chart of accounts.

Myanmar. There were weaknesses in almost every aspect of PFM. The incremental budget formulation process was incapable of allocating resources to the emerging government policies. The treasury management function was rudimentary—budget deficits were routinely monetized, contributing to macroeconomic instability; and more transparent and market-oriented procedures for cash and debt management were needed, with a more strategic perspective. The financial reporting was incapable of meeting the increased demand from the legislature, decision-makers, and other stakeholders. Some key institutional reforms were implemented in a well-structured and gradual approach. In 2014, the government established a new Treasury Department, structured along the lines of a modern treasury, and a system of faster (weekly) settlement of government funds with the central bank was introduced. In 2015, the government started auctioning treasury bills, and a top-down approach to budgeting was introduced in the formulation of the 2015–16 budget. Revisions to the 1986 Financial Rules and Regulations are being finalized, and at the initiative of the new government an organic PFM law is under development.

South Sudan. PFM institutions were nonexistent or extremely weak in the wake of the country's independence in 2011, and most of the senior government staff were drawn from the diaspora, with little PFM experience. There was no systematic budget planning or policy development, and ad hoc decisions were taken to use surplus oil revenues to expand government activities and progressively increase government expenditure. There were no in-year and end-of-the-year fiscal reports/accounts to inform decision-making and enhance transparency and accountability, including in the use of oil revenues. Considering the weak starting point, the initial focus of reforms was on budget execution control, accounting and reporting systems, including monitoring and reporting on accumulation of payment arrears; developing macro-fiscal analysis capacity; and putting in place the necessary institutional framework for a comprehensive budget planning and preparation process. There was progress in the PFM area until 2014, albeit slow and somewhat timid, but the nascent PFM institutions and routines largely broke down during the ensuing economic and political turmoil.

basic budget process, such as the structure of budget presentation, content of the budget circular, specification of the roles and functions of various agencies, and the budget preparation calendar. Integrating planning and budgeting functions should receive priority. As fragile states move toward more democratic structures, the role of parliaments in the budget process becomes more important.

Measures to strengthen basic budget execution controls should go hand-in-hand with budget preparation reform to establish the credibility of the budget. This can be done by developing or restoring basic fiscal controls through cash-based expenditure management, defining key controls at various stages of budget execution,[37] monitoring and reporting on accumulation of payment arrears, equipping the ministry of finance with the legal and regulatory powers to define how the expenditure chain will operate, and providing operational guidance to line ministries and other government agencies. When approved budgets in fragile states are not credible and expenditures cannot be financed within the available resource envelope, the budget and spending program must be reprioritized in-year during execution so that it is affordable. This reprioritization should take account of

[37] IMF (2016).

any emerging payment arrears. In post-conflict situations, in the initial stages partial amendments to existing PFM legislation could be adopted by eliminating wartime exemptions from financial regulations and piloting and rolling out prioritized reform measures. An annual budget law could also be used for this purpose.

Developing the capacity to produce basic fiscal reports on budget execution should be a priority to ensure accountability to the public and donors (see Box 11.1 for example of Haiti).[38] Initially these reports do not have to be very detailed. They should aim to provide an indication of whether fiscal developments are on track and explain deviations relative to the budget. More detailed reporting could, initially, be on a semiannual or annual basis. As reporting improves, these reports should be produced quarterly or monthly. There may be windows of opportunity to start computerizing budget accounting and reporting systems at an early stage in fragile states (for example, Afghanistan and Kosovo). Automated accounting systems could substitute for weak human capacity and could be an effective way to reduce the scope for corruption and the misuse of public funds. Donors should report to recipient governments on the expenditure of aid funds using the governments' own accounting classification, so that recipient governments can incorporate this information into their own budget processes and fiscal reports.

Full and timely recording of the government's cash inflows and outflows and consolidating cash resources for treasury oversight should be a key objective. Government banking arrangements in fragile states typically remain diffuse; operating cash resources are dispersed across many accounts, including in the commercial banking sector, outside the control of the ministry of finance and the treasury. Cash surpluses in accounts and funds which are not readily available to the treasury make it difficult to pay for priority expenditures in a timely manner and could lead to expenditure arrears. In addition, several off-budget entities could continue to exist with cash resources and/or the right to have direct access to certain revenue streams and use them. It is necessary to identify these entities, their nature, rights and obligations, and their cash holdings, and implement a program to reduce the number of bank accounts (including extrabudgetary accounts) by closing them and returning their balances to a treasury single account (TSA) (see Box 11.1 for examples of Afghanistan and Kosovo).[39] This could take time and will need to be phased;[40] for example, bringing all tax receipts into a single account of the treasury could be one of the initial steps.

[38] Donors often require assurance on behalf of their governments that donor funds are being used in an effective and transparent manner.

[39] In countries where an effective treasury single account structure exists, all monies at the control of the government should be contained within it and available to the treasury as fungible liquid assets.

[40] The absence of well-developed modern banking system in fragile states complicates the setting up of a treasury single account system. As a first step, the information on cash balance and cash inflows and outflows in multiple bank accounts (some owned by the treasury, some by other agencies, and some by donors) should be collected on a regular basis to get a consolidated view of cash resources and facilitate the prioritization of payments.

Training on fiscal issues can help the future leaders rebuild institutions and cope with immediate crises. Training groups of officials on macroeconomic and fiscal issues complements more technically-focused capacity building support, and builds sustainable institutional capacity over the long term. This also helps strengthen the ownership of reforms and the authorities' capacity to manage the capacity building support that various development partners/donors provide. For example, in Haiti, the Ministry of Finance partnered with Haiti's School of Administration to mainstream PFM training into their curriculum.

Political priorities that are core to rebuilding a fragile state should be taken into account. Such priorities may have been specified in a post-conflict peace agreement. For example, in Mali, fiscal decentralization was central to the peace agreement. The authorities prepared a three-year strategy to boost regional development projects, and accompanied subnational governments in their budget execution, while providing training and technical assistance to local administrations.

Building capacity at the subnational level should go together with devolution of spending authority under a post-conflict peace agreement. Administrative weaknesses in general and PFM weaknesses in particular may limit subnational governments' capacity to spend the devolved resources. In countries where subnational PFM systems do not meet minimum standards, strengthening PFM arrangements should be a prerequisite for increasing decentralization.[41] Several elements of good PFM and governance are critical at the subnational level. Among these are a realistic budget envelope prepared in a timely manner; an adequate budget classification system, preferably compatible with international standards (especially for economic and functional classifications), and an accounting framework consistent with such classification; effective audit and control mechanisms, with a high probability of detection of, and penalties for, misuse of public funds; and firmly enforced requirements for timely and accurate reporting. Establishing and maintaining subnational debt registries is also recommended.

3.2 Second-Stage Reforms: Expansion and Modernization

For countries that have moved out of immediate fragility, the objective should be to modernize fiscal institutions incrementally through medium-term PFM strategies. In these cases, the PFM institutional capacity-building strategy may be similar to that adopted for low-income countries, with close attention paid to the sequencing of reforms over the next three to five years and taking into account country-specific circumstances and conditions, including the country's capacity to absorb external assistance and advice. A graduated approach, building successive

[41] This was the position taken in the Democratic Republic of the Congo, Kosovo, and Liberia. For more information, see IMF (2010a).

coherent layers of increasing sophistication, is more likely to succeed. The ordering of reforms in the second stage could usefully be guided by the following principles: progressively expanding the horizon of budget forecasts; modernizing PFM systems by leveraging IT-based solutions; and incrementally strengthening the control and accountability frameworks.

The medium-term PFM strategy's main components could include:

- *Establishing a medium-term budget framework that takes into account the impact of policies over the longer term.* The medium-term budget framework should incorporate recurrent costs of development spending and other fiscal pressures.[42] The objective is to ensure that budget appropriations in future years are consistent with meeting the government's medium-term fiscal objectives, given the expected level of available resources. The recurrent and development budgets should be integrated into the medium-term budget framework.[43] Experience from other countries suggests that medium-term budgeting reforms should be introduced progressively over at least 10 years, starting with the preparation of a medium-term fiscal framework (MTFF) that provides forecasts of budget aggregates.
- *Implementing PFM-related IT systems that support planning and implementation of the budget.* This can be the first step in introducing an integrated financial management information system (IFMIS), bearing in mind the country's capacity for implementation. Too frequently, complex, resource-intensive solutions have been implemented with inadequate planning or oversight and a lack of political commitment—all prerequisites for successful implementation. Well-designed solutions that consider capacity constraints have the best chances of success (Kosovo, Afghanistan).
- *Ensuring the creation of an internal control framework to manage the budget execution and reporting processes.* Building capacity to reduce budget overruns and unauthorized expenditures is a core element of second-stage reforms in fragile states. Payment arrears are a common feature of fragile states, caused, to a certain extent, by the absence of a robust internal control framework.[44] Introduction of commitment controls to regulate the pre-cash stages of the expenditure process is a crucial element of efforts to prevent the accumulation of payment arrears, to be accompanied by efforts to improve the accountability of budget institutions for execution of the budgets under

[42] For example, it was critical in Afghanistan to take account of the potential impact of operational costs of the large inventory of donor-created physical assets and the increase in security spending after 2014, when security responsibilities were gradually being transferred from the international community to the government.

[43] As fragile states receive significant donor aid focused on development, it is not uncommon for the preparation of the recurrent and development budgets to follow two separate and uncoordinated processes, with institutional separation both at the central and line ministry and agency levels.

[44] The absence of a credible budget also contributes to the accumulation of arrears.

their control.[45] Integrity checks in fiscal reports and interim audits of fiscal transactions should also be introduced.

- *Enhancing accounting and reporting practices in accordance with international standards.* Once a basic fiscal reporting system has been established, the next phase is to introduce a reporting framework that complies with international standards for coverage and comprehensiveness. Preparation and implementation of a chart of accounts that meets these standards is a key element of second-stage reforms. In the accounting area, a key objective should be to expand the coverage of annual accounts which may be limited to the budget sector. The reporting framework should adequately cover all levels of government to ensure that a full picture of the public finances is available.[46]
- *Strengthening cash and debt management arrangements.* This includes the gradual establishment of a treasury single account (TSA),[47] a comprehensive electronic government payment system, developing cash forecasting capacity, introducing a debt recording and reporting system, and developing an integrated cash and debt management function. Processes and procedures to enable the treasury to meet payment obligations in an efficient and transparent manner should be developed; they should include the ability to plan ahead for expected cash shortages and surpluses, and to satisfy the cash needs during times of cash shortage through drawdown of liquid assets or efficient borrowings.
- *Developing state audit institutions that have a key role to play in enforcing accountability.* There will, inevitably, be tensions between audit institutions, parliaments, and ministries of finance, but the potential role of audit institutions has been illustrated in some fragile states. For example, with donor finance and support, the Audit Commission was established in Liberia and its role has been built upon its independence from the president, its operational independence, its ability to hire, fire and remunerate staff, and its financial independence.
- *In the case of resource-rich fragile states,*[48] *introducing a framework to smooth the effects of the volatility of resource revenues and provide for the eventual depletion of natural resources.* Although infrastructure needs in fragile states are large and will require financing from resource revenues, their absorption capacity is likely to be limited at the outset and there could be a strong case for intergenerational savings beyond whatever buffer is needed for predictable revenue stabilization needs. The stabilization and savings portfolios should be fully integrated into the fiscal policy framework. If a sovereign wealth fund (SWF) is to be created, there will be a need for legal and

[45] See IMF (2014). [46] IMF (2011b). [47] IMF (2011c).
[48] A significant proportion of FS in 2017 (18 out of 42) were resource-rich countries.

governance reforms regarding the SWF structure and operation (see Box 11.2 for example of Timor-Leste).[49] The SWF should be prohibited from direct spending, from providing guarantees or loans, from borrowing, or from pledging its assets.

Box 11.2 Focus of Second-Stage Public Financial Management Reforms in Selected Fragile States

Afghanistan. Soon after PFM improvements in the first stage, organizational reforms were undertaken to streamline the Ministry of Finance's structure and consolidate its core functions. The Ministry of Finance prepared a five-year strategic plan in 2005 and progressively developed a more efficient organization. In parallel, second-generation PFM reforms were undertaken, including introduction of new PFM laws and financial regulations, gradual implementation of program budgeting, and multi-year budget preparation, mostly at the level of the medium-term fiscal framework. The Afghanistan National Development Strategy was developed to set national priorities to facilitate a more coordinated approach to integrating donors' budgets. These reforms were all supported by the donor community and led to increased confidence in the government's capacity for financial management.

Kosovo. Following the country's independence in 2008, the government produced a comprehensive and integrated PFM reform plan for which the IMF provided technical assistance in a diverse range of areas such as cash management, expenditure arrears management, and the design and implementation of a fiscal rule.

Timor-Leste. The first stage of reform, started in 1999 under the United Nations Transitional Administration to establish a Central Fiscal Authority, was followed by preparing the strategy for setting up modern budgetary and treasury functions. The initial emphasis was on the effective management of the country's substantial oil and gas wealth, including the creation of a Petroleum Fund (July 2005) and a comprehensive public investment program. The Petroleum Fund's strong governance is one of the cornerstones of Timor-Leste's PFM system. The focus of the work in the second stage was to strengthen expenditure management, treasury operations and fiscal reporting, including advising on how to maintain fiscal discipline after devolving expenditure assignments to line ministries and subnational governments.

[49] For example, in Timor-Leste the Petroleum Fund was created in 2005 and its strong governance is one of the cornerstones of Timor-Leste's PFM system.

Once PFM institutions make progress, a new overarching PFM law could be introduced to cement the results of the reform and move to more advanced PFM practices. A comprehensive PFM law typically includes provisions that regulate: the roles and responsibilities of the various actors in the budget process; the process and timeline surrounding the development of the fiscal framework and the preparation and approval of the budget; budget execution procedures; management of debt and cash; accounting and fiscal reporting; and ex-post control and audit functions.[50] More recently, overarching PFM legislation typically includes provisions that require governments to be fiscally responsible and manage fiscal risks. However, a legislative framework at this level of comprehensiveness requires a high level of capacity for even partial implementation.

Though the appropriate legal framework is important, it is necessary to ensure that the implementation capacity exists to back up the legal provisions.[51] Legal reform without institutional capacity is meaningless. A country's inability to implement legislation fully can undermine its credibility. In some post-conflict states where the rule of law has suffered a complete collapse, it is necessary to establish a basic respect for legal procedures and some form of social contract before it is possible to put a legal framework in place. In the interim, many problems can be solved without recourse to legal reform. Administrative regulations can often be effective. It is better to keep legislation concise, focusing on those changes that can be implemented in the short to medium term, and to introduce detailed secondary regulations that can be activated as capacity increases and processes and procedures evolve.

It is important to link PFM reform to wider civil service reform. In most fragile states, pay levels in the public sector are too low to attract and retain qualified staff. At the same time, this reform is not straightforward since increasing public service salaries not only has fiscal implications but also has knock-on effects in the private sector.[52] Sometimes this is an exogenous problem when there is a significant gap in the levels of remuneration offered by the administration in comparison with those offered by the donors or contracting organizations. This often leads to a heavy reliance on international experts and contracted technical assistance. In some fragile states (for example, Afghanistan), several efforts have been made to address pay incentives for key finance ministry staff through forms of salary supplementation (funded by donors).

For building sustainable PFM capacity, it is important to manage the delivery of technical assistance as the medium-term PFM strategy gets implemented. The

[50] IMF (2010b).

[51] For example, it is not uncommon to see that some PFM-related laws in fragile states are simply imported from other countries and translated from another language, rather than being drafted to be relevant to local conditions.

[52] In this regard, the policymakers are faced with a difficult choice between retaining qualified staff and ensuring a sustainable fiscal position, without impeding private sector development.

emphasis should be to increase government leadership of PFM reforms and to place donors and technical assistance providers in a supportive rather than a driving role. In particular, the role of long-term international experts and advisors needs to be defined and managed carefully to ensure internal capacity building and skills transfer to local staff or officials. Though it is recognized that some of the PFM tasks may have to be done initially by international experts especially in areas that require years of experience and training such as policy analysis and the development of information technology (IT) systems,[53] several steps could usefully be taken for making the most of PFM technical assistance: (1) senior ministry management should coordinate technical assistance to ensure that there is appropriate distribution of support; (2) a suitable emphasis should be placed on skills transfer relative to getting the job done; (3) appropriate staff should be identified to act as counterparts and be trained by international experts; and (4) long-term experts should be held accountable through clear specification of skills transfer. The oversight of the PFM technical assistance program should be given to one of the senior staff in the ministry of finance.[54]

Finally, political leadership and commitment are critical to ensure that PFM reforms are institutionalized and that sustainable capacity is built in this area. Continued political commitment is a challenge because PFM reforms are likely to spread across several political cycles. It is, therefore, important to build wider political convergence on key reform priorities and show tangible results and quick wins along the entire reform process, to keep momentum and encourage reforms to move forward. For example, in Afghanistan, progress in implementing a financial management information system (FMIS), which was acquired as an off-the-shelf system, was remarkable despite resistance from several stakeholders. A key factor in the success was the acceptance and commitment by the authorities to implement the system without too much customization. Similarly, the early success in the IMF-led PFM technical assistance program in Myanmar during 2014–16 reflects leadership commitment and willingness to learn from international good practice.

4. Fiscal Conditionality in IMF Programs and Fragile States

Conditionality in IMF programs covers the design of macroeconomic and structural policies as well as specific tools to monitor progress toward program goals as

[53] Experience also shows that expatriates taking over line management tasks could lead to distortions and a lack of sustainability. Outsiders can lower morale among local staff. The expertise of some "experts" is also often felt to be quite shallow, leading them to try to implement best-practice reforms without an understanding of the local context and a focus on form rather than function.

[54] These observations regarding the use and design of external advice are also applicable to tax policy and revenue administration.

defined by country officials in cooperation with the IMF. The program goals and underlying policies to achieve them vary across countries, but the overarching objective is to restore or maintain balance-of-payments viability and macroeconomic stability, while, in low-income countries and in the majority of fragile states, reducing poverty.

IMF program conditions take varied forms: quantitative performance criteria (QPC), indicative targets, structural benchmarks, or prior actions. QPC are conditions that are under the control of government officials and could be measured by economic indicators. Examples of QPCs include the maximum level of domestic financing, a minimum level of international reserves, or a certain range for the fiscal balance. Indicative targets are also quantitative measures, established in addition to QPCs to assess progress in meeting the program objectives; they are set when QPCs cannot be met because of data unreliability. These targets might be converted into QPCs, with some modifications, as uncertainty lessens. Structural benchmarks, on the other hand, are not quantifiable and are used as critical markers to assess the implementation of the program. Finally, prior actions are actions that the authorities agree to take before the IMF Executive Board approves the program. Unmet QPCs require formal waivers from the Executive Board to mark the review as complete, while indicative targets and structural benchmarks are assessed in the context of the overall program and do not require a formal waiver if unmet.

Revenue and expenditure conditions are invariably present in all IMF programs, including those in fragile states. A large and growing proportion of such conditions are structural in nature, many drawn from the IMF's technical assistance, which has grown exponentially in recent years. Revenue conditionality has mostly taken the form of structural benchmarks (80 percent), with the remainder of the conditionality taking the form of prior actions (Crivelli and Gupta, 2016). This differs from expenditure conditionality, which is spread across QPCs, indicative targets, prior actions, and structural benchmarks (Gupta, Schena and Yousefi, 2020). Roughly 80 percent of revenue and expenditure conditionality for all IMF programs was met during 1992–2016. The nature of conditionality varies across fragile states, depending on its starting conditions, capacity to implement institutional reforms, availability of a diagnosis identifying institutional weaknesses and willingness of its leadership to accept conditions. Thus, there are no standard conditions found in all fragile states in the two-step approach enumerated above.

4.1 Revenue Conditionality

The bulk of revenue conditionality in IMF programs during 1993–2016 has centered on taxes on goods and services (more than half), followed by conditionality on taxes on income (about one-third) and on international transactions (about one-tenth) (Crivelli and Gupta, 2016). Revenue conditionality has increased in low-income countries since 2008, reflecting the desire of these countries to strengthen the revenue base in the aftermath of the financial crisis. More recently, with declining external concessional flows, low-income countries are turning increasingly to mobilizing more tax revenues from domestic sources. Table 11.2 provides an example of how conditionality is divided between tax policy and tax administration actions and whether it is specific or general.

Countries that have implemented revenue conditionality under IMF programs are associated with higher tax revenues. Figure 11.5 shows tax-to-GDP ratios in countries where tax reform was supported by a period of at least two consecutive years of revenue conditionality. In more than 75 percent of such cases, the tax ratio increased as compared to the year prior to the inclusion of the revenue

Table 11.2 Examples of Tax Policy and Tax Administration Conditionality

	Specific	General
Tax Policy	-Introduce a VAT/increase the VAT rate to 18 percent;	-Submission to cabinet of a tax reform proposal;
Tax Administration	-Create a large VAT taxpayers unit;	-Adopt a new IT system in the revenue agency;

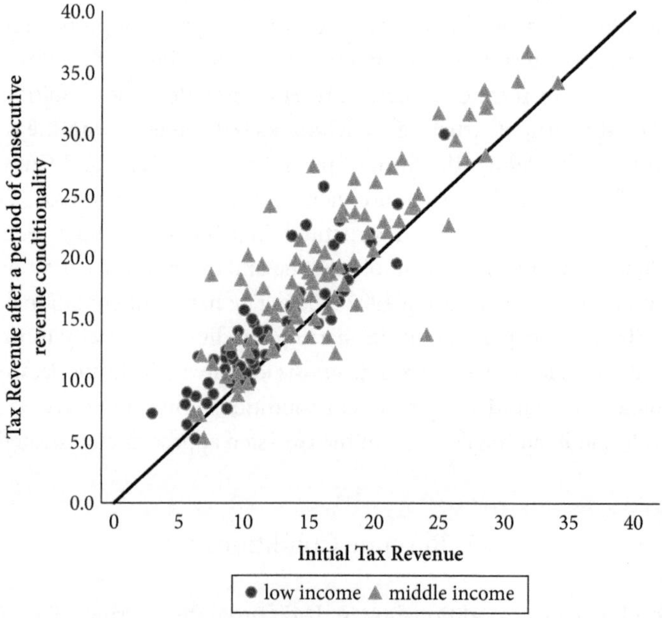

Figure 11.5 IMF Conditionality and Tax Revenue
(126 low- and middle-income countries, 1993–2013)
Source: IMF WoRLD, SSA and MENA Databases and IMF Staff.

conditionality. This result is particularly strong for low-income countries, with resulting revenue growth of twice as much compared to the sample as a whole.

The above conclusion is supported by detailed econometric tests. Revenue conditionality has the potential of raising tax revenue ratios by about one percentage point of GDP in a given year and matters more in low-income countries than in middle-income ones, particularly those countries where tax revenue ratios are below the group average (Crivelli and Gupta, 2016). It has the maximum impact on taxes on goods and services as well as the VAT. The latter is attributable to the fact that the VAT tends to help strengthen the overall tax administration, thereby improving tax collection in the aggregate.

The preceding results do not hold for fragile states. When these results are tested for a sub-sample of fragile states, revenue conditionality does not have a significant impact on tax revenue outcomes. This result could be attributable to weaknesses in basic institutions and administrative capacity, which make it difficult for these states to implement major tax revenue reforms. This also suggests that revenue conditionality for fragile states should be designed differently, with an explicit focus on long-term capacity development.[55] A similar result emerges when countries are separated on the basis of institutional strength as proxied by the International Country Risk Guide (ICRG) index of corruption. Countries with weak institutions are those with a score below 3.[56]

4.2 Expenditure Conditionality

The key expenditure conditions in IMF programs during 1992–2016 are in the areas of social protection (for example, increasing spending on education, health and poverty), budget execution and control (for example, establishing commitment control and Treasury Single Account systems), budget preparation (for example, approving the government budget), accounting and financial reporting (adopting a comprehensive chart of accounts) and institutional design (centralizing public revenues) (Gupta, Schena and Yousefi, 2020). Expenditure conditions can be grouped into nine spending categories and seven public financial management categories.

The bulk of expenditure conditions are structural benchmarks. On average during 2005–16, about 50 percent of all conditions fell in this category (Figure 11.6).

The econometric results suggest that expenditure conditionality on social spending in the form of safeguards or floors appears to be ineffective in the

[55] The recent evaluation by the IMF's Independent Evaluation Office (2018b) concluded that the IMF has treated fragile states using IMF-wide norms rather than as countries needing special attention.

[56] This grouping is almost equivalent to considering the 50th percentile of the distribution with less and more corrupt countries, respectively, on the basis of the International Country Risk Guide ranking of corruption.

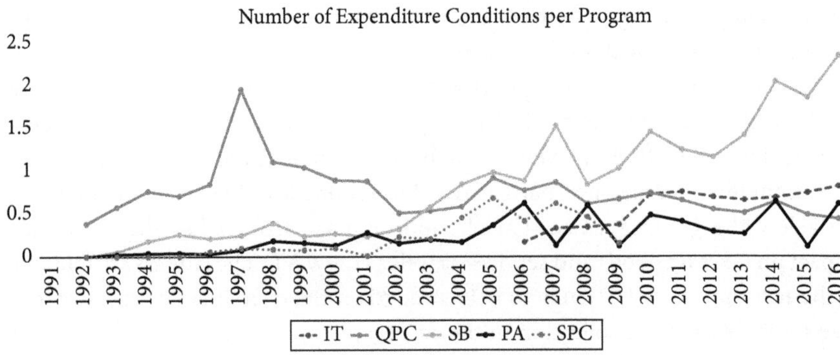

Figure 11.6 Number of Expenditure Conditions per Program
Source: IMF Staff Estimates.

medium term (Gupta, Schena, and Yousefi, 2020). In contrast, structural conditionality (such as accounting and financial reporting) is associated with higher social spending. For instance, such improvements have helped countries raise the share of education expenditures in the total by about 0.9–2.0 percent in the long term. In a similar vein, implementation of structural conditionality (accounting and financial reporting, budget execution and control) has further helped spur public investment. Finally, conditionality on increasing public investment in the short term can exert downward pressure on the share of health spending in the budget, implying that there is a tradeoff between spending categories even when overall spending remains unchanged.

The regressions covering a smaller sample of fragile states yield a few results that are statistically robust. They show that general PFM conditionality (such as developing a PFM strategy, monitoring operations and financial performance of public enterprises) has a positive impact on public investment; a reduction in expenditure arrears creates fiscal space for more productive spending in the long term; and improved budget preparation systems help increase the share of the education sector in total budget outlays. These results contrast with the lack of impact of revenue conditionality on tax revenue performance in fragile states. The results relating to PFM conditionality suggest that a longer-term institutional development has a positive impact on expenditure outcomes.

5. Concluding Remarks

Several key lessons can be drawn from the IMF's experience with building fiscal capacity in fragile states:

First, it is important to set priorities and pay attention to the sequencing of reforms. The focus during the early stages should be on easy-to-implement measures which do not overburden a country's limited capacity. On the revenue side, more complex reforms such as setting up an integrated revenue authority should be considered only once a sound organizational structure has been established in both the tax and customs administrations, and core processes are in place and operating in both administrations. On the expenditure side, more advanced reforms such as medium-term budgeting should be introduced only when basic PFM systems are in place. Setting priorities is effective when multiple players providing technical assistance coordinate their work. This is easier when country authorities lead coordination efforts, with donors and technical assistance providers playing a supportive role.

Second, there is value in a focus on medium-term reform; efforts to design and implement formal MTRS and PFM reform strategies may help countries exit fragility. The approach may be similar to that adopted for low-income countries, with close attention paid to the sequencing of reforms to reflect low, but gradually improving, administrative capacity. A medium-term approach on both revenue and spending reforms is also consistent with medium-term budget frameworks.

Third, natural resource revenues can provide time and resources for institutional reconstruction. Angola and Lao P.D.R. are examples of countries that, after having taken advantage of their natural resource revenue to escape fragility, are now engaging in a reform of their tax system to respond to the pressures of lower commodity prices and competition from neighbors for foreign investment. In some natural resource–rich countries, there could be a strong case for intergenerational savings to provision for the eventual depletion of natural resource wealth.

Fourth, more attention should be paid to reforming and strengthening customs—especially when revenue from taxes collected at the border is significant in fragile states. Customs is often a bellwether for the degree of corruption and arbitrariness in a country; effective reform of customs can help improve public perceptions of fiscal institutions.

Finally, the design of fiscal conditionality in fragile states with an IMF program should focus more on the medium- and long-term aspects of institution building. Given the weakness in basic institutions and administrative capacity of fragile states, it is difficult for these countries to implement major revenue mobilization reforms in the short term, and conditionality that seeks to improve revenue performance during this period is not as effective as in nonfragile states. Expenditure conditionality, however, appears more effective in achieving desired expenditure outcomes.

References

Acosta-Ormaechea, S. and J. Yoo. 2012. "Tax Composition and Growth: A Broad Cross-Country Perspective." IMF Working Paper No. 257. International Monetary Fund, Washington, DC.

Besley, T. and T. Persson. 2014. "Why Do Developing Countries Tax So Little?" *Journal of Economic Perspectives*, 28(4): 99–120.

Bird, R. and E. Zolt. 2010. "Dual Income Taxation and Developing Countries." *Columbia Journal of Tax Law*, 1(2): 174–217.

Brautigam, D., F. Odd-Helge, and M. Moore (Eds). 2008. *Taxation and State Building in Developing Countries.* Cambridge: Cambridge University Press.

Brun, J.-F., G. Chambas, and M. Mansour. 2015. "Tax Efforts of Developing Countries; An Alternative Measure," in M. Boussichas and P. Guillaumont (Eds.), *Financing Sustainable Development—Addressing Vulnerabilities.* London: Economica.

Cilliers, J. and T. Sisk. 2013. "Assessing Long-Term State Fragility in Africa: Prospects for 26 'More Fragile' Countries." Pretoria: Institute for Security Studies, Monograph no. 188.

Crivelli, E. and S. Gupta. 2014. "Resource Blessing, Revenue Curse? Domestic Revenue Effort in Resource-Rich Countries." *The European Journal of Political Economy*, 35(5).

Crivelli, E. and S. Gupta. 2016. "Does Conditionality in IMF-Supported Programs Promote Revenue Reform?" *International Tax and Public Finance*, 23: 550–79.

Everest-Phillips, M. 2010. "State-Building Taxation for Developing Countries: Principles for Reform." *Development Policy Review*, 28(1): 75–96.

Gaspar, V., L. Jaramillo, and P. Wingender. 2016. "Political Institutions, State Building and Tax Capacity: Crossing the Tipping Point." IMF Working Paper 16/233. International Monetary Fund, Washington, DC.

Gelbard, E., C. Deléchat, E. Fuli, M. Hussain, U. Jacoby, D. Glaser, M. Pani, G. Ramirez, and R. Xu. 2015. *Building Resilience in Sub-Saharan Africa's Fragile States.* International Monetary Fund, Washington, DC.

Gupta, S., M. Keen, A. Shah, and G. Verdier. 2017. *Digital Revolutions in Public Finance.* Washington, DC: International Monetary Fund.

Gupta, S., M. Schena, and S.R. Yousefi 2020. "Revisiting IMF expenditure conditionality." *Applied Economics*. 52(58): 6338–59.

IMF. 2010a. "Making Fiscal Decentralization Work: Cross-Country Experiences." Occasional Paper 271.

IMF. 2010b. "Reforming Budget System Laws." FAD Technical Notes and Manuals 10/01.

IMF. 2011a. "Revenue Mobilization in Developing Countries." IMF Policy Paper.

IMF. 2011b. "Chart of Accounts: A Critical Element of the Public Financial Management Framework." FAD Technical Notes and Manuals 11/03.

IMF. 2011c. "Treasury Single Account: An Essential Tool for Government Cash Management." FAD Technical Notes and Manuals 11/04.

IMF. 2014. "Prevention and Management of Government Expenditure Arrears." FAD Technical Notes and Manuals 14/01.

IMF. 2015. "The Commodity Roller-Coaster: A Fiscal Framework for Uncertain Times." IMF *Fiscal Monitor.*

IMF. 2016. "Expenditure Control: Key Features, Stages, and Actors," FAD Technical Notes and Manuals 16/02.

IMF. 2017a. "Building Fiscal Capacity in Fragile States." IMF Executive Board Paper.

IMF. 2017b. "Multi-Country Report: Building Fiscal Capacity in Fragile State - Case Studies." IMF Executive Board Paper.

IMF. 2018a. "Sub-Saharan Africa: Domestic Revenue Mobilization and Private Investment." *Regional Economic Outlook: Sub-Saharan Africa*, April 2018.

IMF. 2018b. "The IMF and Fragile States." Independent Evaluation Office.

Mansour, M., and J-L. Schneider. 2019. "How to Design Tax Policy in Fragile States." IMF How-to-Note 19/04.

Matheson, T., and P. Petit. 2017. "Taxing Telecommunications in Developing Countries." IMF Working Paper No. 247.

World Bank. 2011. *World Development Report—Conflict, Security, and Development.*

Zee, H. 2004. *Taxing the Financial Sector: Concepts, Issues, and Practice.* Washington, DC: International Monetary Fund.

Annex

Table A11.1 Evolution of Total and Tax Revenues in Permanent versus Former Fragile States

	(Percent of GDP)				(Percent of Tax Revenue)			
	PFSs		FFSs		PFSs		FFSs	
	2005-07	2013-16	2005-07	2013-16	2005-07	2013-16	2005-07	2013-16
Total Revenue	20.92 (15.77)	24.70 (18.53)	26.31 (25.93)	26.19 (23.72)				
Tax Revenue	11.89 (10.92)	13.28 (12.11)	17.80 (18.7)	17.41 (17.31)	100.00 100.00	100.00 100.00	100.00 100.00	100.00 100.00
Income Tax Revenue	2.75 (2.46)	4.14 (3.66)	2.74 (2.34)	3.81 (3.39)	23.09 22.53	31.18 30.22	15.42 12.51	21.89 19.58
PIT	1.26 (1.09)	2.04 (1.53)	1.14 (0.77)	1.72 (1.47)	10.60 9.98	15.36 12.63	6.42 4.12	9.86 8.49
CIT	1.28 (1.29)	1.81 (1.48)	1.40 (1.28)	1.89 (1.49)	10.73 11.81	13.65 12.22	7.85 6.84	10.87 8.61
Payroll Taxes	0.14 (0.18)	0.63 (0.17)	0.73 (0.03)	0.03 (0.03)	1.18 1.65	4.75 1.40	4.08 0.16	0.16 0.17
Property Taxes	0.06 (0.05)	0.25 (0.19)	0.20 (0.14)	0.25 (0.22)	0.53 0.46	1.88 1.57	1.11 0.75	1.46 1.27
Goods and Services Taxes	3.21 (3.25)	4.38 (4.19)	7.32 (5.46)	9.08 (8.54)	27.00 29.76	32.97 34.60	41.13 29.20	52.13 49.34
VAT	2.54 (2.16)	3.02 (2.83)	4.45 (3.06)	6.77 (4.88)	21.35 19.78	22.70 23.37	25.00 16.36	38.87 28.19
Excises	0.57 (0.51)	1.20 (1.03)	1.55 (1.44)	1.87 (2.5)	4.80 4.67	9.01 8.51	8.72 7.70	10.74 14.44

Trade Taxes	2.93	3.73	2.00	1.64	24.63	28.07	11.21	9.43
	(2.91)	(2.23)	(1.72)	(1.31)	26.65	18.41	9.20	7.57
Other Taxes	2.18	1.91	4.73	3.13	18.36	14.39	26.60	17.98
	(0.22)	(0)	(0.51)	(0.18)	2.01	0.00	2.73	1.04
Total Resource Revenue	11.75	8.50	18.34	9.37	56.19	34.41	69.71	35.79
	(5.9)	(2.05)	(20.31)	(4.61)	37.41	11.06	78.33	19.44
Number of Countries	30		12		30		12	

Note: CIT = corporate income tax; PIT = personal income tax; PFS = permanent fragile state; FFS = former fragile state.

Source: IMF WoRLD, SSA and MENA databases.

12

Establishing a New Currency and Central Bank in Fragile States

Warren Coats

1. Introduction

The fragility of economies and, in particular, of their monetary and financial sectors can arise from quite different factors. My experience in establishing or advising central banks has been primarily in post-conflict countries (Afghanistan, Bosnia and Herzegovina, Croatia, Iraq, Kosovo, South Sudan, West Bank and Gaza) and in centrally planned countries transitioning into market economies (Bulgaria, Kazakhstan, Kyrgyz Republic, Moldova, Slovakia). Fragility in these countries reflected the urgent need to reestablish and rebuild or transform monetary and financial systems that were sometimes weak to begin with.

The most basic and critical functions of the monetary authority of any country are providing a currency (another country's or its own), stabilizing and maintaining its value, and establishing the legal foundations on which these activities are performed. The next steps of developing (or restoring) non-cash payment and credit systems (that is, banks) follow quickly. This chapter will draw on my experience in the above countries in: (a) establishing a central bank and banking laws; (b) establishing and maintaining a currency; (c) establishing an efficient and accountable central bank organizational structure and staff; and (d) establishing or reforming non-cash payment systems. Though it will not directly address the development of credit and other financial markets, the requirements for their development should always be kept in mind by anyone designing the instruments and policies for controlling the central bank's supply of base money.

The first and overriding lesson from these experiences is that no country is a blank slate on which established Western best practice can be dropped without regard to the history and economic, political, and cultural legacies upon which anything must be built, though the West Bank and Gaza experience comes close. Thus the first step in assisting post-conflict or transition economies is to understand what was or is already in place.

Another lesson is that political considerations cannot be ignored. By the early 1990s the case for central bank independence was so firmly established globally that we rarely encountered the traditional tension between finance ministries and

Warren Coats, *Establishing a New Currency and Central Bank in Fragile States* In: *Macroeconomic Policy in Fragile States.* Edited by: Ralph Chami, Raphael Espinoza, and Peter Montiel, Oxford University Press (2021). © International Monetary Fund. DOI: 10.1093/oso/9780198853091.003.0012 the central banks over low interest rates and easy money and thus the legal provisions to protect central bank operational independence. However, there were often issues about central bank capital and the accounting of its income and income remittance to the treasury. It was always appropriate to adhere to international accounting standards for these (and other) purposes. As we learned in Bosnia, political considerations with regard to governance and even currency design could also be quite intense.

Another lesson is that developing the instruments, systems, and capacities needed for successful monetary and financial policy requires more resources and time than the IMF alone can offer. One or more resident advisors are often essential. Thus close collaboration and cooperation with the World Bank, USAID, and other development agencies is essential.

2. Central Banks' Law and Organizational Structure

Unless a central bank is being created where none existed before—the creation of the Palestine Monetary Authority was the only such case I know of[1]—the modernization and improvement of its legal foundation and organizational structure are not the most urgent priorities. This is not to say that they are not critically important, but they can be undertaken after putting out the fires and can benefit from deepening the IMF team's understanding of the existing legal and political environment. Nonetheless, because the central bank law and the actual existence of the institution logically precede anything it might do, I take them up first.

2.1 Laws

During the 1990s central bank and banking laws converged to a considerable extent, so as to contain relatively standard functions and features built around the consensus that central banks should be protected from government interference. This central bank independence is reconciled with democratic oversight by establishing in the law the politically determined objectives of monetary policy—almost universally price stability (whether external or domestic)—while leaving to the central bank the discretion as to how best to achieve those objectives within the instruments given to it in the law. This relative operational autonomy should be balanced with central bank accountability to the legislature that established it. Policy transparency not only contributes to accountability but also facilitates more effective market-based monetary policy implementation.

[1] The creation of the Central Bank of Bosnia and Herzegovina was a case of creating one central bank out of three. For details see Coats (2007b).

Traditionally, central bank laws established the legal status of the bank, its governance (oversight board, governor, and other officers and their duties), objectives and responsibilities, financial provisions (capital, allocation of net income, reserves, accounting standards and reporting), relations with government (fiscal agent, limited or no credit to government), relations with banks and other financial institutions (credit facilities, supervision powers and responsibilities), authority to issue and regulate currency, relations with payment systems (supervision powers and responsibilities), foreign exchange reserves and transactions, and general powers (what it is allowed and not allowed to do as a legal entity).

In 1995 IMF lawyer Henry Schiffman and I introduced a new structure for the central bank law of Moldova (*Law on the National Bank of Moldova*) that explicitly consolidated into a new section on *Monetary and Foreign Exchange Policy* the central bank's instruments of monetary and exchange rate policy. This explicit treatment of the central bank's policy role is now a common feature of central bank laws.[2] For example, the *Law on the National Bank of Serbia* contains a chapter on "Determination And Implementation Of Monetary Policy" that incorporates the central bank's monetary policy and financial and payments supervisory powers and responsibilities. Previously these instruments were established in sections dealing with Relations with Government and Relations with Banks and other Financial Institutions without explicit consideration of their monetary policy implications.

During this same period banking laws have strengthened the bank regulator's bank resolution tools to reduce the moral hazard of government bailouts and to clarify and strengthen their oversight powers and obligations. Borrowing from US banking laws,[3] bank resolution requirements and tools (prompt corrective action) have been increasingly adopted in more modern banking laws. Banking laws increasingly strengthened the regulator's prudential focus, especially capital adequacy, while relaxing economic regulations.[4]

Our missions spent considerable time explaining and promoting these principles to our counterparts. While the former Soviet Republics were eager to replace centrally directed credit allocation and to establish monetary policy with market based instruments (open market operations, standing credit and deposit facilities, etc.), they were not generally familiar with how these policy tools should be designed and used to achieve those policy objectives while also promoting the development of market liquidity management and credit allocation.

[2] Coats and Schiffman (1995).

[3] The Federal Deposit Insurance Corporation Improvement Act of 1991 required prompt corrective action by undercapitalized banks and their takeover and resolution by the Federal Deposit Insurance Corporation if they became critically undercapitalized, thus correcting a moral hazard of deposit insurance.

[4] Coats and Liuksila (1999).

For parties arriving at agreement on the many options possible in new central bank and banking laws, it is essential that these laws conform to the basic legal traditions and practices of the country and that they be drafted in close cooperation with the local legal authorities who will implement them. Parliaments usually adopted the laws proposed to them by their central banks, but their successful implementation depended on the understanding and commitment of central bank management.

2.1.1 Kosovo

My IMF team arrived in Pristina, the capital of Kosovo, on August 18, 1999—two months after Yugoslav President Slobodan Milosevic agreed to withdraw his troops and NATO ended its air strikes. Kosovo's several commercial banks had suspended operations. The National Bank of Kosovo (NBK), a branch of Yugoslavia's central bank, had also ceased operations. The recently built headquarters of the NBK in Pristina had been severely damaged in NATO bombings on April 6–7, 1999, and could not be used. Its modern vaults in the building's basement were inaccessible and the supply of Yugoslav dinars in the NBK's other vaults were very limited and declining. The Payment Bureau of Kosovo (the SDKK[5]), the local branch of the Yugoslav Service for Social Bookkeeping (SDK), the highly centralized payment system of Yugoslavia, which operated outside of and separately from banks and from the central bank, had also largely ceased to function during the war from 1998–99.

Following the end of fighting in Kosovo, the United Nations Interim Administration Mission in Kosovo (UNMIK), established in the fall of 1999, administered its government functions until September 2012 when Kosovo became fully responsible for its own governance. Thus our work, including the drafting of relevant laws, fell under the supervision of UNMIK.

Being heavily dollarized with German marks (DM) and cut off from Serbia by choice, UNMIK made the use of DM legal in Kosovo (alongside the Yugoslav dinar) on September 2, 1999. It adopted a regulation formally giving it control of the SDKK, the Kosovo branch of the Yugoslav payment system, on October 15. Following a big debate in Washington about whether to create separate banking supervision and payment institutions, the IMF, World Bank, and the US Agency for International Development (USAID) quickly prepared legislation to establish one new institution, the Banking and Payment Authority of Kosovo (BPK) to take over the SDKK's payment functions and to license and regulate banks. The BPK was to be an autonomous authority with most of the powers of a central bank, including bank licensing, supervision, and regulation (but without the power to issue its own currency and to extend credit).

[5] The branch of the Yugoslav payment bureau system in Kosovo—Sherbimi I Kontabilitetit Shoqeror I Kosoves—or the Public Accounting Service of Kosovo.

The new institution was temporarily allowed to accept deposits from the public and provide payment services for those deposits, inventory DM banknotes and coins, and provide local DM settlements between banks. As a practical matter this more or less continued the existing practice of the SDKK. This was a controversial measure that ran the risk of building up (or prolonging) a commercial function that the SDKK should shed as quickly as private banks could be established to take it over. In fact, I replaced the first IMF-funded Managing Director of the BPK because of his over-enthusiasm for building up these commercial functions.

Foreign advisors prepared the "Regulation" of the BPK (as UNMIK's laws were called). The first draft of the law was prepared in the summer of 1999 in Washington by the IMF in consultation with the World Bank, the US Treasury, and USAID advisers. This draft was reviewed and modestly amended by the UN's New York lawyers. The UN High Representative presented the resulting draft to an Economic Policy Review Committee of local leaders. My IMF team then traveled to Pristina and spent many hours answering questions about the draft. On the basis of those meetings and written comments from Kosovars, the draft was revised and issued by UNMIK on November 15, 1999.

This procedure was below the minimum amount of local consultation the IMF considered desirable; but it seemed acceptable and more or less unavoidable in that environment. A similar procedure was followed with the Regulation on Bank Licensing, Supervision, and Regulation. These regulations reflected the UNMIK policy decision, strongly supported by local Kosovar leaders, that banks operating in Kosovo would be licensed and supervised in Kosovo rather than in Belgrade.

These "Regulations" functioned well until they were replaced by a law making the BPK a central bank on September 22, 2006, changing its name to the Central Banking Authority of Kosovo (CBAK), but still without currency issuing powers.

2.1.2 Bosnia and Herzegovina

After three and a half years of some of the most brutal fighting ever seen in Europe, the war between Bosnia and Herzegovina's three "ethnic" regions[6] (three nations within one country, it was sometimes said) "ended" on October 10, 1995 with the General Framework Agreement for Peace in Bosnia and Herzegovina (the Dayton Agreement). The Agreement, which became the constitution of Bosnia and Herzegovina, provided for the establishment of a new central bank operating under currency board rules to replace existing monetary institutions in the three sections of the country.

The discussions that produced the Central Bank of Bosnia and Herzegovina law were like no other. They dragged on for almost two years and were more a continuation of the peace negotiations than are our usual discussions with more

[6] The three regions were religiously rather than ethnically distinguished (Catholic, Orthodox, and Muslim).

unified counterparties. Bosnia's three Presidents (a Bosniak, a Croat, and a Serb) each appointed their member of the future central bank's board to represent them in the discussions (negotiations) with us of the draft law.

As with other areas of state administration, the leaders of the three "ethnic" regions of Bosnia were primarily concerned with determining how the responsibilities for governing and administering the central bank would be defined and distributed among them. Thus, for example, in addition to the three board members, one from each region, the bank had three vice governors similarly distributed and reporting to a governor chosen by the IMF from a noncontiguous country (first France then New Zealand) for the first six years of its existence. The very contentious issues of the currency design and distribution are discussed in section 2.4.

Our recommendation of a currency board monetary regime was never challenged or in doubt. In fact it is doubtful that the three factions would have trusted each other with any other regime. However, its technical details specified in the law (for example, the definition of the central bank's monetary liabilities that must be fully backed by foreign assets) gave rise to arguments with the US Treasury, which wanted a very hard, rigid specification. I preferred limited elements of flexibility that, in my view, would make the law more enforceable in times of stress. In the end the Republika Srpska representative presented us language (which I suspected had been provided to him by the US Treasury), which the Bosniak and Croat representatives accepted under strong pressure. However, in changing the concepts of monetary liabilities and monetary assets, the US Treasury's draft had destroyed the needed symmetry between the two, a problem also recognized by David Lipton, Assistant Secretary of the US Treasury. After considerable internal anguish we determined that adding one word in the draft ("resident" account holder) would restore coherence. We quietly added the word to the law, claiming that we were correcting a typo, and all was well.[7]

2.1.3 Iraq

The United States invaded Iraq on March 20, 2003. Following the surrender of Saddam Hussein's regime on April 9, 2003, the so-called Coalition Provisional Authority (CPA) of Iraq administered Iraq's government affairs for 14 months. As the Senior Monetary Policy Advisor to the Central Bank of Iraq after my

[7] Coats (2007b). The required foreign asset backing of the Central Bank of Bosnia and Herzegovina's (CBBH's) monetary liabilities had been changed from "gross" to "net" foreign assets. A foreign loan to Bosnia would normally take the form of a deposit to the CBBH's account in New York or London (a foreign asset) and an equivalent increase in the CBBH's liability to the lender (that is, an increase in its *gross* but not its *net* foreign assets). However, the liability created by a loan from the IMF would take the form of an increase in local currency deposits by the IMF in the CBBH. Such a loan would leave Bosnia's net foreign assets unchanged but would increase its monetary liabilities that needed to be backed with foreign assets. We changed the deposit liabilities to be covered from "Credit balances of all accounts... [of] all account holders," by inserting "resident" before "account holders."

retirement from the IMF, I was a member of the CPA during its final two months. The process of producing the central bank and banking laws under the CPA was unfortunately the worst I had ever experienced.

After I retired from the IMF in May 2003, I was asked to join an exploratory IMF mission to Baghdad in July 2003 during which Peter McPherson, Director of Economic Policy for the Office of Reconstruction and Humanitarian Assistance in Iraq, asked us (the IMF) to urgently prepare a Bank Licensing Law that would make it possible to license foreign banks to operate in Iraq as quickly as possible.[8] He gave us two weeks. We agreed that it would be very desirable to have American and/or other foreign banks set up in Iraq, but convinced him that no reputable bank would seek a banking license without first reviewing the (rest of the) banking law. Mr. McPherson reluctantly agreed and gave us until the end of August to produce a full draft banking law. Despite our urging, it was never discussed with the local authorities and was adopted as Order #40 of the CPA on September 24, 2003.

The law reflected the international state of the art at the time but was largely ignored in Iraq. The President of the Private Bankers Association of Iraq told me a year later that the Arabic translation was of very poor quality and that "no one understands what the law says."

The development of the central bank law followed a more normal path, though as a result of the IMF's refusal to travel to Iraq after the Canal Hotel bombing, for security reasons the draft was largely prepared by a lawyer from the New York Federal Reserve Bank on loan to the CPA, Raleigh Tozer, whose desk was next to mine in Saddam's Republican Palace. The law was decreed by the CPA and entered into force on March 1, 2004.

A dispute with the Iraqi government, which assumed full control from the CPA after June 2004, over the application of these laws to the resolution of insolvent-state-owned banks, illustrates the difficult tradeoff between international best practice and local political reality.

The US Treasury bank supervision team in Iraq from the Office of the Comptroller of the Currency (OCC) had locked horns with their Iraqi counterparts in the Finance Ministry over the resolution of Iraq's insolvent state-owned banks. The OCC team insisted that, as required by the banking law, all insolvent-banks, including those owned by the state, should be closed and liquidated and that those whose regulatory capital had fallen below 50 percent of the minimum required amount must be put into conservatorship. Though they were correct both about the law and about best practice, their dogmatic insistence on the most extreme implementation of these principles (liquidation) had resulted in the

[8] The bombing of the Canal Hotel (UN headquarters at the time) in Baghdad one month later on August 19, 2003, which killed 22 people including the United Nations' Special Representative in Iraq, Sérgio Vieira de Mello, and injured several IMF staff, ended IMF missions in Iraq.

Ministry of Finance's refusal to deal with them. USAID by whom my work was paid via BearingPoint, asked me if I would intervene and deal with the Ministry of Finance on this issue. I agreed only on the condition that the US Treasury accept this arrangement, which it promptly did.

As background, all foreign accounts of Iraqi banks had been frozen for some time as a result of Iraq's earlier default on its external debt. Any new export revenue, such as from the sale of Iraqi oil, normally would be immediately impounded in these frozen accounts. The Oil for Food program provided a partial circumvention of the embargo on oil revenue by setting it aside for humanitarian purposes. Thus in order to enable Iraqi companies and the Iraqi government to pay for imports until Iraq's foreign debts could be renegotiated and its deposits unfrozen, the CPA had established a temporary bank for this sole purpose—the Trade Bank of Iraq. The Trade Bank of Iraq took over the operations of the Oil for Food program and was run in New York by a consortium of American banks headed by J.P. Morgan Chase. The traditional state-owned Iraqi banks, the largest and most important of them being Rafidain and Rasheed, were insolvent and barely functioning.

My goal was to reach an agreement with the Finance Minister, Ali Allawi, and the Central Bank on resolution strategies for the state-owned banks that respected the spirit and essence of the US Treasury proposals but also respected Iraqi political sensitivities. Ali Allawi, who I grew to respect a great deal, was Deputy Prime Minister Ahmed Chalabi's sister's son and a cousin of the former, Interim Prime Minister, Iyad Allawi. Ali Allawi had previously served as the Defense Minister and the Trade Minister. He was wrapping up his term as Finance Minister and told me that he had accomplished all that he had committed to do except the resolution of the state-owned banks. And he was now running out of time.

After preliminary meetings with Minister Allawi, we gathered a larger group on November 23, 2005 in the section of the Green Zone Conference Center reserved for Iraqi officials. Minister Allawi had invited the President of the Trade Bank of Iraq, Hussein Isam Al Uzri, who is a nephew of Ahmed Chalabi. I presented my 18-slides PowerPoint presentation (which had been printed out and distributed because no projector was available), summarizing a wide range of resolution options. I placed the greatest stress on the "good bank" versus "bad bank" split resolution for Rafidain and Rasheed, because this would be less disruptive than simply closing and liquidating them. This approach creates a new bank from the good assets of the insolvent bank and assumes all of its deposit liabilities that it has the assets to support (a "purchase and assumption"). The original bad bank is then closed and liquidated without most depositors even noticing what had happened.

As the meeting got under way the infamous Ahmed Chalabi walked in uninvited and immediately took it over. He flipped through my PPP and without a pause said "there is no way we are going to break up and privatize these banks.... The public would not understand why the government could not take care of its own banks." He left without mentioning that his grandfather had started Rafidain in 1941. The meeting was over.

Minister Allawi was now caught between what he knew needed to be done one way or another and his uncle Chalabi's limitations on what those ways might be. We began to discuss alternative means to the same ends and essentially agreed on a compromise approach that was unfortunately never implemented because, I would like to believe, the Minister's term ended a few weeks later.

2.1.4 Summary

International monetary and banking standards and modern central bank and banking legislation adopted in most advanced economies embody best practices that all countries should endeavor to adopt. However, if their merits are not well understood and embraced by the local bodies that must administer them, and if they do not conform to the underlying legal foundations of the adopting country, they will be misapplied, ignored, or will fail to live up to their potential to establish a sound monetary and financial system.

Clear rules provide monetary and supervisory authorities and the markets they operate in with a reliable framework of operation and the basis for the accountability of the central bank. However, if rules are not realistic/or are overly costly to implement, they will be ignored. For many decades, for example, the legal requirement to close insolvent banks was ignored throughout most of the world via state bailouts until the procedures for insolvent bank resolution were made less painful and disruptive, an area in which the United States provided the leadership.

Local political realities must be weighed and considered and can't be simply ignored even if they prevent the adoption of best practice.

2.2 Central Bank Organizational Structure

As with every area of central bank technical assistance, the first requirement is to determine what is in place (the structure of management and departments and the functions and staffing of each) and the background or reasons for the existing structure. These are the people, possibly with the additional support of external experts, who are available to address all of the urgent emergency needs of the central bank. Significant changes to the bank's organizational structure, job descriptions, and personnel policies are disruptive and should take a few years to develop and implement.

The central bank law should protect the independence and provide for the accountability of the central bank via the composition, and terms of appointment and removal of the oversight board, the governor, and the senior management. The reporting lines of departments to deputy governors should separate the policy and operational functions from accounting and administrative and support functions in order to provide some checks and balances and the internal auditor should report directly to the Board.

The existing structure should be reviewed against the functions assigned to the central bank in the existing and/or prospective central bank law. With due regard for what is in place, the desired structure should be developed in consultation with existing management. Job descriptions and staff qualifications should be formally adopted as part of a merit-based hiring and promotion human resources policy. The implementation of new structures and policies needs to be carefully planned to avoid undue hardship on existing staff.

Many post-conflict and transition economy central banks were overstaffed with employees who had neither clearly defined functions nor training for performing them. Many employees were the friends or relatives of parliamentarians or other important people. These nepotistic practices are generally deep-seated and very difficult to reform and are often sources of significant corruption. Transparent reports to parliament on employment and operational outcomes are a helpful tool. Unlike policy accountability, the central bank's requirement to report to parliament on its operations (budget and its execution, staffing and compliance with human resources standards, procurement practices and outcomes) is not legally mandated (other than audited financial statements) in many central bank laws and has not been easy to establish.

2.2.1 West Bank and Gaza

The Oslo Accords between the State of Israel and the Palestine Liberation Organization (PLO) were signed in the White House on September 13, 1993, and with several follow-on agreements established the Palestine Authority (PA) to administer a limited number of government functions. These included the establishment of a Palestine Monetary Authority (PMA) in December 1994 that would have the usual powers of a central bank but without the right to issue its own currency.

My first mission to assist with the development of the PMA arrived on July 25, 1995 to meet with Governor Dr. Fouad Bseiso, who had been appointed by the PA seven months earlier. Several resident advisors were already in place from Jordan, Tunisia, and the United Kingdom. However, trust was not easily established in a land that had been at war for decades if not centuries. Yasser Arafat, who headed the PA, seemed to trust no one and traditionally did not share with his right hand what he was doing with his left hand. We immediately encountered frictions between two of our advisors and the governor that were sufficiently severe that we had to replace the advisors. Gaining trust, and hence effectiveness as advisors, proved our primary challenge in building a monetary authority totally from scratch.

Because our technical assistance missions were at the invitation of the Israeli government, which was the member in the IMF representing the West Bank and Gaza, our missions initially began and ended with a meeting at the Bank of Israel.

Three days after our arrival on February 22, 1996 for what turned out to be my last mission to the West Bank and Gaza for several years, I was eating breakfast at about 6:30 a.m. in the American Colony Hotel in Jerusalem when I heard a boom that silenced the room and sent a chill down my spine. We later learned that a terrorist's bomb had destroyed a commuter bus, killing 26 and injuring 46 people. One week later a bus on the same line (bus #18) was bombed, killing 19. The following day our debriefing in the Bank of Israel was interrupted by the announcement that yet another bomb had exploded in Tel Aviv, killing 13. No one said anything and we slowly walked out of the room and the Bank to our hotel where we packed up and drove to Amman, Jordan, changing cars at the Allenby Bridge at the Jordan River. Governor Bseiso's home is in Amman and we finished up our mission there with great sadness.

2.2.2 Afghanistan

"At the end of 2001, Afghanistan's formal financial system had largely ceased to exist. The country had become almost entirely cash-based. Banks had essentially stopped functioning during the Taliban years and whatever financial infrastructure had survived the many years of conflict was in very poor condition. What remained was the informal Hawala system that people could use to change and transfer money. Confidence in the national currency, the Afghani, was low, as it had lost much of its value following years of high inflation."[9]

The central bank, Da Afghanistani Bank (DAB), was divided into 20 departments at its headquarters in Kabul with 89 branches across the country, six desks in hotels and other public places, and four toll desks on the highway. It had 3,471 employees, many of them performing functions not usual for central banks. It was overstaffed with underqualified employees. DAB needed to establish new central bank functions (monetary policy and banking supervision), eliminate activities inconsistent with the new central bank law (such as commercial banking, tax collection), establish requirements for each position and criteria for promotion (that is, a modern human resources policy), and undertake recruiting and training to match staff capacities to its requirements.

The international efforts to assist the Afghan government and its central bank were extensive and included a large number of resident foreign advisers and expatriate Afghan nationals returning for temporary resident assignments. We collaborated closely with the World Bank teams, USAID contractors (BearingPoint) and the US and Canadian embassies. The USAID contractor BearingPoint (later purchased by Deloitte) had a large presence of resident experts in DAB. Among other things they prepared the human resources policies and job descriptions.

[9] IMF (2003), p. 97.

DAB's restructuring took almost a decade. Starting with the Monetary Policy, Financial Supervision, Human Resources Departments, and the Chief Information Office, BearingPoint installed resident advisors, expatriate Afghans where possible, as department heads and to develop the details of their new functions. Young Afghans were recruited and employed by BearingPoint to work in each of these and other departments for two years, after which they were invited to join DAB's regular staff, which most did. The program was a stunning success, producing a young cadre of well-educated and increasingly well-trained and motivated staff. Now almost every department head in DAB is one of these so-called BearingPoint Afghans, including the second Deputy Governor.

Though the modern HR policies developed by BearingPoint and the position descriptions and their qualifications were adopted in the mid-2000s, they were only implemented gradually. Traditionally, many positions were filled with unqualified relatives and friends of Parliamentarians and other "important" people. A complete culture change was required and having the unqualified so-called zombie employees sitting around in the same building with the new hard-working staff was awkward.

When Abdul Fitrat returned as governor in 2008 he quickly undertook the full implementation of the bank's reorganization and human resources policies. "Under this program, the Central Bank employees were reduced from nearly 2,550 persons to only 1,500."[10] Governor Fitrat's successor, Noorullah Delawari, was less firm about adhering to hiring standards and the number of so-called "legacy" hires (friends of someone, who did not meet the position's requirements) rose from about zero to about a third of the employees in just a few years, demonstrating how difficult it is to overcome decades of relationship favoritism. I was impressed with how quickly the new staff, especially the young BearingPoint Afghans, embraced the revolutionary merit-based hiring and promotion system and resented failures to fully implement it.

Khalil Sediq returned to DAB's governorship in July 2015 and DAB continues to grow in its professionalism and competence.

2.2.3 Bosnia and Herzegovina

During the Bosnia civil war from March 1992 to November 1995 the Croatian region was artificially joined with the Bosnian region to form the so-called Federation. In drafting the central bank law and developing the organizational structure of the Central Bank of Bosnia and Herzegovina (CBBH) between its branches in the two (actually three) regions, consideration was given to a distribution of its functions that would take into account the reality of animosities and nationalistic pressure while promoting cooperation and integration.

[10] Fitrat (2018), p. 78.

While the two branches in the Republika Srpska (in Banja Luka and Pale) and the two branches in the Federation (in Sarajevo and Mostar) all performed normal central bank banking operations and cash handling, we assigned the entire research department to Pale. Though in the Republika Srpska, Pale was effectively a suburb of Sarajevo in the Federation. This facilitated easy physical interaction between the research staff in Pale with the main office in Sarajevo. This interaction was also promoted and encouraged by the Serbian Vice Governor, Ljubiša Vladušić, who headed the Pale office. With his agreement I assigned Marko Škreb as a resident research advisor to the Pale office. Marko had taught monetary policy at the University of Zagreb Faculty of Economics, had been the Governor of the National Bank of Croatia, and was an irresistibly likeable man. The assignment worked very well.

The first joint meeting of the heads of the payment bureaus in the Bosniak, Croat, and Serb regions then being absorbed into the CBBH following the end of their civil war was a moving reunion of old colleagues and friends for the first time in five years. These are the events that give us hope.

2.2.4 Iraq

The restructuring of the Central Bank of Iraq's departments that I proposed to Governor Sinan Shabibi in 2003 combined the research and statistics functions into two sections of one department. The lady who headed the existing Research Department came to me and pleaded to keep them as two separate departments. She said that she simply would not be able work with the woman who headed the Statistics Department. I accepted her request. There was no overriding need to combine the two that would justify ignoring staff sensitivities.

2.2.5 Kazakhstan

After the newly independent National Bank of Kazakhstan issued its own currency in November 1993, the monetary policy needed to closely monitor the central bank's creation of reserve money contributed to revolutionary changes in the central bank's accounting systems. The wise head of the National Bank of Kazakhstan's Accounting Department approached the challenge by segregating a dozen young women from the rest of the accounting staff for special training in what would be required to produce daily reports on bank reserve balances with the National Bank. Ms. Abdullina's undertaking was very successful.

2.2.6 Summary

The development of new functions or a new central bank takes many years. In addition to the IMF's normal technical assistance missions, resident advisors, expats where possible, are very helpful, often funded by USAID and other development agencies, as are outside training programs such as the IMF's regional training centers. Whatever the level of international support to central bank reorganization and staff development, explicit agreement on the assignment of lead roles and coordination of efforts with other assistance organizations are critical for maximizing the benefits of such assistance. The wisdom of international best practices with regard to what central banks should do and how they should organize staff and reporting lines to most efficiently and safely deliver their services needs to take account of local customs and personalities and the pace with which they can be reasonably reformed.

2.3 Currency

The most urgent priority for any central bank is providing its economy with the means of payment, starting with currency. This is particularly urgent and challenging for a new or a post-conflict central bank. The former Soviet Republics initially continued to use the Soviet ruble until each introduced its own currency. The same was true for the six republics that had made up Yugoslavia. The experiences of Afghanistan and Iraq were rather different; and Kosovo and West Bank and Gaza still have no currency of their own and need to maintain the condition and stock of foreign banknotes.

Issuing a new currency, generally in exchange for another one, requires very careful planning and clear communications with the public about the process. Security measures to prevent multiple exchanges of the same notes are critical. Several countries failed to receive value for the currency they replaced because of the lack of advance agreement with its issuer but proceeded to issue their new currency anyway.

2.3.1 Kosovo, West Bank and Gaza, and Zimbabwe

Neither Kosovo, the West Bank and Gaza, nor Zimbabwe have their own currency; thus, they also have no monetary policy or need to develop the data and analytics generally required for implementing monetary policy (more on that later). Dollarization (the use of another country's currency) is ideal for small, open economies with very limited institutional and administrative capacity (think of California's use of US dollars). Its simplicity, stability, and credibility have served economies very well, even in well-established economies such as Panama, which has successfully used the US dollar as its official currency for 90 years.

When a country uses the currency of another country it is free of the need to design its notes and coins and to arrange for their printing, but it is not generally free of the need to arrange for replacing old and damaged notes with new ones and to safe keep them (generally performed by banks) until they are demanded by the public. It also forgoes the seigniorage of issuing its own currency.

2.3.2 Kosovo

The official currency of Kosovo was still the Yugoslav dinar, but the country had largely spontaneously dollarized into DM, US dollars, and Swiss francs over the previous decade. UNMIK, effectively an interim government, removed the existing Yugoslavian legal restriction on the use of currencies other than the Yugoslavian dinar in September 1999, and the DM quickly became the dominant currency. However, no formal agreement or arrangement existed with the German Bundesbank for the use of DM in Kosovo, including arrangements for the supply of DM banknotes and coins. I visited the Bundesbank in Frankfurt to discuss these arrangements. The Bundesbank did not object to Kosovo's use of the DM, but preferred to keep their "agreement" informal.

Our mandate was to assist the authorities in providing and maintaining a physical currency, maintaining its value, and reestablishing non-cash payment systems. While we operated under the authority of UNMIK as the interim administrative authority, we consulted regularly with the competing local political parties, the outgrowths of Kosovo's government in exile: the Democratic League of Kosovo (LDK) headed by Ibrahim Rugova, and the Kosovo Liberation Army (KLA) headed by Hashim Thaçi. In effect, Kosovo had two competing shadow governments.

After intense discussions abroad and locally, general agreement was reached that the SDKK should not be revived and rebuilt, and should be replaced with more standard bank-based payment systems of the type common in market economies. This departed from our usual practice of starting with the system in place and modernizing or reforming it over time as appropriate, as we had done in Bosnia, Croatia, and Serbia. We concluded that this was appropriate, given the high cost of resuscitating the SDK system, the rapid decline in the use of the Yugoslav dinar, and the incompatibility of the Yugoslav payment system approach with those of existing market economies. However, this approach complicated the urgent need for money and payment services.

It was also agreed that the National Bank of Kosovo would be dissolved and that Kosovo's new monetary authority, the Banking and Payment Authority of Kosovo (BPK), would not issue its own currency. Though there was a strong political desire among the Albanian majority to replace the Yugoslav dinar with a currency of their own, this could not be permitted by the UN administration because Kosovo formally remained a province of Serbia. It was wiser, in any event, to continue and formalize the use of the DM, which would have been unavoidable for a transition period under any circumstances. Though dollarization with the DM was the simplest course it still demanded urgent interim measures to restore payment systems.

In the decade before the war of 1998–99 dollarization occurred through market practice without any official support to the supply of currency. Payments of DM in the market were supplemented with Yugoslav dinar for small change. Without replenishment after the war the local supply of dinars evaporated quickly. The most immediate manifestation of the currency situation was the lack of small change, either DM or Yugoslav dinar coins. Small change in local shops was often made in candy bars or similar merchandise. Our discussions concluded that the high cost of transporting DM coins to Kosovo did not justify doing so. Merchants frequently brought relatively large amounts of coins with them when returning to Kosovo from Germany and the DM coin shortage gradually dissipated.

The above narrative obscures the chaos of the early months and year following the end of hostilities. President Milosevic had rescinded Kosovo's autonomy and imposed marshal law in 1989. Kosovar institutions were replaced or absorbed by Yugoslav institutions and Serbs replaced Albanian Kosovars in management positions. When the Serbian Army withdrew on June 11, 1999, Serbian management and trained staff departed as well, leaving nothing behind—neither operating manuals, nor vault or any other keys. Telecommunication lines had been cut and electricity was sporadic. When the former ethnically Albanian management and staff returned (most had moved to Albania) they were 8–9 years removed from current operations. They returned to empty, looted buildings and Albanian Kosovar employees expecting a reset to a decade earlier.

The ownership of public assets also presented challenges. Ownership of the office facilities of the now defunct SDKK was transferred by UNMIK, in its capacity as interim civil administrator for the government, to the new BPK. However, when former employees of the SDKK demonstrated outside the building (which we were occupying) to protest the theft of their building, their spokesperson explained to us that the building was not "public" property but rather "social" property. According to him, they had worked for many years at reduced wages in exchange for a share in the ownership of the building and related assets (IT equipment, etc.). Thus we learned of a new form of ownership under Yugoslav law.

There was an urgent need to reestablish the capacity to make payments for UNMIK and enterprises and to provide cash safekeeping and other payment services in DM. Thus, until a new authority could be legally established, UNMIK provided for the urgently needed monetary services (such as safekeeping of border taxes and making pension payments) by hiring the staff and management and leasing the facilities and equipment needed for the entire operation from the former SDKK.

The SDKK's (now BPK's) vault procedures for accepting, safeguarding, and transporting currency were reviewed and revised. Even relatively simple operational changes, such as replacing the multiple teller windows required to deposit or withdraw cash or to issue a payment order with a single Universal Teller Window, proved difficult not just because procedures had to be rewritten, staff retrained, and Teller Window equipment changed, but mainly because old managers resisted adapting to new ways.

Tensions existed not only between former Kosovo management wanting to retain familiar functions and procedures and the desire of reformers to adapt institutions to market economy norms as quickly as possible, but also between the pressing need to fulfill basic payment functions by having UNMIK and BPK undertake them on a temporary basis and the longer-term development of more permanent systems. We were concerned that basic functions taken on by state institutions (BPK) risked becoming permanent. The unshakable enthusiasm of the IMF-recruited General Manager of the BPK to expand its commercial activities resulted in my replacing him.

Building modern electronic payment systems is a multi-year undertaking. Fortunately, the banking sector revived more quickly than expected as new banks were licensed by the BPK, and most of the deposit and payment services initially performed by the BPK moved rather quickly to banks. The functions of maintaining and safe keeping DM currency were also taken up and performed primarily by banks rather early on. When allowed, the private sector almost always moves more quickly than the public sector.

The BPK was transformed into the Central Banking Authority of Kosovo in September 2006 and was replaced by the Central Bank of Kosovo in June 2008, the year Kosovo became independent. Kosovo unilaterally adopted the euro in January 2002—it is not a member of the European Union (EU)—but with the cooperation of the European Central Bank so that it enjoyed the usual currency services provided by the issuing central bank (replacing old and damaged notes with new ones, and the desired supply of coins).

2.3.3 West Bank and Gaza

When my IMF missions established the PMA there was no predecessor institution to build on and it issued no currency of its own. The Israeli shekel (NIS) was the main currency for the PA's fiscal accounts. The PA's main revenue source was and remains taxes collected by the Israeli authorities from a VAT and import duties. These account for about 70 percent of revenues and are transferred to the PA in NIS. Expenditures, including wages and pensions, are made in NIS. Palestinian workers in Israel remit in NIS and the NIS is the main transactional currency. Goods from Israel are paid for in NIS and the main Consumer Price Index (CPI) calculation is in NIS.

The US dollar is used by the banking system as its main unit of account: all reporting to the PMA is in US dollars; loans and deposits are commonly denominated in US dollars. The PMA balance sheet is in US dollars and its staff is paid in US dollars. The PA receives donor support in US dollars. Most remittances from outside the region (that is, from the United States, Europe, and the Gulf) are in US dollars.

The Jordanian dinar (JD), which is pegged to the US dollar, is used for large-value transactions, especially property transactions in the West Bank. Aid flows and remittances from the EU are in euros. The Egyptian pound is also used in Gaza.

The currency responsibilities of the PMA were initially limited to exchanging old and damaged shekel notes for new ones. The PMA had an agreement with an Israeli commercial bank to purchase new Israeli banknotes and to replace old and damaged NIR banknotes with new ones. Given the border restrictions imposed by Israel, Israeli armored cars would unload their currency at the border with the West Bank and Palestinians would reload it into a Palestinian bank armored car for delivery to the vaults of banks operating in the West Bank and Gaza. The PMA did not have its own vaults until the completion of its new headquarters in Ramallah in 2011, at which time cash handling and security measures were developed and implemented.

The challenges of managing the supply of currency in the West Bank and Gaza were illustrated in 2006 by the threatened termination of the arrangement with Israeli banks to supply banknotes. The Israeli banks were concerned that the PMA might not be sufficiently compliant with international Anti-Money Laundering (AML) norms. The governor of the Bank of Israel, Stanley Fischer, and the governor of the PMA, George Abed, met to resolve the threatened cutoff. Both had been colleagues at the IMF and quickly determined that Palestinian banks were in better compliance with AML regulations than were the Israeli banks. The threatened termination was withdrawn.

2.3.4 Zimbabwe

After averaging about 20 percent per annum in the 1990s, Zimbabwe's inflation rate gradually rose to 239 percent in 2005, to over 1000 percent in 2006, and to 10,000 percent in 2007. In 2008 it exploded and "is estimated to have peaked in September 2008 at about 500 billion percent per annum." This incomprehensible rate of inflation means that in September prices were doubling every eleven-and-a-half days. When the Zimbabwe Stock Exchange stopped trading the Zimbabwean dollar in Nov 2008, its exchange rate to the US dollar was estimated by the UN to be 35 quadrillion (35×10^{15}). This was the rate generally used for 2008 year-end financial statements.

The Reserve Bank couldn't print new currency notes fast enough to keep up with their demand as people spent Zimbabwean dollars faster and faster before prices went up even more. This is what happens in hyperinflations. The velocity of circulation of money accelerates, reflecting rising expectations of further inflation with the result that the real value of the money supply shrinks. The total amount of Zimbabwean dollar currency in circulation at the end of 2008 was Z $22,400,000,000,000,000. Its value in US dollars was 64 cents! I checked that figure twice with our accountant Ken Sullivan.

Because the Reserve Bank could not print banknotes quickly enough to keep up with the demand, it imposed a limit on the amount of cash that depositors could take out of their bank accounts at one time. At one point this amount was not enough to pay for a gas tank fill-up, thus requiring multiple trips to the bank. Zimbabweans could write checks on their bank accounts; but paying for gasoline with a check would entail a much higher price reflecting the inflation expected over the next several days that it would take the gas station to collect the money via the check.

To help their customers pay for gasoline, wholesalers issued coupons denominated in liters of gasoline. These were purchased months before the holder intended to use them to pay for gasoline, and they locked in the real gasoline value of the later actual purchase. Some firms bought large quantities and used these coupons to pay their employees. The coupons circulated as currency. The early sale of coupons for cash and its immediate use to pay for imported gasoline protected the wholesaler just as well as holding the inventory of gasoline for subsequent sale at a higher ZIM dollar price.

Restaurants put the prices of menu items on a sheet at the back that could be replaced every day with new prices. Some menus stated prices in "units" where the ZIM dollar value of a unit was updated every day.

The game ended when the Central Bank ran out of enough foreign exchange (euros) to pay its German note printer to keep printing. Obviously the note printer wasn't about to accept payment in the notes it was printing. Near the end of 2008 the economy spontaneously dollarized, which was legally recognized by the new "inclusive" government in February 2009. During the year before the collapse of the currency many firms had already established financial accounts in US dollars for internal management purposes.

The inability of the Reserve Bank to print more currency ended government "borrowing" from the Reserve Bank and limited its disbursements to cash on hand as tax revenues were received. However, for some time this meant that many obligations could not be honored. Government employees could not be paid their salaries (all received monthly stipends of $100 for the time being). The Reserve Bank could not repay all depositors, etc. The economy could only earn foreign currency by exporting, and many of its industries were operating at one-third capacity because they did not have the money to pay for electricity and other imported inputs needed to operate. Private banks could not lend to them because significant amounts of their money was deposited with the Reserve Bank, which could not repay it at that time.

This was the situation when our five-person mission from the IMF visited Harare in May 2009 to advise on monetary policy. Contrary to our expectation that Zimbabweans would dollarize with the South African rand, they did so with US dollars. Our immediate concern was how the supply and condition of US dollar banknotes would be maintained.

Local banks purchased US currency from a secondary market in South Africa. We asked them whether it would be helpful for the Reserve Bank to import these banknotes, becoming a local warehouse and source of supply to the banks. Their response was: "Absolutely not. We want nothing to do with the Reserve Bank."

2.3.5 Bosnia and Herzegovina

Most countries choose to issue their own currency. The newly independent countries of the former Soviet Union chose to issue their own currencies, in part to establish a clear national symbol and patriotic identity. Introducing their own currencies also had the advantage of generating profits (seigniorage) from the monopoly issue of banknotes (or more broadly, "base money"). Issuing its own currency also gave the monetary authority control over its supply and thus the ability and need to implement its own monetary policy.

The key decisions with regard to currency note design are:

- note size, security features (paper, ink, printing technologies, micro threads, watermarks, etc.), themes (national heroes, buildings, art, etc.), text, colors, durability;[11]
- the number and amount of note denominations (1, 5, 10, 20, 50, 100 or 2, 5, 25, 100, 500, etc.), the aggregate and relative numbers of each to print initially;
- the initial value of one unit in relation to typical domestic household purchases; and
- whether to issue coins and the breaking point between the highest-value coin and the lowest-value bank note.[12]

The value of the new unit should be simple in relation to the old currency it replaces (a round number) and have convenient purchasing power. Security features consist of those that help the general public identify the authenticity of the notes, those designed for people more specialized in detecting counterfeits (bank tellers and sorting machines) and those known only to and used by the central bank itself. The issuer of a new currency must adequately inform the public about all of these features.

After redenominating prices, contracts, and bank deposits from the old to the new monetary unit by the adoption of the appropriate law, the easiest way to introduce a new currency is for the government to start using it for all of its salary and pension payments (which are usually in cash) and for banks to pay out deposit withdrawals in the new currency after exchanging the old for the new in their vaults. Thus merchants would withdraw new currency from their banks with

[11] These and other aspects of note design are reviewed in more detail in Abrams (1995).
[12] Abrams (1995).

which to make change and would deposit old currency with their banks at the end of the day. To the extent that the exchange takes place in this gradual way, the cash distribution, storage, handling, and accounting systems in place can and should be used.

Generally, however, including for the exchange of national European currencies for the new euro, designated exchange points and rules for direct exchanges have also been used. Exchange points must be established and provided with adequate security. These might be limited to banks and/or post offices or they might also include temporary storefront locations or mobile teller facilities. Clear rules for the exchange must be developed and communicated effectively to the public. These would include the hours of operation, any limits on the amounts that may be exchanged, and identification documents required by the person making the exchange, if any. Exchange staff must be trained, and vault, procedural, and accounting safeguards and security must be reviewed and or established. Existing banking facilities, staff, and procedures should be relied upon to the extent possible.[13]

Procedures are also needed for securing and ultimately destroying redeemed old notes to ensure that they are not redeemed a second or third time. Where new notes replace notes of another country, as was the case with former Soviet Union countries replacing the Soviet and the Russian rubles, agreement should be sought with the issuer of the currency redeemed for its repatriation and recovery of value without which the new central bank currency liabilities will have no asset backing.

In Kazakhstan, the Kyrgyz Republic, and other former Soviet Union countries, local officials carried out the tasks of note design and related issues with the help of international note printers, without input from IMF missions. Our local counterparts were quite capable of organizing and executing the note exchanges once we had advised them on what was needed. Bosnia and Herzegovina was a very different case.

Bosnia and Herzegovina replaced the Yugoslav dinar with its own Bosnian dinar when it gained independence from the Soviet Federal Republic of Yugoslavia in March 1992, but civil conflict between its Serbian, Croatian, and Bosnian citizens began immediately escalating into full-scale war with Serbia. The war ended October 10, 1995 with the Dayton Peace Agreement.

The branches of the National Bank of Yugoslavia located in Mostar for the Catholic-Croatian region, Banja Luka for the Orthodox-Serbian region, and Sarajevo for the Muslim-Bosnian region, had functioned as independent central banks during their civil war. Each dealt with a different currency within its area.

[13] For a more detailed discussion see the IMF note on: "Introduction of a New National Currency: Policy, Institutional, and Technical Issues," prepared by Richard K Abrams and Hernán Cortés-Douglas, June 1993.

In addition to the Bosnian dinar, the German mark was also widely used throughout the entire country, but the Croatian-majority region also used the Croatian kuna and the Serbian-majority area also used the Yugoslav dinar. Neither of these areas issued a currency of their own, and the Bosnian dinars, which were fixed to the German mark, were generally used only in the Bosnian majority region. By the end of the war, these Bosnian dinars were in poor and deteriorating condition but most transactions were made in German marks. The arrangements in place could be continued for several years without serious hardship. As it turned out those extra years were needed.

Twenty-two months of stressful negotiations over a new central bank law stretched from the end of fighting to the opening of the new Central Bank of Bosnia and Herzegovina on August 11, 1997.[14] Our Serb, Croat, and Bosniak counterparts (the members of the future Board of the CBBH appointed by the Presidents of the three ethnic regions) barely mentioned the core currency board rules featured in the law we were negotiating. In fact, they would not have been able to trust any other policy rule. It was completely uncontroversial.

The issues that dominated the discussions over the details of the central bank law for more than a year were the provisions on the voting powers of the members of the Board, the role and powers of the branches of the central bank (one in each of the three regions), and the name and design of the currency notes.

Manojlo Ćorić, the Serb member of the future Board, sought to distinguish everything possible about the central bank's operations and currency in his region from the rest of the country, while our objective, and that of the international community, was to create a single central bank and currency indistinguishable among the three regions.

The Bosnian Serbs sought their own version of the new currency in their Cyrillic alphabet. It would be issued by their branch of the central bank but would be legal tender throughout the country. They even wanted their branch of the central bank to separately own the foreign exchange reserve backing of the new currency that it would issue. This, in their view, was consistent with the essence of a single monetary area and system. A compromise was finally reached: each region would have its own version of the currency, which would circulate freely throughout the country with equal legal tender status. The two versions,[15] however, would look as much as possible like the same currency, generally having "common design elements," as well as "distinct design elements for the Federation of Bosnia and Herzegovina and the Republika Srpska." Mr. Ćorić was all too familiar with the structure of the American system in which 12 separate regional

[14] For details, see Coats (2007a).

[15] In the later stages of the civil war the Croatian and Bosnian regions joined into the so-called Federation and jointly fought against the Republika Srpska. Thus the three regions became (notionally at least) two entities.

central banks notionally issued distinguishable currency notes (this is no longer the case).

Each of the three ethnic groups put forward its proposed design, which was knocked down by one of the other two groups. In a few cases "national" heroes of one ethnic group or the other were proposed, which was clearly objectionable to the other two. Generally, however, designs were objected to because there was still no political support for moving forward with the new currency. No design would have been acceptable and any excuse might be offered. This exercise was repeated a number of times. As a practical matter the growing delay was only a problem for the Bosniak area because of the old and worn condition of the Bosnian dinars, which would be replaced by the new notes.

In February 1998, the new CBBH governor selected by the IMF, Peter Nicholl from New Zealand, took the latest set of objections from each side to the current round of proposals for note designs and unilaterally decided which he felt were justified and which were not, and made his own proposal to the CBBH Board. When the Board could not agree to act, he submitted the resulting designs to the UN Office of the High Representative (OHR). The High Representative approved the designs and presented it to the Joint Presidency, which also approved them.

This proved to be a very well-timed intervention. No one really objected. It would not have been possible to force any of the political leaders to take actions they strongly opposed. There were times when it was politically difficult for the three groups to explicitly agree to something they might otherwise find acceptable. At those times, an externally imposed decision might be acceptable (and probably welcomed). This was one of those times.

The Serb and Federation versions of the new banknotes were initially issued in their respective areas. The governor decided that no effort would be made to sort circulating or returned notes into their two versions in order to return them to the "proper" Entity. The differences between the two versions of the currency were more noticeable than were the 12 versions for each US currency note (one for each of the 12 Federal Reserve Banks) but only modestly so, and after a few years the two versions were thoroughly mixed without public notice (or concern).

The search for a name for the currency followed a similar pattern. To put off that debate, we referred to the future currency by the temporary name "glasses" in successive drafts of the banking law and in our discussions. ("Glasses"—referring to a pair of eyeglasses—appeared the most innocuous word we could think of at the time because it had no reference to any single party's history or cultural affinity.)

Between November 1996 and May 1997, each member of the Board had made interesting and worthy suggestions for the name of the new currency. Before there were political will and commitment to move forward, however, no name would be acceptable to all three groups. When that time was reached in May, all of the good names had already been rejected. At that point David Lipton of the US Treasury (and at that time the First Deputy Managing Director of the IMF), suggested the pedestrian but descriptive name Convertible Marka (KM), which was immediately accepted.

The new currency name and design were not agreed until the political leadership of the previously warring groups were ready politically to move forward with the implementation of the new central bank. Gentle but persistent international pressure played a key role.

The new banknotes were first issued on June 15, 1998 and the Bosnia and Herzegovina dinars were demonetized on June 30, two weeks later. The introduction of the new notes and the redemption of the old Bosnia and Herzegovina dinars went relatively smoothly and the CBBH was finally fully established and operating in all areas of the country.

Almost four years later, when a new 200 KM note was introduced, it had only one version for both the Federation and the Republika Srpska. The CBBH board approved the single design without controversy.

2.4 Case Studies of Issuing a New Currency

2.4.1 Bosnia and Herzegovina

When setting up the new CBBH and liquidating the old National Bank of BH (NBBH), the new CBBH only accepted liabilities from the NBBH that reflected the deposits of banks and Bosnian dinar currency in circulation (the best estimate thereof).[16,17] Foreign exchange assets of equivalent value were also transferred (DM balances in Frankfurt) from the NBBH to the new central bank. These banknotes were redeemed by the CBBH for its new currency, which was thus fully backed by its DM assets. Because the amount of old currency actually redeemed was less than the DM assets transferred to the CBBH for that purpose, the surplus DM assets were returned to the NBBH as part of its liquidation. A special trust account had been set up for this purpose, reflecting the expectation that some of the old notes had been lost, destroyed, or taken away as souvenirs.

2.4.2 Republika Srpska

The population of the Republika Srpska had not embraced the Bosnian dinar issued by the NBBH in 1992 and continued to use the Yugoslav dinar issued by the National Bank of Yugoslavia. As a result, few residents of the Republika Srpska had Bosnian dinars to exchange for the new currency of the CBBH (Convertible Markka—KM) and Yugoslav dinars were not accepted by the CBBH. Moreover, the National Bank of Yugoslavia cut the Republika Srpska off, refusing to redeem its currency there and refusing to send more. Thus depositors could not withdraw

[16] For fascinating details of the complex currency situation in Afghanistan, see IMF (2003).
[17] For details, see Coats (2007b).

their dinar balances in cash to spend in Serbia and it was no longer possible to transfer dinar balances via the payment system operated by the National Bank of Yugoslavia.

To help preserve the value of these dinars held by its citizens, the government of the Republika Srpska accepted dinars in payment of taxes. In about two years all dinars vanished from the Republika Srpska, having been spent in Serbia or in the Republika Srpska for taxes, and the National Bank of the Republika Srpska accumulated claims on the National Bank of Yugoslavia that were never collected. The Republika Srpska now uses KM from the countrywide central bank (CBBH) that it acquired the hard way (exports for DM with which holders could buy KM).

2.4.3 Croatia

The Croatian dinar was released into circulation on the December 23, 1991 as the legal tender in the Republic of Croatia, marking the end of the country's process of gaining monetary and political independence from the Socialist Federal Republic of Yugoslavia. The Yugoslav dinar was exchanged for the Croatian dinar at the ratio of 1:1 from the December 23–31, 1991. In an effort to prevent Yugoslav dinars from outside of Croatia participating, the exchange was done quickly. The initial exchange rate of the Croatian dinar for German marks was set by the National Bank of Croatia on the January 1, 1992 at 1 German mark equal to 55 Croatian dinars.

The National Bank of Croatia had no arrangements with the National Bank of Yugoslavia, which issued the dinars, to receive credit for the dinars it had collected.

2.4.4 Slovenia

The Bank of Slovenia was established on June 25, 1991 as part of its separation from the Socialist Federal Republic of Yugoslavia by taking over the assets and liabilities of the National Bank of Slovenia from the National Bank of Yugoslavia, of which it was a branch. The Constitution stipulates that the Bank of Slovenia be independent and responsible directly to the Parliament.

The Bank of Slovenia replaced the Yugoslav dinar with it own currency, the tolar, on October 8, 1991 by redeeming dinars one for one with the tolar. The Yugoslav dinar notes that were collected were returned to the National Bank of Yugoslavia in Belgrade, which accepted a claim on the National Bank for the same amount on the books of the Bank of Slovenia. The subsequent hyperinflation of the dinar reduced the value of this dinar claim to almost nothing.

2.4.5 The Kyrgyz Republic

In 1991 the Soviet Union dissolved peacefully into 15 independent countries, of which the Kyrgyz Republic was one. Initially the Gosbank's—then the new Central Bank of Russia's—rubles were the only currency in the 15 newly independent republics. On May 10, 1993, the Kyrgyz Republic's new central bank (the National Bank of the Kyrgyz Republic) issued its new currency, the som, and exchanged it for whatever Russian and Soviet rubles its people cared to redeem at the rate of 200 rubles per som for an official exchange period of two weeks (extended to three weeks in special cases). The large number of rubles collected in the process were returned to the Central Bank of Russia and credited against amounts owed to the Central Bank of Russia by the National Bank of the Kyrgyz Republic.[18] Remaining rubles continued to circulate in the Kyrgyz Republic for eventual use in Russia; however, as public confidence in the som increased, most "unredeemed" rubles still in the country were exchanged in the market at the prevailing ruble/som rate.

2.4.6 Summary

Commercial currency printers can and should be relied upon for assisting central banks in making key technical decisions about note denominations and design. Where political aspects influence note designs, patience is essential. The design of a note is a national symbol and most often has an emotional significance related to historical and cultural contexts that must be considered.

Similarly, central bank facilities (such as vaults) for managing the currency supply (adequate inventories, procedures for replacing old and damaged notes, secure transport to and from banks), and procedures to protect cash handling from theft (vault and teller window procedures) are technical in nature and are generally satisfactorily provided by market specialists (usually the note printers).

Existing organizations and staff can generally be relied upon to implement a well-specified plan for introducing and maintaining a new currency. However, the tension between what is expedient in the short term with what is desirable in the long term can be difficult to manage. For example, the failure to secure advance agreement with the issuing central bank for the return of its currency when that is being replaced by a new national currency has resulted in unnecessary and costly losses. Every effort should be made to address urgent needs with an eye to their compatibility with sound long-term development. For example, any temporary provision of banking services to the public by the central bank should be phased out as quickly as possible.

2.5 Non-Cash Payment Systems, Central Bank Credit, and Money Markets

When the Soviet Union dissolved, the IMF had no expertise in payment systems. It was a part of the transmission of monetary policy that worked behind the scenes

[18] However, the agreement and its terms for the return of and credit for these Soviet and Russian rubles was struck only after the exchange was completed.

well enough in most places that we paid it no attention. We quickly learned that in the USSR and Yugoslavia the design of their deposit payment systems was an integral part of their overall central planning approach to economic management. A first lesson was that payments by transfer of deposit balances were made without regard to the payer's deposit balance. Payments were made on the authority of budgets. Thus the accounting systems were not designed to closely monitor deposit balances, which were only consulted and reconciled at the end of each year. This came as quite a surprise to us until we understood the procedure in budget execution terms.

All payments between the republics of the Soviet Union ultimately went through the accounts in the Central Bank of Russia in Moscow, which had been the currency issuer for the entire USSR. When Western payment system advisors told the Central Bank of Russia that it should process a payment only when the payer had sufficient funds in its account, the system froze up and the payment backlog in Moscow quickly extended to several months. It took several years to completely clear the logjam.

The capacity of the IMF to offer advice and of the new central banks of the former Soviet Union and of post-conflict countries to implement it was stretched almost to the breaking point. In the initial years of independence (1992–93) our missions almost reached World Bank sizes (10–12 people). Banking and financial markets were not at the top of our priorities list. The development of prudential regulations and supervision was largely neglected for the first year or two, though countries were encouraged to license foreign banks so as to take advantage of their banking and risk management expertise.

The same can be said for payment systems development. The reform of central bank credit instruments to the requirements of market-directed credit allocation and of the interrelated management of liquidity by banks received more immediate attention.

The Soviet system used central bank allocation of credit as an element of the governments' overall central economic plans. In Kazakhstan and the Kyrgyz Republic (and in the other former Soviet Union countries) the allocation of credit to designated firms and sectors according to the central plan was phased out by gradually (over about two years) replacing allocated central bank credit with central bank credit auctions to banks as the primary tool for increasing the money supply.[19] This required helping former Soviet Union central banks develop the credit auction rules and procedures and to explain them to their banks. It also required commercial banks to develop market-based lending criteria and capabilities. We did not provide assistance in that area.

[19] The critically important and—for the former Soviet Union central banks—totally new function of determining the size of such auctions, that is, monetary policy, is not discussed in this chapter.

In parallel with the development of credit auctions, we helped central banks develop the legal and regulatory foundations for issuing tradable government debt securities, the rules and procedures for auctioning them, and the rules regulating secondary trading of such securities. Generally, the central bank provided the central registry of government securities. These registries recorded the issuance (ownership) and trading (transfer of ownership) of treasury securities and/or their pledge as collateral.

Starting initially as simple spreadsheets, proper registries with payment versus delivery integrated with real-time gross settlement payment systems were developed after several years. We generally recommended the development of a two-tiered system in which the central bank maintained the ownership records of commercial banks (held on their own account and on their customers' accounts) and on the second tier, the banks held the ownership records of their retail customers.

Initially our counterparts didn't always appreciate the importance of facilitating the development of private sector money markets where banks could manage their liquidity in the face of fluctuating deposits and withdrawals. It would have been easy to keep all liquidity adjustments between each individual bank and the central bank rather than between banks (by transferring their reserve balances with the central bank between them). However, forcing liquidity management into the private market incentivized banks to monitor the soundness of their fellow bank counterparties, increased the sensitivity of money market interest rates to liquidity conditions, and strengthened the central bank's control over base money. Central bank policy instruments needed to be designed to control the evolution of reserve money and limit the volatility of short-term interest rates while keeping the central bank as a source of bank liquidity of second choice, with money market transactions between banks as the first choice for liquidity management.

For central banks with fixed exchange rates, foreign exchange was bought or sold with a small spread around the fixed rate. Generally, banks should be able to get a better rate from the market than from the central bank but central bank intervention (actively or passively) would keep the rate close to the fixed target.

For central banks with floating exchange rates and a monetary or inflation target—invariably implemented via interest rate targets—this meant allowing a spread around its interest rate target. Generally, banks should be able to get a better rate from the market than from the central bank.

Thus we recommended a standing deposit facility with an interest rate a fixed amount below the policy target rate and a standing credit facility with an interest rate charge a fixed amount above the policy rate. A change in the policy rate moved the whole structure of rates automatically. It often took a while to convince central banks of the need to float these rates around the policy rate. In addition to these, central banks established clear rules for their "lender of last resort" assistance to solvent but illiquid banks not otherwise able to use the collateralized standing credit facility. These simple and transparent instruments swept away multiple facilities that were often offered with considerable central bank discretion. They also replaced lending rates that often remained fixed for long periods, growing increasingly out of line with changing policy and market rates. Redesigning reserve requirement regulations to allow reserve averaging (the requirement was based on daily average rather than absolute amounts over a period of several weeks or a month) further incentivized banks to carefully manage their daily liquidity.

Initially many banks continued to borrow from or deposit with the central bank rather than looking for better rates in the market and ignored their ability to vary their reserve balances within the reserve requirement-averaging period. Over time, however, the better-managed banks profited from developing liquidity trading relationships with other banks, and money markets began to develop.

2.5.1 South Sudan

In July 2011 South Sudan separated from Sudan and became an independent country.[20] It immediately replaced the Sudanese pound with its own South Sudanese pound but initially inherited (adopted) the overvalued exchange rate and accompanying exchange controls of the Sudanese pound. The government's revenue before and after independence resulted almost exclusively from its exports of oil. The US dollars received by the government were sold to the central bank for local currency, which the government spent into the economy. Because the resulting increase in the local currency money supply would have exceeded the public's demand with stable prices, the central bank sold sufficient amounts of these dollars to the private market to slow the growth in South Sudanese pounds to a noninflationary rate.

Prior to independence the overvalued pound and exchange controls needed to keep it there resulted in a depreciated "street" exchange rate below the official rate. As the central bank did not have all of the USD the market desired at the pound's overvalued exchange rate, it rationed the weekly sales among the exchange dealers who then reaped the profit of the large spread between the official rate and the street rate. On foreign exchange allocation days there was always a line of dealers in the hall outside the office of the central bank official responsible for the allocation. The system provided a strong incentive for corruption.

We pressed hard and quite successfully to keep exchange control authority out of South Sudan's new central bank law. I drafted simple auction rules that replaced the allocation of scarce US dollars with twice-weekly auctions of the policy-determined amount of US dollars to the highest bidders and participated in

[20] Having retired from the IMF, I worked in South Sudan under a BearingPoint contract with USAID.

executing the first three auctions. With each auction the official exchange rate (now determined by the auction outcome) depreciated, while the now legal street rate remained more or less unchanged. By the third auction the spread between the official and the street rates had almost vanished, still with no significant change in the street rate. We couldn't have hoped for a better result.

For the fourth auction the acting governor, responding to political pressure, capped the exchange rate above the rate of the previous auction. That was the end of the emerging clean market determination of the exchange rate. While the man on the street had seen no change in the value of the South Sudanese pound, government officials, who were allowed to purchase dollars at its official rate, had suffered from its depreciation. I resigned in disgust.

2.5.2 Afghanistan

When Afghanistan's Taliban government was replaced by the Hamid Karzai government on December 22, 2001 such banking system as had existed had stopped functioning. The three state-owned commercial banks, Bank Millie, Pashtaney, and the Export Promotion Bank, had been largely government pay-masters that counted out the cash to pay government employees, handled the government's foreign payments, and lent their depositors' money to the government and state-owned enterprises, and so on. I joined the IMF Afghan program team as a consultant from the Middle East and Central Asia Department. The inclusion of central bank experts in program teams to fragile states followed the recommendations of the Independent Evaluation Office.

The establishment of the first new private bank was welcomed. Kabulbank was established in 2004 by Sherkhan Farnood, one of Afghanistan's biggest and most successful *hawala* dealers. During the next five years Kabulbank had acquired three times more deposits than the next largest bank in Afghanistan, and more than one-third of all deposits in the banking system. Unfortunately, Mr. Farnood's bank had lent almost all of its nearly $US1 billion worth of deposits to himself and his friends through various dummy companies; when world financial markets went sour, Mr. Farnood's investments soured as well and Kabulbank became deeply insolvent. The failure of Kabulbank was an economic and political crisis of world-class magnitude.[21]

Following a drop in Kabulbank's deposit base of US$1.3 billion by one-third in the first week of September 2010 in reaction to a public feud between its two largest shareholders, President Karzai announced that all depositors' funds in Kabulbank would be protected (guaranteed somehow) and central bank Governor Fitrat assured the public that the central bank would provide Kabulbank with all of the liquidity it needed to honor public demands for their money.

[21] Fitrat (2018).

Though corrupt, Kabulbank had developed an extensive branch network and an electronic deposit capacity that allowed the government to pay its workers via direct deposit to their accounts at Kabulbank. These direct deposits made a major contribution to eliminating ghost workers and salary skimming when wages were paid out in cash. No other bank had yet developed this capacity. In light of President Karzai's announcement of a full deposit "guarantee" and to preserve this valuable electronic deposit capacity we advised DAB to execute a good bank–bad bank split. Thus Kabulbank's deposits with matching assets from the central bank ("lender of last resort" loans) were ultimately transferred to New Kabul Bank along with its electronic salary payment capacity. The split took more than six months to achieve.

The deposit guarantee was a fait accompli, and DAB did not have the expertise to quickly implement an orderly liquidation, but we were determined to instill as much resolution good practice into the process as politically possible. I recommended that the IMF recruit Kat Woolford, a bank resolution expert with whom I had worked in Baghdad, and she moved to Kabul a few weeks later; she remained there for several years.

With Governor Fitrat's encouragement we began to hold regular meetings in the IMF offices in DAB with the World Bank and the US Treasury teams to develop joint recommendations for stemming the run on Kabulbank and for its resolution. At the end of our September 2010 mission we submitted a joint report (a unique and difficult achievement) with our recommendations to our respective head offices. Speaking with one voice added considerable power to our recommendations. The World Bank undertook to fund the development of a more modern payment system (automated clearing house) in which other banks could participate, thus providing an alternative to and competition with Kabulbank.

The underdevelopment of Afghanistan's economy and financial sector made the development of the existing level of electronic messaging and payments a slow process. It had taken DAB, with assistance from BearingPoint/USAID, more than five years to establish electronic communications and reporting between all of its branches and its headquarters in Kabul. The World Bank–funded system was launched in 2013–14.

Moreover, the deep-seated corruption surrounding the scandal (President Karzai's brother was a major shareholder of Kabulbank) seriously impeded the bank's resolution.

In a meeting at the IMF guesthouse near the end of our September mission Kabulbank's internal auditor Raja Gopalakrishnan gave a thoroughly shocking presentation in which he bragged about the skill with which he had designed the fraud and covered up the bank's crimes (insider lending), providing us with a number of detailed examples. He ended with the defiant challenge that: "This is Afghanistan. Kabulbank will never be put into conservatorship. Never! Not as long as we are alive." It was put into conservatorship the next day but without a public announcement (contrary to our recommendations).

The IMF made a new lending program contingent, among other things, on a forensic audit of Kabulbank, an independent public review of the Kabulbank crisis, putting the bank under receivership and its controlled liquidation by selling off its good assets, a serious effort at asset recovery from "borrowers," and prosecuting wrongdoers if criminal activity at Kabulbank were found.

Achievement of these benchmarks came slowly and the approval of a new program with the IMF was significantly delayed. Kabulbank was not put into receivership until April 20, 2011, seven months after it was put into conservatorship, at which time it was split into a good bank and bad bank—Kabulbank in liquidation and a successor New Kabul Bank. Karzai commissioned a quick and dirty report by an Investigative Commission Evaluation of Kabulbank submitted six weeks later, but it was not acceptable to the IMF.

New Kabulbank, "temporarily" owned by the government, was not allowed to extend new loans. Two efforts were made to sell it to private banks with the technical assistance of outside experts. The first produced no acceptable buyers and the second did but was rejected by the government. The bank has continued to improve and expand its electronic payment and deposit capabilities and remains Afghanistan's largest bank.

2.5.3 Summary

The payment capacity of banks to transfer their reserve account deposits at their central bank and the structure of the central banks' lending and deposit facilities for banks, provide the foundation in which interbank money markets develop (or don't). Developing and implementing interbank payment systems, securities registries, and settlement systems takes a few years; the adoption of the instruments by which central banks influence the liquidity of their banks (standing deposit and credit facilities, open market operations, and mandatory reserve requirements) can and should be implemented early on. The development of, or evolution to, market allocation of credit and management of liquidity requires the adoption of central bank instruments and facilities that promote such developments by making central bank credit and deposits the second choice to the market alternatives. But it also requires that banks develop systems for evaluating the creditworthiness of their customers and for managing their exposures to default risk.

Coordinating assistance and policy advice with other international bodies, such as the World Bank, is always wise, to maximize the benefit of given assistance resources and to help fill gaps in counterpart capabilities. But where there is political resistance, often associated with corruption, to desirable reforms or measures, coordinating policy advice with other aid agencies can be very helpful in gaining counterparty agreement, while conflicting advice can be very detrimental.

References

Abrams, R.K. 1995. "The Design and Printing of Bank Notes: Considerations When Introducing a New Currency." IMF Working Paper 95/26. International Monetary Fund, Washington, DC.

Coats, W. 2007a. "Monetary Policy Issues in Post-Conflict Economies," in J.K. Boyce and M. O'Donnell (Eds.), *Peace and the Public Purse: Economic Policies for Postwar Statebuilding*. London: Rienner.

Coats, W. 2007b. *One Currency for Bosnia: Creating the Central Bank of Bosnia and Herzegovina*. Ottawa, IL: Jameson Books.

Coats, W. and A. Liuksila. 1999. "Institutional and Legal Impediments to Efficient Insolvent Bank Resolution and Ways to Overcome Them." Paper presented at the USAID/Barents Conference on Banking Supervision in Sofia, Bulgaria, July 9, 1999. https://works.bepress.com/warren_coats/17/ (last accessed July 16, 2020).

Coats, W. and H. Schiffman. 1995. "Key Issues in Reform of Central Bank Legislation," International Monetary Fund, Washington, DC.

Fitrat, A.Q. 2018. *The Tragedy of Kabul Bank*. New York: Page Publishing.

IMF (International Monetary Fund). 2003. Islamic State of Afghanistan: Rebuilding a Macroeconomic Framework for Reconstruction and Growth. IMF Country Report No. 03/299 (September).

13

Monetary and Exchange Rate Policy in Fragile States

Christopher Adam and James Wilson

1. Introduction: The Stabilization Challenge in Fragile States

An effective monetary policy framework is one that delivers a credible anchor for low and stable inflation, provides a capacity to balance the desire to insulate and smooth consumption in the face of external and domestic shocks against adjustment when required, and does so in a manner that supports efficient domestic revenue mobilization, public investment, and the deepening of domestic financial markets.

Though this summary may describe monetary regimes in many mature, stable economies, it is a more challenging standard for fragile states where state capacity is limited and/or political legitimacy is challenged and where the risks of full-blown state failure, in which the rule of law has limited traction, the normal functioning of the state can no longer be presumed, and economic, social, and political anarchy prevails. Most fragile states are assailed by frequent and sizeable economic shocks and often exist on or close to the margins of open conflict and state failure. State fragility and failure are also highly correlated with low average incomes, thin markets in goods and assets, widespread market failure and limited technical and regulatory capacity. These associated economic distortions alter the stabilization challenge in three main ways. First, and most obviously, the magnitude and composition of shocks differ. In addition to the conventional terms-of-trade and/or climate-related shocks, fragile states are more likely to have to deal with shocks that emanate from, and interact with, the risks and consequences of civil or cross-border conflict. Moreover, these shocks and their effects will be amplified by weak state capacity—most obviously in the macroeconomic domain by the absence of effective institutions of fiscal control—which, in turn, undermines resilience.

Second, the capacity for countercyclical action is often severely compromised. Automatic fiscal stabilizers, which are typically a product of broad and mature fiscal systems, are absent; access to international private capital markets is generally limited; while domestic debt markets tend to be extremely thin. As a consequence,

Christopher Adam and James Wilson, *Monetary and Exchange Rate Policy in Fragile States* In: *Macroeconomic Policy in Fragile States.* Edited by: Ralph Chami, Raphael Espinoza, and Peter Montiel, Oxford University Press (2021).

DOI: 10.1093/oso/9780198853091.003.0013

capital flows to and from fragile states are often highly procyclical: liquidity drains from debt markets, often dramatically in the form of "sudden stops," while the risk premiums demanded by investors move sharply against debtors. This is true not just for debt markets but also for non-debt sources of private financing, including remittances. One important implication is the opportunity for official capital flows to lean against the procyclicality of private capital flows, by directly providing public funds and by offering implicit partial guarantees to private capital. The issue for donors and the international financial institutions (IFIs), of course, is one of adequate safeguards. As concerns about corruption and transparency have increased, and as donors have become more risk averse in the face of taxpayers' aid fatigue, bilateral official flows have themselves become more procyclical. Effective countercyclical official flows to low-income and fragile states are only feasible if recipient governments can commit to a politically credible and economically coherent macroeconomic framework, a task which, as history suggests, is extremely difficult in times of state fragility and limited capacity.

This difficulty reflects, in part, the third important difference. Fragility shortens horizons, undermining policymakers' incentives to balance current against future outcomes. Hence arises the temptation to increase borrowing on unattractive terms and to pursue macroeconomic stabilization through short-term political expediency, for example by scaling back spending on operations and maintenance of the public capital stock (where there are few votes), exploiting low-hanging fruit in terms of tax grabs, and discounting the adverse effects of future inflation on growth and investment in favor of short-term seigniorage revenue.

In chronically weak states, choices made by governments and their central banks over the exchange rate regime and the conduct of monetary policy will rarely be fundamental drivers of deep structural fragility, although they may present as the proximate causes. Nor are choices in this domain likely to be decisive in driving the recovery from conflict or extreme fragility: the factors leading to sustainable exits lie elsewhere, principally in the political settlement and in the fiscal domain. The argument we wish to make in this chapter, however, is that although the roots and fundamental determinants of state fragility lie elsewhere, decisions around monetary and exchange rate policies do play an important role in affecting movements into fragility, they shape exit options, and they can directly influence the risks of falling back into fragility and conflict. Moreover, choices in the monetary and exchange rate domain also affect the likely distribution of rents, including those generated by policy distortions themselves. In doing so, they alter the balance of power and can decisively shift the points of influence for policy, including by outside agents.

Our aim in this chapter is to offer a brief review of monetary and exchange rate policy aspects of countries' descent into, and exit from, fragility (as well as relapses back into fragility) and to use this to draw out some key normative policy lessons for fragile countries and their external partners. This task is not straightforward, for at least two reasons. First, in a short chapter like this we cannot do justice to individual country cases, all of which differ in important and less important ways. Second, there is relatively little evidence and data on sustained exits from fragility, at least from those countries currently classified by the World Bank and others as fragile (in some sense the raw material for this volume). With these caveats in mind, section 2 starts with a brief statistical description of monetary and exchange rate regimes amongst those countries currently classified as fragile states, and section 3 offers simple analytical narratives on how formerly stable monetary regimes are undermined in the face of increased state fragility. Section 4 describes policy choices in the context of the exit from fragility, including post-conflict settings where the priority is on the restoration of macroeconomic balance. The chapter concludes in section 5 by recapping some key policy lessons.

2. Summary Evidence: Monetary and Exchange Rate Regimes in Fragile States

To set the scene for the discussion to follow, we start by describing the evolution of *de facto* exchange rate and monetary policy choices in those fragile and non-fragile states that make up the 84 low- and lower-middle-income countries around the world for the period from 2005 to 2018,[1] using data from the IMF's *Annual Report on Exchange Arrangements and Exchange Restrictions* and the World Bank's Harmonized List of Fragile Situations.[2] We subdivide this set into four mutually exclusive groups, the first of which consists of the 32 countries that have never been classed as fragile throughout this period—denoted as *Never Fragile*. Of the remaining 52 countries that have been classified by the World Bank as fragile in at least one year, 17 are classified as fragile over the entire period—the *Always Fragile* group—while the remainder are further divided between those that, on average, have experienced an improvement in their Country Policy and Institutional Assessment (CPIA) rating in the second half of the period compared to the first half—*Improvers* (18 countries)[3]—and those that have seen deterioration—*Decliners* (17 countries). Individual countries are listed in the Annex.

A natural way to classify monetary and exchange rate instruments and policy choices is in terms of the trilemma—the idea that beyond the short-run, policy-makers cannot simultaneously target the nominal exchange rate, run an activist

[1] Using "World Bank Country and Lending Groups" classifications: https://datahelpdesk.worldbank.org/knowledgebase/articles/906519-world-bank-country-and-lending-groups (last accessed July 16, 2020).

[2] From 2004–08, the World Bank classification was known as Low-Income Countries Under Stress (LICUS) List. In 2009–10, it was renamed the Fragile States List, before taking its current form in 2011.

[3] *Improvers* are those countries where their average Country Policy and Institutional Assessment score for the period 2012–18 is higher than in the period 2005–11, and vice versa.

monetary policy and maintain an open capital account. They must ultimately choose which objective to abandon. In practice, experience suggests it is hard to limit *de facto* cross-border private capital flows, both inflows and particularly outflows, even when official capital controls are in place. Hence the resolution of the trilemma boils down to the strength of policymakers' commitment to a choice between targeting the nominal exchange rate—an external anchor—or letting the exchange rate float as a complement to an activist monetary policy (a domestic anchor). In terms of stabilization policy, this choice has a direct corollary in the debate between the relative efficacy of exchange rate-based stabilization (ERBS) versus money-based stabilization (MBS) as described in Calvo and Vegh (1999), amongst others.

In reality, however, as Ghosh et al. (2016) and others have noted, the choice of anchor is much less stark in fragile states where cross-border capital flows behave in a rather different manner than our textbook description of the trilemma suggests. Cross-border private capital flows play an important role in fragile states but do so in highly asymmetric and segmented ways. First, in the context of macroeconomic stabilization and monetary policy, formal *de jure* financial capital mobility tends to be relatively inelastic with respect to return differentials, so that portfolio investors do not appear to react aggressively to arbitrage opportunities that emerge between domestic and foreign assets. Low *de facto* substitutability in these cases reflects in part structural weaknesses in domestic financial markets. The first weakness is what Mishra and Montiel (2013) describe as the weak and unreliable transmission mechanism in low-income countries, which means that movements in policy interest rates are very imperfectly transmitted even into the short end of domestic asset markets. The second is that foreign investors face prohibitive liquidity risks, such that it may be difficult to repatriate capital inflows and thereby realize arbitrage gains; hence even if the transmission mechanism is weak, the interest sensitivity of capital inflows is low. In the textbook trilemma, when domestic and foreign bonds are imperfect substitutes, domestic monetary policy actions are not immediately and fully neutralized by offsetting private capital flows, which creates space for authorities to run an activist monetary policy *and* target the exchange rate in pursuit of macroeconomic stabilization over the short to medium term as described by Ghosh et al. (2016). As we discuss, this "domestic-anchor-with-exchange-rate-management" remains a popular, if not the dominant, *de facto* regime choice in a range of former fragile lower-income frontier economies such as Ghana, Uganda, and Kenya.

But this is only part of the story. The bigger element of *de facto* capital mobility in fragile states is capital flight. In the sense discussed by Collier et al. (2001) and Ajayi and Ndikumana (2015), the consequences of capital flight are primarily felt in the real economy via the impact on investment (in human and physical capital) and the external balance, rather than on short-term macroeconomic management. The element of capital flight which is decisive from a macroeconomic management perspective is, however, expectations-driven shifts in the demand for domestic money. Adverse shifts in the demand for money—whether this is the asset demand or transactions demand—are frequently decisive proximate elements in the collapse of currencies and/or severe inflation, but, equally, positive shifts are often central to supporting recovery from fragility.

Before turning to the choices confronting fragile states, we describe prevailing trends among low- and lower-middle-income countries that have never been categorized as fragile, those which may be expected to have enjoyed an associated level of political, institutional, and macroeconomic stability. During the past decade there has been a modest shift from external exchange rate anchors towards domestic anchors, although the former remain the predominant choice for low- and lower-middle-income countries. Among those adopting a domestic anchor, however, there has been a shift away from conventional money aggregate anchors to hybrid (interest-rate based) and full-fledged inflation targeting regimes. By 2018 nearly 20 percent of the sample were operating inflation targeting regimes, compared to only 3 percent in 2005 (see also IMF, 2015).

At the same time, however, as shown in Figure 13.1 these same countries have drifted towards greater exchange rate management, with only 20 percent of countries adopting a *de facto* floating regime. There has been a marked move towards operating with a soft peg, at the expense of more discretionary managed arrangements, although it is likely that this behaviour, which is marked from 2015 onwards, reflects resistance to nominal exchange rate adjustment as the commodity supercycle came to an end.

Among the *Always Fragile* group, almost 60 percent of countries declare an explicit exchange rate anchor for monetary policy on a *de jure* basis. Unsurprisingly, no *Always Fragile* countries have moved to adopt inflation-targeting regimes. But

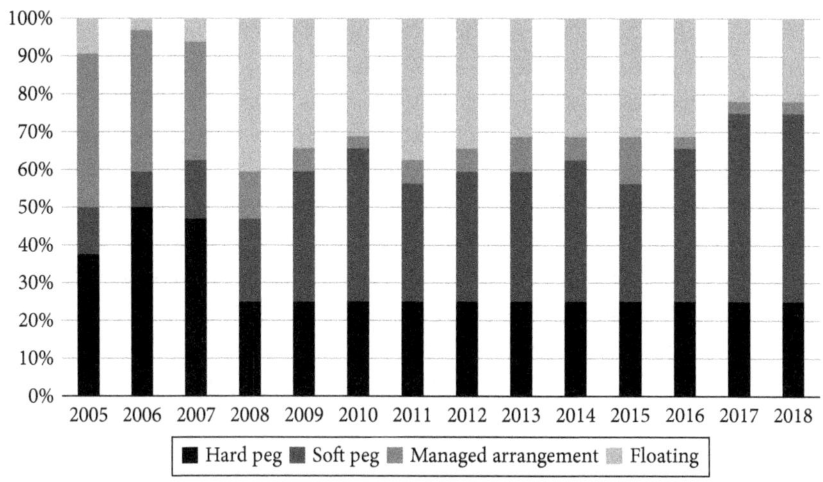

Figure 13.1 De Facto Exchange Rate Regimes: "Never Fragile" Countries

Notes: The exchange rate regime classifications taken from the IMF's Annual Report on Exchange Arrangements and Exchange Restrictions. 'Hard peg' covers regimes where there is no separate legal tender or a currency board arrangement; 'soft peg' covers conventional pegs, pegs within horizontal bands, stabilised arrangements, crawling pegs, and crawl-like arrangements; 'floating' covers floating and free-floating regimes; while 'managed arrangement' captures the residual group where flexible exchange rates are actively managed through regular central bank interventions.

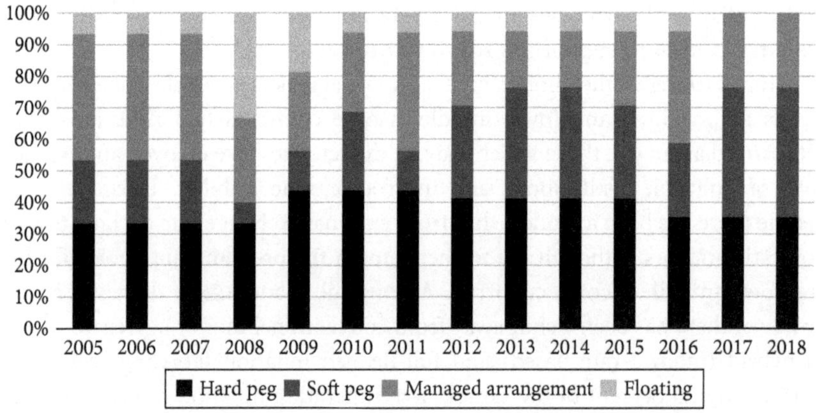

Figure 13.2 De Facto Exchange Rate Regimes: "Always Fragile" Countries

Notes: 'Hard peg' covers regimes where there is no separate legal tender or a currency board arrangement; 'soft peg' covers conventional pegs, pegs within horizontal bands, stabilised arrangements, crawling pegs, and crawl-like arrangements; 'floating' covers floating and free-floating regimes; while 'managed arrangement' captures the residual group where flexible exchange rates are actively managed through regular central bank interventions.

again, as the *de jure* classification presented in Figure 13.2 indicates, there has been a decisive shift towards fixed regimes on a *de facto* basis, with the proportion of soft and hard peg exchange rate regimes increasing over the period. This move away from managed floating regimes towards greater management of the exchange rate suggests an even stronger "fear of floating" (or "inability to float") motive in fragile states. As we discuss below, this increasing reluctance to let the nominal exchange rate fluctuate may be a function of the high domestic liability dollarization among many of these countries.

For those countries that have transitioned out of and into fragility, the picture is as we would expect. In terms of the broad stance of monetary policy regimes, the *Improver* group displays a (weak) convergence towards the patterns observed in the *Never Fragile* group, while the *Decliners* converge on the *Always Fragile* group. However, both groups show the same strong tendency towards fixed exchange rate regimes, suggesting that the transition out of fragility is likely to be extended because rebuilding the institutional framework necessary to support a *de facto* floating exchange rate regime takes time.

Broadly speaking, however, these data suggest that fixed or heavily managed exchange rates remain the predominant nominal anchor for fragile states, either by choice or by default. In some cases, this is due to their membership in long-standing institutional monetary structures, notably the CFA Franc zones in West and Central Africa; but even accounting for these countries, the evidence suggests increasing divergence between fragile states and broader global trends towards greater reliance on domestically anchored and discretionary monetary policy frameworks (IMF, 2015).

3. Descent into Fragility: Alternative Monetary and Exchange Rate Pathologies

The origins and drivers of state fragility are varied, but their manifestation in the monetary policy domain has a number of common features. A recognizable narrative runs as follows.[4] As state structures come under stress and the broader economic policy regime becomes increasingly distorted, monetary policy regimes become dysfunctional. The monetary authorities—usually national central banks—are progressively asked to do "too much" and eventually (and inevitably) fail to deliver on most if not all of these multiple objectives, including the core monetary objective of providing an effective nominal anchor for prices. Thus central banks typically get drawn into administering heavily managed exchange rates (often in situations of severe rationing so that parallel markets in foreign exchange emerge); setting administered interest rates, typically far below market-clearing values; directing the allocation of domestic credit between sectors, in many cases through state-dominated and oligopolistic banking systems whose operations are often limited to mobilizing private savings for on-lending to government and state-owned enterprises at highly repressed rates;[5] and—crucially—providing direct monetary financing of the budget deficit. High and variable inflation becomes pervasive and parallel markets for foreign exchange flourish, further distorting incentives for investment and encouraging widespread rent-seeking. Central to this failure is the pressure on central banks to finance fiscal deficits from their own balance sheets. As capital flight and currency substitution take hold, the capacity for noninflationary deficit financing disappears and the monetary system risks collapse under the pressure of fiscal dominance, which renders ineffectual any formal distinction between fiscal and monetary policy.

Whether starting from an external or domestic anchor, the proximate cause of an unravelling is usually a loss of fiscal control, which in turn reflects deeper pressures on the state. On the one side, state fragility is associated with falling private investment, lower incomes, and the diversion of economic activity into subsistence and barter shrinking the tax base while the erosion of the social contract around taxation will lead to increased corruption and tax evasion, further lowering revenue mobilization. On the other side of the ledger, increased short-term fiscal needs (which are likely to be extreme in the case of conflict) and/or increased predation of fiscal resources by the elite or other groups mean increased spending pressures. These may initially be accommodated by reallocation of public expenditure away from infrastructure investment and its operation and

[4] See, for example, Honohan and O'Connell (1997).

[5] Collier and Gunning's (1991) description of the banking system in Tanzania in the early 1980s perfectly captures this dysfunctionality.

maintenance, but invariably aggregate spending pressures also build as the institutions of control erode. At the same time, access to external finance diminishes, both from the domestic private sector and from official and creditors. What happens next in these circumstances is well understood, although the precise pathology will depend on the nominal exchange rate regime.

3.1 From Managed/Flexible Rates to Crisis

Adam (1995) and Adam et al. (2008) describe these dynamics in situations from an initial configuration of a (managed) floating regime, where the fiscal shock of fragility worsens the trade-off between seigniorage revenues and the pursuit of low and stable inflation. Fragility triggers two forces. First, the combination of the pressure to spend and a rise in the discount rate (which dampens the disutility from future inflation) tilts government preferences in favor of higher inflation and higher seigniorage. The higher rate of growth of base money raises seigniorage revenue in the short term, but this is temporary; agents adjust their demand for money in response to higher actual and expected inflation. Second, as fragility increases, private agents disengage from the formal economy and seek opportunities for capital flight and currency substitution. These effects induce a further shift out of domestic currency and an increase in the inflation elasticity of the demand for money. As a result, transitional seigniorage revenue shrinks further. As Adam et al. (2008) show, the economy can suddenly experience an explosive path for inflation expectations, which lays the foundations for an incipient hyperinflation cycle and eventual dollarization, such as was observed in Zimbabwe in the early 2000s (see Box 13.1).

Box 13.1 Fragility and Currency Collapse: Zimbabwe

Following almost 20 years of steady growth since independence in 1980, macroeconomic stability began to unravel in the late 1990s. Fiscal control weakened substantially, fuelled in part by Zimbabwe's involvement in the conflict in the Democratic Republic of Congo. A widening fiscal deficit, accompanied by the rapid buildup of quasi-fiscal losses by the Reserve Bank of Zimbabwe, (Munoz, 2007) saw capital flight—both financial and human—accelerate. Following a number of failed attempts at conventional stabilization (Kovanen, 2004), Zimbabwe was by the mid-2000s in the grip of a full-blown hyperinflation (Coorey, 2007) as money demand collapsed, leading to eventual demonetization of the economy.

In 2009 the government abandoned the Zimbabwean dollar and authorized several foreign currencies as legal tender, with the US dollar quickly emerging as the *de facto* dominant currency. The stabilizing effects of dollarization were dramatic and quickly felt: inflation rapidly settled at below 5 percent per annum; real GDP rebounded and returned to a reasonable growth path, while previous capital outflows were reversed and the banking system enjoyed a period of significant re-monetization.

However, significant structural problems soon started to emerge. The appreciation of the US dollar against the South African rand led to a large overvaluation of the real exchange rate—approximately 75 percent of exports were going to South Africa—and the resulting trade deficit triggered dollar outflows. The continued fragility of the political situation meant that diaspora remittances, foreign aid, and foreign investment remained weak so that as the current account deteriorated, dollar liquidity was squeezed. With stubbornly high public expenditure and weakening revenue mobilization, the authorities lacked the capacity and will to engineer the internal devaluation required to restore macroeconomic stability. The fiscal balance began to deteriorate, declining from a nearly balanced budget in 2009, when dollarization commenced, to a deficit of close to 15 percent by 2017/18 (Mlambo, 2018).

Absent sufficient fiscal adjustment and access to external debt markets, the government returned to forms of domestic financing that in effect re-introduced a domestic currency, predominantly in the form of "real term gross settlement" (RTGS) balances: direct electronic reserve money deposits to bank accounts, which could be used for settlement but could not be withdrawn as physical cash. Through this, the monetary base quickly exceeded the underlying official foreign reserve holdings. Unsurprisingly, private agents increasingly called into question the credibility of the new alternative currency.

Parallel markets started to show the RTGS money trading at a large discount to US dollars, and in 2019 official annual inflation figures accelerated to beyond 100 percent. In response, the central bank governor announced that the newly created near money would be merged into a new currency called the RTGS dollar, which would operate as a managed float against the US dollar; and ultimately the use of foreign currency was abolished, ending the multicurrency system and reversing the dollarization policy 10 years after its introduction. The RTGS dollar became the sole legal tender in Zimbabwe, acting as a bridge to the introduction of a sovereign currency, despite very low foreign exchange reserves.

The severe negative consequences of full dollarization are starkly illustrated here. Faced with an overvalued real exchange rate, a lack of structural reforms, and rapidly deteriorating public finances, the government of Zimbabwe has been unable or unwilling to impose the fiscal discipline required by the monetary regime. Fiscal dominance re-emerged through the back door: parallels with the mid-2000s re-emerged, in particular the steep rise in central bank liabilities to the domestic banking sector and central bank claims on the government. As at the time of writing, it remains unclear whether the authorities will be successful in stabilizing the value of the new currency.

3.2 From Fixed Rates to Crisis

In many fragile states the exchange rate remains the notional nominal anchor for the system, even if the authorities are unable or unwilling to submit to the fiscal discipline of an exchange rate anchor. As a result, when fiscal discipline fails, the familiar dynamics of a speculative attack on the currency take over. As fiscal incompatibility becomes entrenched (in the sense that holders of domestic financial assets do not expect an immediate and sufficient restoration of the fiscal balance), the demand for foreign exchange at the prevailing official rate increases in anticipation of a run on reserves and/or a discrete devaluation. Absent a credible nominal (and real) devaluation, the central bank will typically move to restrict net foreign exchange demand—increasing surrender requirements on exporters and rationing foreign exchange to importers—which, in turn, leads to the emergence of parallel (black) markets in foreign exchange, fueled by both current account and capital market factors. As fiscal imbalances persist and are monetized, the real and nominal official rates become progressively overvalued, foreign exchange becomes increasingly scarce and the parallel market premium increases. Domestic inflation then tends to track the parallel market exchange rate so that the system loses its nominal anchor. With adjustment to external shocks coming through the (endogenous) rationing of foreign exchange and goods, the central bank is drawn into administrative allocation of foreign exchange, leaving the ground fertile for pervasive rent-seeking, with the official exchange rate becoming an instrument of patronage rather than one of macroeconomic management.

These quasi-rents (transfers from those selling foreign exchange at the official rate to those granted access to buy at that rate) can be large. In aggregate the realized value of rents will equal the parallel market premium times the volume of *net* sales of foreign exchange to importers (or re-sellers) at the official exchange rate. Data on net sales are difficult to estimate but some historical estimates may give a sense of the scale. Morris' (1995) classic paper on parallel markets, exchange rate unification, and inflation in Uganda suggests that on the eve of exchange rate unification net sales by Bank of Uganda to the private sector were on the order of 30 percent of exports which in turn were approximately 15 percent of GDP. With the premium at that stage between 100 percent and 200 percent of the official rate this suggests the value of rents transferred to those with access to the official market of between 5 percent and 10 percent in GDP. Absent detailed microeconomic evidence on the structure and operation of foreign exchange markets as the parallel market emerges, it is difficult to generalize from Morris (1995). Nonetheless, similar work by Pinto (1989) and Kiguel and O'Connell (1995) for Ghana and Tanzania at the time would put the value of rents in the same ballpark.

3.3 Denouement: Domestic Currency Recovery or *de facto* Dollarization

Extremely high parallel exchange rate premiums, and the quasi-rents they generate, are, as with hyperinflation episodes, self-limiting and hence relatively temporary. Clearly one possible end point, which we discuss in section 4, is that policy measures are put in place and/or external factors change sufficiently to eliminate the excess supply of domestic money and restore exchange rate stability in the context of a market-clearing rate (which could entail the restoration of either a domestic anchor or credible external anchor). If policy changes are not forthcoming, however, inflation will continue to accelerate and/or the premium will continue to increase as a progressively smaller share of export earnings passes through the official foreign exchange market. The natural culmination of both processes is the effective marginalization of the domestic currency and *de facto* dollarization of the economy as firms and households turn to foreign currencies to hedge their savings against inflation (dollarization) and as a means of exchange (currency substitution).

Dollarization may be total and formalized where the domestic currency is replaced in its entirety as legal tender, as in the cases of Zimbabwe or Ecuador or, more commonly, *de facto* in the sense that the use of foreign currency is sufficiently widespread that domestic monetary policy is effectively powerless. Both are common occurrences in fragile states: even outside of the CFA franc zones, a large proportion of fragile states operate with high and highly persistent levels of *de facto* dollarization (Mecagni et al., 2015).

By effectively removing the domestic deficit financing option—the key instrument of fiscal dominance—dollarization typically delivers powerful inflation stabilization, at least in the short term. The bigger question is how effective (enforced) dollarization is in laying the foundations for broader macroeconomic, political, and institutional stabilization and recovery. Success in this respect requires navigation of two major challenges. The first concerns the process of stabilization itself while the second, related issue concerns the process of dedollarization and the challenges of exiting from dollarization towards the re-introduction of a renewed domestic monetary regime, assuming this is an objective.

We discuss the latter in the next section. On the former, the key feature of dollarization is that it removes the scope for an independent monetary policy, eliminates seigniorage revenues, and curtails the central bank's ability to fulfil its "lender of last resort" function. But the key challenge, as is well understood from the literature on exchange rate-based stabilization, is that dollarization leverages up the pressure on fiscal policy by delegating to it primary responsibility for ensuring macroeconomic stabilization through its influence on aggregate demand (that is, the internal devaluation channel). Once authorities deviate from the strict fiscal policy path that dollarization demands, whether voluntarily or involuntarily, the consequences can become severe. Moreover, the effects can be felt acutely; whereas large fiscal mismanagement in a floating regime would be immediately punished through movements in the exchange rate, under the dollarized arrangement it is able to persist and real exchange rate imbalances are allowed to build until the situation becomes untenable. Once the policy can no longer be sustained, the ensuing crisis can often have severe consequences for macroeconomic, political, and social stability. The fiscal space available will depend partly on the vulnerability of the economy to shocks, while the ability to stay within this space will depend upon the institutional capacity to manage a sustainable fiscal policy; two features, as noted above, that are conspicuous by their absence in fragile states. Political fragility, combined with persistent external imbalances, has contributed to the recent failure of dollarization in Zimbabwe to successfully and credibly discipline economic policy and anchor the system, resulting in renewed fiscal dominance—exactly what the policy was intended to prevent (see Box 13.1).[6]

4. Exiting, Recovery, and Relapse

The next step in the analysis is to examine monetary and exchange regimes of countries that exit from fragility. This is easier said than done since while around two thirds of the countries ever classed as fragile in the World Bank's sample have moved in and out of fragility at some point—in the sense that their fragility "score" moved from one side to the other of the cut-off used by the World Bank—there are very few cases of sustained exit. Of those countries that were classified as fragile at some point in the sample period, 13 countries have graduated from fragility.[7] Of these, five reverted to hard-peg external anchors (including currency boards and institutional hard pegs such as the CFA franc) and the remainder have adopted some form of domestic anchor, four of which have adopted monetary targets.

An alternative perspective on the recovery from currency crises can be taken from data on the *de facto* exchange rate arrangements that countries followed immediately prior to and in the aftermath of exchange rate crises, using the data from Ilzetzki et al. (2017). Lacking comparable data on fragility, a country is deemed to be in crisis if it is classified by Ilzetzki et al. (2017) as having a currency that is "freely falling," which corresponds to cases where the 12-month inflation

[6] Not all dollarization episodes have played out in this manner, with Ecuador standing as the key counter-example, although this probably owes more to the greater political stability and pre-existing institutional framework as well as the crucial establishment of credible fiscal prudential rules and fiscal stabilization funds at the outset of dollarization (see Anderson, 2016; Del Cristo and Gomez-Puig, 2016).

[7] Where graduation implies three or more years of "non-fragile" Country Policy and Institutional Assessment scores.

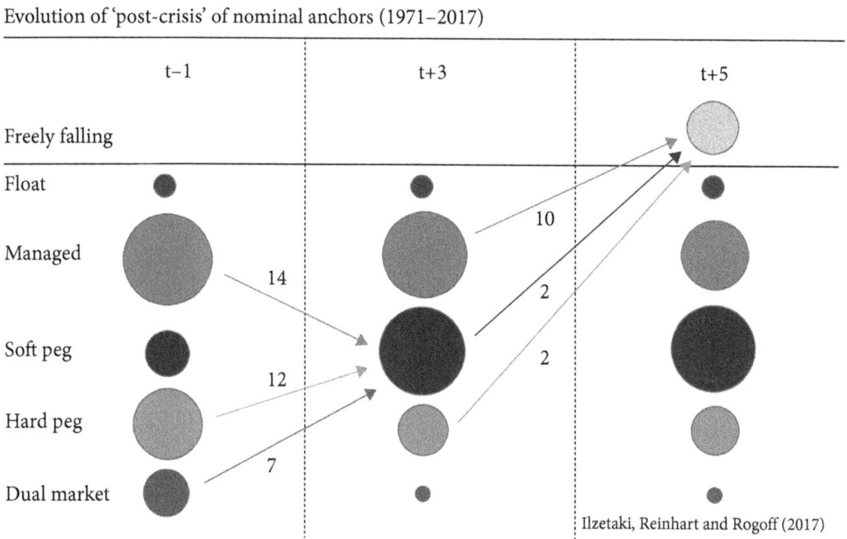

Figure 13.3 Evolution of "Post-Crisis" of Nominal Anchors (1971–2017)
Note: The areas of the circles are scaled to represent the number of countries in each group and the numbers indicate the number of transitions between groups.

rate exceeds 40 percent[8] and hence provides a reasonable proxy for macroeconomic fragility. To be classified as "exiting fragility" the final period of crisis must be followed by three consecutive years where the country doesn't fall back into a freely falling regime.[9]

Figure 13.3 shows the distribution of regimes immediately prior to the freely falling period (period t-1), and the evolution of *de facto* nominal anchors three and five years after the exit. The sample tracks the post-Bretton Woods era (1971–) and consists of 106 separate cases of lapses into monetary/exchange rate crisis or fragility, and subsequent exits.[10] The freely falling periods recorded vary in length from 1 to 28 years,[11] and the median length of a freely falling regime is three years.

Three features emerge from Figure 13.3. First, managed floats are the regime type most associated with currency crises, representing 42 percent of pre-crisis instances in the sample, even though managed floats only register 19 percent of the unconditional sample[12] in the post-Bretton Woods era. Within five years of the last freely falling episode, 15 percent of countries fell back into free fall. When this period is extended to 10 years, 25 percent of countries had experienced another

[8] This may be a country with a floating exchange rate or a fixed official rate with either multiple devaluations and/or a growing parallel market premium.

[9] In other words, a freely falling country at period t exits fragility if and only if there is no freely falling episode in periods $t+1$, $t+2$, and $t+3$.

[10] These numbers are not the same because some countries have not exited their freely falling phase, while some countries were already in a freely falling phase at the beginning of the sample period.

[11] Democratic Republic of Congo from 1975–2002.

[12] Once freely falling cases are excluded.

freely falling episode. Second, after the exit from a currency crisis, the most common regime choices are for a soft exchange rate peg and a managed float (by construction, freely falling is not an option in period t+3). Notably the tendency to adopt a soft peg is more than double what it was for the pre-crisis period. The first set of arrows shows how the growth in soft pegs has come from both ends of the spectrum: failed hard pegs and failed managed regimes. Soft pegs are seen as desirable in a post-crisis because of the increased exchange rate stability while the economy remains vulnerable as it attempts to recover from the high inflation episode. Finally, managed regimes in the post-crisis period appear more likely to precipitate a fall back into fragility. The data indicate that countries are sometimes too quick to move back to more of a market-determined exchange rate. Countries that adopt a soft peg post-crisis appear to reduce their risk of slipping back into a freely falling regime. The desire to quickly adopt or return to a floating regime may be part of a signalling measure by the state to demonstrate that monetary conditions have stabilized, or may be influenced by structural adjustment programs that encourage flexible exchange rates. Figure 13.3 suggests that often this decision is made prematurely and that countries should be careful not to accelerate this process. It is likely that there is persistence in some of the factors that precipitated the initial crisis, such that the economy remains vulnerable for several years in the aftermath. As a result, in many cases there will be an absence of the institutional capacity and stability necessary to support a managed float in the short to medium term.

4.1 De-dollarization and the Transition from Fixed Exchange Rates

Given the difficulties that high levels of dollarization present, countries may look to reduce its extent and restore a more central role for the domestic currency. Flexible exchange rates provide a greater degree of monetary policy autonomy, allowing for greater flexibility in responding to external shocks. But flexible rates also reduce the risks of one-way bets against currencies, dampening incentives for destabilizing short-term capital flows; they eliminate the build-up of quasi-rents that are generated by (misaligned) pegged rates; and by discouraging the accumulation of unhedged exchange rate risks they demand more effective management of exchange rate and relative price risks by the private sector.

However, the historical evidence does not point to many successful de-dollarizations. Reinhart et al. (2003) examine 85 cases over 1980–2001 where countries sought to dedollarize, finding only four cases where countries managed to achieve large and lasting declines in domestic dollarization,[13] and in two of these cases there were heavy costs in financial disintermediation or capital flight.

[13] Israel (1985), Mexico (1982 – forced conversion), Poland (1990), and Pakistan (1999).

Likewise, Mongardini (1999) and Mecagni et al. (2015) find strong evidence for "ratchet effects" in deposit dollarization, such that beyond a certain threshold the ratio remains stubbornly high. Mecagni et al. (2015) observe this persistence across Sub-Saharan Africa, with *Always Fragile* countries seeing an increase in their deposit dollarization ratios during the period 2001–12. The notable dedollarization success stories of the past two decades have been in Latin America, with progress attributed to macroeconomic stability, prudential measures, and development of the local capital market (Catão and Terrones, 2016; García-Escribano, 2010, 2011). Some of the prudential measures include higher provisioning and capital requirements for US dollar loans, asymmetric reserve requirement ratios, higher liquidity requirements on US dollar liabilities, and tightening limits on banks' net open positions.

This evidence suggests that moving from heavily dollarized and pegged regimes towards more flexible exchange rate regimes is difficult and often extremely protracted, even though the objectives for doing so seem clear, particularly in post-fragile settings. The literature is replete with lessons on the requirements for successful exchange rate transitions (for example, Ötker-Robe and Vávra, 2007; Maehle et al., 2013).

Aside from the fundamental requirement that the authorities establish and communicate a coherent alternative domestic anchor for inflation, the first key element of a transition to flexible rates is the development of a deeper and more liquid foreign exchange market, in which the central banks progressively exit from market-making. For many fragile states, the central bank will remain a key market participant on the sell side in the foreign exchange market, managing government budget support and other official aid flows, which requires a coherent policy on foreign exchange intervention that clearly distinguishes between structural interventions to manage aid flows and conventional discretionary actions aimed at managing exchange rate volatility.

There is a deep and difficult chicken-and-egg problem with exchange rate transitions: flexibility requires deep markets but deep markets are lubricated and supported by flexibility. As the lessons from successful transitions show (Ötker-Robe and Vávra, 2007), this tension requires time to resolve: successful transitions tend to emerge not from crisis but from intent, and they occur gradually by providing increasingly more flexible forms of intermediate regimes in the interim period so as to prepare for an orderly exit, thereby reducing the scope for policy reversals. By contrast, a premature introduction of exchange rate flexibility can be damaging. Advance preparation is essential in ensuring a smooth and successful regime change, and though too much emphasis on meeting all preconditions may unduly prolong the move to a float, the experiences with disorderly exits underscore the high premium assigned by markets to the need for the transition to be built around a coherent domestically anchored macroeconomic framework. We now turn to this challenge.

4.2 Reserve Money Programs and the Exit from Fragility

One of the striking themes in the economic history of Sub-Saharan Africa is how many of the successful exits from fragility have been built around money-based stabilization programs, often away from severely distorted regimes characterized by heavily administered official exchange rates. In particular, Reserve Money (RM)-based programs have played a central role in the stabilization efforts of many fragile and post-fragile low-income countries during the 1990s and early 2000s including Ghana, Zambia, Uganda, Nigeria, Tanzania and Mozambique (see Adam et al., 2018; IMF, 2015; Coorey et al., 2007). Few RM programs have proceeded smoothly—most RM-based country programs with the IMF suffered setbacks and re-negotiation, with not a few going severely off track—but it remains the case that the successful ones have played a decisive role in anchoring inflation (and inflation expectations) in the aftermath of periods of weak economic performance. In doing so, they have cleared the ground for the authorities to put in place broader reform measures to support the exit from fragility.

RM programming is a rule-based and essentially non-discretionary approach to the conduct of monetary policy (see Box 13.2). Among fragile states, RM programs are characterized by an overwhelming weight placed on the price stabilization objective relative to concerns about output stabilization and the use of simple, if unsubtle, mechanisms of fiscal control, such as cash budget mechanisms (see Adam and Bevan, 1999 and Stasavage and Moyo, 2000). RM programming is well designed for anchoring inflation in flexible or managed exchange rate regimes in which the transactions of government play an important role in the structural generation of liquidity and where the latent risk of fiscal dominance is large and ever-present. The corollary to the focus on inflation control is, of course, that the authorities place relatively little weight on output stabilization and are less concerned about instrument volatility (which might be the case if the weight on output stabilization is small, even in the short-run). The low weight on output stabilization makes sense in post-conflict settings in particular, where economies are often in a period of decompression following the removal of the pervasive distortions and in the influx of aid and private capital. In such circumstances it is extremely difficult to determine potential (non-inflationary) output, so that any attempt to stabilize short-term output around this unknown quantum is not just irrelevant but may be a source of volatility in its own right. This low weight is also justified when macroeconomic data, especially on the real economy, are problematic (see for example, Jerven, 2013), and when it is extremely difficult to determine potential (non-inflationary output). The measurement errors here are not just an unknown but may be a source of volatility in their own right.

Moreover, the RM framework functions well when financial markets, particularly interbank markets, are in an embryonic state and are dominated by banks

Box 13.2 Reserve Money Programming

Reserve Money Programming is a consistency framework built around a simple open-economy monetarist representation of the transmission mechanism. The framework combines a simple quantity theory of money, with broad money the nominal anchor and intermediate target for monetary policy, and reserve money (H), the operational target for the central bank. From the quantity theory, the target growth of the money supply can be defined as

$$\widehat{M}_t^* = \pi_t^* + (\tilde{y}_t - \tilde{v}_t) \qquad [1]$$

where the percentage growth rate of a variable is denoted by a hat (^), the *projected* percentage growth rate by tilde (~) and a target by a star (*). Substituting in the monetary identity, $\widehat{M}_t = \tilde{m}_t + \widehat{H}_t$, where m_t denotes the money multiplier, gives an inflation target–consistent reaction function for the path of reserve money, given forecast values for the growth of real output (y_t), the velocity of circulation (v_t) and the money multiplier

$$\widehat{H}_t^* = \pi_t^* + (\tilde{y}_t - \tilde{v} - \tilde{m}_t). \qquad [2]$$

Equation [2] links directly to the fiscal stance, the key proximate driver of internal and external disequilibrium in fragile state environments, through the liability side of the central bank's balance sheet. Simplifying only slightly to isolate reserve money, the central bank's balance sheet can be written as

$$\widehat{H}_t = \underbrace{\widehat{DC}_t^g + \widehat{DC}_t^p}_{\text{Net domestic assets}} + E_t\widehat{NIR}_t + \widehat{NOA}_t \qquad [3]$$

where DC^g is central bank credit to the government, DC^p central bank credit to the private sector (including banks), NIR denotes net official international reserves (measured in US$ terms), E is the exchange rate, and NOA net other assets (including exchange rate revaluation effects on NIR).

The standard RM program designed for low-income countries typically sets a floor under net international reserves, measured in terms of import coverage or of the outstanding short-term external sovereign debt, and a ceiling on the growth of net domestic assets (NDA). If the floor is binding (and assuming that the growth in net other assets is stationary or otherwise accommodated in the target for reserve money), the NDA ceiling ties down the path for reserve money. Moreover, assuming that central bank credit to the private sector is zero, which would normally be the case except when the central bank is drawn into lender-of-last-resort obligations, the ultimate control instrument is the growth of domestic credit to government, in other words the money financing of the government deficit.

that rely heavily on transactions with the central banks for their funding and liquidity, and so the transmission mechanism is not well understood, either by market players or the central bank. Likewise, the technical capacity of the central bank, in terms of both economic analysis and forecasting as well as market-based surveillance and banking sector regulation, is typically weak.

As section 4.3 discusses, there are meaningful shortcomings of the RM approach once economic and political conditions have stabilized, but in environments of significant fragility and limited capacity, this limited and non-discretionary approach to monetary policy is, arguably, not just feasible but also probably optimal. Most importantly, from a political economy perspective it places fiscal control at the center of the macroeconomic debate and in doing so helps to lean against severe fiscal dominance. As has been shown in many circumstances, the substantial and rapid leverage on inflation (and as a consequence the stabilization of nominal exchange rate depreciation) has powerful demonstration effects beyond simply anchoring inflation expectations. Quick wins in inflation stabilization are themselves not sufficient in restoring broader macroeconomic stabilization and recovery, but they can play a decisive role at critical times in securing the post-fragility settlement.

Two features of this framework stand out. The first is the lack of feedback from market conditions, in particular interest rates, onto the operational target. This gives RM programming its non-discretionary flavor. In practice, the discretionary element of monetary policy is exercised at low frequency, often in the context of quarterly reviews of the country's IMF program: but otherwise discretion is distinctly *ex post*.

The second is the emphasis on fiscal control that embodies a simple but powerful diagnosis of the macroeconomic stabilization challenges facing most fragile states. RM programming sees the stabilization challenge as being the interplay of structural problems of fiscal dominance, the proximate cause of high and variable inflation (and associated external imbalances and low growth) which, in turn, is manifest as excess domestic credit to government, and the fragility of the demand for domestic money (as summarized by the velocity of circulation and the money multiplier).

This focus on the fiscal channel has a number of implications. First, it led to the adoption by a number of countries—including Tanzania, Uganda, and Zambia—to reinforce the balance sheet logic of the reserve money program with simple "cash-budget" arrangements that sought to provide a legislative lock on the growth of domestic credit to government. This created the space to crowd-in credit provision to the private sector and at the same time build up external reserve coverage. The second concerns broader questions of the role of fiscal policy and fiscal institutions in exiting fragility. Clearly, generalized budget support can be a key element in financing of incipient fiscal deficits, but the difficult policy questions surround whether and how donor leverage can be deployed to influence the associated debate around the nature of fiscal policy and fiscal consolidation. Two aspects of this debate are particularly challenging. First, the authorities must take a view around the balance between prioritising revenue mobilization, which may be politically difficult in settings where the underlying social contract between the state and the people is frayed but which, if successful, is likely to underpin sustained fiscal consolidation, and expenditure management. Second, they must also balance competing claims of social protection spending and the maintenance of public investment with the protection of politically sensitive transfers and entitlements, including public sector salaries.

The third is the role of aid in supporting stabilization efforts. Much of the literature on aid flows to fragile states is concerned with the role of aid in securing the peace in post-conflict settings (see Collier and Hoeffler, 2004) and with the broader macroeconomic and institutional consequences of large capital inflows. These latter tend to center on questions of managing aid inflows where absorptive capacities are limited (see Bevan, 2006; and Aiyar et al., 2006) and where institutions of governance are fragile (Johnson and Subramanian, 2006), and on the perennial question of Dutch Disease effects of aid (Adam, 2006). There are few simple results emerging from this literature other than the obvious point that the effectiveness of aid in supporting the emergence from fragility is primarily determined by the political settlement in play; in other words, whether aid inflows strengthen the hands of those opposing reform and recovery or undermine this opposition. But when aid does support the reform tendency, the evidence suggests that inflows can play a decisive role in supporting macroeconomic stabilization, through two channels, the first of which is to augment typically weak domestic tax revenues to finance elements of recurrent and investment expenditure that are deemed critical to the restoration of a functioning state.

The second channel is by substituting for domestic deficit financing, which serves to support the reconstruction of domestic money demand, particularly in environments where incentives for dollarization and/or currency substitution are high. To the extent that donor flows directly support the government budget, aid reduces the pressure for the authorities to extract seigniorage revenue which, by the "unpleasant monetarist arithmetic" of Sargent and Wallace (1981), acts to lower the expected future rate of inflation, other things being equal, anchoring current inflation expectations and thereby strengthening the demand for money. Over time, the more strongly inflation expectations are anchored, the more strongly the portfolio switch into domestic money and the more rapidly the demand for domestic money can be reconstructed. Examining only post-conflict situations, Adam et al (2008) find strong substitution effects—their central elasticity of substitution between aid and domestic seigniorage revenue in (successful) post-conflict settings was approximately 0.3—but effective aid-based stabilization occurs elsewhere. The successful stabilization episode in countries such as Ghana, Tanzania, Uganda, and Zambia in the 1990s and early 2000s were all supported by strong aid inflows, including debt relief (see Box 13.3 on Uganda, and Buffie et al., 2004).

Box 13.3 Uganda: Aid-Based Stabilization and Recovery with a Floating Exchange Rate

In the 30 years since President Yoweri Museveni's National Resistance Army overthrew the regime of President Milton Obote in 1986, Uganda achieved a steady recovery from extreme fragility and effective state collapse in the 1970s and early 1980s. A key feature of both recovery and the sustained growth that followed was a progressive and technocratic approach to macroeconomic management built around a Ministry of Finance and Economic Development and a central bank, the Bank of Uganda, noted for their high levels of capacity and expertise and an increasing degree of functional independence.

The stabilization trajectory in Uganda, which is an exemplar of aid-based stabilization built around strong fidelity to a reserve money (RM) program, can be divided into three phases. By about 1992, the fixed exchange rate regime was failing to anchor inflation, which was far in excess of 100 percent per annum, and a large parallel market in foreign exchange had developed. Led by technocrats in the Ministry of Finance, the government implemented a successful unification of the exchange rate, eliminating the parallel market premium and bringing inflation rapidly to single-digit levels (see Morris 1995 and Henstridge and Kasekende, 2001). A critical factor in the success of exchange rate unification was that the Ugandan government enjoyed substantial aid support so that government was a net seller of foreign exchange to the private sector. As a consequence, exchange rate unification was budget-improving; domestic monetary finance requirements fell, and because domestic prices were already being set by the parallel market exchange rate, the fiscal balance improved and inflation fell sharply.

This set the scene for Phase II, which was an extended period when the Bank of Uganda operated a tight RM program. Again with the support of significant of aid flows in the form of budget support and bolstered by a "cash budget" at the heart of fiscal structures (Stasavage and Moyo, 2000), the RM program was successful in anchoring inflation, in the context of a flexible exchange rate and an open capital account, at least until about 2010 (Byaruhanga et al., 2010).

By the eve of the global financial crisis in 2008, it was becoming clear to the Bank of Uganda that strict RM programming was losing its effectiveness. Already by 2009, Uganda was employing their RM program in a flexible manner. The Bank of Uganda altered its short-term liquidity management,

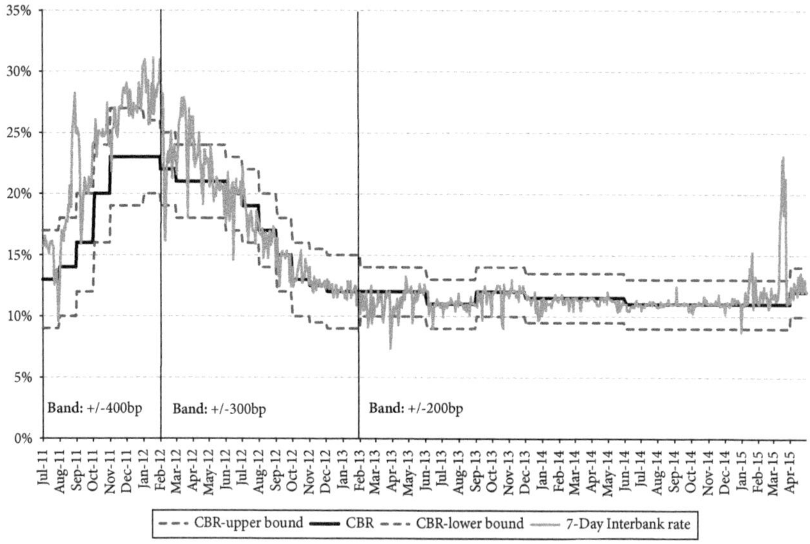

Figure 13.4 Bank of Uganda Policy Rate: July 2011–April 2015

and in July 2011 introduced an inflation targeting "lite" regime, with the Bank's operational target switching from RM to a policy interest rate. The implementation of the inflation targeting "lite" regime has been supported by improvements in policy communication, measures to tighten government's access to central bank advances, and ongoing efforts to strengthen the Bank of Uganda's inflation forecasting capabilities.

Even though Uganda has only recently made the switch, the impact on interest rate volatility in particular is dramatic (see below). The policy-rate system was introduced in July 2011 and by mid-2013 market interest rates had converged into a very tight pattern around the policy rate [CBR].

By 2017/18, approximately 30 years after the end of civil war, Bank of Uganda had effectively transited to an inflation target regime.

4.3 Transiting from Reserve Money Programming in the Medium Term

By the early 2000s a number of countries including Ghana, Kenya, Nigeria, Tanzania, Uganda, and Zambia, that had experienced crisis and state fragility since the early 1980s, were beginning to enjoy sustained growth with low and stable inflation (Box 13.3 describes in some detail Uganda's transition from extreme fragility to stability). In all these cases, RM programming had played an important role in containing fiscal dominance and supporting the restoration of macroeconomic stability (Coorey et al., 2007; Adam et al., 2016). As stability was restored, however, there was a growing sense that the benefits of RM programming as a monetary framework—principally when it was being applied in a non-discretionary manner—were starting to diminish and increasingly constrain rather than support macroeconomic stabilization. Three key shortcomings started to emerge.

First, the lack of flexibility and discretion in the framework meant that supply-side shocks were being poorly managed. Unlike demand shocks, where output and inflation movements require the same optimal monetary policy response in RM programs, for supply shocks this "divine coincidence" property is not present. The authorities are faced with a trade-off between accommodating the supply shock and letting inflation rise (or fall), or stabilizing inflation at the risk of exacerbating output volatility. This trade-off is less of a concern when the principal source of disequilibrium is on the demand side, coming from a lack of fiscal discipline, as in the fragile situations discussed in previous sections. However, as the challenges of tackling extreme inflation begin to wane and the balance of shocks changes, the trade-off occurs more frequently and the willingness to ignore output volatility becomes less readily tolerated. Faced with such shocks, one option is to move towards greater discretion, allowing RM to expand more rapidly than the initial targets, in order to partially accommodate the inflation consequences of the supply-side shock.[14]

Second, tight adherence to RM programs has often come at the cost of high interest rate volatility. This reduces the capacity for effective stabilization of output in the *short run* and acts as a brake on the development of the financial sector and its capacity to mobilize and allocate savings and to price and intermediate financial risk. By design, strict RM programming makes currency highly inelastic in supply in the short run with the result that the money market is characterized by extremely high volatility in short-run interest rates and in banks holding high levels of (unremunerated) reserves, in excess of statutory requirements. This can create excessive noise in the market, impairing price discovery, hampering efficient liquidity management by the banking system and severely compromising the monetary transmission mechanism, in particular the interest rate channel.[15]

[14] This is consistent with a simple *ex post* form of nominal GDP targeting. Nominal GDP targeting entails exactly the same response as under reserve money programming but generates a stronger countercyclical element in the face of supply-side shocks.

[15] The transmission from changes in short-term policy interest rates to aggregate demand requires price signals from policy intervention at the short end do in fact translate to changes in the longer-dated market interest rates that matter for the interest-sensitive components of aggregate demand. This pass-through is brought about by arbitrage, to the extent that movements in short-rates are expected to persist. Clearly, the more volatile and less predictable are short interest rates the less impact on long-dated rates. Moreover, low levels of competition in the banking system, combined with other factors that might make long-term interest rates sticky, will also exacerbate the weakness of this transmission channel.

The third factor confounding effective liquidity management is aid, particularly since fragile and post-conflict states are often recipients of large aid inflows. The domestic portion of aid-financed spending causes an injection of domestic liquidity, which, other things equal, must be sterilized in order for RM targets to be hit. This process generates two challenges. First, as the central bank sells foreign currency into the market as part of its sterilization mechanism, the domestic currency appreciates, and undesirable Dutch Disease effects can arise from the aid-induced real exchange rate appreciation. Fearing this, the authorities are often reluctant to allow the nominal exchange rate to take the full burden of sterilization. Second, even if the aid inflow is fully absorbed through the current account over the medium term, large periodic sales of aid may generate destabilizing effects, given the thinness of domestic foreign exchange markets.

Strict RM targeting has served emerging-from-fragility economies well; however, as inflation expectations become more firmly anchored post-fragility and economies operate closer to their potential, the conditions that favored a non-discretionary RM program are less relevant and the case for moving towards a policy-rate system is compelling. The argument for proceeding with the transition to a forward-looking interest rate-based monetary framework is thus a strong one. As O'Connell (2013) argues, though some form of policy-rate system necessarily underpins full-fledged inflation targeting regimes, moving towards such a system does not imply a commitment to inflation targeting. But a policy-rate system—which is about the operational target for monetary policy—is also warranted, even if the intermediate target of policy, that is, the nominal anchor, remains the growth of broad money. This is necessary if financial markets are to continue to deepen and support a more effective monetary policy transmission. However, as with exiting fragility, the historical evidence demonstrates that a gradual approach is essential.

4.4 Monetary Policy Management in Periods of Fragility

Successful exits from fragility are protracted and vulnerable to reversal, and often the factors precipitating such reversals lie outside the control of the monetary and fiscal authorities. Macroeconomic conditions will often be volatile; private capital and external aid flows are also likely to be volatile and procyclical, especially amongst aid donors whose support tends to be short-term and highly conditional;[16] while accurate measurement and assessment of economic developments are often

[16] There are some important exceptions where donors have made long-term commitments in an attempt to reduce volatility and support new administrations. One of the more celebrated cases was the extended support to post-genocide Rwanda which saw major donors such as the United Kingdom, the United States, Canada, and the Netherlands make unprecedented multi-year aid commitments.

impaired by highly imperfect data that are subject to serious delay. In these circumstances, the question is whether there are obvious lessons for those executing monetary and exchange rate policy? A number of general lessons appear to be germane.

The first lies outside the narrow monetary and exchange rate domain: as we have already stressed, coherence in monetary and exchange rate policy and management is impossible without a compatible fiscal position. Some of the structural demands on fiscal policy have already been discussed; the key additional requirement is the challenge of maintaining a sufficient degree of flexibility that will allow the authorities to accommodate volatility in revenue and aid flows and to support the management of aggregate demand. This latter point is particularly important when the limits of monetary policy are recognized. Unlike monetary policy in economies with developed financial markets, monetary policy in situations of fragility will be unable to carry much of the burden of aggregate demand management. While domestic monetary markets remain thin, the conventional transmission mechanism of monetary policy is relatively weak, which hands back a larger portion of the adjustment burden to fiscal policy. And with improvements to revenue mobilization likely to be relatively slow, the heavy lifting will fall on the expenditure management side. Expenditure management is extremely difficult and intensely political; there are few quick wins, especially when public expenditure per capita is already low, needs are high, and priority areas of expenditure need to be protected. A key implication is that, given that access to external credit is likely to be compromised and fiscal space is limited, in the sense of its ability to absorb adverse fiscal shocks without jeopardising its already fragile debt position, efforts to rebuild fiscal buffers, primarily through official reserve accumulation, become critical.

Second, two key aspects of fiscal policy require close monitoring to ensure that monetary policy is not overwhelmed by (quasi-) fiscal incompatibility. The first concerns the absorptive capacity of systems of public expenditure in times of fragility, particularly in the presence of potentially large and often uncoordinated aid inflows from donors, NGOs, and others. Public expenditure plans that confront limited or distorted institutional capacity can quickly lead to a severe loss of fiscal control. Recognizing capacity constraints and the emergence of points of rent capture is not straightforward, but as Bevan (2006) notes, improved public expenditure management strategies that aim at "satisficing" rather than achieving best practice, combined with greater external pressures for transparency, can make early adjustments to spending plans more feasible. The second area where close scrutiny is essential in environments of fragility (as elsewhere) is in the monitoring of quasi-fiscal liabilities that arise from actions by central banks and the state-owned enterprise sector. Moves towards liberalization of domestic financial markets that fail to account for and accommodate these liabilities run the risk of placing unsustainable pressure on the fiscal balance as and when these liabilities crystalize. Failing to monitor and account for these effects can be very costly to putative recovery processes, the prime example, as noted above, being the case of Zimbabwe in the early 2000s (see Box 13.1).

Third, key structural developments that are likely to be required to support the move towards a more flexible exchange rate regime and domestically anchored macroeconomic framework will take time. On the exchange rate side, moves towards a more flexible regime require the development of mechanisms of price discovery, increasing the incentives for firms and households to manage foreign exchange risks, and for the public sector to step back from being a market maker in foreign exchange. On the money market side, developing the short-term interbank money market lays the ground for the eventual introduction of monetary policy instruments that can allow the central bank to use a range of monetary policy instruments (short-term interest rates and standing facilities) to help steer short-term market interest rates and, hence, start to build an effective transmission mechanism. And on the domestic asset market side, domestic bond and money markets need to be developed by progressively removing controls on domestic interest rates; moving away from non-market credit allocation; introducing debt instruments across the maturity spectrum, from which a yield curve can emerge which then can help underpin risk pricing by commercial banks and other private sector financial institutions. These developments are necessary elements of building an effective domestic monetary policy framework, for which "letting the water run through the pipes" is an essential element in ensuring the financial infrastructure functions; but the risks of moving in a precipitate manner are high. In particular, moves towards liberalization of residual controls on cross-border capital flows, particularly on the debt side, should be avoided. Countries that have pursued rapid capital account liberalization, either as a policy choice or, as in the case of Zambia in the early 1990s, as a perceived means to signal commitment to broader economic reforms, have found the attendant volatility that open capital accounts have brought to thin domestic markets very difficult to deal with, with no measurable offsetting benefits. The priority in market development should be on progressive unification of the exchange rate and deliberate but gradual moves to unwind repression in domestic financial markets.

Finally, the general theory of the second best will always apply. Policymakers therefore need to recognize the importance of, as Deng Xiaoping put it, "crossing the river by feeling the stones." While it may be reasonably clear what sorts of macroeconomic adjustments and policy choices are required, the deep uncertainties about likely responses of the different groups of private sector actors, interest groups, and external creditors, a gradualist approach to unwinding macroeconomic imbalances is required, one that is guided by a tatonnement process that fine-tunes as it goes, so as to balance decisive and coherent progress against the risks of going too quickly and being forced into costly and undesirable policy reversals.

5. Conclusions: Key Lessons

State fragility is complex and multifaceted. The origins and manifestation of emerging state fragility are highly context- and time-specific, and how fragility plays out in a particular country and at a particular time depends on the political settlement and on local and international events. These conditions, in turn, shape the broad strategic and policy options for exit, rendering the process profoundly path-dependent. To a large degree this path dependency applies equally to choices in the monetary and exchange rate domain as countries seek to chart an exit from fragility: it is therefore a fool's errand to attempt to summarize the insights from the evidence reviewed in this chapter. We therefore close by reprising three key lessons that appear relevant to countries seeking to manage a route out of fragility.

The first and most obvious is the primacy of establishing and maintaining a degree of fiscal control. If fiscal dominance is not tethered—on an ongoing basis—macroeconomic stabilization cannot be achieved. This is fundamentally a political problem and holds true regardless of the nominal anchor the authorities seek to deploy, and in both cases the effects of weak fiscal control can be highly non-linear, with extended periods of apparent stability quickly tipping into open crisis. Nonetheless, failure to manage the pressures from fiscal dominance is arguably more problematic with exchange rate anchors. Conditions may look favorable in the short term, but the buildup of distortions around pegged rates, from the accumulation of unsustainable quasi-fiscal liabilities on central bank balance sheets to the emergence of *de facto* dual exchange rate regimes, ultimately deprives exchange rate anchors of their functionality. Moreover, the rents generated through these markets can be corrosive to social cohesion and, by entrenching gains to favored groups who can control access to distorted foreign exchange markets, can represent a road block to reforms that otherwise may drive the exit from fragility.

Regimes operating with a domestic anchor with some form of flexible exchange rates are, of course, equally vulnerable to fiscal dominance, but its manifestation tends to be much more transparent and public; sharply depreciating nominal rates and rising inflation offer a very public demonstration of weak fiscal control and lay responsibility for this clearly at the door of government. The important corollary is that the evidence of success in restraining fiscal dominance is also very public: as has been shown in a number of cases from Sub-Saharan Africa, inflation stabilization can be achieved very rapidly and hence can deliver early political payoffs, even if other factors, including external aid from donors, may have played a decisive role. But we should not be too naïve about the virtues of flexible exchange rates in these circumstances. Though they may remove the open rents that emerge around parallel markets in foreign exchange, heavy management of flexible rates, whether fuelled by fiscal dominance and/or financial repression, will nonetheless generate "hidden" rents from real exchange rate overvaluation that accrue to net importers who are often the same well-connected political elites that otherwise stand to benefit from black market rents.

Second, all the evidence we have on stabilization and economic recovery suggests that processes of recovery are gradual. As noted, the restoration of an initial degree of price stability, for example, may be rapid and dramatic; this is often built through expedients such as simple but draconian fiscal rules that require significant political capital to install. The challenge is to consolidate these advances once the initial existential threats to the regime diminish (see Adam and O'Connell, 1999).[17] Still, the evidence suggests that the exit from fragility is slow and incremental and that efforts to accelerate the process may be self-defeating. This seems particularly true for those regimes seeking to dedollarize and move away from fixed exchange rates. Even in examples of success, such as Uganda, the time scale is measured in decades, not years or months, not least because the move from a tentatively adequate initial stabilization to the creation of a resilient and flexible macroeconomic framework involves substantial investment in technical capacity, the progressive deepening of markets (particularly asset markets), and a political environment where central banks have the independence to move, stepping-stone by stepping-stone, towards more discretionary policy environments.

Third and finally, the evidence highlights how aid-based stabilization efforts, delivered at critical moments, can play a decisive role in both supporting the stabilization of fragile and post-conflict regimes and post-stabilization recovery. In an era of aid fatigue and hyper-accountability, many bilateral donors have, however, become increasingly risk-averse and are wary of favoring aid in the form of necessarily fungible generalized budget support provided under broad macroeconomic conditionality (an IMF program) over highly focussed and earmarked transfers supporting noncompetitive imports. Providing aid to fragile states is a risky business—as it should be—and it clearly needs to be done with a careful understanding not just of the prevailing political environment on the ground but also of the effect that aid may have on that political economy. But if the evidence from those countries that have emerged from situations of state fragility suggests anything, it is that the (general equilibrium) returns from sustained and fungible aid flows are high.

[17] They develop a model that shows how as existential threats diminish it becomes progressively more likely that previously committed polities are more likely to drift towards rent extraction and distribution.

References

Adam, C. 2006. "Exogenous Inflows and Real Exchange Rates: Theoretical Quirk or Empirical Reality?" in Peter Isard, Leslie Lipschitz, Alexandros Mourmouras, and Boriana Yontcheva (Eds.), *The Macroeconomic Management of Foreign Aid.* Washington, DC: International Monetary Fund.

Adam, C., A. Berg, R. Portillo, and F. Unsal. 2018. "Monetary Policy and Central Banking in Sub-Saharan Africa," in P.C. Brown and R.M. Lastra (Eds.), *Research Handbook on Central Banking.* Cheltenham: Edward Elgar.

Adam, C., P. Kessy, and B. Langford. 2016. "Evolving Monetary Policy Frameworks in Low-Income Countries: The Case of Tanzania," in D. Cobham (Ed.), *Monetary Analysis at Central Banks.* Basingstoke: Palgrave MacMillan.

Adam, C., P. Collier, and V. Davies. 2008. "Post-Conflict Monetary Reconstruction." *World Bank Economic Review,* 22(1): 87–112. Washington, DC: World Bank.

Adam, C. and D. Bevan. 1999. "Fiscal Restraint and the Cash Budget in Zambia," in P. Collier and C. Patillo (Eds.), *Risk and Investment in Africa.* London: Macmillan.

Adam, C. and S. O'Connell. 1999. "Aid, Taxation and Development in Sub-Saharan Africa." *Economics and Politics,* 11(3): 225–53.

Adam, C. 1995. "Fiscal Adjustment, Financial Liberalization and the Dynamics of Inflation: Some Evidence from Zambia." *World Development,* 23(5): 735–50.

Aiyar, S., A. Berg, M. Hussain, A. Mahone, and S. Roache. 2006. "High Aid Inflows: The Case of Ghana," in Peter Isard, Leslie Lipschitz, Alexandros Mourmouras, and Boriana Yontcheva (Eds.), *The Macroeconomic Management of Foreign Aid.* Washington, DC: International Monetary Fund.

Anderson, A. 2016. "Dollarization: A Case Study of Ecuador." *Journal of Economics and Development Studies,* 4(2): 56–60.

Ajayi, S.I. and L. Ndikumana. 2015. *Capital Flight from Africa: Causes, Effects, and Policy Issues.* New York: Oxford University Press.

Bevan, D. 2006. "An Analytical Overview of Aid Absorption: Recognizing and Avoiding Macroeconomic Hazards," in P. Isard, L. Lipschitz, A. Mourmouras, and B. Yontcheva (Eds.), *The Macroeconomic Management of Foreign Aid.* Washington, DC: International Monetary Fund.

Byaruhanga, C., M. Henstridge, and L. Kasekende. 2010. "Exchange Rate, Fiscal and Monetary Policy," in F. Kuteesa, E. Tumusiime-Mutebile, A. Whitworth, and T. Williamson (Eds.), *Uganda's Economic Reforms: Insider Accounts.* Oxford: Oxford University Press.

Buffie, E., C. Adam, S. O'Connell, and C. Pattillo. 2004. "Exchange Rate Policy and the Management of Official and Private Capital Flows." *Africa IMF Staff Papers,* 51: 126–58.

Calvo, G. and C. Vegh. 1999. "Inflation Stabilization and BoP Crises in Developing Countries," in J.B. Taylor and M. Woodford (Eds.), *Handbook of Macroeconomics.* Amsterdam: Elsevier North-Holland.

Catão, L. and M. Terrones. 2016. "Financial De-Dollarization: A Global Perspective and the Peruvian Experience." IMF Working Paper WP/16/97. International Monetary Fund, Washington, DC.

Collier, P. and J. Gunning. 1991. "Money Creation and Financial Liberalization in a Socialist Banking System: Tanzania 1983–88." *World Development*, 19(5): 533–8.

Collier, P. and A. Hoeffler. 2004. "Aid, Policy and Growth in Post-Conflict Societies." *European Economic Review*, 48(4): 1125–45.

Collier, P., A. Hoeffler, and C. Pattillo. 2001. "Flight Capital as a Portfolio Choice." *World Bank Economic Review*, 15(1): 55–79.

Coorey, S., J. Clausen, N. Funke, S. Muñoz, and B. Ould-Abdallah. 2007. "Lessons from High-Inflation Episodes for Stabilizing the Economy in Zimbabwe." IMF Working Paper WP/07/99. Washington, DC: International Monetary Fund.

Del Cristo, M., and M. Gómez-Puig. 2016. "Sustainability and Dollarization: The Case of Ecuador." *Applied Economics*, 48(23): 1–17.

García-Escribano, M. 2011 "What Is Driving Financial De-dollarization in Latin America?" IMF Working Paper No 11/10. International Monetary Fund, Washington, DC.

García-Escribano, M. 2010. "Peru: Drivers of De-dollarization." IMF Working Paper WP/10/169. International Monetary Fund, Washington, DC.

Ghosh, A., J. Ostry, and M. Chamon. 2016. "Two Targets, Two Instruments: Monetary and Exchange Rate Policies in Emerging Market Economies." *Journal of International Money and Finance*, 60(C): 172–196

Henstridge, M. and L. Kasekende. 2001. "Exchange Reforms, Stabilization and Fiscal Management," in R. Reinikka and C. Pattillo (Eds.), *Uganda's Recovery–The Role of Farms, Firms, and Government.* Washington, DC: World Bank.

Honohan, P. and S. O'Connell. 1997. "Contrasting Monetary Regimes in Africa." IMF Working Papers 97/64. International Monetary Fund, Washington, DC.

Ilzetzki, E., C. Reinhart, and K. Rogoff. 2017. "Exchange Arrangements Entering the 21st Century: Which Anchor Will Hold?" NBER Working Paper 23134.

IMF Staff Report. 2015. "Evolving Monetary Policy Frameworks in Low-Income and Other Developing Countries." (Draft Board Paper, 23 October 2015). Washington, DC: International Monetary Fund.

Jerven, M. 2013. *Poor Numbers: How We Are Misled by African Development Statistics and What to Do about It.* Ithaca, NY: Cornell University Press.

Johnson, S. and A. Subramanian. 2006. "Aid, Governance and the Political Economy: Growth and Institutions," in Peter Isard, Leslie Lipschitz, Alexandros Mourmouras, and Boriana Yontcheva (Eds.), *The Macroeconomic Management of Foreign Aid.* Washington, DC: International Monetary Fund.

Kiguel, M. and S. O'Connell. 1995. "Parallel Exchange Rates in Developing Countries." *The World Bank Research Observer*, 10(1): February, 21–52.

Kovanen, A. 2004. "Zimbabwe: A Quest for a Nominal Anchor." IMF Working Paper WP/04/130.

Maehle, N., H. Teferra, and A. Khachatryan. 2013. "Exchange Rate Liberalization in Selected Sub-Saharan African Countries: Successes, Failures and Lessons." IMF Working Paper WP/13/32. International Monetary Fund, Washington, DC.

Mecagni, M. et al. 2015. *Dollarization in Sub-Saharan Africa: Experience and Lessons.* African Department, International Monetary Fund, Washington, DC.

Mishra, P. and P. Montiel, P. 2013. "How Effective is Monetary Transmission in Developing Countries? A Survey of the Empirical Evidence." *Economic Systems*, 37(2): 187–216.

Mlambo, K. 2018. "Central Banking in a Dollarised Environment: Insights from Zimbabwe." Distinguished Guest Lecture, Centre for Global Finance, SOAS University of London, October 9, 2018.

Mongardini, J. 1999. "Ratchet Effects in Currency Substitution: An Application to the Kyrgyz Republic." IMF Working Paper WP/99/102. International Monetary Fund, Washington, DC.

Morris, S. 1995. "Inflation Dynamics and the Parallel Market for Foreign Exchange." *Journal of Development Economics*, 46(2): 295–316.

O'Connell, S. 2013. "The Bank of Tanzania: A Monetary Policy Framework in Transition." Mimeo, International Growth Centre, London.

Ötker-Robe, I., and D. Vávra. 2007. "Moving to Greater Exchange Rate Flexibility: Operational Aspects Based on Lessons from Detailed Country Experiences." IMF Occasional Paper No. 256. International Monetary Fund, Washington DC.

Pinto, B. 1989. "Black Market Premiums, Exchange Rate Unification and Inflation in Sub-Saharan Africa." *World Bank Economic Review*, 3(3): 321–38.

Sargent, T. and N. Wallace. 1981. "Some Unpleasant Monetarist Arithmetic." *Federal Reserve Bank of Minneapolis Quarterly Review*, Fall, 5(3): 1–17.

Stasavage, D. and D. Moyo. 2000. "Are Cash Budgets a Cure for Excess Fiscal Deficits (and at What Cost)?" *World Development*, 28(12): 2105–22.

Appendix

Table A13.1 Countries That Have Been Classified as Fragile 2005–17 – Fragility Status

	Countries in Fragile Situations (x denotes fragility in a given year)												
	2005	2006	2007	2008	2009	2010	2011	2012	2013	2014	2015	2016	2017
Afghanistan	x	x	x	x	x	x	x	x	x	x	x	x	x
Angola	x	x	x	x	x	x	x	x					
Bosnia & Herzegovina					x	x	x	x	x	x	x		
Burundi	x	x	x	x	x	x	x	x	x	x	x	x	x
Cambodia	x	x	x	x									
Cameroon				x	x								
Central African Republic	x	x	x	x	x	x	x	x	x	x	x	x	x
Chad	x	x	x	x	x	x	x	x	x	x	x	x	x
Comoros	x	x		x	x	x	x	x	x	x	x	x	x
Congo, Dem. Rep.	x	x	x	x	x	x	x	x	x	x	x	x	x
Congo, Rep.	x	x	x	x	x	x	x	x	x				x
Côte d'Ivoire	x	x	x	x	x	x	x	x	x	x	x	x	x
Djibouti	x	x	x	x	x							x	x
Eritrea	x	x	x	x	x	x	x	x	x	x	x	x	x
Gambia, The	x	x	x	x	x						x	x	x
Georgia					x	x							
Guinea	x	x	x	x	x	x	x	x					
Guinea-Bissau	x	x	x	x	x	x	x	x	x	x	x	x	x
Haiti	x	x	x	x	x	x	x	x	x	x	x	x	x
Iraq						x	x	x	x	x	x	x	x
Kiribati			x	x	x	x	x	x	x	x	x	x	x
Kosovo	x	x	x	x	x	x	x	x	x	x	x	x	x
Laos	x	x	x	x									
Lebanon											x	x	x
Liberia	x	x	x	x	x	x	x	x	x	x	x	x	x
Libya								x	x	x	x	x	x

Continued

Table A13.1 *Continued*

	Countries in Fragile Situations (x denotes fragility in a given year)												
	2005	**2006**	**2007**	**2008**	**2009**	**2010**	**2011**	**2012**	**2013**	**2014**	**2015**	**2016**	**2017**
Madagascar									x	x	x	x	
Malawi									x				
Mali									x	x	x	x	x
Marshall Islands							x	x	x	x	x	x	x
Mauritania		x											
Micronesia, Fed. Sts							x	x	x	x	x	x	x
Mozambique													x
Myanmar	x	x	x	x	x	x	x	x	x	x	x	x	x
Nepal					x	x	x	x	x				
Nigeria	x	x											
Papua New Guinea	x	x	x		x							x	x
Sao Tome & Principe	x	x	x	x	x	x							
Sierra Leone	x	x	x	x	x	x	x	x	x	x	x	x	x
Soloman Islands	x	x	x	x	x	x	x	x	x	x	x	x	x
Somalia	x	x	x	x	x	x	x	x	x	x	x	x	x
South Sudan								x	x	x	x	x	x
Sudan	x	x	x	x	x	x	x	x	x	x	x	x	x
Syria								x	x	x	x	x	x
Tajikistan	x			x	x	x							
Togo	x	x	x	x	x	x	x	x	x	x	x	x	x
Tonga	x	x	x	x	x								
Tuvalu								x	x	x	x	x	x
Uzbekistan	x	x	x	x									
Vanuatu	x	x	x										
Yemen, Rep.				x	x	x	x	x	x	x	x	x	x
Timor-Leste	x	x	x	x		x	x	x	x	x	x		
Zimbabwe	x	x	x	x	x	x	x	x	x	x	x	x	x
Number of countries	34	34	32	34	34	31	30	34	35	32	34	34	35

Table A13.2 Countries That Have Been Classified as Fragile 2005–17 – Monetary Policy Frameworks

	Monetary Policy framework (1=exchange rate anchor, 2=monetary aggregate target, 3=inflation-targeting regime, 4=other)												
	2005	**2006**	**2007**	**2008**	**2009**	**2010**	**2011**	**2012**	**2013**	**2014**	**2015**	**2016**	**2017**
Afghanistan	4	4	2	2	2	2	2	2	2	2	2	2	2
Angola	4	1	1	1	1	1	4	4	4	4	4	1	2
Bosnia & Herzegovina	1	1	1	1	1	1	1	1	1	1	1	1	1
Burundi	4	4	2	2	2	2	2	2	2	2	2	2	2
Cambodia	2	4	1	4	1	1	1	1	1	1	1	1	1
Cameroon	1	1	1	1	1	1	1	1	1	1	1	1	1
Central African Republic	1	1	1	1	1	1	1	1	1	1	1	1	1
Chad	1	1	1	1	1	1	1	1	1	1	1	1	1
Comoros	1	1	1	1	1	1	1	1	1	1	1	1	1
Congo, Dem. Rep.	2	2	4	2	2	2	2	2	2	2	2	2	2
Congo, Rep.	1	1	1	1	1	1	1	1	1	1	1	1	1
Côte d'Ivoire	1	1	1	1	1	1	1	1	1	1	1	1	1
Djibouti	1	1	1	1	1	1	1	1	1	1	1	1	1
Eritrea	1	1	1	1	1	1	1	1	1	1	1	1	1
Gambia, The	2	4	2	2	2	2	2	2	2	2	2	2	2
Georgia	4	4	2	1	3	3	3	3	3	3	3	3	3
Guinea	4	4	2	2	2	2	2	2	2	2	2	2	2
Guinea-Bissau	1	1	1	1	1	1	1	1	1	1	1	1	1
Haiti	2	2	2	4	4	4	4	4	4	4	4	4	4
Iraq	1	1	1	1	1	1	1	1	1	1	1	1	1
Kiribati	1	1	1	1	1	1	1	1	1	1	1	1	1
Kosovo					1	1	1	1	1	1	1	1	1
Laos	1	2	1	4	4	1	4	4	4	4	4	4	4
Lebanon	1	1	1	1	1	1	1	1	1	1	1	1	1
Liberia	4	4	1	1	1	1	1	1	1	1	1	1	1
Libya	1	1	1	1	1	1	1	1	1	1	1	1	1
Madagascar	2	2	2	2	2	2	2	2	2	2	2	2	2

Continued

Table A13.2 *Continued*

	Monetary Policy framework (1=exchange rate anchor, 2=monetary aggregate target, 3=inflation-targeting regime, 4=other)												
	2005	2006	2007	2008	2009	2010	2011	2012	2013	2014	2015	2016	2017
Malawi	2	2	2	1	2	1	2	2	2	2	2	2	2
Mali	1	1	1	1	1	1	1	1	1	1	1	1	1
Marshall Islands	1	1	1	1	1	1	1	1	1	1	1	1	1
Mauritania	1	1	1	1	1	4	4	4	4	4	4	4	4
Micronesia, Fed. Sts	1	1	1	1	1	1	1	1	1	1	1	1	1
Mozambique	4	2	2	2	2	2	2	2	2	2	2	4	4
Myanmar	4	4	1	1	4	4	4	4	2	2	2	2	2
Nepal	1	1	1	1	1	1	1	1	1	1	1	1	1
Nigeria	1	4	2	2	2	2	2	2	2	2	2	2	2
Papua New Guinea	4	4	2	2	2	2	2	2	2	4	4	2	4
Sao Tome & Principe	4	4	2	1	1	1	1	1	1	1	1	1	1
Sierra Leone	2	1	2	2	2	2	2	2	2	2	2	2	2
Soloman Islands	1	1	1	1	1	2	4	4	4	4	4	4	4
Somalia	4	4	4	4	4	4	4	4	4	4	4	4	4
South Sudan								1	1	1	4	4	4
Sudan	2	4	2	2	2	1	4	4	4	4	4	4	4
Syria	1	1	1	1	1	1	1	1	1	1	1	1	1
Tajikistan	2	2	1	2	2	2	2	2	2	2	2	2	2
Togo	1	1	1	1	1	1	1	1	1	1	1	1	1
Tonga	1	1	1	1	1	1	1	1	1	1	4	4	4
Tuvalu						1	1	1	1	1	1	1	1
Uzbekistan	1	1	1	1	1	2	2	2	2	2	2	2	2
Vanuatu	1	1	1	1	1	1	1	1	4	4	4	4	4
Yemen, Rep.	2	1	1	1	1	2	2	2	2	2	2	2	2
Timor-Leste	1	1	1	1	1	1	1	1	1	1	1	1	1
Zimbabwe	1	1	1	1	1	1	1	1	1	1	1	1	1

Table A13.3 Countries That Have Been Classified as Fragile 2005–17—Exchange Rate Regime

	De facto exchange rate regime (1=hard peg, 2=soft peg, 3=managed float, 4=floating)												
	2005	2006	2007	2008	2009	2010	2011	2012	2013	2014	2015	2016	2017
Afghanistan	3	3	3	4	4	4	4	4	4	4	4	4	2
Angola	3	2	2	2	3	3	2	2	2	2	3	2	2
Bosnia & Herzegovina	1	1	1	1	1	1	1	1	1	1	1	1	1
Burundi	3	3	3	4	2	2	3	3	2	2	2	2	2
Cambodia	3	3	3	4	2	2	2	2	3	2	3	3	3
Cameroon	1	1	1	1	1	1	1	1	1	1	1	1	1
Central African Republic	1	1	1	1	1	1	1	1	1	1	1	1	1
Chad	1	1	1	1	1	1	1	1	1	1	1	1	1
Comoros	1	1	1	1	1	1	1	1	1	1	1	1	1
Congo, Dem. Rep.	4	4	4	4	4	2	3	2	2	2	2	3	3
Congo, Rep.	1	1	1	1	1	1	1	1	1	1	1	1	1
Côte d'Ivoire	1	1	1	1	1	1	1	1	1	1	1	1	1
Djibouti	1	1	1	1	1	1	1	1	1	1	1	1	1
Eritrea	2	2	2	2	2	2	2	2	2	2	2	2	2
Gambia, The	3	3	3	4	4	4	4	4	3	4	3	3	3
Georgia	3	3	3	3	3	4	4	2	4	4	4	4	4
Guinea	3	3	3	4	3	3	3	3	2	2	3	3	2
Guinea-Bissau	1	1	1	1	1	1	1	1	1	1	1	1	1
Haiti	3	3	3	4	3	2	2	2	2	2	3	3	2
Iraq	2	2	2	2	2	2	2	2	2	2	2	2	2
Kiribati	1	1	1	1	1	1	1	1	1	1	1	1	1
Kosovo					1	1	1	1	1	1	1	1	1
Laos	3	3	3	3	2	2	2	2	2	2	2	2	2
Lebanon	2	2	2	2	2	2	2	2	2	2	2	2	2
Liberia	3	3	3	3	3	3	3	3	3	3	3	3	3
Libya	2	2	2	2	2	2	2	2	2	2	2	2	2
Madagascar	3	3	3	4	4	4	4	4	4	4	4	4	4
Malawi	3	3	2	2	3	2	3	3	4	4	4	2	2

Continued

Table A13.3 *Continued*

	De facto exchange rate regime (1=hard peg, 2=soft peg, 3=managed float, 4=floating)												
	2005	2006	2007	2008	2009	2010	2011	2012	2013	2014	2015	2016	2017
Mali	1	1	1	1	1	1	1	1	1	1	1	1	1
Marshall Islands	1	1	1	1	1	1	1	1	1	1	1	1	1
Mauritania	2	2	3	3	3	3	3	3	3	2	2	2	2
Micronesia, Fed. Sts	1	1	1	1	1	1	1	1	1	1	1	1	1
Mozambique	3	3	3	4	4	4	4	4	4	4	4	4	4
Myanmar	3	3	3	3	3	3	3	3	3	3	3	3	2
Nepal	2	2	2	2	2	2	2	2	2	2	2	2	2
Nigeria	3	2	3	3	3	3	3	3	3	3	2	2	2
Papua New Guinea	3	3	3	4	4	4	4	4	4	2	2	2	2
Sao Tome & Principe	3	3	3	2	2	2	2	2	2	2	2	2	2
Sierra Leone	4	2	2	4	4	4	4	4	4	4	4	3	2
Soloman Islands	2	2	2	3	3	3	3	2	2	2	2	2	2
Somalia	4	4	4	4	4	4	4	4	4	4	4	4	4
South Sudan								2	2	2	3	3	2
Sudan	3	3	3	4	4	3	3	3	3	3	2	2	3
Syria	2	2	2	2	2	2	3	3	3	3	3	3	3
Tajikistan	2	3	2	3	2	2	2	2	2	2	3	2	2
Togo	1	1	1	1	1	1	1	1	1	1	1	1	1
Tonga	2	2	2	2	2	2	2	2	2	2	2	2	2
Tuvalu						1	1	1	1	1	1	1	1
Uzbekistan	3	2	2	2	2	2	2	2	2	2	2	2	2
Vanuatu	2	2	3	3	3	3	3	3	3	3	3	3	3
Yemen, Rep.	3	2	2	2	3	3	3	2	2	2	2	2	2
Timor-Leste	1	1	1	1	1	1	1	1	1	1	1	1	1
Zimbabwe	2	2	2	3	1	1	1	1	1	1	1	3	3

Table A13.4 Low- and Lower-Middle-Income Countries That Have Never Been Classified as Fragile 2005–17

A. Monetary policy framework

	Monetary Policy framework (1=exchange rate anchor, 2=monetary aggregate target, 3=inflation-targeting regime, 4=other)												
	2005	**2006**	**2007**	**2008**	**2009**	**2010**	**2011**	**2012**	**2013**	**2014**	**2015**	**2016**	**2017**
Bangladesh	2	2	1	1	1	2	2	2	2	2	2	2	2
Benin	1	1	1	1	1	1	1	1	1	1	1	1	1
Bhutan	1	1	1	1	1	4	1	1	1	1	1	1	1
Bolivia	1	1	1	1	1	4	4	4	4	2	2	2	2
Burkina Faso	1	1	1	1	1	1	1	1	1	1	1	1	1
Cabo Verde	1	1	1	1	1	1	1	1	1	1	1	1	1
Egypt	1	1	4	4	4	4	4	4	4	4	4	4	4
El Salvador	1	1	1	1	1	1	1	1	1	1	1	1	1
Ethiopia	2	1	1	1	1	1	1	1	2	2	2	2	2
Ghana	2	3	3	3	3	3	3	3	3	3	3	3	3
Honduras	1	1	1	1	1	1	1	1	1	1	1	1	1
India	4	4	4	4	4	4	4	4	4	3	3	3	3
Indonesia	2	3	3	3	3	3	3	3	3	3	3	3	3
Kenya	4	4	2	2	2	2	2	2	2	4	4	4	4
Kyrgyz Republic	4	4	1	1	4	4	2	2	4	4	4	4	4
Lesotho	1	1	1	1	1	1	1	1	1	1	1	1	1
Moldova	2	2	2	2	2	3	3	3	3	3	3	3	3
Mongolia	2	1	1	2	2	2	2	4	4	4	4	4	4
Morocco	1	1	1	1	1	1	1	1	1	1	1	1	1
Nicaragua	1	1	1	1	1	1	1	1	1	1	1	1	1
Niger	1	1	1	1	1	1	1	1	1	1	1	1	1
Pakistan	4	4	4	4	4	2	2	4	4	4	4	4	4
Philippines	3	3	3	3	3	3	3	3	3	3	3	3	3
Rwanda	4	1	1	2	2	2	2	2	2	2	2	2	2

Continued

Table A13.4 *Continued*

	Monetary Policy framework (1=exchange rate anchor, 2=monetary aggregate target, 3=inflation-targeting regime, 4=other)												
	2005	2006	2007	2008	2009	2010	2011	2012	2013	2014	2015	2016	2017
Senegal	1	1	1	1	1	1	1	1	1	1	1	1	1
Sri Lanka	2	2	1	4	4	2	2	2	2	2	4	4	4
Swaziland	1	1	1	1	1	1	1	1	1	1	1	1	1
Tanzania	4	2	2	2	2	2	2	2	2	2	2	2	2
Tunisia	2	2	1	2	2	1	4	4	4	4	4	4	4
Uganda	2	2	2	2	2	2	2	2	3	3	3	3	3
Vietnam	1	1	1	1	1	1	1	1	1	1	1	1	1
Zambia	2	2	2	2	2	2	2	2	4	4	4	4	4

B. Exchange rate regime

	De facto exchange rate regime (1=hard peg, 2=soft peg, 3=managed float, 4=floating)												
	2005	2006	2007	2008	2009	2010	2011	2012	2013	2014	2015	2016	2017
Bangladesh	3	3	1	2	2	2	3	3	2	2	2	2	2
Benin	1	1	1	1	1	1	1	1	1	1	1	1	1
Bhutan	1	1	1	1	1	1	1	1	1	1	1	1	1
Bolivia	2	1	2	2	2	2	2	2	2	2	2	2	2
Burkina Faso	1	1	1	1	1	1	1	1	1	1	1	1	1
Cabo Verde	1	1	1	1	1	1	1	1	1	1	1	1	1
Egypt	1	1	3	3	3	2	2	2	2	2	3	4	2
El Salvador	1	1	1	1	1	1	1	1	1	1	1	1	1
Ethiopia	3	1	2	2	2	2	2	2	2	2	2	2	2
Ghana	3	3	3	4	4	4	4	4	4	4	4	4	4

Honduras	1	1	1	2	2	2	2	2	2	2	2	2	2
India	3	3	3	4	4	4	4	4	4	4	4	4	4
Indonesia	3	3	3	4	4	4	4	2	4	4	4	4	2
Kenya	3	3	3	4	4	4	4	4	4	4	4	2	2
Kyrgyz Republic	3	3	3	3	3	3	3	3	3	3	3	3	3
Lesotho	1	1	1	1	1	1	1	1	1	1	1	1	1
Moldova	3	3	3	4	4	4	4	4	4	4	4	4	4
Mongolia	3	1	1	4	4	4	4	4	4	4	4	4	4
Morocco	1	1	1	1	1	1	1	1	1	1	1	1	1
Nicaragua	2	2	2	2	2	2	2	2	2	2	2	2	2
Niger	1	1	1	1	1	1	1	1	1	1	1	1	1
Pakistan	1	1	3	4	4	2	4	4	3	3	3	2	2
Philippines	4	4	4	4	4	4	4	4	4	4	4	4	4
Rwanda	3	1	1	3	2	2	2	2	3	2	3	2	2
Senegal	1	1	1	1	1	1	1	1	1	1	1	1	1
Sri Lanka	3	3	1	4	2	2	4	4	2	2	2	2	2
Swaziland	1	1	1	1	1	1	1	1	1	1	1	1	1
Tanzania	4	3	3	4	4	4	4	4	4	4	4	2	2
Tunisia	3	3	1	4	2	2	2	2	2	2	2	4	2
Uganda	4	3	3	4	4	4	4	4	4	4	4	4	4
Vietnam	1	1	1	3	2	2	2	2	2	2	2	2	2
Zambia	3	3	4	4	4	4	4	4	4	4	4	4	4

14
Exports, Exchange Regimes, and Fragility

Ibrahim Elbadawi, Raimundo Soto, and Isaac Z. Martínez

1. Introduction

In fragile environments, economic growth is significantly slower than and twice as volatile as in other emerging economies.[1] Backwardness also shows in foreign trade. The share of exports in GDP of fragile economies has remained stagnant since the 1980s, while in other emerging economies it has risen significantly—by about 10 percentage points—reflecting their increased integration into global markets and higher value chains.

One key determinant of exports is the real exchange rate, that is, the relative price between traded and nontraded goods. Because it largely determines the relative profitability of investment in traded and nontraded sectors, this economy-wide relative price signals intersectorial resource transfers and factor movements in the economy, particularly capital accumulation. Exchange rate misalignment and instability have been frequently associated with the choice of exchange regimes: misalignment is more often observed in economies that peg their currency to the euro or the US dollar, while instability is usually linked to floating exchange regimes. Though the choice of an inflexible exchange regime does not automatically imply a tendency of the currency to misalign, there is significant evidence of real exchange rate appreciation in fragile economies.

In this chapter we revisit the role of exchange regimes in fostering exports and economic growth in fragile economies and, thereby, in reducing political fragility. For this purpose, we use a dynamic, stochastic, general equilibrium (DSGE) model. Two reasons justify the use of this methodology. First, our DSGE model is tailored to replicate the structural features of fragile economies, in particular the presence of frictions in market adjustment, the influence of external shocks (for example, foreign aid), and the roles of the government in providing public goods (public investment) and delivering social transfers to the population. The former

[1] We would like to thank the editors of this book for excellent comments and suggestions, the IMF Institute for its support, as well as suggestions received from participants in the seminar "Macroeconomic Policy in Fragile States," Blavatnik School of Government, University of Oxford, December 10 and 11, 2018. The usual disclaimer applies.

Ibrahim Elbadawi, Raimundo Soto, and Isaac Z. Martínez, *Exports, Exchange Regimes, and Fragility* In: *Macroeconomic Policy in Fragile States.* Edited by: Ralph Chami, Raphael Espinoza, and Peter Montiel, Oxford University Press (2021).

DOI: 10.1093/oso/9780198853091.003.0014

are instrumental in supporting sustained growth while the latter may determine the support of the government and, thereby, its political fragility. In a context of limited government resources, fulfilling these roles poses a key political dilemma to the government. Second, and most important, our DSGE model allows us to track the response of variables associated with fragility to shocks that are likely to be important in fragile economies. The simulations we perform below illustrate the types of general-equilibrium interactions that may complicate the analysis of the effects of shocks that typically affect fragile economies on endogenous variables that may influence fragility.

In an influential paper, Rodrik (2008) calls for an undervalued exchange rate as a mechanism for export promotion and sustained economic growth. His observation is that producers of traded goods suffer disproportionately from the government or market failures that keep poor countries from converging toward those with higher income. Collier and Gunning (1999) make a similar point, asserting that high transaction costs resulting from a poor policy environment become a source of comparative disadvantage for fragile economies in exporting manufacturing, which is one of the most transaction-intensive sectors.

The presence of frictions and externalities is the main theoretical justification for deviating from policy neutrality. Learning externalities from exports could justify export subsidies; knowledge spillovers from foreign companies could justify tax breaks for foreign direct investment (FDI); production externalities in "advanced" sectors could justify infant-industry protection or other measures to expand those industries. However, as noted by Harrison and Rodriguez-Clare (2010), the theoretical justification for protection requires at a minimum either that the country have a latent comparative advantage in the protected industry or that the international price for this industry is higher than warranted by the true opportunity cost of this good in the rest of the world.

In section 2 of this chapter we discuss the main political characteristics of the 51 fragile countries. Political fragility plays an important role in determining the fate of fragile countries, interacting frequently with economic aspects. Governments in fragile economies frequently lack authority and legitimacy and are unable to manage their populations' expectations through the political process. The evidence suggests that the incidence of violent civil conflicts is significantly higher in fragile economies, both before and since 1990. Political regimes in fragile economies are not only less democratic than in other emerging economies but also significantly less accountable. The executive in fragile economies is significantly less constrained in its ability to engage in arbitrary practices.

The interaction between political and economic factors in fragile economies is a relatively new topic of analysis. Most of the literature has focused on violent political and social conflicts, particularly civil wars. But there are a number of fragile economies where large-scale armed conflict is not present and where the insights of the economics of civil war do not necessarily apply. In these economies, authoritarian governments do not rely on repression but on enticing the different groups to support the government, that is, an implicit arrangement between ruling elites and citizens whereby citizens relinquish political influence in exchange for public spending. In section 3 we summarize the nature and main insights of the political economy model by Soto (2019) which links political fragility with the transfers and non-pecuniary goods given by the ruling coalition to its own constituency and to opposition groups. We subsequently use this model to justify the type of analyses using the DSGE model we develop in section 2. Although the political economy model is not embedded into the DSGE model, it provides a general framework for understanding how economic variables—and, particularly, the different government policies—may affect fragility.

Section 4 provides a summary presentation of our DSGE model which is designed to understand the role of different policies in both inducing exports and economic growth and affecting political fragility. The type of government policies that we would like to study relate to government transfers to the population (which have direct effect on political fragility), the level of government expenditures (which links to Dutch disease problems), and the allocation of public investment (which can be instrumental in reconstruction of conflict-affected economies as well as in fostering exports). We also consider the role of external debt levels and foreign aid surges, the latter being an important external force that might help support government finances but can be seriously damaging to the external competitiveness of a small economy if not properly managed.

Among the most interesting and novel features of the model is its ability to track transfers given by the ruling coalition to the population to entice political support, the fact that these transfers cannot be arbitrarily set but are limited by the available financing, and the intertemporal restrictions that governments must obey to implement sustainable policies. A second feature is the presence of quadratic costs to the relocation of physical capital from one sector to another, a realistic friction that shapes the speed at which an economy returns to sustained growth after a policy shock. The third and most unique feature is the explicit modeling of learning by exporting, which occurs in most industries even when exports are largely concentrated on commodities. Learning, as opposed to total factor productivity (TFP) gains, is the result of accumulating knowledge of previous export activities and, therefore, is an endogenous externality.

Finally, because our aim is to understand the impact on exports and growth of the choice of exchange regimes, the proposed model allows for markets to clear continuously under two alternative closures. One closure allows the nominal exchange rate to freely float in response to the supply and demand of foreign liquidity. In this case, the nominal exchange rate is endogenous and foreign reserves of the Central Bank are kept constant. The other closure imposes rigidities on the adjustment of the nominal exchange rate which, in the limit, can mimic a fixed exchange rate regime. In the latter case, reserves are used to manage the exchange rate.

Section 5 collects the main results and the policy implications from our analyses. Our conclusions complement and support those from Chami et al. (2019) who also use a DSGE model to study issues related to shorter-term macroeconomic stabilization in fragile states.

2. Exports and Growth

As shown in Figure 14.1, there has been a tendency to adopt fixed exchange regimes in all emerging economies in the period 1990–2017 and dismiss managed floats and other intermediate regimes. Such a trend, nevertheless, has been much more marked in fragile economies: two-thirds of fragile economies had implemented fixed exchange regimes during the period 1990–2017 as opposed to only one-third in the period 1960–89. Nonfragile economies with inflexible exchange regimes increased from 45 percent to less than 60 percent in the same time span. Though the choice of an inflexible exchange regime does not automatically imply a tendency of the currency to misalign—as amply demonstrated by the experience

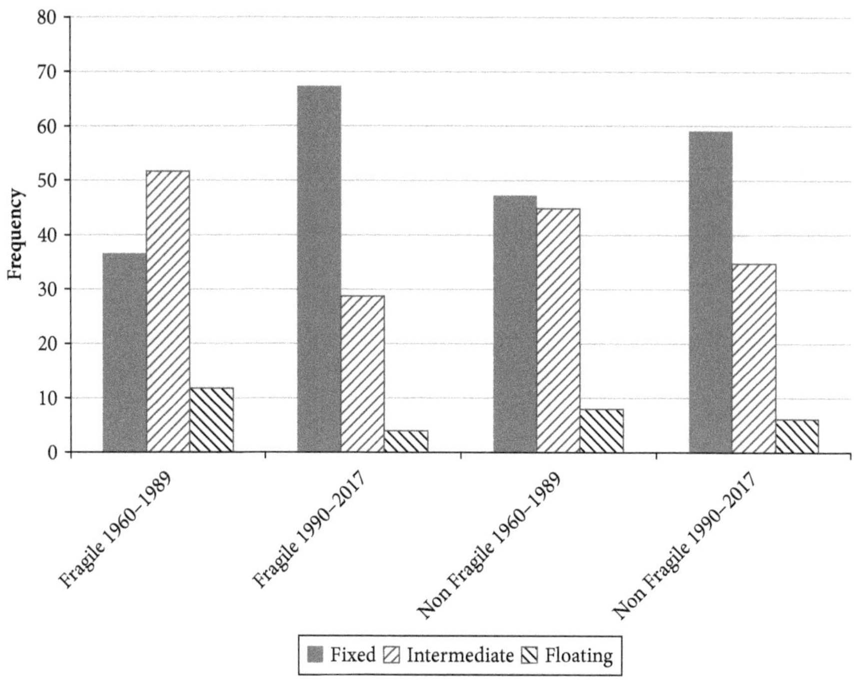

Figure 14.1 Exchange Regimes in Fragile and Non-Fragile Economies
Source: Authors' own elaboration based on data from Ilzetsky et al. (2016).

of the European Union since the adoption of the euro—there is significant evidence of currency appreciation in fragile economies. Estimates by Couharde et al. (2017) show that fragile states are more likely to have an overvalued currency (55 percent) than nonfragile economies (45 percent).

2.1 Productivity Gains and Learning by Exporting

The evidence suggests that key determinants of development in fragile economies relate to (a) investment levels, in particular public investment as the main provider of infrastructure and other public goods; (b) exports and the inability of fragile economies to become competitive in international markets; and (c) the growing proclivity of governments toward conducting monetary policy under fixed exchange regimes.

Consequently, a key issue for fragile economies would be to determine which exchange regime is more conducive to a virtuous circle of higher levels of investment and exports, given the structural and political restrictions that characterize fragility.

The notion that exporting may increase the productivity of firms and thereby support sustained economic growth has been at the roots of economic development for long time. Successful cases of export-led growth are Germany and Japan in the 1950s and 1960s and the four East Asian "Tigers" (South Korea, Hong Kong, Singapore, and Taiwan) in the 1970s and 1980s. However, what exactly constitutes export-led growth is ambiguous. As noted by Weiss (2005), the precise mechanism through which countries can benefit from openness to trade and rising exports has been the subject of much discussion. Possible mechanisms include:

- If economies can break into export markets they will be able to overcome the constraints on sales imposed by the absolute size and dynamism of the domestic market. Insofar as increasing returns to scale in production are important this will reinforce the advantage of operating at higher output levels needed for exporting (see Bartelme et al., 2018).
- Exporting can lead to productivity gains that arise from exposing firms to foreign competition, technology and marketing and that would otherwise not be obtainable from selling only to domestic markets. Participating in export markets brings firms into contact with international best practice and fosters learning and productivity growth (World Bank, 1997).
- Exports allow access to imports that can be purchased with the foreign exchange they generate. For individual producers, gains from imports can be both static, if they cost less than competing domestic production, and

dynamic, where capital and intermediate imports embody superior technology that allows productivity gains (Halpern et al., 2015).

- An export-oriented strategy attracts foreign direct investment (FDI) that would not have come to the economy under an import substitution regime, and insofar as this FDI generates positive externalities for the domestic economy, there will be further benefits that go beyond the monetary value of increases in exports (Kimura and Kiyota, 2006).

Empirical studies tend to agree that exporters have, on average, higher productivity levels than non-exporting firms. Naturally, correlation is not causality; therefore, a still ongoing debate ensued as to whether exporting has a *causal impact* on measures of firm performance. Two causal mechanisms are often used to explain the higher productivity of exporters as compared to non-exporters. The first hypothesis is self-selection, where only the more productive firms will self-select into the export market (for example, Bernard and Jensen, 1999). An alternative but not mutually exclusive explanation is learning by exporting, which argues that export participation can be a source of productivity growth, enabling exporting firms to become more productive relative to non-exporters (e.g., Van Biesebroeck, 2005). In our empirical work, we focus on the latter as the key causal mechanism linking exports and sustained growth. The DSGE model we develop lends itself to studying learning by exporting using a representative exporting firm; to study the self-selection mechanism the DSGE model would have to extended to consider the distribution of productivity of potentially exporting firms—information that is unlikely to be available for fragile countries.

Learning by exporting has been identified as an important mechanism whereby firms can increase productivity if they access information to which they would otherwise not be privy (Salomon and Shaver, 2005). Indeed, it refers to a variety of mechanisms that might induce productivity gains when firms start exporting, such as investing in marketing, upgrading product quality, innovating, or dealing with foreign buyers (Eaton et al., 2016). Evidence regarding the learning-by-exporting hypothesis is controversial, because proper measurement would require controlling for other firm-level actions such as R&D, technology adoption, and quality upgrading (de Loecker, 2013). According to a recent survey by Martins and Yang (2009), the evidence is conclusive in that exporting does increase productivity and that the impact is higher for developing than for developed economies. They also find that the export effect tends to be higher at the initial stages of exporting (compared to later years).

The evidence suggests that there is a strong correlation between exporting and productivity gains, and empirical studies linking exports and economic growth abound. The successful experience of some countries with export-led growth and the abundant microeconomic evidence of a positive correlation between exports and both higher productivity and sustained growth has revamped the importance of trade and trade-promoting policies (see, for example, Frankel and Romer, 1999) and has whetted the appetite of the supporters of active industrial policies (for example, Hausman et al., 2008). Trade and industrial policies have diverse instruments available for these purposes. At the micro level, tax incentives, subsidies, government purchasing, contracting of services, soft loans, guarantees, tariffs, and regulations are considered to be playing an export-fostering role. At the macroeconomic level, exchange regimes are considered a key component of the export-promoting strategy, and real exchange undervaluation—be it transitory or long-lasting—features prominently in most empirical and policy-oriented studies.

Aizenman and Lee (2010) focus on how different forms of learning-by-doing externalities call for different first-best policy interventions (in the absence of policy intervention, externalities are suboptimally produced). Depending on the nature of the learning-by-exporting externality, it may call for subsidizing the cost of capital, subsidizing the cost of labor, or both. Real exchange rate undervaluation—as proposed, for example, by Rodrik (2008)—would be the suggested policy only if the learning-by-exporting externality calls for subsidizing employment in the traded sector, and if this end cannot be accomplished through more effective means. They claim that activist exchange rate policies may generate competitive gains through keeping the real exchange undervalued, and the resultant increase in exports will promote economic growth. Korinek and Serven (2016) propose that a long-lasting undervaluation of the currency can be achieved by accumulating foreign reserves, as opposed to expansionary monetary policies that can only depreciate the exchange rate in the short term. In the DSGE model we allow for temporary undervaluation of the currency but impose the restriction that the real exchange rate must return to equilibrium in steady state.

3. Political Fragility

As mentioned, economic fragility is but one of the two crucial aspects of fragility we consider: political fragility plays an equally important role in determining the fate of fragile countries, interacting frequently with economic aspects. In this section we summarize a theoretical model by Soto (2019), that links political fragility with the transfers and nonpecuniary goods given by the ruling coalition to its own constituency and to opposition groups. We subsequently use its insights to justify the type of analysis we undertake using the DSGE model we develop in section 2. Although the political economy model is not embedded into the DSGE model, it provides a general framework to understand how economic variables—in particular, the different government policies—may affect fragility. Political fragility, in this context, would correspond to an unstable political environment (characterized by the risk of a coup d'état or a civil conflict) and weak state capacity, made only worse by a high propensity to destabilization by external shocks.

The model posits a simple game between the governing coalition and opposition groups. Political power entails control of government rents (taxation, natural resources, etc.), as well as the authority to choose a preferred set of nonpecuniary policies (for example, the degree of political participation and civil liberties). Government rents are stochastic; in every period, their level is known to the government but unknown to the population, which has to form expectations based on private and publicly available signals. The informational asymmetry is used by the government to its own advantage to maximize the probability of staying in power.

The key insight is that although the ruling coalition would prefer to keep all available rents for its constituency and set nonpecuniary policies according to their own preferences, it will find it desirable to share rents and accommodate, to some degree, its policies to the preferences of the opposition so as to limit popular discontent or contain the threat of an uprising. Rent sharing is modelled in the form of direct transfers to the population but it could include guaranteed public jobs at a wage premium, labor market protection in the private sector, or subsidies for schooling, housing, and utilities.

The government offers each group in the opposition a bundle comprising a share of total rents (the rest goes to its constituency) and an attractive nonpecuniary policy (that may or may not be the preferred policy of its constituency). When evaluating the bundle, the opposition has two alternatives: (a) accept the bundle, or (b) reject the bundle and attempt to overthrow the ruling coalition. The outcome is uncertain. If the overthrow is successful, the opposition captures all rents and imposes its preferred policy. If it is unsuccessful, then the ruling coalition does not give any transfer to the opposition and enacts its ideal policy. The ruling coalition will successfully appease the opposition when the value of the bundle for the population exceeds the expected value of overthrowing the government. The equilibrium takes the form of an authoritarian bargain (Desai et al., 2009).

The uprising is successful with a probability that depends inversely on the political support given to the ruling coalition by the population. The model assumes that such political support depends on the *relative size* of the transfer offered to a group in the opposition vis-à-vis the rest of the individuals (that is, its *share of the pie*). Each group observes the transfer being offered but is uncertain about the total size of rents and must form a conjecture as to whether their relative position has improved or deteriorated. Their conjecture is based on available *public* information and the *private* signal received in the bundle offered. Public information includes all available information, except the total rent.

In this context of incomplete information, political support for the governing coalition increases with the *expected* share of the pie: whenever transfers are lower than expected, political support dwindles. Consider the situation when government rents dwindle (for example, as a result of falling prices of natural resources) and the ruling coalition is forced to reduce the total transfer to society. Each group in the opposition observes the proposed cut in its transfers but not the total decline in government rents and, therefore, must guess whether the offered transfer maintains its share of the pie. If not, they withdraw their support of the government. Likewise, during a commodity price boom the individual would assess whether they are getting their fair share of the windfall.

Because both private and public information are noisy, when forecasting the total available transfer, each opposition group must decide how much to trust each signal. They use a Bayesian rule that weighs the relative uncertainty of each signal: the lower the relative uncertainty of one type of information, the higher its informational value. A group that has historically received a very predictable share of the pie would put significantly more trust in the transfer offered by the government than in public signals. Governments in more unstable economies, that is, where the relative uncertainty of public information is higher, would face lower political support than more stable economies for the same level of transfers. In this case, even smaller shocks can be destabilizing.

This political economy theory provides a number of insights that guide the design of the structure of our empirical DSGE model and identifies the main policies one would like to study in the context of fragile economies. Among others:

- For any level of rents and given the ideal policies of the governing coalition, an increase in transfers to the opposition lowers the consumption and utility of the ruling coalition but it raises their political support, thereby reducing the probability of a successful overthrow of the regime. Transfers reduce fragility. This is the capital trade-off for the ruling coalition. This would explain the generous transfers given to opposition groups during political turmoil (Manacorda and Vigorito, 2011).
- For any level of rents and given the ideal policies of the governing coalition, it is costlier to collect political support in societies where individual transfers are more uncertain than total transfers. Stable transfers reduce fragility. Ruling coalitions would like to have opposition groups significantly trust the information value of individual transfers. For example, when transfers come in the form of public employment and subsidies, as is the case in most fragile economies, the ruling coalition would avoid changing current expenditures (public wages, social programs) during the business cycle and focus on adjusting capital spending. Evidence indicates that fiscal adjustment episodes tend to be accompanied by disproportionate public investment cuts, a characteristic behavior in developing countries related to the fact that capital expenditure cuts may prove to be more politically palatable than cuts in current expenditure (Ardanaz and Izquierdo, 2017).

- An increase in government rents improves the welfare of the ruling coalition but it also increases the payoff of a successful overthrow, additional transfers are then called for to lower the probability of success. Sharing fiscal bonanzas reduces fragility. This would explain, for example, the generous transfers given to citizens by oil exporters during price booms (Diamond and Mosbacher, 2013).
- Aligning the ideal policy of the ruling coalition to that of the nationals would reduce the cost of securing political allegiance. Transfers are used by the ruling coalition to counterbalance the political cost of imposing their ideal policies over those of the opposition. When the cost of such transfers is too high, governments are forced to yield to popular demands and re-align their preferred policies (Lacroix and Filiu, 2018). Likewise, during the Arab Spring, Gulf Cooperating Council monarchies massively expanded transfers to maintain political support but chose to crack down rapidly on any political demand (Kamrava, 2012).

4. Modeling Fragility, Exports, and Exchange Regimes

In this section we present a stylized description of our DSGE model, identifying its key characteristics and providing a snapshot on how to solve it and simulate its dynamic properties (a description of the full model is available upon request). The model extends the standard DSGE macroeconomic model to account for (a) costly relocation of resources between sectors; (b) learning by exporting; and (c) the presence of capital goods provided freely by the public sector (for example, infrastructure). The model is calibrated to mimic the case of fragile economies and used to study its response to different types of policy shocks.

An alternative methodology is employed by Chami et al. (2019): they set up a nonstandard DSGE framework specifically intended to describe what they perceive as a typical macroeconomic setting in fragile states. These include (a) the tendency to monetize fiscal deficits (itself the result of small domestic debt markets and closed financial accounts), as well as (b) labor market frictions that create unfair wage distributions. When appropriate, we identify the differences and complementarities between both models.

4.1 The Model

We focus on a small open economy. Most fragile countries are small economies by international standards, in that their internal markets are not sizable and they cannot affect international markets in a systematic manner. Most conflict countries are also *de facto* open economies even if from a *de jure* perspective they may appear relatively closed, simply because frontiers liquefy as a result of the conflict and/or because of their very weak state capacity.

The model is designed to understand the role of different policies in inducing exports and economic growth and affecting political fragility. The types of government policies that we would like to study relate to government transfers to the population (which have a direct effect on fragility as discussed in section 1), the level of government expenditures (which links to Dutch disease and debt service problems) and the allocation of public investment (which can be instrumental in fostering exports and supporting sustained growth). We also consider the role of external debt levels and foreign aid surges, the latter being an important external force that might help government finances and the balance of payments but can seriously damage the external competitiveness of a small economy if not properly managed.

Crucially, in our model the level of transfers given by the ruling coalition to the population to entice political support cannot be arbitrarily set and, in fact, it results from the choices of the authorities regarding such policies and the fact that the choices are limited by the available financing and the intertemporal restrictions that the government must obey to implement sustainable policies. Contrary to CCEM, we do not link explicitly government transfers to the probability of the government remaining in power. Nevertheless, we compute a second-order approximation to the change in welfare induced by the different policies and, therefore, obtain an indirect measure of their effect on political fragility.

Our specification comprises the following elements, which we discuss in more depth in what follows. Given our interest in the role of exports and exchange regimes we consider three markets –nontraded, exported, and imported goods— so that we can identify separately terms-of-trade from the real exchange rate. Without loss of generality, we assume that exported goods are not consumed domestically and that imported goods are not produced in the country. Production of exportable and nontraded goods uses private capital, public capital, and employment with different intensities, according to standard production functions.

We assume that labor markets clear continuously (that is, we abstract from unemployment issues) but we impose that relocating physical capital from one sector to another is subject to a quadratic cost. Chami et al. (2019), on the contrary, make public employment the key policy variable that influences fragility. In their case, public employment must be solved for explicitly, as in a Ramsey model, to maximize the utility of the policymaker (which is a composite of the utility of the representative agent, public consumption, and the probability and cost of state failure).

A salient feature of our model is the explicit modeling of learning by exporting, which occurs in most industries even if exports are largely concentrated in commodities. Learning, as opposed to TFP gains, is the result of accumulating knowledge of previous export activities and is subject to depreciation. Consequently, exporting knowledge operates as an endogenous externality.

The households, which are the ultimate owners of all firms in the economy, receive both profits from firms as well as the returns on renting capital to produce goods and services. Households supply labor to the market and collect wages and are also the holders of government bonds and foreign assets. Finally, households hold money and, as mentioned, receive a transfer from the government.

The third component of our model is the government, which comprises the fiscal and monetary authorities. The fiscal authority is in charge of collecting taxes from the sales of exports and nontraded goods, spending on government consumption and public investment, and issuing and repaying government debt. The government is not entitled to issue external debt. The fiscal authority is also the recipient of foreign aid. The Central Bank issues money and collects seigniorage, which is passed on directly to the financing of the government and maintains foreign reserves for which it earns the international risk-free rate of return.

The setup of our model allows for studying the effects of an important type of external shock: foreign aid. As discussed, aid flows to fragile economies, particularly those in post-conflict situations, is usually massive and occasionally untimely. In effect, these financial flows usually come at times when the absorptive capacity of the fragile economy is unable to cope with them. It is not unusual to observe that in those cases the real exchange rate appreciates and most of the resources are devoted to financing consumption booms.

Finally, because our aim is to understand the impact on exports and growth of the choice of exchange regimes, the proposed model allows for markets to clear continuously under two alternative closures. One closure allows the nominal exchange rate to freely float in response to the supply and demand of foreign liquidity. In this case, the nominal exchange rate is endogenous and foreign reserves of the Central Bank are kept constant. The other closure imposes rigidities on the adjustment of the nominal exchange rate which, in the limit, can mimic a fixed exchange rate regime. In the latter case, reserves are used to manage the exchange rate.

One key difference between our model and that of Chami et al. (2019) is in the time horizon. They adopt a shorter time perspective because their model does not allow for capital accumulation or intersectoral capital reallocation, while we allow for accumulation of public capital and (costly) intersectoral reallocation of private capital as well as learning by exporting. These features produce marked differences between short-term and long-term responses to policy shocks.

4.1.1 Production Frontier

We consider three markets: nontraded, exported, and imported goods. Without loss of generality, we assume that exported goods are not consumed domestically and imported goods are not produced in the country. Production of the two domestic industries (exportable goods, *X*, and nontraded goods, *N*) uses private capital (*Kn, Kx*), public capital (*Kg*), and employment (*Ln, Lx*) with different intensities (as reflected in parameters ϕ, φ, η *and* λ, according to standard production functions as described in equations (1) and (2).

$$N_t = An_t Kg_{t-1}^{\phi}(Kn_{t-1})^{\varphi} Ln_t^{1-\varphi}$$

$$X_t = Ax_t Kg_{t-1}^{\eta}(H_t Kx_{t-1})^{\lambda} Lx_t^{1-\lambda}$$

Public capital enters directly the production function of the firms and, being provided freely by the government (such as infrastructure), it lowers costs and enhances TFP. This feature is not present in Chami et al. (2019). Technology (denoted by *An* and *Ax*) evolves in an exogenous but stochastic and independent manner in each industry according to a standard AR(1) process. We also assume that the capital share in the tradable sector is greater than in the nontradable sector, that is $\lambda > \phi$. Because the tradable sector employs relatively more capital, it will also draw more investment and will generate greater learning-by-exporting externalities, as we discuss in more detail.

The first salient feature of our model is the explicit modeling of learning by exporting, as indicated by variable H_t in equation (2). As discussed, exporting in most industries is subject to learning even if exports are largely concentrated in commodities. Learning, as opposed to TFP gains, is the result of accumulating knowledge of previous export activities and it is subject to time depreciation (at a rate of ϑ).[2] Consequently, knowledge of exporting operates as an endogenous externality. We model the learning externality in exports as:

$$ln(H_t) = (1-\vartheta)ln(H_{t-1}) + \vartheta ln(Kx_{t-1})$$

The second salient feature of the model is the presence of adjustment costs to capital accumulation. Following Chatterjee and Mursagulov (2016), firm owners in the nontraded sector pay a quadratic cost to capital adjustment of the form $\Gamma(Z_t) = Z_t + \frac{h}{2}Z_t^2$ is total private investment. Whenever parameter *h* is positive, the total cost of investment exceeds the value of capital goods. This assumption allows us to have different short-term and long-term elasticities of capital supply, because the finite speed of adjustment to investment precludes the capital stock to reach equilibrium instantaneously. Adjustment costs to capital accumulation play an important role in contemporary DSGE models. The stock of capital in both

[2] Note the difference between our modeling of learning by exporting and that in Clerides et al. (1998). Their critical assumption is that learning by exporting depends only on a firm's previous participation in foreign markets and not, as we assume, on the cumulative volume of its exports. Their specification better allows for fixed costs to exporting while ours better reflects dynamic efficiency gains from participating in foreign markets.

industries evolves according to the perpetual inventory method. The accumulation of private capital in each sector is given by:

$$Kn_t = Z_t + (1 - \delta_T)Kn_{t-1}$$

$$Kx_t = I_{x,t} + (1 - \delta_T)Kx_{t-1} - \Gamma(Z_t)$$

Firms maximize the discounted present value of profits over an infinite horizon. In both industries, sales are valued at domestic prices net of government taxes denoted by τ_X and τ_N. Costs include both the payment of labor at nominal wage W_t and renting capital at a cost of rx_t^K per unit. We abstract from capital and labor taxes. Note that we assume that factor markets clear at every instant and, therefore, capital is not idle and there is no unemployment.

$$\underset{Kx_{t-1},Lx_t}{\Pi xt} = (1 - \tau_X)Px_tX_t - rx_t^K(Px_tKx_{t-1}) - W_tLx_t$$

$$\underset{Kn_{t-1},Ln_t}{\Pi nt} = (1 - \tau_N)Pn_tN_t - rn_t^K(Pn_tKn_{t-1}) - W_tLn_t$$

The domestic price of exported goods (as well as that of imported goods) follows the law of one price $P_t^x = s_tP_t^{x*}$ *where* P_t^{x*} is the international price and s_t is the endogenous, nominal exchange rate. The price of nontraded goods is also endogenous, determined by the interaction of supply and demand. Consequently, the real exchange rate—the relative price of traded goods to non-traded goods—is endogenously determined.

Production decisions are made by forward-looking individuals and are aimed at maximizing the discounted present value of real profits over an infinite horizon at discount rate $\tilde{Q}_{t+j} = \beta^j \frac{UMgC_{t+j}}{UMgC_t}$. Optimization by exporters indicates that in equilibrium the following important condition holds:

$$\lambda(1 - \tau_X)\left[(1 + \vartheta)\frac{Y_{X,t}}{K_{X,t-1}} + (1 - \vartheta)\vartheta E_t\tilde{Q}_{t+1}\left(\frac{Y_{X,t+1}}{K_{X,t}}\frac{\frac{K_{X,t}P_{X,t+1}}{P_{t+1}}}{\frac{K_{X,t-1}P_{X,t}}{P_t}}\right)\right] = r_{X,t}^K$$

When there is no learning by exporting, $\vartheta = 0$, and equation (8) yields the standard result for a Cobb-Douglas specification whereby firms equate the marginal value of the productivity of capital to its real rental cost: $(1 - \tau_X)\left[\lambda\frac{Y_{X,t}}{K_{X,t-1}}\right] = r_{X,t}^K$. However, with learning by exporting, an important external effect occurs: by expanding capital and exports today, the firm learns how to be more productive *tomorrow* (because it increases knowledge of how to export), generating a future extra benefit in expected terms, which is internalized by the firm and discounted at rate $\tilde{Q}_{t+1}$. This extra effect is not considered in Chami et al. (2019) but it will make important differences in the response of the economy to government policies. In this way, our model complements their analysis.

4.1.2 Demand Possibilities

The representative household consumes nontraded and imported goods, while it supplies labor to the market. For simplicity, we assume that households supply inelastically one unit of labor to both sectors, so that $1 = Lx_t + Ln_t$. Wages, nevertheless, are endogenously determined by the combined labor demand of the nontraded and exported sectors. Given that labor is nonspecific, wages equalize at all times. Unemployment is thus excluded from our analysis. In addition to consuming goods and supplying labor, households hold real money balances which, again for simplicity, we model using a "money-in-the-utility function" specification. Chami et al. (2019) motivate money holding thorough a transactions technology.

The representative household is infinitely-lived and discounts the future using the discount factor β. Hence:

$$U_t = \max_{C_t, M_t} E_t \sum_{j=0}^{\infty} \beta^j \left[\frac{C_{t+j}^{1-\theta}}{1-\theta} + \frac{1}{1-\chi} \left(\frac{M_{t+j}}{P_{t+j}} \right)^{1-\chi} \right]$$

Our specification reflects the notion that households value having a stable path of consumption over time and that they will attempt to smooth out consumption in response to policy shocks. We thus assume that agents are not liquidity constrained. Such a possibility is not allowed in Chami et al. (2019), again indicating the shorter-term horizon of their specification.

Consumption comprises both imported and nontraded goods which we represent using a CES function:

$$C_t = \left((1-\alpha)^{\frac{1}{\varepsilon}} Cm_t^{\frac{\varepsilon-1}{\varepsilon}} + \alpha^{\frac{1}{\varepsilon}} Cn_t^{\frac{\varepsilon-1}{\varepsilon}} \right)^{\frac{\varepsilon}{\varepsilon-1}}$$

where ε is the elasticity of substitution and α is the share of nontraded goods in total consumption.

The representative household owns all firms in the economy and thus collects profits Π_t^x and Π_t^n as well as real wages. Being also the owner of all physical capital in the economy, it earns returns of the form $r_t^K(P_t K_{t-1})$ and decides investment in the exportable and nontraded sectors. Crucially for the political support of the government, it also receives a lump-sum transfer which we denote by TR_t.

As for assets, in addition to money, the representative household holds domestic bonds B_t earning a nominal return t_i, and external bonds denominated in foreign currency, denoted by F_t, earning a nominal return of i_t^*. The latter includes a risk premium, $\Psi\left(\frac{S_t F_t}{P_t}\right)$, which grows with the existing stock of foreign debt. External assets are expressed in local currency using the spot exchange rate. The household arbitrages the risks and returns of domestic and foreign assets. Note that because of imperfect capital mobility, weak uncovered interest parity holds as $(1+i_t) = E_t \frac{S_{t+1}}{S_t}(1+i_t^*)\Psi\left(\frac{S_tF_t}{P_t}\right)$ where $\Psi\left(\frac{S_tF_t}{P_t}\right)$ is the country risk premium.

4.1.3 The Government

The government is designed in a simple manner so as to analyze the role that different policies have on exports and the growth path of the economy and, thereby, on transfers, welfare and political fragility. It comprises of two authorities—fiscal and monetary—which we assume to operate in full in coordination and in a consistent manner: whenever any of these authorities enact a policy of their choice, they must obey their short- and long-term budget constraints, as well as the consolidated government constraints.

The government in this model is different from that in Chami et al. (2019). In their specification, the government is a planner that sets policies taking into account the risk of state failure. It encompasses a range of relevant situations, including governments that can be myopic and/or corrupt, as well as those that optimize social welfare. In our specification, we impose the rule that the government must obey its intertemporal budget constraint and is, therefore, always solvent. This would rule out myopic and corrupt governments that base their political support on irresponsible policies. Our assumption is justified on the grounds that households in this model internalize the short-term and long-term financial needs of the government.

Regarding the fiscal authority, and without loss of generality, we assume that the government consumes only nontraded goods and that the level of its current expenditures is exogenous, thus becoming its first policy variable. Note that government spending does not enter the household utility function and, consequently, it is pure waste. This is a standard hypothesis in the real business cycle literature (e.g., Baxter and King, 1993) and new Keynesian models: private and government consumption are separable in preferences or government consumption is a pure waste of resources.[3]

In our case, two considerations motivate this assumption. First, because our focus is on exchange regimes, our interest is in the issue of the appreciation of the real exchange rate as a result of increased government expenditures and the subsequent penalizing effect of exports. This, as discussed, has occupied a prominent role in policy discussions in fragile economies. Second, as discussed in our political economy model, one characteristic of fragile economies is that

[3] Our assumption also allows us to avoid the issue of whether public consumption is a complement of or a substitute for private consumption. The empirical evidence is not conclusive. Aschauer (1985) finds a significant degree of substitutability between the two variables of interest in the case of the United States, whereas Amano and Wirjanto (1998) find weak complementarity. Karras (1994), examining the relationship between private and public consumption across 30 countries, finds that the two types of goods are best described as complementary (but often unrelated).

government expenditures are allocated usually to the government constituency to the neglect of the population: government purchases of nontraded goods benefit only the policymakers themselves and, from the perspective of society, this spending is simply waste.

A positive shock to government expenditures in our model, nevertheless, must be financed in the short and long term by foreign aid (A_i, raising taxes, and/or issuing domestic debt. In our simulations we keep tax rates—but not tax collection—fixed and consider foreign aid to be exogenous. Consequently, any fiscal imbalance must be financed by issuing domestic bonds which are purchased by the households. Arbitrage between domestic and foreign assets occurs, making external debt the adjustment variable.

The government decides on the level of public investment, which we denote G_t^I. The stock of public capital (such as roads, ports, telecoms, etc.) evolves according to

$$K_{G,t+1} = G_{X,t}^I + G_{N,t}^I - (1 - \delta_G)K_{G,t}$$

The government must also decide on its third policy variable, namely the level of tax rates to be levied separately on the consumption of nontraded (τ_N) and traded goods (τ_X). Actual tax collection is endogenous and depends on the levels of consumption and exports.

Regarding the monetary authority, its main policy variable is that of money issuing and the collection of seigniorage. The Central Bank determines the rate of monetary expansion—and in the long term, inflation—but seigniorage is actually endogenous because it will depend on the levels of money demand and economic activity resulting from the decisions of consumers and producers. In addition to seigniorage, the Central Bank transfers to the government the full return on holding foreign reserves. The total transfers is denoted by Q_t.

As mentioned, at every instant in time the government must obey its nominal budget constraint, which also includes servicing its existing debt (B_{t-1}) and transferring resources (TR_t) to its constituency and the general population. Therefore:

$$\begin{aligned} &P_{X,t}G_t^I + P_{N,t}(G_{N,t}^C) + TR_t + B_{t-1}(1 + i_{t-1}) \\ &= A_tS_t + B_t + \tau_N Y_{N,t}P_{N,t} + \tau_X Y_{X,t}P_{X,t} + Q_t \end{aligned}$$

To have an intertemporally consistent budget balance we impose the restriction that in the steady state transfers (TR_{SS}) must be in line with the level of debt that is sustainable (B_{ss}). The latter is determined from the no-Ponzi conditions of our dynamic model. Equation (13) indicates that there exists a level of long-term transfer of resources to the public TR_{ss} that is consistent with the steady-state level of the government's debt (B_{ss}): whenever the current level of public debt is in excess of its sustainable level, transfers must be adjusted downwards to its sustainable level with a dynamic pattern controlled by the decay parameter, ρ. Parameter γ_b controls how much the government relies on debt for short-term financing.

$$log\ TR_t = (1-\rho)log\ TR_{ss} + \rho\ log\ TR_{t-1} + \gamma_b(B_{ss} - B_t)$$

4.1.4 Exchange Regimes

Key for our chapter is the monetary authorities' choice of the exchange regime. We focus on the two polar cases of a freely floating exchange rate and a fixed parity of the local currency to the US dollar. In both cases, we assume that once chosen, the exchange regime cannot be changed. In other words, we assume that the exchange regime—particularly the fixed parity rate—is fully credible. We therefore abstract from the fact that in real life such credibility may falter. Chami et al. (2019) assume a floating exchange rate regime that allows for central bank intervention to influence the rate.

In the floating exchange regime, the nominal exchange rate is freely determined by market forces without any intervention from the monetary authorities. The fixed exchange regime is modelled by imposing rigidities on the adjustment of the nominal exchange rate which, in the limit, can mimic the case of a totally fixed exchange regime. In this case, the foreign reserves held by the Central Bank are used to manage the exchange rate. The adjustment friction δ_t determines the evolution of the nominal exchange rate, such that:

$$S_t = \delta_t S_{t-1}$$

$$\delta_t = \left(\frac{P_{t-1}}{P_t}\right)^{\sigma_2 - 1}\left(\frac{S_t}{S_{t-1}}\right)^{\sigma_2}$$

When parameter $\sigma_2 = 1$, the nominal exchange rate is flexible (that is, it is determined endogenously every period), while if $\sigma_2 = 0$, the nominal exchange rate adjusts to match exactly the evolution of the domestic price index.

4.1.5 Parameterization

To solve and simulate our DSGE model we need to parameterize its equations. We use a set of about 31 parameters chosen to describe adequately the case of fragile economies. We estimate a number of parameters using data from World Economic Indicators (World Bank, 2019). Some of the parameters are obtained from previous studies, which we identify in Table 14.1. Other parameters are obtained from the constraints imposed by the model and its solution, usually from the first-order conditions governing the decision-making processes of consumers, producers, and investors. The model also solves from some built-in parameters, such as the shares of factor payments on value added. Finally, some

Table 14.1 Parameterization

Parameter		Source
β =0.96	Discount factor	Levin et al. (2005)
$\theta = 1$	Constant relative risk	Authors' estimates
$\psi_B = 0.01$	Parameters of sensibility risk premium	Authors' estimates
$\chi = 8$	Inverse of demand of money elasticity	Adam (2000)
$\delta_T = 0.1$	Depreciation of capital, tradable sector	Levin et al. (2005)
$\delta_N = 0.1$	Depreciation of capital, non-traded sector	Levin et al. (2005)
$\delta_G = 0.1$	Depreciation of capital, public sector	Levin et al. (2005)
$\tau_X = 0.12$	Tax, tradable sector	Authors' estimates
$\tau_N = 0.05$	Tax, non-traded sector	Authors' estimates
$\alpha = 0.6$	Share of consumption, non-traded sector	Castillo et al. (2009)
$\varepsilon = 0.75$	Elasticity of tradable sector/non-traded sector	Castillo et al. (2009)
$\lambda = 0.4$	Share of capital, tradable sector	Authors' estimates
$\varphi = 0.4$	Share of capital, non-traded sector	Authors' estimates
$\eta = 0.15$	Share of public capital, tradable sector	Chatterjee and Mursagulov (2016)
$\phi = 0.15$	Share of public capital, non-traded sector	Chatterjee and Mursagulov (2016)
$\gamma_b = 5$	Sensibility of transfer to government debt	Authors' estimates
$\vartheta = 0.001$	Elasticity of externality, private capital	Authors' estimates
$h = 0.001$	Capital adjustment cost, non-traded sector	Levin et al. (2005)
$i^* = 0.06$	Nominal International interest rate	Authors' estimates
$\mu = 0.5$	Persistency of monetary shock	Authors' estimates
$\rho = 0.5$	Persistency of transfer to consumer	Authors' estimates
$P_X^* = 1$	International price of exported goods (normalized)	Authors' estimates
$P_M^* = 1$	International price of imported goods (normalized)	Authors' estimates
$M_{ss} = 1$	Money holdings in steady-state (normalized)	Authors' estimates
$A_{X,ss} = 1$	TFP in exported sector (normalized)	Authors' estimates
$A_{M,ss} = 1$	TFP in nontraded sector (normalized)	Authors' estimates

Note: The value of some parameters has been imposed to be coherent with the data in steady-state (*SS*): TFP (A_{ss}), transfers (A_{ss}), government consumption of nontraded goods ($G_{N,ss}^C = 0.3$), government investment ($G_{ss}^I = 0.1$), and $\sigma_2 = [0, 1]$.

parameters were chosen to secure a parsimonious representation of the responses of the endogenous variables.

In addition to the equations, we need to parameterize the structure of the stochastic shocks of policy variables that are later used in the simulations. Following the common practice in the literature, for each stochastic variable we posit models of the form: $\ln x_t = \alpha + \rho \ln x_t + \varepsilon_t$, where ε_t is a pure i.i.d. innovation. Table 14.2 presents the estimated values for the uncertainty in shocks (as measured by their standard deviation of innovations) as well as their persistence (as measured by coefficient ρ).

Table 14.2 Estimated Stochastic Processes for Shocks, 1990–2018

Shocks	Standard Deviation	AR (1) coefficient
General government expenditure (percent of GDP)	0.766	0.531
Gross fixed capital formation (percent of GDP)	0.801	0.470
Net official foreign aid received (percent of GDP)	1.031	0.285

Source: Authors' estimation using data for the period 1990–2018 obtained from World Bank (2019).

4.2 Model Solution and Simulations

As described, the model is highly nonlinear and does not lend itself to closed-form solutions. The solution, therefore, is undertaken using simulations of the toolbox DYNARE in Matlab. In total, the model has 45 equations.

The dynamic properties of nonlinear models are best described using impulse response functions. Nevertheless, before discussing the response of our model to policy shocks, it is useful to describe some of the key characteristics of our model that shape the findings of the chapter.

Consider, first, that in our model there is imperfect capital mobility and that, therefore, weak uncovered interest parity holds. Domestic interest rates depend on the country risk premium, itself inversely determined by the stock of foreign assets or debts and the real exchange rate. An increase in net foreign assets naturally lowers the country risk while a depreciation of the real exchange rate makes repayment of foreign obligations more expensive vis-à-vis domestic prices and thus increases the country risk. The key issue is that the stock of foreign assets and the exchange rate—real and nominal—are endogenously determined in our model by the combined decisions of the government and the private sector, so that the long-term steady state and the trajectories toward equilibrium depend on the nature of the shock affecting the economy. Needless to say, different steady states and trajectories to equilibrium will induce dissimilar levels of transfers and real wages, affecting political support for the government.

Second, consider the existence of frictions in the reallocation of capital between sectors in the economy. Because reallocating is costly, the marginal value of capital does not equalize the alternative cost of resources; there will always be a wedge. Consequently, future relocations of capital will have an effect on today's investment that goes beyond the expected changes in the cost of capital. This restriction, by itself, will make adjustments in production more difficult than in the case where there is no friction, and will induce differential trajectories toward adjustment, distorted output levels and taxes paid vis-à-vis the no-frictions case, and, ultimately, an altered pattern of transfers.

Third, recall that learning by exporting changes the dynamics of the exporting firms because current investment and production decisions have significant effects on future production costs and profitability. Because exporters are forward-looking, entrepreneurs anticipate that higher exports today will lower production costs for the entire future and increase profitability. The return on capital, therefore, will be more than just today's value of the marginal productivity of capital because it will include the discounted shadow value of tomorrow's cost reductions derived from today's production. All else being equal, this externality will induce, in equilibrium, higher levels of private capital accumulation in traded sectors than the no-externality case and, because of complementarity, higher levels of investment by the public sector.

Note, finally, that in the absence of adjustment costs to capital and learning externalities, our model collapses to the standard intertemporal model of production and consumption of an open economy. It is precisely this feature of our model—that it encompasses the distortion-free economy as a special case—which allows us to identify and isolate the role of frictions and externalities on exports, wages, transfers, and economic growth under different exchange regimes. We therefore start our analysis from the distortion-free case where markets clear and all prices are free to adjust within the boundaries of a floating exchange regime. We focus then on the dynamics of the three types of shocks that we think are the most common and important for fragile economies: aid shocks, government expenditure shocks, and public investment shocks. We compute the model solution and simulate the dynamic effects on key macroeconomic variables, such as the real exchange rate, exports, consumption, and investment, but we focus more closely on three variables closely linked to fragility. First, we consider real transfers from the government to the population which, according to our political economy model, directly affect political support for government. Second, real wages which, being an important determinant of welfare, also determine political support for the government. Third, we also scrutinize sovereign country risk, which signals to a large extent the financial fragility of an economy.

4.2.1 Aid Shocks

One of the classical phenomena in fragile economies, particularly those coming out of violent civil conflicts, is the sudden inflow of unrequited external aid given to governments. International donors and multilateral organizations pour resources into the fragile economy in an attempt to promote development, foster exports, and combat poverty. Geopolitical considerations are often also present. Aid can involve a transfer of financial resources or commodities (such as food or military equipment) or technical advice and training, and it may take the form of grants, concessional credits, or official development assistance.

In our model, foreign aid can be used basically for two purposes. First, to buy back government debt, saving on its service and reducing an eventual debt overhang. A debt overhang reduces the incentives for investment, both foreign and domestic, because of the threat of future taxes. In principle, efficiency gains resulting from a reduction in debt overhang could be quite significant. Bulow and Rogoff (1989) argue, nevertheless, that when market prices correctly reflect the probability of repayment, these schemes typically result in a waste of valuable resources. The problem is that a buyback raises the market value of the debt left outstanding, and consequently it may not improve the net asset position of the sovereign. We call this case the *aid-for-debt swap*. Second, resources can be used to finance an expansion in government expenditures. Though in principle aid should help support development, evidence indicates that a significant fraction of received aid is squandered in nonproductive uses, such as military expenses (Collier and Hoeffler, 2007). Bueno de Mesquita and Smith (2009), however, found that aid is used for the provision of public goods despite leakages and waste. For a survey on the use and effectiveness of aid in fragile economies see Dreher et al. (2017). We call this case the *aid-for-government expenditures* case.

We simulate the effects of a once-and-for-all shock (one-period lump-sum transfer) of foreign aid to a fragile economy using our DSGE model and compute the trajectories of the variables of interest as deviations from their steady-state level. We focus first on the aid-for-debt swap and then on the aid-for-government-expenditures case.

4.2.1.1 Aid-for-Debt Swap

The aid-for-debt swap corresponds to the case where all of the aid inflow is used to retire government debt. That is, it corresponds to a pure wealth shock. The results of our simulations are displayed in Figure 14.2. We start our analysis from the distortion-free case where there are no frictions, no learning by exporting, and where all prices—including the nominal exchange rate—are free to adjust. The causal mechanism is as follows. Upon receiving the inflow of foreign aid, the government uses all resources to reduce its debt. The lowering of the internal debt and the readjustment of the portfolio of the private sector lead to a decline in country risk and an expansion in perceived permanent wealth by the households. In turn, this leads to an expansion in the demand for nontraded goods and also in the demand for imports: both effects amount to a consumption boom. To fulfil the demand for nontraded goods, production must expand, which requires relocating capital from the traded to the nontraded sector. Investment in the nontraded industries expands at the cost of lowering capital in the traded sector and exports, thus leading to a trade account deficit.

The most interesting results are those for the variables linked to political fragility. As a result of the expansion in the demand for nontraded goods and the relocation of capital from exports to nontraded industries, the demand for labor expands and initially real wages increase. Wages decline in the medium term because as a result of the frictionless relocation of capital from the traded to the

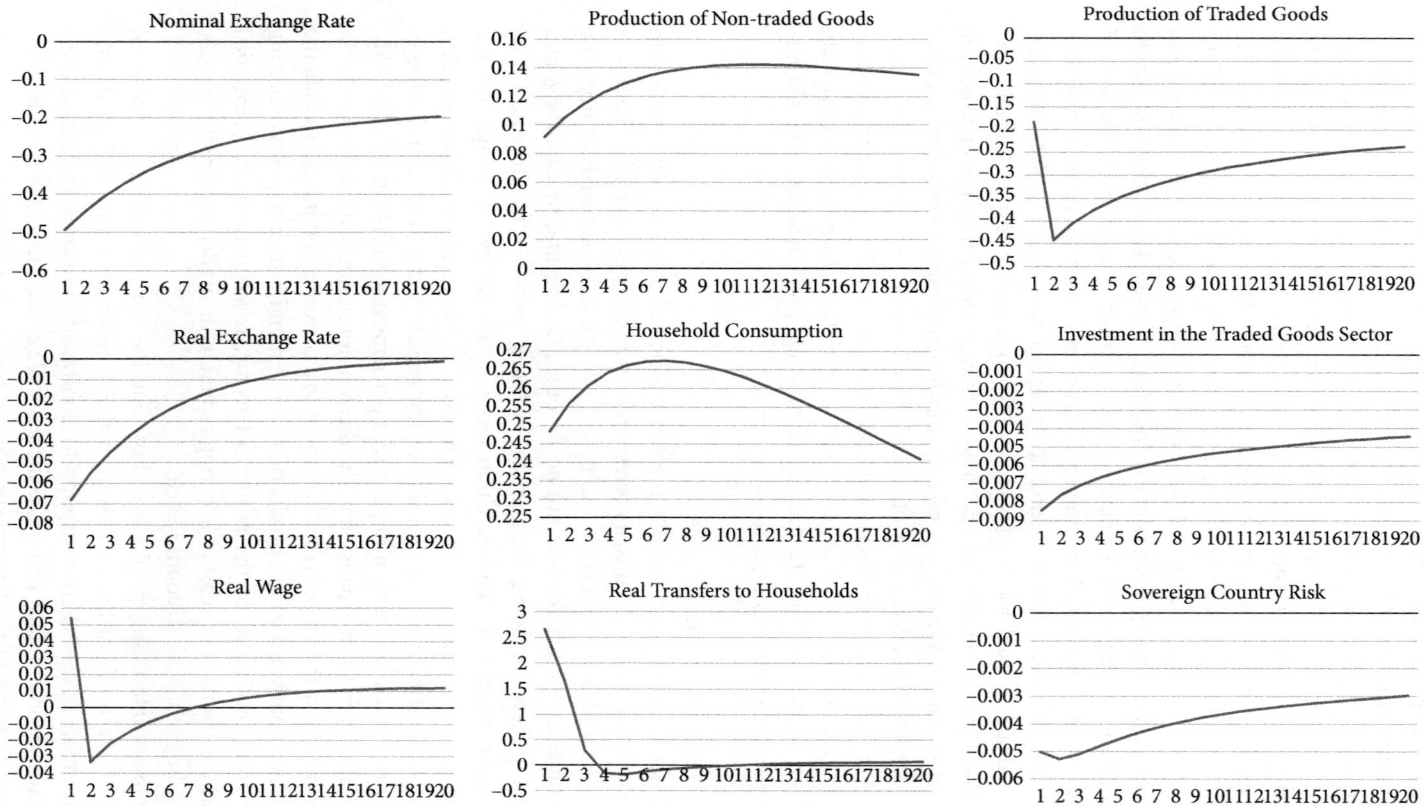

Figure 14.2 Aid-for-Debt Swap Shock

(Floating Exchange Regime, No Frictions, and No Learning by Exporting)

non-traded sector, workers are employed in the transitorily less productive sector. The population perceives this as an increase in welfare which, coupled with the consumption boom, raises political support for the government, at least in the short term. More important, the aid shock improves the government's budget and allows for a significant expansion in transfers to the population, thereby raising additional political support. However, the expansion in transfers is short-lived, because the aid shock is a once-and-for-all event, and it reverts to equilibrium in the long term because government finances worsen as a result of the reduced tax collection that follows the relocation of activities from the traded to the nontraded sectors. Political support for the government is limited in time. Finally, because the aid shock was used to buy back government bonds (inducing by arbitrage a lowering of the external debt), there is a significant and permanent decline in country risk that reduces the external fragility of the economy.

We now turn to the analysis of the aid shock in a context of frictions to capital adjustment and learning externalities but still in the floating exchange regime. We confine our discussion only to the evolution of the fragility-related variables, but full results are available upon request. As shown in Panel A of Figure 14.3, when frictions are introduced to capital adjustment and learning-by-exporting externalities, the general message remains qualitatively intact but the magnitude and phase of the responses to the aid shock is somewhat changed. First, note that the general dynamics of our three variables of interest are relatively similar. This is not unexpected; the shock corresponds basically to a wealth shock that does not induce a significant adjustment in the margin to the decisions made by households and the government. Nevertheless, the frictions in the capital market make the relocation of resources toward the nontraded industries costlier than it would be in the absence of such frictions. In addition, extracting workers from the traded sector to relocate to nontraded goods industries is now costlier because there is a sacrifice: future cost reductions that are foregone as a result of lower learning-in-exporting activities. Because the pull of demand in the nontraded sector cannot be serviced as quickly as in the baseline case, real wages initially rise more—and subsequently decline much more slowly, in the frictions case. Though this would imply additional political support for the government and lower fragility levels, the government fiscal position worsens more under frictions because tax collection suffers more from the decline in exports during the consumption boom than in the no-frictions case. Transfers are thus smaller. Finally, the presence of learning externalities in exporting indicate that the economy is more capable of servicing its foreign debt in the long run, thus allowing for a more appreciated real exchange than in the non-frictions scenario. The aid-for-debt swap shock, then, benefits the economy more than proportionally in the short and medium term.

Panel B of Figure 14.3 also shows the results of the model simulations in the fixed exchange regime scenario. As shown, the trajectories of the variables in response to the wealth shock are qualitatively similar to the case of the floating

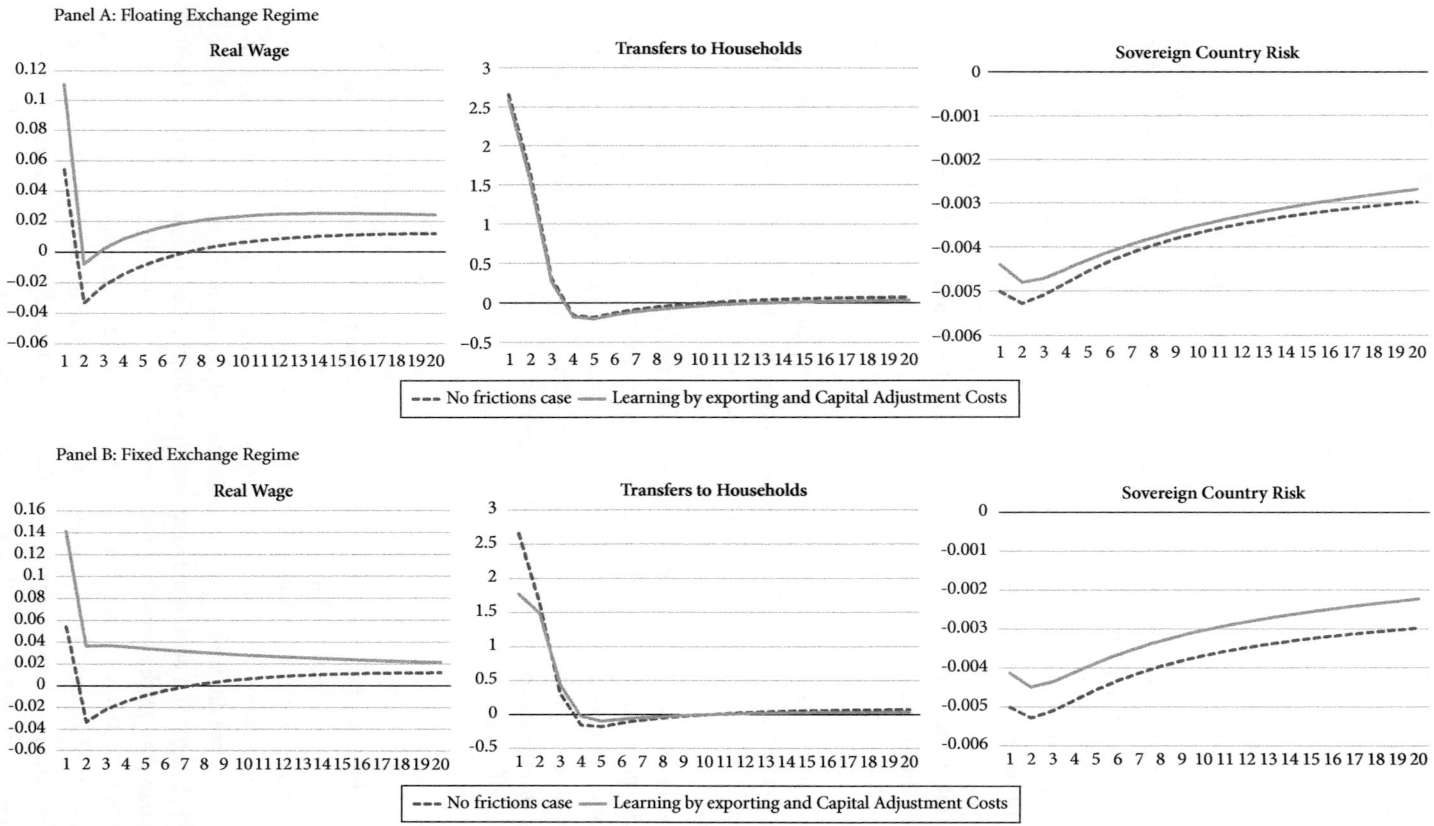

Figure 14.3 Aid-for-Debt Swap Shock

Panel a. Floating Exchange Regime; Panel b. Fixed Exchange Regime

exchange regime, except that in the steady state under the fixed exchange regime real wages are higher and decline slowly, transfers are lower and the decline in country risk is less significant. The underlying reason for the less dynamic response of the economy in this case is that the drop in the relative price of exported to nontraded goods is much smaller since the exchange rate is fixed and, therefore, the relocation of resources between the traded and nontraded sectors is also dampened.

4.2.1.2 Aid-for-Government-Expenditure

The aid-for-government-expenditures shock corresponds to the case where 50 percent of the aid inflow is used to retire government debt and the other 50 percent is used to finance government expenditures. The 50–50 shares were chosen for expositional purposes only. The results of our simulations are displayed in Figure 14.4 and, again, we focus only on the three fragility variables which are compared to the no-frictions case. Consider first the case of the floating exchange regime, as depicted in Panel A. Now, the wealth effect is much weaker, as shown in the less dramatic decline in the sovereign country risk. Because the government purchases only nontraded goods, there is a demand shock that translates into a concurrent higher demand for labor—with a significantly higher increase in real wages vis-à-vis the no-friction case—and a higher investment flow from the traded sector to the nontraded sector. Inevitably, the trade balance worsens. Foreign aid, in this case, does not allow the fiscal authority to pass on some of the resources to the population in transfers; as shown, contrary to the aid-for-debt case, the government uses external and internal resources to finance the purchases of nontraded goods. Note that the latter do not increase the welfare of society, so this policy is definitely worse than the previous case. Below we compute a quantitative measure of the welfare changes of these different policies using the expected households utility over the simulation horizon.

Panel B of Figure 14.4 shows the results of our simulations for the alternative fixed exchange regime. It can be seen that the impact on real wages is significantly stronger in this case, not only because the government induces a demand shock for nontraded goods and thereby for labor, but also because the price level adjusts only very slowly upwards. The latter effect occurs because the price of traded goods in domestic currency increases very slowly as the nominal exchange rate adjusts sluggishly toward equilibrium. As expected, the sovereign country risk improves less than when all of the aid support is used to retire government debt. The more interesting results are in the transfers to the population. In the absence of frictions, transfers are slightly negative, because the wealth is weaker. In the frictions case, transfers are initially very negative (becoming a substantial tax on consumers) because the increased government demand for nontraded goods raises their price and crowds out private demand, thus lowering tax collection. In order to finance the deficit, the government issues bonds, raising the sovereign

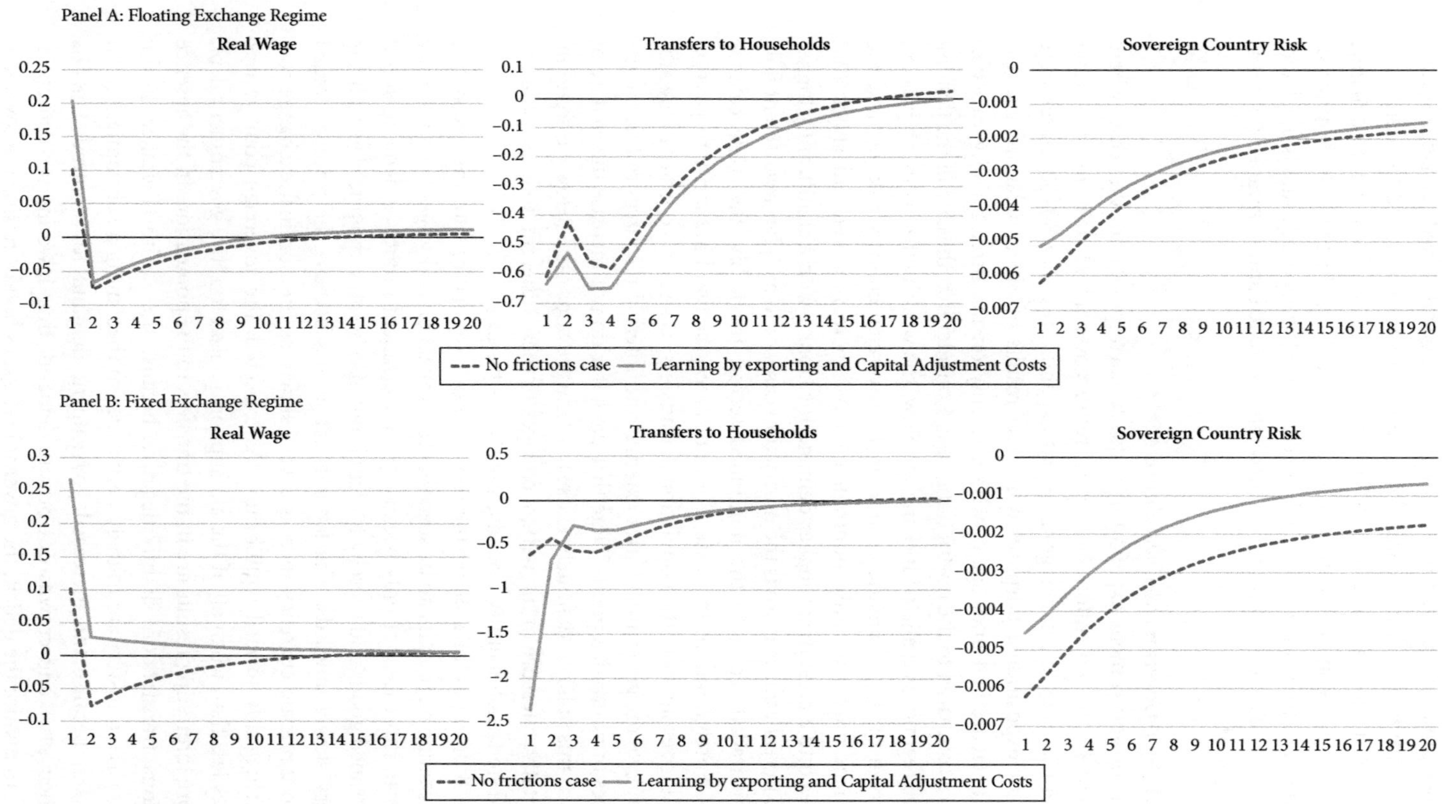

Figure 14.4 Aid-for-Government Expenditures Shock

Panel a. Floating Exchange Regime; Panel b. Fixed Exchange Regime

country risk and the domestic interest rate, which incentivize households to postpone consumption, thus further reducing tax revenue. Transfers become the adjustment variable. Because aid is a once-and-for-all shock, the crowd-out effect government demand is transitory and, as the fiscal stance improves, transfers return to equilibrium.

4.2.2 Government Expenditures Shock

In this exercise we give a once-and-for-all shock to the current expenditures of the government, that is, a demand shock to the nontraded sector because, as mentioned, the government does not consume imports. The main difference between this case and the previous exercise is that here the additional government expenses must be financed out of internal resources and not by recourse to foreign aid. Financing by the government can be achieved by raising taxes, lowering capital expenses, issuing debt, and/or reducing transfers to the population. To keep comparability with previous cases we keep tax rates and capital expenses fixed. The results of our simulation for the case of an economy with no frictions and conducting monetary policy in a floating exchange regime are shown in Figure 14.5.

The shock to government expenditures bears some resemblances to the previous case but differs in a significant dimension. Note, first, that the shock has an appreciating effect on both the nominal and real exchange rate. This is expected, but the response is much smaller (about one-third) and it is noticeably short-lived. The reason is that the government has to obey its intertemporal budget constraint and must finance the expansion of expenses somehow. As expected, production of nontraded goods increases, albeit only transitorily, and exports decline as a result of the relocation of capital and workers. Second, the differences with the previous case are nonetheless manifest: because the government is competing with the private sector for resources, consumption declines as a result of negative transfers needed to finance the budget in the absence of foreign resources. Fragility is most likely to increase, and in a significant manner. Note also that the sovereign country risk increases and then returns to its previous level. The reason is that by financing the expansion of expenditures while curtailing transfers, the government will not change either its internal debt or the country's external debt.

The results do not change significantly when allowing for adjustment costs to capital relocation as well as learning by exporting. As shown in Panel A of Figure 14.6, the trajectories of the real wage and government transfers show clearly that the drop is slightly less acute—because of frictions—and that the adjustment to equilibrium is now slower. Interestingly, the negative effects on the sovereign country risk are smaller in this case, because frictions retard the relocation of capital from the traded to the nontraded sector and the government is not required to issue as much debt as in the no-frictions case. As expected, *because* this government policy is transitory, all real variables return to equilibrium in the long term.

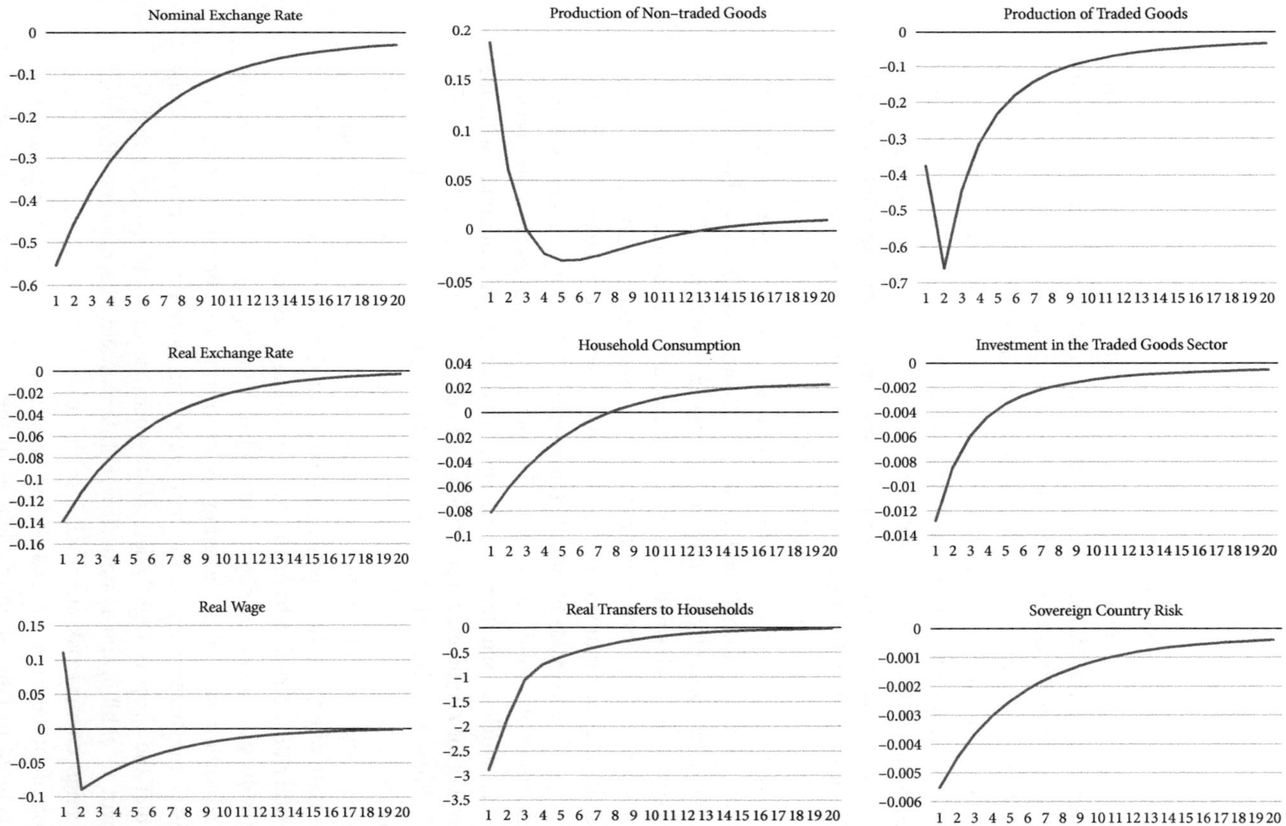

Figure 14.5 Shock to Government Expenditures
(Floating Exchange Regime, No Frictions, and No Learning by Exporting)

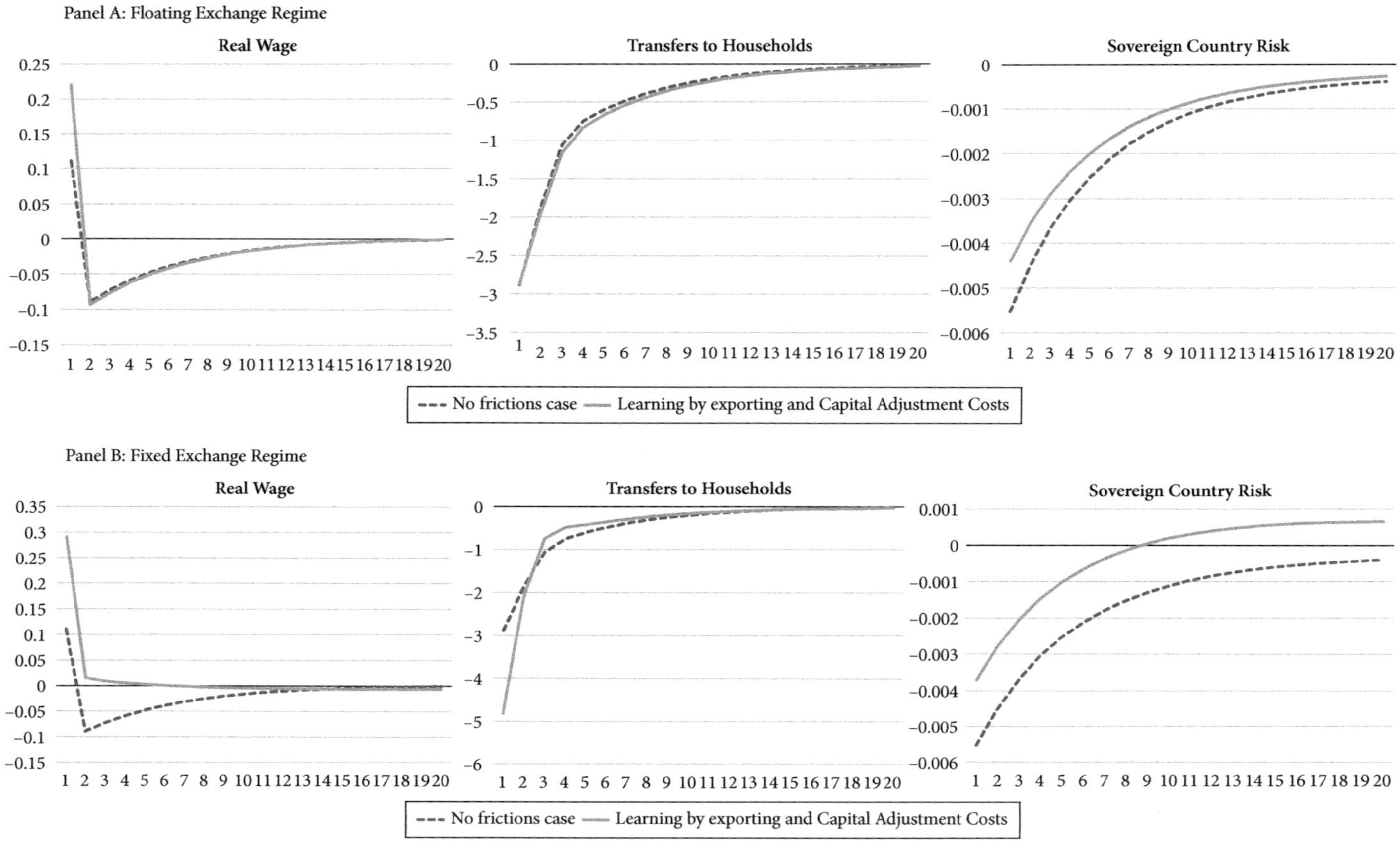

Figure 14.6 Positive Shock to Government Expenditures

Panel a. Floating Exchange Regime; Panel b. Fixed Exchange Regime

The case of the fixed exchange regime is displayed in Panel B of Figure 14.6. As it can be seen, there are important differences vis-à-vis an economy conducting monetary policy under a floating exchange regime. Consider first the no-frictions case. Because the government is financing domestically its higher demand for nontraded goods, there is no pressure on the exchange market and consequently no unsustainable appreciation of the real exchange rate. Wages, as before, drop initially before slowly returning to equilibrium. Because the government must finance its expenditures domestically, its transfers to the households ostensibly drop and it issues debt that, ultimately, is to be paid by the consumers. Households internalize this fact, anticipate the future payment of such government debt, and make arbitraging decisions accordingly.

In the presence of frictions, the effects on the wages and transfers remain very similar but the sovereign country risk increases in the long term, because the relocation of capital toward the nontraded sector destroys export knowledge and the ability to repay the external debt of the economy.

What drives the results in our model, and it might be in dissonance with the observed negative experiences of fragile countries attempting to jump-start their economies with an expenditure shock, is that in our case the government is restricted to obeying its intertemporal budget constraint, thereby making its policies sustainable. The often-encountered situation of a government that engages in an expansionary fiscal policy to gain popularity and political support at the (usually hidden) cost of expanding the public debt beyond sustainability is not taken into account in our model. Using a similar DSGE model, Evans et al. (2013) study the point where an unsustainable fiscal policy can no longer be maintained and collapses (dubbed the *game over point*). Their very long-term, closed-economy model, calibrated to replicate the US economy, is ill designed to study the cases of fragile economies.

4.2.3 Public Investment Shocks

Our final exercise consists of studying the effects of a positive impulse to public investment financed with domestic sources. Public investment freely provides public goods to producers that reduce costs and enhance productivity and production of traded and nontraded goods. Note, however, that the effects of this shock to public investment depreciate over time. The results of the simulations are presented in Figure 14.7. We assume that there is no time-to-build in public goods, so that the impulse immediately augments the production of traded goods. Because the share of public goods in the traded sector is larger than that in the nontraded sector, exports expand and the nontraded sector shrinks. Capital flows from the latter to the exporting sector, which also benefits from the relocation of workers, transitorily at lower real wages. Note that because there is learning-by-exporting, the expansions in exports and investment in the traded sector are long-lasting and quite significant. This reflects a type of "virtuous circle"

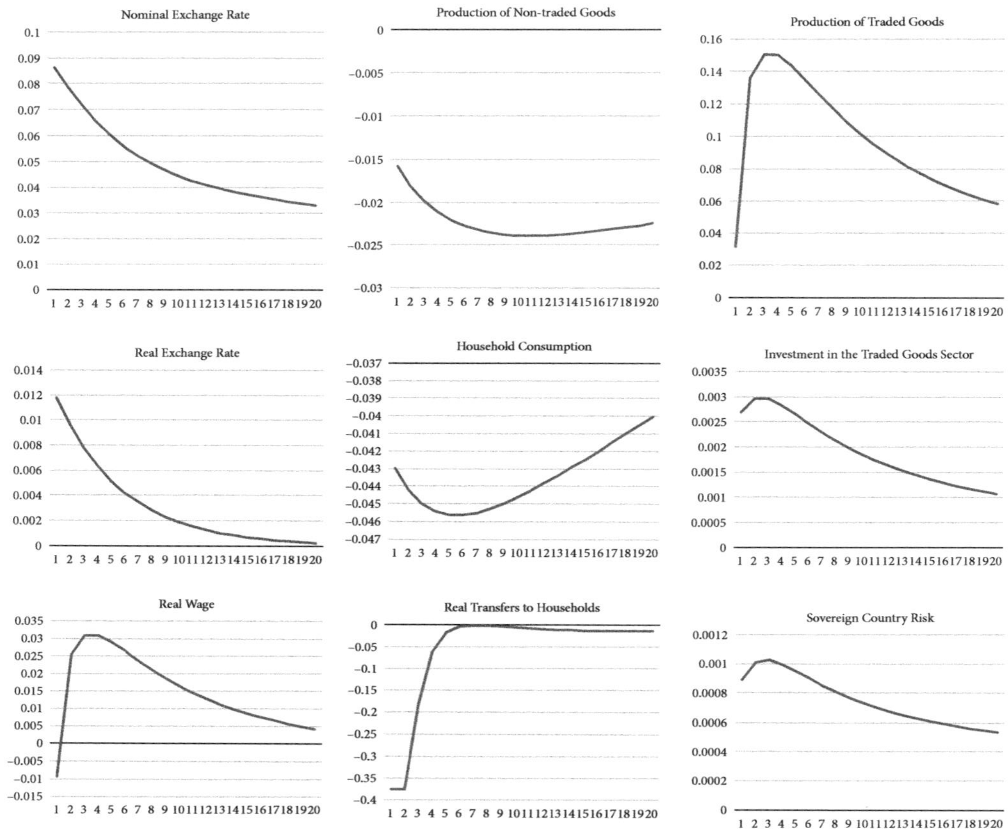

Figure 14.7 Positive Shock to Public Investment
(Floating Exchange Regime, No Frictions, and No Learning by Exporting)

between public investment and exports: a higher stock of public capital lowers costs in the traded sector and expands exports which, in turn, further lower production costs because of learning. Higher exports provide for increased tax revenue which allows for financing subsequent expansions in public investment.

Note also that the decline in the demand for nontraded goods and consumption, brought on by the negative transfers needed to finance the expansion in public investment, induces significant nominal and real depreciation. The nominal depreciation increases the sovereign country risk because the stock of debt is denominated in foreign currency and thus becomes more difficult to service; nonetheless, valuation returns to equilibrium as the expansion in exports causes the nominal value of the currency to appreciate. In other words, there is a transitory and relatively mild increase in external fragility as a result of the revaluation of the debt that eases in time until it returns to equilibrium. Note that though real wages and consumption take a relatively long term to return to equilibrium (indicating a deterioration in confidence in the government), real transfers to the population are greater in the medium term as a result of the higher taxes collected from the traded sector. Here the traded sector provides for sustained growth derived from the higher export levels achieved by the lower production cost sinduced by public infrastructure.

The latter effect is softened, as expected, when we allow for frictions. As shown in panel A of Figure 14.8, the combined effect of adjustment costs to capital relocation and learning externalities induces a less pronounced hike in real wages as a response to the public investment shock. It also allows for a less significant initial drop in transfers but sustains higher transfers in the medium term, thus reducing long-term fragility even if in the short term there is a transitory adverse effect.

Panel B suggests that the choice of exchange regime is relatively innocuous, a feature that derives from the sustainability of the fixed exchange regime in our model: the country never gets into the position of having to devalue the currency to achieve balance in its foreign accounts.

4.3 Welfare Implications

The ultimate purpose of our analysis would be to indicate which exchange regime is preferred for the three types of government policies discussed abovein our model. Such measures ought to rely on changes in welfare. Because our DSGE model is micro-founded, maximizing a measure of welfare of the representative household may be an appropriate instrumental objective to guide the choice of policies. Welfare is thus measured using the utility function of the households, as described in equation (9).

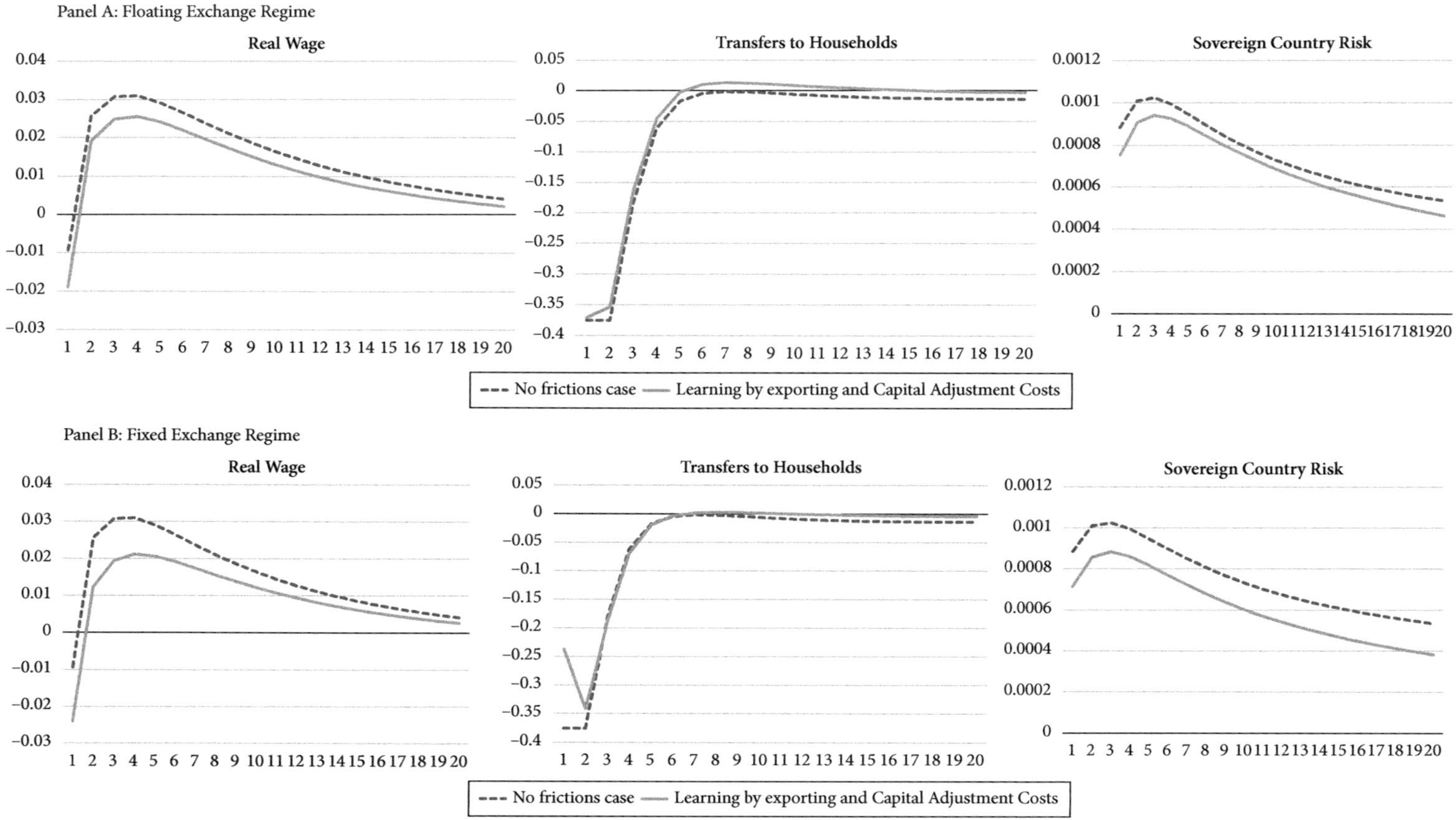

Figure 14.8 Positive Shock to Public Investment

Panel a. Floating Exchange Regime, Frictions, and Learning by Exporting

Panel b. Fixed Exchange Regime, Frictions, and Learning by Exporting

Computing welfare levels under optimal and non-optimal policy shocks is not straightforward, given the highly nonlinear nature of the DSGE model. As discussed in Benigno and Woodford (2012), it is relatively easy to approximate the welfare implications of policies of a simple, linear quadratic model if one specifies an ad hoc quadratic loss function on the basis of informal consideration of the kinds of instability in the economy that one would like to reduce, and posits linear structural relations that capture certain features of economic time series without requiring these relations to have explicit choice theoretic foundations. But it is highly unlikely that the analysis of optimal policy in a DSGE model will involve either an exactly quadratic utility function or exactly linear constraints. This is not the case for our model. Nonetheless, linear quadratic problems can usefully be employed as approximations to exact optimal policy problems in a fairly broad range of cases, when the solution to the problem represents a local linear approximation to the actual optimal policy and as long as the policy shocks are small enough.

We rely on a second-order approximation of the equilibrium conditions around the nonstochastic steady state to obtain reliable welfare level measures. Households' welfare in the economy is measured, to a second-order approximation, as the discounted expected sum of each period's utility value. Consider the value function of the utility of the household:

$$V_t = max\left\{\frac{C_t^{1-\theta}}{1-\theta} + \frac{m_t^{1-\chi}}{1-\chi} + \beta E(V_{t+1})\right\}$$

Let the value function in steady-state: $V_{ss} = \frac{1}{1-\beta}\left[\frac{C_{ss}^{1-\theta}}{1-\theta} + \frac{m_{ss}^{1-\chi}}{1-\chi}\right]$

We thus define an index of welfare as the deviation of the Expected Value of $E(V_t)$ with respect to its steady-state value, V_{ss}. When the deviation $E(V_t) - V_{ss}$ is highest, we say that this framework generates the least loss of welfare. Note that the second-order approximation is necessary because in the first-order approximation the expected value is equal to the value function in the steady state. The discount factor β in Table 14.1 is used when computing the discounted sum of each period's expected utility value.

The results are presented in Table 14.3. Consider, first, the welfare effects of the external aid shocks. As discussed, this shock amounts to a pure wealth shock, used by the government to reduce the public debt. The highest welfare gain of such debt reduction obtains in the absence of frictions to capital relocation in the economy and endogenous learning externalities in exporting. In such case, a credible fixed exchange rate regime provides a higher welfare gain vis-à-vis the floating exchange regime. Welfare gains in the case of frictions and externalities are noticeably lower, as expected, and suggest again that the best regime would be the credible fixed exchange regime. It is important to bear in mind that, contrary to many real life

Table 14.3 Estimates of Welfare Levels and Changes

One Standard Deviation Shock to:		Floating Exchange Regime		Fixed Exchange Regime	
		No Frictions No Learning by Exporting	Frictions and Learning by Exporting	No Frictions No Learning by Exporting	Frictions and Learning by Exporting
External Aid	$E(V_t)$	−10.2	−29.2	−5.2	−20.8
	V_{ss}	−23.9	−25.6	−23.9	−25.6
	$E(V_t) - V_{ss}$	13.7	−3.6	18.7	4.8
Government Expenditure	$E(V_t)$	−20.5	−29.9	−24.7	−29.9
	V_{ss}	−23.9	−25.6	−23.9	−25.6
	$E(V_t) - V_{ss}$	3.4	−4.3	−0.8	−4.4
Public Investment	$E(V_t)$	−24.9	−26.6	−24.7	−26.3
	V_{ss}	−23.9	−25.6	−23.9	−25.6
	$E(V_t) - V_{ss}$	−0.9	−1.1	−0.8	−0.8

Note: Welfare levels are expressed in net present value terms.

Source: Authors' own estimates.

situations in fragile economies, in our DSGE model the fixed exchange regime is credible because the government is forced to fully internalize all of its policies in an infinite horizon set up.

Consider now the case of a shock to government spending in nontraded goods financed domestically by a combination of public debt issuing and lowering transfers to the population. In a number of cases this policy has been linked to the Dutch disease phenomenon, particularly when the economy operates in a fixed exchange regime. It can be seen that the preferred policy in this case is the floating exchange regime, precisely because the flexible exchange regime allows the households quick and efficient adjustment of expenditures in the face of a drop in wealth. Recall that government expenditures in our model are a complete waste and, therefore, consumers anticipate the future increase in taxes needed to repay public debt and/or face immediately the drop in government transfers that is concomitant with higher government spending. Next, notice that under frictions and externalities, both regimes imply an equally negative utility in net present terms. This, naturally, arises from the adjustment costs that an economy has to pay for a policy that is essentially wasteful and transitory.

Finally, consider the policy of expanding public investment financed by issuing domestic debt. It can be seen that there are virtually no differences between exchange regimes in the no-frictions case and when there are learning by exporting and capital adjustment costs. The underlying reason for this result is that in both exchange regimes the government and the private sector fully internalize the positive yet transitory effects of public investment in exports as well as the cost of financing such investment.

5. Conclusions

State fragility has emerged as a rallying point in recent development policy debates. This in part reflects the widely held view that the state has a central role in the development process, which has been further reinforced following the 2008 global economic recession. The definition of fragility and the symbiotic cause-and-effect relationship between state fragility and underdevelopment have been the focus of these debates.

In this chapter we revisit the role of exchange regimes in fostering exports and economic growth in fragile economies and, thereby, in reducing political fragility. A comparison between fragile and emerging countries reveals that slower growth in fragile countries is linked to lower levels of private and public gross fixed capital formation, an inability to compete successfully in exporting markets, and reliance on much higher levels of external aid. Likewise, fragile economies show significant political differences vis-à-vis other emerging economies. Political regimes in fragile economies are not only less democratic than in other emerging economies but also significantly less accountable. The executive in fragile economies is significantly less constrained in its ability to engage in arbitrary practices. Nevertheless, authoritarian governments in fragile economies do not rely exclusively on repression but also on enticing the different groups to support the government. This is an implicit arrangement between ruling elites and citizens whereby citizens relinquish political influence in exchange for public spending. Political fragility thus depends on the amount of transfers and nonpecuniary goods given by the ruling coalition to its own constituency and to opposition groups.

Our analysis is based on a DSGE model, tailored to replicate some of the structural features of fragile economies, in particular the presence of frictions in market adjustment, the influence of external shocks (for example, foreign aid), and the roles of the government in providing public goods (public investment) and delivering social transfers to the population. The former are instrumental in supporting sustained growth; the latter may determine the support of the government and, consequently, its political fragility. Fragile economies are usually plagued by distortions, frictions and externalities that render the standard first-best prescriptions inapplicable. In addition to economic distortions, political issues and institutional weaknesses are key elements to consider in the evaluation of exchange regimes.

A key issue for fragile economies, therefore, would be to determine which exchange regime is more conducive to a virtuous circle of higher levels of investment and exports, given the structural and political restrictions that characterize fragility. The DSGE model allows us to track the response of variables associated with fragility to shocks that are likely to be important in fragile economies. We treat fiscal variables—government spending and fixed capital formation—as exogenous and study the response of the economy to shocks in such policies. Our simulations illustrate the types of general-equilibrium interactions that may complicate the analysis of the effects of shocks that typically affect fragile economies on endogenous variables that may influence fragility.

Our analyses complement those by Chami et al. (2019). In their model the link between fiscal policy and political fragility is explicitly modelled via public employment, while in ours the link operates implicitly via transfers to households. Their model adopts a shorter time perspective because they do not give a role to capital accumulation, intersectoral capital reallocation, or the potential role of increased export competitiveness derived from learning by exporting.

Before briefly summarizing the model simulation results, we note that in the absence of adjustment costs to capital and learning externalities, our model collapses to the standard intertemporal model of production and consumption of an open economy. It is precisely this feature of our model—that it encompasses the distortion-free economy as a special case—which allows us to identify and isolate the role of frictions and externalities on exports, wages, transfers, and economic growth under different exchange regimes. We have, therefore, started our analysis from the distortion-free case where markets clear and all prices are free to adjust within the boundaries of a floating exchange regime. We focused then on the dynamics of the three types of shocks that we think are the most common and important for fragile economies: aid shocks, government expenditure shocks, and public investment shocks.

- *Aid shocks.* Fragility decreases with foreign aid when the government decides to improve its asset stance by retiring public debt, because this reduces the sovereign country risk, real interest rates, and servicing the public debt. In turn, this liberates resources to transfer to the population, thus raising political support for the government. The latter effect is reinforced by the consumption boom and the concurrent rise in wages brought about by the higher permanent income of consumers. These effects, obtained in the context of a floating exchange rate, remain qualitatively comparable in the fixed exchange regime. However, when the government chooses to spend part of the foreign aid in the domestic markets the effects can change dramatically, depending on the exchange regime. In a floating exchange regime, the fraction of the aid from the donors used to reduce the public debt will improve the sovereign country risk but significantly less than in the other case (country risk is a nonlinear function of the stock of debt). Internal fragility will improve in response to higher wages, which in this case do not increase as much as before because the improvement in permanent income is only partial. Furthermore, transfers to the population will be much reduced as a result of the government's decision to spend a fraction of tax revenues for purchasing nontraded goods.

- *Government expenditure.* A pure shock to government expenditures, where responsible authorities engage in sustainable fiscal policies, has very little effect on the medium- to long-term working of the economy or the welfare of the households. This is the result of having to finance such shock with domestic resources coming in the form of a reduction in transfers to the population or by issuing debt that, ultimately, had to be paid by the households in the form of taxes. Consequently, this type of policy cannot be used to gain political support for the government and lower fragility in the medium to long term. In the short term, some transitory gains can be achieved when rigidities and frictions delay the response of the private sector. However, such gains are neither significant nor persistent. Strikingly, there are no differences in the response of the economy to shocks between having a floating exchange regime or a hard peg to another currency. The sustainability of fiscal policy and the fact that households are forward-looking guarantee that the fixed exchange regime is sustainable and, therefore, choosing to have a fixed exchange regime becomes irrelevant.
- As a corollary, one should conclude that only in the short term can governments engage in significant expansions of government expenditures to placate political discontent in a manner that is inconsistent with their long-term budget constraint. In the long term, such populist policy is to be undone by the need to finance the budget and by the realization on the part of households, creditors, and financial markets that the policy stance is unsustainable. Hence, short-term policies might increase popularity and fragility at the same time.
- *Public investment.* An increase in public investment in the form of making public goods available to firms induces a far more favorable fiscal stance in the long term, allowing for expanded transfers to households even if in the short term there is a mild deterioration required to finance such capital expenditures. Note that because there is learning-by-exporting, the expansions in exports and investment in the traded sector are long-lasting and quite significant. This reflects a type of "virtuous circle" between public investment and exports: a higher stock of public capital lowers costs in the traded sector and expands exports which, in turn, further lower production costs because of learning. Higher exports provide for increased tax revenue, which allows for financing subsequent expansions in public investment. Long-term fragility is thus reduced, regardless of the choice of exchange regimes. In the short term, the government will have to shore up the decline in political support that results from the responsible financing of higher public investment.

The ultimate purpose of our analysis would be to indicate which exchange regime is preferred in terms of welfare for the three types of government policies discussed above. Because our DSGE model is micro-founded, maximizing a measure of welfare of the representative household may be an appropriate instrumental objective to guide the choice of policies. We rely on a second-order approximation of the equilibrium conditions around the nonstochastic steady state to obtain reliable welfare level measures. We define an index of welfare as the deviation of the expected value of utility after a shock with respect to its steady-state value.

Consider, first, the welfare effects of an external aid shock used to retire public debt. As expected, the highest welfare gain obtains in the absence of frictions to capital relocation in the economy and endogenous learning externalities in exporting. In such case, a credible fixed exchange rate regime provides a higher welfare gain vis-à-vis the floating exchange regime. It is important to bear in mind that, contrary to many real-life situations in fragile economies, in our DSGE model the fixed exchange regime is credible because the government is forced to fully internalize all of its policies in an infinite horizon set-up.

Consider, next, the case of a shock to government spending financed domestically. In a number of cases this policy has been linked to the Dutch disease phenomenon, particularly when the economy operates in a fixed exchange regime. We find that the preferred policy is the floating exchange regime, precisely because the flexible exchange regime allows the households quick and efficient adjustment of expenditures in the face of a drop in wealth. Recall that government expenditures in our model are a complete waste and, therefore, consumers anticipate the future increase in taxes needed to repay public debt and/or face immediately the drop in government transfers that is concomitant with higher government spending.

Finally, consider the policy of expanding public investment financed by issuing domestic debt. We found that there are virtually no differences between exchange regimes, even when there is learning by exporting and capital adjustment costs. The underlying reason for this result is that in both exchange regimes the government and the private sector fully internalize the positive yet transitory effects of public investment in exports as well as the cost of financing such investment.

References

Adam, C. 2000. "The Transactions Demand for Money in Chile." *Economía Chilena*, 3(3): 33–56.

Aizenman, J. and J. Lee. 2010. "Real Exchange Rate, Mercantilism and the Learning by Doing Externality." *Pacific Economic Review*, 15: 324–35.

Amano, A.R. and T.S. Wirjanto. 1998. "Government Expenditures and the Permanent-Income Model." *Review of Economic Dynamics*, 1(3): 719–30.

Ardanaz, M., E. Cavallo, A. Izquierdo, and J. Puig. 2017. "Growth-Friendly Fiscal Rules? Safeguarding Public Investment from Budget Cuts through Fiscal Rule Design," Interamerican Development Bank Discussion Paper IDB-DP-698, Washington, DC.

Aschauer, D.A. 1985. "Fiscal Policy and Aggregate Demand." *American Economic Review*, 75(1): 117–27.

Bartelme, D., A. Costinot, D. Donaldson, and A. Rodriguez-Clare. 2018. "Economies of Scale and Industrial Policy: A View from Trade," mimeo, UC Berkeley.

Baxter, M. and R. King. 1993. "Fiscal Policy in General Equilibrium." *American Economic Review*, 83(3): 315–34.

Benigno, P. and M. Woodford. 2012. "Linear-quadratic Approximation of Optimal Policy Problems." *Journal of Economic Theory*, 147(1): 1–42.

Bernard, A.B. and J.B. Jensen. 1999. "Exceptional Exporter Performance: Cause, Effect, or Both?" *Journal of International Economics*, 47(1): 1–25.

Bueno de Mesquita, B. and A. Smith. 2009. "A Political Economy of Aid." *International Organization*, 63(2): 309–340.

Bulow, J. and K. Rogoff. 1989. "Sovereign Debt: Is To Forgive To Forget?" *American Economic Review*, 79(1): 43–50.

Castillo, P., C. Montoro, and V. Tuesta (2009): "Un modelo de equilibrio general con dolarización para la economía peruana". Documento de Trabajo BCRP.

Chami, R., T. Cosimano, R. Espinoza, and P. Montiel (2019): "The Challenge of Macroeconomic Stabilization in Fragile States", mimeo, International Monetary Fund.

Chatterjee, S. and A. Mursagulov (2016): "Fiscal Policy and the Real Exchange Rate." *Macroeconomic Dynamics*, 20(7): 1742–70.

Clerides, S., S. Lach, and J. Tybout. 1998. "Is Learning By Exporting Important? Micro-Dynamic Evidence from Colombia, Mexico, and Morocco." *The Quarterly Journal of Economics*, 113: 903–47.

Collier, P. and A. Hoeffler. 2007. "Unintended Consequences: Does Aid Promote Arms Races?" *Oxford Bulletin of Economics and Statistics*, 69(1): 1–27.

Collier, P. and J.W. Gunning. 1999. "Explaining African Economic Performance." *Journal of Economic Literature*, 37(1): 64–111.

De Loecker, J. 2013. "Detecting Learning by Exporting." *American Economic Journal: Microeconomics*, 5(3): 1–21

Desai, R., A. Olofsgard and T. Yousef. 2009. "The Logic of Authoritarian Bargains." *Economics and Politics* 21(1): 93–125.

Diamond, L. and J. Mosbacher (2013): "Petroleum to the People. Africa's Coming Resource Curse—And How to Avoid It." *Foreign Affairs*, September/October, 12–24.

Dreher, A., V. Lang and S. Ziaja. 2017. "Foreign Aid in Areas of Limited Statehood", CESIFO Working Paper No. 6340, February.

Eaton, J., S. Kortum, B. Neiman, and J. Romalis. 2016. "Trade and the Global Recession", *American Economic Review*, 106(11): 3401–38.

Evans, R.H., L.J. Kotlikoff, and K.,L. Phillips. 2013. "Game Over: Simulating Unsustainable Fiscal Policy", in A. Alesina and F. Giavazzi (Eds.), *Fiscal Policy after the Financial Crisis*. Chicago, IL: University of Chicago Press.

Frankel, J.A. and D. Romer. 1999. "Does Trade Cause Growth?" *American Economic Review*, 89(3): 379–99.

Halpern, L., M. Koren, and A. Szeidl. 2015. "Imported Inputs and Productivity." *American Economic Review*, 105(12): 3660–3703.

Harrison, A.E. and A. Rodríguez-Clare. 2010. "Trade, Foreign Investment, and Industrial Policy for Developing Countries", Vol. 5 of *Handbook of Development Economics*, Elsevier.

Hausman, R., D. Rodrik, and A. Velasco. 2008. "Growth Diagnostics", in N. Serra and J.E. Stiglitz (Eds.), *The Washington Consensus Reconsidered Towards a New Global Governance* (pp. 324–355). Oxford: Oxford University Press.

Kamrava, M. 2012. "The Arab Spring and the Saudi-Led Counterrevolution." *Orbis*, 56(1): 96–104.

Karras, G. 1994. "Government Spending and Private Consumption: Some International Evidence." *Journal of Money, Credit and Banking*, 26(1): 9–22.

Kimura, F. and K. Kiyota. 2006. "Exports, FDI, and Productivity: Dynamic Evidence from Japanese Firms", *Review of World Economics*, 142(4): 695–719.

Korinek, A. and L. Servén (2016): "Undervaluation through Foreign Reserve Accumulation: Static Losses, Dynamic Gains." *Journal of International Money and Finance*, 64: 104–36.

Lacroix, S. and J.P. Filiu. 2018. *Revisiting the Arab Uprisings: The Politics of a Revolutionary Moment*. London: Hurst.

Levin, A.T., A. Onatski, J.C. Williams and N. Williams. 2005. "Monetary Policy Under Uncertainty In Micro-Founded Macroeconometric Models", NBER Working Paper 11523, National Bureau of Economic Research, Cambridge, MA.

Manacorda, M., E. Miguel, and A. Vigorito (2011): "Government Transfers and Political Support." *American Economic Journal: Applied Economics*, 3(July): 1–28.

Martins, P. and Y. Yang. 2009. "The Impact of Exporting on Firm Productivity: A Meta-Analysis of the Learning-By-Exporting Hypothesis", *Review of World Economics*, 145: 431–45.

Rodrik, D. 2008. "The Real Exchange Rate and Economic Growth: Theory and Evidence." *Brookings Papers on Economic Activity*, Fall: 365–412.

Salomon, R. and J.M. Shaver. 2005. "Learning by Exporting: New Insights from Examining Firm Innovation." *Journal of Economics & Management Strategy*, Summer, 14(2): 431–60.

Soto, R. 2019. "Fiscal Institutions and Macroeconomic Management in the United Arab Emirates", in K. Mohaddes, J.B. Nugent, and H. Selim (Eds.), *Institutions and Macroeconomic Policies in Resource-Rich Arab Economies.* Oxford: Oxford University Press.

Van Biesebroeck, J. 2005. "Exporting Raises Productivity in Sub-Saharan African Manufacturing Firms." *Journal of International Economics*, 67(2): 373–91.

Weiss, J. 2005. "Export Growth and Industrial Policy: Lessons from the East Asian Miracle experience", ADB Institute Discussion Paper No. 26.

World Bank. 1997. *World Development Report 1997: The State in a Changing World.* New York, Oxford University Press.

World Bank. 2018. *Pathways for Peace: Inclusive Approaches to Preventing Violent Conflict.* Washington, DC: World Bank and United Nations.

World Bank (2019): *World Economic Indicators Database.* Washington, DC: World Bank and United Nations.

15
Do Financial Flows Make a Difference in Fragile States?

Ralph Chami, Ekkehard Ernst, Connel Fullenkamp, and Anne Oeking

1. Introduction

Because of their size, financial flows in the form of foreign direct investment (FDI), official development assistance (ODA), and workers' remittances may have important economic impacts on the countries that receive them. In the case of low- and middle-income countries, these flows add up to approximately one trillion dollars per year. In addition, each flow is individually significant: FDI to low- and middle-income countries reaches $600 billion per year, remittances more than $300 billion per year, and ODA another $100 billion. And on a per country basis, each type of flow can be quite large relative to the size of the economy that receives it (measured by GDP). Thus, understanding what determines the amounts of the three main financial flows, and how these flows affect the economies that receive them, are important questions in development economics and policy making. Finding the answers to these questions is even more important for fragile states, given recent estimates that 80 percent of the world's poorest citizens will be living in fragile states by the year 2030 (OECD, 2018, p. 7). In addition to the possibility that financial flows can facilitate (or hinder) economic development in these countries and situations, there also exists the possibility that these flows can support (or work against) fragile states' efforts to overcome the sources of their fragility. Therefore, determining how fragility affects financial flows, and how these flows affect symptoms or determinants of fragility, can make a significant contribution to reducing the fragility of many states and situations.

Because the importance in economic development has been recognized quite recently, there is only a limited literature that focuses directly on its interaction

The views expressed in this chapter are those of the authors and do not necessarily represent the views of the International Labour Organization, or those of the IMF, its Executive Board, or IMF management. Comments by Antoine Bonnet, Floriana Boriano, Peter Montiel, and participants at the Oxford Expert Meeting on "Macroeconomic Policy in Fragile States" in December 2018 are gratefully acknowledged. All remaining errors are ours.

Ralph Chami, Ekkehard Ernst, Connel Fullenkamp, and Anne Oeking, *Do Financial Flows Make a Difference in Fragile States?*
In: *Macroeconomic Policy in Fragile States.* Edited by: Ralph Chami, Raphael Espinoza, and Peter Montiel,
Oxford University Press (2021).
DOI: 10.1093/oso/9780198853091.003.0015

with financial flows. Adding to this literature by investigating the two-way relationship between fragility and financial flows is the goal of this chapter. There are good reasons to expect that fragility does alter both the amount of financial flows that a country receives, as well as the effects that these flows have on the recipient economy. As we show in section 2, fragile countries are on average less productive, less open, and more unequal than other countries, and also have higher incidences of poverty. They experience strong demographic pressures, which also manifest as higher rates of unemployment, especially among young males. At the same time, fragile states are generally characterized by low government stability and effectiveness, and they are subject to more social unrest. We expect that these conditions not only affect the mixture of financial flows that fragile states receive, but also interact with the flows in ways that significantly alter their economic and social impacts.

In section 3, we consider the effect of fragility on financial flows. In addition to examining the size and volatility of these flows to fragile contexts, we ask whether the degree of country fragility appears to be related to the size (measured as percent of GDP) of any of the three financial flows. On average, fragile countries attract larger shares of ODA and remittances than FDI. But heterogeneity among fragile countries is high with respect to the amounts of financial flows received. For example, not all fragile countries receive ODA and some may receive it sporadically. Similarly, the bulk of remittances or FDI to fragile states tends to flow to a subset of countries. Nonetheless, we find that ODA flows tend to show a positive relationship with the degree of fragility. Although FDI flows to fragile states are lower than ODA, they tend to be more stable over time. They tend to decline as fragility increases, however. The data do not suggest a simple proportional relationship between the quantity of remittance flows and fragility, but a more complex one cannot be ruled out.

Ideally, we would also like to estimate the effect of financial flows on fragility, or on the causes of fragility. We estimate correlations between each financial flow and underlying dimensions of fragility and report these results in section 3. These correlations also motivate bivariate Granger causality tests between the financial flows and dimensions of fragility. The tests reveal that FDI seems to be causally related to a reduction in fragility across a range of fragility dimensions, whereas ODA seems to undermine country stability. The impact of remittances on fragility is ambiguous and depends on the specific fragility dimension. Overall, the results from these estimations are mixed and indicate that the causal relationships between financial flows and fragility are in general too complex to be captured using relatively simple techniques, especially given the limited data we currently have on fragile states.

An equally important way that fragility may interact with financial flows is by changing the way that these flows affect the economies that receive them. We investigate this possibility in section 4. The literature argues that any type of financial flow has the biggest impact once supportive economic conditions and institutions exist; fragility makes it less likely to meet these preconditions. We find that fragility does appear to affect the impacts of the three financial flows on economic growth, poverty, and employment. In terms of economic growth, severe fragility weakens the economic impact of financial flows on growth acceleration or slowdowns, except that of FDI on growth accelerations. ODA leads to growth accelerations in non-fragile countries but not in fragile countries; at the same time, it lowers the prevalence of employment growth slowdowns but less so in fragile than in non-fragile countries. In line with our earlier findings (see Chami et al., 2018), remittances both lower the prevalence of growth accelerations and increase the probability of employment growth slowdowns for non-fragile countries. But these effects disappear for fragile countries. Fragility also alters the impact of financial flows on poverty. We find that both FDI and ODA have only minimal impact on economic inequality and poverty in fragile countries, while remittances have none at all. This stands in contrast to all three flows' strong impact on poverty in non-fragile countries. Finally, we also estimate the impact of financial flows on sectoral employment, because shifts in employment among sectors can show more explicitly how financial flows affect growth and poverty. We find that ODA and remittances drive employment shares in construction and public services for low-fragility countries, whereas FDI increases employment shares in manufacturing for these countries. But none of these effects persist in fragile countries. In fact, from a sectoral employment perspective, all flows lose their capacity to impact structural adjustment in highly fragile countries.

The basic message from the exercises in this chapter is that fragility does matter for financial flows. It affects both how much flows to a country and the forms taken by those flows. And it affects how these flows in turn interact with the recipient country's economy. In the conclusion of this chapter, we reflect on what our findings imply both for policy and for future research on financial flows to fragile states.

Before proceeding with the analysis, it is important to clarify the definition(s) of fragility that are being used in this chapter, since several different ones have been created by organizations that work with or are concerned with fragile situations, and the differences may affect the outcomes of the analyses. We rely on data from the Fund for Peace (FFP) to classify fragile countries.[1] The overall fragility indicator is based on 12 sub-indicators with a maximum value of 10 (that is, most fragile), covering the following dimensions: security apparatus; factionalized elites; group grievance; economic decline; uneven economic development; human flight and brain drain; state legitimacy; public services; human rights and rule of law; demographic pressures; refugees and internally displaced people; and external intervention.[2] On the basis of these data, a fragility assessment is available for the period 2006 through 2017 for 164 countries. Fragility scores are highly persistent with an autocorrelation

[1] Data on fragility ranking of countries and the underlying sub-indicators are available here: http://fundforpeace.org/fsi/data/ (last accessed July 16, 2020).

[2] See https://fragilestatesindex.org/indicators/ for a detailed description of these 12 dimensions.

coefficient of almost 83 percent in the first year; autocorrelation becomes insignificant only after eight years.

Another frequently used definition of fragility comes from the Organisation for Economic Co-operation and Development (OECD).[3] The OECD fragility indicator covers the same number of countries but only for the years 2014 through 2017. The sub-indicators are organized around major topics, covering economic, environmental, political, security and societal fragility.[4] The World Bank Group also uses a Harmonized List of Fragile Situations, based mainly on the Country Policy and Institutional Assessment (CPIA) country ratings assigned by the World Bank Group and regional development banks (Asian Development Bank, etc.). Whenever possible, we try to specify which definition of fragility is being used by the researchers cited in this chapter.

2. What Is Special about Fragile Countries?

Many low- and middle-income countries not classified as fragile also receive hundreds of billions of dollars in financial flows each year. Thus, a fundamental question that we investigate in this chapter is whether fragility significantly alters the patterns of financial flows or their effects on recipient countries. We argue that fragile countries share a number of characteristics that affect their ability to attract various financial flows, and that make them react differently to financial flows than their non-fragile counterparts. In this section, we summarize the evidence on fragile countries and country characteristics associated with country fragility, and then argue why these characteristics should affect the quantities or impacts of financial flows. The section starts by giving an overview of the data and methods we use here and in the rest of the chapter.

2.1 Data and Methods

2.1.1 Data

We use the fragility data from FFP to group countries into quintiles according to their level of fragility, as reported in Annex Table A15.1.

Information on economic development, GDP per capita, labor productivity, the fiscal balance, trade openness and the (real effective) exchange rate, is taken from the IMF's World Economic Outlook database. Remittances are taken from the

[3] We used information from the Organisation for Economic Co-operation and Development's States of Fragility Framework to test the robustness of our analysis in the annex.

[4] See OECD, States of Fragility, 2018, pp. 265–79 for a methodological discussion of the indicator, available at https://read.oecd-ilibrary.org/development/states-of-fragility-2018_9789264302075-en. (last accessed July 16, 2020).

IMF's Balance of Payments Statistics, and data on FDI and ODA come from the World Bank's World Development Indicators database.

The Human Development Index is taken from the United Nations Development Programme.[5] Labor market information on unemployment, employment (both sectoral and aggregate), labor force participation, status in employment and employment by economic class is taken from ILOSTAT.[6] Because labor market information is patchy for most fragile countries, data has been completed using imputation methods.[7] Social unrest is based on newspaper data collected in the GDELT database and aggregated to the International Labour Organization (ILO) Social Unrest indicator.[8] Information on governance quality is taken from the Worldwide Governance Indicator database compiled by the World Bank.[9]

2.1.2 Methodology

The FFP and the OECD indicators on fragility offer a continuous index of fragility rather than a sharp cut but are truncated both from below and above. Countries' ranking and fragility scores evolve gradually over time. This allows us to treat these scores as if they were similar to other continuously measured regressors rather than applying discontinuity analysis. We introduce (arbitrary) cutoff points for fragility only in cases where a more granular analysis of the impact of financial flows on distributional outcomes prevented us from using the full continuum of fragility. Our analysis is based on panel data approaches, with different methods applied depending on the type of research question.

2.2 Characteristics of Fragile Countries

Country fragility spans a heterogeneous set of countries, including countries in or emerging from conflict, countries with prolonged political crises, or those slowly exiting fragility. Although the context varies in these countries, many of them share some common characteristics. Fragility is highly correlated with weak economic and social outcomes. Average (labor) productivity is lower, not least because of lack of investment and underdeveloped or destroyed infrastructure (see Figure 15.1, Panel A). Also, trade relationships and the share of exports in GDP is lower than in non-fragile countries, reflecting the fact that fragile countries

[5] Data are available here: http://hdr.undp.org/en/data (last accessed July 16, 2020).

[6] Available here: http://www.ilo.org/ilostat (last accessed July 16, 2020).

[7] For an overview of the imputation techniques used see https://www.ilo.org/empelm/projects/WCMS_114246/lang–en/index.htm.

[8] See ILO (2019) for a presentation of the indicator and a discussion of how the social unrest index is constructed.

[9] The WGI database can be downloaded here: https://info.worldbank.org/governance/wgi/.

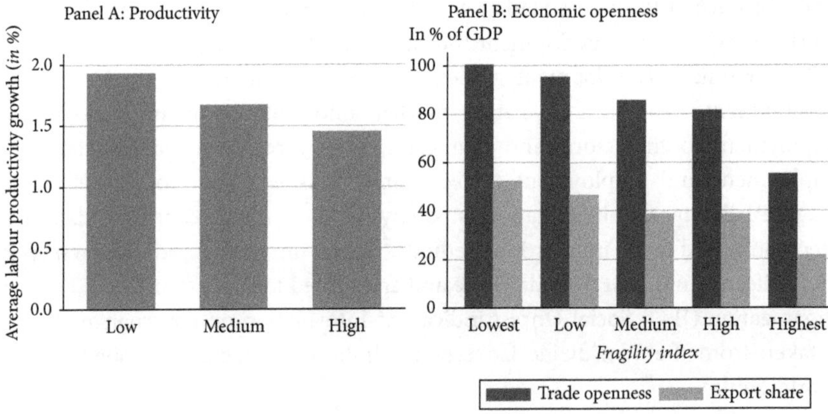

Figure 15.1 State Fragility and Economic Performance
Sources: World Bank, World Development Indicators; Fund for Peace, Fragile States Index.

often rely on primary commodity exports with little value added (see Figure 15.1, Panel B).

Not only are fragile countries less developed and less open on average, they often also face severe inequalities (see Figure 15.2). One indicator of social outcomes concerns vulnerable employment, which comprises own-account workers and contributing family workers.[10] In developing countries particularly, such workers often lack social protection, face unstable employment and earnings opportunities, and experience inferior working conditions. As panel A in Figure 15.2 shows, there is a strong correlation between the incidence of vulnerable employment and a country's fragility, with a particularly strong increase, reaching vulnerability levels of more than 80 percent of employment, in the most fragile countries. An alternative way of looking at social outcomes is to consider employment by economic class (panel B in Figure 15.2).[11] Using quantile regression to establish cross-country correlations between the share of employment across 14 different consumption levels and fragility demonstrates that the share of poorer workers is strongly positively correlated with fragility, whereas the share of more affluent workers is strongly negatively correlated with fragility.

Table 15.1 summarizes our main results regarding factors correlated with state fragility. The estimates are based on panel data across the 164 countries that could be classified according to their level of fragility. Because the country coverage of

[10] For a detailed definition of various forms of employment, see https://www.ilo.org/ilostat-files/Documents/description_STE_EN.pdf (last accessed July 16, 2020).

[11] Employment by economic class is an indicator of employment shares for 14 different consumption levels based on poverty surveys. The lowest category corresponds to workers in extreme poverty, whereas the highest category reflects workers with consumption levels at advanced economy middle- and upper-income household levels. In the absence of earnings data for large parts of the informal economy in many developing countries, this indicator is a close proxy for such information.

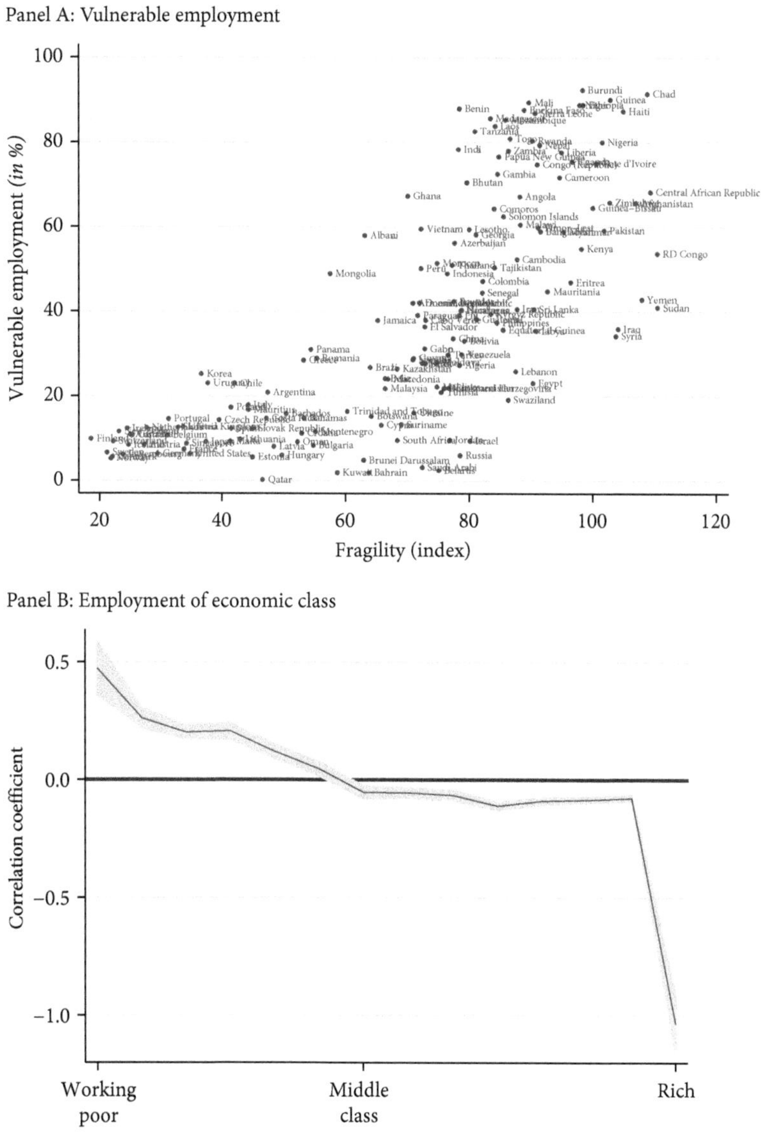

Figure 15.2 Country Fragility, Poverty, and Inequality

Note: Panel A shows the share of vulnerable employment in total employment (in %) against the average fragility index over the period 1995-2012. Panel B displays correlation coefficients (red line) and confidence intervals (grey area) between country fragility and employment by economic class, using quantile regression estimations of the equation: $fragIndex_i = \alpha + \beta^j \times empClass^j_i + \varepsilon_i$ where *fragIndex*: the average fragility index of country i between 2012 and 2017; $empClass^j_i$: the average share of employment in consumption class $j \in [1, \ldots, 14]$ between 2012 and 2017 in country i. The chart reports the estimate β^j as well as the confidence interval. To avoid that results are driven by outliers given the particular nature of fragile countries, estimates have been established using quantile regression rather than standard least-squares. Employment by economic class used as a measure for (consumption) inequality, distinguishing 14 different levels of inequality.

Source: Fund for peace, ILO.

Table 15.1 Determinants of Country Fragility

	(1)	(2)	(3)	(4)	(5)	(6)	(7)
Social unrest (lagged)	0.0306** (0.0133)	0.0161* (0.00881)	0.0180* (0.00960)	0.0202** (0.0102)	0.0179* (0.00983)	0.0176* (0.00989)	0.0177* (0.00990)
Human Development Index		−79.01*** (13.79)	−82.00*** (15.13)	−73.76*** (17.34)	−69.40*** (17.28)	−72.60*** (17.35)	−55.74*** (17.40)
Government effectiveness		−2.531*** (0.846)	−2.436*** (0.877)	−2.361*** (0.852)	−2.152** (0.840)	−2.225*** (0.840)	−2.177** (0.858)
Government stability		−2.056*** (0.691)	−2.085*** (0.736)	−1.909*** (0.676)	−1.907*** (0.682)	−1.929*** (0.682)	−1.811*** (0.682)
Population trend			0.0498** (0.0216)	0.0504** (0.0225)	0.0461** (0.0213)	0.0483** (0.0220)	
GDP per capita (in logs)				−1.584* (0.815)	−1.451* (0.835)	−1.439* (0.819)	−1.481* (0.861)
Unemployment					0.189** (0.0916)		
Youth unemployment						0.0737* (0.0114)	
Male unemployment							0.222*** (0.0776)
Male youth unemployment		0.0850** (0.0371)					
Youth participation (lagged)							0.143** (0.0675)
Constant	69.17*** (0.300)	122.1*** (9.801)	123.4*** (10.16)	131.3*** (9.404)	125.8*** (9.169)	128.1*** (9.402)	112.0*** (11.94)
Observations	1,758	966	961	961	961	961	961
R-squared	0.007	0.285	0.223	0.231	0.241	0.238	0.250
Number of countries	162	161	161	161	161	161	161

	(8)	(9)	(10)	(11)	(12)	(13)	(14)
Social unrest (lagged)	0.0225** (0.0109)	0.0199* (0.0105)	0.0200* (0.0102)	0.0208** (0.0102)	0.0177* (0.00997)	0.0175* (0.00993)	0.0197* (0.0106)
Human Development Index	−36.27* (20.62)	−56.78*** (16.81)	−72.65*** (17.31)	−59.60*** (17.49)	−54.87*** (17.37)	−60.81*** (18.02)	−61.65*** (17.47)
Government effectiveness	−2.566*** (0,979)	−2.131*** (0.810)	−2.234*** (0.848)	−2.327*** (0.846)	−2.086** (0,856)	−2.052** (0.850)	−2.017** (0.807)
Government stability	−1.758*** (0.648)	−1.786*** (0.657)	−1.986*** (0.676)	−1.897*** (0.674)	−1.875*** (0,682)	−1.889*** (0.678)	−1.858*** (0.652)
Population trend	0.0478*** (0.0181)		0.0508** (0.0218)			0.0546** (0.0212)	0.0522** (0.0201)
GDP per capita (in logs)	−2.205*' (0.872)	−0.640 (0.745)	−1.693** (0.823)	−1.794** (0.838)	−1.589* (0.868)	−1.616* (0.860)	−0.781 (0.760)
Male unemployment	0.312** (0.141)	0.216*** (0.0823)			0.209*** (0.0771)	0.203*** (0.0765)	0.199** (0.0822)
Youth participation (lagged)	0.179** (0.0771)	0.153** (0.0668)		0.127* (0.0670)	0.145** (0.0675)	0.155** (0.0666)	0.163** (0.0660)
Employment in mining	0.277** (0.132)						
Fiscal position (lagged)		−0.0895** (0.0348)					−0.0878** (0.0350)
Exchange rate regime (10 categories)			−0.156** (0.0728)	−0.163** (0.0753)	−0.133* (0.0703)	−0.136* (0.0698)	−0.124* (0.0694)
Constant	103.1*** (12.83)	104.9*** (11.93)	132.5*** (9.341)	120.8*** (11.78)	113.2*** (11.89)	114.9*** (11.96)	107.6*** (12.05)
Observations	739	961	961	961	961	961	961
R-squared	0.281	0.275	0.236	0.240	0.253	0.258	0.283
Number of countries	124	161	161	101	161	161	161

Note: Robust standard errors in parentheses; p<0.01, ** p<0.05, * p<0.1. Dependent variable: Fragile states score, taken from the Fund for Peace, higher scores indicate more fragile countries. Government effectiveness and government stability as measured by the World Government Indicators are scaled from -2.5 to +2.5.

the co-variates is limited, the number of countries in each regression is slightly less than 164 except for regression (8) where we also consider sectoral employment. Estimation is carried out using the standard within estimator that removes country fixed effects.

As the table demonstrates, a country's level of fragility is negatively associated with its level of human development, per capita GDP, government effectiveness and stability. Higher levels of unemployment (especially among men) and social unrest foster fragility, as do stronger population growth and a larger share of young people in the labor force. Moreover, fragile countries are characterized by a larger share of workers in extractive industries, lower levels of productivity, a weaker fiscal position, a less open economy, and fixed exchange rate regimes.

2.3 How Drivers of Fragility May Affect the Quantities and Impacts of Financial Flows

The characteristics identified above that are significantly associated with fragility, such as high unemployment and low government effectiveness, are also present in many low-income and some middle-income countries. But the distinguishing feature of fragile states is the intensity of these characteristics, either individually (that is, a country is fragile because its government is among the least stable) or collectively (a country is fragile because it is afflicted by multiple economic and governance problems of moderate to severe intensity). The intensity of these issues implies that they play a defining role in how a particular country's economy functions and how it is perceived by the rest of the world. Therefore, it is reasonable to expect both that financial flows to fragile states will differ in type and quantity from those to nonfragile states, and that these flows will affect fragile states in ways that differ in outcome and intensity from their typical impacts on nonfragile states.

In the case of flows to fragile states, the poor economic outcomes that are important drivers of fragility are likely to motivate increased levels of altruistically motivated flows such as remittances. Thus, we should expect remittances to rise with the degree of country fragility, all else being equal; however, remittances require labor migration, which very poor families can ill afford. To the extent that ODA is also at least partially motivated by altruism, we should also expect fragile states to attract elevated ODA flows. Regardless of motivation, ODA also represents compensatory transfers that are intended to ameliorate the symptoms or causes of poor economic and social outcomes, which again suggests that the degree of fragility should positively affect ODA flows.

FDI flows tend to respond to economic opportunity. Some countries may be fragile and yet offer good economic opportunities for some types of foreign firms, especially those in extractive industries. In other countries, however, fragility may imply lack of sufficient legal guarantees of property rights and contract enforcement, which would discourage FDI. Or the poor economic performance of a fragile economy simply means that there are no attractive economic opportunities for foreign firms or investors.

The extreme economic and social weaknesses that characterize fragile states may also influence how financial flows affect the economies that receive them. Countries that have extremely weak economic or governance systems may simply not be able to use the flows they receive in the ways that were intended, or problems such as corruption may divert significant shares of these flows to unintended beneficiaries. Yet weak or underdeveloped economies may also reduce the potential harm associated with financial flows. For example, a fragile state with a critically underdeveloped export sector may be much less susceptible to Dutch disease effects associated with remittances (see Chami et al., 2018). Thus, it is very difficult to form a clear prediction of how fragility should affect the economic and social impacts of financial flows.

3. Is There a Relationship between Fragility and Financial Flows?

3.1 Level and Volatility of Financial Flows in Fragile Countries

As mentioned in the introduction to this chapter, there is only a nascent literature focused on the amounts and determinants of financial flows to fragile states. One of the most significant contributions is Lomoriello (2018), which describes and compares all three types of financial flows to fragile states. The discussion in Lomoriello (2018) focuses first on the relative sizes of the flows, noting that total financial flows to the 58 situations identified as fragile by the OECD amounted to US$240 billion in 2016. Remittances account for the largest share of flows to fragile states at 45 percent of the total, ODA accounts for 28 percent of the total, and FDI for 22 percent of total flows (the remaining 5 percent were Other Financial Flows).

But one striking feature is that these flows are quite unevenly distributed across fragile states. In the case of FDI, 10 states receive over half of overall FDI flows to fragile states, while for the case of remittances, five countries receive more than 70 percent of all remittance flows to fragile states. Lomoriello and Scott (2018) show that this is also true in the case of ODA to fragile states: 10 "aid darlings" receive half of all ODA to fragile states. Meanwhile, the group of states rated extremely fragile receives a very small share of both remittances and FDI, according to Lomoriello (2018). On the other hand, Lomoriello and Scott (2018) report that extremely fragile states receive nearly half of total ODA flowing to fragile states, primarily because of a large increase in the amount of humanitarian aid being directed to these states during the past several years.

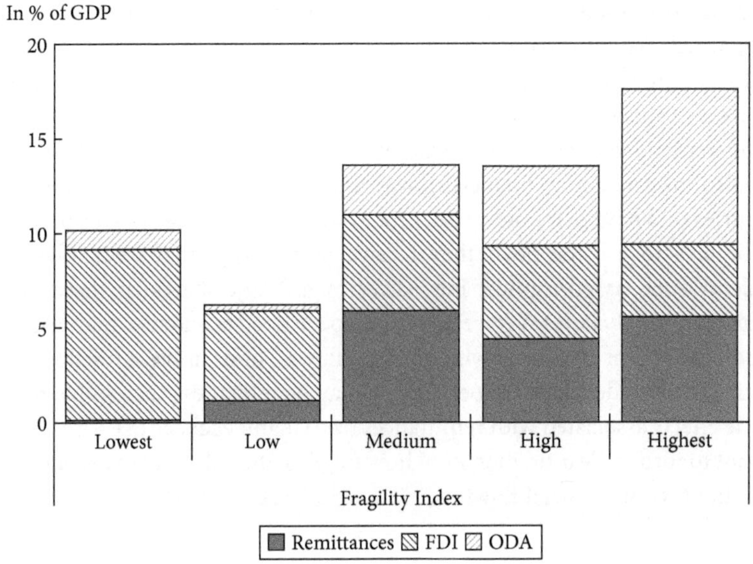

Figure 15.3 Financial Flows by Fragility

Note: Financial flows in percent of GDP for fragility quintiles. Country averages over the years 2012 to 2017.

Source: Fund for peace, IMF, WDI.

Keeping this uneven distribution of financial flows in mind, we decompose the aggregate flow data according to the degree of fragility of the recipient country or situation, using five levels of fragility (lowest, low, medium, high, and highest; see the country groupings in Annex Table A15.1). When we do this, we find that the sizes of financial flows differ significantly, depending on a country's fragility (see Figure 15.3). FDI represents the largest share of financial flows in lowest and low fragile countries but its share diminishes gradually as fragility rises, representing only about 20 percent of the total sum of flows in highly fragile states. Remittances are the largest financial flow only in countries of medium fragility, though they are still relatively large in high and highest fragility countries. And as Lomoriello and Scott (2018) suggest, ODA is the largest financial flow for the most-fragile countries and situations. Interestingly, the three flows are nearly equal to each other in size in high-fragility countries.

The relationships in Figure 15.3 are generally consistent with the other existing research on the causes of financial flows to fragile states. Scott (2018), which uses the OECD definition of fragility, also relates financial flows to different dimensions of fragility, finding that FDI tends to flow to countries with low economic fragility, while the portion of ODA that is not humanitarian aid is positively related to economic fragility. Ragoussis and Shams (2018), using the World Bank

Group's definition of fragility, examine FDI in fragile and conflict-affected states, focusing on what steps these states can take to attract more FDI. This paper notes that FDI to fragile and conflict-affected states currently represents only 1 percent of global financial flows and mostly goes to middle-income and resource-rich fragile states.

In Figure 15.3, remittance flows do not appear to have a proportional relationship with the degree of fragility. Ragoussis and Shams (2018) also find that remittances do not show strong correlations with most dimensions of fragility, although they are highest in countries with high social fragility. They are negatively correlated with political fragility, however. McPeak (2012) examines how fragility can be a driver of remittances. Countries whose economies are in decline receive more remittances as a share of GDP, and increased flight from a country increases per capita remittances.

The volatility of financial flows also reveals interesting differences according to the type of the flow and the country's fragility. We calculated the volatility of each flow (relative to GDP) for a large set of countries including both fragile and nonfragile contexts, as well as for the subset of highly fragile countries. The results are displayed in Figure 15.4. In both the full set of countries as well as fragile contexts considered separately, remittances show the lowest degree of volatility. This suggests that remittances provide a relatively stable source of income, especially for fragile countries, given their large size compared with other flows (see Figure 15.4). In contrast, volatility of both ODA and FDI is significantly higher: in some cases they are more than five times as volatile as remittances. Relative volatility changes depending on the status of a country: Whereas ODA is most volatile in fragile countries, FDI shows the highest degree of volatility in the overall sample of countries (see Figure 15.4, panel A).

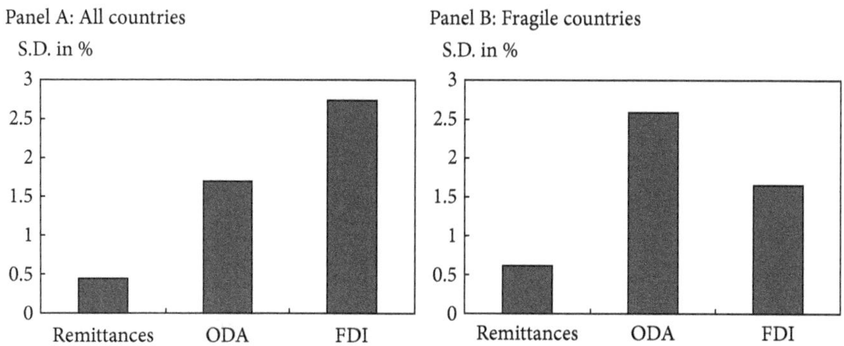

Figure 15.4 Volatility of Financial Flows

Note: Volatility is defined as the standard deviation of the HP de-trended ratio of each variable to GDP, 1990-2017. Fragile countries defined as the highest quintile based on FFP data.

Source: Fund for peace, IMF, WDI.

The evidence from the extant literature and the further exercises described above suggests that two of the three main financial flows appear to be related to the degree of country fragility. FDI tends to decline as country fragility increases, though this effect also appears to be offset at least somewhat in the case of countries with large natural resource industries. For example, the group of highly fragile countries include the four major oil-exporting nations (Iran, Angola, the Russian Federation, and Venezuela), which do attract significant foreign investment given their large petroleum extraction industry. If we examine the criteria that go into the FFP fragility index, at least two dimensions—state legitimacy and rule of law—have strong and well-known effects on the investment climate of a country. Therefore, it seems reasonable to find a negative relationship between fragility and FDI. In the case of ODA, the relationship tends to be positive, with more development assistance flowing to higher-fragility situations. Again, because several of the indicators that make up the FFP fragility index reflect direct motivations for providing development assistance, including economic decline, uneven economic development, public services, demographic pressures, and refugees and internally displaced people, the negative relationship seems reasonable.

Remittances, however, do not seem to have a clear relationship with the degree of fragility. But again, if we examine the components of the FFP fragility index, we uncover some clues that help explain this finding. Although several of the components could be argued to have some impact on households' migration and remittance decisions, none of them appear to have a direct and unambiguous or unconditional impact on these decisions. For example, the economic decline of a country could, and likely does, motivate more families to send members abroad in search of work to fund remittances, but this decision also depends on additional factors such as family resources and the costs of taking advantage of potential remittance corridors available to a particular country. In the literature on remittance determination, one of the strongest predictors of remittance flows is the income differential between a remittance-receiving country and the country that is the source of remittances, which is not included in (and does not belong to) fragility indexes. Thus, the relationship between remittance flows and fragility indexes reflects multiple indirect relationships that are relatively weak determinants of remittances, and which may offset each other.

3.2 Financial Flows and Fragility

Table 15.2 further breaks down the relationship between (different dimensions of) fragility and the three financial flows. Setting up a fixed-effects regression with the various dimensions of fragility as a dependent variable, we estimate the simultaneous association of FDI, ODA, and remittances. We also distinguish between remittances in per capita terms and as a share of GDP. As the table demonstrates,

Table 15.2 Financial Flows and Fragility Dimensions

Type of fragility	FDI	ODA	Remittances	
	(in % of GDP)	*(per capita)*	*(per capita)*	*(in % of GDP)*
Security apparatus	0	+	0	0
Factionalized elites	0	0	+	0
Group grievance	0	0	+	0
Economic decline	0	+	0	0
Economic inequality	+	0	–	+
Human flight and brain drain	0	–	0	+
State legitimacy	+	+	–	0
Public services	+	0	–	+
Human rights	0	+	0	+
Demographic pressures	+	+	–	+
Refugees/IDP	0	0	+	+
External intervention	0	0	+	+

Note: IDP = internally displaced people. The table displays the signs of (significant) correlations between the three types of financial flows and the different fragility indicators. Correlation coefficients are taken from a multi-variate, fixed effects regression where alternatively remittances as a share of GDP or remittances in per persons income is being considered. Significance level at 5 per cent. Results are essentially the same even when running censored regressions given the truncated nature of the fragile states sub-indices.

Source: Fund for Peace Fragile States Index; IMF Balance of Payments.

in a majority of cases no significant contemporaneous association can be established between these fragility dimensions and any of the three financial flows. Where there is a significant association it is more often positive, suggesting that the flow is associated with higher fragility levels. Only when measuring remittances in per capita terms can one detect some negative associations, in particular as regards countries with low state legitimacy, weak public services, high economic inequality, and strong demographic pressures.

These results suggest that financial flows and fragility might enter a complex, bi-directional relationship that potentially depends on the lag structure of the effects considered. To understand further how fragility and financial flows are related, we proceed to a series of Granger causality tests that should help not only to identify associations but also the direction in which fragility and financial flows affect each other. Figures A15.7 to A15.15 in the annex summarize the evidence on causal relations between financial flows and different types of fragility, using the panel vector autoregression approach based on the generalized method of moments (GMM) developed by Abrigo and Love (2016). Granger causality is being established on the basis of bivariate panel vector autoregression estimates with different forms of fragility estimated against the three different financial flows using various lag lengths (up to six years). To select the appropriate lag length we use the standard information criteria appropriate in the GMM context as suggested by Andrews and Lu (2001). The estimates with the optimal lag length for our different panel vector autoregressions are indicated by dark-shaded bars in the figures. Statistically significant Granger causalities are indicated by asterisks over/under the bars.

Looking through the different fragility dimensions, some broad conclusions can be drawn: First, in none of the cases analyzed do remittances and fragility enter a causal relationship when analyzed at the optimal lag length. Under most forms of fragility remittances are negatively correlated with fragility, except in the cases of (violent) conflicts such as external interventions, factionalized elites, and group grievances. Second, ODA weakly causes fragility based on human flight and brain drain (see Figure 15.13); most importantly, ODA enters a bi-directional causal relationship with fragile state legitimacy (see Figure 15.15), echoing long-standing criticism about current forms of development cooperation. Finally, a complex picture emerges as to the causal relationship between FDI and fragility. Different forms of fragility seem to cause (albeit often only weakly) FDI (see Figures 15.7, 15.9, 15.13, and 15.15). Nonetheless, FDI is a source of stabilization because it helps to reduce some other fragility dimensions (see Figures 15.8 and 15.9). This seems to suggest that while FDI is an alternative form of capital mobilization in countries with high levels of fragility, it has the potential to reduce some forms of fragility, especially economic ones.

4. How Does Fragility Influence the Effects of Financial Flows on Growth and Jobs?

Fragile countries share a number of characteristics that affect how they react to financial flows. In this section, we will summarize the available evidence, looking into a variety of economic, labor, social, and governance issues, starting with an overview of existing evidence. We then develop a framework for understanding the impact of financial flows on growth, employment structural change, and working poverty in fragile countries in comparison to their non-fragile counterparts.

4.1 Existing Evidence

As yet, there is no literature devoted specifically to the impacts of financial flows on fragility. Nonetheless, the large literature on the impacts of financial flows on the economies that receive them provides benchmarks and stylized facts that give a useful frame of comparison for any examinations (including our own) of the effects of financial flows on fragility. In addition, some of the insights from this literature have implications for the effects of financial flows on fragility. Moreover, as we discuss, several strands of this literature examine the impact of financial flows on economic and social characteristics that are strongly associated with fragility.

The impact of financial flows on economic growth has been extensively studied, and each type of capital flow has its own large literature examining its effects on economic growth and development. These literatures consist of hundreds of single-country studies and regional studies, but we focus on the relatively small number of cross-country studies because we believe they present the most convincing evidence regarding the true tendencies of these capital flows to affect the recipient economies. Even though these literatures have developed quite separately, each one finds mixed evidence regarding the respective flow's impact on development.

In the case of FDI, the work of Prasad et al. (2003) and Carkovic and Levine (2005) finds that FDI does not promote economic growth in recipient countries; however, later research such as Iamsiraroj (2016) finds a positive connection between FDI and economic growth. Much recent research finds that FDI has a conditionally positive impact on growth. Shen and Lee (2010) find evidence that FDI's growth impact is positive, given the appropriate conditions in the recipient economy. Slesman et al. (2015) find that FDI contributes positively to growth in countries that have passed a threshold of institutional quality.

Similarly, the literature on ODA often finds that these flows have no positive impact on growth, as in Boone (1996) and Rajan and Subramanian (2008). Burnside and Dollar (2000) and many subsequent papers, however, find that aid can help growth in countries with sufficiently supportive economic policies or institutions. Clemens et al. (2011) argue that when the empirical methods allow for lags between aid and subsequent growth, and avoid the use of weak instruments, ODA has a positive association with economic growth, although the amount of subsequent growth associated with a given amount of ODA is modest.

Workers' remittances also have a mixed empirical record. Barajas et al. (2009) find that remittances have an insignificant and often negative relationship to economic growth. As in the cases of the other financial flows, however, other researchers have found that remittances are positively associated with growth provided that supportive conditions exist. Giuliano and Ruiz-Arranz (2009) find evidence that a moderate degree of financial development appears to facilitate a positive impact of remittances on growth, while Catrinescu et al. (2009) find that higher institutional quality is associated with a positive effect of remittances on growth. In more general terms, Rao and Hassan (2011, 2012) show evidence that the direct effect of remittances on economic growth is insignificant, but the indirect effects can be positive though small.

Some strands of the literature on financial flows have compared the effects of multiple flows. For example, several papers on the relationship between financial flows and the Dutch Disease compare the effects of remittances and ODA across multiple countries. Magud and Sosa (2010) review the literature linking ODA and remittances to Dutch Disease outcomes such as real exchange rate appreciation and decline in the ratio of tradables to nontradables. Rajan and Subramanian (2011) find that both ODA and remittances are associated with Dutch Disease effects, but Nsor-Ambala (2015) finds that many of these effects disappear when there are more countries in the sample and a fixed-effects approach is used. Lartey et al. (2012) compare the effects of remittances and FDI on the real exchange rate and the ratio of tradables to nontradables in a panel of 109 countries, finding evidence that both types of flows are associated with real exchange rate appreciation and a decrease in the ratio of tradables to nontradables. Ben Naceur et al. (2012) compare all three financial flows' impacts on real exchange rates in a 57-country panel, finding that remittances and ODA are associated with real exchange rate appreciation while FDI is not.

Relatively few papers have compared the effects of all three financial flows on economic growth and development. Benmamoun and Lehnert (2013) include all three flows in a typical growth model equation, estimated using annual data on 182 countries from 1990 through 2006. This paper also compares the impacts of these flows across income levels, finding that although all three flows contribute to economic growth in low-income countries, none of them contribute significantly to growth in middle-income countries. Only ODA, moreover, was found to contribute positively to growth in highly indebted low-income countries. Driffield and Jones (2013) also compared the impacts of FDI, ODA, and remittances on economic growth in a sample of developing economies measured between 1984 and 2007, using a system of equations approach. They found that FDI and remittances were significantly positively associated with economic growth, and ODA was significantly negatively associated with growth when using annual data, while remittances became insignificant when five-year averages were used.

In addition to examining the impact of financial flows on economic growth and development, researchers have studied the effects of financial flows on some of the symptoms of fragility as identified in Collier (2019). For example, there is a large literature relating FDI to inequality. Earlier papers in this literature include Basu and Guariglia (2007), which finds that FDI increases inequality, and Milanovic (2005), which finds no effect of FDI on inequality. Later papers show a more nuanced effect. Wu and Hsu (2012) find that FDI increases inequality in countries that have poor "absorptive capacity," the ability to adopt and integrate new technologies into their economy's production. Similarly, Majeed (2017) finds that FDI can reduce inequality, but only in countries that have sufficient human capital and labor market development, as well as higher income levels; otherwise, FDI increases inequality.

The findings on the relationship between ODA and inequality are mixed. Chong et al. (2009) find weak evidence that ODA reduces inequality in countries with strong enough institutions. Herzer and Nunnenkamp (2012), however, find that ODA increases inequality when using panel co-integration techniques to estimate the long-run relationship between ODA and inequality. More recently, Kasuga and Morita (2018) find evidence that ODA generally reduced inequality up to the mid-2000s, provided the share of pro-poor aid in ODA transfers was high enough. There are also many papers on remittances' impacts on inequality, generally finding that remittances reduce inequality in most, but not all, countries. Cross-country studies in this literature include Portes (2009) and Ebeke and LeGoff (2009).

There is also a substantial literature investigating the effects of financial flows on governance and related issues such as corruption, mostly investigating the impacts of ODA. Much of this has been driven by the question of whether a "political resource curse of aid" exists that has negative effects on governance similar to those associated with the better-known natural resource curse. Busse and Gröning (2009) do find a negative effect of ODA on governance, using panel methods on multiple countries. But subsequent research has tended to contradict these findings. Altincekic and Bearce (2014) find no effect of aid on dependent variables that proxy for political appeasement or repression. Kersting and Kilby (2014) find that ODA has a positive effect on democracy, while Jones and Tarp (2016) find that ODA has a small, positive impact on governance, which they attribute to more stable flows of ODA that are specifically targeted at improving governance. Dadsov (2017) finds that multilateral aid from EU institutions has generally had a positive impact on governance in recipient countries, while bilateral aid from large European country donors has not.

Other researchers have investigated the effect of ODA on corruption. Okada and Samreth (2012) use quantile regressions that find ODA reduces corruption, but the effect is greatest in countries that already have less corruption. Menard and Weill (2016) perform panel Granger causality tests of ODA and corruption and find no causality in either direction. Dijkstra (2018) performs an extensive literature review on the relationship between ODA and various measures of governance and finds that most studies document that ODA's impacts on democracy, governance, and corruption have improved over time. Like other researchers, Dijkstra suggests that donor targeting of aid matters and has improved.

In the case of FDI, there is relatively little research on its effects on governance and corruption, despite a large literature that examines the causality running in the opposite direction. But Farooque and Yarram (2013) do find evidence of two-way causality running between FDI and six governance measures in a cross-country sample. Similarly, there are relatively few papers documenting the effect of remittances on governance. Abdih et al. (2012) show that remittances lower the quality of institutions in countries that receive significant remittance inflows, or that there is evidence of a "remittances curse" similar to a natural resources curse. Berdiev et al. (2013) find that remittances increase measures of corruption. By contrast, Hassan and Faria (2015) find evidence that remittances reduce social violence and may therefore reduce symptoms of social fragility.

Despite the limited amount of direct evidence on the relationship between financial flows and fragility, two messages do emerge from relevant research. First, fragility, especially extreme fragility, does seem to matter for some types of financial flows. One question, however, is the apparent lack of strong response of remittances to fragility, especially given that remittances are motivated by altruism. The second message is that financial flows appear to have significant interactions with several symptoms of state fragility. Much of the literature investigating financial flows' impacts on growth finds that the size or direction of these impacts depends on characteristics of the recipient economies, such as institutional quality, that are also associated with fragility. Similarly, other research suggests that financial flows directly affect some of the symptoms of fragility, which in turn suggests that financial flows may affect fragility through these economic and social characteristics. It should be noted, however, that all of these messages are preliminary in nature. Much more research is needed to refine (or perhaps rebut) these findings, such as that presented in the remainder of this chapter.

4.2 Do Financial Flows Make a Difference in Fragile Countries?

4.2.1 Country Fragility and Growth

Analyzing the impact of financial flows on economic growth suffers from endogeneity bias (see, for instance, Benmamoun and Lehnert, 2013; Kosack and Tobin, 2006; Li and Liu, 2005). To address this problem, we follow ILO (2015) and Eichengreen et al. (2013) in defining episodes of growth and employment accelerations and slowdowns. In particular, growth accelerations are measured as the starting year of seven-year growth spurts at 3.5 percent p.a. after an acceleration of at least 2 percentage points with respect to the previous seven years. Similarly, growth slowdowns are measured as the starting year of a drop of average growth by 2 percentage points after a period of growth at 3.5 percent p.a. over the previous seven years. This leaves us with 78 episodes of growth spurts and 32 episodes of growth slowdowns in our country sample, including countries that experience more than one growth spurt or deceleration over the observation period. We implement our empirical strategy, using a probit estimation on the pooled sample, controlling for lagged growth, population growth, and (average) country fragility (see estimates in Table 15.2). To address heteroscedasticity we use robust standard errors. Specifically, we use maximum likelihood to estimate and report the β-coefficients of the following pooled-countries equations:

$$Pr(GDP\_accelerations_{i,t}) =$$

$$\alpha + \beta^1 \cdot \Delta\overline{\mathrm{GDP}^7_{i,t}} + \beta^2 \cdot \Delta \mathrm{Pop}_{i,t}$$

$$+\beta^{FSI} \cdot \overline{FSI}_i \times (\beta^{FDI} \cdot FDI_{i,t} + \beta^{ODA} \cdot ODA_{i,t} + \beta^{REM} \cdot REM_{i,t}) + \varepsilon_{i,t}$$

and

$$Pr(EmploymentGrowth\_slowdowns_{i,t}) =$$

$$\alpha + \beta^1 \cdot \Delta\overline{E^7_{i,t}} + \beta^2 \cdot \Delta Pop_{i,t}$$

$$+\overline{FSI}_i \times (\beta^{FDI} \cdot FDI_{i,t} + \beta^{ODA} \cdot ODA_{i,t} + \beta^{REM} \cdot REM_{i,t}) + \varepsilon_{i,t}$$

where $Pr(GDP\_accelerations_{i,t}), Pr(EmploymentGrowth\_slowdowns_{i,t})$: the probability of GDP per capita accelerations, respectively, the slowdowns in employment growth in country i at starting year t; $\Delta\overline{GDP^7_{i,t}}$: average GDP per capita growth over the seven years prior to t; $\Delta\overline{E^7_{i,t}}$: average employment growth over the seven years prior to t; $\Delta Pop_{i,t}$: population growth; $\overline{FSI_i}$: average fragility index; $FDI_{i,t}, ODA_{i,t}, REM_{i,t}$: FDI as a share of GDP, ODA per capita and remittances per capita respectively; and $\varepsilon_{i,t}$: i.i.d. error terms.

Results of the impact of financial flows on growth accelerations and slowdowns over different levels of fragility are depicted in Figure 15.5 and estimated coefficients displayed in Table 15.3. Figure 15.5 demonstrates a consistent positive impact of FDI on the probability of growth accelerations at all levels of fragility and a negative impact on the probability of growth slowdowns, but only for low and intermediate levels of country fragility. The positive impact of FDI on growth accelerations, even for higher levels of fragility, can be related to the importance of the role that FDI plays in resource-rich countries. Indeed, as shown by Table 15.3, employment in the mining sector is positively associated with the level of country fragility, indicating that even in very fragile countries, firms are ready to invest, provided their investment focuses on extractives that can be monetized easily.

Remittances, however, increase the chances for growth decelerations and lower the probability of growth accelerations for all but the most fragile countries. This confirms earlier research that point to the pernicious effects of remittances on growth (see Barajas et al., 2009; Chami et al., 2005, 2018). In contrast, official development aid helps support growth accelerations, although not in highly fragile countries, and prevents growth slowdowns across the fragility spectrum.

Estimated coefficients hide large differences in how significant changes in any of the financial flows would affect growth probabilities. Taking one standard deviation as the benchmark for changes in the three flows and calculating the

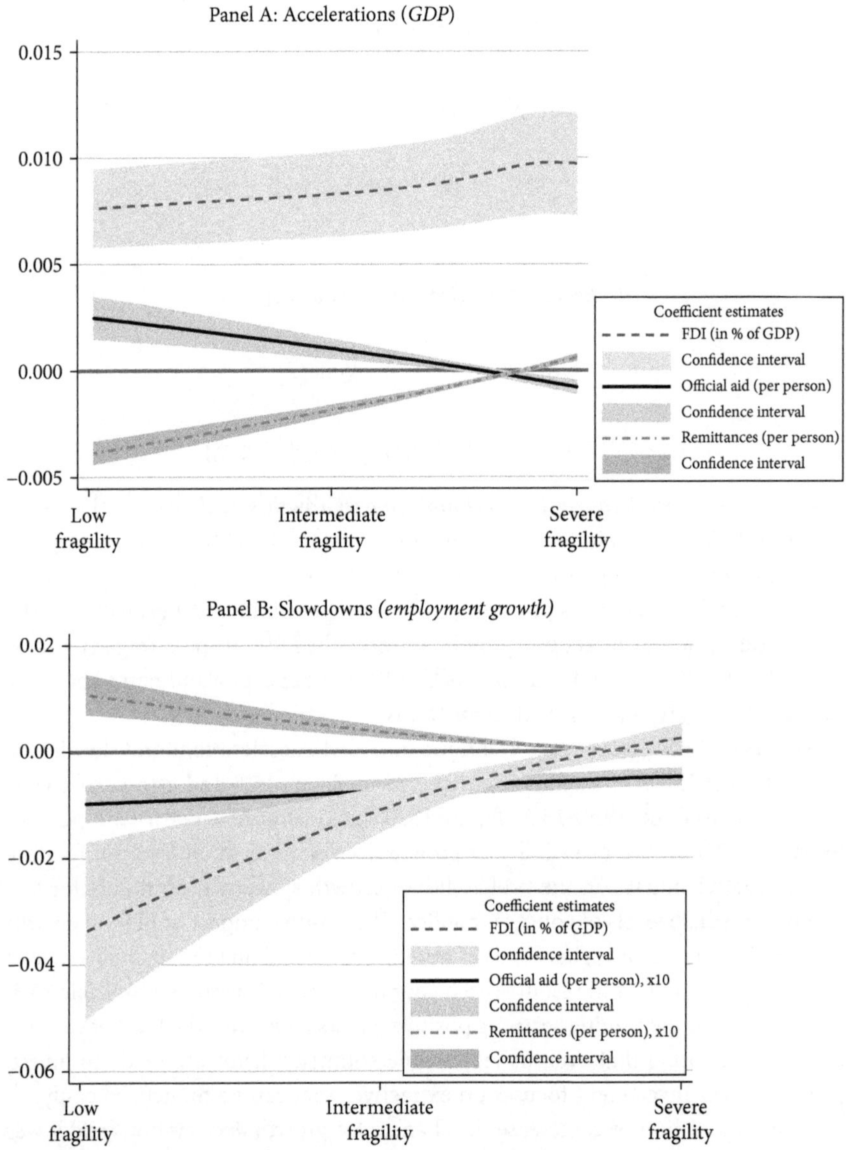

Figure 15.5 Financial Flows and Growth Accelerations and Slowdowns

Note: The charts display the estimated coefficients of foreign direct investments, official development aid and remittances to increase (+) or decrease (-) the probability of growth accelerations and slowdowns for different levels of country fragility. Growth accelerations are measured as seven-year growth spurts at 3.5 per cent p.a. after an acceleration of at least 2pp with respect to the previous seven years. Similarly, growth slowdowns are measured as a drop of average growth by 2pp after a period of growth at 3.5 per cent p.a. over the previous seven years (see ILO (2015) and Eichengreen *et al.* (2013)). Growth slowdowns refer to slowdowns in employment growth.

Source: Capital and income flows: IMF Balance of Payment statistics, employment: ILO Global Employment Trends database, own calculations

Table 15.3 Financial Flows and Growth Accelerations and Slowdowns: Estimation Results

	Coefficient estimate	Standard error
Pre-slowdown growth	−0.3378372***	0.0294346
Population growth	−0.249947***	0.0508086
Level of fragility	−0.0030315	0.0039916
Foreign direct investment (in % of GDP)	0.0388498***	0.0095248
FDI x fragility	–	
Official development aid (per person)	0.0126453**	0.0049625
ODA x fragility	−0.0001595**	0.0000607
Remittances (per person)	−0.01968***	0.002592
Remittances x fragility	0.0002233***	0.0000307
Constant	0.5802508*	0.3098105
Number of observations	1202	
Pseudo R^2	0.2504	
	Coefficient estimate	**Standard error**
Pre-slowdown growth	1.514295***	0.1499478
Population growth	−0.6583071***	0.1231291
Level of fragility	−0.015155*	0.0090239
Foreign direct investment (in % of GDP)	−0.397462***	0.1524093
FDI x fragility	0.0046023**	0.0019969
Official development aid (per person)	−0.0114871***	0.0029493
ODA x fragility	–	
Remittances (per person)	0.0126181***	0.0028674
Remittances x fragility	−0.0001382***	0.0000337
Constant	−4.068697***	0.7181027
Number of observations	1170	
Pseudo R^2	0.5233	

Note: Probit estimations with robust standard errors.

effects at the mean of country fragility, the probability of growth accelerations would increase by 11 percent for FDI, more than double for ODA, and decrease by 40 percent for remittances. Similarly, the probability for growth slowdowns would be divided by a factor of 3 for FDI, decline by 76 percent for ODA, and more than double for remittances, at the average level of country fragility.

Estimates are also subject to measurement issues related to the assessment of fragility. Nevertheless, in the annex, we provide evidence that using the OECD fragility indicator instead of the one provided by the FFP does affect our estimates only marginally and leaves unchanged the broad conclusion about the impact of fragility on the effectiveness of financial flows for growth accelerations and slowdowns unchanged, except, notably, the impact of FDI under certain forms of fragility (see "Robustness check" in annex).

4.2.2 The Impact of Financial Flows on Poverty

Not only do financial flows have different effects on growth depending on the level of fragility; their effect on poverty alleviation also changes significantly between highly fragile countries and the rest. To understand the impact of financial flows on socioeconomic outcomes, we analyzed their effect on employment shares at different levels of consumption for different country groups. Employment by levels of consumption provides proxy information for earnings distribution, which in most cases is not available.[12] Figure 15.6 demonstrates that large differences exist between the impact of financial flows on employment shares by consumption level in fragile countries and their impact in non-fragile countries. In particular, in non-fragile countries remittances alleviate the worst forms of working poverty, whereas FDI allows employment to shift into higher levels of consumption. None of these effects exist in fragile countries, however.

In Figure 15.6, fragile countries have been identified as those with a fragility index ranking them among the 30 percent most fragile ones whereas all other countries were classified as nonfragile. Coefficient estimates in the chart are derived from the following estimation equation:

$$E_{i,t} = \alpha_i + \beta_1 \cdot E_{i,t-1} + \beta_2 \cdot \Delta GDP_{i,t} + \beta_2 \cdot FDI_{i,t} + \beta_3 \cdot ODA_{i,t} + \beta_4 \cdot Remittances_{i,t} + u_t + \varepsilon_{i,t}$$

where u_t: time dummies, α_i: country fixed effect, $E_{i,t}$: employment by economic class, $\Delta GDP_{i,t}$: GDP growth, $FDI_{i,t}$: FDI as a share of GDP, $ODA_{i,t}$: ODA per person and $Remittances_{i,t}$: remittances per person. Estimations have been carried out using panel-correction standard errors to account for heteroscedasticity and contemporaneous correlation.[13]

4.2.3 Financial Flows and Sectoral Specialization

The aggregate growth and employment effects shown in the previous subsections are driven by differences in the impact of financial flows across different sectors. Using the ILO's global employment estimates by sector, a simple analysis of variance of sectoral shares across levels of fragility has been conducted in Figure 15.7. Following the analysis in Chami et al. (2018), the chart depicts the association of different financial flows with employment shares in manufacturing, construction, real estate and business services, and in public services. Confirming our earlier results, the chart demonstrates that remittances lift the share of employment in construction and, to a lesser extent, related business services for

[12] Most countries outside the group of advanced economies are characterized by large shares of the population working in the informal economy, for which no earnings information is available. Employment by economic class (that is, consumption level) is derived from combining labor force information with that available in poverty surveys (see Kapsos and Bourmpoula, 2013, for a detailed description of the methodology).

[13] Detailed regression output available from the authors upon request.

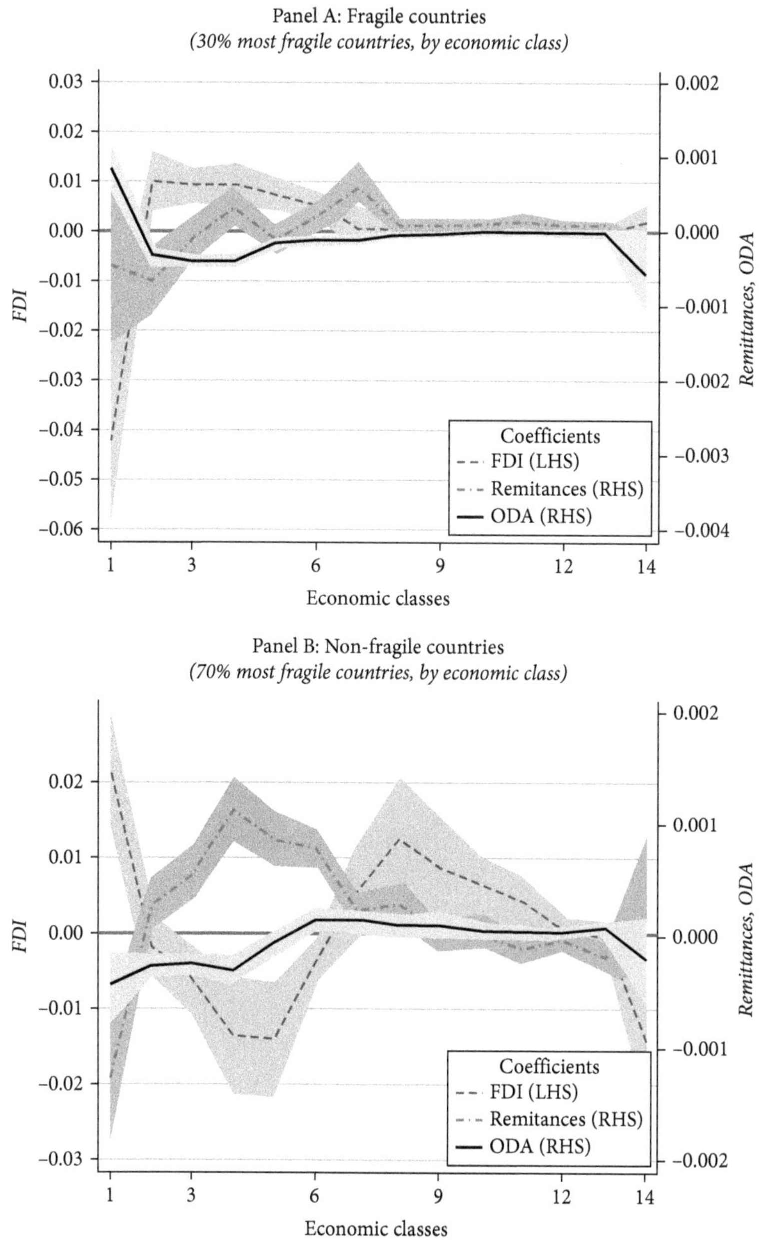

Figure 15.6 Financial Flows and Employment by Economic Class

Note: The chart displays coefficient estimates for FDI (in % of GDP), remittances (per capita) and ODA (per capita) for employment by economic class. The model estimates distinguishes 14 different economic classes: (1) Extreme working poor at less than \$1.9 per capita and per day, (2) Moderately working poor between \$1.9 and \$2.4, (3) Moderately working poor between \$2.5 and \$3.1, (4) Near poor between \$3.1 and \$4, (5)-(14) Economic class by one dollar increment between \$4 and \$14. Employment by economic class is expressed in per cent of total employment. Estimates control for auto-correlation and heteroscedasticity.

Source: ILO, own estimates.

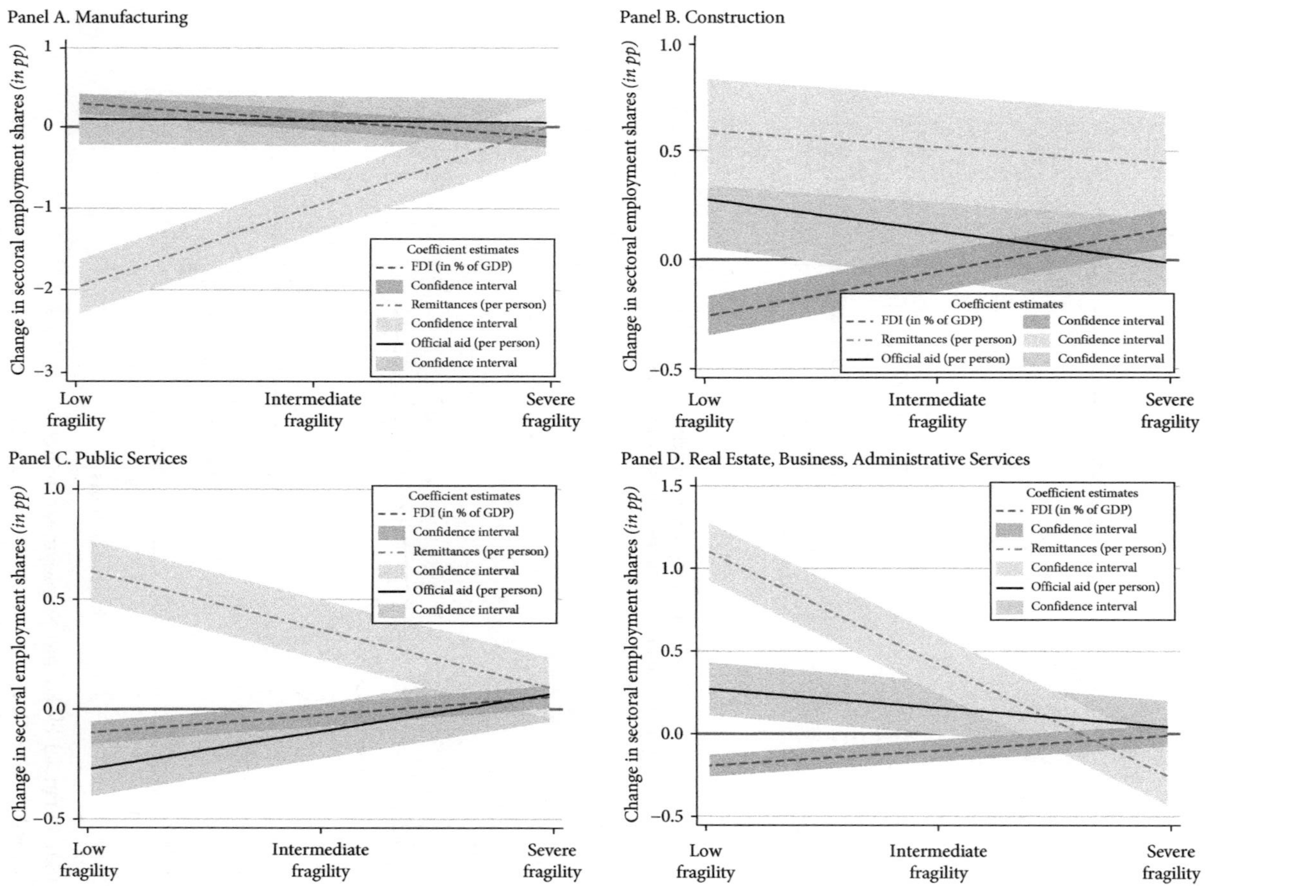

Figure 15.7 Sectoral Employment Changes, by Level of State Fragility

Note: The chart displays coefficient estimates for FDI (in % of GDP), remittances (per capita) and ODA (per capita) for employment by economic class. The model estimates distinguishes 14 different economic classes: (1) Extreme working poor at less than \$1.9 per capita and per day, (2) Moderately working poor between \$1.9 and \$2.4, (3) Moderately working poor between \$2.5 and \$3.1, (4) Near poor between \$3.1 and \$4, (5)-(14) Economic class by one dollar increment between \$4 and \$14. Employment by economic class is expressed in per cent of total employment. Estimates control for auto-correlation and heteroscedasticity.

all levels of fragility; at the same time, remittances reduce the share of manufacturing employment but mostly for lower levels of fragility. The associations between sectoral employment changes and FDI or ODA, respectively, are much more limited, particularly for higher levels of fragility.

5. Interpretation and Conclusion

The main message of this chapter is that fragility matters: fragile countries' characteristics make them likely to receive different amounts of financial flows than their non-fragile peers, and these flows are likely to affect fragile countries in ways that are substantially different from the ways they affect non-fragile countries. In particular, our findings suggest that though remittances do not seem to be (causally) related to fragility, FDI appears negatively and ODA positively correlated with the level of fragility. On causality, some evidence points to ODA causing several dimensions of fragility, while the direction of causality between FDI and fragility shifts for different fragility dimensions. Importantly, though, the amounts of these financial flows are unevenly distributed across the set of fragile states, and the specific type of fragility seems to have a part in determining the size and composition of the different flows.

Looking beyond the magnitude and drivers of these flows, fragility influences the effects that financial flows exert on recipient economies. It is often presumed that more financial flows to fragile states are always better. Our results shed more light on this idea. In the case of FDI, this presumption still seems accurate, considering the evidence produced in this chapter. FDI increases the likelihood of growth accelerations across all degrees of fragility, and increases employment in the manufacturing sector, which generally has higher productivity and wages. In addition, FDI does not appear to exacerbate inequality in fragile states, as it often does in non-fragile states.

With respect to remittances, our findings suggest that in the most fragile countries, they do not show the negative growth impact identified elsewhere. Even though the direct impact of remittances on growth might be limited, they might provide benefits in fragile states not captured in our analysis amid less negative side-effects. At the same time, their effects on poverty reduction and structural adjustment seem limited for fragile states.

The evidence on ODA is more mixed, however, reinforcing some conclusions of research that is skeptical about the effectiveness and even the positive impacts of ODA. While ODA reduces the probability of employment growth slowdowns across different levels of fragility, the finding that it increases the occurrence of growth accelerations does not hold for highly fragile countries. Evidence suggests that politics interferes with the effectiveness of ODA. This can be seen in the volatility of ODA and in the positive correlation between state legitimacy and ODA. Unfortunately, ODA does not appear to affect poverty or inequality in fragile states; nor does it appear to cause sectoral shifts of employment.

To distill some specific recommendations from the exercises in this chapter for policymakers and researchers, our findings suggest that providing answers to what fragile countries can do to attract FDI and remittances should be a top priority. Can industries other than mining or other natural resource extraction attract FDI to fragile states? Why do remittances fall dramatically from medium- to high-fragility countries, and how difficult would it be to mitigate these obstacles to increased remittances? In particular, are remittances the return on an investment in migration that especially fragile countries cannot afford, at least on the part of the private sector? The results further support the growing sentiment that ODA must be more carefully designed and non-humanitarian aid better targeted to fragile states. Both the economics and the political economy of the determinants of financial flows to fragile states need to be investigated further for the design of effective policies.

Our work implies several areas for future research. A somewhat troubling aspect is raised by results of our causality exercise; these suggest that some forms of fragility cause higher FDI. Whether these forms of fragility make FDI the only practical way to raise investment capital in a country, or whether they make it easy for a company to earn economic rents, are two questions that should be investigated. The political economy of ODA and fragile countries also needs to be much better understood. What are the main reasons why only a few "aid darlings" receive a large share of ODA to fragile states? What is the relationship between humanitarian aid and other ODA? What are the main causes of the relatively high volatility of ODA? Finally, future research could focus on identifying the specific channels by which fragility influences the effects of financial flows on recipient economies.

Annex 1

Fragility and Financial Flows: Causality Analysis

The following figures present a summary of the coefficient estimates of a bivariate vector autoregression between financial flows (FDI, remittances, ODA) and different indicators of country fragility, using the Fund for Peace Fragile States Index. The bars indicate the (sum of) estimated coefficients whereas the asterisk(s) indicate the significance level of Granger causality (if any). Detailed overviews of the underlying characteristics of each fragility dimension can be found on the Fund for Peace website.

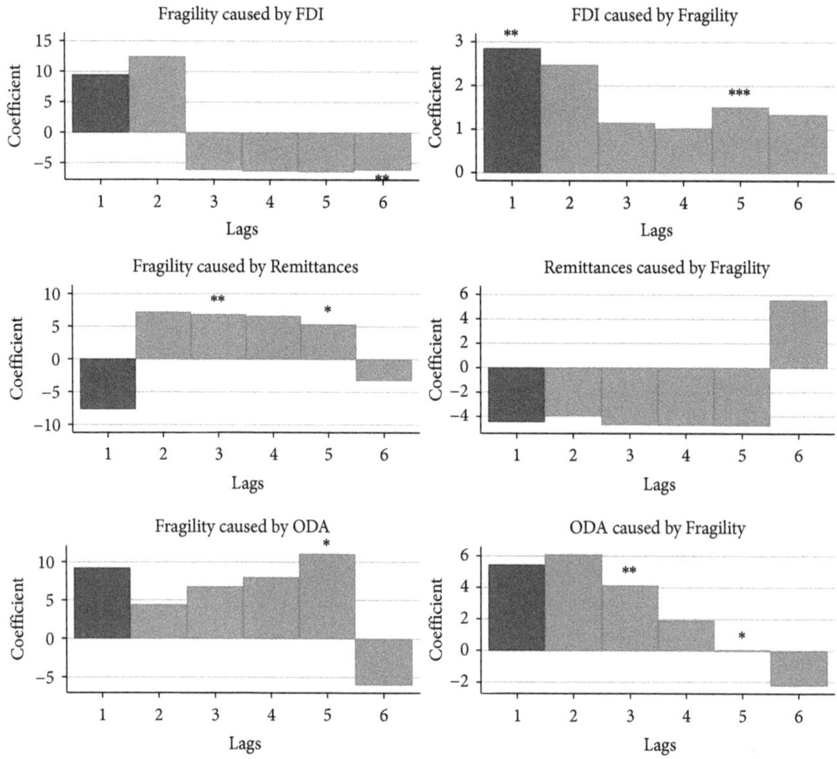

Figure A15.1 Security Apparatus Fragility and Financial Flows

(Bivariate vector autoregression)

Note: The graph displays the (sum of the) coefficient estimates of the bi-variate panel vector autoregression between the security apparatus fragility score and different financial flows for different lag lengths (maximum 6 years). The left column indicates the impact of different financial flows on the fragility score, the right column the impact of the fragility score on different financial flows. Higher fragility scores indicate higher levels of fragility. Significant causality relations in the Granger sense are indicated by an asterisk: *=10%, **=5%, ***=1%. Bars in red indicate estimates using optimal lag length criteria, based on Andrews and Lu's (2001) approach.

Robustness Check

The extent to which a country is considered to be fragile is often based on a subjective assessment because no commonly agreed measure exists. To assess to what extent our estimates on the impact of financial flows on growth accelerations and slowdowns depend on the particular fragility measure we use, we have conducted some robustness checks.

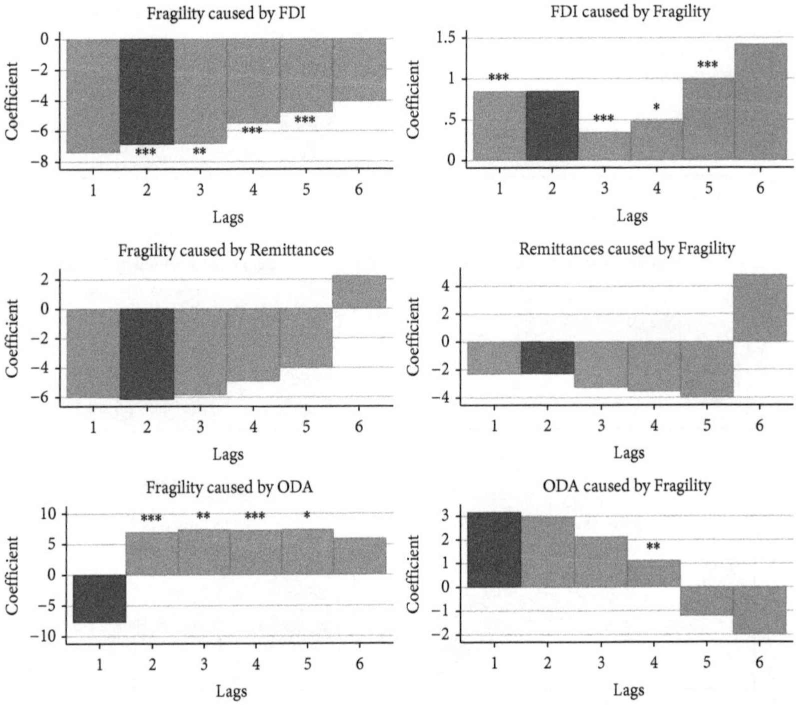

Figure A15.2 Demographic Pressure, Fragility and Financial flows

(Bivariate vector autoregression)

Note: The graph displays the (sum of the) coefficient estimates of the bi-variate panel vector autoregression between the demographic pressure fragility score and different financial flows for different lag lengths (maximum 6 years). The left column indicates the impact of different financial flows on the fragility score, the right column the impact of the fragility score on different financial flows. Higher fragility scores indicate higher levels of fragility. Significant causality relations in the Granger sense are indicated by an asterisk: *=10%, **=5%, ***=1%. Bars in red indicate estimates using optimal lag length criteria, based on Andrews and Lu's (2001) approach.

Specific Fragility Dimensions

A first robustness check concerns the particular fragility dimension we have used previously. For the estimates in Figure 15.4, the aggregate fragility indicator developed by the Fund for Peace was used. When specific fragility dimensions are used instead, the picture changes slightly (see Figure A15.9). Estimating the impact of financial flows on growth accelerations looking specifically at economic fragility, two effects can be observed (see Figure 17, panel A): First, FDI no longer has a positive impact on growth accelerations for countries with high levels of economic fragility.[14] Second, the negative impact of remittances on growth accelerations disappears for low levels of economic fragility.

[14] Economic fragility refers to the degree of economic inequality in a country, see http://fundforpeace.org/fsi/ (last accessed July 16, 2020).

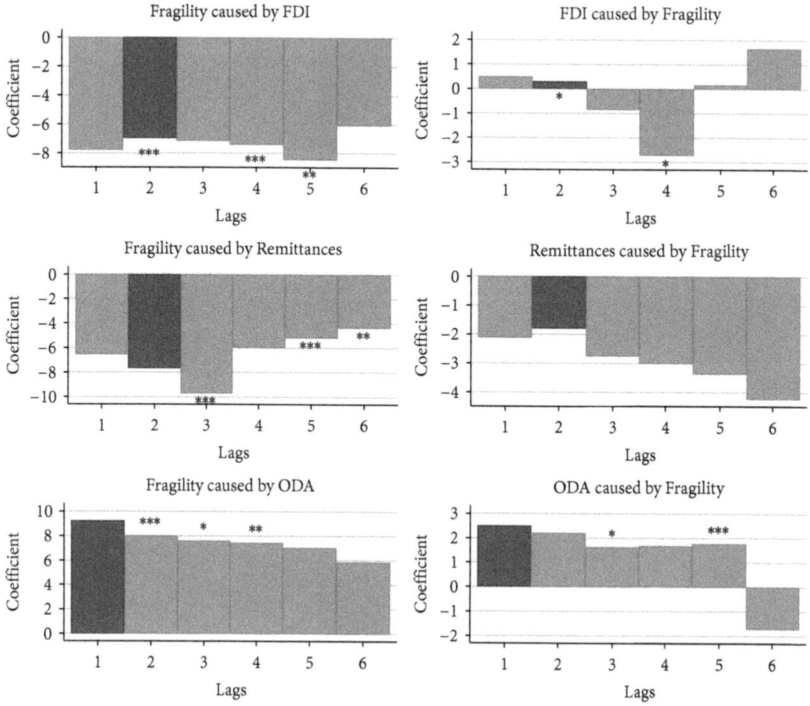

Figure A15.3 Uneven Economic Development Fragility and Financial Flows

(Bivariate vector autoregression)

Note: The graph displays the (sum of the) coefficient estimates of the bi-variate panel vector autoregression between the uneven economic development fragility score and different financial flows for different lag lengths (maximum 6 years). The left column indicates the impact of different financial flows on the fragility score, the right column the impact of the fragility score on different financial flows. Higher fragility scores indicate higher levels of fragility. Significant causality relations in the Granger sense are indicated by an asterisk: *=10%, **=5%, ***=1%. Bars in red indicate estimates using optimal lag length criteria, based on Andrews and Lu's (2001) approach.

Another fragility dimension reported by the Fund for Peace concerns public services fragility, that is, the extent to which essential services such as health care and education are being provided by public institutions. On this fragility dimension (Figure A15.10, panel B), ODA increases rather than decreases the risk of slowdowns at low levels of this type of fragility; effects for both remittances and FDI remain broadly in line with those reported in Figure 15.4. The degree of public services fragility raises the likelihood that ODA will increase rather than decrease the probability of growth slowdowns at low levels of fragility; this suggests that ODA is indeed competing for public resources to the detriment of economic growth, like the results suggested by our causality analysis discussed earlier.

OECD Fragility Indicator

Rather than looking at specific fragility dimensions, we replace the measure of fragility with that reported by the OECD in Figure A15.11 (see OECD, 2018). Results for the effect of FDI

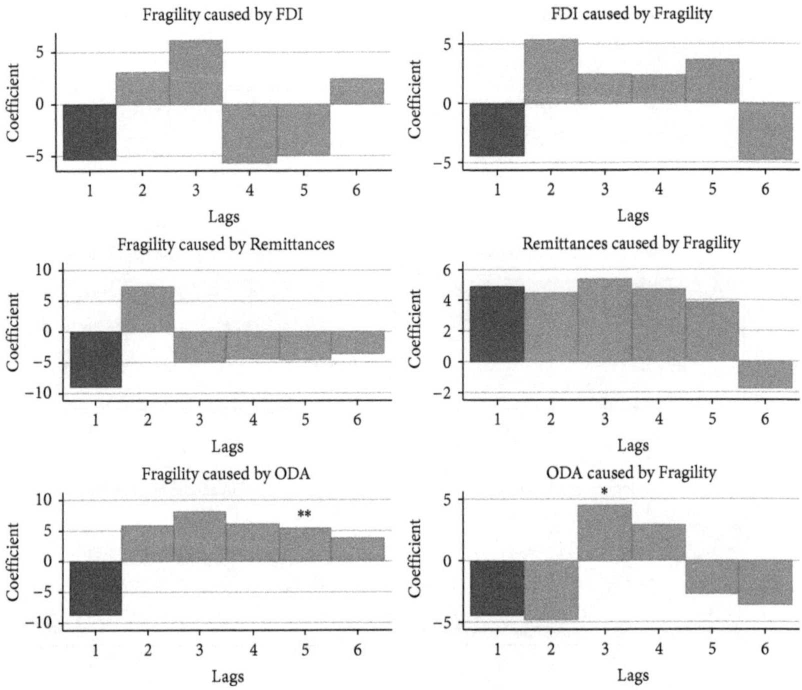

Figure A15.4 External Intervention Fragility and Financial Flows

(Bivariate autoregression)

Note: The graph displays the (sum of the) coefficient estimates of the bi-variate panel vector autoregression between the external intervention fragility score and different financial flows for different lag lengths (maximum 6 years). The left column indicates the impact of different financial flows on the fragility score, the right column the impact of the fragility score on different financial flows. Higher fragility scores indicate higher levels of fragility. Significant causality relations in the Granger sense are indicated by an asterisk: *=10%, **=5%, ***=1%. Bars in red indicate estimates using optimal lag length criteria, based on Andrews and Lu's (2001) approach.

on either growth accelerations or slowdowns are broadly in line with those presented in Figure 15.4. However, results for both ODA and remittances are different. For ODA, no significant results are being reported at any level of fragility. This is most likely because of the significantly reduced size of the sample: the OECD fragility indicator is only available for a much shorter time. As to the impact of remittances, the impact on growth accelerations is negative but this time increasingly so for countries with higher levels of fragility. No significant effect of remittances can be detected for slowdowns, again most probably because of the short sample period.

In sum, our robustness analysis shows that the impact of FDI on either growth accelerations or growth slowdowns is broadly confirmed, irrespective of the particular fragility indicator used. In contrast, when the impact of either remittances or ODA is considered, estimated coefficients depend both in sign and size on the type of fragility and

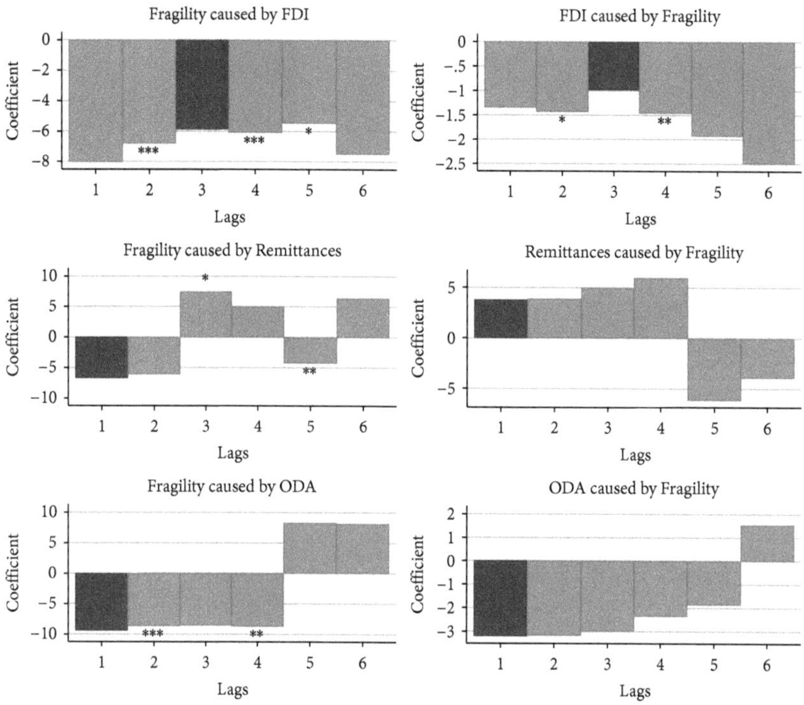

Figure A15.5 Factionalized Elites Fragility and Financial Flows

(Bivariate vector autoregression)

Note: The graph displays the (sum of the) coefficient estimates of the bi-variate panel vector auto-regression between the factionalized elites fragility score and different financial flows for different lag lengths (maximum 6 years). The left column indicates the impact of different financial flows on the fragility score, the right column the impact of the fragility score on different financial flows. Higher fragility scores indicate higher levels of fragility. Significant causality relations in the Granger sense are indicated by an asterisk: *=10%, **=5%, ***=1%. Bars in red indicate estimates using optimal lag length criteria, based on Andrews and Lu's (2001) approach.

the source of the fragility indicator. The choice of the source has a particularly strong effect because the sample size is significantly reduced when the OECD indicator, covering only the period 2014 through 2017, is used. In contrast, the fact that the type of fragility, even from the same source, influences the sign of the estimated coefficient indicates that a closer look at the nature of fragility is necessary to fully grasp the transmission mechanism through which financial flows affect the real economy.

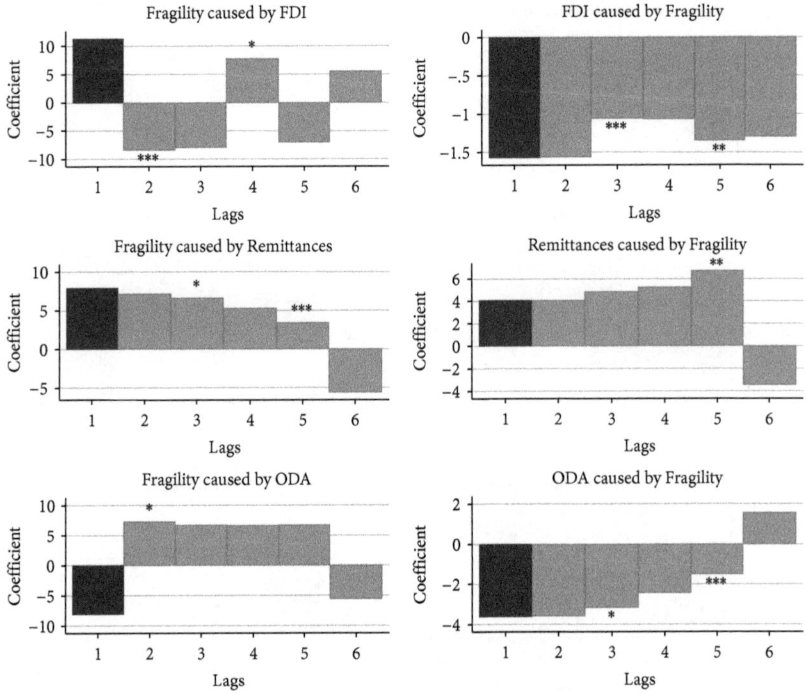

Figure A15.6 Group Grievances, Fragility and Financial Flows

(Bivariate vector autoregression)

Note: The graph displays the (sum of the) coefficient estimates of the bi-variate panel vector autoregression between the group grievances fragility score and different financial flows for different lag lengths (maximum 6 years). The left column indicates the impact of different financial flows on the fragility score, the right column the impact of the fragility score on different financial flows. Higher fragility scores indicate higher levels of fragility. Significant causality relations in the Granger sense are indicated by an asterisk: *=10%, **=5%, ***=1%. Bars in red indicate estimates using optimal lag length criteria, based on Andrews and Lu's (2001) approach.

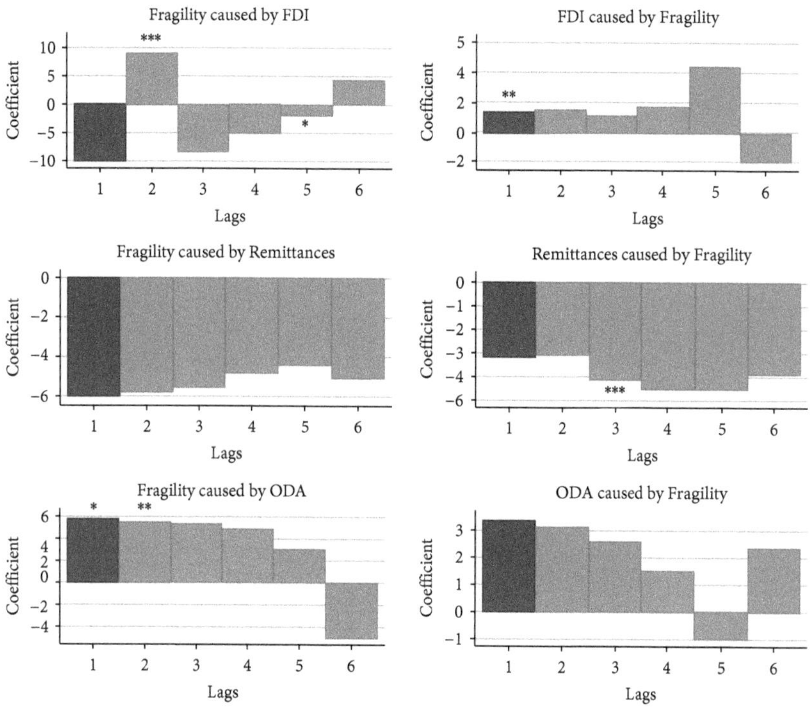

Figure A15.7 Human Flight and Brain Drain Fragility and Financial flows

(Bivariate vector autoregression)

Note: The graph displays the (sum of the) coefficient estimates of the bi-variate panel vector autoregression between the human flight and brain drain fragility score and different financial flows for different lag lengths (maximum 6 years). The left column indicates the impact of different financial flows on the fragility score, the right column the impact of the fragility score on different financial flows. Higher fragility scores indicate higher levels of fragility. Significant causality relations in the Granger sense are indicated by an asterisk: *=10%, **=5%, ***=1%. Bars in red indicate estimates using optimal lag length criteria, based on Andrews and Lu's (2001) approach.

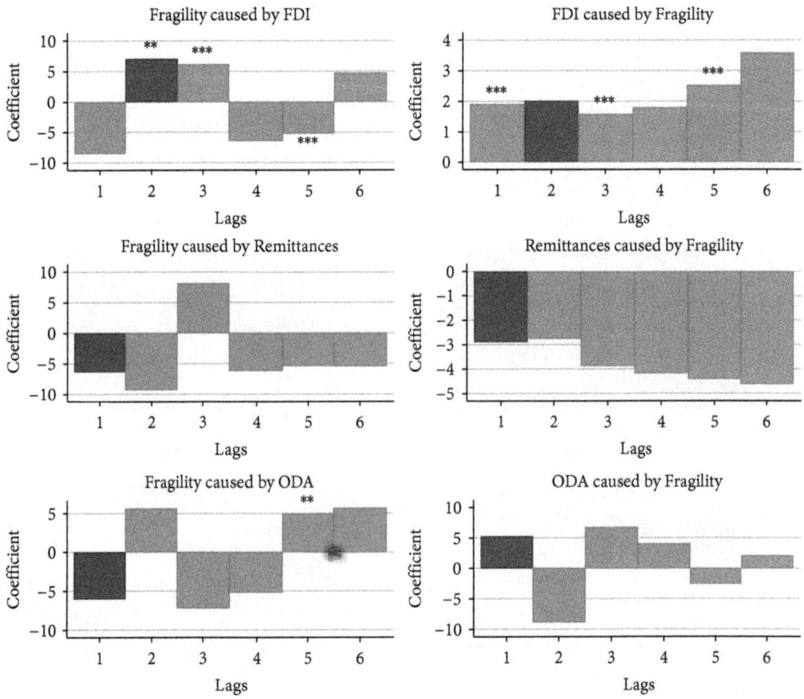

Figure A15.8 Public Services Fragility and Financial Flows

(Bivariate vector autoregression)

Note: The graph displays the (sum of the) coefficient estimates of the bi-variate panel vector autoregression between the public services fragility score and different financial flows for different lag lengths (maximum 6 years). The left column indicates the impact of different financial flows on the fragility score, the right column the impact of the fragility score on different financial flows. Higher fragility scores indicate higher levels of fragility. Significant causality relations in the Granger sense are indicated by an asterisk: *=10%, **=5%, ***=1%. Bars in red indicate estimates using optimal lag length criteria, based on Andrews and Lu's (2001) approach.

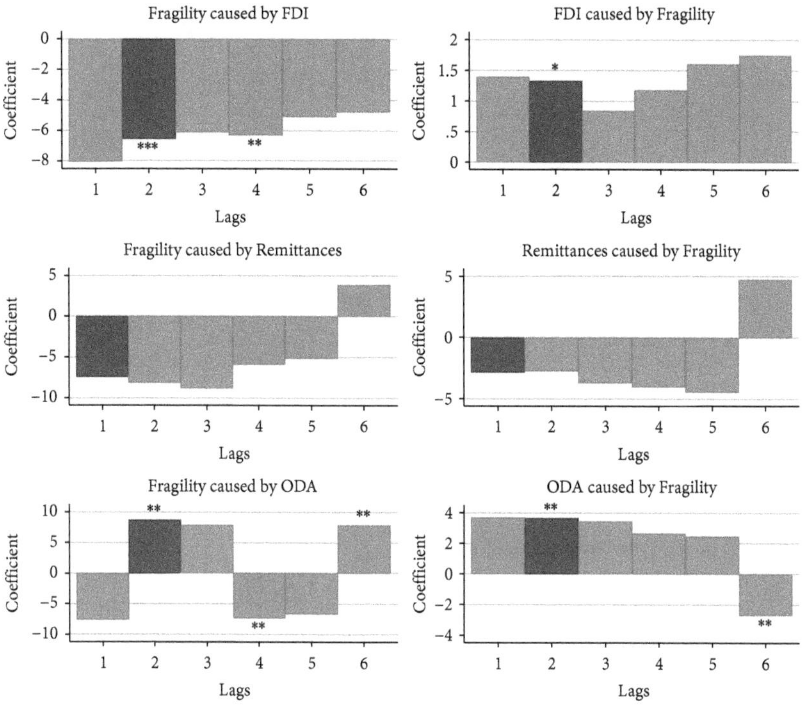

Figure A15.9 State Legitimacy Fragility and Financial Flows

(Bivariate vector autoregression)

Note: The graph displays the (sum of the) coefficient estimates of the bi-variate panel vector auto-regression between the state legitimacy fragility score and different financial flows for different lag lengths (maximum 6 years). The left column indicates the impact of different financial flows on the fragility score, the right column the impact of the fragility score on different financial flows. Higher fragility scores indicate higher levels of fragility. Significant causality relations in the Granger sense are indicated by an asterisk: *=10%, **=5%, ***=1%. Bars in red indicate estimates using optimal lag length criteria, based on Andrews and Lu's (2001) approach.

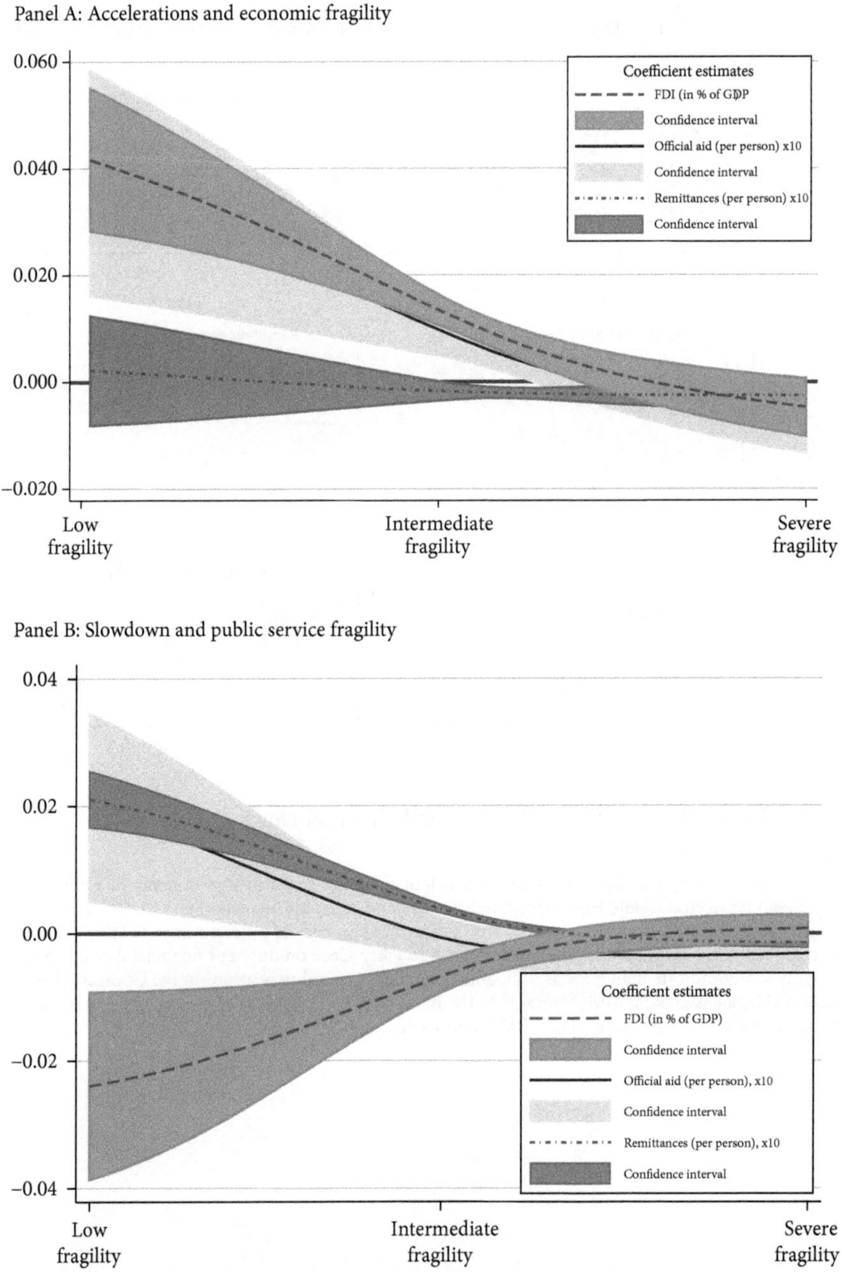

Figure A15.10 Growth and Slowdown Effects of Financial Flows—Specific Fragility Dimensions

Note: The charts show the estimated coefficients of foreign direct investments, official development aid and remittances to increase (+) or decrease (-) the probability of growth accelerations and slowdowns for different levels of specific forms of fragility. Panel A depicts the impact of financial flows on growth accelerations along economic fragility; panel B shows the impact of financial flows on growth slowdowns along public services fragility. Growth accelerations are measured as seven-year growth spurts at 3.5 per cent p.a. after an acceleration of at least 2pp with respect to the previous seven years. Similarly, growth slowdowns are measured as a drop of average growth by 2pp after a period of growth at 3.5 per cent p.a. over the previous seven years (see ILO (2015) and Eichengreen *et al.* (2013)). Growth slowdowns refer to slowdowns in employment growth.

Source: Capital and income flows: IMF Balance of Payment statistics, employment: ILO Global Employment Trends database, own calculations

Panel A: Accelerations (GDP)

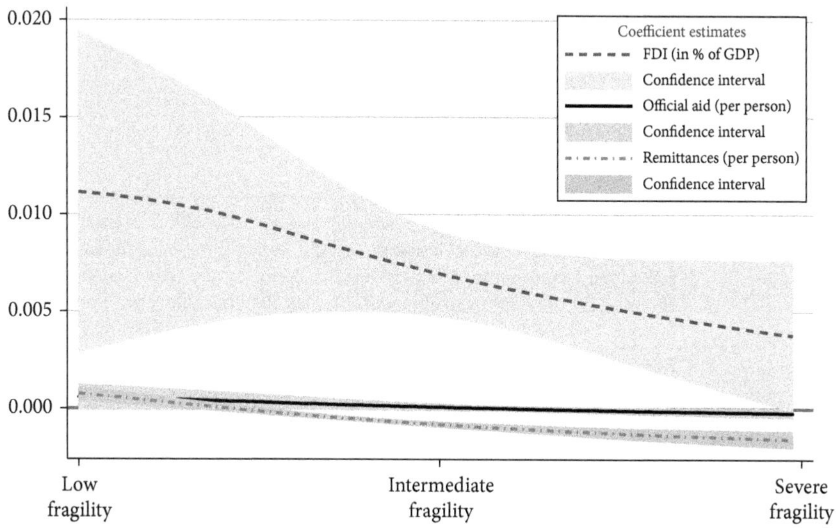

Panel B: Slowdowns (Employment)

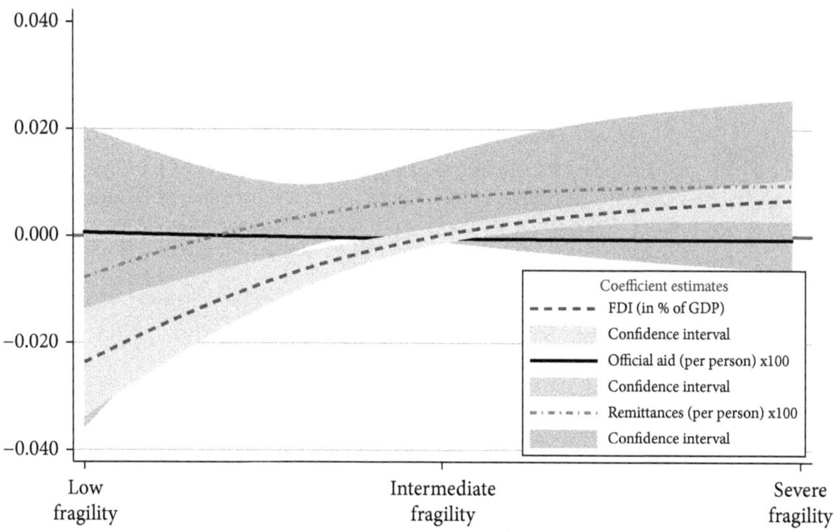

Figure A15.11 Estimated Coefficients of Financial Flow Effects on Accelerations and Slowdowns—OECD Economic Fragility Indicator

Note: The charts show the estimated coefficients of foreign direct investments, official development aid and remittances to increase (+) or decrease (-) the probability of growth accelerations and slowdowns for different levels of the OECD indicator of economic fragility- Growth accelerations are measured as seven-year growth spurts at 3.5 per cent p.a. after an acceleration of at least 2pp with respect to the previous seven years. Similarly, growth slowdowns are measured as a drop of average growth by 2pp after a period of growth at 3.5 per cent p.a. over the previous seven years (see 1LO (2015) and Eichengreen *et at.* (2013)). Growth slowdowns refer to slowdowns in employment growth.

Source: Capital and income flows: IMF Balance of Payment statistics, employment: ILO Global Employment Trends database, OECD State Fragility Index; own calculations

Annex 2

Country Fragility Groupings

Table A15.1 Countries by Level of Fragility (average 2013–17)

Fragility level	Countries
Lowest	Australia, Austria, Belgium, Canada, Chile, Czech Republic, Denmark, Estonia, Finland, France, Germany, Iceland, Ireland, Italy, Japan, Korea, Lithuania, Luxembourg, Malta, Mauritius, Netherlands, New Zealand, Norway, Poland, Portugal, Singapore, Slovak Republic, Slovenia, Spain, Sweden, Switzerland, United Kingdom, United States, Uruguay
Low	Albania, Argentina, Armenia, Republic of Bahamas, Bahrain, Belize, Botswana, Brazil, Brunei Darussalam, Bulgaria, Costa Rica, Croatia, Cyprus, Ghana, Greece, Hungary, Jamaica, Kazakhstan, Kuwait, Latvia, Macedonia (FYR), Malaysia, Mongolia, Montenegro, Namibia, Oman, Panama, Qatar, Romania, South Africa, Suriname, Trinidad and Tobago
Intermediate	Algeria, Azerbaijan, Belarus, Benin, Bolivia, Bosnia and Herzegovina, Cabo Verde, China, P.R., Dominican Republic, Ecuador, El Salvador, Fiji, Gabon, Guyana, India, Indonesia, Jordan, Maldives, Mexico, Moldova, Morocco, Nicaragua, Paraguay, Peru, Saudi Arabia, Serbia, Thailand, Tunisia, Turkey, Turkmenistan, Ukraine, Vietnam
High	Angola, Bhutan, Burkina Faso, Cambodia, Colombia, Comoros, Egypt, Equatorial Guinea, Gambia, Georgia, Guatemala, Honduras, Iran, Israel, Kyrgyz Republic, Laos, Lebanon, Lesotho, Madagascar, Malawi, Mozambique, Papua New Guinea, Philippines, Russian Federation, Senegal, Solomon Islands, Sri Lanka, Swaziland, Tajikistan, Tanzania, Togo, Venezuela, Zambia
Highest	Afghanistan, Bangladesh, Burundi, Cameroon, Central African Republic, Chad, Congo, Congo (RDC), Cote d'Ivoire, Eritrea, Ethiopia, Guinea, Guinea-Bissau, Haiti, Iraq, Kenya, Liberia, Libya, Mali, Mauritania, Myanmar, Nepal, Niger, Nigeria, Pakistan, Rwanda, Sierra Leone, Sudan, Syria, Timor-Leste, Uganda, Yemen, Zimbabwe

References

Abdih, Y., R. Chami, J. Dagher, and P. Montiel. 2012. "Remittances and Institutions: Are Remittances a Curse?" *World Development*, 40(4): 657–66.

Abrigo, M.R.M. and I. Love. 2016. "Estimation of Panel Vector Autoregression in Stata." *The Stata Journal*, 16(3): 778–804.

Altincekic, C., and D.H. Bearce. 2014. "Why There Should Be No Political Foreign Aid Curse." *World Development*, 64: 18–32.

Andrews, D.W.K. and B. Lu. 2001. "Consistent Model and Moment Selection Procedures for GMM Estimation with Application to Dynamic Panel Data Models." *Journal of Econometrics*, 101(1): 123–64.

Barajas, A., R. Chami, C. Fullenkamp, M. Gapen, and P. Montiel. 2009. "Do Workers' Remittances Promote Economic Growth?" Working Paper 09–153. Washington, DC: International Monetary Fund.

Basu, P. and A. Guariglia. 2007. "Foreign Direct Investment, Inequality and Growth." *Journal of Macroeconomics*, 29: 824–839.

Benmamoun, M. and K. Lehnert. 2013. "Financing Growth: Comparing the Effects of FDI, ODA, and International Remittances." *Journal of Economic Development*, 38 (2): 43–65.

Ben Naceur, S., D. Bakardzhieva, and B. Kamar. 2012. "Disaggregated Capital Flows and Developing Countries' Competitiveness." *World Development*, 40(2): 223–37.

Berdiev, A.N., Y. Kim, and C.P. Chang. 2013. "Remittances and Corruption." *Economics Letters*, 118: 182–185.

Boone, P. 1996. "Politics and the Effectiveness of Foreign Aid." *European Economic Review*, 40(2): 289–329.

Burnside, C. and D. Dollar. 2000. "Aid, Policies and Growth." *American Economic Review*, 90(4): 847–68.

Busse, M. and S. Gröning. 2009. "Does Foreign Aid Improve Governance?" *Economics Letters*, 104: 76–78.

Carkovic, M. and R. Levine. 2005. "Does Foreign Direct Investment Accelerate Growth?" in M. Blomstroem, E.M. Graham, and T. Moran (Eds.), *Does Foreign Direct Investment Promote Development*? New York: Columbia University Press.

Catrinescu, N., M. Leon-Ledesma, M. Piracha, and B. Quillin. 2009. "Remittances, Institutions, and Economic Growth." *World Development*, 37(1): 81–92.

Chami, R., C. Fullenkamp, and S. Jahjah. 2005. "Are Immigrant Remittance Flows a Source of Capital for Development?" *IMF Staff Papers*, 52(1): 55–81.

Chami, R., E. Ernst, C. Fullenkamp, and A. Oeking. 2018. "Are Remittances Good for Labor Markets in LICs, MICs and Fragile States?" Working Paper 18/102 (IMF, Washington, DC).

Chong, A., M. Gradstein, and C. Calderon. 2009. "Can Foreign Aid Reduce Income Inequality and Poverty?" *Public Choice*, 140: 59–84.

Clemens, M.A., S. Radelet, R.R. Bhavnani, and S. Bazzi. 2011. "Counting Chickens When They Hatch: Timing and the Effects of Aid on Growth." *Economic Journal*, 122: 590–617.

Dadsov, R. 2017. "European Aid and Governance: Does the Source Matter?" *European Journal of Development Research*, 29: 269–88.

Dijkstra, G. 2018. "Aid and Good Governance: Examining Aggregate Unintended Effects of Aid." *Evaluation and Program Planning*, 68: 225–32.

Driffield, N. and C. Jones. 2013. "Impact of FDI, ODA and Migrant Remittances on Economic Growth in Developing Economies: A Systems Approach." *European Journal of Development Research*, 25(2): 173–96.

Ebeke, C. and M. LeGoff. 2009. *Why Migrants' Remittances Reduce Income Inequality in Some Countries and Not in Others*, CERDI Working Paper 2009–19 (Auvergne, France, University of Auvergne).

Eichengreen, B., D. Park, and K. Shin. 2013. "Growth Slowdowns Redux: New Evidence on the Middle-Income Trap." NBER Working Paper 18673 (Cambridge, MA, National Bureau of Economic Research).

Farooque, O.A. and S.R. Yarram. 2013. "Evidence on Two-Way Relationships between Foreign Direct Investment Inflows and Country-Level Individual Governance Indicators." *Singapore Economic Review*, 58(2): 1350013.1–1350013.26.

Giuliano, P. and M. Ruiz-Arranz. 2009. "Remittances, Financial Development, and Growth." *Journal of Development Economics*, 90: 144–52.

Hassan, G.M., and J.R. Faria. 2015. "Do Remittances Diminish Social Violence?" *Journal of Development Studies*, 51(10): 1309–25.

Herzer, D. and P. Nunnenkamp. 2012. "The Effect of Foreign Aid on Income Inequality: Evidence from Panel Cointegration." *Structural Change and Economic Dynamics*, 23: 245–55.

Iamsiraroj, S. 2016. "The Foreign Direct Investment-Economic Growth Nexus." *International Review of Economics and Finance*, 42(C): 116–33.

ILO (International Labour Organization). 2015. *World Employment and Social Outlook*. Trends. Geneva: International Labour Organization.

ILO (International Labour Organization). 2019. *World Employment and Social Outlook: Trends 2019*. Geneva: International Labour Organization.

Jones, S., and F. Tarp. 2016. "Does Foreign Aid Harm Political Institutions?" *Journal of Development Economics*, 118: 266–81.

Kapsos, S. and E. Bourmpoula. 2013. *Employment and Economic Class in the Developing World*, Research Paper 6. Geneva: International Labour Organization.

Kasuga, H. and Y. Morita. 2018. "Does Aid Affect Inequality?" *Applied Economics*, 50 (58): 6249–62.

Kersting, E. and C. Kilby. 2014. "Aid and Democracy Redux." *European Economic Review*, 67: 125–43.

Kosack, S. and J. Tobin. 2006. "Funding Self-Sustaining Development: The Role of Aid, FDI and Government in Economic Success." *International Organization*, 60: 205–43.

Lartey, E.K.K., F.S. Mandelman, and P.A. Acosta. 2012. "Remittances, Exchange Rate Regimes and the Dutch Disease: A Panel Data Analysis." *Review of International Economics*, 20(2): 377–95.

Li, X. and X. Liu. 2005. "Foreign Direct Investment and Economic Growth: An Increasingly Endogenous Relationship." *World Development*, 33(3): 393–407.

Lomoriello, R.S. 2018. "What Sources of External Development Finance Are Available to Fragile Contexts?" *States of Fragility 2018*. Paris: OECD, chap. 6.

Lomoriello, R.S. and R. Scott. 2018. "What Official Development Assistance Went to Fragile Contexts?" *States of Fragility 2018*. Paris: OECD, chap. 4.

Magud, N. and S. Sosa. 2010. "When and Why Worry about Real Exchange Rate Appreciation? The Missing Link between Dutch Disease and Growth." Working Paper 10/271. Washington, DC: IMF.

Majeed, M.T. 2017. "Inequality, FDI and Economic Development: Evidence From Developing Countries." *Singapore Economic Review*, 62(5): 1039–57.

McPeak, J. 2012. "Remittances and Fragile states: What Do We Know?" in S. Brown (Ed.), *Transnational Transfers and Global Development*. New York: Palgrave Macmillan, chap. 3, pp. 56–75.

Menard, A R. and L. Weill. 2016. "Understanding the Link between Aid and Corruption: A Causality Analysis." *Economic Systems*, 40(2): 260–72.

Milanovic, B. 2005. "Can We Discern the Effect of Globalization on Income Distribution? Evidence from Household Surveys." *World Bank Economic Review*, 19(1): 21–44.

Nsor-Ambala, A. 2015. *Foreign Transfers, Manufacturing Growth, and the Dutch Disease Revisited*, Discussion Paper 15/663. Bristol: University of Bristol.

OECD (Organisation for Economic Co-operation and Development). 2018. *States of Fragility 2018*. Paris: OECD.

Okada, K. and S. Samreth. 2012. "The Effect of Foreign Aid on Corruption: A Quantile Regression Approach." *Economics Letters*, 115: 240–43.

Portes, L.S.V. 2009. "Remittances, Poverty and Inequality." *Journal of Development Economics*, 34(1): 127–40.

Prasad, E.S., K. Rogoff, S.-J. Wei, and M.A. Kose. 2003. *Effects of Financial Globalization on Developing Countries: Some Empirical Evidence*. Occasional Paper 220. Washington, DC: IMF.

Ragoussis, A. and H. Shams. 2018. "FDI in Fragile and Conflict-Affected Situations." *Global Investment Competitiveness Report 2017–2018: Foreign Investor Perspectives and Policy Implications*. Washington, DC.: World Bank, chap. 5.

Rajan, R. and A. Subramanian. 2011. "Aid, Dutch Disease, and Manufacturing Growth." *Journal of Development Economics*, 94(1): 106–18.

Rajan, R.G., and A. Subramanian. 2008. "Aid and Growth: What Does the Cross-Country Evidence Really Show?" *The Review of Economics and Statistics*, 90(4): 643–65.

Rao, B.B. and G.M. Hassan. 2011. "A Panel Data Analysis of the Growth Effects of Remittances." *Economic Modelling*, 28(1–2): 701–09.

Rao, B.B. and G.M. Hassan. 2012. "Are the Direct and Indirect Growth Effects of Remittances Significant?" *The World Economy*, 35(3): 351–72.

Scott, R. 2018. "What Do Financial Flows Look Like Using a Multidimensional Lens?" *States of Fragility 2018*. Paris: OECD.

Shen, C.H. and C.C. Lee. 2010. "What Makes International Capital Flows Promote Economic Growth? An International Cross-Country Analysis." *Scottish Journal of Political Economy*, 57(5): 515–46.

Slesman, L., A.Z. Baharumshah, and M.E. Wohar. 2015. "Capital Inflows and Economic Growth: Does the Role of Institutions Matter?" *International Journal of Finance and Economics*, 20: 253–75.

Wu, J.Y. and C.C. Hsu. 2012. "Foreign Direct Investment and Income Inequality: Does the Relationship Vary With Absorptive Capacity?" *Economic Modelling*, 29: 2183–9.

16
Aid Effectiveness in Fragile States

Francesca G. Caselli and Andrea F. Presbitero

1. Introduction

In 2017 foreign aid to developing countries—measured by official development assistance (ODA) grants—amounted to more than US$140 billion.[1] A large (and increasing) share of these flows have been directed to fragile states, which received US$68 billion in 2016 (OECD, 2018). In fragile states, aid inflows account for a much larger share of GDP than in other developing countries and, on average, are the most important source of external finance. Fragile states are highly dependent on foreign aid and are also characterized by several features that impair their economic and social performance: weak governance, limited administrative capacity, low legitimacy, chronic humanitarian crises, polarized societies and persistent social tensions, and, often, violence or the legacy of armed conflict and civil war (OECD, 2018; Commission on State Fragility, Growth and Development, 2018). Thus, two questions arise: how predictable and, more important, effective are aid inflows to fragile states?

The experience of Malawi is a case in point. Foreign aid amounted to 17 percent of GDP between 2005 and 2008 and in the same period the country grew at 6.3 percent per year (in real terms), a rate significantly higher than in previous years.[2] Commentators praised Malawi for "its sound economic policies and a supportive donor environment" (Wroe, 2012). However, in 2009 the situation changed dramatically as aid money was used for personal expenditures and human rights and international observers raised governance concerns (IMF, 2012). These events triggered a reaction by the international community and a steady decline in foreign assistance (aid averaged 12.5 percent of GDP in 2009–11, the decline in Malawi was bigger than the decline in aid that resulted from the financial crisis in some donor countries), which created mounting pressure on the exchange rate

The views expressed in this chapter are those of the authors and do not necessarily represent the views of the IMF, its Executive Board, or IMF management. We would like to thank Axel Dreher, Chris Lane, Valentin Lang, and Peter Montiel for helpful comments and feedback. We also thank Kai Gehring, Lennart Kaplan, and Melvin Wong for sharing subnational data on conflicts and World Bank projects.

[1] Data are from the OECD, http://www.oecd.org/newsroom/development-aid-drops-in-2018 especially-to-neediest-countries.htm (last accessed: June 2019).

[2] Data are from the World Bank's World Development Indicators (last accessed: June 2019).

Francesca G. Caselli and Andrea F. Presbitero, *Aid Effectiveness in Fragile States* In: *Macroeconomic Policy in Fragile States.* Edited by: Ralph Chami, Raphael Espinoza, and Peter Montiel, Oxford University Press (2021).
DOI: 10.1093/oso/9780198853091.003.0016

and led to significant negative real effects and a growth slowdown in subsequent years. The case of Malawi would suggest that aid can be a key driver of sustained growth, even in fragile states; however, weak governance can undermine aid effectiveness and lead to volatile inflows, which are likely to adversely affect fragile states.

Given that fragile countries are at the risk of being left behind—it has been estimated that by 2030 more than 80 percent of the world's poorest will live in fragile countries (OECD, 2018)—there is ground to advocate for additional and increasing aid inflows to fragile states. For instance, in 2015 the UK's Department for International Development (DFID) made the commitment to allocate 50 percent of its budget to fragile states and regions (DFID, 2015). Similarly, the United States—which is the largest donor to fragile states—is scaling up its effort to tackle fragility (D'Alelio, 2018). Multilateral institutions are also taking steps in the same direction. The World Bank agreed to double its funding for fragile, conflict, and violence-affected countries,[3] while the IMF (2018b) has published a comprehensive review of its technical assistance programming in fragile states with a set of recommendations for improving fiscal capacity.

However, the literature on the effects of foreign aid on growth and poverty reduction has not yet reached a consensus on aid effectiveness, and fragile states are characterized by elements (such as weak institutions, conflicts) which could weaken aid effectiveness. Moving from similar concerns, and to maximize aid effectiveness and lift countries out of fragility, the Commission on State Fragility, Growth and Development (2018) recommends developing aid strategies specific to fragile states so as to channel aid flows to strategic sectors, finance key public investment projects necessary to emerge from political and economic fragility, and promote job creation.

Building on these considerations, this chapter reviews the literature on aid effectiveness with a focus to issues specific to fragile states (section 2). The existing literature on aid and growth has not yet reached a consensus on aid effectiveness, mostly because of severe methodological challenges that complicate the identification of causal effects in macro data. Bringing new evidence is beyond the scope of this chapter, which instead discusses several aspects of aid assistance that may affect the effectiveness of aid flows to promote inclusive growth in fragile states.

Then, the chapter presents several stylized facts on aid flows to fragile states, looking both at country-level and sector-level data (section 3). Plotting aggregate trends in aid flows shows three main features. First, the data highlight the aid dependency of several fragile states, where aid inflows account, in a few cases, for more than 10 percent of GDP. These flows have been declining over time and are not countercyclical, suggesting that they cannot really serve as a shock absorber. However, on the bright side, the data indicate that aid flows to fragile states have

[3] See: https://www.worldbank.org/en/topic/fragilityconflictviolence/overview#2 (last accessed: June 2019).

become less unpredictable over time. Third, there is a clear increasing trend in aid fragmentation over time, coupled with a stable share of multilateral aid flows and a recent increase in the share of aid delivered as budget support rather than project aid. Because a large number of donors can overburden the local institutional capacity and result in less efficient spending (Djankov et al., 2009), the recent increase in budget support, maximizing the ownership of aid flows, could mitigate the potentially negative effects of donor fragmentation (Dreher et al., 2018b).

The final part of the chapter takes advantage of project-level data to provide novel evidence on aid effectiveness in fragile states (section 4). The analysis of a large dataset of aid projects funded by seven large donors over the period 1980–2012 shows that the success rate of a project is significantly lower in fragile states (and if the projects are implemented during a conflict), even after controlling for a large set of country- and project-specific characteristics, and a granular set of fixed effects which absorb the impact of unobserved factors on differences in the project success rates across sectors and over time. Our results are economically sizable and indicate that a project implemented in a fragile state is about 8 percentage points less likely to be successful than a similar project financed in another developing country.

For a sub-sample of aid projects financed by the World Bank we can extend our analysis at the sub-national level, focusing on the conflict dimension of fragility, and exploiting the variation of conflict within countries and over time. In this case we can strengthen the identification of the effects of (conflict) fragility on aid effectiveness by controlling for country fixed effects, which absorb any cross-country variation that may affect project outcomes. The results indicate that the likelihood that a project is successful is lower in conflict (subnational) regions, further strengthening our argument that aid effectiveness could be weaker in fragile states than in comparable countries. Finally, we find that the project success rate increases with stronger control of corruption, showing that polices targeted at curbing corruption could contribute to increase aid effectiveness.

2. Aid Effectiveness: A Brief Literature Review

Does aid help countries grow? The economic literature on foreign aid is extremely broad (see, among others, the seminal contributions by Alesina and Dollar, 2000; Boone, 1996), but it has not yet reached a consensus on whether aid is effective in promoting growth in the recipient country (see, among others, Rajan and Subramanian, 2008; Clemens et al., 2012; Dreher and Lohmann, 2015; Arndt et al., 2015; Galiani et al., 2017; Dreher et al., 2018a; and Addison et al., 2017 for an overview of the macroeconomics of aid). Existing studies find that the success of aid in boosting the recipient country's economy is conditional on donor characteristics and their motivations (Kilby and Dreher, 2010; Dreher et al.,

2018a), and on the quality of policies and institutions in recipient countries (see Burnside and Dollar, 2000), although the evidence on the importance of sound policies and institutions is far from clear (Easterly et al., 2004). In this section, we briefly review the characteristics of aid flows, donor, and recipient countries which the literature has identified as elements that can influence the effectiveness of aid for economic development. For a comprehensive review of these factors and the role they have played in countries with limited statehood, see also Dreher et al. (2018b).

A first key element is the notion that large aid inflows can put pressure on the exchange rate, with negative effects on external competitiveness, exports, and manufacturing growth (Arellano et al., 2009; Rajan and Subramanian, 2011). Related to this issue, a more general concern is that the capacity to absorb foreign aid is impaired by various types of bottlenecks, implying that there are diminishing returns to aid (Clemens and Radelet, 2003; Clemens et al., 2012).[4] Consistent with this conjecture, the empirical literature at the macro-level shows decreasing marginal returns to aid (Clemens et al., 2012). Focusing on project-level data, Presbitero (2016) finds that World Bank investment projects are less likely to be successful if implemented during periods of public investment booms, because of absorptive capacity constraints in recipient countries. Carter (2014) shows that, when recipients face absorption constraints, aid allocations that favor poorer recipients are not always optimal and a sizable portion of aid could be wasted. In line with this evidence, Feeny and McGillivray (2009) show that a number of fragile countries receive more aid inflows than they can efficiently absorb, weakening the impact of these flows on growth and poverty reduction. On the other hand, and focusing only on the conflict dimension of fragility, Collier and Hoeffler (2004) document that absorptive capacity is greater than normal in post-conflict countries, suggesting that more aid could be channeled to these countries, under the conditions that could put policies are in place.

Large inflows are also often associated with a multitude of international agencies, including regional development banks, emerging bilateral donors, global funds, philanthropic foundations, and nongovernmental organizations (NGOs). Donor proliferation and aid fragmentation across donors (or sectors) is a second factor that has been largely investigated as potentially harmful for aid effectiveness (see, for instance, Easterly and Pfutze, 2008 and Kimura et al., 2012). When aid is fragmented, transaction costs become generally higher (Anderson, 2012; Acharya et al., 2006), and the quality of public sector bureaucracy declines because of corruption (Djankov et al., 2009; Knack and Rahman, 2007). At the same time,

[4] More generally, Besley and Mueller (2019) discuss the role of institutions and state capacity as a key constraint in fragile states. While their focus is on fiscal capacity, the notion that weak state capacity acts as a bottleneck to raise revenue has similar implications for the capacity to absorb and use effectively aid inflows.

while most of the literature focuses on the negative effect of aid fragmentation, recent studies stress that the participation of several donors and a greater diversity can help developing better policies. Kimura et al. (2012), for instance, use a donor-concentration index to capture a low degree of donor proliferation and find that aid proliferation has a negative effect on the economic growth of recipient countries, especially in Africa.[5] By contrast, Han and Koenig-Archibugi (2015) and Koeln (2019) argue that a larger number of donors can bring a more diverse set of views that in turn can generate better policies. Consistent with this hypothesis, Han and Koenig-Archibugi (2015) find a U-shaped relationship between the number of donors and the effectiveness of health aid, while Koeln (2019) shows that diversity provided by a multitude of donors helps improve a recipient country's democracy. Gehring et al. (2017) also find that the effects of fragmentation are not universally negative. Rather, they stress significant heterogeneity across sectors and channels of influence, with the so-called "social sectors" benefiting from aid fragmentation and the lack of a lead donor triggering the negative effect.

A third aspect that could reduce the growth dividend of foreign aid is its unpredictability (and volatility), which could be the consequence of uncoordinated and fragmented donors. Aid unpredictability is generally measured as the deviation of aid disbursements from commitments and captures potential shortfalls in aid flows which could generate pressures on public finances (Celasun and Walliser, 2008; Kodama, 2012). Unpredictable and volatile aid can reduce aid effectiveness (Arellano et al., 2009; Bulir and Hamann, 2008) and can have asymmetric negative effects on the level and composition of government expenditures, given that aid shortfalls are likely to reduce investment projects, while windfalls are often spent on consumption rather than investment.

Donors provide aid through the financing of specific projects (project finance) or delivering general support to the recipient country (budget support), imposing conditionality on how the funds are allocated to avoid granting full control to recipient government on how to spend the money. The pros and cons of these two different approaches to delivering international aid have long been debated in the literature without reaching a settlement on what is preferable. Cordella and Dell'Ariccia (2011) show theoretically that budget support is preferable when the donors' preferences are aligned to those of the recipients and the disbursements are small relative to the recipient country's domestic resources. Similarly, Morrissey (2006) shows that it is safe to provide budget support when recipients agree to spend the funds in line with donors' preferences. Eifert and Gelb (2005) favor budget support regardless of governance levels in recipient countries because reducing the number of projects lowers transaction costs for the donors. Gupta et al. (2006),

[5] Recent evidence by Davies and Klasen (2019) seems to suggest that herding is a key feature of the interaction of donors when making aid allocation choices, so that more coordination could be beneficial and favor the transmission of information.

instead, argue that project aid is preferable as it is less volatile than aid channeled through general budget support. More recently, Dreher et al. (2017) argue in favor of budget support aid in democratic countries, because it attributes full responsibility to recipient governments, while project aid generates lower ownership.

Another aspect that is generally recognized as influencing aid effectiveness is whether the funds are allocated through multilateral agencies or bilateral donors. The literature traditionally identifies multilateral aid as being more targeted to support development outcomes, while bilateral aid is seen as linked to donor strategic interests (Alesina and Dollar, 2000; Burnside and Dollar, 2000). On the other hand, recent studies find evidence suggesting that flows allocated through multilateral agency are also guided by political interests: Dreher et al. (2009), for instance, find that UN Security Council membership influences World Bank loans. A recent meta-analysis by Biscaye et al. (2017) on 45 empirical studies find no consistent evidence that either bilateral or multilateral aid is overall more effective in improving development outcomes.

Finally, several studies also focus on the sectoral allocation of aid and find that ODA is often used for different purposes than those originally decided. For instance, Collier and Hoeffler (2007) and Langlotz and Potrafke (2019) find that aid is correlated with higher military expenses in receiving countries, even though ODA excludes military use. In terms of sectoral allocation, there is also no agreement in the literature on whether foreign aid is more successful in improving outcomes in certain sectors than in others. There is some encouraging evidence that aid disbursed toward the education sector has positive impact (Dreher et al., 2008; Christensen et al., 2011; Birchler and Michaelowa, 2016), while there is no conclusive evidence as far as the health sector is concerned (Williamson, 2008; Nunnenkamp and Öhler, 2011).

3. Is Aid in Fragile States Different? Stylized Facts

What is the role of each of the factors discussed in the previous section in fragile states? While the empirical evidence focusing specifically on aid in fragile states is still limited because of data limitations (Dreher et al., 2018b), we now turn to the data and investigate how the characteristics of aid flows differ between fragile and non-fragile states to try to understand which factors are more likely to undermine aid effectiveness in fragile states.[6] The following analysis is predominately based

[6] We use the definition of fragile states from the IMF Independent Evaluation Office (IEO) (IMF 2018a). For the complete list see https://www.imf.org/en/Publications/Policy-Papers/Issues/2017/06/14/pp041817building-fiscal-capacity-in-fragile-state (page 45). The countries considered are: Afghanistan, Angola, Bosnia and Herzegovina, Iraq, Burundi, Central African Republic, Chad, Comoros, Democratic Republic of the Congo, Eritrea, Guinea, Guinea-Bissau, Haiti, Kiribati, Kosovo, Liberia, Libya, Madagascar, Malawi, Mali, Marshall Islands, Tuvalu, Micronesia, Myanmar, Nepal, Congo Republic of, Côte d'Ivoire, São Tomé and Príncipe, Solomon Islands, Sudan, Sierra

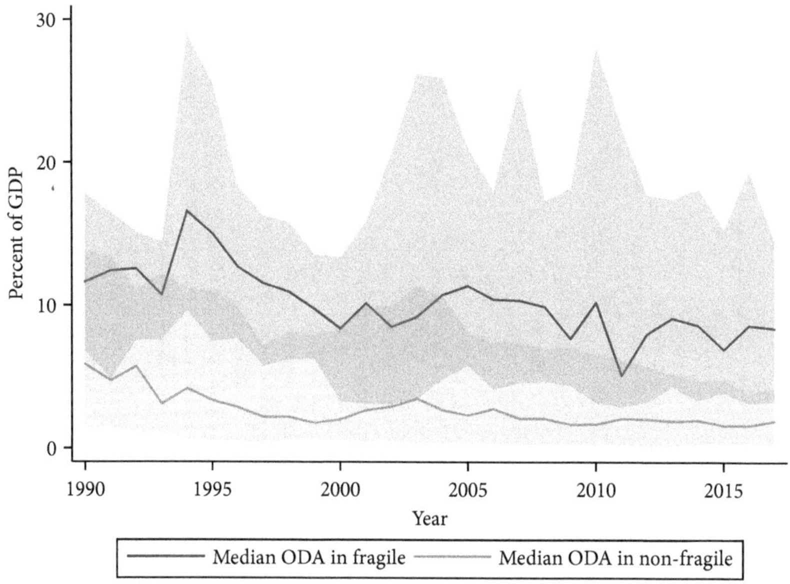

Figure 16.1 Median Official Development Assistance over Time
(Percent of GDP)

Notes: the chart reports the median net official development assistance received over GDP from the World Bank World Development Indicators over the sample 1990 to 2018. The shaded areas correspond to the 25th and 75th percentiles. We exclude countries with population less than 1 million. See text for the sample of countries.

Source: World Bank World Development Indicators

on Organisation for Economic Co-Operation Development Assistance Committee (OECD DAC) data.

Fragile countries receive about three times more aid as a share of their GDP than non-fragile states that receive DAC ODA flows. A first inspection of the aggregate data since 1990 reveals that fragile states are highly dependent on foreign assistance. Considering countries with complete aggregate data on net ODA (in percent of GDP) over the period 1990–2017 and comparing 25 fragile states with 75 low- and middle-income countries shows that, on average, net ODA account for almost 15 percent of GDP in fragile states, while the average ODA-to-GDP ratio is 6 percent in the other countries (Figure 16.1).[7] Zooming in at the country level reveals significant heterogeneity in degree of exposure to aid. Afghanistan and Liberia exhibit the highest levels of ODA to GDP, followed by Burundi, West Bank and Gaza, Eritrea and Somalia (Figure 16.2). All the fragile

Leone, Somalia, South Sudan, Syria, Timor-Leste, Togo, West Bank and Gaza, Yemen, Zimbabwe. We exclude countries with population less than 1 million.

[7] The median values are, respectively, 9.8 and 3.2 percent. A caveat to keep in mind when working on low-income countries is data quality, which could be weakened by limited funding and weak capacity of local statistical agencies (Devarajan, 2013; Klasen and Blades, 2013).

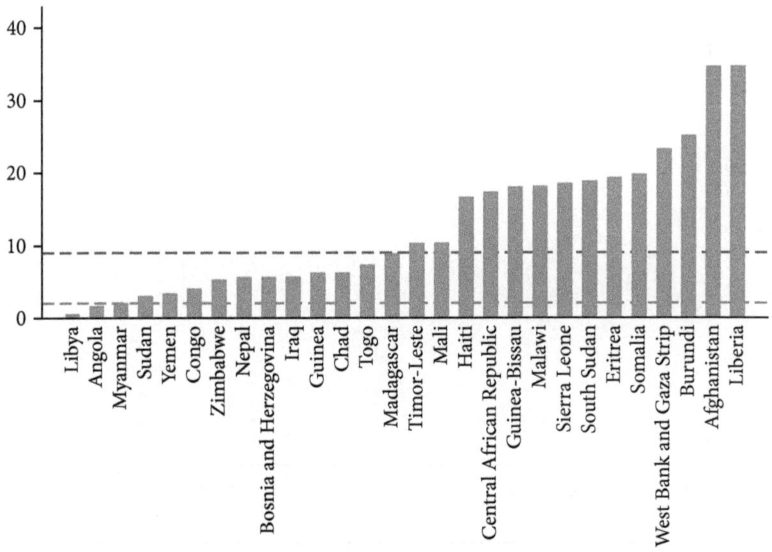

Figure 16.2 Official Development Assistance to GDP, by Country

Note: the bars report the median ODA to GDP over the period 1990–2017. The dashed red (blue) line corresponds to the median ODA to GDP in fragile (non-fragile) states. We exclude countries with a population below 1,000,000 inhabitants.

Source: OECD DAC database

countries, except Libya, Angola and Myanmar received more aid (as a ratio to GDP) than the median levels for non-fragile countries.[8]

Aid dependency is also evident when net ODA inflows are compared with two other key sources of external financing, remittance inflows and net foreign direct investment (FDI). In the broad sample of low- and middle-income countries, remittances and FDI are the two major sources of foreign exchange earnings (World Bank, 2018); in fragile states aid inflows are still much larger than remittances and FDI (Figure 16.3).

The literature on aid effectiveness points out the importance of not only the volumes but the volatility, cyclicality and predictability of aid inflows. Contrary to a common perception, aid flows in fragile states are not more volatile than in other developing countries (the average coefficient of variation is 0.64 in fragile states and 0.74 in the other developing countries).[9] Though year-on-year changes could have a number of adverse consequences on macroeconomic management, aid volatility is not necessarily a bad thing. Especially for countries exposed to a large variety of shocks, one would expect high volatility if aid is able to respond to negative economic shocks. For this reason, looking at aid cyclicality can provide a

[8] Discussing the reasons behind donors' aid allocations, especially to fragile states, is beyond the scope of this chapter. For a review of donors' motives, including geo-political interests, see Alesina and Dollar (2000), Berthelemy (2006), and Fuchs et al. (2014).

[9] The median values are, respectively, 0.64 and 0.55.

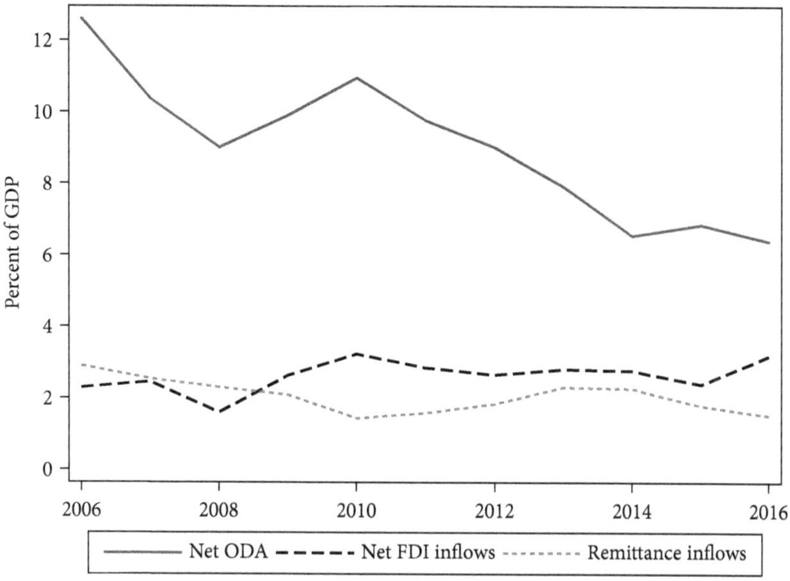

Figure 16.3 Aid, Foreign Direct Investment, and Remittances to Fragile States
Note: the chart reports the median ratios of net ODA, net FDI inflows and remittance inflows, as percent of GDP, for a sample of 31 fragile states, selected to have a minimum of 6 observations (jointly for the three ratios) over the sample period 2006–2016.
Source: OECD DAC database

better measure of the capacity of aid to mitigate negative shocks. A simple inspection of the macroeconomic data shows that aid to developing countries is, on average, moderately counter-cyclical. However, the negative correlation between aid as a share of GDP and the cyclical component of GDP is driven mostly by non-fragile states, while it is very close to zero for fragile states.[10] Overall, the macro data suggest that aid inflows have a limited capacity to act as a shock absorber in developing countries, but less in fragile states. Finally, we consider aid unpredictability, which can have adverse effects on the level and the composition of government spending, undermining aid effectiveness and jeopardizing growth. This could be especially the case for fragile states which often lack access to international capital markets and have limited foreign reserves to serve as buffers. Figure 16.4 shows the evolution over time of a standard proxy for aid unpredictability, the difference between commitments and disbursements, both measured as a share of GDP. At the beginning of the sample fragile countries presented significantly higher level of unpredictable aid (almost double) than non-fragile countries. However, there is a marked downward trend throughout the

[10] The cyclical component of GDP is computed using the Hodrick-Prescott filter to the annual series of the logarithm of real GDP. The correlation between this cyclical GDP component and aid (as a share of GDP) is equal to -0.15 for nonfragile developing countries and -0.03 for fragile states. The sample includes 23 fragile states with 74 low- and middle-income countries with full data on aid and real GDP between 1990 and 2017.

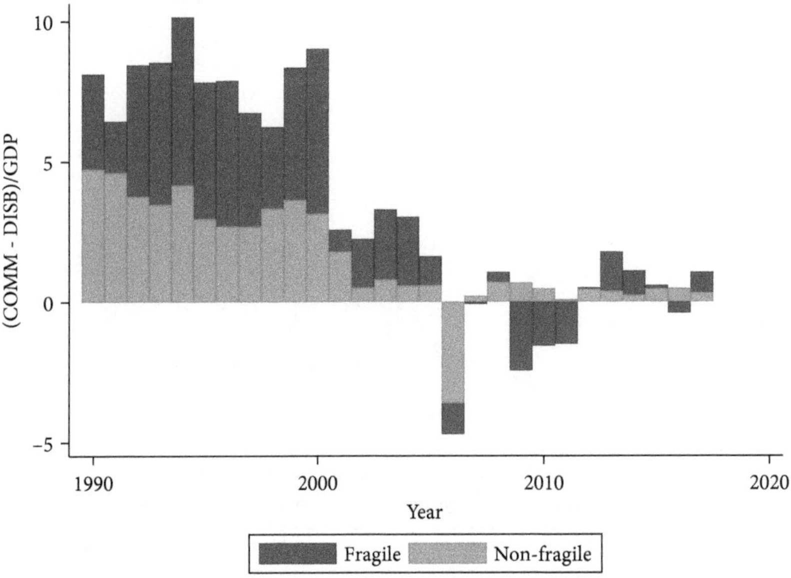

Figure 16.4 Unpredictability of Aid

Note: the chart reports the ratio of the difference between commitments and disbursement (a proxy for unpredictability) to nominal GDP for both fragile and nonfragile countries.

Source: OECD DAC database

sample for both country groups, suggesting improvements in the predictability of flows across all recipients.

Moving to the granularity of aid inflows, we start by investigating the degree of aid fragmentation across donors in our sample. We follow Gehring et al. (2017) and build two different measures of fragmentation. First, we build the Herfindahl index of aid concentration across donors in each country over time:

$$HI_{ct} = \sum_{d=1}^{D} share_{dct}^{2}$$

where d=1,...,D are donors and $Share_{dct}^{2}$ is the share of disbursements from donor d in recipient country c in year t. We compute fragmentation as $1-HI_{ct}$. The second proxy for fragmentation is the number of donors per country. We observe an increasing degree of fragmentation in fragile states since the beginning of the 1990s, with the fragmentation index flattening at the beginning of the 2000s (Figure 16.5). This trend is similar to the one observed in the rest of ODA recipients, that present a comparable number of donors, with the median being 33 across the sample considered. In sum, the rising trend in donor fragmentation indicates another potential source of concern for aid effectiveness in fragile states. Related to this issue, we observe that the bulk of ODA is delivered by bilateral donors and there is no upward trend in the share of multilateral aid, which would be consistent with a change in aid allocation—specifically targeted towards fragile states—by multilateral agencies. In our sample, on average since the 2000s, both

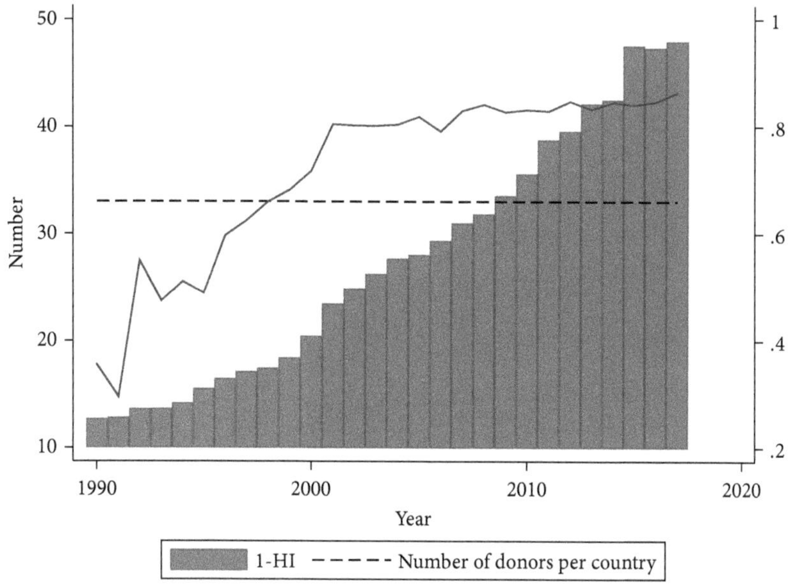

Figure 16.5 Different Measures of Donor Fragmentation in Fragile States

Note: the grAy bars report the average number of donors in fragile states. The red line corresponds to fragmentation across donors computed as 1 – the Herfindahl Index. The dashed line is the median average of donors in nonfragile countries.

Source: OECD DAC database

non-fragile and fragile countries received about 70 to 80 percent of total disbursements through bilateral flows.

A final important aspect to consider when moving beyond aid aggregates is the sectoral composition of aid and its type. In our sample of fragile states, the three largest recipient sectors are the government, action related to debt (aid for debt relief or restructuring, reflecting the bilateral and multilateral debt relief initiatives of the mid-1990s and early 2000s) and emergency response (Figure 16.6), consistent with the vulnerability of fragile states to external shocks. When looking at aid type, we focus on budget support, as a measure of how much aid is given directly to the government to increase ownership. Budget support flows are also less volatile than other aid flows.[11] The share of budget support disbursements over total disbursements in fragile states shows a steep decline in the late 1990s and a recent pick-up in the mid-2000s (Figure 16.7, see also Dreher et al. 2017). On the contrary, nonfragile DAC countries present steadily decreasing budget support flows. The recent increase in the share of total disbursements in budget support in fragile states might come as a surprise, because donors tend to trust governments less in fragile states (see Dreher et al., 2018b).[12] However, looking at

[11] The average coefficient of variation for budget support aid in fragile countries is 2, while in nonfragile states it is 7.

[12] Dreher et al. (2018b) adopt a different fragile states classification that includes 19 countries.

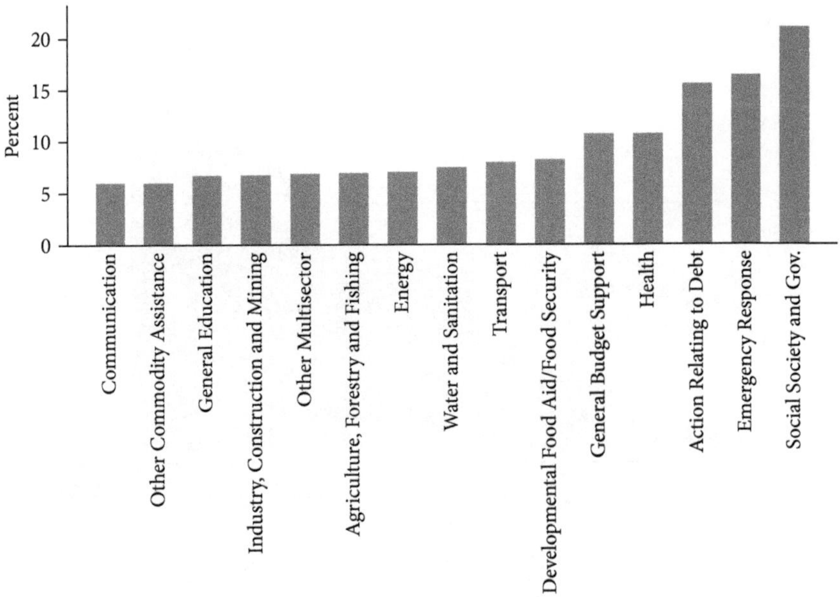

Figure 16.6 Sectoral Allocation in Fragile Countries

Note: The sectoral allocation is based on the DAC CRS classification. We consider the 3-digit classification and we group several subsectors to ease visualization. We exclude sectors that are classified as "Unallocated."

Source: OECD DAC database

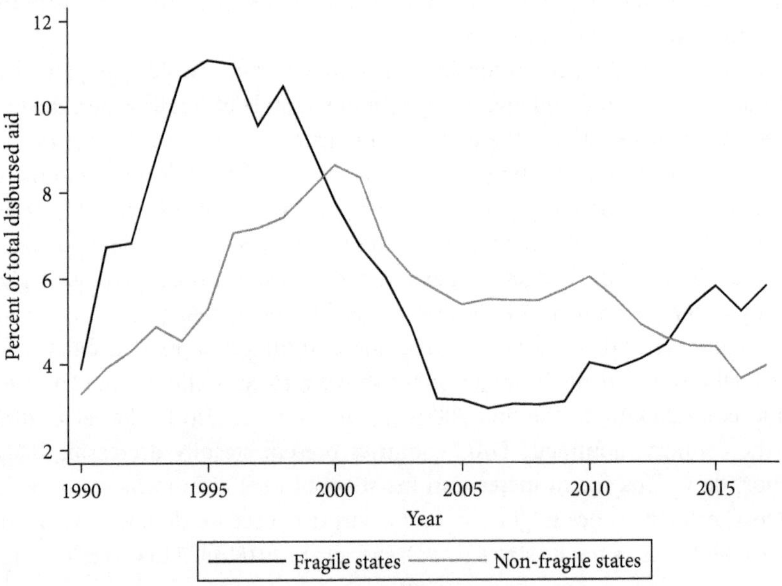

Figure 16.7 Evolution of Budget Support versus Project Aid

Note: the chart reports the 5-year moving average of budget support disbursements as a share of total disbursed aid in fragile and nonfragile states. Budget support aid corresponds to the CRS code 510.

Source: OECD DAC database

the channels of delivery, Dreher et al. (2018b) find that less aid is allocated through governments in fragile states.

Overall, our reading of the literature and of the evidence on aid effectiveness in fragile states suggests that the growth dividend of aid flows could be limited by several factors (such as high aid dependency coupled with limited absorptive capacity, limited propensity to act as a shock absorber, rising donor fragmentation), which are common to several recipients, but are often more prevalent in fragile states. This does not imply that aid to fragile states should be reduced across the board (Dreher et al., 2018b). By contrast, this evidence would point to an approach tailored at targeting the key bottlenecks to promote aid effectiveness. First, non-aid-specific policies directed at promoting state building and stability would also contribute to better aid effectiveness. Then, aid polices should consider the extent to which absorptive capacity constraints, lack of donor coordination, aid unpredictability, or the modalities of aid delivery (budget support versus project aid, for instance) act as a major constraint to aid effectiveness.

4. Aid Effectiveness: Project-Level Analysis

Overall, the literature on aid effectiveness, reviewed in section 2, does not provide a clear answer on the extent to which aid can promote growth in fragile states. Similarly, the set of stylized facts discussed in section 3 shows conflicting trends: aid flows are large, but their effectiveness could be weakened by absorptive capacity constraints, aid dependency, and donor fragmentation. Thus, in this section we look explicitly at aid effectiveness in fragile states, by exploiting a large dataset on project-level data which brings together other 14,000 projects funded by 8 donor agencies[13] in 176 countries approved since 1956 until 2012. For each project, the data collects information on the dates of approval, completion and evaluation; the sector of the project; the presence of the funding donor in the country with an office; and, most importantly, the rating of the project's overall success, measured on a scale from 1 (highly unsatisfactory) to 6 (highly satisfactory).[14] Then, depending on the donor, other project-specific information is available, including the lending instrument and the project cost, in the case of World Bank's projects.

[13] The Asian Development Bank, the UK's Department for International Development, the Global Fund for AIDS, TB, and Malaria, the German Society for International Cooperation (GiZ), the International Fund for Agricultural Development, the Japanese International Cooperation Agency, the German Development Bank (KfW), and the World Bank.

[14] Following Presbitero (2016), Bulman et al. (2015) and Kilby (2015), we classify a project as successful if it has been evaluated as "highly satisfactory", "satisfactory" or "moderately satisfactory" and as unsuccessful if it has been evaluated as "moderately unsatisfactory", "unsatisfactory" or "highly unsatisfactory". In line with existing literature (Deninzer et al. 2013; Presbitero 2016), in the case of a 0/1 dependent variable we estimate a linear probability model, which can more flexibly accommodate a large set of granular fixed effects than a probit model. See also Briggs (2019) for a recent analysis of aid success using these data.

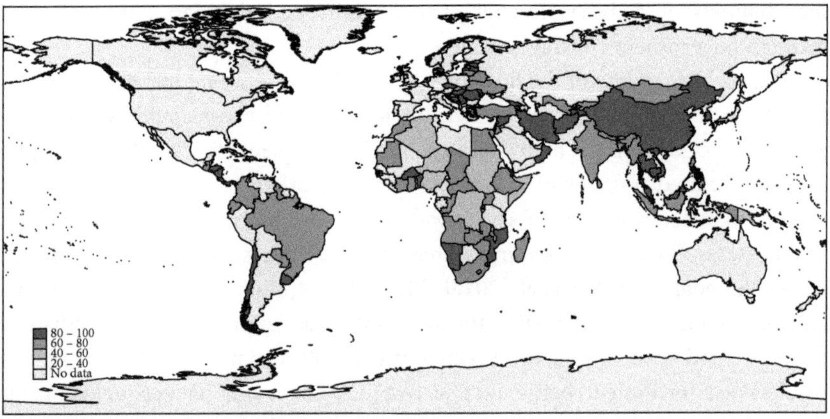

Figure 16.8 Aid Disbursed through NGOs

Note: The map reports the number of successful projects as a share of total projects by country. We consider only country that reports at least three projects. Data are from Honig (2018) and available here: Project Performance Database February 2019, https://doi.org/10.7910/DVN/444GNW, Harvard Dataverse, V1.

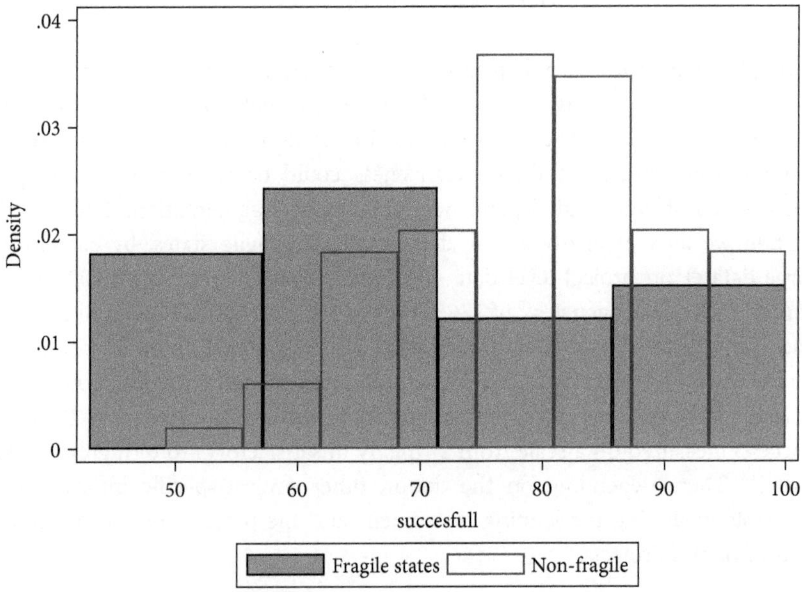

Figure 16.9 Share of Successful Projects

Note: The chart reports the share of successful projects to total projects calculated at the country level. We consider only countries where at least three projects were implemented.

Source: Honig (2018)

Figure 16.8 shows the distribution across countries of the average share of successful projects. The map clearly points out the relatively poorer performance in many Sub-Saharan African countries compared to countries in Eastern Europe and Asia. The distribution of successful projects across fragile and non-fragile

Table 16.1 Project Characteristics, Fragile versus Non-Fragile Countries

	Non-fragile			Fragile		
Variable	Obs.	Mean	St. dev	Obs.	Mean	St. dev
Project duration	8127	6.5	2.7	1392	6.1	2.9
Lag to evaluation	8255	2.3	2	1418	2.5	2.3
Office presence	7974	0.8	0.4	1263	0.7	0.5

Notes: the table reports the summary statistics of the project level characteristics.

states indicates that projects undertaken in fragile states are less likely to be successful, with a large share of countries below the 50 percent success rate (Figure 16.9). As the observable project characteristics do not appear to be systematically different between projects undertaken in fragile and non-fragile states (see Table 16.1), differences in project success rates are likely to be driven by country characteristics (such as fragility).

The availability of project-level data with information on project outcomes allows us to directly test whether the success rate in fragile states is significantly different from the success rate in other countries, controlling for a set of project-specific characteristics and a variety of granular fixed effects, which absorb unobserved heterogeneity. To run this exercise, we estimate the following linear model, which is similar in spirit to existing works done by Denizer et al. (2013) and Presbitero (2016) in a similar context:

$$OUTCOME_{ijt} = \beta FS_j + \delta Country_{jt} + \gamma Project_{ijt} + \varepsilon_{ijt} \tag{1}$$

where the dependent variable $OUTCOME_{ijt}$ is, alternatively, the rating of project i undertaken in country j at time t, measured on the 1 to 6 scale, or by a dummy equal to one if the investment project is evaluated as satisfactory and zero otherwise. The key explanatory variable is FS_j, a dummy equal to one for fragile states, defined according to the IMF classification. Since the *FS* dummy does not vary over time and we cannot include country fixed effects, we control for a set of macroeconomic variables which should absorb cross-country heterogeneity and add region and income-level fixed effects.[15] The set of country-specific variables ($Country_{jt}$) includes the logarithm of real per capita GDP, the growth rate and the variability of real GDP, and the ratios of foreign aid and private capital inflows over GDP. Country-specific variables are measured as averages over the length of the project, computed as the difference between the completion and the start year. The vector of project-specific characteristics ($Project_{ijt}$) includes: (1) the duration of the projects, measured (in years) as difference between date of project

[15] We follow the World Bank classification and we include: six regional dummies for East Asia and Pacific, Europe and Central Asia, Latin America and the Caribbean, Middle East and North Africa, South Asia, and Sub-Saharan Africa; and four income-level dummies for high-income, upper-middle-income, lower-middle-income, and low-income countries.

completion and date of project start; (2) the lag to project evaluation, measured (in years) as difference between date of project evaluation and date of project completion; and (3) a dummy to identify projects for which the donor agency had an office in the country during the length of the project. We also include donor fixed effects to allow for donor-specific unobserved differences in project evaluation. Fixed effects for the start and evaluation years and a set of 36 sector fixed effects, based on 3-digit purpose classification code used by the Creditor Reporting System (CRS) of the OECD-DAC, absorb sector-specific and time-specific unobservable differences in project outcomes. In the most demanding specification, we introduce sector x evaluation year and sector x start year fixed effects, to control for external (sector-specific) aggregate shocks and unobservable changes in the evaluation standards over time. We cluster the standard errors at the country level to allow for the potential correlation of the residuals within country.

Results show that the fragile state dummy is consistently associated with a lower probability of project success (Table 16.2). This is true for the full sample that includes all donors and the sample restricted to World Bank projects; in this case we can also control for project size—proxied by the logarithm of the project cost (in US dollars). To quantify the economic magnitude of this correlation, our findings indicate that, on average, the rating of a project in a fragile state is 0.2 points lower than a similar one in non-fragile countries (column 2). When we consider the dummy variable for successful projects, our results indicate that a project carried out in *FS* is 8 percentage points less likely of being successful than a similar one in non-fragile developing countries (column 4). Given that the average in-sample success rate is 73 percent, this effect is relatively large.[16]

The volatility of growth also has a negative effect on the likelihood of project success, while overall GDP growth is associated with positive outcomes. Consistent with the evidence presented in Presbitero (2016), Kilby (2015), and Denizer et al. (2013), projects are more likely to be successful when they are undertaken during periods of higher growth rates at the country-level. Other macro variables (non-reported in the table) such as overall aid to GDP, net capital flows as a percent of GDP, and GDP per capita are not playing a significant role in explaining project success in our sample; nor do we find significant evidence that project duration, its cost, the presence of a local office, and the time needed to evaluate it matter for the probability of its success, after controlling for a large set of fixed effects.[17]

[16] The summary statistics show that the difference in the success rate between fragile (61 percent) and nonfragile (74 percent) states is 13 percentage points.

[17] Denizer et al. (2013) and Presbitero (2016) find mixed evidence on the correlation between the proxies for project complexity and outcomes: smaller projects are generally more likely to be successful than larger (i.e., more complex) ones, but these results lose significance when country fixed effects are included in the estimation.

Table 16.2. Project Outcomes in Fragile States

	(1)	(2)	(3)	(4)	(5)	(6)	(7)	(8)
VARIABLES	**Project rating (1-6)**		**Project success (0/1)**		**Project rating (1-6)**		**Project success (0/1)**	
Fragile states dummy	−0.1768***	−0.1975***	−0.0735***	−0.0808***	−0.1748*	−0.1985*	−0.0742**	−0.0786*
	(0.058)	(0.064)	(0.022)	(0.024)	(0.097)	(0.115)	(0.037)	(0.045)
Growth	0.0789***	0.0750***	0.0226***	0.0216***	0.0726***	0.0777***	0.0211***	0.0234***
	(0.007)	(0.008)	(0.003)	(0.003)	(0.011)	(0.013)	(0.004)	(0.005)
Volatility of growth	−0.0273***	−0.0299***	−0.0069**	−0.0076**	−0.0218*	−0.0298**	−0.0044	−0.0071
	(0.008)	(0.008)	(0.003)	(0.003)	(0.011)	(0.014)	(0.004)	(0.006)
Project duration	0.0093	−0.0186	0.0026	−0.0072	0.0661	0.0154	0.0050	−0.0130
	(0.036)	(0.040)	(0.013)	(0.015)	(0.063)	(0.074)	(0.023)	(0.028)
Lag to evaluation	−0.0047	−0.0333	−0.0031	−0.0134	0.0189	−0.0378	−0.0154	−0.0360
	(0.036)	(0.040)	(0.013)	(0.015)	(0.065)	(0.078)	(0.024)	(0.029)
Office presence	0.0119	0.0664	0.0036	0.0105	−0.0866	−0.0698	−0.0159	−0.0221
	(0.058)	(0.068)	(0.021)	(0.026)	(0.093)	(0.125)	(0.033)	(0.045)
WB project cost					0.0394*	0.0442	0.0080	0.0072
					(0.021)	(0.028)	(0.008)	(0.010)
Observations	7,995	7,717	7,995	7,717	2,747	2,565	2,747	2,565
R-squared	0.158	0.282	0.104	0.229	0.145	0.351	0.120	0.331
Region & income FE	Yes	Yes	Yes	Yes	Yes	Yes	Yes	Yes
Donor FE	Yes	Yes	Yes	Yes	Yes	Yes	Yes	Yes
Time & sector FE	Yes	No	Yes	No	Yes	No	Yes	No
Approval year X sector FE	No	Yes	No	Yes	No	Yes	No	Yes
Evaluation year X sector FE	No	Yes	No	Yes	No	Yes	No	Yes
Evaluation year FE	Yes	No	Yes	No	Yes	No	Yes	No
Lending type FE	No	No	No	No	Yes	Yes	Yes	Yes
Project vars	Yes	Yes	Yes	Yes	Yes	Yes	Yes	Yes
Sample	All	All	All	All	WB	WB	WB	WB
R2adj	0.1456	0.1587	0.0914	0.0964	0.1121	0.1302	0.0865	0.1022

Robust standard errors in parentheses *** p<0.01, ** p<0.05, * p<0.1

Note: The table reports the results from Equation (1). Standard errors are clustered at the country-approval year level. Column (1)-(4) reports the results for the full sample, while Column (5)–(8) report the results for World Bank projects only.

4.1 The Conflict Dimension of Fragility

The analysis presented in Table 16.2 confirms that, even controlling for project and country factors and a large set of fixed effects, investment projects are less likely to be successful when carried out in fragile states than elsewhere. However, even controlling for several macroeconomic variables does not exclude the possibility that this correlation could be owing to several unobservable country characteristics that are different between fragile and other developing countries. In other words, the FS_j dummy could capture several unobserved country characteristics other than fragility, which may explain differences in the likelihood of project success. To overcome this concern, we focus on the conflict dimension of fragility and we run two additional exercises, which exploit the variation of conflicts over time and within countries.

First, we modify model (1) replacing the time-invariant FS_j dummy with a time-varying indicator of the presence of a conflict in country j at time t ($ConflictS_{jt}$):[18]

$$OUTCOME_{ijt} = \beta Conflict_{jt} + \delta Country_{jt} + \gamma Project_{ijt} + \psi_j + \varepsilon_{ijt} \qquad (2)$$

In this way we can augment the model with country fixed effects (ψ_j) and estimate the effect of a conflict on the likelihood of project success within-country (and also controlling for time-varying sector specific shocks).

The results, reported in Table 16.3, are consistent with our baseline and show that the likelihood that a project is successful is lower in conflict periods, even after controlling for any time-invariant dimension of country fragility, project characteristics, and time-varying sector-specific unobservable heterogeneity. The economic size of the reduction of the project rating is similar to what was discussed in the baseline (Table 16.2), while the likelihood of project success is 4.8 percentage points lower in conflict years than in tranquil periods (column 4).

Second, we take advantage of georeferenced data on World Bank investment projects and conflicts and we zoom in on the role played by conflicts at the subnational level.[19] We rely on the data collected by Gehring et al. (2019), which

[18] The indicator variable $Conflict_{jt}$ equals to one if during the length of the project the country experienced a war conflict defined as causing at least 1000 battle-related deaths in one calendar year (Intensity level=2).

[19] The literature on aid and conflict progressively used georeferenced data to investigate subnational dynamics. In a recent paper, Gehring et al. (2019) aim at bridging the gap between analyses at the country level and specific country studies using more disaggregated data. They combine data on georeferenced projects by the World Bank and China and different stability measures at the regional level. Such include the Uppsala Conflict Data Program's (UCDP) georeferenced event dataset (Sundberg and Melander, 2013; Croicu and Sundberg, 2015), the Social Conflict Analysis Database (Salehyan, 2012), and Afrobarometer (2018). Their findings suggest that there is no systematic evidence that aid triggers outright conflict at the regional level. On the contrary, they find that aid by both donors reduces lethal violence against civilians initiated by the state.

Table 16.3 Project Outcomes and Conflicts

	(1)	(2)	(3)	(4)
Dependent variable:	**Project rating (1-6)**		**Project success (0/1)**	
Conflict	−0.2761***	−0.2402**	−0.0725**	−0.0685**
	(0.091)	(0.095)	(0.032)	(0.034)
Growth	0.0538***	0.0528***	0.0122***	0.0117***
	(0.010)	(0.010)	(0.004)	(0.004)
Volatility of growth	−0.0216**	−0.0253**	−0.0077**	−0.0088**
	(0.010)	(0.010)	(0.004)	(0.004)
Observations	7,990	7,850	7,990	7,850
R-squared	0.141	0.231	0.105	0.191
Country FE	Yes	Yes	Yes	Yes
Sector X Year	No	Yes	No	Yes
Evaluation year FE	Yes	Yes	Yes	Yes
Year FE	Yes	No	Yes	No
Project vars	Yes	Yes	Yes	Yes
Sample	All	All	All	All
R2adj	0.1188	0.1427	0.0820	0.0979

Robust standard errors in parentheses *** p<0.01, ** p<0.05, * p<0.1

Note: The table reports the results from Equation (2). Standard errors are clustered at the country-approval year level.

provide information on whether an ADM2 region in a certain year experienced a conflict, and on AidData for the geocoded World Bank projects.[20] To maximize coverage, in the empirical analysis we collapse the conflict data at the ADM1 level and we restrict the data to all the ADM1 regions where a World Bank project is recorded. A first inspection of the data at the subnational level reveals that the presence of conflicts across ADM1 regions seems to be correlated with a higher presence of unsuccessful projects (see, for instance, the case of Uganda, Figure 16.10).

To formally test this hypothesis, we estimate a model that exploits the within-country variation of conflicts' incidence and World Bank project success. The specification is similar to equation (1) with the difference that the dependent variable $OUTCOME_{irjt}$ measures the outcome of the project i undertaken in the ADM1 region r of country j at time t:

$$OUTCOME_{irjt} = \beta Conflict_{irjt} + \delta Country_{jt} + \gamma Project_{irjt} + \varepsilon_{irjt} \qquad (3)$$

The key explanatory variable—$Conflict_{rjt}$—is a dummy equal to one if a region r experiences at least one conflict in a given year. Given that the conflict dummy varies by region and time, we can again augment the estimation with country fixed effects, to absorb all those time-invariant characteristics that might make fragile countries different. In addition, we can also saturate the model with ADM1 region

[20] A conflict is defined as an event in which there are more than 25 casualties: see Gehring et al. (2019) for further details. ADM1 corresponds to the first level of subnational administrative division ("provinces," "states," or "regions"). ADM2 corresponds to lower-level administrative regions.

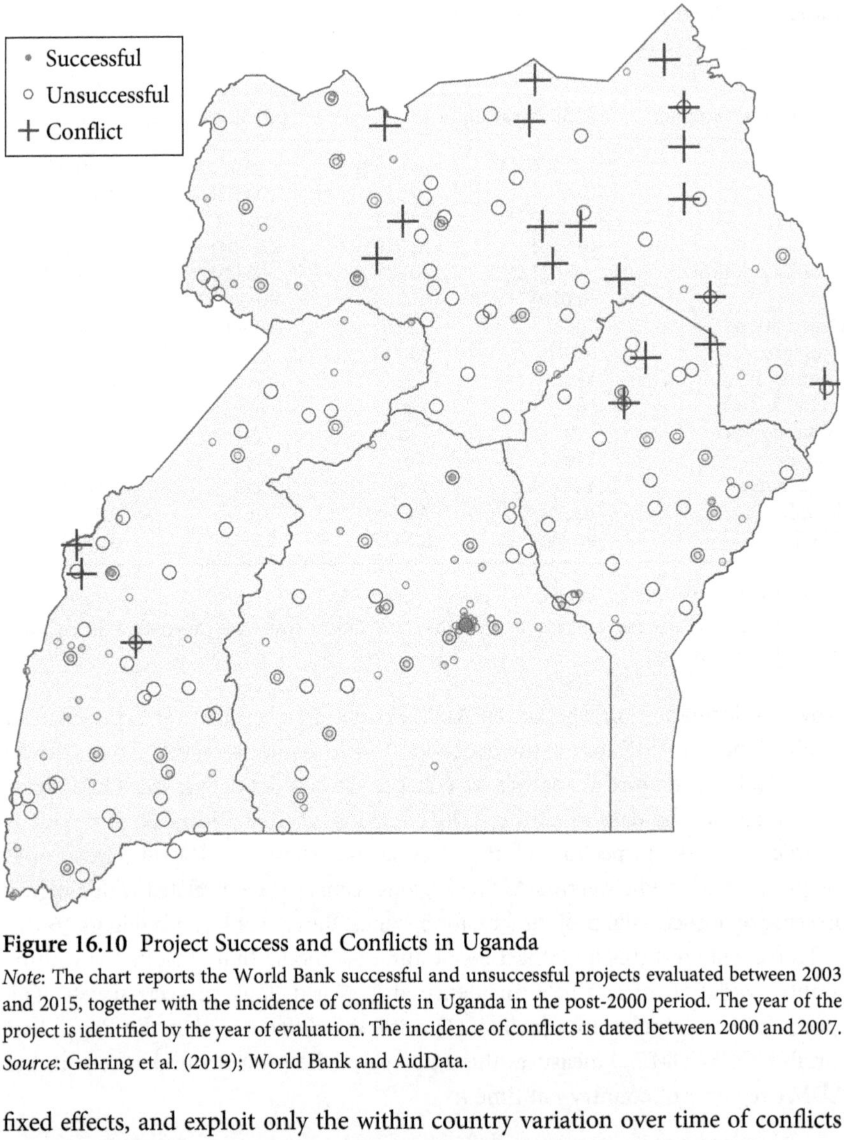

Figure 16.10 Project Success and Conflicts in Uganda

Note: The chart reports the World Bank successful and unsuccessful projects evaluated between 2003 and 2015, together with the incidence of conflicts in Uganda in the post-2000 period. The year of the project is identified by the year of evaluation. The incidence of conflicts is dated between 2000 and 2007.

Source: Gehring et al. (2019); World Bank and AidData.

fixed effects, and exploit only the within country variation over time of conflicts and World Bank projects. The set of control variables at the country- and project-level are the same as in equation (1). As we focus on World Bank projects, we can also control for project size as in Table 16.2 (columns 5–8).

The results are reported in Table 16.4 and confirm that fragility is associated with a lower project success rate, notwithstanding the significant reduction in sample size and the more demanding empirical design. The coefficient on the regional conflict dummy is negative, but not significant, when we measure project success with the continuous rating variable (columns 1–2). However, it becomes statistically significant when project success is measured by the dummy indicator (columns 3–4). The economic magnitudes are comparable to what we found in the previous exercises.

Table 16.4 Project Outcomes and Conflicts at the Regional Level

	(1)	(2)	(3)	(4)
Dependent variable:	**Project rating (1-6)**		**Project success (0/1)**	
Dummy for conflict in the region	−0.0376	−0.0684	−0.0534**	−0.0641*
	(0.056)	(0.086)	(0.025)	(0.035)
Project cost	0.0782***	0.0858***	0.0226***	0.0243***
	(0.020)	(0.021)	(0.008)	(0.008)
Project duration	−0.0437**	−0.0408**	−0.0081	−0.0075
	(0.019)	(0.018)	(0.007)	(0.007)
Growth	0.0657***	0.0725***	0.0187**	0.0220***
	(0.022)	(0.022)	(0.008)	(0.008)
Volatility of growth	−0.0322	−0.0387	−0.0059	−0.0084
	(0.026)	(0.026)	(0.010)	(0.011)
Observations	3,145	3,054	3,145	3,054
R-squared	0.311	0.339	0.238	0.268
ADM1 FE	No	Yes	No	Yes
Country FE	Yes	No	Yes	No
Year FE	Yes	Yes	Yes	Yes
Evaluation Year FE	Yes	Yes	Yes	Yes
Sector FE	Yes	Yes	Yes	Yes
R2adj	0.2812	0.2175	0.2052	0.1337

Robust standard errors in parentheses *** p<0.01, ** p<0.05, * p<0.1

Note: The table reports the results from Equation (3). Standard errors are clustered at the ADM1 level.

The model of column 3 with country fixed effects indicates that a project is 5.3 percentage points less likely to be successful if it has been implemented in a conflict region than a similar project in the same country (but implemented in a non-conflict region). The specification with region fixed effects shows that a project in a conflict region is 6.4 percentage points less likely to be successful than a similar project in the same region but started in a non-conflict year (column 4).

4.2 The Role of Corruption

The evidence discussed in the previous sections clearly indicates that aid is likely to be less effective in fragile states than in other developing countries, with conflict being a key element that could reduce projects' success rate. However, state fragility is a multidimensional concept (IMF, 2018; OECD, 2018) and aid effectiveness could be improved in implementing policies along many dimensions. Because it is oftentimes difficult to map policies into outcomes in a rigorous setting, here we limit our attention to the role of corruption, which we can measure in a precise way through the World Governance Indicators. In particular, "control of corruption captures perceptions of the extent to which public power is exercised for private gain, including both petty and grand forms of corruption, as well as 'capture' of the state by elites and private interests" (Kaufmann et al., 2010).

Because the number of fragile states is too low to rigorously investigate the effect of corruption on aid effectiveness across fragile and nonfragile states, we look at the association between corruption and project success in the whole sample of developing countries. We estimate equation (1) on a subsample of country-year pairs for which we can match our data with the control of corruption variable.[21] Notwithstanding the small sample and the rich set of fixed effects, the results—reported in Table 16.5—show a clear and positive association between the strength of the control of corruption and project success. In economic terms, the most conservative estimates show that one standard deviation change in the control of corruption index (equal to 1, as the variable is standardized) is associated with 0.15 increase in project rating (column 2) and with an increase of 6 percentage points in the likelihood of project success (column 4).

In the spirit of Dreher et al. (2018b), we combine this information with the observation that the control of corruption is weaker in fragile countries than in other developing countries (Figure 16.11) to argue that investing in policies to curb corruption is likely to improve aid effectiveness in fragile states.[22]

5. Conclusions and Policy Discussion

Aid dependency is a feature of several fragile states, where aid inflows account, in a few cases, for more than 10 percent of GDP. Can these flows promote growth and development? Methodological issues severely limit our capacity to answer this question, especially when looking at macro data and when zooming in on a relatively small sample of fragile states. Also for this reason, the literature on aid effectiveness has not yet reached a consensus, because results often depend on several concurrent factors, ranging from the type of aid flows, donors' policies, and recipient countries' institutional and macroeconomic characteristics.

In a recent survey on aid effectiveness in fragile states, Dreher et al. (2018b) overcome these limitations by combining information on how different types of aid, motives for granting it, recipient country policies and characteristics, and modalities by which aid is delivered shape aid effectiveness with differences of

[21] We end up with a sample that starts in 1996 of 121 countries, only 24 of which are fragile states.

[22] Figure 16.11 reports the distribution of the variable control of corruption for the two groups, showing higher level of control in non-fragile countries. A t-test on the difference of the means suggests that the average level of corruption in fragile states is significantly lower than in nonfragile states.

Table 16.5 Project Outcomes and Corruption

	(1)	(2)	(3)	(4)
VARIABLES	**Project rating (1-6)**	**Project rating (1-6)**	**Project success (0/1)**	**Project success (0/1)**
Fragile states dummy	−0.0746	−0.1164	−0.0227	−0.0268
	(0.113)	(0.133)	(0.043)	(0.052)
Growth	0.0807^{***}	0.0747^{***}	0.0221^{***}	0.0193^{***}
	(0.012)	(0.014)	(0.004)	(0.005)
Volatility of growth	−0.0141	−0.0124	−0.0007	0.0006
	(0.014)	(0.017)	(0.005)	(0.006)
Control of corruption	0.2261^{***}	0.1495^{*}	0.0831^{***}	0.0571^{*}
	(0.067)	(0.079)	(0.027)	(0.030)
Observations	1,988	1,843	1,988	1,843
R-squared	0.204	0.376	0.111	0.289
Region & income FE	Yes	Yes	Yes	Yes
Donor FE	Yes	Yes	Yes	Yes
Time & sector FE	Yes	No	Yes	No
Approval year X sector FE	No	Yes	No	Yes
Evaluation year X sector FE	No	No	No	Yes
Evaluation year FE	Yes	No	Yes	No
Lending type FE	No	No	No	No
Project vars	Yes	Yes	Yes	Yes
Sample	All	All	All	All
R2adj	0.1695	0.2043	0.0727	0.0925

Robust standard errors in parentheses *** p<0.01, ** p<0.05, * p<0.1

Note: The table reports the results from Equation (2) augmented with a term that capture the level of control of corruption. Standard errors are clustered at the country-approval year level

these characteristics across fragile and nonfragile states, to conclude that, on average, aid given to fragile states is less likely to be effective than elsewhere.

We confirm this conclusion looking at a large sample of investment projects and showing that a project implemented in a fragile state is about 8 percentage points less likely to be successful than a similar project financed in another developing country. Though we are not able to identify the effect of fragility on aid effectiveness, using project-level data allows us to control for a large set of observable and (time-varying) unobservable characteristics which could be correlated with fragility and could affect project outcomes. We also focus on the conflict dimension of fragility to further substantiate our conclusion at a sub-national level.

On the policy side, we concur with Dreher et al. (2018b) that our analyses do not imply that aid to fragile states should be reduced across the board. It could be that in specific cases, absorptive capacity constraints bind and weaken aid effectiveness. In other cases, lack of donor coordination, aid unpredictability, or the modalities of aid delivery (budget support vs project aid, for instance) could be the

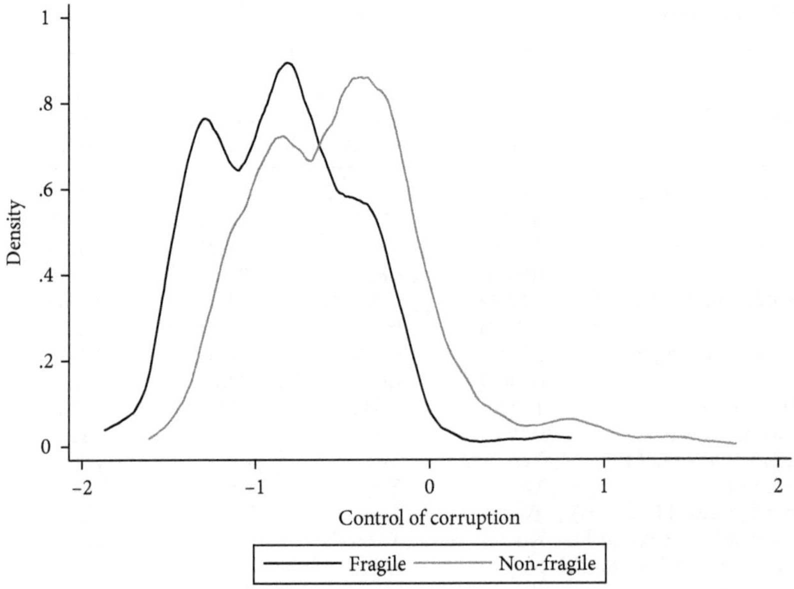

Figure 16.11 Control of Corruption: Fragile and Non-Fragile States

Note: the figure reports the distribution of the variable control of corruption from the World Bank "Worldwide Governance Indicators" for both fragile and nonfragile countries.

most important factor hampering the growth dividend of aid flows, although, on average, some of these factors do not seem to be specific to fragile states. One aspect that seems to be particularly important for project outcomes is corruption, an area where fragile states, on average, look weaker. However, more research—and more granular data—are needed to better identify the constraints to aid effectiveness and inform policy making, not only in fragile states. For the time being, aid polices and aid projects in fragile states should be carefully tailored around the large set of country-specific factors that are likely to undermine aid effectiveness. At the same time, given limited aid effectiveness, policies for fragile states should generally be directed at building the support structure—the *scaffolding*, in the words of Collier (2019)—which is the key condition to building an effective state. However, policymakers should keep in mind the challenges of engineering appropriate strategies to promote stability and escape state fragility (see Acemoglu and Robinson, 2019). Institutions and state building—as discussed extensively by Besley and Mueller (2019)—can contribute to mitigate fragility and generate growth through several channels (such as enhanced revenue mobilization, better governance, less political instability). In this way, state-building could strengthen aid effectiveness, thanks to better absorptive capacity, more accountability, and less corruption.

References

Acemoglu, D. and J.A. Robinson. 2019. *The Narrow Corridor*. New York: Penguin.

Acharya, A., A.T. Fuzzo de Lima and M. Moore. 2006." Proliferation and Fragmentation: Transactions Costs and the Value of Aid." *The Journal of Development Studies*, 42(1): 1–21.

Addison, T., O. Morrissey, and F. Tarp. 2017. "The Macroeconomics of Aid: Overview." *Journal of Development Studies*, 53(7): 987–97.

Alesina, A. and D. Dollar. 2000. "Who Gives Foreign Aid to Whom and Why?" *Journal of Economic Growth*, 5(1): 33–63.

Anderson, E. 2012. "Aid Fragmentation and Donor Transaction Costs.", *Economics Letters*, 117(3): 799–802.

Arellano, C., A. Bulir, T. Lane, and L. Lipschitz. 2009. "The Dynamic Implications of Foreign Aid and Its Variability." *Journal of Development Economics*, 88(1): 87–102.

Arndt, C., S. Jones, and F. Tarp. 2015. "What Is the Aggregate Rate of Return of Foreign Aid?" *World Bank Economic Review*, 30(3): 446–74.

Berthelemy, J-C. (2006). "Bilateral Donors' Interest vs. Recipients' Development Motives in Aid Allocation: Do All Donors Behave the Same?" *Review of Development Economics*, 10(2): 179–94.

Besley, T. and H. Mueller. 2019. "Fiscal Capacity and State Fragility," in R. Chami, R. Espinoza, and P. Montiel (Eds.), *Macroeconomic Policy in Fragile States*. Oxford: Oxford University Press.

Birchler, K. and K. Michaelowa (2016). "Making Aid Work for Education in Developing Countries: An Analysis of Aid Effectiveness for Primary Education Coverage and Quality." *International Journal of Educational Development*, 48: 37–52.

Boone, P. 1996. "Politics and the Effectiveness of Foreign Aid." *European Economic Review*, 40(2): 289–329.

Bulíř, A. and A.J. Hamann. 2008. "Volatility of Development Aid: From the Frying Pan into the Fire?" *World Development*, 36(10): 2048–66.

Biscaye, P.E., T.W. Reynolds and C.L. Anderson. 2016. "Relative Effectiveness of Bilateral and Multilateral Aid on Development Outcomes." *Review of Development Economics*, 21(4): 1425–47.

Briggs, R.C. 2019. "Results from Single-Donor Analyses of Project Aid Success Seem to Generalize Pretty Well Across Donors." *Review of International Organizations*. https://link.springer.com/article/10.1007/s11558-019-09365-x (last accessed July 16, 2020).

Burnside, C. and D. Dollar. 2000. "Aid, Policies, and Growth." *American Economic Review*, 90: 847–68.

Carter, P. 2014. "Aid Allocation Rules." *European Economic Review*, 71: 132–51.

Celasun, O. and J. Walliser. 2008. "Predictability of Aid." *Economic Policy*, 23(55): 545–94.

Christensen, Z., H. Dustin, and D.L. Nielson. 2011. "Dodging Adverse Selection: How Donor Type and Governance Condition Aid's Effects on School Enrollment." *World Development*, 39(11): 2044–53.

Clemens, M.A. and S. Radelet. 2003. "Absorptive Capacity: How Much Is Too Much?" in S. Radelet (Ed.), *Challenging Foreign Aid: A Policymaker's Guide to the Millennium Challenge Account*. Washington, DC: Center for Global Development.

Clemens, M.A., S. Radelet, R.R. Bhavnani, and S. Bazzi. 2012. "Counting Chickens When They Hatch: Timing and the Effects of Aid on Growth." *The Economic Journal*, 122: 590–617.

Collier P. and A. Hoeffler. 2004. "Aid, Policy and Growth in Post-Conflict Societies." *European Economic Review*, 48(5): 1125–45.

Collier P. and A. Hoeffler. 2007. "Unintended Consequences: Does Aid Promote Arms Races?" *Oxford Bulletin of Economics and Statistics*, 69(1): 1–27.

Collier, P. 2019. "Transition Programs: A Theory of the Scaffolding Needed to Build out of Fragility," in R. Chami, R. Espinoza and P. Montiel (Eds.), *Macroeconomic Policy in Fragile States*. Oxford: Oxford University Press.

Commission on State Fragility, Growth and Development. 2018. *Escaping The Fragility Trap*, London. https://www.theigc.org/wp-content/uploads/2018/04/Escaping-the-fragility-trap.pdf (accessed July 16, 2020).

Croicu, M. and R. Sundberg. 2015. UCDP Georeferenced Event Dataset Codebook Version 4.0.

D'Alelio, D. 2018. *US Aid to Fragile States: Where Does the Money Go?, Center for Global Development*, June 11.

Davies, R.B. and S. Klasen. 2019. "Darlings and Orphans: Interactions across Donors in International Aid." *The Scandinavian Journal of Economics*, 121(1): 243–77.

Denizer, C., D. Kaufmann, and A. Kraay. 2013. "Good Countries or Good Projects? Macro and Micro Correlates of World Bank Project Performance." *Journal of Development Economics*, 105: 288–302.

Devarajan, S. 2013. "Africa's Statistical Tragedy." *Review of Income and Wealth*, 59(S1): S9–S15.

DFID. 2015. "UK Aid: Tackling Global Challenges in the National Interest," Department for International Development and HM Treasury.

Djankov, S., J.G. Montalvo, and M. Reynal-Querol. 2009. "Aid with Multiple Personalities." *Journal of Comparative Economics*, 37(2): 217–29.

Dreher, A., P. Nunnenkamp, and R. Thiele. 2008. "Does Aid for Education Educate Children? Evidence from Panel Data." *World Bank Economic Review*, 22(2): 291–314.

Dreher, A., J-E. Sturm, and J.R. Vreeland. 2009. "Development Aid and International Politics: Does Membership on the UN Security Council Influence World Bank Decisions?" *Journal of Development Economics*, 88(1): 1–18.

Dreher, A. and S. Lohmann. 2015. "Aid and Growth at the Regional Level." *Oxford Review of Economic Policy*, 31: 420–46.

Dreher, A., S. Langlotz, and S. Marchesi. 2017. "Information Transmission and Ownership Consolidation in Aid Programs." *Economic Inquiry*, 55: 1671–88.

Dreher, A., V. Eichenauer, and K. Gehring. 2018a. "Geopolitics, Aid and Growth: The Impact of UN Security Council Membership on the Effectiveness of Aid." *World Bank Economic Review*, 32: 268–86.

Dreher, A., V. Lang, and S. Ziaja. 2018b. "Foreign Aid," in T. Risse, T. Börzel, and A. Draude (Eds.), *The Oxford Handbook on Governance and Limited Statehood*. Oxford: Oxford University Press.

Easterly, W., R. Levine, and D. Roodman. 2004. "Aid, Policies, and Growth: A Comment." *American Economic Review*, 94(3): 774–80.

Easterly, W. and T. Pfutze. 2008. "Where Does the Money Go? Best and Worst Practices in foreign Aid." *Journal of Economic Perspectives*, 22(2): 29–52.

Feeny, S. and M. McGillivray. 2009. "Aid Allocation to Fragile States: Absorptive Capacity Constraints." *Journal of International Development*, 21(5): 618–32.

Fuchs, A., A. Dreher, and P. Nunnenkamp. 2014. "Determinants of Donor Generosity: A Survey of the Aid Budget Literature." *World Development*, 56: 172–99.

Galiani, S., S. Knack, L. Xu, and B. Zou. 2017. "The Effect of Aid on Growth: Evidence from a Quasi-experiment." *Journal of Economic Growth*, 22(1): 1–33.

Gehring, K., K. Michaelowa, A. Dreher, and F. Sporri. 2017. "Aid Fragmentation and Effectiveness." *World Development*, 99: 320–34.

Gehring, K., L. Kaplan, and M. Wong. 2019. Aid and Conflict at the Subnational Level—Evidence from World Bank and Chinese Development Projects in Africa, AidData Working Paper 70.

Gupta, S., C. Pattillo, and W. Smita. 2006. "Are Donor Countries Giving More or Less Aid?" *Review of Development Economics*, 10(3): 535–52.

Han, L. and M. Koenig-Archibugi. 2015. "Aid Fragmentation or Aid Pluralism? The Effect of Multiple Donors on Child Survival in Developing Countries, 1990–2010." *World Development*, 76: 334–58.

IMF. 2012. Malawi: 2012 Article IV Consultation and Request for a New Arrangement Under the Extended Credit Facility, IMF Country Report No. 12/221.

IMF 2018a. The IMF and Fragile States, Independent Evaluation Office, International Monetary Fund.

IMF 2018b. Implementation Plan in Response to the Board-Endorsed Recommendations for the IEO Report—"The IMF and Fragile States", *Policy Paper*, International Monetary Fund.

Kaufmann, D., A. Kraay, and M. Mastruzzi. 2010. The Worldwide Governance Indicators: Methodology and Analytical Issues, *World Bank Policy Research Working Paper*, No. 5430.

Kodama, M. 2012: "Aid Unpredictability and Economic Growth." *World Development*, 40(2): 266–72.

Kilby, C. and A. Dreher. 2010. "The Impact of Aid on Growth Revisited: Do Donor Motives Matter?" *Economics Letters*, 107(3): 338–40.

Kilby, C. 2015. "Assessing the Impact of World Bank Preparation on Project Outcomes." *Journal of Development Economics*, 115: 111–23.

Kimura, H., Yuko M., and Y. Sawada. 2012. "Aid Proliferation and Economic Growth: A Cross-Country Analysis." *World Development*, 40(1): 1–10.

Klasen, S. and D. Blades. 2013. Issues and Challenges in Measuring National Income, Wealth, Poverty, and Inequality in Sub-Saharan African Countries: An Introduction, Review of Income and Wealth, 59(S1):S1–S8

Knack, S. and R. Aminur. 2007. "Donor Fragmentation and Bureaucratic Quality in Aid Recipients." *Journal of Development Economics*, 83(1): 176–97.

Langlotz, S. and N. Potrafke. 2019. "Does Development Aid Increase Military Expenditure?" *Journal of Comparative Economics.*

Nunnenkamp, P. and H. Öhler. 2011. "Throwing Foreign Aid at HIV/AIDS in Developing Countries: Missing the Target?" *World Development*, 39(10): 1704–23.

OECD. 2018. States of Fragility, http://www.oecd.org/dac/states-of-fragility-2018-9789264302075-en.htm (last accessed July 16, 2020).

Presbitero, A. 2016. "Too Much and Too Fast? Public Investment Scaling-Up and Absorptive Capacity." *Journal of Development Economics*, 120: 17–31.

Rajan, R. and A. Subramanian. 2008. "Aid and Growth." *Review of Economics and Statistics* 90(4): 643–65.

Rajan, R. and A. Subramanian. 2011. "Aid, Dutch Disease, and Manufacturing Growth." *Journal of Development Economics*, 94(1): 106–18.

Sundberg, R. and E. Melander. 2013. "Introducing the UCDP Georeferenced Event Dataset." *Journal of Peace Research*, 50(4): 523–32.

World Bank. 2018. Migration and Remittances—Recent Developments and Outlook, Migration and Development Brief.

Williamson, C. 2008. "Foreign Aid and Human Development: The Impact of Foreign Aid to the Health Sector." *Southern Economic Journal*, 75(1): 188–207.

Wroe, D. 2012. "Donors, Dependency, and Political Crisis in Malawi." *African Affairs*, 111(442): 135–44.

17

Assessing the Role of the IMF in Fragile States

Charles Collyns, Kevin Kuruc, and Shinji Takagi

1. Introduction

This chapter presents an overview and assessment of the IMF's role in countries in fragile and conflict-affected situations (FCS), drawing on the findings of a recent evaluation report by the Independent Evaluation Office (IEO, 2018).[1] It addresses two aspects of the IMF's work in fragile states: (i) country engagement primarily through program lending and capacity development,[2] and (ii) the institutional frameworks and procedures for FCS work. The internal methodology adopted by the IMF identifies about 20 percent of the IMF's total membership, and about 45 percent of its low-income members, as fragile.

The IMF has repeatedly recognized the importance of its work on fragile states. In October 2007, the Managing Director joined the heads of multilateral development banks in recognizing fragility as "one of the highest priorities of the development community" and agreeing to "deepen [their] efforts" to make their engagement with fragile states more effective, including by adopting "a shared approach to identifying fragility" and, to the extent possible, programming "resources through joint assistance strategies."[3] In 2012, the Fund issued a Staff Guidance Note (SGN) on its engagement with fragile states, outlining how best the staff should design and conduct its operational work in these countries. In

[1] The views expressed in the chapter are the authors' own and do not necessarily represent the views of the Independent Evaluation Office, the IMF, its Executive Board, or IMF management.

Presented at the conference "Macroeconomic Policy in Fragile States," Oxford, December 10–11, 2018. The authors thank Ralph Chami and other conference participants for useful comments on an earlier draft of this chapter. All remaining errors are theirs alone.

[2] The chapter does not explicitly discuss surveillance, the other principal activity of the IMF. The policy advice role of surveillance is highly integrated with the other activities in fragile states. Fragile states in which the IMF is not involved in program lending or capacity development often do not hold Article IV consultations, the main vehicle of IMF bilateral surveillance, because of instability and security concerns.

[3] https://www.iadb.org/en/news/development-banks-commit-closer-collaboration-working-fragile-situations (last accessed July 16, 2020).

Charles Collyns, Kevin Kuruc, and Shinji Takagi, *Assessing the Role of the IMF in Fragile States* In: *Macroeconomic Policy in Fragile States.* Edited by: Ralph Chami, Raphael Espinoza, and Peter Montiel, Oxford University Press (2021).

DOI: 10.1093/oso/9780198853091.003.0017

2015, the IMF called it "imperative" that fragile states are "not left behind in the development process," renewing its commitment to ramping up capacity development work (IMF, 2015b).

Even so, the IMF's role in fragile states has been a controversial one. Though it is generally recognized that, with its crisis response and prevention mandate, the IMF has a key role to play in international efforts to help these countries, many of the issues that demand attention in these countries are outside its core competence. Some critics say that the IMF does not sufficiently appreciate the deep-rooted nature of the difficulties such states face, nor does it provide financial and technical resources commensurate with their challenges. Others say that, given the fundamental nature of the Fund as a monetary institution focused on balance-of-payments financing, its role should be limited to helping fragile states build their long-term institutional capacity in the areas of its technical expertise.

The rest of this chapter is organized as follows. Section 2 discusses the key features of fragile states, including the persistence of fragility and the macroeconomic performance of fragile states as a group. Section 3 presents an overview of the IMF's engagement with fragile states in three areas: policies and approaches, program engagement, and capacity development. Section 4 assesses the impact of IMF involvement in fragile states, including in helping to build institutional capacity, promoting growth, and catalyzing official aid inflows. Section 5 discusses obstacles to IMF effectiveness in these and other areas. Section 6 concludes. The Appendix describes the details of the event study approach we use as our main analysis.

2. Key Features of Fragile States

2.1 Definition of Fragility

Even though the IMF maintains no formal list of fragile states, for internal purposes it has at least since 2015 relied broadly on the approach taken by the World Bank to identify such countries. First, a low-income country (LIC), eligible for International Development Association (IDA) assistance,[4] is considered fragile if the three-year moving average of its Country Policy and Institutional Assessment (CPIA) scores, prepared by the World Bank, is 3.2 or lower.[5] Second, and in addition, any country is considered fragile if there has been a United Nations or regional peace-keeping or peace-building operation there

[4] The International Development Association is a concessional arm of the World Bank. It provides loans and grants to the world's poorest countries.

[5] A country is assigned an annual Country Policy and Institutional Assessment (CPIA) rating from 1 (low) to 6 (high) against a set of 16 criteria in 4 clusters: economic management, structural policies, policies for social inclusion, and public sector management and institutions.

during the previous three years or if the CPIA has not been computed because of conflict.[6] The IMF's list is updated about once a year, but only the 2015 list has been made public. Our study uses this list when aggregating numbers to obtain statistics for *current* fragile states. When we discuss the IMF's experience with FCS members, we base our assessment primarily on case studies of 24 countries characterized as fragile by the IMF in 2008 or 2015.[7,8]

For conducting quantitative analyses, we use a "dynamic" definition, that is, a classification of fragile states that changes from year to year. If the only countries classified as fragile over the previous years are the countries that are still fragile at the end of the period, the true underlying distribution of growth outcomes will be underestimated (for example, an end of conflict could see a surge in economic activity). The countries that exited fragility must therefore be included to obtain a truly representative average. For estimating the trajectories of fragile states, the dynamic definition allows countries to transition into and out of fragility. To create a dynamic list of fragile states, our study uses the IMF's current definition to identify fragile states retroactively to the year 2000, irrespective of how the IMF actually identified such countries in any given year. This identifies a total of 63 countries that have been classified as fragile at some point during these years, with the number fluctuating between 36 and 48 from year to year (Table 17.1).

State fragility tends to be persistent. Of the 63 countries that our dynamic definition would have identified as fragile between 2000 and 2018, 24 remained fragile over the entire 19-year period (that is, for 18 years), and eight more were still considered fragile in 2018, after having been in that state for a decade or more (Figure 17.1). Though these data cannot be used to calculate the average duration of fragility, they highlight the importance of using a dynamic definition for analysis of fragility.[9] Several academic works conclude that the level of state capacity is a highly persistent variable (Collier and Chauvet, 2008; Pritchett et al., 2010). The

[6] The IMF's definition differs from the World Bank's in two respects. First, the IMF uses the three-year CPIA average, while the World Bank uses the annual score. Second, the World Bank uses a "Harmonized Average," which is an average of its CPIA score and the CPIA score produced by the Asian or African Development Bank for the country concerned.

[7] The IMF's 2008 list was not based on the current approach. It consisted of (i) countries that had appeared on the World Bank's list of low-income countries under stress (LICUS) at least twice during 2000–05; (ii) countries in conflict in any year during 1995–2005; and (iii) countries that had received Emergency Post-Conflict Assistance from the IMF during 1995–2005. The list excluded non-IMF member countries.

[8] *Africa*: Angola, Central African Republic, Chad, Côte d'Ivoire, Democratic Republic of the Congo, Liberia, Rwanda, Sierra Leone, South Sudan; *Asia-Pacific*: Cambodia, Kiribati, Lao PDR, Myanmar, Solomon Islands, Timor-Leste; *Europe*: Bosnia and Herzegovina, Kosovo; *Middle East-Central Asia*: Afghanistan, Iraq, Somalia, Sudan, West Bank and Gaza (a territory that is not an independent member), Yemen; *Western Hemisphere*: Haiti.

[9] Suppose that a country has been classified as fragile for the entire 19-year period. We cannot determine the "true" length of fragility until it ends. Therefore, the observed sample does not allow computation of the true average length.

Table 17.1 Number of Fragile States by Year, 2000–18

Year	Number of Fragile States
2000	48
2001	44
2002	43
2003	41
2004	42
2005	42
2006	41
2007	41
2008	40
2009	41
2010	37
2011	36
2012	37
2013	38
2014	41
2015	40
2016	44
2017	42
2018	43

Source: Authors' calculations.
Notes: Based on the authors' dynamic definition. The number in any given year may not equal the number on the IMF's internal list.

fluid nature of fragility shown in Figure 17.1 is not meant to challenge these claims. Transitions will artificially look more common when an arbitrary cutoff point (such as 3.2), derived from an underlying continuous input, is used, especially if the input variable has high-frequency fluctuations.

2.2 Macroeconomic Performance of Fragile States

Every fragile state is unique in the characteristics of its fragility. Some fragile states are middle-income countries (MICs), though the overwhelming majority are low-income countries (LICs).[10] A few have good administrative capacity; most do not. Nevertheless, fragile states tend to be less diversified in economic structure and more susceptible to shocks, and to experience more volatile aid flows, than the average for their nonfragile peers. Among LICs, fragile states on average have lower standards of living, as reflected in lower GDP per capita; less access to electricity; and higher mortality rates, than their nonfragile peers, although the difference diminishes when weighted by population size (Table 17.2).

[10] Low-income countries (LICs) are defined throughout this chapter as those eligible for IMF concessional financing; Middle-income countries (MICs) are those classified by the IMF's *World Economic Outlook* (WEO) as emerging market and developing countries (EMDCs) but excluding LICs.

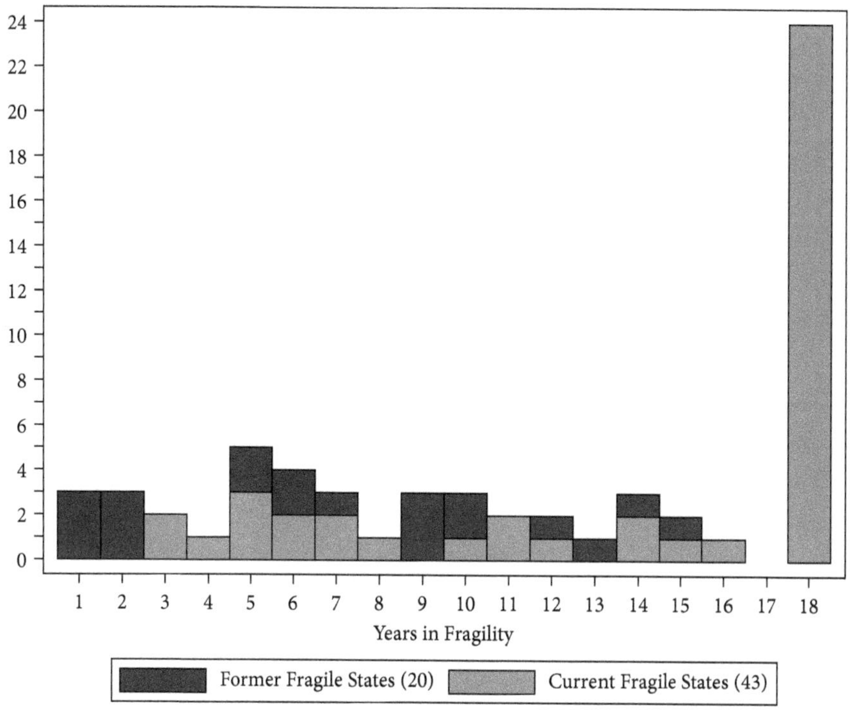

Figure 17.1 Persistence of State Fragility, 2000–18

(Number of Countries)

Notes: The IMF definition was applied retroactively to 2000.

Source: Authors' estimates.

Table 17.2 Standards of Living in Fragile versus Nonfragile States, 2014 (Low-Income Countries Only)

	Variable	Fragile low-income states (NOB = 30)	Non-fragile low-income states (NOB = 33)
Unweighted	GDP per capita (PPP $)	2,240	4,534
	Access to electricity (%)	42.3	62.3
	Mortality rate (per 1,000)t	8.9	7.5
Weighted by population	GDP per capita (PPP $)	2,311	2,631
	Access to electricity (%)	42.9	44.7
	Mortality rate (per 1,000)	9.1	7.3

Notes: Includes only low-income countries for which data on all three variables were available for 2014. NOB = number of observations; PPP = purchasing power parity.

Sources: Authors' estimates based on IMF. World Economic Outlook database; and World Bank, World Development Indicators.

Table 17.3 Key Economic Characteristics of Fragile versus Nonfragile States, 2000–16

	Fragile low-income states	Non-fragile low-income states
GDP growth (percent)	3.8	4.5
Variance of growth rates	30.9	13.1
Inflation (percent)	9.4	6.3
External debt (percent GDP)	73.1	54.7
Tax revenue (percent GDP)	12.4	16.0
Current account balance (percent GDP)	−6.6	−8.9
Number of observations	459	540

Note: Includes all country-year observations.

Source: Authors' estimates based on IMF. World Economic Outlook database.

Fragile states that are LICs tend to display weaker macroeconomic performance (Table 17.3). During 2000–16, compared to the averages for their nonfragile peers, their average inflation was 3.1 percentage points higher, external debt larger by 18.4 percentage points of GDP, and tax revenue lower by 3.6 percentage points of GDP. Their average current account deficit was smaller by 2.3 percentage points of GDP, pointing to their more limited access to external financing.[11] We also find the volatility of growth rates is substantially higher in fragile states. However, one thing to keep in mind is that the quality of their national income data is generally considered to be questionable, making the observed larger growth volatility indistinguishable from the noise inherent in estimates of GDP (Jerven, 2013). Our own past work using satellite images of light visible from space as a proxy for economic activity confirms that measurement error does not drive the differences in variability found here (Kuruc, 2018).[12]

3. Overview of the IMF's Engagement in Fragile States

3.1 Institutional Guidance on FCS Work

Since 2008, IMF staff have conducted three reviews of its work on fragile states. The first of these observed that although the IMF's engagement with fragile states had been broadly favorable, there was room for strengthening program implementation in fragile states (IMF, 2008). The 2011 review was a landmark document that signaled an intensification of the IMF's efforts to improve its

[11] None of these qualitative observations change if the median numbers are used instead of the mean.

[12] Kuruc (2018) further shows that greater fragility (as measured by a lower CPIA score) was associated with greater variability of GDP growth.

engagement with fragile states (IMF, 2011). It concluded that greater flexibility was needed in program design, along with fuller attention to the political context. A gradual and realistic approach to reforms was to be maintained, even after transition to an upper-credit-tranche program.[13] To give staff an incentive to work on fragile states, the review called for "a clear signal that the institution values the work done on fragile states," which it said required the institution to "change its mindset."

The 2011 review led to the 2012 issuance of a "Staff Guidance Note on the Fund's Engagement with Countries in Fragile Situations" (IMF, 2012). Among the key points in the Guidance Note are:

- Work should be guided by (i) attention to the political economy; (ii) the content and pace of reforms that reflect security and social needs as well as capacity constraints; (iii) approaches conducive to sustained engagement; and (iv) close coordination with donors.
- Effective engagement requires identification and regular updates of the country's main fragilities and of the authorities' capacity and commitment.
- Strong outreach by mission teams and resident representatives with local civil society, parliamentarians, and academics can help build support for the reform program.
- Capacity building is to be guided by: (i) close attention to absorptive capacity; (ii) well–tailored technical assistance aligned with program objectives; (iii) involving authorities in preparing a medium-term plan; (iv) reliance on resident advisors; and (v) donor coordination.
- Documentation should address the nature of fragility, political and social context, and aspects of donor coordination, and should include a brief discussion of the overall strategy that would help the country transition out of fragility.

The 2015 review, the last of the three, was a "stocktaking" exercise to assess how the 2012 Guidance Note had been implemented in practice (IMF, 2015a).

3.2 Program Engagement

The IMF has provided financing to FCS through various facilities, some of which are dedicated to LICs; other facilities are specially designed to provide rapid financing for countries in the wake of conflict or a natural disaster. No

[13] Upper-credit tranche refers to access above the first 25 percent of a member's quota; it requires higher standards of conditionality.

Table 17.4 IMF Commitments and Disbursements to Fragile versus Nonfragile States, 2010–17(In SDR billion; percent)

Country Grouping		Commitments (percent share in each category)	Disbursements (percent share of commitments)
Low-income	Fragile	4.38 (22.9)	3.22 (73.5)
	Non-fragile	14.74 (77.1)	11.50 (78.0)
Middle-income	Fragile	5.58 (7.3)	2.99 (53.6)
	Non-fragile	70.77 (92.7)	16.62 (31.4)

Notes: All arrangements approved or ongoing as of January 1, 2010 and ended by December 31, 2017; excludes undrawn precautionary arrangements. Fragile states are identified by the 2015 SPR list.

Sources: Independent Evaluation Office (IEO) estimates based on Strategy, Policy and Review Department (SPR), Fund Arrangements since 1952; LIC Arrangements and Instruments Approved on, or after, November 1998; and IMF Members' Financial Data by Country.

specific facility is dedicated to FCS. Between 2006 and 2017, the incidence of borrowing from the IMF (including under emergency facilities) by fragile LICs differed little from that by nonfragile LICs, though the incidence was significantly higher among fragile MICs. The incidence of countries borrowing under the quick-disbursing, low-conditionality Rapid Credit Facility (RCF) was somewhat higher among fragile LICs.[14] Some fragile states gained access to Fund resources only after complicated arrears-clearance operations. Others, such as Cambodia, Somalia, and Sudan have not had access to Fund resources for many years; long-standing arrears to official creditors (if not to the IMF itself) have limited the IMF's role in these countries.

Among LICs, access to Fund resources (as a share of a member country's quota) has typically been considerably lower for FCS than for non-FCS.[15] As a share of the IMF's total LIC financing under arrangements between 2010 and 2017, fragile states accounted for 22.9 percent in terms of commitments (or about 4.4 billion SDRs) (Table 17.4). The four MICs that feature in the list of fragile states represented a very small fraction of total IMF lending commitments to MICs (7.3 percent; 5.6 billion SDRs). The amount disbursed as a share of total commitments was 73.5 percent for fragile LICs—similar to the 78.0 percent disbursed for

[14] From its inception in 2010 through 2017, the Rapid Credit Facility had 10 FCS and 7 non-FCS low-income country borrowers.

[15] In nearly 40 percent of the Extended Credit Facility (ECF)-supported arrangements with fragile states between 2010 and 2016, the access level was 20–40 percent below the applicable norms, while in most ECF arrangements with non-FCS during the same period the access level was on par with the applicable norm. By contrast, in 2017, access levels for FCS arrangements exceeded the applicable norms.

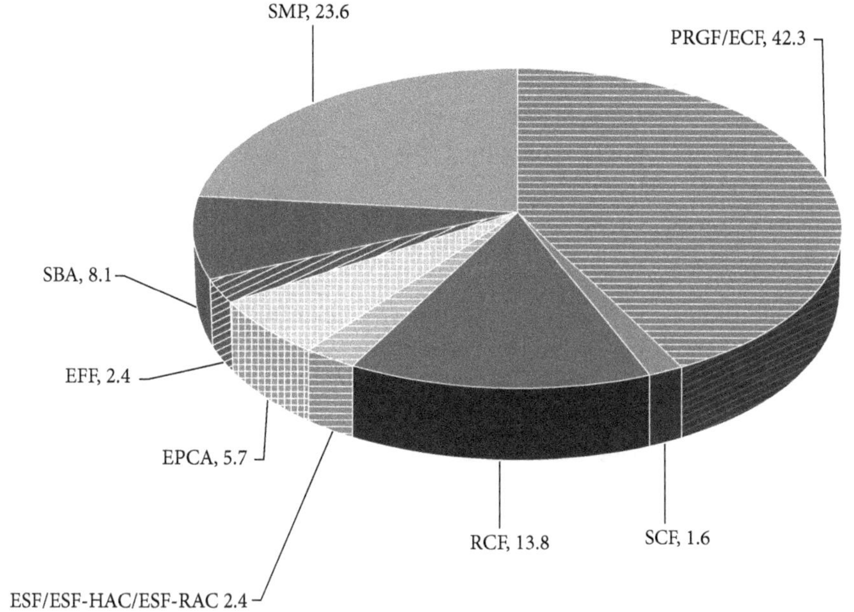

Figure 17.2 Distribution of Fragile State Arrangements or Instruments, by Type, 2006–17 (Percent)

Note: All arrangements approved or ongoing as of January 1, 2006.

Sources: IEO estimates based on SPR, Fund Arrangements since 1952; SPR, LIC Arrangements and Instruments approved on or after November 1998; IMF Members' Financial Data by country.

nonfragile LICs—and was 53.6 percent for fragile MICs—compared to 31.4 percent for nonfragile MICs.

During the period 2006–17, roughly one-fifth of the IMF's program engagement in fragile states used rapid access facilities that did not require upper-credit-tranche conditionality (Figure 17.2). In about a quarter of FCS cases, program engagement took the form of Staff-Monitored Programs (SMPs),[16] which involve no financing and are typically used to build a track record of policy performance to pave the way for use of Fund resources. Nearly 60 percent of the FCS programs used concessional facilities dedicated to LICs under what is now known as the Poverty Reduction and Growth Trust (PRGT).[17] Reforms of the PRGT and other lending facilities, undertaken in 2015, increased access for fragile LICs, including

[16] Under a Staff-Monitored Program, countries formulate a macroeconomic policy framework to be monitored by staff. In addition, the IMF maintains another nonfinancing instrument called the Policy Support Instrument, which functions as a signaling device of good economic performance to facilitate a country's access to external financing.

[17] These included the Poverty Reduction and Growth Facility (PRGF)/Extended Credit Facility (ECF), the Stand-by Credit Facility (SCF), and the Rapid Credit Facility (RCF). In 2009, all concessional facilities were placed under the umbrella of a single trust (PRGT), and streamlined into three: the ECF, the SCF, and the RCF.

by: raising access norms by 50 percent across the concessional facilities for all PRGT-eligible countries; by taking steps to focus concessional financing to support the poorest and most vulnerable PRGT-eligible countries; by increasing access to fast-disbursing support under the RCF and Rapid Financing Instrument (RFI); and by setting the interest rate on RCF loans at zero percent.

3.3 Capacity Development

In the area of capacity development, the IMF increased its technical assistance allocations to FCS from fewer than 40 person-years of field delivery in FY 2009 to more than 60 person-years in FY 2017, although the fragile states' share in the Fund's total technical assistance remained about 20 percent (Figure 17.3). The IMF's capacity development role in FCS has been most prominent in public finances, including tax administration and public financial management. During the period FY 2009–17, about half the amount of IMF technical assistance, as measured in person-years, was given by the Fiscal Affairs Department. This was followed by the Monetary and Capital Markets Department, whose technical assistance focused on banking supervision, monetary policy and central bank

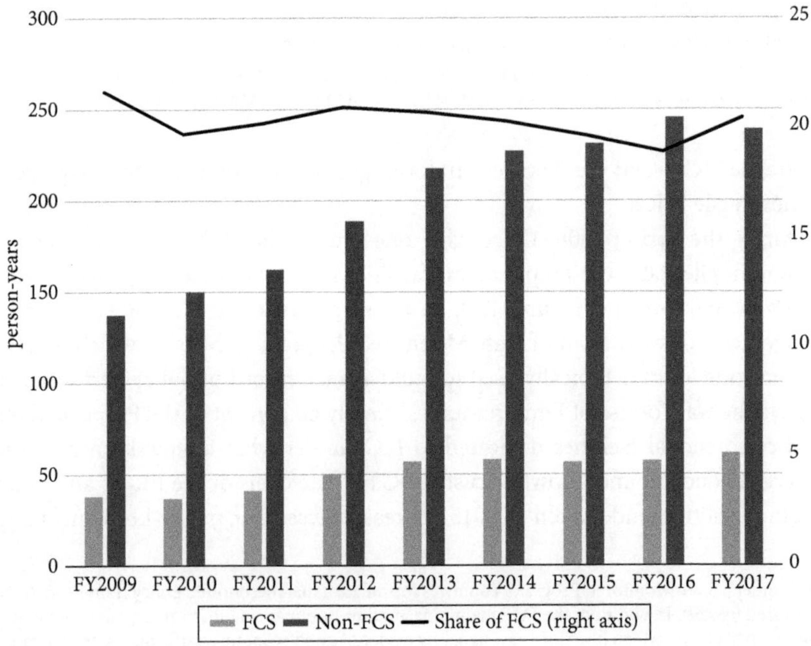

Figure 17.3 IMF Technical Assistance to Fragile versus Non-Fragile States, FY 2009–17
(Person-years of field delivery; percent)

Notes: Fragile states are identified by the 2015 SPR list; TA delivered to multiple countries and regional institutions is excluded.

Sources: IEO estimates based on ICD data.

operations, and currency reform in an early stage of post-conflict reconstruction (Kim, 2018b).

4. Assessing the Impact of IMF Involvement in Fragile States

How effective has the IMF's work in fragile states been? In what follows, we use a simple event study methodology to provide quantitative evidence on the impact of IMF engagement on institutional capacity (as proxied by tax revenue), macroeconomic performance (as reflected in GDP growth), and official inflows (as measured by official development assistance (ODA)). The methodology is designed to track the trajectory of summary statistics at a yearly frequency before and after the inception of an IMF-supported program (see the Appendix for technical details). This allows us to (i) examine whether these variables increased after a typical IMF-supported program and, if so, (ii) whether the trend before a program would have suggested that this increase was likely even in its absence. For this exercise, we use the sub-sample of IMF-supported programs with fragile states for the period 2000–12; the cutoff year of 2012 ensures that we have an adequate number of post-event years. In our event studies, we look at performance in the four years after approval of a new IMF lending arrangement. Although some benefits (or costs) may take longer to materialize, the longer the time horizon, the more difficult it becomes to attribute outcomes to IMF financial support as opposed to other factors.

Admittedly, a simple event-study is an imperfect way to estimate the impact of IMF engagement. Estimating such an impact comes with well-known challenges, especially when the sample is small.[18] The main difficulty is that the impact of IMF engagement cannot be isolated from the effects of other important political and economic factors, such as a ceasefire in the case of a post-conflict state. Econometric techniques attempting to overcome this difficulty typically rely on finding a sufficient number of cases where IMF intervention was uncorrelated with these other factors. These techniques require many more data points than we have access to. We instead take the view that an event study, though less ambitious, produces a transparent and interpretable analysis that can nonetheless be very useful. In this context, Kuruc (2019), using more observations and a state-of-the-art technique for causal analysis, studies the effects of IMF program engagement during macroeconomic crises.[19] Although the context of his

[18] There were only about 50 new lending arrangements (defined as those initiated in a year that was not immediately preceded by any IMF disbursements) to fragile states over the 2000–12 horizon considered.

[19] Kuruc (2019) uses the newly developed Synthetic Control Method for his causal analysis.

analysis is different, it comes close to confirming the results of our event study for fragile states.

4.1 Impact on Institutional Capacity

The IMF has rightly highlighted its capacity development work as the "front and center" of its engagement with FCS. The severe lack of capacity in many fragile states implies large potential gains from IMF technical assistance, including in the building of inclusive, effective institutions. At the same time, the lack of institutional capacity also means that the ability to absorb and implement technical assistance is generally limited. There are wide variations across countries in national ownership, and, hence, in the authorities' willingness to implement technical assistance recommendations, and in institutional continuity.

Authorities in post-conflict states widely acknowledge that the IMF has played a crucial role in building capacity at the central bank and the ministry of finance during the early phases of reconstruction, by, for example, introducing new currencies, basic central banking operations, and a budgetary execution and monitoring framework. In these areas, the IMF is uniquely qualified to support the design of core macroeconomic institutions. Officials in many countries also value the role the IMF plays as an external advocate in supporting the reformers against stiff domestic political opposition, in such areas as revenue mobilization and banking supervision. Yet, evidence is mixed on the effectiveness of IMF technical assistance when a country is in a prolonged state of fragility. A recent study prepared by the Fiscal Affairs Department finds some evidence of improved revenue and expenditure management performance in fragile states receiving IMF technical assistance, but the impact seems to have been quite small (IMF, 2017).

In what follows, an event study is used to shed additional light on the IMF's contribution to capacity building in fragile states, with the tax-to-GDP ratio used as a proxy for institutional capacity. To be sure, one cannot easily identify the precise timing of when technical assistance begins or when it should be expected to have impact. To get around this problem, we use approval of an IMF arrangement, with or without financing, as coincidental with technical assistance. IMF-supported programs often use tax revenue as a policy objective and, to support this policy objective, the IMF typically provides technical assistance on tax administration.

Displayed in Figure 17.4 are the results from this exercise, where the value is set to zero in the year the program begins ($t = 0$). The y-axis measures the average difference in tax revenue (as a share of GDP) in the years before ($t < 0$) and after ($t > 0$) the onset of the program. Only *new* (as opposed to *successive*) arrangements for fragile states were considered. Tax revenue appears to be significantly higher following the start of an IMF arrangement, while it is *lower* before the

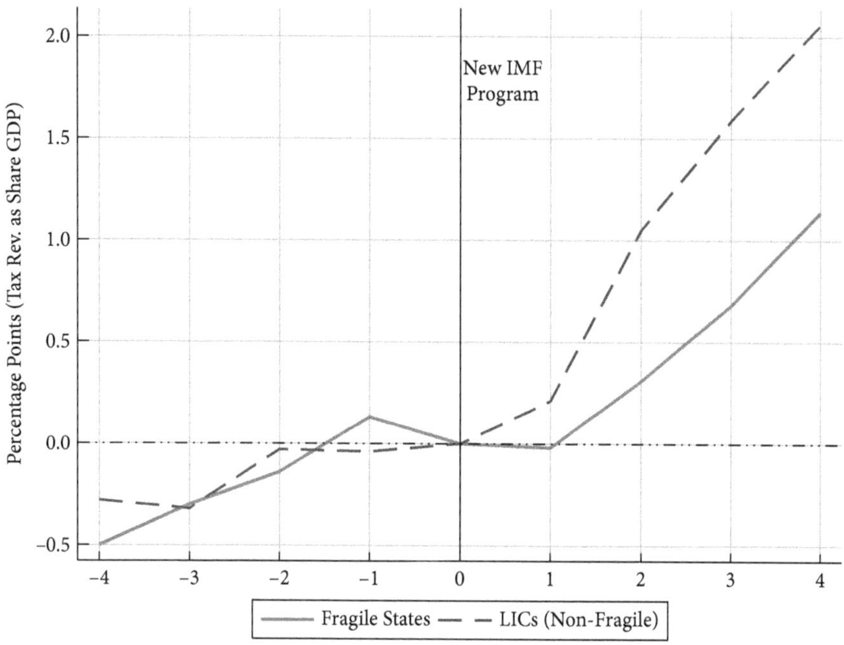

Figure 17.4 Evolution of Tax Revenue Surrounding IMF Arrangement, 2000–12

Notes: Simple averages of relative tax revenue computed across all new IMF arrangements, including non-lending instruments. Countries are included if they are identified as fragile in the year the arrangement began.

Source: Authors' calculations based on revenue data from WEO; dates of arrangements from IMF Finance Department.

arrangement begins. To the extent that a trend growth was observed, the post-event increase in tax revenue may not be entirely attributable to IMF technical assistance.

We have compared these results with the estimated responses for nonfragile LICs. For these LICs, an increase in tax revenue is also observed, but the increase appears to be stronger; the pre-trend also appears to be less suggestive that this would have happened even in the absence of a program. If anything, the IMF seems to be more effective in helping nonfragile states build capacity, perhaps because the benefits feed through more quickly where initial institutional conditions are stronger. Overall, these results broadly seem to support the findings of the recent Fiscal Affairs Department study—IMF technical assistance may positively contribute to building institutional capacity in fragile states, but the impact is numerically small, at least initially.

4.2 Impact on GDP Growth

An IMF-supported program can benefit GDP growth by stabilizing the economy, raising confidence, and increasing access to external resources. To assess such an

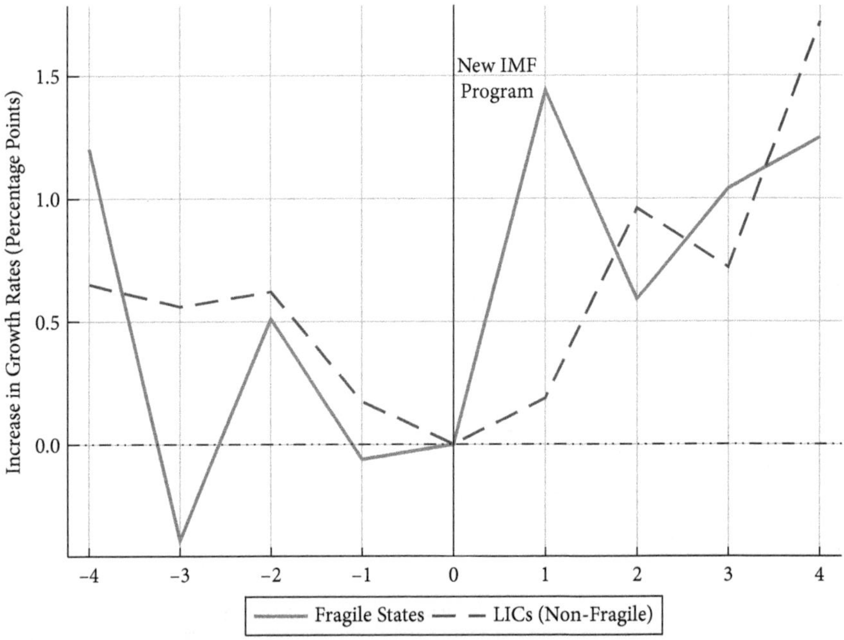

Figure 17.5 Evolution of GDP Surrounding IMF Financing, 2000–13

Notes: Median changes in GDP growth relative to the year an IMF arrangement began. Countries are included if they are identified as fragile in the year the arrangement began.

Source: Authors' calculations based on GDP from World Bank, World Development Indicators; dates of financing agreements from IMF Finance Department.

impact, we use GDP growth numbers from the World Bank's World Development Indicators.[20] Only 48 fragile state arrangements fall within this time period and have the growth data necessary for constructing estimates. In the case of countries that received multiple successive IMF arrangements, each arrangement is counted as an independent event if there is at least one intervening year without a disbursement. Likewise, countries with programs that have gone "off-track" due to non-compliance are retained in the sample. These choices serve to ensure that we do not spuriously conclude that IMF financial engagement is growth-enhancing by arbitrarily omitting less successful programs.[21]

The main results are depicted in Figure 17.5 in terms of *median* outcomes.[22] In the years following program approval most programs see growth rates that are about 1 percentage point higher than were experienced at their inception. The

[20] The use of a non-IMF data source is meant to avoid any possible implicit correlation between measurement error in *World Economic Outlook* GDP and lending decisions for countries with limited national GDP data.

[21] In both cases, the arrangements are plausibly less likely to be successful than the average arrangement (so dropping these observations would increase the average reported change in growth) and hence should not be the cause of a spuriously observed increase in growth outcomes. For the sake of increasing sample size, and with the aim of being objective, these cases are included.

[22] Even though using averages is the standard approach for event-studies, there are large outliers that make inference by averages especially challenging in this case. Use of medians allows for identifying whether *most* programs were followed by increased growth rates.

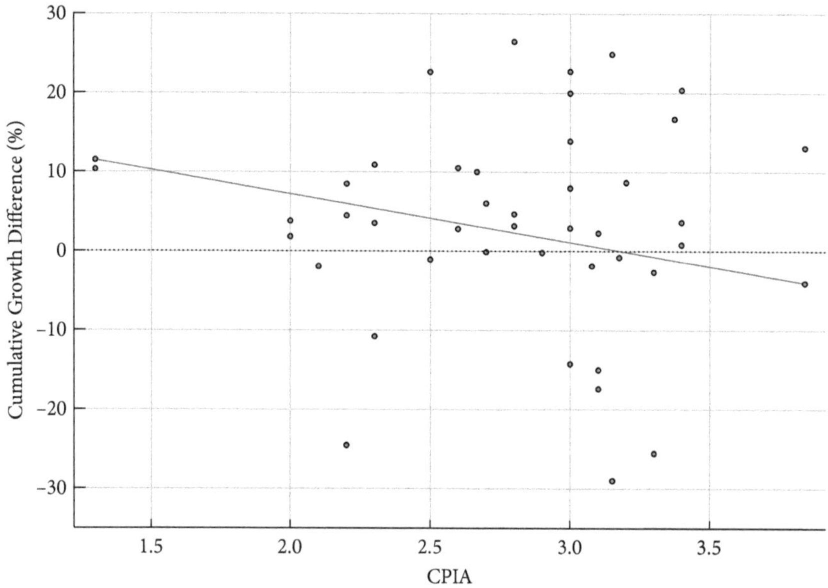

Figure 17.6 The Growth Impact of IMF Financial Arrangement in Low-Capacity Countries

Notes: Estimated GDP effect, measured on the y-axis as the percent difference between the actual observation and its counterfactual, three years following an IMF arrangement. The counterfactual is estimated by the Synthetic Control Method.

Source: Kuruc (2019)

pre-period trends do not suggest that this increase would have been expected: in the three years preceding the program growth rates are approximately level. We of course cannot rule out factors that happen simultaneously, but we consider this a broadly positive finding for the IMF, especially considering the additional evidence presented in Kuruc (2019).

These results are similar to those for nonfragile LICs, although one difference relates to the pre-period reduction in growth rates observed for nonfragile LICs relative to fragile states. This reduction may reflect the greater likelihood that nonfragile LICs will approach the IMF in the context of a cyclical downturn. Whatever the reason, evidence appears to be strong that, in the case of fragile states at least, growth rates do in fact increase following the inception of an IMF-supported program while there is no obvious pre-trend to suggest that these increases would have been anticipated.

These results are corroborated by those obtained by Kuruc (2019) based on a more rigorous event study, which explicitly models the counterfactual (of no IMF program).[23] This analysis shows that, in the case of low-capacity countries (for

[23] The broader focus of Kuruc (2019) is on recovery from macro-crises (primarily of a financial or monetary nature) using a technique called the Synthetic Control Method (SCM). The SCM looks for other crises that can replicate the pre-trend of the crises with an IMF program so that their outcomes can serve as a reasonable estimate of what would have happened in its absence.

which CPIA scores are calculated), there is a large positive association of economic output with IMF financing. This is seen in the average value of the scattered points (in Figure 17.6 the *y*-axis measures the cumulative growth effect). Among this group, approximately 2.7 percent of GDP was gained in the first three years of recovery from a macroeconomic crisis by participating in an IMF program. Importantly for this analysis, the average effect size is especially large and positive in the range of CPIA scores below the 3.2 fragility cut-off (about 4 percent), and the effect size is estimated to *increase* as CPIA scores *decrease.*

4.3 Catalytic Effect on Official Aid Inflows

The IMF's direct financing role is generally limited in fragile states, compared to total DAC ODA. The IMF is not the cheapest source of concessional financing. Even though the IMF can lend interest-free from the PRGT, many fragile states have recourse to more concessional sources of donor money, including much longer-term loans and grants.[24] Moreover, the IMF's obligation to safeguard its resources has in some cases limited its willingness to increase exposure to fragile states, whose capacity to fulfill an agreed economic program and to service debt is uncertain.[25]

IMF financing to FCS has an important signaling role. Approval of an arrangement provides the donor community with a degree of assurance that a country's public finances are benefitting from IMF guidance and monitoring, and that donor financial assistance would be used in a transparent and sustainable macroeconomic framework, thereby catalyzing additional official aid inflows. Development partners often consider IMF involvement in a country—especially in the context of a financing arrangement—as a *de facto*, if not *de jure*, precondition for their own financial engagement. Given this special role with a country's development partners, the IMF has typically exercised considerable influence with the authorities well beyond the amount of financing it provides, including in situations where countries have preferred not to access IMF financing.

A similar event study can be used to test this "catalytic" effect by observing the evolution of ODA inflows before and after the approval of an IMF arrangement. Here, we only consider new arrangements because the mechanism for catalytic financing presumably relies on the signal associated with the commencement of a new engagement by the IMF. Moreover, what should matter is the signaling an IMF arrangement provides, not the actual disbursements. Staff-Monitored Programs (SMPs), which involve no financing, are therefore also included in the sample.

[24] Currently, interest rates charged by the Extended Credit Facility and Rapid Credit Facility under the Poverty Reduction and Growth Trust (PRGT) are set at zero with a grace period of 5.5 years and a repayment period of up to 10 years. The Stand-by Credit Facility also carries a zero interest, but its grace and repayment periods are shorter at four and eight years, respectively.

[25] As of November 2017, the average outstanding credit balance of 23 FCS borrowers was 20 percent of the access limit under the PRGT's upper-credit-tranche facilities.

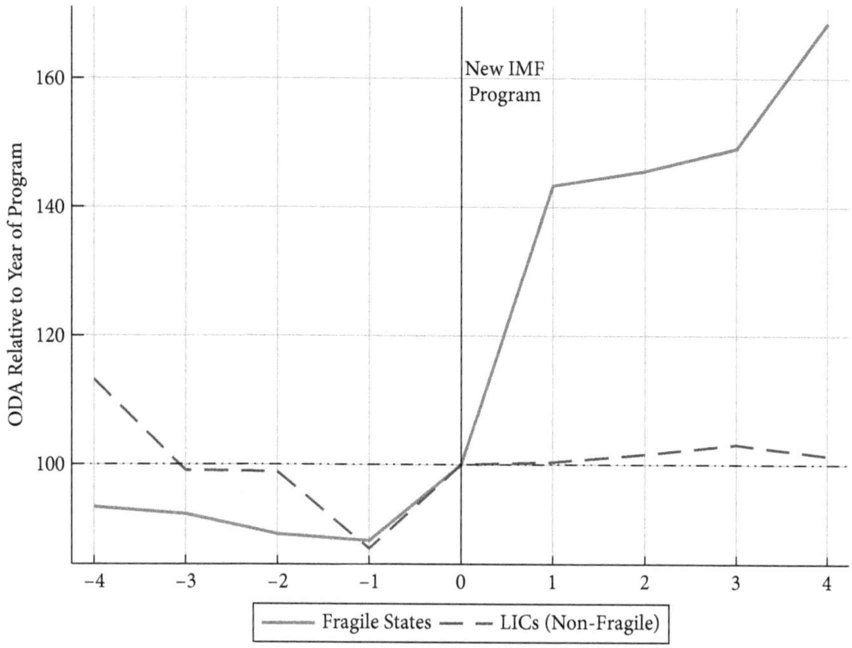

Figure 17.7 Evolution of Official Development Assistance Inflows Surrounding IMF Arrangement, 2000–12

Notes: Simple averages of relative ODA inflows computed across all new IMF arrangements, including non-lending instruments. Indexed to 100 at year of arrangement's start. Countries are included if they are identified as fragile in the year the arrangement began.

Source: Authors' calculations based on ODA data from OECD; dates of arrangements from IMF Finance Department.

The results are plotted in Figure 17.7, where the normalization is in percentage terms rather than levels: 100 represents ODA flows at the approval of an IMF arrangement (with or without financing); 150 would represent 50 percent more ODA than at time zero.[26] These results strongly support a "catalytic" effect of IMF engagement. The pre-period does not exhibit any trend of improvement that could suggest that the observed 45–60 percent increase would have happened in the absence of an IMF arrangement.

Also shown in Figure 17.7 is the evolution of ODA inflows surrounding approval of an IMF arrangement for nonfragile LICs. It is striking that the sharp pickup in ODA inflows observed for fragile states is not at all present in the case of nonfragile states. Though not reported here formally, a similar strong catalytic role of an IMF arrangement was observed for fragile, but not for non-fragile, middle-income countries. This finding fits squarely with the view that the

[26] Kuruc (2018) shows that the results are robust to an alternative specification in which the sample included overlapping arrangements but excluded non-lending arrangements, even though the response becomes weaker. However, this is exactly what would be expected if only new arrangements mattered for "catalyzing" aid.

Fund is particularly influential with the international community's concerted effort to engage with fragile states.

5. Obstacles to IMF Effectiveness

5.1 Tailoring of Policy Advice and Conditionality

Fragile states typically have lower lending program completion rates than nonfragile state counterparts (Table 17.5). During the period 2010–17, only 27 percent of IMF lending arrangements with all fragile states were fully completed (30 percent of those with fragile LICs and 17 percent of those with fragile MICs). In contrast, the completion rate for all nonfragile countries was much higher, at 67 percent (75 percent of the arrangements with nonfragile LICs and 57 percent of those with nonfragile MICs). This contrast suggests that programs with fragile states are less well tailored to their specific circumstances, such as limited implementation capacity, unstable politics, and security challenges. The conditionality applied to FCS has not been very different from that applied to non-FCS. From 2006 to 2017, the number of conditions (including prior actions, quantitative performance criteria, structural performance criteria, and structural benchmarks) was in fact generally higher for fragile states (Table 17.6).

Table 17.5 IMF Lending Arrangements Completion, 2010–17: Fragile versus Non-Fragile States (Percent of Total)(Average number of conditions per completed review)

	Low-income countries		Middle-income countries		All low–and middle-income countries	
	Fragile	Non-fragile	Fragile	Non-fragile	Fragile	Non-fragile
Concluded	30	75	17	57	27	67
Not fully concluded	30	0	33	7	31	3
Cancelled	35	19	0	29	27	23
Off-track	0	6	17	7	4	3
Quickly off-track	5	0	33	0	12	3
Total	100	100	100	100	100	100

Notes: All arrangements approved as of January 2010 and ended by end-December 2017, under the ECF, SCF, SBA, and ESF, but excluding undrawn precautionary arrangements and rapid disbursement facilities. "Concluded" means programs for which all scheduled reviews were completed; "off-track" are those with no more than two reviews completed; and "quickly off-track" those with no or one review completed. Sums may not add up to 100 because of rounding.

Sources: IEO estimates based on SPR, IMF Arrangements since 1952; Monitoring of Fund Arrangements (MONA) database; IMF Members' Financial Data by Country; country staff reports.

Table 17.6 Conditionality in Fragile versus Nonfragile State Arrangements, 2006–17

Type of conditions	2006–09		2010–13		2014–16		2017 (preliminary)	
	Fragile[1]	Non-Fragile	Fragile[1]	Non-Fragile	Fragile[1]	Non-fragile	Fragile[1]	Non-fragile
Low-income countries								
Total conditions Of which:	18.9	14.9	18.6	15.3	18.8	19.1	24.1	20.5
Performance criteria	7.9	7.1	7.9	6.7	8.0	6.2	11.2	8.0
Structural benchmarks[2]	7.5	5.6	6.2	4.8	6.0	6.9	4.1	1.9
Others	3.5	2.2	4.5	3.8	4.8	6.0	8.8	10.6
Middle-income countries								
Total conditions Of which:	18.9	19.1	20.7	13.8	23.7	18.4	35.3	18.8
Performance criteria	10.9	0.2	10.9	7.0	11.7	6.8	10.0	7.7
Structural benchmarks[2]	6.7	6.8	6.9	4.3	4.0	6.3	3.5	3.8
Others	1.3	12.1	2.9	2.5	8.0	5.3	21.8	7.3

[1] Fragile states are identified by the 2015 SPR list.

[2] Includes structural performance criteria through 2009.

Sources: IEO estimates based on IMF, Monitoring of Fund Arrangements (MONA) database.

The need to tailor policy advice or conditionality to country circumstances, important for any country, assumes even greater importance for fragile states. This is well recognized by the 2012 Staff Guidance Note, which suggests that setting fewer conditions would be appropriate in the context of upper-credit-tranche conditionality. For fragile states, however, there appear to be tensions within the IMF staff concerning the right balance between the need to tailor conditionality to country circumstances and the need to preserve the signaling role of IMF program financing. Clearly, there is a gap between the low-conditionality emergency financing facilities (RCF/RFI) and the more stringent upper-credit-tranche conditionality arrangements.

Area department staff reported cases in which their efforts to incorporate greater country specificity in their policy advice or conditionality were undermined by the Fund's interdepartmental review process. In their view, the process imposed too much uniformity (for example, in terms of data requirements, analysis, topic coverage, or even table format) where more differentiated treatment would have been warranted. Some referred to the culture of the institution where, in the case of a Fund-supported program, the ability to negotiate tough conditionality measures is prized. When asked by the IEO staff survey why the principles advocated in the Staff Guidance Note had not been applied in specific instances, 39 percent of respondents attributed the failure to an "IMF culture that places value on best international practice," while 61 percent of them attributed it to "pressure from review departments" (de Las Casas, 2018).

5.2 Mode of Technical Assistance Delivery

Judgments as to effectiveness vary; but there is a near consensus that the IMF's technical assistance delivery has improved in recent years. The IMF's general mode of operation in earlier years typically was to send a team of technical experts to the field for a brief period, prepare a report outlining what was needed, and leave a copy with the authorities. This approach was particularly ineffective for fragile states. Often, the report would sit in a desk drawer and little follow-up would take place. In more recent years, IMF technical assistance has become more hands-on, with deployment of long-term resident experts and, increasingly, experts assigned from the IMF's regional technical assistance centers.[27]

Also showing improvement is the integration of technical assistance with surveillance and program work. IMF country teams have made serious efforts in the past few years to integrate their policy advice in surveillance and program work with the technical assistance provided by functional departments. Several area departments now have a process in which they strategically map medium-term capacity development needs to technical assistance delivery by functional departments, in close consultation with the authorities of the countries concerned. Even so, most fragile states, especially those with weak capacity, have a large unmet demand for resident experts as a source of easily accessed advice and support—a finding that echoes previous IMF staff reviews (for example, IMF, 2015a) and the view of 64 percent of the IEO staff survey respondents (de Las Casas, 2018).

As noted previously, IMF technical assistance to fragile states as a group has plateaued in recent years. IMF staff involved in technical assistance administration have suggested that this largely reflects concerns about the low absorptive capacity of fragile states, as reflected in a lack of progress in implementing technical assistance recommendations, set against competing priorities. Under these circumstances, the volume of technical assistance to fragile states has reached

[27] At present, the IMF operates a network of 15 regional technical assistance centers located in the Africa, Asia- Pacific, Europe and Central Asia, Middle East, and Western Hemisphere regions. Their activities are funded by member and host countries, external development partners, and the IMF. See Kim (2018b).

roughly the capacity limit. As a matter of practice, moreover, the IMF has sought to limit the overall technical assistance budget so as to maintain the quality of its technical assistance. Because the IMF does not outsource the delivery of technical assistance to third parties, the limited ability to hire backstop staff could potentially place an additional constraint on the amount of technical assistance it can deliver (Kim, 2018b).

5.3 Collaboration with Development Partners

The need for collaboration and coordination among development partners in FCS work is well recognized within the IMF. Given the limited capacity of many fragile states, all bilateral donors and multilateral agencies need to collaborate and coordinate, but the need is particularly relevant for the IMF, which is a relatively minor player both as a source of financing and as a provider of technical assistance. While the IMF's share in the total technical cooperation expenditures by OECD-DAC countries for fragile states has increased every year since FY 2011, it still accounted for only about 2 percent in FY 2015. The IMF's share is larger in the areas of its core competence, but even there it must rely on other donors for implementation support (Kim, 2018b).

Collaboration occurs at multiple levels—on the ground, at headquarters, and at the institutional or global level. Wherever a resident representative is assigned, a good deal of collaboration takes place on the ground, at least in the area of information exchange. IMF resident representatives meet regularly with the local representatives of development partners; in almost all cases there exists a formal or informal mechanism of information exchange, with or without host government involvement. The IMF is regularly invited to brief development partners whenever a mission visits the country. Yet, partners often express concern that communication with the IMF tends to be one-way and not sufficiently interactive; the IMF would brief them on the outcome of negotiations but show less interest in an open discussion of strategy.

Beyond information exchange, the depth of collaboration among development partners is quite varied. Collaboration typically works better where the host government's capacity is well developed, allowing the government to identify needs and set priorities, help to coordinate donors, and request specific assistance from development partners as it sees fit. In the many fragile states that lack these conditions, there was a fair amount of duplication and wasted effort in the delivery of technical assistance, where both IMF teams and teams from other agencies were involved in the areas of public finance and financial sector regulation. In the IEO staff survey, 59 percent of the respondents considered that coordination with partners on the delivery of technical assistance was either strong or adequate, but 30 percent considered it weak (De Las Casas, 2018).

Effective collaboration on technical assistance delivery requires broad agreement among development partners on the objectives, tasks, and responsibilities of each provider, but such collaboration has been rare in fragile states for understandable reasons. First, it is often not clear which donor should assume the leadership or coordinating role in a country. In the view of most stakeholders, the IMF is not the right organization to play that role, given its limited mandate, except perhaps in capacity building in the areas of its core competence. Second, development partners have different budget cycles and planning horizons. Third, each donor has its own mandate and agenda. For these reasons, collaboration and coordination have rarely gone much beyond information sharing, and donors have continued to work separately, even though in principle they have agreed to work together.

5.4 Resource Allocation

Poor data quality, weak implementation capacity, quickly shifting local conditions, and the greater need to consider the political economy context all make FCS work particularly labor-intensive. Even so, fragile states tend to receive fewer human resources from the IMF. As of the end of FY 2016, for example, non-small fragile states were allocated on average about three full-time staff equivalents (FTEs) of resources per country, compared to the average of nearly five FTEs of staff resources allocated to G20 countries or the average of four FTEs for all program countries. Looking at program cases only, FCS teams received an average of three FTEs, compared to a Fund-wide average of four.

5.5 Staff Incentives

Even though senior country officials generally give high marks for the caliber of the IMF mission chiefs and resident representatives assigned to their countries, the IMF has experienced long-standing, systematic difficulties in recruiting experienced staff to work on fragile states, especially as desk economists and other country mission members, including from functional departments. As a result, FCS missions have been routinely staffed with junior economists, external mid-career economist hires, and even research assistants. Without questioning the innate competence of such staff, their lack of IMF experience diminishes the quality of support the institution can provide to fragile states while increasing the workload of mission chiefs, who can be required to do the work normally performed by other mission team members.

Several reasons have been offered to explain why it is so difficult to recruit experienced staff members to work on fragile states. First, most IMF economists have advanced degrees in macroeconomics or finance, with less interest in development issues. Second, given their professional background, many of them do not find it intellectually interesting or challenging to work on FCS where economic diversity is limited, quality data are not available, or financial markets are not well developed. Third, there is a tendency within the IMF to consider that the mark of a good economist is an ability to do analytical work on complex economies, with less attention paid to the ability to make a difference to countries' policy making on the ground. Fourth, conditions in FCS can be personally risky, even dangerous, and typically less comfortable than in other IMF assignments, while workloads and travel requirements are often heavy.

On top of these factors, FCS work has developed a certain stigma. Country assignments in the IMF are heavily affected by personal preferences: when a position becomes open, it is advertised and then filled through a competitive process. In this environment, there is a natural tendency for high performers to gravitate toward working on large or advanced economies and away from small or fragile states. The IMF's human resources data confirm that FCS positions have attracted far fewer applicants than have other positions (Kim, 2018a). Moreover, staff members assigned to work on FCS, especially at the economist level, on average have received a lower than average rating on their annual performance reviews; the promotion rates have also been considerably lower for those who work on fragile states (Kim, 2018a). The need to incentivize staff to work on FCS has been recognized by the IMF for some time, but practical steps have yet to be taken.

5.6 Security policy

The IMF is widely considered to be among the most risk-averse of major global institutions when it comes to staff security. The safety of staff must be an overriding interest of any organization, but the IMF's security policy has on occasion caused the IMF to be absent where bilateral donors and other multilateral institutions continue to operate on the ground. The threshold of safety was tightened further following the murder of its resident representative in Kabul in 2014. No technical assistance, program, or consultation mission has visited the countries classified as having the highest risk (under the three-tier classification system) since the current policy was put in place.

Development partners often question why the IMF is physically absent in countries where their own people are present. Several explanations are offered. First, the IMF staff primarily consists of macroeconomists who tend to be more risk averse because they are less attracted by the challenges of working on development issues. Second, much of the work the IMF does on the ground is limited to dialogue with senior officials at finance ministries and central banks. There is a presumption within the IMF that, unlike the work of multilateral development banks, which often requires staff presence at project sites, field presence is not as critical, and that in-country interactions can, if required, be replaced by dialogue with the authorities in other locations. Third, IMF management has made it clear that they take an extremely cautious approach to putting the safety of staff members at risk.

Fragile state authorities, in contrast, offer a very different perspective, seeing engagement with the IMF outside the country as disruptive and far less effective. Moreover, in their view, by not visiting the country, the IMF staff becomes much less attuned to local conditions and political constraints, and much less able to coordinate effectively with other partners on the ground or to play an advocacy role in the broader community.

6. Conclusion

This chapter has presented an overview and assessment of the IMF's role in countries in fragile and conflict-affected situations, drawing on the findings of a recent evaluation report by the Independent Evaluation Office. Following a review of the key features of fragile states and an overview of the IMF's engagement with them, an event study methodology was used to quantify the impact of IMF program engagement. The novel feature of our empirical work was the use of a dynamic definition of fragile states, coupled with a transparent analysis of outcomes. The empirical evidence pointed to a positive, albeit numerically small, impact of the IMF's program engagement on tax revenue and GDP growth and a strong catalytic effect on official aid inflows. Though caution must be exercised in interpreting these results, there is good statistical evidence to suggest that IMF engagement has made a positive overall contribution to the economic performance of fragile states.

The chapter's overall assessment is that the IMF has made significant contributions to helping build core economic policy institutions, achieve macroeconomic stability, and promote macro-critical reforms in fragile states. The Fund's expertise and effectiveness, especially during the early phases of reconstruction following conflict, are widely acknowledged.

Even so, the IMF's business model, with its short-term focus, has a tendency to treat fragile states like any other country and does not always fit well with their long-term sustained development needs. The lack of a full consensus within the IMF on its mandate meant that past efforts to adapt IMF policies and practices to FCS needs were not sufficiently bold or adequately sustained. The chapter argues that the IMF is yet to achieve its full potential to support fragile states by identifying areas where it could increase its effectiveness, including in tailoring of policy advice and conditionality, closer collaboration with development partners, and adapting human resources policy and practice.

References

Collier, P. and Chauvet, L. 2008. "What Are the Preconditions for Turnarounds in Failed States?" *Conflict Management and Peace Sciences*, 25(4): 332–48.

De Las Casas, M. 2018. "The IMF and Fragile States: IEO Survey of IMF Staff," IEO Background Paper No. BP/18-01/06. Washington, DC: International Monetary Fund.

IEO (Independent Evaluation Office) of the International Monetary Fund. 2018. "The IMF and Fragile States," Evaluation Report. Washington, DC: International Monetary Fund.

International Monetary Fund. 2008. "The Fund's Engagement in Fragile States and Post-Conflict Countries—A Review of Experience—Issues and Options". Washington, DC: International Monetary Fund.

International Monetary Fund. 2011. "Macroeconomic and Operational Challenges in Countries in Fragile Situations". Washington, DC: International Monetary Fund.

International Monetary Fund. 2012. "Staff Guidance Note on the Fund's Engagement with Countries in Fragile Situations". Washington, DC: International Monetary Fund.

International Monetary Fund. 2015a. "IMF Engagement with Countries in Post-Conflict and Fragile Situations– Stocktaking," May 7. Washington, DC: International Monetary Fund.

International Monetary Fund. 2015b. "The Role of the IMF in Supporting the Implementation of the Post-2015 Development Agendas," August 19. Washington, DC: International Monetary Fund.

International Monetary Fund. 2017. "Building Fiscal Capacity in Fragile States—Case Studies," prepared by the Fiscal Affairs Department, April 18. Washington, DC: International Monetary Fund.

Jerven, M., 2013. *Poor Numbers: How We Are Misled By African Development Statistics and What to do About It.* Ithaca, New York: Cornell University Press.

Kim, J-Y. 2018a. "The IMF and Fragile States: Human Resources Issues," IEO Background Paper No. BP/18-01/03. Washington, DC: International Monetary Fund.

Kim, J-Y. 2018b. "The IMF and Fragile States: Capacity Development Issues," IEO Background Paper No. BP/18-01/04. Washington, DC: International Monetary Fund.

Kuruc, K. 2018. "The IMF and Fragile States: Assessing Macroeconomic Outcomes," IEO Background Paper No. BP/18-01/05. Washington: International Monetary Fund.

Kuruc, K. 2019. "Are IMF Rescue Packages Effective? A Synthetic Control Analysis of Financial Crises," Doctoral Dissertation (Chapter 1), The University of Texas at Austin, Austin, Texas.

Pritchett, L., M. Woolcock, and M. Andrews. 2010. "Capability Traps? The Mechanisms of Persistent Implementation Failure." Washington, DC: Center for Global Development.

Appendix: Event Study Methodology

This appendix outlines the event study methodology used in the text to estimate the impact of IMF engagement on tax revenue, GDP growth, and ODA inflows. An event study does not necessarily establish causality, which requires knowing the relevant counterfactual: "what would have been the outcome had the IMF not been engaged?" Given the challenges of establishing the counterfactual, in this chapter, we appeal to graphical evidence on potential causal linkages without making precise quantitative statements.

The numerical technique is to compute the average (or median) path surrounding the approval of an IMF arrangement for some variable of interest (tax revenue, GDP growth, or ODA inflows) relative to its value at the time of approval. Our procedure normalizes the year of the "event," approval of an IMF arrangement, to be year $t = 0$ for all countries that have such an event. The average increase in the variable of interest across countries the year following an arrangement, $t + 1$, is then computed.

In particular, we estimate the following regression equation:

$$W_{i,t} = C_i + \Sigma a_j IMF_{t-j} + u_{i,t} j \Sigma j$$

where $W_{i,t}$ is an outcome for the variable of interest t years from IMF arrangement i, that had value C_i in the year of the arrangement. The outcome follows a non-parametric path as summarized by a_j, where j indicates how many years from an arrangement the observation is. The set J runs from $\{-4,4\}$ excluding 0. IMF_t is an indicator variable for whether a lending arrangement began in time t. Suppose, as an example, $a_l = A$. The prediction of this model is that one year following $(t + 1)$ the start of arrangement i, the outcome is $W_{i,t+l} = C_i + A$. When looking at one year following an arrangement, only $IMF_{i,t-l}$ will be non-zero, so only a_l survives.

In the case of GDP growth rates, we find that estimating a_j by ordinary least squares leaves the results particularly susceptible to outliers. Though it is in itself informative that the average path is very noisy, this is also a setting where use of median estimators is equally appropriate. It should be noted that the results are not necessarily robust, which is not surprising given the low-power inherent in a setting with small samples and large volatility in $u_{i,t}$.

18

Tailoring IMF-Supported Programs to Fragile and Conflict-Affected States' Needs

What Works?

Chris Lane, Rima Turk, Ermal Hitaj, and Paulomi Mehta

1. Motivation

We seek to understand the impact of IMF program engagement with fragile and conflict-affected states (FCS) along two dimensions: (i) ascertaining whether successful program engagement acts to catalyze official development assistance (ODA) flows in FCS and, if so, (ii) determine what factors are associated with program success in FCS. The empirical work approaches these questions using three definitions of fragility and two indicators of program success (completion of program reviews and a new metric that assesses performance against broad program objectives). We seek to learn lessons about what works that could increase the probability of program success and the related catalytic financing effect in FCS. The structure of the chapter is as follows: (i) summarize relevant literature on the impact of IMF programs and recent focus on programs in FCS; (ii) present stylized facts regarding the extent of FCS program engagement and the policy content of programs; (iii) conduct an empirical analysis of the catalytic effect of program engagement and the key determinants of program success and failure; and (iv) draw some tentative conclusions for program engagement and design in FCS.

2. Background

The unique challenges facing fragile states require sustained IMF engagement. Concerns about preserving peace and security in fragile states, as well as the risk of

The views expressed in this chapter are those of the authors and do not necessarily represent the views of the IMF, its Executive Board, or IMF management. The authors thank participants at a conference on "Macroeconomic Policy in Fragile States," Oxford, December 10–11, 2018, and Peter Montiel, Raphael Espinosa, and Ralph Chami for comments on earlier drafts of this chapter.

Chris Lane, Rima Turk, Ermal Hitaj, and Paulomi Mehta, *Tailoring IMF-Supported Programs to Fragile and Conflict-Affected States' Needs: What Works?* In: *Macroeconomic Policy in Fragile States*. Edited by: Ralph Chami, Raphael Espinoza, and Peter Montiel, Oxford University Press (2021). © International Monetary Fund.
DOI: 10.1093/oso/9780198853091.003.0018

spillovers to neighboring countries, have made sustained engagement with fragile states a priority for the international community, including the IMF. To help restore macroeconomic stability, build core macroeconomic policy institutions, and catalyze donor support, the IMF has provided unique and essential services, playing a critical role in fragile states (Independent Evaluation Office (IEO), 2018).

An extensive literature assesses the impact of IMF programs on economic and social outcomes (see Bird and Rowlands, 2017; and Atoyan and Conway, 2006). Many studies focus on the impact on growth, concluding that the short-term impact is somewhat negative but that longer-term engagement can be beneficial, at least for low-income countries across both economic and social outcomes (Bal Gunduz et al., 2013). Bird and Rowlands (2017) and Bal Gunduz et al. (2013) employ propensity score matching approaches to make comparisons of similarly situated countries with and without IMF engagement. Empirical analysis has mainly considered program engagement in low-income countries as distinct from middle-income countries.

Analysis has also focused on the impact of IMF programs in FCS, a concept and country grouping that has been widely used at the IMF since 2008. A review of IMF engagement in FCS found that program implementation in fragile low-income countries during 2000–10 has been "bumpy" with lower program completion rates and weaker performance on structural reform objectives (IMF, 2011). A second review of program engagement during 2005–14 found that the overall success rate for FCS programs is "broadly similar" to non-FCS peers although when programs go "off track" they tend to do so more quickly for FCS (IMF, 2015). However, neither of these analyses empirically test their findings. Collyns, Kuruc, and Takagi (Chapter 17) use an event study approach to compare economic performance before and after program approval in FCS, finding a positive, though small impact on tax revenue and GDP growth, and a strong catalytic effect on official aid flows.

The IMF's IEO finds that "over the period 2010–17, only 27 percent of IMF lending arrangements with all fragile states were fully completed" and "the completion rate for all non-fragile countries was much higher at 67 percent" (IEO, 2018). The IEO offers two possible explanations for the low FCS success rate: (i) the IMF was prepared to take more risks up front in approving arrangements for FCS, thus raising the probability of program failure; and (ii) the programs were not sufficiently tailored to the specific circumstances of FCS such as limited implementation capacity, divisive politics, or security challenges. The Report of the Commission on State Fragility, Growth, and Development (2018) leans firmly toward the latter view—that the IMF "has encouraged over-ambitious policy change," has become associated and blamed for program failures in FCS, and has impeded the process of social learning by which societies learn from their mistakes.

3. Design of IMF Conditionality in FCS versus Non-FCS

In designing programs in FCS there is a tension between addressing higher levels of risk through strong conditionality and reflecting weaker institutional capacity through a weaker or less demanding conditionality. In undertaking higher risks, the IMF would normally require stronger safeguards to ensure repayment which, in particular, would suggest stronger application of conditionality, notably in the use of prior actions, the strongest form of conditionality. Stronger conditionality coupled with weaker institutional ability for implementation would imply a lower success rate. At the other end of the spectrum, if conditionality is tailored in line with institutional capacity, that is, fewer conditions and reduced load, to support program completion and catalytic financing, we might reasonably expect similar rates of program completion, albeit with weaker economic outcomes. Conversely, a lack of tailoring would lower rates of program completion compared to non-FCS.

To understand program engagement in FCS, we first examine whether the design of program conditionality is inherently different from design for non-FCS. In particular, we focus on the number of prior actions, quantitative performance criteria, and structural benchmarks in programs for fragile and non-fragile countries. We also gauge differences in the depth of structural benchmarks to understand the nature of conditionality and ease of implementation.

We rely on the sample of programs from the IMF's 2018 Review of Conditionality (IMF, 2019a). We restrict the sample of the review of conditionality (ROC)—which covers ongoing programs between September 2011 and December 2017—to 61 countries that are eligible for ODA. We classify countries as FCS and non-FCS using the IMF definition of fragility for analytical purposes. This definition is based on the World Bank's harmonized list, calculated as a threshold for the World Bank Country Policy and Institutional Assessment (CPIA), or the presence of UN or regional peacekeepers. The IMF analytical definition included 43 fragile and conflict-affected countries in 2017.

Prior actions are less common in arrangements for FCS than non-FCS. During the period covered by the 2018 ROC, the average annual number of prior actions was slightly lower in programs for FCS than non-FCS (Figure 18.1). That said, more pronounced differences are depicted when considering other analytical groupings, as the number of prior actions varied significantly by the country's economic conditions and type of arrangement. Further, more prior actions and off-track programs tend to go hand-in-hand. Fragile state programs that went off track had on average more than 50 percent additional prior actions than completed programs, suggesting that greater use of prior actions did not translate into higher completion rates. This finding is in line with IMF (2019a) which uses a broader sample of all arrangements during the same period. Lower program

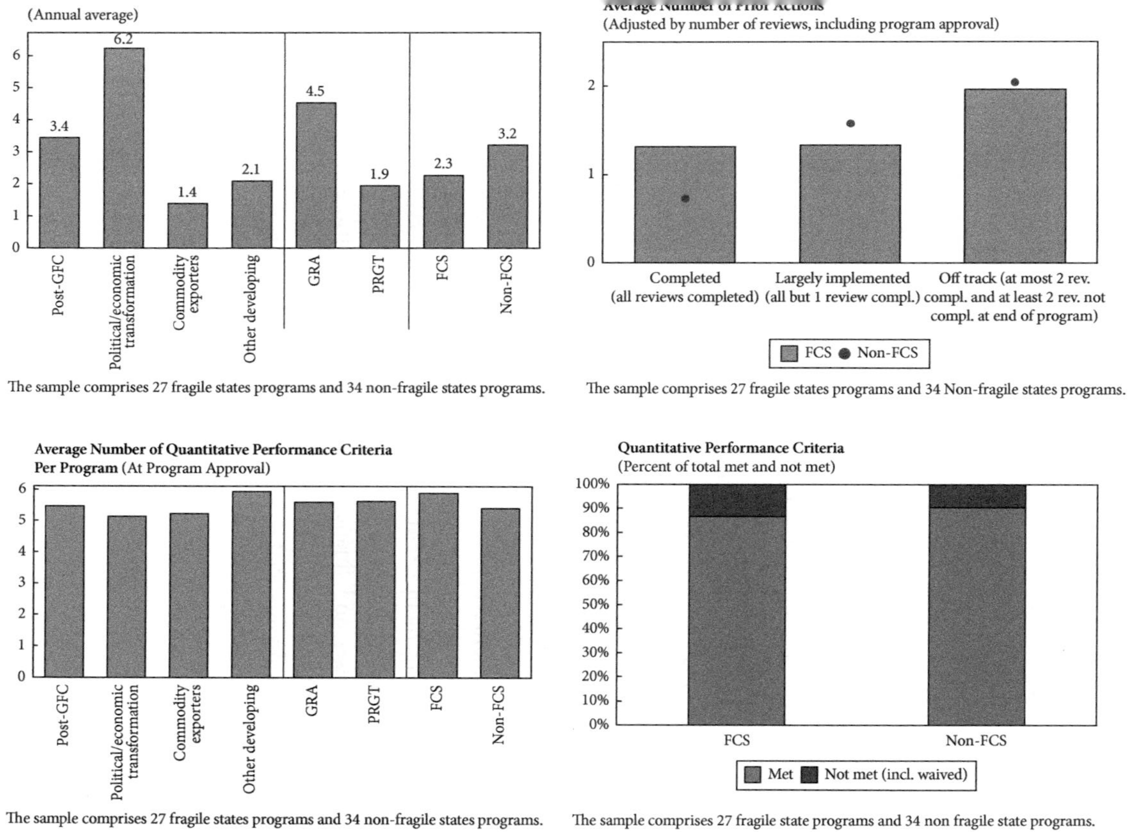

Figure 18.1 Prior Actions and Quantitative Performance Options

Panel a. Number of Prior Actions (Annual average);

Panel b. Average Number of Prior Actions (Adjusted by number of reviews, including program approval)

Panel c. Average Number of Quantitative Performance Criteria per Program (At program approval)

Panel d. Quantitative Performance Criteria (Percent of total met and not met)

Note: GFC = global financial crisis; GRA = General Resources Account; PRGT = Poverty Reduction and Growth Trust.

Source: IMF 2018 Review of Conditionality and IMF staff calculations completion rates suggest increasing issues with ownership, though prior actions were likely required in more challenging cases.[1]

The number of quantitative performance criteria at program approval was slightly higher for fragile than for non-fragile states, and it was greater than for other analytical groups.[2] Also, the implementation rate of quantitative performance criteria was lower for fragile than for non-fragile states, possibly reflecting unique challenges that these countries face. Similar to the IEO (2018) finding, and abstracting from differences in performance criteria, it seems that IMF programs have in practice often treated fragile states almost like any other country rather than requiring distinctive treatment. Nonetheless, because balance-of-payments adjustment contributes a significantly smaller share of overall program financing in FCS programs than in non-FCS programs, it seems fair to conclude that the intensity of quantitative performance criteria is lower in FCS (see subsequent discussion on financing sources).

We next examine structural conditionality giving particular attention to three dimensions: frequency, depth, and focus (Figure 18.2).[3] The "load" of structural conditionality was lower for fragile than non-fragile states, but the number of conditions was higher than for other peer groups: Poverty Reduction and Growth Trust (PRGT) arrangements and "other developing countries." The overall depth of structural conditions in FCS programs during this period was broadly in line with the average for the overall sample, notwithstanding calls for a strict, prioritized, and gradual structural agenda in the presence of capacity constraints or specific sources of fragility (IMF, 2012). However, the design of structural conditionality across groups included some tailoring to reflect salient economic characteristics of countries. In particular, FCS had relatively more conditions relating to public financial management (PFM) and revenue administration (RA), while political/economic transformation programs put more emphasis on reform of state-owned enterprises and financial sectors. Structural conditionality was slightly less likely to be modified in FCS than non-FCS, with the most frequent areas of modification being financial sector conditions. Finally, the overall record of structural conditions implementation is very similar in FCS to non-FCS with 15–20 percent of conditions not met.

[1] Evidence suggests that strong ownership occurred where programs incorporated national reform plans, there was a robust communication strategy, and/or implementation capacity was strong (IMF, 2019a).

[2] Quantitative performance criteria set time-bound ceilings or floors on key variables, typically including: net international reserves of the central bank, net domestic assets of the central bank, a measure of the fiscal balance, and limits on debt accumulation, as well as other criteria, depending on country circumstances.

[3] Depth is defined by the degree and durability of the structural conditionality. It is classified as high, medium, or low based on the degree and durability of the condition. A condition with high depth will lead to permanent institutional changes, whereas conditions with low depth do not themselves bring about change but are steps toward a change (IMF, 2019a).

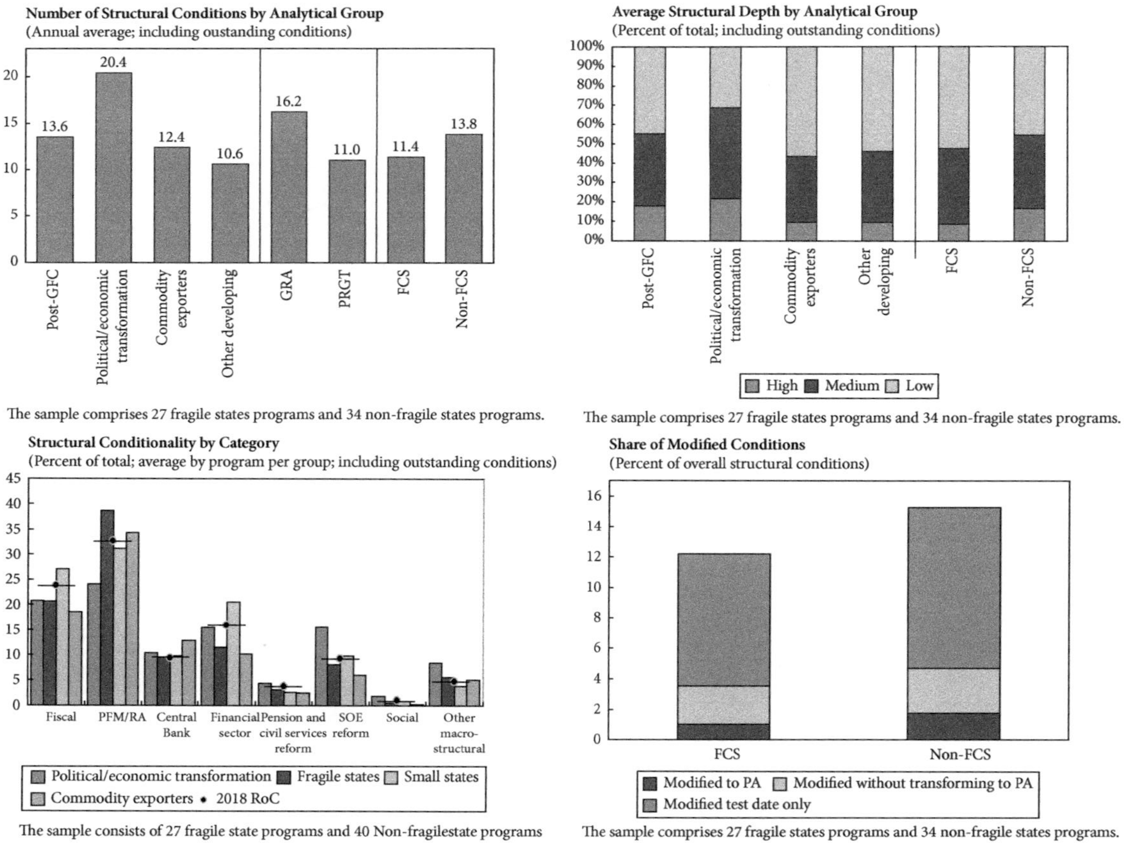

Figure 18.2 Structural Conditionality

Panel a. Number of Structural Conditions by Analytical Group (Annual average, including outstanding conditions)
Panel b. Average Structural Depth by Analytical Group (Percent of total, including outstanding conditions)
Panel c. Structural Conditionality by Category (Percent of total, average by program per group, including outstanding conditions)
Panel d. Share of Modified Conditions (Percent of overall structural conditions)

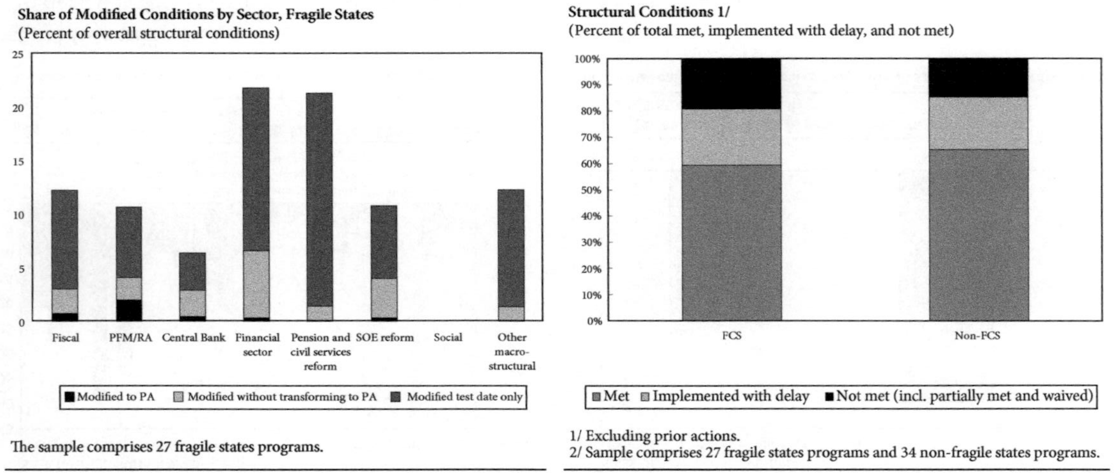

Figure 18.2 Continued

Panel e. Share of Modified Conditions by Sector, Fragile States (Percent of overall structural conditions)
Panel f. Structural Conditions (Percent of total met, implemented with delay, and not met)

Note: PA = prior action; PFM = public financial management; RA = revenue administration; RoC = Report on Conditionality; SOE = state-owned enterprise.

Source: IMF 2018 Review of Conditionality and IMF staff calculations

3.1 Catalytic Role of the IMF

3.1.1 Stylized Facts

FCS continue to attract more ODA than other countries, and such financing is generally higher when the country has a financial arrangement with the IMF (Figure 18.3). Between 2010 and 2017, ODA flows decreased from 6.6 percent to 4.1 percent of GDP for the countries in our sample. Yet, ODA was generally higher for FCS than for other countries, especially in the presence of an IMF program.

The IMF's direct financing is more limited in FCS relative to non-FCS, but its catalytic role is more pronounced in FCS. When a country enters into a financial arrangement with the IMF following a balance-of-payments need, the gap is filled via a mix of adjustment and financing. The decomposition of the balance-of-payments need shows distinctive patterns of financing and adjustment across FCS and non-FCS.[4] Programs in FCS entail less current account adjustment, on average, as a percent of their balance-of-payments need than programs in non-FCS. They also attract a lower share of private financing (other financial flows)

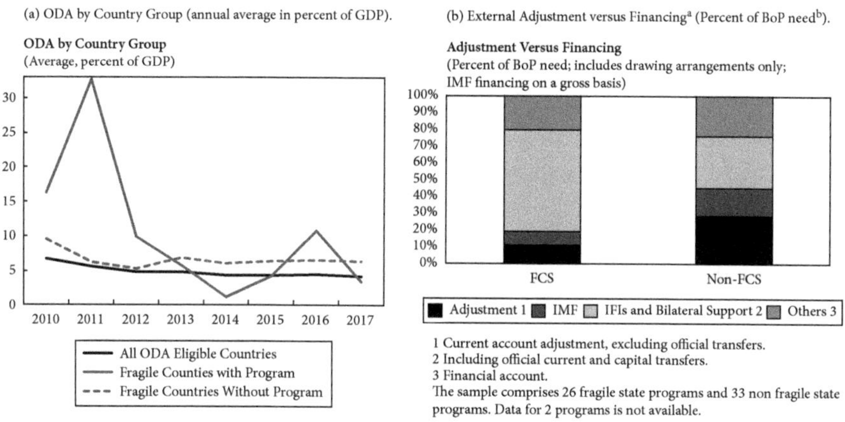

Figure 18.3 Catalytic Role of the IMF

Panel a. ODA by Country Group (Annual average in percent of GDP); Panel b. External Adjustment versus Financing (Percent of BoP need includes drawing arrangements only; IMF financing on a gross basis)

Note: BoP = balance of payments; IFE = international financial institutions; ODA = official development assistance

[4] This decomposition follows IMF (2019b). For any program approved at year *t*, the BoP need and adjustment/financing to cover it during *t* to *t+h* (where *h*=0,1,2,3) is decomposed into a targeted current account adjustment between *t-1* and *t+h*, IMF financing between *t* and *t+h*, financing by other international financial institutions between *t* and *t+h*, and residual balances between *t* and *t+h*. For more details, please see IMF (2019b).

because they have weaker market access. Further, IMF financing in FCS covers a lower share of the balance-of-payments need alongside a larger share that is provided by international financial institutions and bilateral donors. The greater reliance on non-IMF donor financing in FCS is suggestive of a catalytic impact in such countries compared with non-FCS.

3.1.2 Empirics

We examine the catalytic role of the IMF in a multivariate setting. We extend the 2018 ROC sample to cover ongoing programs between 2010 and April 2019 as well as other ODA-eligible countries with no IMF program.[5] The starting year of the sample reflects a reform of the architecture of lending facilities for low-income countries. During this period, 45 countries had 61 non-precautionary Fund-supported arrangements. We investigate whether FCS are able to attract more ODA than non-FCS and investigate the role of IMF-supported programs as catalyzer for FCS to receive ODA. In particular, we estimate the following regression models:

$$ODA_i = \alpha + \beta FCS_i + \gamma X_i + \delta_j \sum\nolimits_{j=1}^{3} \textit{Macro Fundamentals} + \varepsilon_i \qquad (1)$$

$$ODA_i = \alpha + \beta FCS_i x X_i + \delta_j \sum\nolimits_{j=1}^{3} \textit{Macro Fundamentals} + \varepsilon_i \qquad (2)$$

Where *ODA* is the ratio of official development assistance to GDP; *FCS* is an indicator for fragile and conflict-affected states; $X_i \in \{0, 1\}$ for either having a program or a completed program; and *Macro Fundamentals* are the ratio of public debt to GDP, GDP per capita, and real GDP growth (see Table A18.1 in the Annex for variables definition).

We use three definitions of country fragility in our analysis. Because no single definition is employed by all key stakeholders, we identify FCS using two sources other than the IMF: (i) the Organisation for Economic Co-operation and Development (OECD), which defines fragile situations based on a multidimensional indicator of up to 51 input variables aggregated using principal components analysis (58 countries in 2018);[6] and (ii) the Stockholm Peace index of fragility,

[5] The sample comprises Stand-by Credit Facility, Extended Credit Facility, Stand-by Arrangement and Extended Fund Facility arrangements that have an upper-credit-tranche standard of conditionality and were not envisaged as precautionary at program approval. It excludes Staff-Monitored Programs and the Policy Support Instrument (nonfinancial instruments), the Precautionary Credit Line, and Flexible Credit Line (precautionary arrangements which FCS are unlikely to qualify for), as well as Rapid Credit Facility and Rapid Financing Instrument (one-off disbursements with no subsequent reviews or ex post conditionality). The exclusion of Staff-Monitored Programs is motivated by the observation that they are almost only applied to FCS given an assessment that institutional weakness precludes an upper-credit-tranche program.

[6] The Organisation for Economic Co-operation and Development (OECD) group of fragile situations includes several countries that are not included in the IMF analytical group: Bangladesh, Burkina

which comprises 12 conflict risk indicators in 4 areas and ranks most countries without applying a numerical threshold to identify FCS. Because the IMF definition of fragility is narrower than the OECD definition, a smaller proportion of the programs in our sample are identified as being in FCS under the IMF definition (44 percent versus 52 percent) (see Table A18.2).

The catalytic role of IMF engagement is significant, and it is even more prominent in FCS. The multivariate results presented in Table A18.3 Panel A indicate that FCSs receive more ODA from the international community than non-FCS ODA-eligible countries, confirming the findings elsewhere in this volume of Collyns, Kuruc, and Takagi (Chapter 17). Across all specifications, having a financial arrangement with the IMF is associated with more ODA. Also, a FCS with a program is able to attract significantly more external donor official financing than a FCS without a program (columns 2, 4, and 6). These results are maintained using all definitions of fragility, and they indicate that external donor support in FCS is more prominent in conjunction with Fund involvement. Further, completed programs (Panel B) correlate positively with higher ODA, and FCS programs that are completed mobilize more external donor support than FCS with non-completed programs. These findings are maintained regardless of the definition of FCS. Macroeconomic fundamentals also matter for ODA. A country with a higher debt burden is more likely to be an ODA recipient, and so are states with lower levels of income (as in Alesina and Dollar, 2000).

4. Analysis of Program Success

4.1 Stylized Facts

Programs in FCS are less likely to be successful than non-FCS. We provide a brief overview of program success in fragile and non-fragile states using two different assessment methods. For the first approach, we rely on the methodology devised by the IMF (2019a) that identifies two separate program assessment frameworks—non-concessional financing from the General Resources Account (GRA) and the other for concessional financing from the Poverty Reduction and Growth Trust (PRGT)—to classify programs as "Successful," "Partially Successful," and "Unsuccessful."[7] This classification of programs is available

Faso, Kenya, Mauritania, Mozambique, Niger, Pakistan, Rwanda, Tanzania, and Uganda. OECD excludes Kosovo, and São Tomé and Principe and Vanuatu, which are in the IMF group.

[7] The degree of program success for General Resources Account arrangements is assessed using the nature of post-program IMF engagement (as proxy for resolving a balance-of-payments problem) and the evolution of vulnerability indicators (as proxy for achieving medium-term external viability). For Poverty Reduction and Growth Trust arrangements, program success is measured using a set of five

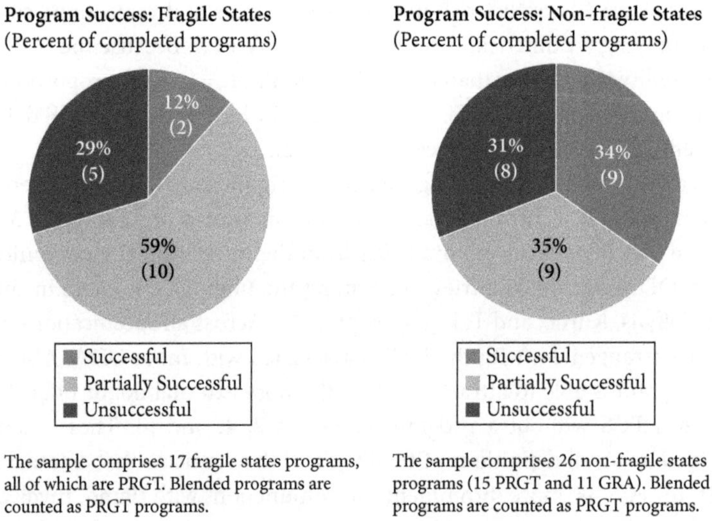

Figure 18.4 Program Success

Panel a. Fragile States (Percent of completed programs); Panel b. Non-Fragile States (Percent of completed programs)

Note: GRA = General Resources Account; PRGT = Poverty Reduction and Growth Trust.

Source: IMF 2018 Review of Conditionality, IMF staff calculations

only for a subset of our sample of 61 IMF-supported arrangements between 2010 and 2019. We find that 12 percent of FCS programs are successful compared with 34 percent for non-FCS (Figure 18.4).[8] Fragile states do, however, have more partially successful programs—59 percent compared with 30 percent for non-FCS, while the proportion of unsuccessful programs is about the same.[9]

FCS concessional programs are more likely to fall short of achieving core program objectives than similar non-fragile programs. In our version of the 2018 ROC sample that is restricted to ODA-eligible countries, all FCS programs are on a concessional basis. A closer look at indicators of success for PRGT programs reveals that FCS had lower implementation rates compared with non-FCS (Figure 18.5) on all five core macroeconomic indicators used in the assessment. The largest difference in performance was on growth and inflation, where fragile states were less likely to meet targets agreed under the program. Because differences in other areas were less significant between FCS and non-FCS, it may be warranted to look more closely into the reasons that made it less likely for FCS to meet core program objectives.

core indicators reflecting the evolution of external debt vulnerabilities, social spending, capital expenditure, revenue mobilization, real GDP growth, and inflation.

[8] In comparison, the 2018 Report on Conditionality sample included 28 General Resources Account programs with success rate of one-third and 50 Poverty Reduction and Growth Trust programs with success rate of one-quarter, which translates into an overall success rate of about 28 percent for the entire sample.

[9] In the 2018 Report on Conditionality sample, about 47 percent of all programs were partially successful, and 25 percent were unsuccessful.

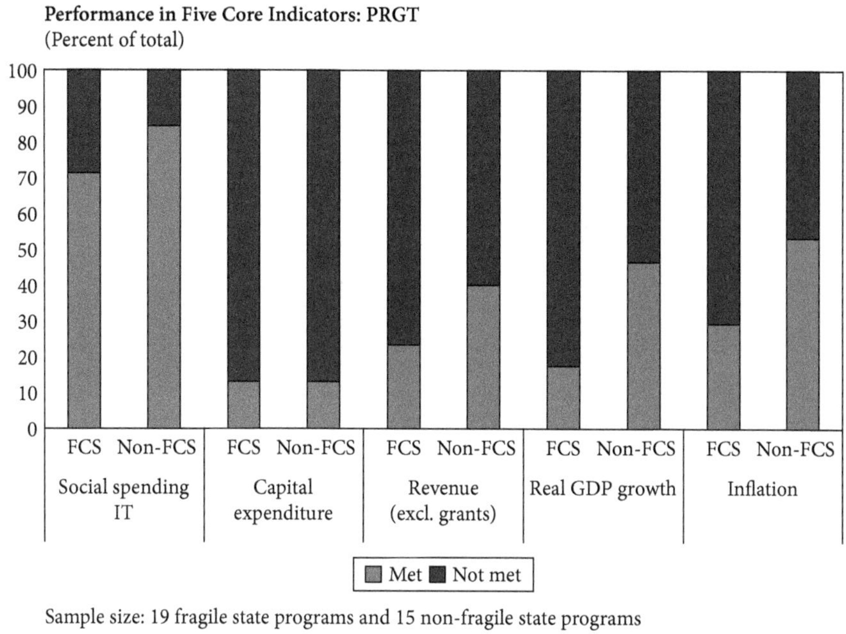

Figure 18.5 Concessional Financing: performance in Five Core Indicators (Percent of total)

Note: IT = [spell out].

Source: IMF 2018 Review of Conditionality, IMF staff calculations

Our second success metric considers the number of program reviews that were completed using our broader sample of 61 programs. We classify programs by completion rates. A fully concluded program has all scheduled reviews completed (which may include delays and/or combined reviews), a partially concluded program has completed at least two but not all reviews, while quickly off-track programs have completed less than two reviews. The program sample is slightly different from that first metric used: it includes programs that concluded or expired in 2018–19 but excludes programs that had not ended by April 2019. We find that programs in FCS have a significantly higher probability of going off track quickly or only partially concluding than programs in non-fragile situations, a finding similar to the finding in the first success metric (Figure 18.6).

A higher risk of conflict or lower political capacity seems to hinder the fulfilment of program requirements. Weaker program performance in FCS is partly because programs go off track owing to civil unrest and/or coup d'état, which is nearly four times more likely to occur in FCS (22 percent of FCS programs compared with nearly 6 percent of non-FCS programs).[10] Removing these country cases from the sample on the basis that conflict is an exogenous

[10] The assessment that conflict is a major factor in program termination is drawn from IMF staff reports. Note, however, that some countries experiencing civil unrest did manage to complete programs, albeit with delay.

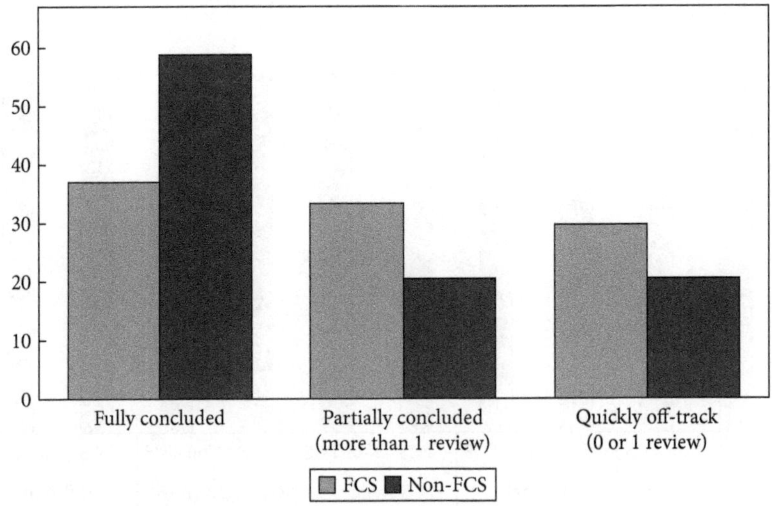

The sample includes 27 FCS and 34 non-FCS.

Figure 18.6 Completion of Reviews: 61 Programs over 2010–19
Source: Monitoring of Fund Arrangements Database and IMF staff calculations

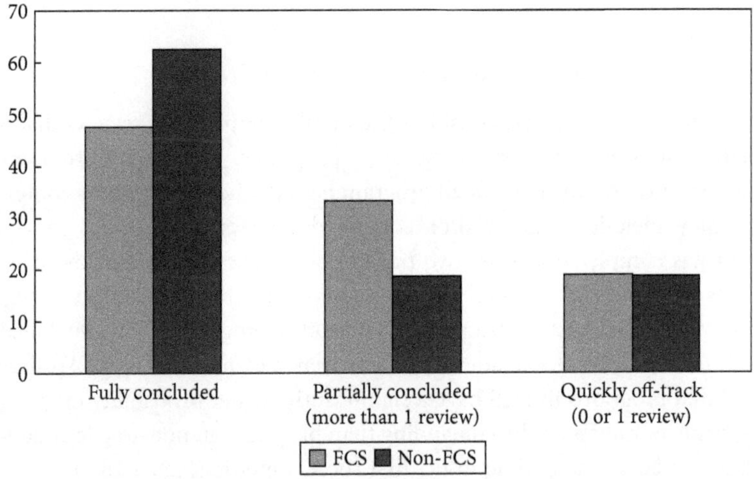

The sample includes 21 FCS and 32 non-FCS.

Figure 18.7 Completion of Review: 53 Programs Excluding Civil Conflicts and Coups
Source: Monitoring of Fund Arrangements Database and IMF staff calculations

factor that has little to do with program design, we find that 45 percent of programs are fully concluded in FCS, against 63 percent in non-FCS, although the proportion of programs that quickly go off track is now equalized at just below 20 percent (Figure 18.7).

4.2 Empirics

We gauge program ownership by investigating the factors associated with completion using a probit model. Following IMF (2019b), we proxy program ownership with strong completion rates. We gather additional key information on countries with programs, including ex ante conditionality from the IMF's Monitoring of Fund Arrangements database and macroeconomic fundamentals from the World Economic Outlook database. We estimate the probability of program completion using the following probit model. In particular, an IMF-supported program i is completed (Completed = 1) when the latent variable $y_i > 0$:[11]

$$Completed_i = \begin{cases} 0 \text{ when } y_i \leq 0 \\ 1 \text{ when } y_i > 0 \end{cases}$$

where the latent variable $y_i = x^{'}\beta + \varepsilon_i, \varepsilon \sim N(0, 1)$, implying that the probability of program completion $\Pr(Completed_i = 1) = \Pr(y_i > 0) = \Phi(x^{'}\beta)$, which is a probability that we estimate through maximum likelihood.

y_i is assumed to be a linear function as follows:

$$y_i = \alpha_0 + \alpha_1 \text{FCS}_i + \beta_j \sum\nolimits_{j=1}^{3} Conditionality_i + \delta_j \sum\nolimits_{k=1}^{3} Initial\ conditions_i + \varepsilon_i \quad (3)$$

where *FCS* is proxied by three variables of fragility: the IMF definition, the OECD definition, both of which $\in\{0, 1\}$, and a continuous score of fragility provided by the Fund for Peace; *Conditionality* measures ex ante program conditionality, entering equation (3) as the number of prior actions, quantitative performance criteria, and structural benchmarks at program approval. *Initial conditions* are the ratio of public debt to gross domestic product (GDP) and GDP per capita, controlling for the initial burden of public debt and the level of income, respectively.

To assess whether conditionality has a differential impact on program completion for FCS and non-FCS, we estimate a variation of equation (3) as follows:

$$y_i = \alpha_0 + \beta_j \sum\nolimits_{j=1}^{3} FCS_i\ x\ Conditionality_i + \delta_j \sum\nolimits_{k=1}^{2} Initial\ conditions_i + \varepsilon_i \quad (4)$$

Programs in FCS countries are less likely to be fully completed than programs in non-FCS countries. The estimation results of equations (3) and (4) presented in Table A18.4 indicate that, using the IMF definition of fragility (Model 1) and controlling for initial conditions, FCS have significantly lower program completion rates than non-FCS. This result is maintained using the continuous fragility

[11] When all reviews or all but one are completed, Completed is coded as 1, whereas off-track or quickly off-track programs are coded as 0.

score (Model 5), though it loses significance using the OECD definition of fragility (Model 3). More broadly, it corroborates the finding from the descriptive analysis that FCS arrangements are more likely to fall short of achieving core program objectives than are non-fragile programs.

Prior actions in FCS are not a substitute for program ownership. We find that a greater number of prior actions at program approval is detrimental to completion rates, using all three definitions of fragility (Models 1, 3, and 5). Though prior actions may be helpful for the implementation of a specific measure, their negative association with completion rates suggests that having many prior actions may signal weak ownership. This finding is in line with IMF (2019a and b).[12] Further, In Models 2, 4, and 6, the coefficient on the interaction between fragile countries and the number of ex-ante prior actions is negative and significant at the 5 percent level, suggesting that prior actions reduce the probability of program completion for fragile states more than they do for non-FCS.

Other types of ex ante conditionality (QPCs and SBs) have no similar differential impact on FCS and non-FCS.[13] More quantitative performance criteria may be helpful for program completion, though the weak association is not maintained across definitions of fragility. The number of structural benchmarks is also not a significant determinant of program completion across all specifications, possibly flagging that meeting or not meeting structural benchmarks is secondary to other types of conditionality in program completion. As would be expected, a higher public debt burden lowers the likelihood of program completion significantly, acting as a proxy for the extent of fiscal adjustment needed to complete program reviews.

The results are maintained in robustness tests. We consider alternative initial conditions including fiscal (net lending to GDP and fiscal adjustment under a program) and external (current account deficit and current account adjustment under a program) indicators, and we incorporate proxies for political stability and the rule of law. Our main results hold.

5. Concluding Remarks

We have analyzed the scope and depth of conditionality in FCS and non-FCS programs. Prior actions are generally less frequent in FCS and their prevalence is negatively correlated with the likelihood of program success. Although the

[12] Whereas one may question whether IMF engagement is warranted at all where ownership is weak, the cost of non-engagement could at times be much higher. It is beyond the scope of this chapter to investigate the factors that influence the adoption of a program for FCS or non-FCS.

[13] Assessing the extent to which conditionality was tailored to country circumstances is challenging.

number of quantitative performance criteria is slightly higher in FCS than non-FCS, the extent of balance-of-payments adjustment is on average lower, indicating some tailoring of performance criteria to FCS circumstances. The scope of structural conditionality also exhibits some tailoring to reflect salient economic features of FCS, but the depth of structural conditions is not significantly different across FCS and non-FCS programs. Summing up these findings, we find some evidence of tailoring of conditionality to FCS circumstances, but room for improvement in structural conditionality. That said, there are tradeoffs involved: more tailoring, or less ambition, in FCS conditionality may prolong the amount of time that macroeconomic imbalances persist, raising risks of reform fatigue and eventual program failure.

Using a subset of programs with concessional financing, we find that core program objectives in FCS are less likely to be achieved than in non-FCS programs. Hence, the consideration of program measures that link directly to better economic outcomes (revenue mobilization, expenditure efficiency and composition, and social protection) could contribute to improving program outcomes.

The pattern of financing and adjustment in FCS also appears quite distinctive, with less private financing and current account adjustment being covered by additional donor flows compared with non-FCS. Our multivariate analysis suggests that not only is IMF engagement key in attracting donor financing, this role is more prominent in FCS with a program. FCS with a program attract more external official financing than FCS without a program. We also empirically confirm the catalytic effect of completed IMF programs on ODA flows in FCS, using three different definitions of FCS.

We also find that programs in FCS have a significantly higher probability of going off track quickly or only partially concluding than programs in non-fragile situations using two metrics of program success based on economic outcomes and on the completion of program reviews. A part of the explanation appears to be a much higher risk of conflict or lower political capacity, which seems to hinder the fulfilment of program requirements. The divergence in performance, however, appears less marked than identified by IEO (2018) with the use of more granular program success metrics that focus not just on reviews completed but also on program outcomes.

Our probit analysis of program completion, employing three definitions of fragility, confirms the above analysis of weaker FCS program completion rates, linked in particular to the use of prior actions which are more detrimental for FCS for than for non-FCS. The number of structural benchmarks at program approval also does not affect program completion, probably because the pattern of compliance does not look different across FCS and non-FCS. We also confirm the strong negative effect of high public debt on program completion. This echoes the finding by IMF (2019) that during the 2011–17 period public debt operations tended to be associated with greater program success.

Returning to the original question posed by IEO (2018) of whether weaker performance is a result of taking additional risks in FCS or a lack of tailoring of program design, we find clear evidence that risks are more elevated in FCS as a result of conflict and political instability. Though the risks of conflict are higher in FCS as a group, in each individual case conflict is essentially exogenous to program design and not foreseeable. This should prompt a greater focus on analysis of the drivers of conflict in FCS that is carried out by other stakeholders, most notably by the World Bank in its Systematic Country Diagnostic and Risk and Resilience Assessments, where available. We also find that usage of prior actions is associated with weaker program performance, suggesting that their use occurs in situations that are perceived as more risky.

A useful extension of our analysis that would illustrate the tradeoffs involved in lowering the strength of program conditionality would be to compare outcomes in FCS programs that have upper-credit-tranche-quality conditionality with outcomes achieved in Staff-Monitored Programs, either on a standalone basis or in conjunction with use of the RCF or RFI. The latter are designed to be better tailored to FCS conditions in terms of conditionality but are likely to provide less IMF financing, have a weaker catalytic impact, and be less ambitious in tackling the roots of macroeconomic imbalances in FCS.

References

Alesina, A. and Dollar, D. 2000. "Who Gives Foreign Aid to Whom and Why." *Journal of Economic Growth*, 5(1): 33–63.

Atoyan, R. and Conway, P. 2006. "Evaluating the Impact of IMF Programs: A Comparison of Matching and Instrumental-variable Estimators." *The Review of International Organizations*, 1(2): 99–124. doi:10.1007/s11558-006-6612-2

Bal Gunduz, Y., Ebeke, C., Hacibedel, B., Kaltani, L., Kehayova, V., Lane, C., et al. 2013. The Economic Impact of IMF Supported Programs in Low-Income Countries (IMF Occasional Paper, 13/277). Washington, DC: International Monetary Fund.

Bird, G. and Rowlands, D. 2017. "The Effect of IMF Programmes on Economic Growth in Low-Income Countries: An Empirical Analysis." *Journal of Development Studies*, 53(12): 2179–96.

Collyns, C., Kuruc, K., and Takagi, S. 2019. "Assessing the Role of the IMF in Fragile States" [Chapter 17 in this volume].

Commission on State Fragility, Growth and Development (2018). Escaping the Fragility Trap. https://www.theigc.org/wp-content/uploads/2018/04/Escaping-the-fragility-trap.pdf (last accessed July 16, 2020).

International Monetary Fund (IMF). 2011. *Macroeconomic and Operational Challenges in Countries in Fragile Situations*. Washington, DC: International Monetary Fund.

International Monetary Fund (IMF). 2012. *Staff Guidance Note on the Fund's Engagement with Countries in Fragile Situations*. Washington, DC: International Monetary Fund.

International Monetary Fund (IMF). 2015. *IMF Engagement with Countries in Post-Conflict and Fragile Situations—Stocktaking*. Washington, DC: International Monetary Fund.

International Monetary Fund (IMF). 2019a. *Review of Conditionality and Program Design*. Washington, DC: International Monetary Fund.

International Monetary Fund (IMF). 2019b. *Review of Conditionality and Program Design—Supplementary Information*. Washington, DC: International Monetary Fund.

Independent Evaluation Office (IEO), International Monetary Fund. 2018. *The IMF and Fragile States*. Washington, DC: International Monetary Fund.

OECD. 2018. *States of Fragility*. https://doi.org/10.1787/9789264302075-en. Paris: OECD Publishing.

Annex

Table A18.1 Variables Definition

Data	Description	Source
FCS – IMF definition	A dummy variable for FCS as identified by the IMF methodology. A country is included if its meets one or both of two criteria: (i) The Country Policy and Institutional Assessment (CPIA) score, averaged over the last three years for which published data are available, is less than 3.20; and (ii) There has been a UN and/or regional peacekeeping or peacebuilding operation in-country during the preceding three years. This list includes only IDA eligible countries and non-member or inactive territories/countries without CPIA data. This FCS dummy identifies 42 states as fragile.	IMF
FCS – OECD definition	A dummy variable for FCS as identified by the OECD's multidimensional framework, which attempts to capture the intrinsic complexity of fragility by framing it as a combination of risks and coping capacities in economic, environmental, political, security and societal dimensions. The OECD defines fragility as "the combination of exposure to risk and insufficient coping capacity of the state, system and/or communities to manage, absorb or mitigate those risks". This FCS dummy identifies 58 states as fragile.	OECD website: http://www.oecd.org/dac/states-of-fragility-2018-9789264302075-en.htm
Fragile States Index	The Fragile States Index (FSI) is an annual ranking of 178 countries reflecting different pressures facing countries that impact their levels of fragility. It is based on The Fund for Peace's proprietary Conflict Assessment System Tool (CAST) analytical approach, using twelve conflict risk indicators in 4 areas (cohesion, economic, political, and social conditions) to measure fragility at any given moment. Lower scores pertain to most stable countries and highest scores are for the most fragile countries.	Fund for Peace website: https://fragilestatesindex.org/category/analysis/fragile-states-index-2019/
Program	A dummy variable that takes the value 1 if the country had a disbursing program in a given year.	IMF (2019)
Program Completion	A dummy variable that takes the value 1 if a program is completed, i.e. it did not go off-track, was not lapsed, or was not replaced by a successor program while another program was still ongoing.	IMF (2019)
Program Success	A categorical variable for the success of GRA and PRGT Fund-supported programs that is devised using 2 different methodologies, classifying programs as "Succesful," "Partially Successful," and "Unsuccessful." It is available for 78 arrangements.	IMF (2019)

Variable	Description	Source
Conditionality	Number of prior actions, quantitative performance criteria, and structural benchmarks at program approval.	IMF MONA Database
Initial conditions/ Macro Funfamentals	The ratios to GDP of of public debt, general governemnt balance, current account deficit, and fiscal and current account adjustments under a Fund-supported prorgam. Other macroeconomic variables include per capita GDP and real GDP growth.	IMF WEO
Official Development Assistance	Net official development assistance (ODA) consists of net disbursements of loans made on concessional terms and grants by official agencies of the members of the Development Assistance Committee (DAC), by multilateral institutions, and by non-DAC countries to promote economic development and welfare in countries and territories in the DAC list of ODA recipients. It includes loans with a grant element of at least 25 percent (calculated at a rate of discount of 10 percent). Data are in percent of GDP.	World Development Indicators: https://data.worldbank.org/indicator/dt.oda.odat.pc.zs

Table A18.2 Descriptive Statistics: IMF Arrangements for FCS and Non-FCS, IMF and OECD Definitions*

	IMF Definition		**OECD Definition**		
Country	**Non-FCS**	**FCS**	**Non-FCS**	**FCS**	
Afghanistan		1		1	
Albania	1		1		
Antigua and Barbuda	1		1		
Armenia	2		2		
Bangladesh	1			1	
Benin	1		1		
Bosnia and Herzegovina	1		1		
Burkina Faso	2			2	
Burundi		1		1	
Central African Republic		1		1	
Chad		1		1	
Cote d'Ivoire		1		1	
Gambia, The		1		1	
Georgia	1		1		
Ghana	1		1		
Grenada	2		2		
Guinea		1		1	
Guinea-Bissau		1		1	
Haiti		2		2	
Iraq		1		1	
Jamaica	2		2		
Jordan	1		1		
Kenya	1			1	
Kosovo		3	3		
Kyrgyz Republic	2		2		
Lesotho	1		1		
Liberia		1		1	
Malawi		2		2	
Mali		2		2	
Mauritania	1			1	
Moldova	1		1		
Mozambique	1			1	
Niger	1			1	
Pakistan	1			1	
Rwanda	1			1	
Sao Tome & Principe		2	2		
Seychelles	1		1		
Sierra Leone		2		2	
Solomon Islands		2		2	
St. Kitts and Nevis	1		1		
Suriname	1		1		
Tanzania	1			1	
Tunisia	1		1		
Ukraine	3		3		
Yemen		2		2	*Totals*
Number of Countries	27	18	20	25	45
In percent of countries	*60*	*40*	*44*	*56*	*100*
Total Arrangements	34	27	29	32	61
In percent of arrangements	*56*	*44*	*48*	*52*	*100*

* See footnote 3 for differences between the IMF and OECD lists.

Table A18.3 Role of the IMF as Catalyzer of External Financing

The dependent variable is ODA-to-GDP

Panel A.	**FCS: IMF Definition**		**FCS: OECD Definition**		**FSC: Fragility Score**	
	(1)	(2)	(3)	(4)	(5)	(6)
FCS	5.17185***	2.26721**	2.91545***	0.69186	0.04769	0.03314
	[5.97]	[2.27]	[3.00]	[0.65]	[1.19]	[0.83]
Program	2.69670***		2.56855***		2.82275***	
	[3.57]		[3.28]		[3.32]	
FCS *x* Program		6.35963***		4.93199***		0.03616***
		[5.32]		[4.71]		[3.74]
Debt-to-GDP	-0.05848***	-0.04997***	-0.07169***	-0.06798***	-0.07949***	-0.07779***
	[-3.87]	[-3.37]	[-4.65]	[-4.48]	[-4.65]	[-4.57]
GDP per capita	-0.00044***	-0.00050***	-0.00046***	-0.00048***	-0.00067***	-0.00066***
	[-3.39]	[-3.94]	[-3.09]	[-3.28]	[-3.81]	[-3.79]
Real GDP growth	-0.05938	-0.05297	-0.11638	-0.13042	-0.09688	-0.09686
	[-0.69]	[-0.63]	[-1.31]	[-1.49]	[-1.03]	[-1.04]
Constant	8.90469***	9.84603***	10.34525***	11.36661***	8.47926**	9.49410**
	[7.60]	[8.98]	[8.02]	[9.29]	[2.09]	[2.38]
Observations	374	374	374	374	342	342
R-squared	0.291	0.319	0.241	0.263	0.225	0.232

Panel B.	**FCS: IMF Definition**		**FCS: OECD Definition**		**FSC: Fragility Score**	
	(1)	(2)	(3)	(4)	(5)	(6)
FCS	9.04514***	7.46034***	6.48437***	5.68598***	0.17635**	0.17465**
	[7.08]	[5.76]	[4.43]	[3.80]	[2.60]	[2.58]
Completed	2.67195**		1.51128		1.19313	
	[2.12]		[1.12]		[0.81]	
FCS *x* Completed		5.91885**		4.52071**		0.01526
		[2.49]		[2.39]		[0.90]
Debt-to-GDP	-0.02394	-0.02548	-0.06739***	-0.07315***	-0.06806**	-0.06793**
	[-1.00]	[-1.09]	[-2.73]	[-2.88]	[-2.35]	[-2.35]
GDP per capita	-0.00056***	-0.00060***	-0.00029	-0.00069***	-0.00046*	-0.00046*
	[-2.98]	[-3.17]	[-1.28]	[-3.31]	[-1.68]	[-1.66]
Real GDP growth	-0.07227	-0.08045	-0.20495*	-0.19095	-0.17190	-0.17409
	[-0.68]	[-0.76]	[-1.78]	[-1.59]	[-1.43]	[-1.45]
Constant	7.96625***	9.11555***	10.02923***	14.80029***	-0.99643	-0.88688
	[4.72]	[5.89]	[5.33]	[10.20]	[-0.14]	[-0.13]
Observations	157	157	157	157	149	149
R-squared	0.431	0.438	0.330	0.269	0.297	0.298

t-statistics in brackets. *** $p<0.01$, ** $p<0.05$, * $p<0.1$

Table A18.4 State of Fragility and Program Completion

Dep. is program completion[1]	**FCS: IMF Definition**		**FCS: OECD Definition**		**FSC: Fragility Score**	
	(1)	(2)	(3)	(4)	(5)	(6)
FCS	-1.48555***		-0.67654		-0.03295*	
	[-3.21]		[-1.47]		[-1.72]	
# PA at prog approval	-0.19674**		-0.17856**		-0.14661**	
	[-2.47]		[-2.42]		[-2.12]	
# QPC at prog approval	0.33697*		0.24441		0.27724*	
	[1.83]		[1.53]		[1.67]	
# SB at prog approval	0.05614		0.05133		0.03812	
	[1.53]		[1.46]		[1.08]	
FCS *x* # PA at prog. approv.		-0.27807**		-0.20734*		-0.00175**
		[-1.98]		[-1.90]		[-2.15]
FCS *x* # QPC at prog. approv.		-0.11667		0.00773		0.00152
		[-1.00]		[0.07]		[1.03]
FCS *x* # SB at prog. approv.		0.04867		0.04192		0.00029
		[1.05]		[1.00]		[0.75]
GDP per capita	0.00013	0.00010	0.00010	0.00012	0.00004	0.00011
	[1.34]	[1.43]	[1.05]	[1.57]	[0.41]	[1.29]
Debt-to-GDP	-0.02354***	-0.01801**	-0.01583**	-0.01230*	-0.01985**	-0.01188
	[-2.72]	[-2.46]	[-2.09]	[-1.80]	[-2.31]	[-1.61]
Constant	-0.00570	1.15233**	-0.18706	0.46573	2.47762	-0.04571
	[-0.01]	[2.56]	[-0.22]	[1.01]	[1.27]	[-0.06]
Observations	61	61	61	61	57	57

[1] Programs where all reviews or all but one were completed are coded as 1, whereas off-track programs are coded as zero. Lapsed or replaced programs and in-progress programs as of May 1, 2019 do not enter the regressions. z-statistics in brackets. *** p<0.01, ** p<0.05, * p<0.1

19

Macroeconomic Policy Challenges in Conflict and Post-Conflict Countries

Experience and Lessons from the Middle East

Mark Griffiths, with Phil de Imus, Kareem Ismail, Gustavo Ramirez, Robert Tchaidze, and Ramzy Al Amine

1. Introduction

Countries in conflict face unique economic and political challenges. Though precise circumstances vary, common features include political division and lack of security. These features in turn reduce the state's legitimacy, weaken its capacity to deliver basic services, and encourage rent-seeking. These outcomes further undermine state legitimacy and increase the risk of violence and conflict. The process feeds on itself. Conflict and the economic fragility that then results impose large costs and hardships on local populations that can also spill over to neighboring countries—through conflict, terrorism, trafficking, and migration, as well as through direct economic linkages.

This chapter examines many of these challenges by presenting case studies of five fragile countries or territories in the Middle East and Africa. All five have conflict as a common denominator. Two are currently in conflict (Libya and Yemen); two are recovering from conflict (Iraq and Somalia); and the fifth, West Bank and Gaza, while treated in this chapter as post-conflict, has its own unique characteristics stemming from its uncertain political status and from its occupation.[1] While it is difficult to generalize from these five case studies to all countries in conflict, in each case conflict has resulted in fragility (or worse, state failure).

We would like to thank Alexander de Keyserling and Jorge de Leon Miranda for research assistance, Philip Barrett for discussions and considerable help with the conflict data, and Taline Koranchelian for extensive comments. The views expressed in this chapter are those of the authors and do not necessarily represent the views of the IMF, its Executive Board, or IMF management.

[1] Syria, despite its more severe conflict, is omitted from this chapter because of insufficient data.

Mark Griffiths, with Phil de Imus, Kareem Ismail, Gustavo Ramirez, Robert Tchaidze and Ramzy Al Amine, *Macroeconomic Policy Challenges in Conflict and Post-Conflict Countries: Experience and Lessons from the Middle East* In: *Macroeconomic Policy in Fragile States.* Edited by: Ralph Chami, Raphael Espinoza, and Peter Montiel, Oxford University Press (2021).

DOI: 10.1093/oso/9780198853091.003.0019

These case studies aim to complement the other more theoretical or broader-ranging chapters in this volume, and to provide a "reality check" on the severity of the challenges these countries face, and of the difficulty in devising and implementing policy recommendations.

The first section describes what makes these economies fragile, taking as a common theme the role of conflict. Characteristics of fragility include loss of physical security, breakdown in the rule of law, and governments and institutions that are divided and ineffective. In some of these countries, hydrocarbon dominance has contributed to fragility by creating substantial economic rents for elites to fight over. Although some patterns are shared, the case studies illustrate that each country is fragile in its own way. Or, to use the terminology of Collier's chapter in this volume, fragility is best thought of as a "syndrome"—a group of signs or symptoms that run together, but where the precise cause (unlike the case of a disease) is unknown. This may limit the usefulness of economic fragility as a diagnosis, in that it may not yield precise recommendations to address the fragility, but fragility may still be a useful way of organizing our thinking concerning these countries' economic problems.

The second section examines some of the macroeconomic consequences of conflict and fragility. These include the humanitarian impact, output collapse, unemployment, destruction of human and physical capital, and spillovers onto neighboring countries. The case studies show that these consequences are large and long-lasting. During conflict, pressures to increase government spending and difficulties raising revenues lead to higher budget and current account deficits, putting pressure on international reserves, the exchange rate, and inflation. The economic imbalances and problems faced by these economies often far exceed those experienced by conventional economies. The case studies also suggest that by taking many things for granted (such as property rights and basic security) or by ignoring fundamental uncertainty (again, a theme developed by Chapter 3 in this volume), conventional macroeconomic models typically fail to capture the characteristics and constraints of conflict and fragility.

The third section considers aspects of the IMF's role in these five countries. The IMF's role has included providing economic policy advice (typically aimed at macroeconomic stabilization) and broader economic assistance, ranging from facilitating discussions between divided institutions, to advising on structural reforms, providing capacity development, and catalyzing international financial support. Consistently with viewing fragility as a syndrome, although some themes are common, policy advice necessarily varies from country to country. The section also includes a more detailed case study of Libya, to provide more specifics on both macroeconomic challenges and the IMF's policy advice for overcoming them. Experience suggests that although the IMF has the potential to make significant contributions to fragile and conflict states, success depends ultimately on being able to end the conflict and on whether policymakers are committed to (and the country ready for) reform—the "pivotal moment."

The final section offers some tentative conclusions. The essential point is that although the challenges facing fragile and conflict-affected economies are immense and overwhelming, so too are the potential benefits of overcoming fragility, both for the people living in these countries (who are some of the world's most vulnerable) and for reducing spillovers to neighboring countries. Thus, despite the obstacles and their apparent intractability, there is no alternative but to try to understand and help solve the economic problems facing fragile and conflict states.

2. Characteristics of Economic Fragility: The Role of Conflict

Each of the five countries considered in this chapter has suffered from conflict. Though the macroeconomic circumstances in each country differ widely, this section describes some of the main mechanisms through which conflict has contributed to economic fragility (Figure 19.1).[2]

Conflict undermines security. In Iraq, security has been dominated by competing militias.[3] Libya has no national army. Instead, Libya's Government of National Accord depends on the support of militias, lacks a monopoly of force, and is in the middle of a protracted civil war (which since April 2019 has intensified).[4] Somalia has suffered from clan-based frictions, territorial disputes between Puntland and Somaliland (which is outside Somalia's Federal Government), and conflict with and terrorism from Al-Shabaab (which controls part of the country).[5] In the West Bank, the Palestinian Authority controls about one fifth of the territory and exercises administrative, but not security control over another fifth; Israel controls the rest. Gaza is controlled by a rival political faction. Yemen's civil war has left local groups loyal to the main sides in the conflict controlling much of the country.

Conflict has led to divided governments and institutions. Although Iraq has a unitary federal government (including the autonomous Kurdistan region), political discourse is fragmented along sectarian and ethnic lines.[6] Libya has two governments and two parliaments, one of each in the West and one of each in the East of the country, and its main economic institutions—the Central Bank, the National Oil Corporation, the Libyan Investment Authority (which holds

[2] Although the focus of this chapter is on conflict, this section's description of fragility is consistent with that in the Commission on State Fragility, Growth and Development (2018) and Chapter 3 in this volume. IMF (2016a) covers the role of conflict in the broader Middle East and North Africa region.

[3] UNHCR (2015), United Nations Iraq(2016) and Gaston and Derzsi-Horvath (2017).

[4] Lacher and al-Idrissi (2018), Wehrey (2017).

[5] Menkhaus (2018).

[6] Al-Qarawee(2014).

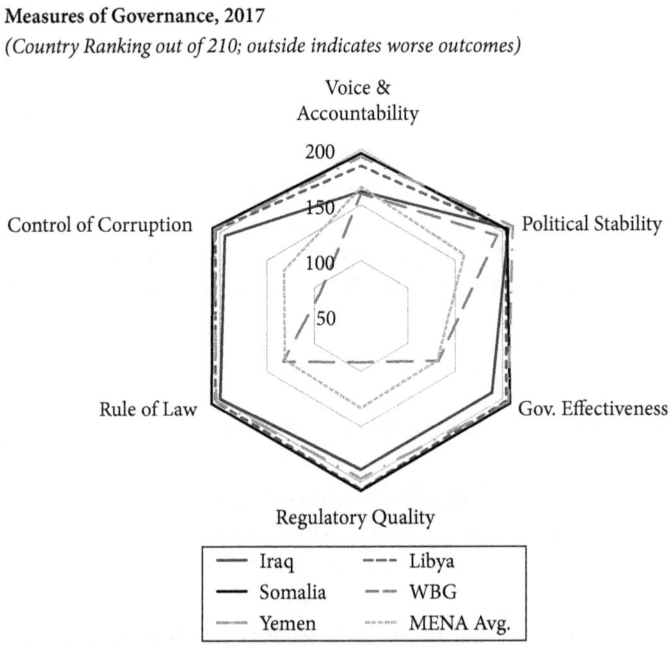

Figure 19.1 Measures of Governance, 2017
(Country ranking out of 210, outside indicates worse outcomes)
Note: MENA = Middle East and North Africa; WBG = West Bank and Gaza.
Source: Worldwide Governance Indicators, World Bank Group.

investments financed from the proceeds of earlier oil sales) and the Ministry of Finance—are divided. Yemen also has two governments and divided institutions. Somalia faces the challenge of building a federal system of government out of the Federal Government (which won international recognition in 2012), the five Federal Member States, and the self-declared independent Somaliland. West Bank and Gaza suffers from political divisions between Fatah (West Bank) and Hamas (Gaza).

Conflict and division weaken government effectiveness and legitimacy. In Iraq, the dismantling of the Baathist-era bureaucracy following the Second Gulf War weakened the effectiveness of the government. Division and incapacity have undermined Libya's provision of public services such as safety and security, health, sanitation, education, water, and power. Somalia suffers from weak institutions and capacity, and from perceived corruption. Yemen's fragmented institutions weaken governance, undermining the provision of health and education. In West Bank and Gaza, dysfunction in government has increased reliance on external providers for public services. Across these cases, division results in questions over government legitimacy, which makes policy implementation more difficult.

Divided governments and institutions, together with the lack of good data, complicate policymaking. Multiple finance ministries or central banks in a single country, often with conflicting objectives, mean that standard macroeconomic models with a single policymaker may be inappropriate. For example, in Libya policymakers in the West and East have divergent objectives, given the conflict between them; thus it has been impossible to reach agreement on a single fiscal or monetary policy (or to monitor either of these ex post), and there are also perceptions that revenues are not being allocated fairly, or that governments exceed their spending plans without penalty. In addition, economic data in each of the five cases is typically of poor quality. What little economic data exists in Libya, Somalia, and Yemen is unreliable and coverage partial. This complicates understanding the economic situation or diagnosing economic problems.

Institutions lack transparency and accountability. In Libya the Government of National Accord prepares the budget, often with delay, but it is neither submitted to nor approved by parliament. The published budget is highly aggregated, making it hard to understand the true allocation of spending or to monitor how the budget is implemented through the year. Spending in the East (about one-sixth of the total) takes place outside any agreed budget or financing mechanism. In Yemen, there is limited auditing of the government, and no information on the economic activities of the de facto Houthi rebel administration. Lack of transparency and accountability allows poor policymaking to persist, and raises popular concerns over how resources are allocated, which can contribute to conflict.

Conflict and fragility may discourage policymakers from investing in economic reform or in sound economic policies. Policymakers may face more pressing problems, such as the humanitarian crisis or ameliorating the impact of the conflict. But, as Collier's arguments in this volume have suggested, policymakers also face radical uncertainty over what will happen to their own positions, their government, or their country; in such circumstances even well-intentioned policymakers find it difficult to make long-term plans. (The same considerations apply to citizens, and these are typically ignored in conventional (optimizing) economic models). And worse, policymakers who are ill-intentioned may use conflict and the absence of rule of law as an opportunity to expropriate rents, and to oppose economic reforms to keep these rents.[7]

In Iraq, Libya, and Yemen, dependence on hydrocarbons increases economic volatility and contributes to fragility (Figure 19.2). Export revenues, tax revenues, and GDP all depend on oil, and are thus vulnerable to changes in world oil prices and—typically for conflict countries—production disruptions. Since 2014, Libya's monthly oil production (and thus the bulk of its GDP) has fluctuated widely,

[7] For examples from Libya, see Eaton (2018).

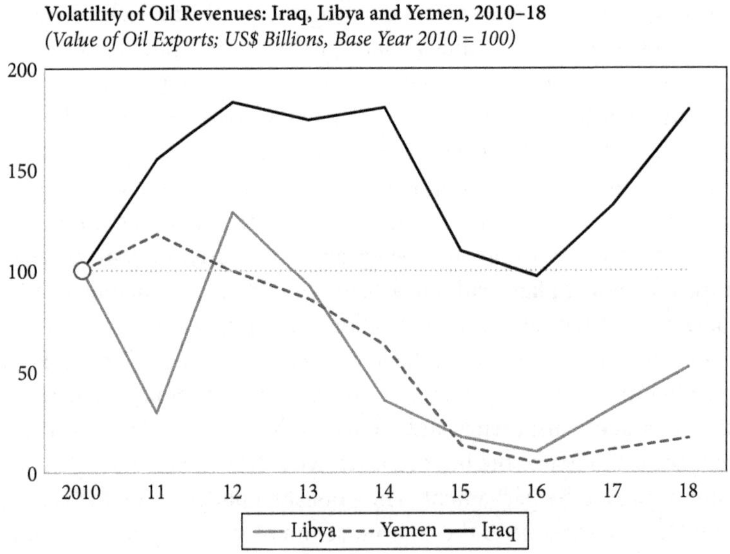

Figure 19.2 Volatility of Oil Revenues: Iraq, Libya, and Yemen, 2010–18
(Value of oil exports, US$ billions, base year 2010 = 100)
Source: National Authorities; and IMF Staff Estimates.

between 0.2 and 1.0 million barrels per day. In Yemen, oil production peaked in 2001 at about 400,000 barrels per day, fell to 170,000 barrels just before the 2014 conflict, and at time of writing is currently negligible.

Hydrocarbon dominance can also undermine economic governance (Collier and Venables, 2009; Besley and Persson, 2013) (Figure 19.3). Without strong institutions and administrative capacity, Iraq's and Libya's oil revenues have encouraged rent-seeking, resulting in excessive public employment and weak investment planning.[8] In Libya, the largest rents come from accessing foreign currency at preferential exchange rates, or from smuggling underpriced fuel.[9] The fight over rents can frustrate economic reform (as successful reform might eliminate the rents) and attempts at political settlement (as this might displace the existing elites and remove their access to the rents).[10]

[8] Estimates of corruption in Iraq vary widely but are large. Global Financial Integrity (2012) estimates that US$65 billion in illicit funds (56 percent of 2011 GDP) left Iraq between 2001 and 2010; Iraq's Board of Supreme Audit puts the figure even higher at about US$40 billion annually (SIGIR, 2013).

[9] Libya has some of the cheapest petrol in the world, costing around US$0.04 per litre (well below the world price), versus US$0.70 in Tunisia and US$1.70 in Italy (February 2019).

[10] Yemen's war economy has created rents through unofficial mechanisms for moving food, fuel, medicines, foreign currency, and weapons. These rents have helped finance the conflict. In Somalia, aside from control of government and ministries, main rents derive from control of seaports, airports, and the telecommunications monopoly (which controls the country's de facto payments system) (Menkhaus, 2018).

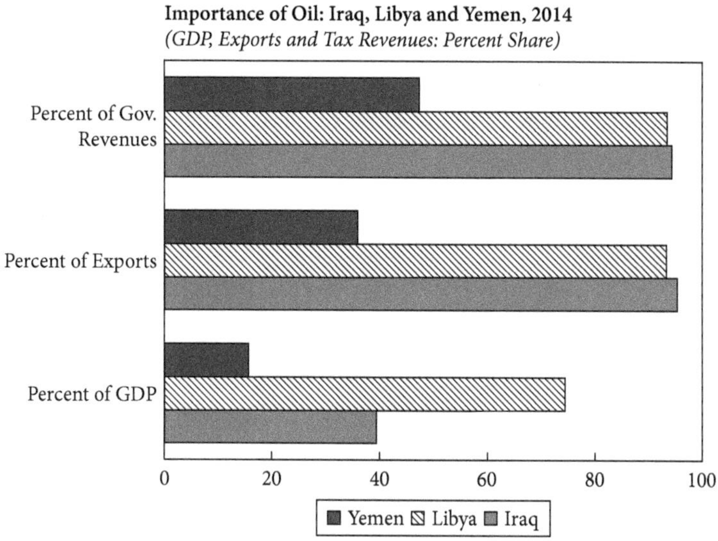

Figure 19.3 Importance of Oil: Iraq, Libya, and Yemen, 2014
(GDP, Exports, and Tax Revenues; percent share)
Source: National Authorities; and IMF Staff Estimates.

- In the worst case, oil revenues can cause or prolong conflict. Oil was central to Iraq's first Gulf war, which started amid accusations of oil theft and against the background of budget deficits following the Iran-Iraq war and the 1980s collapse in oil prices. And although not the original cause, in Libya the fight for oil revenues has contributed to the civil war, as the East and South of the country produce most of the oil, while the revenues are controlled by the government and Central Bank in the West (Gazzini, 2015). Tragically, Libya's oil revenues have financed and helped prolong its civil war.

3. Economic Consequences of Conflict and Fragility

Just as conflict and fragility have many dimensions, their economic consequences also vary widely. Notwithstanding these many differences, one shared theme is that the economic problems that result are typically much greater than those in more conventional economies.[11]

[11] See Barrett (2018) for analysis of the economic costs of conflict, and IMF (2016a) for broader discussions.

3.1 Humanitarian Consequences of Conflict and Fragility

In each of the five countries, conflict has resulted in significant numbers of deaths, large numbers of refugees and internally displaced people, and terrible humanitarian crises (Figure 19.4):

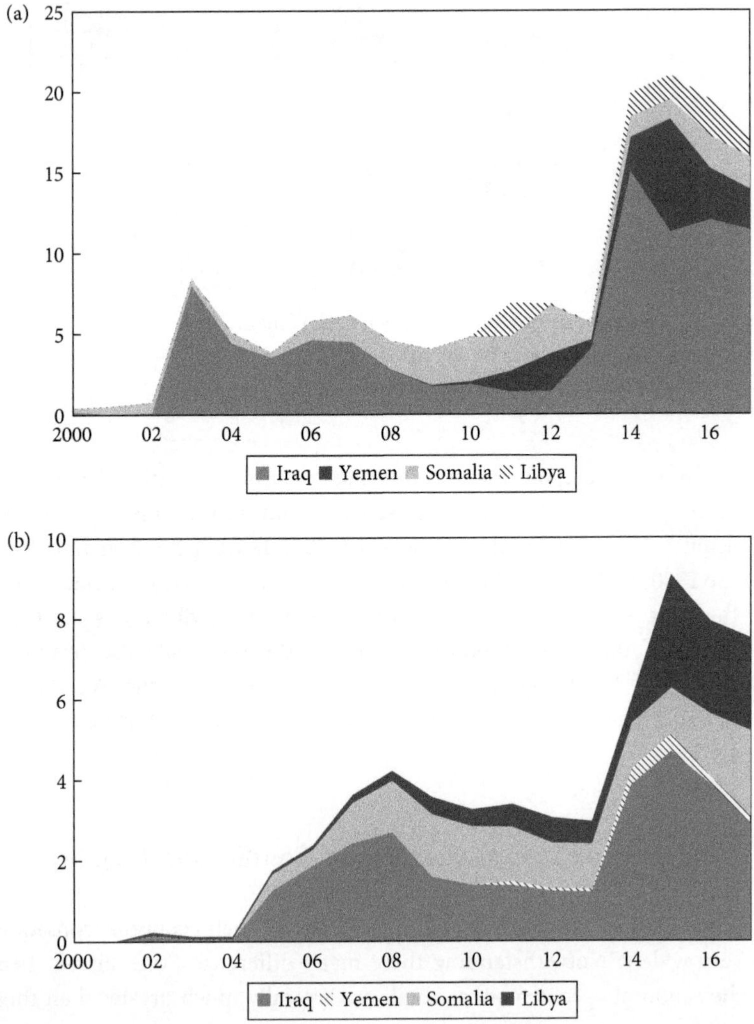

Figure 19.4 Death and Displacement

Panel a. Deaths from Conflict, 2000–17 (Thousands); Panel b. Refugees and Internally Displaced Persons by Host Country, 2000–18 (Millions)

Source: Uppsala Conflict Data Program (UCDP); United Nations High Commission for Refugees (UNHCR).

- At its peak, Iraq's conflict and the subsequent rise of ISIS displaced almost 6 million people. Currently about 2 million are displaced, and about 6.5 million people out of a population of 40 million need some form of humanitarian assistance (UNOCHA, 2019a).
- In Libya, out of a population of 6.6 million (plus an estimated 0.7 million migrants and refugees) an estimated 0.8 million need humanitarian assistance (UNOCHA, 2019b). Half those in need are Libyans, half are refugees and migrants. With the spread of the civil war to Tripoli since April 2019, deaths and displacement have increased further.
- Somalia's civil war and vulnerability to natural disaster (drought and heavy rain) have resulted in repeated population displacement and makes the country prone to humanitarian crisis. At end-2017, about 2.1 million people (14 percent of the population) were internally displaced while Somalia was the source of about 1 million refugees living in other countries (UNHCR, 2017).
- In West Bank and Gaza, the humanitarian challenges in Gaza are particularly deep. The UN Relief and Works Agency for Palestine Refugees in the Near East (UNRWA) provides access to primary health care for 1.3 million people, education for more than 0.25 million children, and food assistance to nearly one million refugees (UNRWA, 2017). More than 90 percent of the domestic water supply in Gaza is undrinkable, while during 2017–18 electricity was available for only 5–7 hours per day.
- Yemen's conflict has heightened the risk of famine. In 2014, before the conflict started, about 40 percent of Yemen's population was already food insecure, reflecting Yemen's dependence on exporting oil for food. Since the start of the conflict, almost 80 percent of the population (24 million people) require humanitarian aid or protection, and 66 percent face food insecurity (World Bank, 2017; UNOCHA, 2019c).

3.2 Macroeconomic Consequences of Conflict and Fragility

Conflict and fragility also have deep macroeconomic consequences, including the collapse of output, destruction of human and physical capital (and thus of potential output), unemployment, inability to raise tax revenues, pressure to increase government spending, and (if financing is available) higher budget deficits, inflation, and balance of payments pressures.

Conflict typically leads to an output collapse. In Libya and Yemen oil production and economic activity fell because of conflict. While conflict-related tensions have held back output growth in the West Bank, the contrasting performance of the West Bank (where real GDP tripled since 1994) compared to the more violent Gaza Strip (where real GDP over the same time period did not even double, and real GDP per capita is less than half that of the West Bank) illustrates that sustained conflict can have a severe impact.[12]

Conflict destroys human capital. This destruction mainly reflects the humanitarian crisis: the large death tolls, internal displacement, and refugees fleeing to other countries. But it also reflects the breakdown in social services. In Iraq, secondary education enrollment has fallen to 50 percent[13] and life expectancy is below the average for the Middle East and North Africa.[14] In Somalia, only 55 percent of the population can read and write, 16 percent have completed primary school (versus 34 percent in low-income Sub-Saharan countries), and 7 percent have finished secondary school (World Bank, 2018a). In Libya and Yemen, conflict has destroyed hospitals, schools, and universities, and delayed salary payments to doctors, nurses, and teachers.[15]

Conflict destroys physical capital, and the uncertainty caused by conflict, together with the lack of security and property rights, deters investment. Destruction of manufacturing plants, public infrastructure, agricultural infrastructure and livestock, and commercial buildings is a direct channel through which conflict hampers economic activity (Collier, 1999). In Iraq, although physical capital is estimated to have doubled from 1980 to 2011, this is half the increase recorded by Middle East and North Africa oil-exporting countries. Decades of conflict and political uncertainty, and restrictions on movement, have discouraged investment in West Bank and Gaza. Though the counterfactual is difficult to construct, IMF staff estimate that in Gaza (where conflict has destroyed much of the capital stock) 2014 GDP per capita could have been 40–130 percent higher had economic performance matched those of its peers or followed Gaza's own pre-1994 trends.[16]

Unemployment tends to increase during and after conflict (Figure 19.5). In West Bank and Gaza, the unemployment rate has increased steadily, and is currently almost 30 percent (more than 50 percent in Gaza). Female labor participation is only about 20 percent. Although Libya's official unemployment rate has remained steady, its youth unemployment rate increased from 28 percent in 2012 to 42 percent in 2015.[17] Reported unemployment rates in conflict countries suffer from data problems (and often have to be generated by models). However, the reliance on the public sector for job creation in many of these countries suggests that they face a severe unemployment problem.

[12] "West Bank and the Gaza Strip—Growing Apart," Annex III of IMF (2018b).

[13] UNICEF Global database.

[14] United Nations Development Programme Human Development Index.

[15] In Libya's case, health professionals have been held hostage and foreign currency restrictions have prevented foreign health workers from sending remittances back home.

[16] "West Bank and Gaza—Estimating the Growth Performance Gap," Box 2 of IMF (2016b). Libya, Somalia, and Yemen lack capital stock data, but each has experienced significant infrastructure damage, including to schools, hospitals, electricity, water supply, sanitation, roads, and telecommunications.

[17] UNFPA (2018), citing Libya Statistics and Census Bureau.

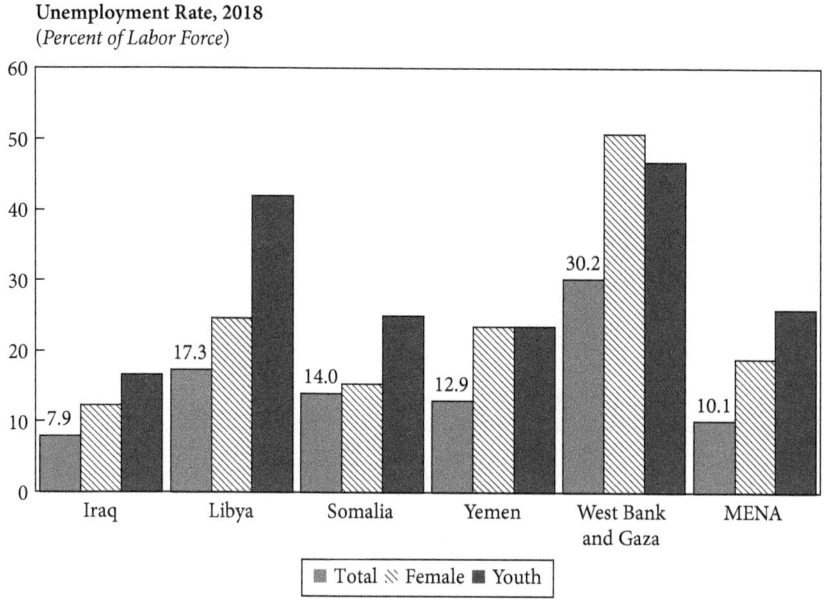

Figure 19.5 Unemployment Rate, 2018 (Percent of labor force)
Source: ILO Modelled Estimates, Nov. 2018.

Poverty in conflict countries tends to rise as job opportunities decline. In Iraq, poverty is estimated to have risen to 20 percent in 2018, from 18.9 percent in 2012. According to the World Bank, nearly 8 out of 10 Somalis live in poverty (World Bank, 2018b). Before the conflict started in 2014, Yemen was already one of the poorest countries in the Arab region, with 34 percent of the population living below the poverty line; by 2016 this had risen to 62 percent (World Bank, 2016). From 2010 to 2017 the poverty rate in the West Bank fell from 18.3 percent to 13.9 percent, but in Gaza it increased from 38 percent to 53 percent.[18]

Conflict-affected and fragile countries tend to have low tax revenues, because of the lack of security, breakdown in the rule of law, and inability to collect taxes (Figure 19.6).

In Libya non-oil taxes have always been minimal, but these fell even further during the conflict.[19] Somalia's conflict has until recently prevented the government from making significant efforts to raise revenues. Customs revenues at Mogadishu port are the Federal Government's main revenue source, while tax collection from large and medium-sized tax payers has only started recently. Total

[18] Palestinian Central Bureau of Statistics.

[19] Libya's non-oil revenues are not taxes proper but Central Bank or telecom profits, or token proceeds from sales of subsidized fuel. This shows Libya's incapacity and inability to levy taxes, and how it lacks one of the defining characteristics of a state.

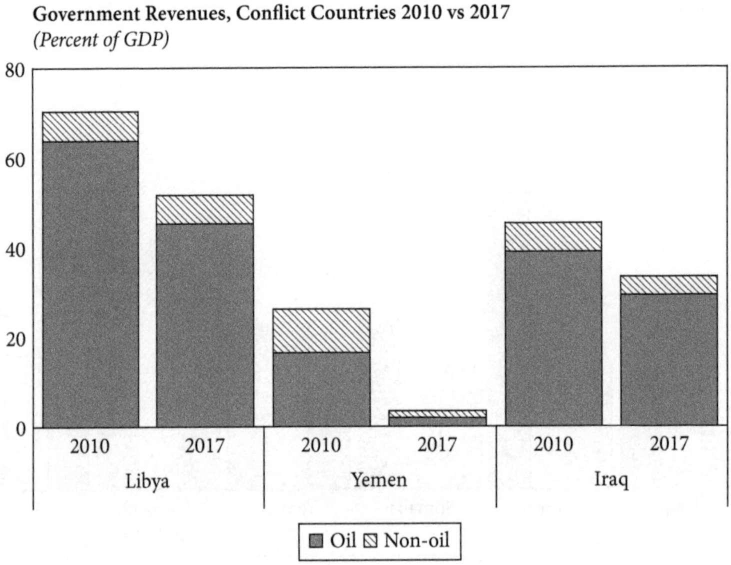

Figure 19.6 Government Revenues, Conflict Countries 2010 versus 2017
(Percent of GDP)
Source: National Authorities; and IMF Staff Estimates.

grants and revenues are only 3.5 percent of GDP, and 40 percent of this comes from foreign grants.[20] In Yemen, conflict caused non-oil revenues to fall from US $4.2 billion in 2014 (about 10 percent of GDP) to about US$0.6 billion in 2018 (less than 2 percent of GDP).

Conflict and fragility put pressure on government spending, either military spending for the conflict, to keep popular support or to substitute for the lack of private sector activity. Wage bills have increased in most countries (Figure 19.7, Figure 19.8).

Libya's government wage bill doubled from 2010 to 2013 because of salary increases to win support for the 2011 revolution, and the (self-defeating) decision to put militias on the government payroll (but without being able to subject them to effective control).[21] Almost 30 percent of Libya's population receives a government salary, but in practice many of these positions are fictitious. Yemen increased public sector salaries in government-controlled areas to compensate for high inflation but has broadly suspended wage payments in rebel-controlled areas.[22]

[20] Total revenues are primarily for Mogadishu only, while GDP is measured for the whole of Somalia. This partly explains the low reported ratios.

[21] Competition between East and West to raise militia salaries has added to budget pressures, and increased wage differentials with other government workers, making militia membership more attractive.

[22] In contrast Libya's government has, for the most part, made wage payments across the whole country, as though it were unified.

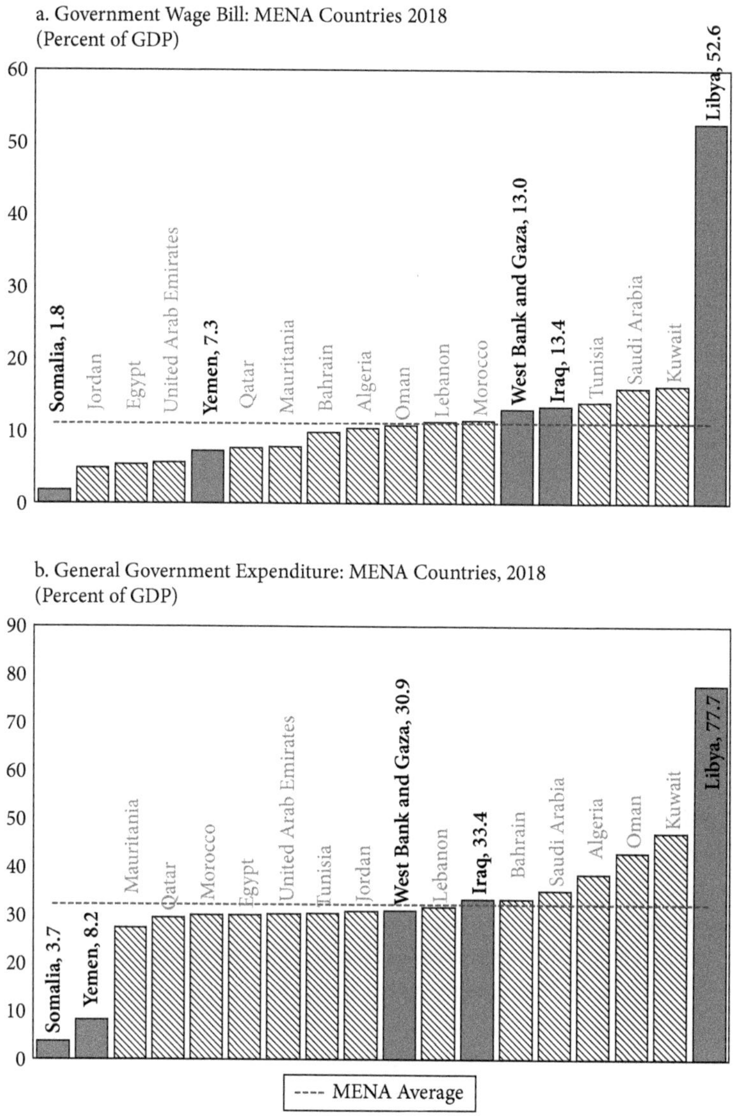

Figure 19.7 Pressure on Government Spending

Panel a. Government Wage Bill: MENA Countries 2018 (Percent of GDP)

Panel b. General Government Expenditures: MENA Countries 2018 (Percent of GDP)

Note: MENA = Middle East and North Africa.

Source: National Authorities; and IMF Staff Estimates.

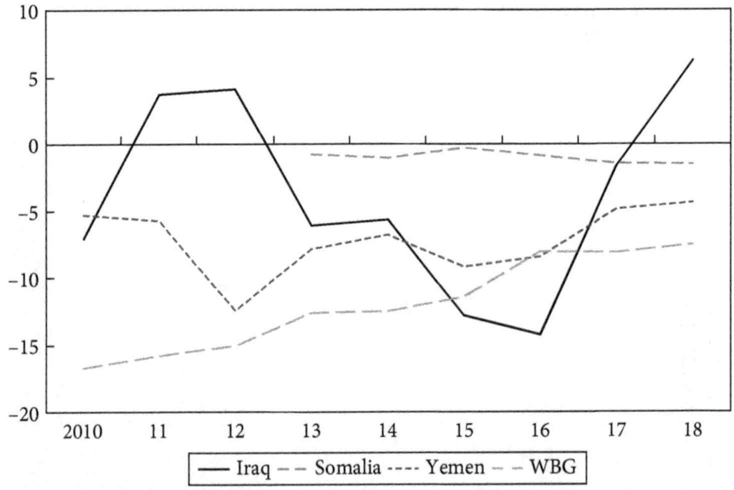

Figure 19.8 Fiscal Balance: Iraq, Somalia, West Bank and Gaza, and Yemen, 2010–18 (Excludes grants; percent of GDP)

Note: WBG = West Bank and Gaza

Source: National Authorities; and IMF Staff Estimates.

The war has also led to higher military spending. In Iraq, the need to finance militia payrolls, provide for internally displaced persons and the families of deceased soldiers, and to raise military spending has increased government spending.[23]

These pressures towards lower revenues and higher spending have increased budget deficits. In the most extreme case, during 2014–16 Libya's budget deficit averaged about 100 percent of GDP (Figure 19.8, Figure 19.9).[24] Yemen's budget deficits have been increasing since 2011, averaging just under 7 percent of GDP, but these would probably have been much higher if financing had been available. In Iraq, current spending has increased steadily, leaving capital spending exposed to oil price volatility and financing constraints, slowing growth and undermining fiscal sustainability.[25]

In the two countries currently in conflict, these large budget deficits resulted in arrears, money financing, high inflation, and balance of payments pressures.[26]

[23] In Somalia, reported spending ratios are low because expenditures are for the Federal Government only, while GDP is for the whole country. Most spending is for payroll (army/security and FGS employees) and goods and services. Social services are primarily grant-funded and routed through the Federal Member States (FMS) directly, not the Federal Government.

[24] These high GDP ratios also reflect denominator effects: the collapse in oil production reduced oil revenues but also GDP.

[25] For example, the 2019 budget envisages a non-oil primary deficit of 56 percent of non-oil GDP, similar to that before the 2014 oil price collapse and related fiscal crisis; the capital budget (expressed as a share of non-oil GDP) is only two-thirds of what it was in 2014.

[26] Reliance on arrears is not exclusively a problem for conflict countries. In West Bank and Gaza arrears have been a constant "financing" source: the data are problematic but these arrears are estimated to exceed 15 percent of GDP.

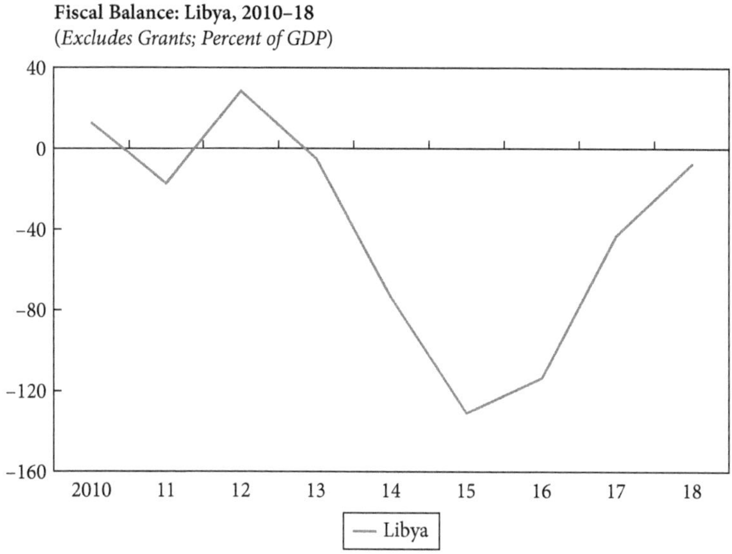

Figure 19.9 Fiscal Balance: Libya, 2010–18 (Excludes grants; percent of GDP)
Source: National Authorities; and IMF Staff Estimates.

Again, Libya's example is the most extreme. At first the central bank financed these budget deficits by printing money. Then in 2016, with reported reserves having fallen from US$110 billion to US$60 billion in three years, the central bank restricted financing of the newly formed Government of National Accord (GNA) (resulting in nationwide wage arrears). Later, responding to international pressure to support the GNA, the central bank quasi-financed the deficits by creating Libyan dinar deposits for the government, but then rationed the supply of banknotes (so that bank reserves and bank deposits could not be converted into cash). In addition, despite having a fixed official exchange rate, the Central Bank also rationed foreign exchange.[27] Although these restrictions protected Libya's international reserves, the parallel exchange rate collapsed, and they created huge and painful cash shortages for the population and new sources of economic rents for militias and elites.

At first Yemen financed its budget deficit by printing money and selling foreign exchange; but with reserves falling quickly to about 1½ months of imports in 2016, the government started to have problems paying pensions and government wages in the whole of the country. In 2018, the government resumed paying salaries in areas it controlled, again by printing money, which led to exchange rate depreciation and price inflation.

[27] Law Number 1 of 2013, passed after the revolution, prevents payment of interest—which would have been a more conventional way to discourage the conversion of bank deposits into cash or foreign exchange.

In Iraq, movements in international reserves also paralleled the government's fiscal activities. After oil prices collapsed in 2014, the government relied on central bank financing of its growing budget deficit. But reserves fell from US$66 billion in 2014 to US$45 billion at end-2016, and the authorities requested an IMF program to stem the decline in reserves.[28]

3.3 Spillovers

In addition to having severe domestic economic consequences, conflicts also create spillovers for neighboring countries. These include the direct economic impact (including on output, inflation, employment, and trade) as well as terrorism, trafficking, and migration. In some cases, spillovers also generate inflationary pressures, partly reflecting additional demand from the large refugee population and a limited short-term supply response.

Somalia's descent towards failed state status led to massive outflows of refugees to neighboring Kenya and Ethiopia, creating some of the largest refugee camps in the world. In addition, Al-Shabaab groups in Somalia have launched terrorist attacks in Kenya, in retaliation for Kenya's participation in the African Union forces that are fighting Al-Shabaab in Somalia. Somalian piracy, again a consequence of state failure, has led to outside intervention to protect international trade. Libya's economic collapse caused exports from both Egypt and Tunisia to more than halve, cutting economic growth. Remittances from migrant workers in Libya also collapsed.

Conflict has resulted in increasing numbers of refugees, which directly spill over into other countries (Figure 19.10). Worldwide the number of refugees has quadrupled since 1980, from about 4 million to 16 million in 2018. More than half of these are from the Middle East and North Africa. The majority of those who have fled the violence are much worse off than before their displacement, often having brought few possessions with them and finding themselves in extreme dependency. In addition, the refugee surge can have a significant economic impact on host communities. Evidence from Lebanon suggests that sizable informal employment among refugees, combined with depressed economic activity, caused a drop in both wage levels and the labor force participation of locals, particularly women and young people.

[28] The subsequent recovery in oil prices allowed reserves to recover to US$62 billion (end-2018).

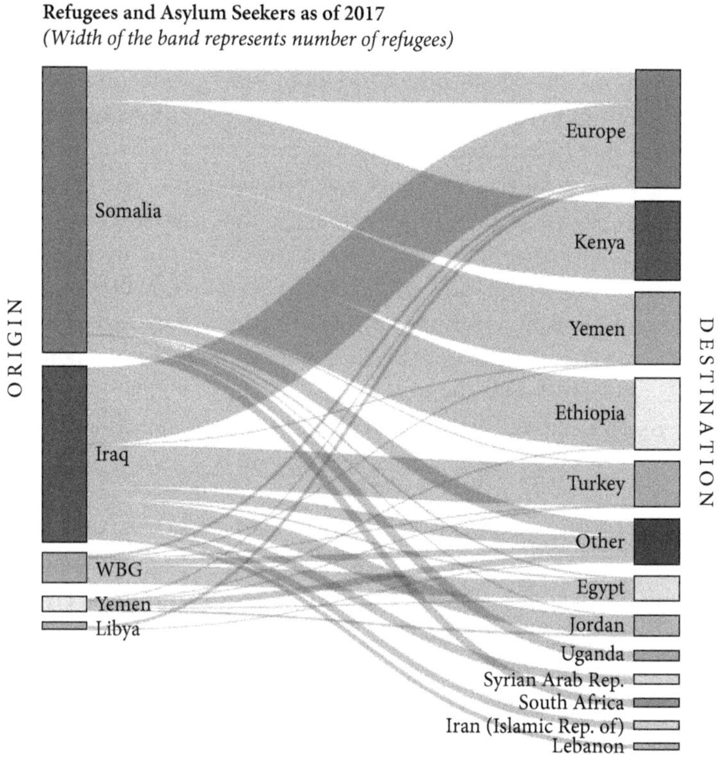

Figure 19.10 Refugees and Asylum Seekers as of 2017 (Width of the band represents number of refugees)

Note: The definition of refugees differs between sources.

Source: United Nations High Commission for Refugees (UNHCR).

4. Addressing Macroeconomic Policy Challenges in Conflict and Fragile Countries: The Role of the IMF

The experience of these five countries makes clear that the nature and consequences of fragility differ considerably. Accordingly, and although some problems are shared, macroeconomic policy advice needs to be country specific, and this is the approach followed by the IMF. For each of its members, fragile and non-fragile alike, the IMF works with country authorities to develop a macroeconomic framework, which provides the basis for the its policy advice. It also provides capacity development to preserve and restore economic institutions. And in post-conflict countries, the IMF has provided financial support, and its endorsement of a sound macroeconomic framework helps to catalyze international assistance. Within this framework, the IMF adopts a tailored approach to respond to country-specific policy challenges, which are different in conflict and post-conflict countries.

4.1 Countries in Conflict

For countries in conflict, getting the basics right—things often taken for granted in conventional economies—is essential.[29] For the countries in conflict considered in this chapter, this includes: (i) improving monetary and exchange rate policies, including removing exchange rate misalignments and freeing up the availability of foreign exchange; (ii) prioritizing public spending and limiting the rise in fiscal deficits to support the exchange rate adjustment and forestall an inflation-devaluation spiral; and (iii) rebuilding (and sometimes re-unifying) economic institutions and promoting greater transparency and accountability (Box 19.1). Even if conflict prevents their implementation, having policy recommendations and a revised strategy ready for when the conflict is over (or what the Commission on State Fragility refers to as a "pivotal moment" is reached) is essential.

Box 19.1 Challenges of Macroeconomic Policymaking Under Conflict—The Case of Libya

Macroeconomic challenges

Oil dominates Libya's economy. Oil and gas revenues make up 80 percent of Libya's GDP, and more than 95 percent of its exports and government revenues. Aside from the recent conflict, many of Libya's macroeconomic problems stem from the dominance of oil, the volatility of oil revenues, and the role of rents from oil revenues in stimulating and perpetuating Libya's conflict.

In 2012, immediately following Colonel Gadhafi's overthrow, Libyan oil production averaged 1.4 million barrels per day, close to previous levels. Oil prices averaged more than US$110 per barrel, oil revenues exceeded US$50 billion, for a population of just over 6 million. Seeking to win popular support, the new government raised salaries, so that by 2013 the wage bill had more than doubled compared to 2010, with victorious militia members now financed from the government payroll.

The revolution was followed by a power struggle among militias. Economic conditions continued to worsen. Militias damaged oil facilities and sought cash for restoring the flow of oil. Oil production fell to only 400,000 barrels a day in 2015 and 2016—a drop of almost three-quarters. On top of this, world oil

[29] IMF (2016a) has a broader discussion for the Middle East and North Africa.

prices halved, falling to less than US$50 per barrel in 2016. Libya's oil revenues collapsed, falling from more than US$50 billion in 2012 to US$5 billion in 2016. Despite large cuts in investment, wage spending remained largely intact, and the budget shifted from a surplus of about US$12 billion in 2012 to deficits of US$20 billion each year between 2014 and 2016 (or roughly 100 percent of GDP, although these high ratios in part reflect the collapse in GDP).

These massive budget deficits created huge monetary problems. At first, the government financed these deficits by withdrawing its central bank deposits, and the central bank offset the monetary impact by selling international reserves, which fell from US$110 billion at end-2013 to US$70 billion at end 2015—an unsustainable path.

Starting in 2016, the central bank took unorthodox steps to protect its reserves. First, despite the fixed exchange rate regime, it restricted sales of foreign exchange. As a result, reserves fell by only US$10 billion in 2016, and in 2017 even stabilized despite the conflict. But the parallel market exchange rate depreciated to around LD 8.5 to the US dollar, well below the LD 1.4 official rate. Second, in part to stem pressure on the exchange rate, the central bank restricted the supply of banknotes, making bank deposit withdrawals difficult, causing widespread cash shortages (which interrupted the functioning of the economy) and long lines outside banks. Both restrictions created new economic rents for the political elites and militias able to access either the foreign exchange or the restricted bank notes.

IMF policy advice

For Libya, the policy advice of IMF staff has focused on policies to reduce these huge macroeconomic imbalances, while being mindful of the way proposed reforms might affect (and also be stymied by) the conflict. This choice was made not because there were no other needs, but simply because policy improvements in the Fund's core areas—balance of payments and macroeconomic adjustment—could generate huge economic benefits (much greater than the benefits of improved economic policy in typical economies) and possibly contribute to a future peace settlement.

First, IMF staff have recommended many improvements to monetary and exchange rate policy. These include devaluing the official exchange rate and making foreign exchange readily available for current transactions, so as to align the parallel and official rates. Although the authorities' tax on foreign exchange purchases, introduced in September 2018, has freed up the supply of foreign exchange, it perpetuates the multiple exchange rate system, distorts the economy, and has created a new and off-budget source of funds for the central bank (which seems to control the revenues). The tax should be replaced by a straight devaluation. Devaluation would boost revenues from oil exports and

Continued

Box 19.1 *Continued*

would eliminate the rents accruing to privileged foreign exchange access. It would also encourage development of a nascent export sector, encouraging diversification away from oil and gas.

The central bank should increase the supply of banknotes to meet depositors' demands for withdrawals. During the transition to full convertibility, limits on conversions into cash could be considered, on a temporary basis, if implemented nationwide and uniformly. The accompanying policy of devaluation would also help reduce cash shortages by making foreign currency more expensive and so reducing the demand for foreign currency and increasing the demand for Libyan dinar deposits. Finally, and of fundamental importance, the central bank in the East should stop issuing its own currency; both sides need to agree on a unified monetary policy.

Second, exchange rate adjustment should be supported by fiscal consolidation. Examples include phasing out fuel subsidies (which have an annual fiscal cost of US$4–5 billion or around 10 percent of GDP) and replacing them with cash transfers. The price of petrol in Libya is fixed at around US$0.03 per liter, well below prices of around US$0.70 in neighboring Tunisia and more than US $1.50 in Malta and Italy. The sheer size of this spread encourages smuggling and illegal activity in Libya and its neighbors. This (together with its huge fiscal cost) argues for a substantial up-front price increase rather than the usual policy recommendation of gradualism, although price increases would need to be accompanied by compensation. Second, Libya's wage bill needs to be reduced. Out of a population of 6.5 million, there are approximately 1.8 million government employees (300,000 of these are reported to work for the Ministry of Interior alone, many of them militia members, whose numbers have dramatically increased since the revolution), or more than one quarter of the whole population. The number of employees needs to be reduced, but with substantial compensation provided for those who lose their jobs, either in the form of a basic income for all, or the introduction of unemployment benefit. Savings should be used to improve security, health, education, other services, and to restore power and water supply.

Third, macroeconomic adjustment should be accompanied by reforms that make policymaking—and how Libya's oil revenues and foreign exchange are shared—more transparent. The government should have its budget debated and passed by parliament (the House of Representatives). If this is not possible (because the House of Representatives is based in the East), then the government should at least publish a detailed budget, and its implementation during the year, to ensure transparency in revenue collection and government spending. If foreign exchange rationing continues, then, to reduce abuses, the central bank and the government should publish a list of all those who apply for Letters of Credit (to access foreign exchange at preferential rates), the amounts, and how much they receive. The integrity, transparency, and accountability of Libya's key national economic institutions need to be restored. The various branches of the Central Bank, the National Oil Corporation, and the Libyan Investment Authority should be unified, and the governance of each institution improved. Regular independent audits should be published. Greater transparency and accountability can improve economic policy. In Libya, such reforms might also promote peace by reducing rents and addressing popular complaints that oil revenues and government spending are not being allocated fairly. (In other countries, reducing rents might be destabilizing by upsetting "elite bargains," but Libya lacks a stable "elite bargain" and the opacity of how oil rents are distributed arguably foments the conflict). A wide range of structural reforms is also needed, but these are probably best left until the conflict is ended and a political settlement reached that generates the will for such reforms.

Challenges of implementation

Although the gains from these kinds of economic reforms are likely to be substantial, the lack of a political settlement (and worse, in 2019, the intensification of the conflict) has prevented reforms from being implemented. The IMF has attempted to reach both sides in the conflict (though mostly to the international recognized government in the West) to promote reform, and to work with Libya's international partners. However, the conflict and the resulting the divergence of interests between the central banks and governments of the West and the East make it difficult to envisage any agreement on policymaking (for example, on an agreed budget deficit, in constraining the spending of each side, or on allocating revenues) until there is a political settlement. And within each government there are powerful and divergent interests (including militias) that stand in the way of reforms such as eliminating fuel subsidies or getting rid of discretionary Letters of Credit. They benefit from the shortage economy and the status quo. Ending salary payments to duplicate or fictitious employees or to militia members (especially now that the conflict has intensified) will be difficult, even if compensation is granted. Likewise, because of the conflict, the two central banks have different interests (including pressure to finance their respective governments), hindering the introduction of a single monetary policy.

Without a political settlement and a strong and committed government, economic reform will not be possible. However, the converse also seems true, that in Libya a political settlement will not be possible or sustained without economic reform and greater transparency. Such circumstances limit what the

Continued

Box 19.1 *Continued*

IMF can achieve, save for sharing its analysis and recommendations with the Libyan authorities and international partners, having these debated and discussed, and for being ready to implement them in case a "pivotal moment" finally arrives.

However, implementing effective economic policies, supported by advice from the IMF and others, has often proven difficult under conditions of conflict or fragility. Implementing unpopular policies (for example, to contain fiscal deficits) is even more challenging in a fragile situation; vested interests can obstruct reforms; policymakers are caught between multiple and often competing objectives; and the fragmentation of government agencies and the presence of multiple and conflicting counterparts hampers policy implementation. Weak institutional capacity limits the depth and breadth of policy discussions, while lack of adequate data hampers the understanding of economic developments and risks.

Given these constraints, the IMF has focused on assessing macroeconomic conditions as input to policymakers and donor agencies. With the country's technical capacity severely weakened by the conflict, the IMF has typically tried to process the limited macroeconomic information available and provide a consistent economic framework. Such a framework can inform policymakers and aid agencies in the design of economic plans for the country, and thus in catalyzing financing which may help address the impact of the conflict. In Yemen, the IMF has designed different macroeconomic scenarios to evaluate the best way to use donor financing to finance essential food imports, to achieve greater economic stability, and to assist urgent humanitarian relief. In Libya, the focus has been on helping the authorities prepare and agree on their annual budgets (including facilitating discussions between rival governments in the country), encouraging greater transparency (to counteract corruption and to promote a fairer allocation of resources), and providing policy advice to address the problems of cash shortages and exchange rate overvaluation. The IMF also works closely with international partners, to inform them of the economic crisis in Libya, in the hope that they too will have the chance to promote better economic policies in Libya.

With limited scope for results in conflict countries, the IMF has often had to focus on a few "quick wins" and to work with a broader set of partners than usual. Achieving sustained macroeconomic stability is difficult during conflict. Instead, IMF policy recommendations are often narrowed to clearly identifiable sets of objectives, defined in coordination with experts from the World Bank, United Nations, aid agencies, and government institutions. In Yemen, in the second half of 2018 IMF policy advice, together with foreign financing and increased central bank issuance of Letters of Credit, helped break the uncontrolled depreciation of the exchange rate, steadied domestic inflation, and increased the availability of essential food imports. In Libya, the IMF and the World Bank have worked together to help country authorities reach agreement on a national budget. Although advice to devalue the exchange rate has been resisted, the authorities have gone halfway towards this goal by introducing a tax on foreign exchange purchases and increasing the availability of foreign exchange.

The IMF has also attempted to preserve economic institutions. Ultimately, in both Libya and Yemen, progress will be difficult until governments and key institutions are unified (which in turn will depend on achieving peace). In the interim, the IMF has worked to preserve these institutions. In Libya, jointly with the World Bank (and before the intensification of the conflict in 2019), the IMF has participated in some of the few technical meetings that bring the finance ministries and economic institutions from the East and West of the country together. Both Libya and Yemen have substantial capacity development needs, but conflict complicates the delivery and absorption of technical assistance (not to mention effectiveness of implementation). In Yemen, IMF technical assistance has helped the central bank assess operational and capacity gaps that have been exacerbated by its relocation from Sana'a to Aden in 2016. The IMF has supported Libya's efforts on anti-money laundering/combating the financing of terrorism (AML-CFT). In both countries, technical assistance would likely need to be expanded considerably if conflict were to end.

4.2 Post-Conflict Countries

Once conflicts subside, one main challenge is how to manage the path back to normalcy. Policy priorities shift to consolidating peace, rebuilding institutions and infrastructure, and creating conditions for sustained economic recovery and growth (IMF, 2015). Economic policy challenges focus on restoring macroeconomic stability, followed by the medium-term objectives of strengthening institutions, and fostering inclusive and sustainable growth.

In Iraq, Somalia, and West Bank and Gaza, the IMF has advised on policies needed for macroeconomic stabilization, given the need to build fiscal and external reserves to protect against shocks (to which post-conflict and fragile countries are particularly susceptible). This is particularly important, given the difficulties for post-conflict or fragile states in securing domestic or external finance. In addition, developing and maintaining credible macroeconomic frameworks can help ease the financing constraint: it enables external donors to step in and provide financial assistance.

The IMF has supplemented its traditional macroeconomic policy advice with extensive technical assistance:

- The IMF has worked with the authorities to improve the effectiveness of public expenditure, to ensure that essential services are provided, and to mobilize domestic revenue to pay for this spending (especially needed given difficulties financing budget deficits). In West Bank and Gaza, these reforms have aimed to improve the formulation and execution of the budget. In Iraq, the Fund has supported public financial management reforms that strengthen expenditure controls and the budgetary process. Similarly, in Somalia, public financial management reforms have aimed at regaining control of the budget, improving cash and treasury management, and enhancing accounting and fiscal reporting.[30]
- IMF technical assistance has sought to improve central bank governance and financial sector oversight, and to combat money laundering and terrorism financing. The IMF assisted Iraq's central bank in addressing deficiencies in AML/CFT compliance that had been identified by the Financial Action Task Force (FATF), which helped move Iraq off the FATF monitoring list. In Somalia, the IMF has supported the reorganization of the central bank, and has helped strengthen regulatory frameworks to preserve correspondent banking relationships and the availability of foreign exchange. In West Bank and Gaza, the IMF has helped improve the Palestine Monetary Authority's capacity to detect and counter risks (implementing risk-based supervision and international financial reporting standards) and to support AML/CFT reforms.

Although improved policies and capacity building can make a difference, in the case of West Bank and Gaza external constraints also pose a fundamental problem. The Palestinian Authority has limited room to maneuver. It has the authority to adopt measures to address government budget pressures and preserve financial stability, but outside constraints are severe. Fundamentally, West Bank and Gaza's prospects depend on achieving freer movement of labor, goods, and capital.[31] But this in turn depends on the Palestinian Authority, Israel, and international partners reaching a peace settlement, and agreeing on and implementing comprehensive reforms.

[30] The finance ministry now publishes its budget, appropriations, revenue and expenditures, and external debt on its website. The Central Bank also publishes its accounts and is making progress towards implementing International Financial Reporting Standards.

[31] For more details, see the section "Key Policy Themes" and Table IV.3 in the September 2018 report to the Ad Hoc Liaison Committee available at https://www.imf.org/en/Publications/CR/Issues/2018/09/17/west-bank-gaza-report-to-the-ad-hoc-liaison-committee (last accessed July 16, 2020).

The IMF has played an active role in this coordination process. Participation in the biannual meetings of the Ad Hoc Liaison Committee (a key international coordination mechanism to support reforms and donor assistance) has been an important vehicle for IMF policy advice. Through its reports as well as its engagement with the authorities and other stakeholders, the Fund aims to be seen—primarily by West Bank and Gaza, but also by Israel and the international community—as a trusted advisor on economic issues. The IMF aims to contribute to the reforms needed to free up the Palestinian economy.

In the case of Somalia, IMF technical assistance has helped strengthen and rebuild key economic institutions and capacity, starting in 2012 when the Federal Government of Somalia was formed. The Somalia Country Fund (SCF) was established in 2015 to finance intensive IMF capacity development in macroeconomic policies and statistics. The SCF has allowed the IMF to double the number of technical assistance missions to about 22 missions per year. This assistance has focused on rebuilding key economic institutions and developing their capacity, supporting macroeconomic stability, and helping the authorities build a track record of policy and reform implementation (which Somalia needed to reach the Decision Point and achieve debt relief under the Highly Indebted Poor Country initiative, and for increased donor financing). These reforms have been designed to be gradual and aligned closely with Somalia's programs with the Fund.

Unlike most fragile states, neither the IMF's technical assistance nor Somalia's successive IMF-supported programs have had to be interrupted. Many factors contributed to this relative success. Somalia's leadership has been reform-minded, and has bought into the goals of the IMF programs and into the reform programs of the World Bank, the European Union, and other development partners. Early programs focused on quick wins that delivered rapid gains and built traction with the authorities and donors. Reforms on budget preparation and execution provide one example. These were guided by a public financial management strategic roadmap that incorporated development partners' comments and fully funded technical assistance. The authorities saw gains from improved government operations, parliamentarians welcomed the improved transparency, and development partners saw better grant management.

The complex environment of post-conflict countries makes it difficult for IMF policy advice to gain traction unless the government owns these reforms. Somalia's experience is a good example. Similarly, in West Bank and Gaza, IMF assistance in creating a credit registry to expand access to finance proved particularly successful because of the strong ownership and commitment of the Palestine Monetary Authority. Today, the Palestine Monetary Authority has an automated, online 24/7 credit registry system that is among the best credit registries in the Middle East and North Africa region.

However, achieving such ownership is often difficult in post-conflict countries. The difficulty reflects the many parties involved during the reconstruction phase, their competing interests, and the changing balance of power over policy decisions. Weak governance and possible corruption that are often associated with post-conflict situations are also factors in decision making. Understanding how to navigate through this political economy is critical to gaining traction. But even with such navigation, results may be difficult to obtain when working with governments whose interests are myopic and faction-centered.

In practice, it has often been easier to rebuild institutions that are less political or more independent. These include statistics offices and central banks (or some parts of these institutions), where the work is more technical. Because turnover tends to be high, the focus needs to be on reforms that are easy to pass on to successor staff, including developing easily accessible manuals for local staff. In contrast, success in PFM reforms may prove more elusive because the government may have an interest in less transparency, and so resist the goals of public financial management.

Even when governments are willing, weak institutions and capacity constraints can make it difficult for reforms to be absorbed. In Iraq, at least 50,000 civil servants are estimated to have been purged following the 2003 Iraq War, in addition to those who were killed or fled the country. It is not easy to rebuild institutions in such circumstances. Appointment of long-term resident advisers can help rebuild institutions, but limits on IMF staff travel to countries lacking security may prevent this. In response, the IMF has created regional technical assistance centers, where experts can help countries implement reforms through a mix of technical assistance and hands-on training.

The IMF also tries to foster donor coordination, to prevent duplication and avoid placing excessive demands on country authorities. In Somalia, the IMF programs' use of roadmaps helped catalyze such coordination and give it structure. However, the donor community needs to recognize that results will take time and will likely be interrupted by setbacks. Announcing large amounts of assistance, and then withdrawing it when results take time to materialize is counterproductive. Large but temporary financial assistance can breed corruption and overheat economies. Thus, donors too need to take ownership of their assistance and to be ready for a long-term commitment.

5. Conclusion

The experience of each of the five countries discussed in this chapter shows how conflict leads to economic fragility, and that conflict can also reveal hidden fragilities in states which before might have appeared stable.

Macroeconomic consequences of conflict and fragility include the destruction of human and physical capital, output collapse, unemployment, and large fiscal and external imbalances. These five case studies show that the costs of conflict and fragility—both humanitarian and economic—are likely to be large and long-lasting. In conflict countries especially, macroeconomic imbalances are likely to be extreme, resulting in loss of international reserves, depreciation, and inflation. Disruption of everyday life (physical threats; uncertain access to food, healthcare, water, fuel, power, and money; lack of property rights) and the types of radical uncertainty faced by people living in fragile states discourage investment and complicate daily economic activity. Aside from capacity constraints, economic policymaking is complicated by the inability to make plans, as well as the presence of policymakers with competing objectives, either within the same government or between rival governments. Although these characteristics and constraints need to be considered when giving policy advice, they do not typically feature in conventional macroeconomic models.

For the IMF, providing policy advice in such circumstances is especially challenging. In conflict countries, implementation of policy advice is weak, either because capacity is lacking, the demands of conflict are more pressing, or because elites benefit from the rents afforded by conflict and thus have little interest in reform. However, the corollary of this is that the sizes of the imbalances and distortions under conflict are such that the benefits from improved macroeconomic policies are likely to be considerable. And if implementation is not possible at present, then the Fund needs to be ready with policy advice in case a "pivotal moment" is reached that is conducive to reform.

Improved policies are likely to be difficult to implement unless the conflict is resolved. But economic disputes (including over the allocation of rents) may also prolong the conflict. Thus, resolution of the conflict will likely depend on reaching a satisfactory bargain over these rents among the competing elites. Greater transparency can contribute to this, both by informing any bargain and, by monitoring its implementation, helping make sure that any bargain is sustained. Any political resolution that does not address economic concerns risks being short-lived. Political and economic reform need to work together.

In post-conflict countries, there are greater prospects that the IMF's policy advice might be implemented. However, the IMF can only succeed if its macroeconomic framework is credible and makes a convincing analysis and diagnosis of the country's economic problems, one that is mindful of the constraints that policymakers face (which will likely be much harsher than elsewhere). The IMF can complement its advisory role by working with other donors to provide (and help coordinate) capacity building, as in Iraq, Somalia, and West Bank and Gaza. Such capacity building is essential for strengthening economic institutions or, in the case of Somalia, in helping create them from scratch. However, such efforts will only succeed if the government genuinely wants and is able to absorb such capacity—strong ownership and political buy-in are essential. At the same time, recovery and reconstruction is likely to be slow and sometimes subject to delay or reversal. This means that the international community needs to be patient and prepared for long-term engagement with these countries, because dealing with fragility requires decades of work.

The many differences between each of the five case studies discussed in this chapter, whether in terms of the nature of their fragility or in the economic challenges they face, is consistent with the view that fragility is best seen as a syndrome. Each country is fragile in its own way; yet some patterns are shared, not least that economic conditions and policymaking challenges are more extreme than those faced in more conventional economies. But the depths of these challenges also mean that the benefits from economic stabilization and reform in fragile and conflict states will likely far exceed gains from reforms in more stable economies. Neighboring countries will also benefit. Thus, despite the apparent intractability of the economic problems facing fragile and conflict states, understanding them better and trying to solve them is imperative. There is no alternative.

References

Al-Qarawee, H.H. 2014. "Iraq's Sectarian Crisis: A Legacy of Exclusion," Carnegie Endowment for International Peace.

Barrett, P. 2018. "Conflict in the Middle East and Central Asia: Costs and Economic Policy Priorities," Box 1.1 of IMF (2018b).

Besley, T. and T. Persson. 2013. "Taxation and Development," in A.J. Auerbach, R. Chetty, M. Feldstein, and E. Saez (Eds.), *Handbook of Public Economics*, Elsevier.

Collier, P. and A. Venables. 2009. "Natural Resources and State Fragility," OxCarre Working Papers 031, Oxford Centre for the Analysis of Resource Rich Economies, University of Oxford.

Collier, P. 1999. "On the Economic Consequences of Civil War." *Oxford Economic Papers*, 51(4): 168–83.

Eaton, T. 2018. "Libya's War Economy: Predation, Profiteering and State Weakness." Chatham House.

Gaston, E. and A. Derzsi-Horvath. 2017. "Iraq after ISIL: An Analysis of Local, Hybrid, and Sub-State Security Forces," Global Public Policy Institute.

Gazzini, C. 2015. "The Prize: Fighting for Libya's Energy Wealth," International Crisis Group.

Global Financial Integrity. 2012. Illicit Financial Flows from Developing Countries: 2001–2010.

International Monetary Fund (IMF). 2015. IMF Engagement with Countries in Post-Conflict and Fragile Situations—Stocktaking.

International Monetary Fund (IMF). 2016a. The Economic Impact of Conflicts and the Refugee Crisis in the Middle East and North Africa.

International Monetary Fund (IMF). 2016b. "West Bank and Gaza, Report to the Ad Hoc Liaison Committee" (September 2016).

International Monetary Fund (IMF). 2018a. "West Bank and Gaza, Report to the Ad Hoc Liaison Committee" (March 2018).

International Monetary Fund (IMF). 2018b. "West Bank and Gaza, Report to the Ad Hoc Liaison Committee" (September 2018).

International Monetary Fund (IMF). 2018c. "Regional Economic Outlook: Middle East and Central Asia."

Lacher, W. and A. al-Idrissi. 2018. "Capital of Militias: Tripoli's Armed Groups Capture the Libyan State," SANA Briefing Paper, Small Arms Survey, June 2018.

Menkhaus, K. 2018. "Somalia Case Study," in Cheng et al. (2018).

Special Inspector General for Iraq Reconstruction (SIGIR). 2013. Final Report—March 2013

United Nations High Commission for Refugees (UNHCR). 2015. Report on the Protection of Civilians in Armed Conflict in Iraq: 11 September–10 December 2014.

United Nations High Commission for Refugees (UNHCR). 2017. "Global Trends: Forced Displacement in 2017."

United Nations Iraq. 2016. "Report on Human Rights in Iraq: July to December 2016"

United Nations Office for the Coordination of Humanitarian Affairs (UNOCHA). 2019a. "Iraq: Humanitarian Needs Overview."

United Nations Office for the Coordination of Humanitarian Affairs (UNOCHA). 2019b. "Libya: Humanitarian Needs Overview."

United Nations Office for the Coordination of Humanitarian Affairs (UNOCHA). 2019c. "Yemen: Humanitarian Needs Overview."

United Nations Population Fund (UNFPA). 2018. "The Libyan Youth Today: Opportunities and Challenges.

United Nations Relief and Works Agency for Palestine Refugees in the Near East (UNRWA). 2017. "Gaza Situation Report 200." https://www.unrwa.org/newsroom/emergency-reports/gaza-situation-report-200 (last accessed July 16, 2020).

World Bank. 2016. Yemen—Country Engagement Note (June 2016).

World Bank. 2018a. "Somalia - Country Partnership Framework for the Period FY19–FY22."

World Bank. 2018b. "Somali Poverty and Vulnerability Assessment."

20

Exiting Fragility

The Experience of Five Sub-Saharan African Countries

Enrique Gelbard, Giorgia Albertin, Lars Engstrom, Jose Gijon, and Clara Mira

1. Introduction

Countries that are considered fragile are characterized by significant limitations in various dimensions, which often lead to instability, underdevelopment, and heightened risks. Their governments often lack legitimacy; a fractious political and social setting heightens security risks; corruption leads to diversion of resources; and government structures lack capacity. These constraints impede the mobilization of resources and the implementation of reforms. More specifically, some or all of the following constraints can play a role:

- Institutions are underdeveloped or impaired in their ability to provide a stable environment, and the rule of law and enforcement of property rights are weak amid corruption and an ineffective judicial system.
- Controls on executive power are ineffective, and the legislative branch of government, the press, or civil society struggle to hold the government accountable.
- Economic and social policies tend to be short-sighted and/or misguided, influenced by lack of a development vision, and by political convenience and corruption.
- Education, health, and social security systems are poorly organized, underfinanced, and unevenly accessible.

The views expressed in this chapter are those of the authors and do not necessarily represent the views of the IMF, its Executive Board, or IMF management. We thank David Robinson and country teams in the African Department for their comments and suggestions. Cleary Haines provided valuable research assistance. We also thank Cristina Carraro Piacentini and Charlotte Vazquez for superb administrative support.

Enrique Gelbard, Giorgia Albertin, Lars Engstrom, Jose Gijon, and Clara Mira, *Exiting Fragility: The Experience of Five Sub-Saharan African Countries* In: *Macroeconomic Policy in Fragile States*. Edited by: Ralph Chami, Raphael Espinoza, and Peter Montiel, Oxford University Press (2021).
DOI: 10.1093/oso/9780198853091.003.0020

- Ethnic, linguistic, or religious divides may undermine the development of a national conscience and awareness of shared interests.
- In a post-conflict or near-conflict environment, there might be violence and extortion.

Given these characteristics and the interactions among them, countries tend to be caught in a "fragility trap," a self-reinforcing equilibrium characterized by underdevelopment, political instability or conflict, and ineffective state capacity (Figure 20.1).[1]

A transition out of fragility is thus complex and lengthy because the country has to move from near state failure and/or conflict to implement coherent policies and improve governance and institutions and, eventually, to a state of relative resilience, along a path beset by challenges and risks of reversals.

At present, there are about 20 countries in these situations in Sub-Saharan Africa.[2] Fragile countries in sub-Saharan Africa have a (weighted) average per

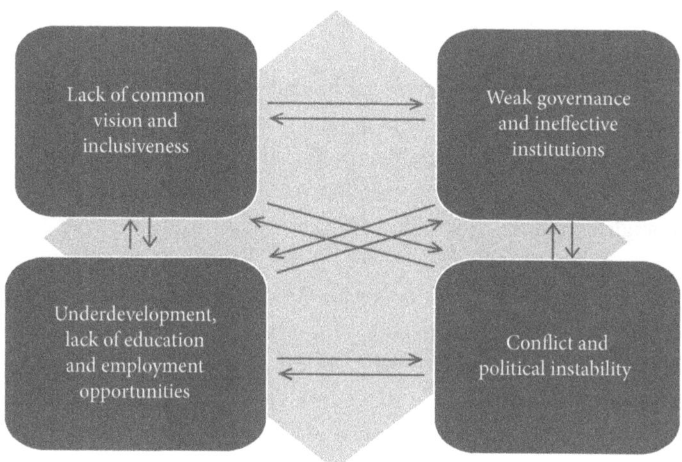

Figure 20.1 The "Fragility Trap"

[1] In the three decades before 2019, the annual per capita GDP growth of all fragile countries was merely 0.6 percent, significantly less than the rate of growth of nonfragile countries (1.7 percent) and their debt-to-GDP ratio was, on average, three times as large compared to nonfragile countries.

[2] For analytical purposes, the classification used is a modified version of the one used by the World Bank. Countries are deemed to be in a fragile situation if the three-year average of their Country Policy and Institutional Assessment rating is less than 3.2 or if they are hosting a UN/regional peace-keeping or peace-building mission. In Sub-Saharan Africa, these are Burundi, Central African Republic, Chad, Comoros, Democratic Republic of Congo, Republic of Congo, Côte d'Ivoire, Eritrea, Gambia, Guinea, Guinea-Bissau, Liberia, Madagascar, Malawi, Mali, São Tomé and Príncipe, Sierra Leone, South Sudan, Togo, and Zimbabwe. Other organizations that compile lists of countries said to be fragile have many more Sub-Saharan African countries in this situation (for example, OECD, 2019; Fund for Peace, 2019).

capita income of about $800, one-fifth of the regional average, and their per capita income rose by 16 percent during the past two decades, compared to a 55 percent increase for nonfragile low-income countries.

2. Case Studies

The underlying causes of fragility are shaped by political and economic conditions as well as by the history of societies, a combination unique for each country; there cannot be a single road to resilience. This chapter therefore takes a more granular approach by examining country experiences that could shed further light on the factors linked to building resilience. It focuses on five countries: the Central African Republic, Côte d'Ivoire, Guinea, Rwanda, and Uganda, to draw insights about the constraints they faced in building resilience, their degree of success thus far, and the possible pathways forward. Rwanda and Uganda are more advanced in this regard; Côte d'Ivoire has made important progress in the 2010s; Guinea and the Central African Republic are showing positive signs in some respects in the past few years; although progress in the Central African Republic remains constrained by the security situation.[3]

We briefly discuss the countries' paths and their periods of highest fragility, analyze what worked and what did not, and consider what can be done to secure more gains and build further resilience. To this end, we compare the historical experience of the five countries after their most recent fragile period across four different angles, to identify commonalities as well as country-specific factors:

1. *Inclusion and checks and balances.* As characterized in Chapter 2, fragile states find themselves outside a narrow corridor (the narrowness of the corridor is related to the political, social, and economic challenges involved in steering fragile states to a zone of resilience) characterized by a virtuous circle where the state and society become stronger, supporting sound policies and instituting checks and balances on executive power. Entering this corridor is quite difficult; it requires, depending on country-specific factors, successful inclusion and a strengthening of the role of society to promote accountability. Successful inclusion requires that the interests of key unrepresented or competing groups be included in the

[3] The countries were chosen to provide a broad spectrum of conditions and progress. Uganda and Rwanda were chosen because they are the countries where most progress has been made since their most fragile periods. Côte d'Ivoire was chosen because of the significant policy reforms applied in the past nine years and their success thus far. Guinea is a country where fragility is still a major issue, though it is not rooted in conflict, and some progress is being made. Lastly, the Central African Republic is one of the most fragile countries in the world, with constant security challenges, a precarious role of the state, and heavily constrained capacity.

development of a vision for the country and in key policy decisions. This is particularly hard to achieve in countries with underlying ethnic tensions, implying heightened risks to peace or sociopolitical stability. Accountability requires some sort of checks and balances on power together with appropriate communication with civil society. In most cases, addressing accountability issues does not mean that the country has to have a well-functioning democracy from the start; this could instead be achieved, for instance, through accords or power-sharing agreements.

2. *Economic stabilization and institutional development.* Economic stabilization refers to the strength and success of macroeconomic (fiscal, monetary, and exchange rate) policies that can correct or prevent serious economic imbalances (that is, financial repression, inflation, and erosion of living standards, exchange rate misalignment, depletion of foreign reserves, and debt distress) and enable economic growth. Institutional development captures the strengthening of economic institutions, which in turn depends on the government's commitment and on technical assistance. These factors are intertwined, because the quality of economic policies and structural reforms and their persistence also depend on the strength of economic institutions.
3. *Fiscal policies and international support.* The quality of fiscal policies can help strengthen the legitimacy of the state, a necessary condition to build resilience. Good fiscal policy, in this context, requires two important elements: resources and appropriate use of the policy space. Fiscal resources stem from effective domestic revenue mobilization (including a level playing field for the private sector), donor support, and debt relief. The effective use of those resources to improve social outcomes and build the public infrastructure is quite a challenge in fragile states; inefficiencies and corruption often thwart such efforts. Consequently, establishing effective Public Financial Management (PFM) systems, which can both control and monitor budget implementation, is critical both to encourage payment of taxes and to encourage donors to channel funds through budgets. Absent such PFM systems, in many countries donors tend to fund social programs directly through civil society organizations and NGOs instead of through government budgets. Although such off-budget spending may be more efficient at the early stages, establishing effective PFM systems is over time is essential in establishing the legitimacy of the state. Lastly, country-specific factors and the effectiveness of public spending should determine the appropriate mix of current and capital expenditure (for example, disarmament and mobilization or other security spending could be critical in some conflict-affected countries while certain types of social spending or public infrastructure could be more appropriate in others).

4. *Private sector.* In the medium to long-term, the role of the private sector is critical to attaining sustained growth, employment creation, and development, particularly as countries begin to emerge from fragility. Private sector investment tends to dry up in the immediate aftermath of a conflict or in a highly unstable political situation. At the same time, the business environment could be stifled by distortive regulations, red tape, lack of access to credit, and an ineffective judicial system. It is only when such risks are more manageable and start to diminish that private sector investment is likely to materialize.

3. Comparative Analysis

The experience of fragile states is varied and country-specific, but the challenges they face could be somewhat similar and lessons may be drawn by looking at these challenges and the paths that countries have followed in an attempt to build resilience. This section aims at identifying these lessons and the countries' degree of success in the years following their most recent fragile periods (even though for some countries such periods have been short) as well as the possible pathways to resilience. The most fragile periods for each country are identified based on the extent of political, economic, and social disruption that they experienced.

Historically, the five countries considered here faced serious instability at least once in the past three decades, with their periods of highest fragility varying from the mid-1980s in Uganda to the early 2010s in the Central African Republic, Côte d'Ivoire, and Guinea (Box 20.1). Their performance in building resilience can be broadly inferred from the Country Policy and Institutional Assessment (CPIA) produced by the World Bank. This index is an aggregate measure of the quality and success of economic policies, reforms, and efforts to strengthen institutions, but it does not capture political and other non-economic factors that are critical for building resilience.[4] Despite its limitations, the index shows that by the mid-2000s, Rwanda and Uganda had made substantial progress, and that since 2011, Côte d'Ivoire has joined them in a zone of relative policy and institutional resilience (Figure 20.2).[5,6] Guinea's CPIA rating deteriorated in the 2000s but gradually

[4] Several authors have used the Country Policy and Institutional Assessment (CPIA) score to define fragility (for example, Bertocchi and Guerzoni, 2010; Chauvet and Collier, 2008). Although there are other indices measuring fragility that use slightly different indicators and aggregation methods, their correlation with the CPIA is above 0.8.

[5] Country Policy and Institutional Assessment (CPIA) data are not available for publication before the mid-2000s, mainly because of methodological changes that makes it very difficult to compare the index across time. Glancing at the pre-2005 CPIA data, however, IMF staff estimate that if the index was computed in the same manner all five countries would have certainly been in a zone of fragility (with a CPIA below 3.2) in the 1980s and early 1990s.

[6] Uganda has experienced a minor decline in its overall Country Policy and Institutional Assessment in the past five years, driven by lower scores on social inclusion and public sector institutions, but overall its relative standing among Sub-Saharan African countries remains strong.

Box 20.1 Identifying the Most Fragile Periods

Central African Republic. The Central African Republic, a resource-rich (mainly diamonds and timber) country, has been mired in repeated spells of political and religious civil conflict—at times driven by desire to control flows from the natural resources—since it gained independence in 1960. Poor governance and very weak institutions have also contributed to a continuous state of fragility. Mostly linked to escalating conflict and/or military coups, the most recent fragile period for the country was 2012–14.

Côte d'Ivoire. Côte d'Ivoire experienced periods of acute political instability driven by different regional groups competing for power and fluctuations in commodity prices; only masked by periods when export prices of commodities were high. The country experienced a collapse of political order in the late 1990s, which degenerated into a civil war in 2002 and an economic recession. The years that followed saw continued instability with occasional conflict which worsened towards the end of the 2000s. The situation improved after 2011 following the creation of a unified army and a new government. For Côte d'Ivoire, the most recent fragile period was 2010–11.

Guinea. Since the mid-1980s, underdevelopment and widespread poverty were exacerbated by decades of autocratic rule, political and social instability, and governance issues. The economic situation worsened in 2008–09 amid a military takeover and sociopolitical upheaval, marking the most fragile period for the country. The political environment improved following the first democratic elections in 2010 and a gradual re-engagement with the international community.

Rwanda. Ethnic divisions in Rwanda are based on tensions between Hutu (85 percent of the population) and Tutsi (15 percent of the population). First the German colonial administration and later the Belgian colonial administration favored the Tutsi minority that was used to enforce colonial rule; ethnic tensions increased. By the late 1980s, following decades of ethnic conflict and violence between the Hutu and the Tutsi, more than half a million people, primarily Tutsi, lived in refugee camps in neighboring countries. The Rwandan Patriotic Front (RPF), founded by the refugees, launched a military offensive against Rwanda's government in 1990. The civil war led to a genocide of up to 1 million people, mainly Tutsi, but also moderate Hutus. It ended when the RPF took control of the capital in 1994. Because of the armed conflict, institutions were closed, the administrative system collapsed, and GDP fell by one-half (IMF, 1999). Though 1993–95 marked the most fragile period for Rwanda, this was not the end of the conflict period; in 1998 Uganda and Rwanda launched an offensive against the Democratic Republic of the Congo in response to security concerns over sanctuary granted to hostile rebel groups responsible for the genocide.

Continued

Box 20.1 *Continued*

Uganda. Uganda experienced recurrent civil strife and external conflicts since the 1970s. Although the civilian government was restored in 1981, an open civil war took place during 1981–85. Shortages of consumer goods and expansionary fiscal and monetary polices led to hyperinflation. Peace and security were restored in late 1986 but living standards fell sharply. The most fragile period for Uganda was 1983–85.

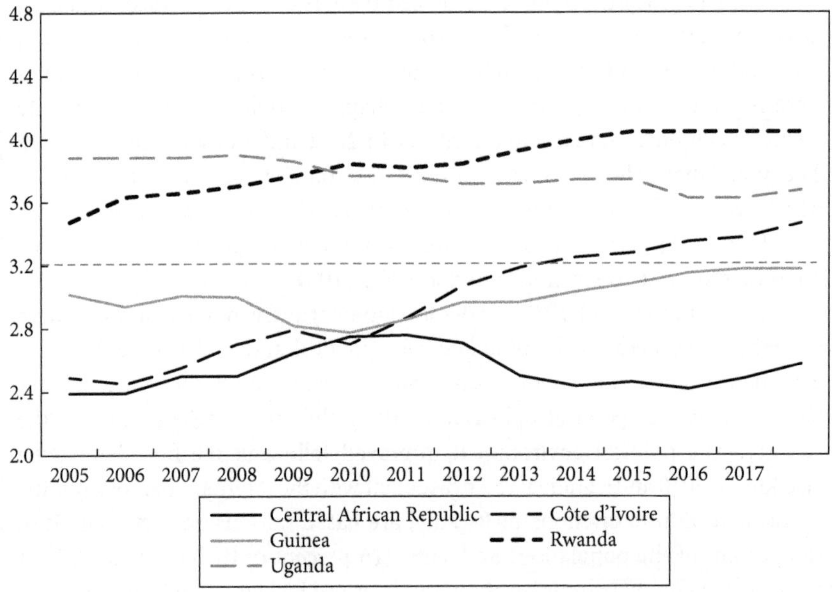

Figure 20.2 Country Policy and Institutional Assessment Index (0–6)
Source: World Bank, World Development Indicators.

improved from 2012 afterwards. Lastly, despite a minor improvement in the 2000s, the Central African Republic has had serious difficulties building resilience.

Figure 20.2 also highlights two important facts: first it takes significant time to improve resilience; and second, that even in those countries that manage to make progress, progress is not smooth or continuous and most countries will experience a period of backsliding or at least a stagnation in progress.

4. Inclusion

This section discusses the experience of the five countries regarding inclusion following their most fragile periods. Rwanda (a resource-poor landlocked country) emerged from conflict in the mid-1990s, and while a single leader (President Kagame) has remained in power since then, an inclusive development path has been pursued that has helped prevent a resurgence of violent conflict.[7]

As in Rwanda, Uganda's political model was based on the strong figure of a leader (President Museveni) who has been in power since 1986 (following decades of political instability and civil strife) and who commands a comfortable majority in the country. The government is credited for the successful implementation of the reform agenda, under a model in which the state plays a critical role driving the process of industrialization and socio-economic transformation. In addition, social fragmentation was addressed by bringing into the ruling party representatives from the main ethnic and religious backgrounds. This process has been broadly successful despite ethnic divisions and instability in neighboring countries (especially South Sudan and the Democratic Republic of the Congo).

In Côte d'Ivoire, conflict and instability were prevalent in the 2000s, with the country controlled primarily by two main groups. Open civil war with possible regional spillovers was averted by the deployment of international peacekeeping forces, which remained in the country until 2017. The winner of the 2010 presidential elections, President Ouattara, took control after a short military campaign against forces supporting former President Gbagbo, reached out to leaders from different political parties, and formed a coalition with a key opposition party that ruled Côte d'Ivoire for almost a decade and ushered in a period of renewed political and economic stability.

Like Côte d'Ivoire, Guinea transitioned to a period of political inclusion following the first democratic elections in the early 2010s. This marked a turning point in the building of democratic institutions and moving towards broad political inclusion. Historically deep political and ethnic differences have resulted in bouts of instability, including a period of violence after the 2013 legislative elections. The situation has improved since then and ethnic tensions have subsided, notably following strides towards broader political inclusion. Nonetheless, risks remain in this area, considering difficult economic conditions and underlying social tensions.[8]

The Central African Republic has had far more difficulty in building resilience. A resource-rich landlocked country, it has been mired in repeated spells of political and civil conflict since it gained independence in 1960, with a long string of coups and civil conflicts. The 2007 peace agreement started a new period of stabilization, but the country fell back into conflict in 2011, erasing much of the

[7] President Kagame has been in power since 1994. He was re-elected President of Rwanda for a third term with 99 percent of the votes in 2017.

[8] Episodes of unrest in the mining region, because of lack of jobs and deficient public services, protests of electricity shortages, and strikes in the public sector, have taken place. Following an increase in fuel prices in 2018, trade union–led strikes and demonstrations took place for several weeks.

progress made. A democratic transition supported by the international community begun in 2015–16 with democratic elections and in 2019 with the signing of a power-sharing agreement between the government and a major rebel group. The reforms envisaged under the peace agreement—such as establishing implementing/monitoring committees—will be critical in the period ahead. Following the ceasefire between the Muslim-rebel coalition and the Christian coalition, prospects begun to improve (albeit slowly) through a demobilization and reintegration process. However, the progress accomplished after the peace agreement remains fragile as some armed groups still have reservations about the process and the recent political arrangements.

In all five countries and in different degrees, there has been a gradual increase in the role of democratic institutions (such as parliaments and the holding of regular elections). However, in many of these countries, systems of checks and balances remain underdeveloped, given the strong power of a presidential figure (partly reflecting traditions and cultural practices), the dominance of leading parties, and the limited roles of civil society and the press. As noted earlier, while this may not be critical at first (and may actually facilitate decision making in the early stages), it becomes more important over time because it helps insure the country against abuses of power and improves policy making.

Lastly, ethnic tensions played a critical role in all countries before and during their most fragile periods, with the process of inclusion in Rwanda, Uganda, and, more recently, in Côte d'Ivoire and Guinea contributing to sociopolitical stability in these countries. The situation in CAR remains quite complicated, as the government only controls 20–25 percent of the country and there are at least 14 active armed groups with different agendas, all of which constitutes a significant challenge to the peace agreement.

Overall, the experience of these countries suggests that political inclusion and determination to pursue sound policies and reforms could be a foundation for peace and building resilience. Absent that, it seems impossible for countries to break the vicious and often recurrent cycle of instability and underdevelopment.

5. Stabilization Policies and Institutions

5.1 Fiscal, Monetary, and Exchange Rate Policies

Economic stability was lost in periods of political instability or conflict in all countries during their most recent fragile periods, leading to higher inflation, loss of foreign reserves and exchange rate pressures, and economic contractions. Stability was at least partially restored within two to four years. Rwanda and Uganda moved quickly to liberalize prices and the exchange rate regime, control monetary growth and the fiscal deficit, and remove other state controls on the economy and

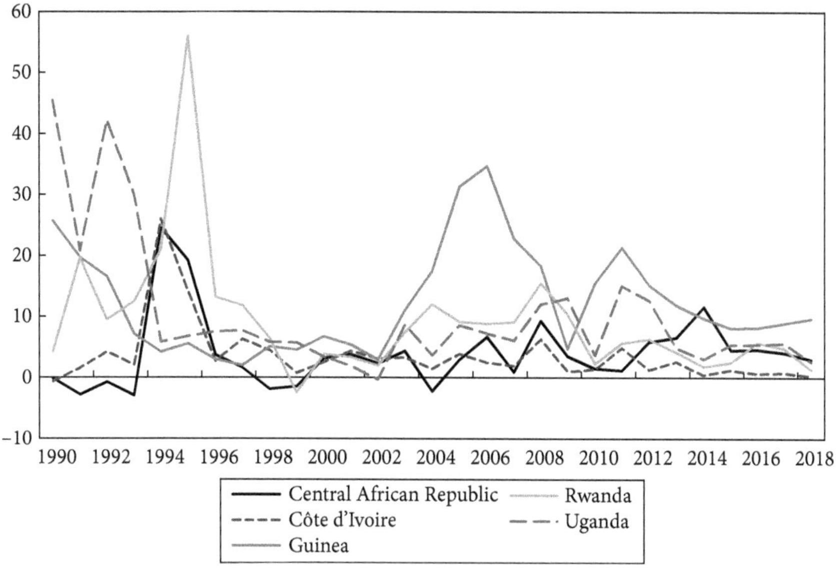

Figure 20.3 Inflation (Percent)
Source: IMF World Economic Outlook Indicators

the financial sector, leading to lower inflation and facilitating a move to a market-based economy. In parallel, economic policy making and capacity were gradually strengthened, setting off a post-conflict rebound with sustained growth accelerations and low inflation in both countries in later years (Figures 20.3 and 20.4).[9]

In Côte d'Ivoire, growth faltered during the 2002–11 political crisis as the result of a decade-long conflict plagued with governance problems and the erosion of key institutions and state functions, including tax collection and public procurement. By the end of the of the conflict in 2011, Côte d'Ivoire's GDP had fallen to 30 percent of the West African Economic and Monetary Union's GDP. Since 2011, the economy has achieved an impressive turnaround, the result of political normalization, a supportive fiscal policy facilitated by Highly Indebted Poor Country debt relief in 2012, business climate reforms, and favorable world cocoa prices.

In Guinea, economic conditions sharply deteriorated during the 2009–10 military regime. After the 2010 elections, the new government started

[9] The return to liberal market systems in Rwanda and Uganda helped not only to restore macroeconomic stability, but also to create policy space. The liberalization of prices resulted initially in an acceleration in inflation, and as market incentives and stabilization policies started to work, inflation abated and real incomes increased. Moreover, the liberalization of the trade regime helped bring in much-needed goods at lower prices. Liberalizing the foreign exchange system also increased policy space and helped bolstering foreign exchange reserves. In contrast, the Central African Republic was not able to create sufficient policy space because fiscal policy could not be adjusted enough, either through revenue mobilization or expenditure reforms, with the recurrence of conflicts making everything more difficult.

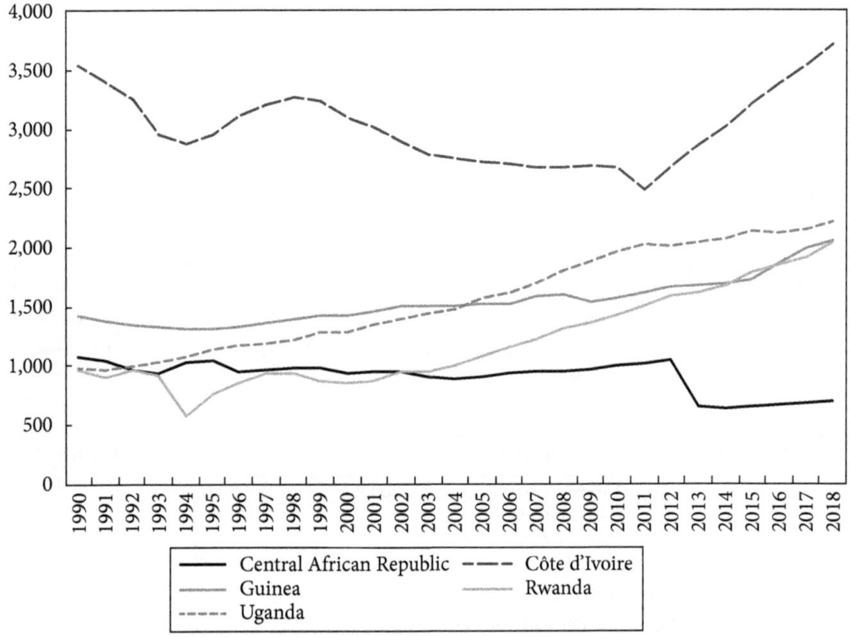

Figure 20.4 Real GDP per Capita (2011 PPP international dollars)
Source: World Bank, World Development Indicators.

implementing sound macroeconomic policies to stabilize the economy. A strong fiscal adjustment significantly reduced the government deficit and its monetization, leading to lower inflation, a more stable exchange rate, and higher official international reserves. Economic growth picked up after the Ebola crisis, reaching about 12 percent during 2016–17.

Lastly, in the Central African Republic, the pervasive risk of conflict, political instability, state ineffectiveness, and a weak environment for the private sector are hallmarks of the challenges the country faced, despite low inflation and exchange rate certainty from membership in the Communauté Financière Africaine (CFA) zone. Notwithstanding these challenges, a reform program has been implemented since 2016 and progress has been achieved in stabilizing the economy, reducing fiscal vulnerabilities while making progress in the implementation of the peace agreement and the strengthening of national security, and improving public financial management. As a result, economic growth is estimated to be about 4–5 percent in 2019.

5.2 Structural Reforms

In both Rwanda and Uganda, a wave of structural reforms was essential to remove distortions, improve the allocation of resources, and raise total factor productivity in the years following their most fragile periods. The main initial reforms comprised restoring competitiveness by liberalizing the exchange rate, removing trade barriers, and eliminating interest rate controls. This was followed by the rationalization of the public service, improvements in budget management and the establishment of revenue authorities, large taxpayers' units, and value-added taxes,[10] as well as the removal of regulations and red tape that impeded the growth of the private sector. Rebuilding PFM systems was particularly important, not only for transparency and accountability, but also for the gradual routing of donor support through national budgets.

Similarly, albeit with different timing compared to Rwanda and Uganda, the Ivorian authorities have pursued an ambitious structural reform agenda since 2011. Building on basic PFM, revenue mobilization, and financial sector reforms instituted in the early 2000s, tax and customs reforms have addressed the efficiency of tax administration and the inclusion of informal activities into the tax base. PFM reforms focused on operationalizing a Treasury Single Account and restructuring public enterprises and public banks, while the business climate was helped by improvements in governance and the removal of red tape (Côte d'Ivoire currently ranks among the top African reformers in the World Bank's Doing Business indicators and the Mo Ibrahim's Governance Index).

1. Guinea has also been moving ahead with a comprehensive package of structural reforms in recent years. The reforms aimed at increasing exchange rate flexibility; improving the anti- corruption framework, the business climate, transparency, and revenue mobilization in the mining sector; setting up a Treasury Single Account; bolstering budget transparency and performance of public enterprises; strengthening the central bank's autonomy and bank supervision; and lowering costs and procedures to establish a business (between 2013 and 2018 the country gained 27 places in the World Bank Doing Business Indicators).
2. The Central African Republic has had a much harder time implementing a structural reform agenda. Financial sector reforms, progress on PFM (computerized tax administration and expenditure management and fiscal revenues) were made at times but derailed often. Some positive signs have however emerged since 2016, with key reforms leading to the strengthening of the treasury single account, better tracking of government spending, streamlining of parafiscal taxes, and improved budget transparency and traceability of fiscal revenue.

[10] Public Expenditure and Financial Accountability (PEFA) Assessments for both countries showed significant improvements since the early 2000s, although some weaknesses remain, notably with respect to the link between annual budgets and the medium-term fiscal framework, lack of performance information on service delivery, and application of accounting standards.

5.3 Capacity

Albeit with different results across countries, efforts at rebuilding economic capacity and institutions focused on three areas: PFM, in particular the budget process and domestic revenue mobilization; and strengthening the central bank and the banking sector. Along with other international financial institutions and bilateral donors, the IMF supported these efforts through technical assistance and training in its core areas of expertise, including through significant increases in technical assistance to Côte d'Ivoire, Guinea, and Uganda in recent years (Figure 20.5).

Most successful among the four countries were Rwanda and Uganda, though they still have some way to go before they fully implement their reform agenda. In both countries, the central bank's effectiveness to run monetary policy has been upgraded significantly, revenue administration reforms were instrumental in achieving a steady increase in government revenue, and budget processes and transparency were improved.

Capacity development was also expanded in Côte d'Ivoire after 2011, leading to important improvements in budget execution and public investment management. In Guinea, technical assistance was provided in key areas, notably to establish a competitive foreign exchange market and foster governance and revenue mobilization, including in the mining sector, and public financial and investment management. The Central African Republic also improved somewhat

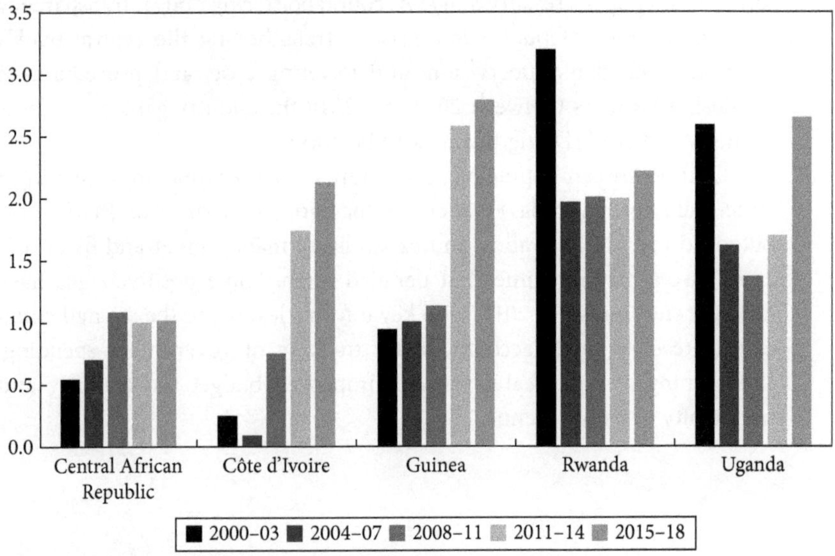

Figure 20.5 Technical Assistance Delivery (Person-years)

Sources: IMF, Travel Information Management System; and staff calculations.

in these areas at first but fell back again with the onset of renewed conflict in the early 2000s and in 2012–14.

5.4 Delivering Public Services

5.4.1 Domestic Revenue Mobilization

Mobilizing additional revenues to create fiscal space for priority spending has been a key objective of most of the countries. In Rwanda, the revenue-to-GDP ratio doubled from 9.1 percent in 1996 to 18.5 percent in 2018. In Uganda, tax revenues rose from 5 percent of GDP in the 1980s to about 15 percent of GDP now, supported by the creation of the Uganda Revenue Authority in 1991 and by substantial changes in the tax system in subsequent years. Despite this progress, Uganda's collection remains below estimates of tax potential and a Medium-Term Domestic Revenue Mobilization Strategy has been prepared to increase revenue.

Tax revenues in Côte d'Ivoire have remained relatively flat at about 17 percent of GDP in recent years, reflecting a depleted tax collection infrastructure and resistance to change (Figure 20.6). Owing to efforts to strengthen tax administration and controls, Guinea's tax revenues rose by about 3 percentage points of GDP in the 2010s, although social tensions in 2017–18 limited revenue mobilization. Lastly, tax revenues in the Central African Republic have remained low, below 10 percent of GDP.

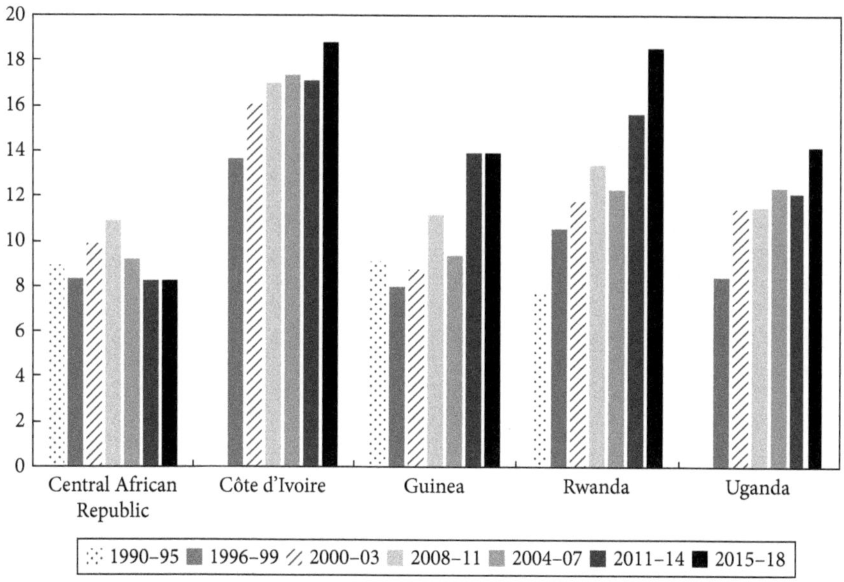

Figure 20.6 Total Revenues Excluding Grants (Percent of GDP)
Source: IMF, World Economic Outlook database.

5.4.2 Donor Support and Debt Relief

Donor support, including debt relief, played an important role, providing fiscal space for priority spending. In the aftermath of their crises, Rwanda and Uganda received sizable financial support from donors. Grants averaged nearly 9 percent of GDP in Rwanda after the mid-1990s, while Uganda approached 7 percent of GDP in the early 1990s and then subsided after 2005 (Figure 20.7). Though fragile countries are not normally able to absorb drastic surges in aid flows, consistently high levels of aid in Rwanda and Uganda seem to have played a positive role in facilitating social and infrastructure investment.

Donor support to Côte d'Ivoire was much smaller as a share of GDP yet still played an important role in post-conflict reconstruction. Similarly, support to Guinea was quite constrained even after it rose in the mid-2010s in response to the Ebola outbreak. In the Central African Republic, donor support increased to about 8 percent of GDP in 2018 and has been important in financing the provision of public services. However, aid levels to the country have fluctuated, reflecting recurrent instability and conflict.

Another important source of support for the five countries was debt relief: all received debt relief under the enhanced Heavily Indebted Poor Countries and the Multilateral Debt Relief Initiatives. Debt relief helped to restore debt sustainability and created additional space to increase budget allocations to poverty-reducing

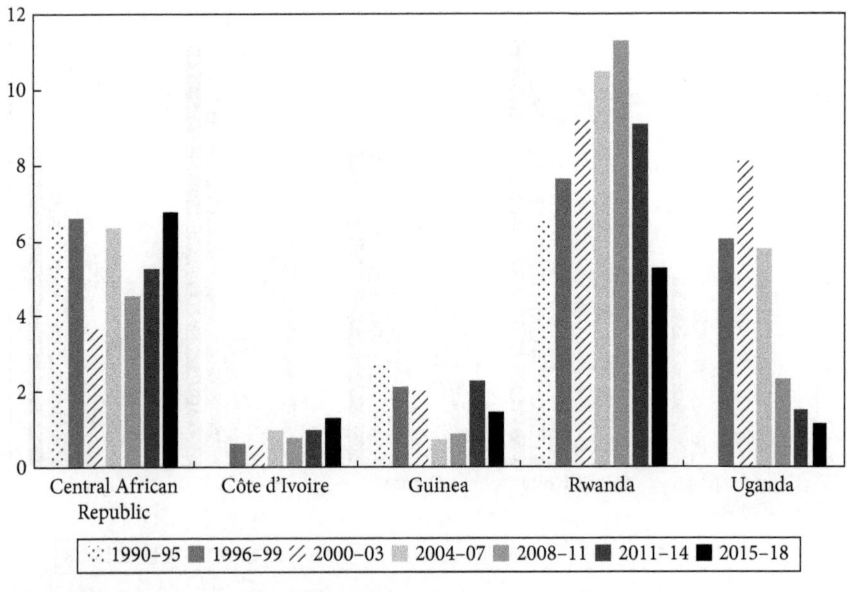

Figure 20.7 Grants (Percent of GDP)

Source: IMF, World Economic Outlook database.

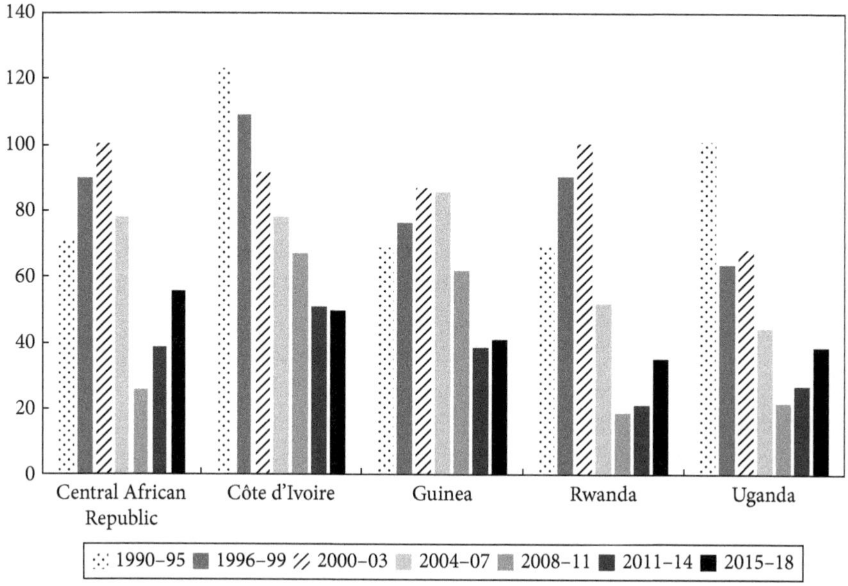

Figure 20.8 Total Public Debt (Percent of GDP)
Source: IMF, World Economic Outlook database.

expenditures (Figure 20.8).[11] In addition, in the wake of the Ebola crisis, the IMF provided further debt relief to Guinea in 2014 to free up resources to increase spending to address the epidemic.

5.4.3 Engagement with the IMF

In all five countries, IMF-supported programs provided financing in support of the authorities' efforts to implement sound macroeconomic policies and reforms to build resilience. The programs played a catalytic role in mobilizing donor support, although such support was in most cases gradual and delivered with a lag. Together with the IMF, the international community has supported countries' efforts to prioritize reforms and generate fiscal policy space aimed at improving living standards and increasing the legitimacy of the state.[12] More recently, in the context of the COVID-19 pandemic, the IMF has provided financial support to all five countries under the Rapid Credit Facility.

Following the genocide in 1994, the IMF was closely engaged with Rwanda, endorsing the authorities' economic strategies through subsequent programs. The

[11] The timing of debt relief was as follows: Uganda (1996), Rwanda (2005), Central African Republic (2009), Côte d'Ivoire (2011), and Guinea (2012).

[12] In recent years, the international community has been re-orienting its engagement in countries in fragile situations by supporting country-led strategies based on good governance and institutional development. New international forums dedicated to supporting fragile states have been established, especially the OECD's International Network for Conflict and Fragility (INCAF).

country was supported through emergency facilities first (1995, 1997), while capacity was being rebuilt to implement programs that included more ambitious structural reforms. Since 1998, the IMF has supported a series of medium-term economic programs with structural adjustment facilities and, more recently, a Policy Support Instrument.

For its part, Uganda also had several programs with the IMF, including successive Poverty Reduction and Growth Facility and, later, Extended Credit Facility programs, and successive Policy Support Instruments. In Côte d'Ivoire, IMF engagement has been substantial since the end of the crisis in 2011 through two subsequent Extended Credit Facilities.

After the end-2010 presidential elections, IMF engagement with Guinea resumed rapidly with a Staff-Monitored Program in 2011 followed by two subsequent three-year Extended Credit Facility programs. The Central African Republic's involvement with the IMF in the past couple of decades has been characterized by several programs and, despite some positive performance (for instance, during the 2006 program) at times, programs were unable to make a significant difference, given the persistent political instability and recurrent conflict. Since 2016, with the help of the international community and IMF-supported programs, the political and the security situation improved, creating a positive environment that helped stabilize the economy and advance some key economic reforms. At the same time, the latest program is taking on board several lessons for IMF engagement with fragile states, notably the paramount importance of peace and reconciliation, the need for parsimony and focus on quick wins, and much less emphasis on private sector reforms that have little chance of success in such a volatile environment (see section 5.9).

5.4.4 Social Spending

Spending on economic, institutional, and human development priorities is a good measure of the government's commitment to development and, more broadly, to building an inclusive society. Though data are scant and of weak quality in most countries, social spending was increased following their most fragile periods to support development priorities, strengthen the provision of social services, and support human capital development.

Rwanda stepped up social spending and allocations to education and health, respectively, by 4.5 percent of GDP and 7.6 percent of GDP during 2000–16. Uganda also increased social spending during the 1990s. Since 2011, Côte d'Ivoire has focused on increasing pro-poor spending and provision of social services, health, and education. In Guinea, poverty-reducing expenditures have gradually increased, though the provision of basic services remains weak and spending in health and education is quite low at about 1 percent of GDP. Expenditure on social safety nets has remained small and mainly donor-financed in Côte d'Ivoire and in Guinea. Similarly, spending in the Central African Republic remained low at about 2 percent of GDP. In the end, however, the main issue is whether the spending and its expansion has been effective (see section 6 below).

5.4.5 Public Investment

Public investment was increased to rebuild and improve basic infrastructure. Both Rwanda and Uganda consistently devoted a large amount of resources to this end, helping to attract private investment and supporting growth in the medium to long term. In Rwanda, public investment averaged 10.5 percent of GDP during 1996–2018, a level well above Africa's average. In Uganda, there was a strong expansion of public investment (to nearly 10 percent of GDP) in the late 1980s with continued relatively high levels thereafter and a further increase after 2014 (Figure 20.9).

In the aftermath of the 2010 crisis in Côte d'Ivoire, the authorities appropriately focused on rebuilding the social and physical infrastructure. Similarly, since 2011, public spending in Guinea has re-oriented towards increasing infrastructure investment. Public investment reached about 6 percent of GDP in 2018. In the Central African Republic, however, public investment remained subdued at 5 percent of GDP. Also, in all countries except the Central African Republic,

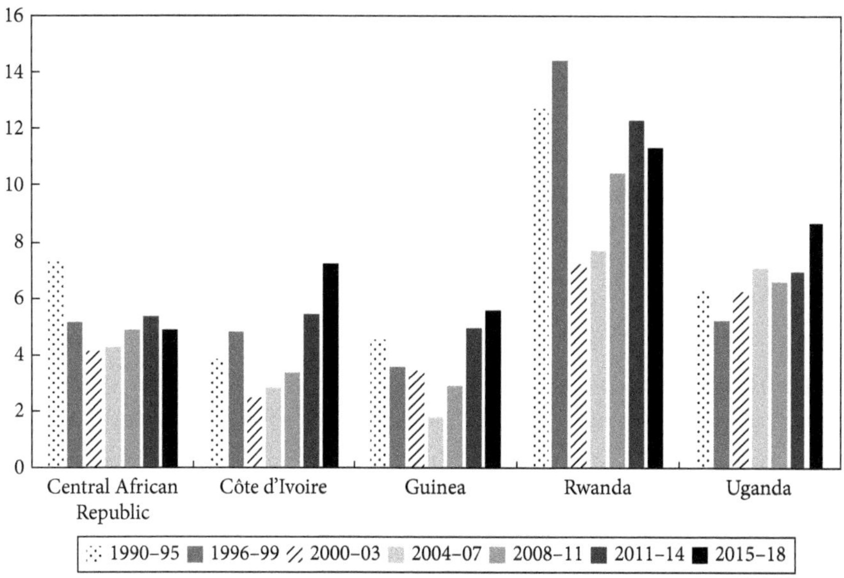

Figure 20.9 Public Investment (Percent of GDP)

Source: World Economic Outlook database.

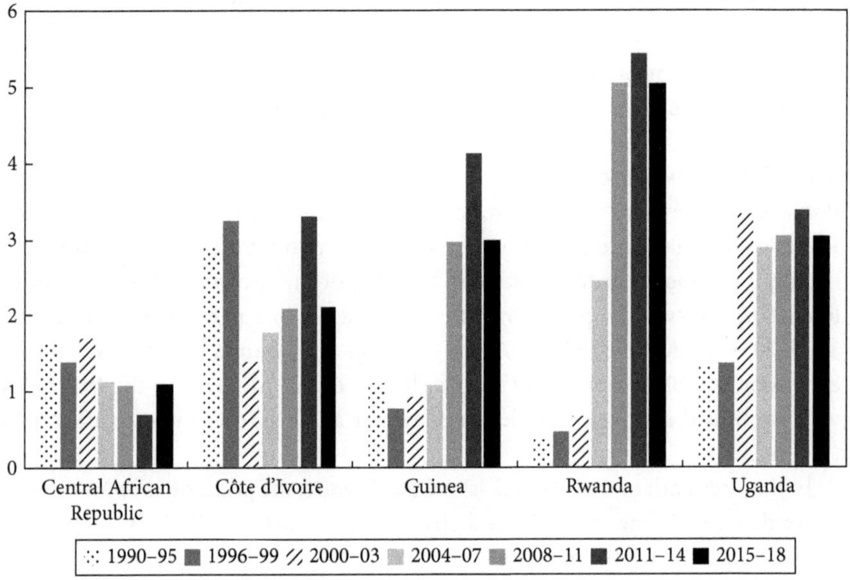

Figure 20.10 Domestically Financed Capital Expenditure (Percent of GDP)
Source: World Economic Outlook database.

domestically financed capital expenditures have increased rapidly since the mid-2000s. This variable shows the governments' commitment to build public infrastructure with its own resources (Figure 20.10).

In addition to the volume of public investment, efficiency matters both in terms of project selection and implementation and in terms of the quality of the outcome. In particular, Rwanda and Côte d'Ivoire display a higher quality of infrastructure compared to many other sub-Saharan African countries (IMF, 2014 *Sub-Saharan Africa Regional Economic Outlook*; Chapter 3, Figure 3.4).

5.5 Private Sector

Reforms to strengthen the business climate and support private sector development were implemented in Uganda, Rwanda, Côte d'Ivoire, and Guinea. Notably, these reforms allowed countries to improve the regulatory environment and the rule of law, although more remains to be done in a number of areas. (Figure 20.11 and Figure 20.12).

In the early 1990s, a new Investment Code was passed in Uganda and an Investment Authority was established as an independent agency to promote private investment and act as a one-stop shop. In Rwanda, a business and land registration program was implemented in 2007 that eliminated registration fees and streamlined procedures for land application, allocation and registration,

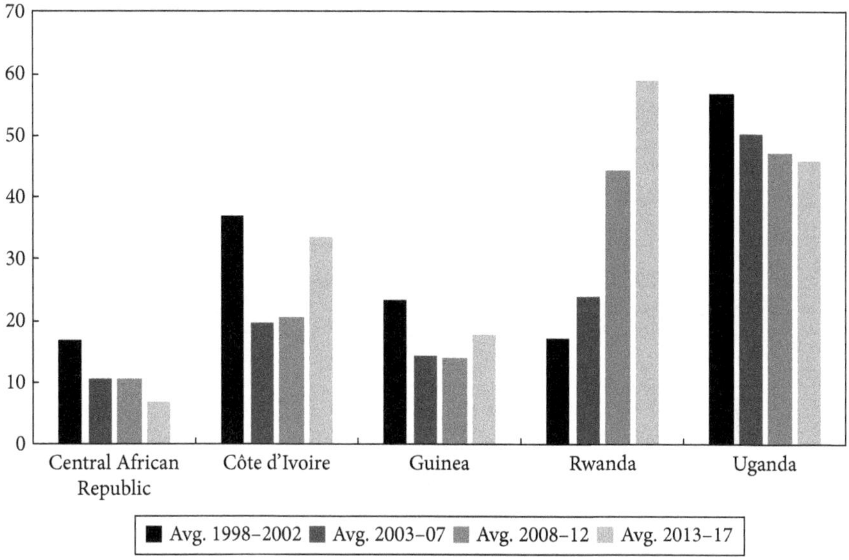

Figure 20.11 Regulatory Quality (Percentile rank)
Source: World Bank, World Governance Indicators database.

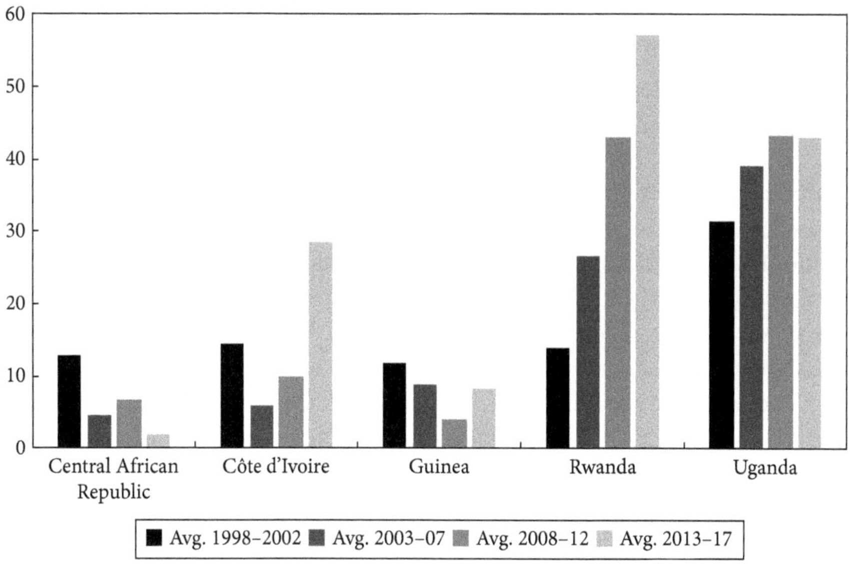

Figure 20.12 Rule of Law (Percentile rank)
Source: World Bank, World Governance Indicators database.

building permits, and international trade. The 2017 Doing Business survey ranked Rwanda as number two in Africa.

During the crisis, Côte d'Ivoire's business climate and key institutions were severely damaged. By 2011, the country ranked at the bottom of international

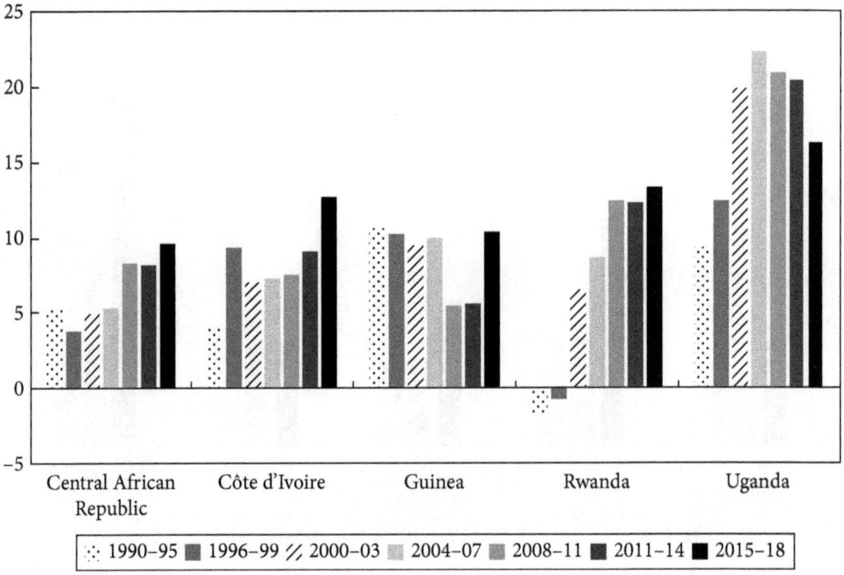

Figure 20.13 Private Investment (Percent of GDP)
Source: IMF, World Economic Outlook database.

Doing Business and governance rankings. As noted before, the process was reversed after 2011 through progress with PFM and revenue reforms and the removal of red tape.

Similarly, reforms to strengthen the business climate improved Guinea's ranking by 27 steps between 2013 and 2018 in the World Bank's Doing Business Indicators. Notably, a specialized Commerce Court was set up in Conakry, procedures to create a business were streamlined, an online business creation platform was launched, and a one-stop-shop for cross-border trade was created. Progress in strengthening the business environment and private sector development was not possible in the Central African Republic because of political instability and insecurity.

As expected, the private sector—at least the formal private sector as captured in the data—did not play a significant role in the immediate period following the countries' major crises but began to so do so a few years later in Rwanda, Uganda, and Côte d'Ivoire (Figure 20.13). In the Central African Republic, private investment has been improving gradually in the past couple of decades but has not yet surpassed 10 percent of GDP.

6. Outcomes

Security, political stability, and governance. Rwanda, Uganda, Côte d'Ivoire, and Guinea followed an approach that avoided conflict and led to political stability and improvements in voice and accountability (Figures 20.14–20.16), On governance, Rwanda and Côte d'Ivoire appears to have made progress (Figure 20.17). The Central African Republic struggled to make progress in all these areas, but the recent peace agreement and gradual improvements in economic management are encouraging signs.

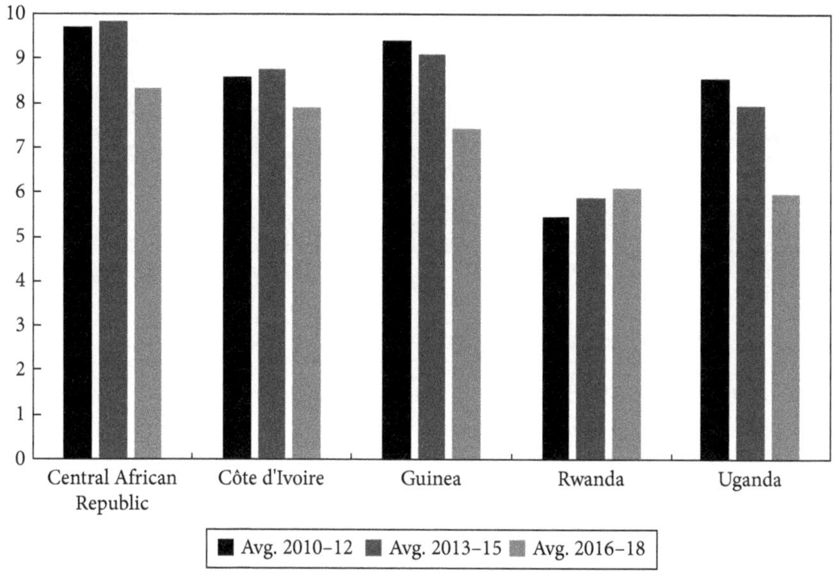

Figure 20.14 Security Apparatus (Index, 1 = lowest threat to 10 = highest threat)
Note: Security apparatus considers the security threats to a state.
Source: Fund for Peace.

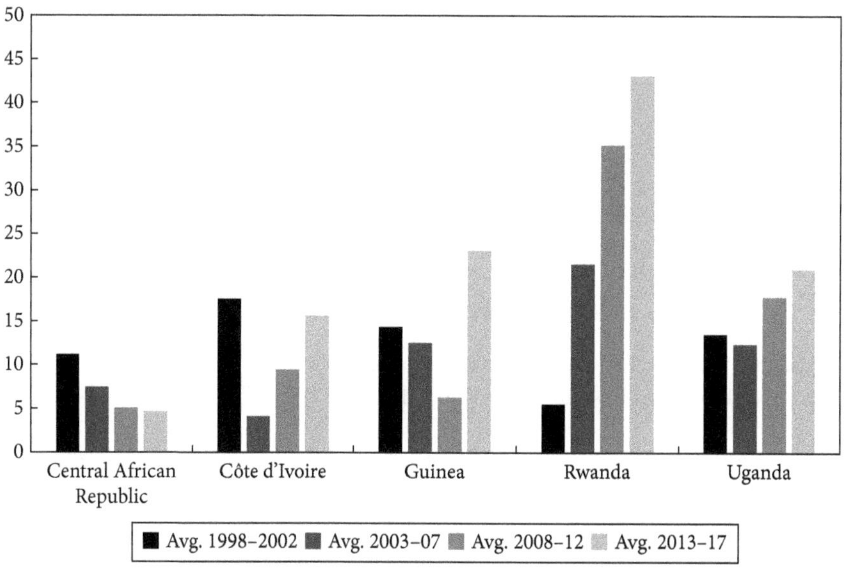

Figure 20.15 Political Stability (Percentile rank)
Source: World Bank, World Governance Indicators database.

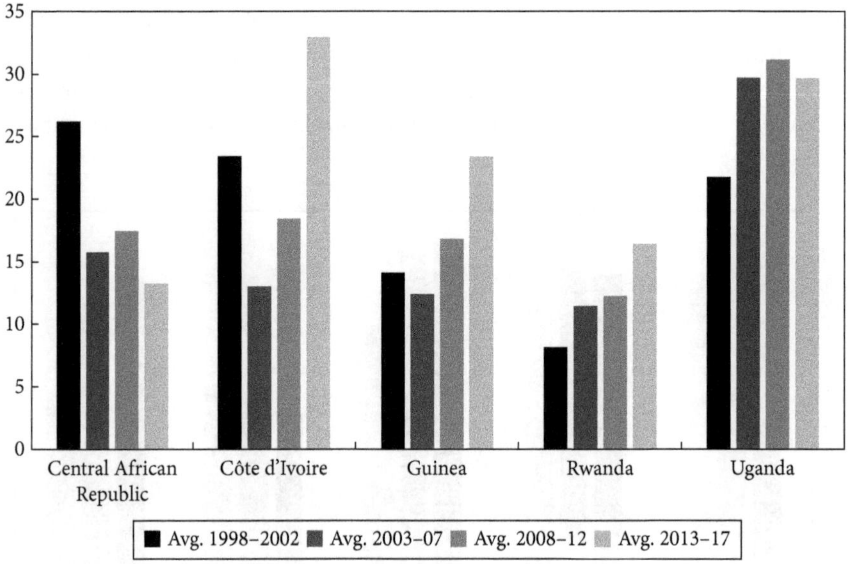

Figure 20.16 Voice and Accountability (Percentile rank)
Source: World Bank, World Governance Indicators database.

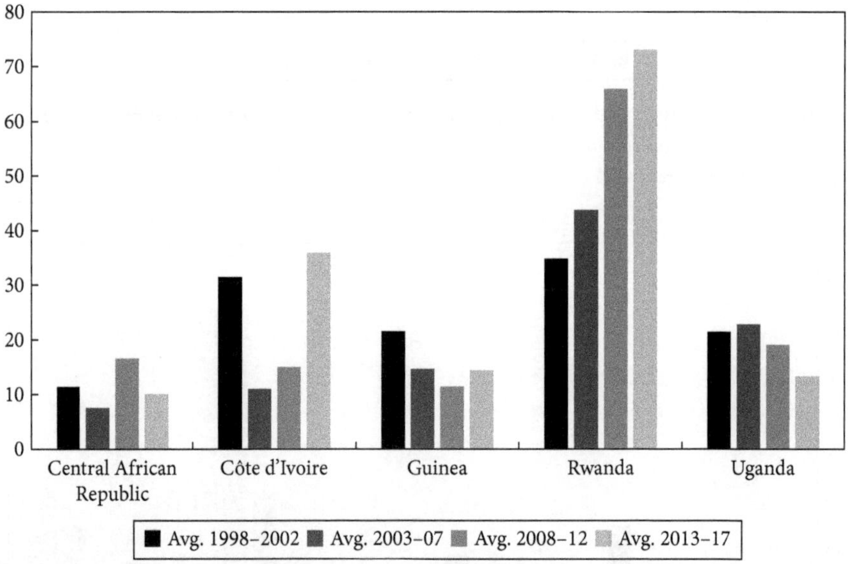

Figure 20.17 Control of Corruption (Percentile rank)
Source: World Bank, World Governance Indicators database.

Economic growth. As noted earlier, Rwanda and Uganda have enjoyed sustained increases in real per capita income since the mid-1990s. Furthermore, since the early 2000s, both countries have embarked on a second generation of economic reforms that seem to have boosted growth beyond the

Table 20.1 Selected Development Indicators

	1990	2017[1]
Primary School Gross Enrolment Rate (percent)		
Central African Republic	70.0	105.7
Côte d'lvoire	69.7	98.8
Guinea	34.8	92.4
Rwanda	73.1	133.4
Uganda	70.4	99.0
Infant Mortally Rate (per 1,000 live briths)		
Central African Republic	114.9	87.6
Côte d'lvoire	104.1	64.2
Guinea	138.6	56.4
Rwanda	92.6	28.9
Uganda	107.2	35.4

[1] Primary school enrolment data of Central Aftican Republic and Guinea are 2016.

Source: World Bank, World Development Indicators.

post-conflict rebound.[13] Nevertheless, though data are scant, some evidence suggests that several countries struggle to make growth more inclusive and create sufficient jobs despite relatively high economic growth, especially in recent years. This, of course, is not only owing to perceived risks of political or social instability and constraints on private sector development but also to the large increase in the labor force propelled by Sub-Saharan Africa's population dynamics. The reasons for such a gap are complex, but further focus on education, training, and labor market reforms could be important to address it.

Social progress. Health and education indicators point to progress in social outcomes in all countries following their most fragile periods, although such progress is much more robust in Rwanda and Uganda than in the Central African Republic (Table 20.1). Clearly, this is a combination of factors such as prudent fiscal and monetary policies, economic reforms, public investment, and improvements in the business climate. Although the data are scant, progress seems to have been made in reducing poverty rates in all countries except the Central African Republic (Table 20.2).

[13] In Rwanda, for instance, reforms to strengthen revenue mobilization and public financial management continued, together with efforts to improve governance, the anticorruption framework and financial sector and legal reforms, boosting trade and diversification, and raising agricultural productivity.

Table 20.2 Poverty Headcount Ratio at $1.90 a Day, 2011 PPP (Percent of population)

	Most fragile period (Closest available data point)	Latest available
Central African Republic	64.8 (2003)	66.3 (2008)
Côte d'lvoire	29.1 (2008)	28.2 (2015)
Guinea	59.7 (2007)	35.3 (2012)
Rwanda	77.2 (2000)	55.5 (2016)
Uganda	57.7 (1989)	41.7 (2016)

Source: World Bank, World Development Indicators.

The connection between the various factors analyzed above and linked to building resilience and the ultimate outcomes can be seen in Figure 20.18, which contains an assessment of the different factors involved in the transition process since the countries' most fragile periods.

6.1 The Road Ahead

Looking ahead, it is important for all countries to ensure that the lessons from their own experience as well as from other countries are taken on board, considering the many examples of cases where countries easily revert to fragility as a result of political instability, lack of inclusion, and counterproductive if well-intended policies.

For both Rwanda and Uganda, the main lessons are the importance of commitment to reforms. As small landlocked countries, their main challenge will be to ensure a transition from being a primary commodity exporter to having a more diversified economic base. This will require a sufficiently open policy towards trade and services, including trade with African countries, to take advantage of economies of scale and specialization in the value chain.

In Guinea, addressing remaining causes of fragility will be key: focusing on strengthening institutions, reducing social and political instability, improving social outcomes and basic service delivery, and fostering economic diversification and good governance. One important lesson from the country's experience (that is also relevant for Côte d'Ivoire and the other countries) is the need to factor in and address capacity constraints while setting up the reform agenda.[14]

[14] In Côte d'Ivoire, because of the postcrisis challenges in tax administration, expected results seemed too ambitious and donor support should have focused on rebuilding this infrastructure and on curbing governance challenges. To this end, recent IMF technical assistance has been focusing on rebuilding fiscal infrastructure by supporting projects such as the update of the taxpayers' database, the digitalization of the directorate general of taxes, and the deployment of a new online tax filing and payment system.

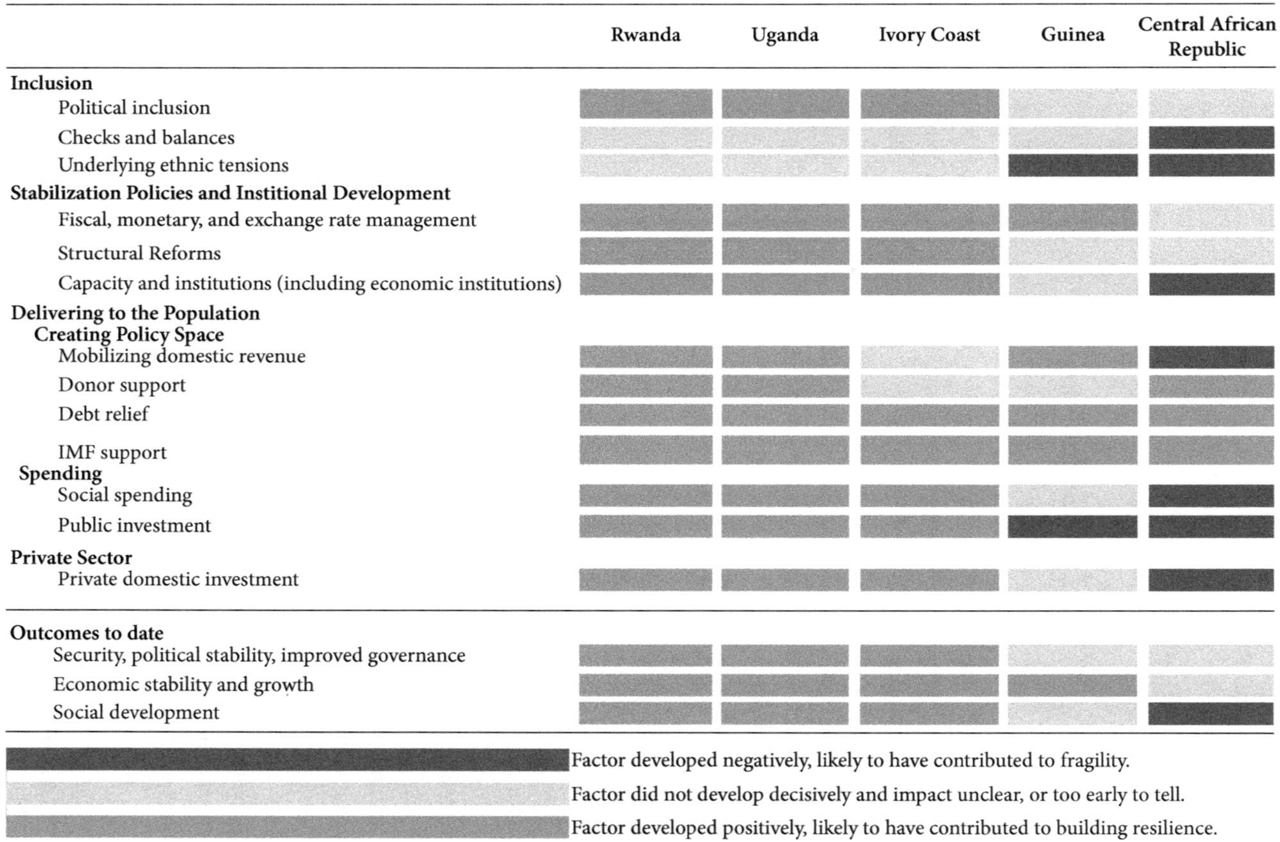

Figure 20.18 Factors in Building Resilience

Source: IMF Staff

Lastly, in the Central African Republic, it is too early to judge the extent of progress since its most fragile period; yet there is clearly a need to continue to work on creating consensus, focusing on establishing peace and security outside the capital as well as the government's role throughout the national territory, and ensuring improvements in taxation, delivery of public services, and investments in the public infrastructure (notably energy).

7. Concluding Comments

Exiting fragility is a difficult challenge for any country. Since the start of the century, only a handful of countries in Sub-Saharan Africa (such as Rwanda, Uganda) have been able to build significant resilience. This success is the outcome of focused policies and political inclusion that fostered economic stability and growth, improved security, and enabled the state to begin delivering basic services.[15] At the same time, for other countries the difficulty of building resilience seems to be related to an uneven evolution of one or more of the above factors or constraints over time. Weak capacity and governance as well as political and social divisions are key factors in these countries' stagnation, and in the vicious cycles that perpetuate low levels of physical and human capital, inadequate public services, and vulnerability to shocks.

The experiences reviewed in this chapter suggest that even when both domestic and external factors are well aligned, building resilience takes a long time. Realism in expectations is needed among among all stakeholders on the pace of progress and for a long-term engagement that balances immediate needs with longer-term priorities. But these experiences have also highlighted that countries can make substantial progress in these efforts and provide valuable insights for others to follow.

Though all five of the countries discussed in this chapter have made progress since the time of their most fragile periods, the experiences of Guinea and the Central African Republic are too recent to draw definitive conclusions. Still, the case studies of the three other countries considered here strongly support the view that countries which manage to adopt a sufficiently inclusive political arrangement can then strengthen their economic policies and, over time, their institutions as well as the business environment, to sustain economic growth.

[15] Gelbard et al., 2015. Based on a panel data logit model (estimating the probability of surpassing the resilience threshold) and a GMM regression, the key variables linked to building resilience were political stability, constraints on the executive, low inflation, avoidance of exchange rate misalignment, revenue mobilization, public spending on education and infrastructure (negative on current and military spending), strength of fiscal institutions, regulatory quality, and presence of IMF-supported programs for three or more years.

This sequence is logical, but the development literature has not paid enough attention to the necessary role played by a strategy that reflects internal consensus and provides a mechanism to mobilize support—financial and technical—from the international community. It is only then that the probability of unleashing a virtuous cycle of events to build resilience increases and fiscal space is created through a combination of domestic revenue mobilization, debt relief, and increased aid, all enabling social and infrastructure investment and increasing the legitimacy of the state. Without the above factors, countries have found it impossible to achieved sustained economic growth and improvements in social indicators.

In sum, there are five main takeaways from this chapter:

1. Sufficient political inclusion and a committed leadership that leads to peace, avoids major political turmoil, and supports the establishment of a national development vision are preconditions for building resilience. Such leadership has to translate this vision into action and implement reforms that promote economic stability, generate policy space to deliver improvements in living standards, and, over time, help strengthen institutions, improve governance and accountability, and build capacity. It also has to foster ownership of the vision and inform the population about the steps being taken to achieve it.
2. Rwanda, Uganda, and Côte d'Ivoire performed better in all dimensions thanks to a leadership strongly committed to political inclusion and appropriate policies, but more progress is needed in making growth fully inclusive. The experiences of Guinea and the Central African Republic offer some encouraging signs, but the improvements noted are still too recent to allow for definitive conclusions as to their long-lasting success.
3. Though not all countries were successful in mobilizing domestic revenue right away, the combination of donor support and debt relief helped most of them deliver results to their populations, including through increased levels of public investment. The most successful countries consistently expanded their priority spending, while the international community, including the IMF, played a supporting role. All in all, beyond the composition of spending, fiscal policy (i.e. tax structure, revenue administration, ways of financing fiscal deficits) played a critical role in helping countries build resilience.
4. The international community can support fragile countries' efforts to prioritize and sequence reforms and to generate fiscal policy space for improvements in living standards and to increase the legitimacy of the state. The IMF should strive to ensure that the policies it supports are parsimonious, adapted to local conditions, and owned by the authorities. At the same time, capacity building has to be better tailored to the circumstances on the ground by focusing more on deploying long-term advisors,

providing more hands-on training, and ensuring ownership by the authorities.

5. Considering the time it takes to build resilience, international stakeholders should be prepared to engage with fragile countries on a long-term basis, provide financial assistance in ways that can improve the effectiveness of the state, coordinate their efforts closely, and focus capacity development efforts on strengthening economic institutions.

Once these conditions are in place, an ensuing process of resource mobilization can enhance the government's financial strength and help establish an implicit contract between the citizens and their government that promotes good governance and accountability. And in the longer term, fostering an environment that promotes the expansion of the private sector—especially in labor-intensive activities and a strong safety net—is required for sustained and inclusive growth.

References

Bertocchi, G. and D. Guerzoni, 2010. "The Fragile Definition of State Fragility," Working Paper 43. Modena: University of Modena.

Chauvet, L. and P. Collier. 2008. "What Are the Preconditions for Turnarounds in Failing States?" *Conflict Management and Peace Science*, 25(4): 332–48.

Fund for Peace. 2019. Fragile States Index. https://fragilestatesindex.org/category/analysis/fragile-states-index-2019/ (last accessed July 16, 2020).

Gelbard et. al., 2015, "Building Resilience in Sub-Saharan Africa's Fragile States," African Departmental Paper. Washington, DC: International Monetary Fund.

IMF (International Monetary Fund). 1999. "Rwanda: Enhanced Structural Adjustment Facility." Policy Framework Paper, 1998/2000–2001/02.."

OECD (Organisation for Economic Co-operation and Development). 2019. *States of Fragility*. Paris: Organisation for Economic Co-operation and Development.

Index

Note: Tables, figures, and boxes are indicated by an italic "*t*", "*f*", and "*b*", respectively, following the page number.